SHARIA INCORPORATED

Law, Governance, and Development

The Leiden University Press series on Law, Governance, and Development brings together an interdisciplinary body of work about the formation and functioning of legal systems in developing countries, and about interventions to strengthen them. The series aims to engage academics, policy-makers and practitioners at the national and international level, thus attempting to stimulate legal reform for good governance and development.

SHARIA INCORPORATED

A Comparative Overview of the Legal Systems of
Twelve Muslim Countries in Past and Present

editor Jan Michiel Otto

Leiden University Press

Grateful acknowledgement is made to the following institutions in The Hague and Leiden for their generous support of this study:

Scientific Council for State Policy (WRR)
Netherlands Organization for Scientific Research (NWO)
Ministry of Foreign Affairs
Leiden University (Faculty of Law; Leiden University Center for the study of Islam and Society (LUCIS); Van Vollenhoven Institute for Law, Governance and Development (VVI)

Cover design: Studio Jan de Boer, Amsterdam
Layout: The DocWorkers, Almere

ISBN 978 90 8728 057 4
E-ISBN 978 94 0060 017 1
NUR 741 / 820

Printed and bound by CPI Group (UK) Ltd, Croydon, CR0 4YY

Table of contents

Acknowledgements

My deep appreciation goes to my fellow researchers, who wrote the country studies constituting the core of this book. It has been a great privilege and pleasure to see this collaborative work developing under the capable hands of Maurits Berger, Léon Buskens, Albert Dekker, Esther van Eijk, Andrew Harding, Mustafa Koçak, Olaf Köndgen, Martin Lau, Ziba Mir-Hosseini, Philip Ostien, Mohammad Hamid Saboory, Dorothea Schulz, Nadia Sonneveld, and Nadjma Yassari.

I am greatly indebted to Jan Schoonenboom and Wendy Asbeek Brusse, who initiated and assigned the project on behalf of the Scientific Council for State Policy (WRR). Without their unwavering support and critical counseling, this project could not have been completed. The intense and stimulating discussions with Maurits Berger, Albert Dekker and Maarten Barends in the initial phase, still fill me with sweet memories.

I am also grateful to Baudouin Dupret and Rudolph Peters, who read the whole manuscript as referees, and provided us with advise. Various chapters of the book were presented to a wider audience at conference panels of the International Law and Society Association, in 2008 in Montreal and in 2009 in Denver. I thank my colleagues from SOAS, Andrew Harding (now at Victoria), and Martin Lau, as well as Philip Ostien and Léon Buskens, for co-chairing those sessions.

For years, the Van Vollenhoven Institute for Law, Governance and Development (VVI) has been the home base for a dozen dedicated academics, who carry out challenging socio-legal research and teaching projects all over the world. Combining the ambitious project of this book with other VVI tasks, notably that of being the institute's director, was challenging in the least. This situation did not only cause considerable delays of the project, but also put quite some stress on my colleagues at the institute. I offer both my apologies and my gratitude to my colleagues, both inside and outside the VVI, who tolerated and supported me, took over the watch, and contributed to the project in many ways. Albert Dekker, my longtime colleague at the VVI, has been a model of generosity and efficacy in an amazing number of capacities, such as librarian, researcher, author, and coordinator. I owe more than thanks to him. For valuable comments and discussions I am grateful to Theo Veenkamp as well as to Adriaan Bedner; thanks to their help and especially to the all-out efforts of Jan van Olden, Ab Massier, and Kari van Weeren, we can finally see this book completed and the VVI still alive and kicking.

I would like to thank Julie Chadbourne for her editorial assistance with regards to the country chapters in this book. Her dedication and meticulous efforts have been crucial for bringing this project close to the finish line. Stijn van Huis also contributed substantively by his careful reading of and commenting on all country chapters, and by composing the glossary, with Julie's help. Nadia Sonneveld helped with the editing of several chapters. At the VVI Marianne Moria, Kora Bentvelsen, Sylvia Holverda, Dennis Janssen, Sandra Moniaga, Tristam Moeliono, Benjamin van Rooij, Myrna Safitri, Ahmed Tawfik, and Janine Ubink were of help for one aspect of the book or another. Hannah Mason edited the introductory and concluding parts of this book, and helped to make all other sections camera ready; she also proofread the manuscript. With her linguistic and organisational skills, she made the completion of this project in its final months both a reality and a pleasure.

To the Faculty of Law, especially to its Dean Carel Stolker, I express my sincere gratitude for creating a supportive environment for our research, similarly to the headquarters of Leiden University. LUCIS, the new Leiden University Center for the Study of Islam and Society, of which the establishment, early 2009, was necessitated by the unfortunate demise of the inter-university ISIM institute, supports many research projects in this field. LUCIS also provided funding for the conference in June 2010, where the authors of this book convened, for the first time, to discuss recent developments in the countries of study, and to launch this publication.

In various stages of this project translations of country studies were made, first from English to Dutch and finally from Dutch to English. I am grateful to Anne Saab, Will Saab, and Kate Delaney for their translation work, and to the Netherlands Organisation for Scientific Research (NWO) for its generous support of the translation. Revisions, updates and other changes made by authors and editor are however considerable, and final responsibility for the text rests with them only.

I record my gratitude to my warmly supportive publisher, Yvonne Twisk of the reborn Leiden University Press as well as to Chantal Nicolaes, Erik van Aert and Saskia de Vries of Amsterdam University Press for their admirable patience and wonderful assistance throughout this project.

Of my dear parents, Will and Ank Otto, my father has not lived to see the completion of this book, but his spirit and my mother's never-ending support have always been there. In a most literal sense, my wife

Marileen and our children, Miriam, Benjamin and Saskia, have joined, supported and taught me more than I could ever expect.

Jan Michiel Otto
Amsterdam/Leiden, March 2010

Editorial note

Transliteration and glossary

As for the transliteration of Arabic terms, the authors of each chapter have followed their own rules regarding the use of diacritical symbols. In the introduction and conclusion I have not used any diacritical symbols, following for example The Oxford Dictionary of Islam. This means that shari'a will appear as 'sharia'. For the meaning of non-English, mainly Arabic, terms, please refer to the Glossary in the back of this book.

Detailed tables of contents

Please note that this book does not contain an index. The clear-cut structure of the chapters combined with the detailed tables of contents at the start of each country study are believed to provide sufficient guidance to the reader.

Tables

The tables in this book, other than those where a source is explicitly mentioned, have been composed by the editor and are based on conclusions drawn by the individual authors. The tables serve to allow the reader to compare countries on specific themes or issues. The tables can be found in the Chapter 1, Chapter 14 and in the Annexe.

Preface

In 2005 a reputed American human rights institute, Freedom House, published a book entitled *Radical Islam's rules. The worldwide spread of extreme Shari'a law.* The book argues that since the 1980s Muslim countries have started replacing their laws with extreme and barbarous 'sharia'. On the basis of seven country studies it claims that sharia, as it has been applied in those countries, undercuts legal systems, frequently employs cruel punishments, threatens Muslims who are not part of the dominant group, and reduces women to secondary status. All states, where such laws have been imposed, it says, produce terrorism (Marshall 2005: 15). In the foreword former CIA director James Woolsey promises: 'We will win this current long war [...] by defeating the Islamist ideology.'

While Freedom House thus advised the United States government to wage war against the Islamist ideology in general and against the forces that supposedly promote sharia in particular, the same problem became the subject of a research project undertaken by an institute in another Western country, based in The Hague in the Netherlands – one which would eventually lead to this book. The Scientific Council for State Policy, a think-tank of the Dutch cabinet (WRR, *Wetenschappelijke Raad voor het Regeringsbeleid*) consulted me in 2003 about the possibility of carrying out a study on sharia. This project would be the third in a series of projects concerning Islam. One stemmed from an inquiry by my colleague Erik-Jan Zürcher about whether EU accession of Turkey would be problematic, because of the fact that most Turks are Muslims. The other sprang forth from a study by another colleague, Nasr Abu Zayd, about reformation of Islamic thought.

The WRR was obviously concerned about deteriorating relations between the West and the Muslim world and had questions about the supposedly increasing role of extreme sharia in the Muslim world. Is sharia really a fixed set of norms that applies to all Muslims as their supreme rule? Do we see an Islamist subversion of national legal systems? Has the legal status of women indeed deteriorated, and have inhuman punishments, such as stoning and hand-cutting, become common practice throughout the Muslim world? Have conservative religious scholars become the key decision makers instead of elected politicians? And, finally, is it really true that in the last 25 years legal systems in the Muslim world have been islamised and moved away from human rights, democracy, and the rule of law?

At the time of the start of the WRR projects, Islam had become a major issue in Dutch politics. Had it hitherto been regarded as a world religion with its good and bad sides like any religion, since the late 1990s maverick politicians had risen to prominence by calling Islam 'backward' (Pim Fortuyn, Ayaan Hirsi Ali) and its Prophet 'a paedophile' (Hirsi Ali). Likewise, filmmaker and columnist Theo van Gogh, before he was brutally murdered by a Moroccan fundamentalist, wrote consistently about Moroccan immigrant Muslims as 'the goatfuckers' or 'the fifth column'. He depicted the mayor of Amsterdam Cohen, admired by many for his capacity to bridge and unite, as soft and naïve, and even called him a 'Nazi-collaborator'. The heated atmosphere in the Netherlands during the years after 9/11 has been captured well by Ian Buruma in his book *Murder in Amsterdam*. The WRR research projects on Islam were to take place in turbulent conditions and could count on sharp criticism, regardless of the results.

Academic research about sharia is usually concerned with studying the classical sources of sharia, notably the *fiqh*-books in which Islamic scholars discuss cases and the application of rules and principles. The focus of such studies is often on the past, on the heyday of sharia, when it was the living law, developed and maintained by religious scholars throughout the Muslim world. However, '[t]o practice law in the modern era is to be an agent of the state' (Hallaq 2009: 549). The main issue at present has become the incorporation of sharia into state law. Which aspects? What exactly? To what extent? Where? When? How? Why? These questions formed the foundations for this study.

A study of this kind seemed to perfectly fit in with the research tradition of the Van Vollenhoven Institute of Leiden University, where since the 1980s my colleagues and I had been studying law and governance in developing countries. Some of the legal systems we had focused on, happened to be situated in Muslim countries, for example Indonesia, Egypt, and Morocco. In the academic domain of 'law, governance and development', which dates back to the study of colonial law and administration, we employ an interdisciplinary tradition, combining legal and social science approaches with language, culture, and history. During thirty years of research, I had become aware of the longstanding political tensions and legal problems surrounding the position and role of sharia within national legal systems. This concern was shared by my colleagues at the School for Oriental and African Studies in London, whose help has proven essential for the undertaking of this project.

On a more personal level, I observed a stark contradiction between what I experienced during in-country field research and what was considered public opinion in the West. With my wife Marileen, a medical anthropologist, I spent years living in Muslim areas, in the mid 1970s near Lucknow, a centre of Shia religion in North India, in the early 1980s in a village in rural Upper Egypt, and ten years later, with our three children, in an urban kampong on the outskirts of Bandung, Indonesia. We had developed personal relations with hundreds of Muslims of many different backgrounds. After 2001, back in the Netherlands, dominant discourses and media reports began to stereotype Islam, Muslims, and sharia in a consistently negative manner. Disturbing news and images related to sharia came in not only from Saudi Arabia, Iran, and Afghanistan, but also from Indonesia, Egypt, and Morocco, countries that had previously been regarded as 'moderate'. It seemed that there was a consistent emphasis in the media on horrifying events happening in the Muslim world, whilst developments in other parts of the world were ignored or paid minimal attention to.

In late 2003, the project started. The first challenge was the selection of countries: in order to cover a considerable, representative part of the Muslim world, I set out to select a number of countries, which together would constitute about two-thirds of the world Muslim population. Next, the selection of countries needed to represent the Muslim world in all its variety, i.e. a wide regional spread; a full range of secular, moderate, and orthodox regimes; and a collection of rich, middle-income, and poor countries, etc. It was decided that the project would focus on the following regions and countries. In North Africa and the Middle East the WRR and I selected five countries, namely Egypt, Morocco, Saudi Arabia, Sudan, and Turkey. The three countries selected in Central and South Asia were Iran, Pakistan, and Afghanistan. In Southeast Asia we opted for Indonesia and Malaysia. And finally, Nigeria and Mali were to represent Sub-Saharan West Africa.

The second challenge consisted of finding authors with sufficient expertise in the law and the socio-political context of the country concerned, who could provide impartial and objective analysis. They needed to be willing to participate in a collaborative research undertaking about a hotly contested issue with an uncertain outcome. I feel privileged to have collaborated with over a dozen authors, who share a longstanding commitment to the study of law and society. All were asked to adhere to the same format, both in terms of subjects as well as historical periods. Much to my relief, they were all willing to go along with the proposed outline.

In 2006 the findings and recommendations of this research were published in three volumes.[1] These books, like other WRR studies, were written in Dutch to serve a Dutch audience. However, given the nature of the subject matter and the diverse backgrounds of the authors, an English language version had to appear. In 2007, we began work on this book. A few new authors joined the team. We took the time to discuss, revise, and rewrite. All authors fastidiously updated their country studies through to early 2010.

The conditions which gave impetus to this project in 2003 have not changed. Since 9/11 the West has been overcome with '[n]egative stereotypes of Islamic law as inflexible, arbitrary, and discriminatory and of legal institutions as oppressive, coercive, and incompatible with democracy' (Hirsch 2006: 168). In Europe, people's fear of terrorist attacks is combined with an anxiety related to signs of islamisation of their own society. Consequently, Europe has seen the rise of new anti-Islam politics, led by populist leaders, such as the Dutch parliamentarian Geert Wilders. Declaring Islam to be the root cause of world problems and depicting sharia as a backward, medieval law has given him and his colleagues enormous popularity and electoral success.

Politicians, such as Wilders, have close connections with a network of publicists and academics, both in Europe and the United States, who have embraced versions of Huntington's clash of civilisations theory, as well as the late work of Bernard Lewis. Huntington had suggested already in the late 1990s that Western civilisation is threatened by Islamic civilisation. In his view, the rule of law, which he describes as a cornerstone of Western civilisation, has come under threat whilst the legal systems of Islamic countries are being increasingly islamicised (Huntington 1998: 116). In the aftermath of 9/11, Lewis produced several short books in which he argued that 'almost the entire Muslim world' can be seen as a 'failure of modernity' (Lewis 2003: 97). He claimed that Muslims recognise sharia as the highest and only norm, and that for them the state is nothing more than an expression of religion (2002: 106).

Whatever may be true of these statements, Lewis, his European epigones, and the neo-conservative architects of Bush's foreign policy, found welcome support in the writings of a few ex-Muslims who had migrated to the West and found a new mission in warning against Islam. For example, Ibn Warraq, author of the much-cited book *Why I am not a Muslim* (1995) stated: 'The truth of the matter is that Islam will never achieve democracy and human rights if it insists on the application of the Sharia.'

While the man in the street in the West believes such allegations to be hard facts, most internationally reputed scholars of Islamic law would argue the opposite. It is a mystery that their solid and thorough work on sharia has hardly been able to counter the abovementioned alarmist, confrontational discourse about sharia. Perhaps this is because academic writing remains nuanced and specialised, – often dealing only with particular aspects or particular countries –, whereas alarmist claims about the rise of extreme sharia are rather absolute and general, always referring to Islam as a whole and to 'the Muslim world', thereby making it difficult to refute their arguments.

In sum, there is a gap, which I hope this book will be able to fill at least partly. It presents a new collaborative effort to lay the groundwork for the analysis of a major question, which will continue to engage many minds and rouse high emotions, both in the Muslim world as well as in the West. How can sharia-based law exist as an integral part of rule-of-law-based national legal systems?

1 Introduction: investigating the role of sharia in national law

Jan Michiel Otto

Table of contents

1.1 Theme, purpose, and approach

What this book is about

This collaborative study intends in the first place to explore the incorporation of sharia-based[1] rules in national legal systems. It tries to answer pertinent questions about islamisation of law throughout the Muslim world: Where? When? To what extent? How? Why? The fact that since the 1970s a number of Muslim countries, notably Iran, Pakistan and Sudan, have followed this course has been a cause for concern, both in Muslim countries and in the West. It has suggested a sidelining of modernising groups, weakening of the legal positions of women and religious minorities, and a return to cruel corporal punishments. One can hardly avoid the impression that islamisation of law equals disrespect for the rule of law and human rights. Yet, the discussion about these developments is hardly based on actual facts; rather, it is filled with controversy, speculation and all sorts of prejudices.

This book provides a factual and comparative overview of the role and position of sharia-based law in the national legal systems of twelve, representative Muslim countries. Each country study consists of two interrelated parts. The first part of each chapter describes the history of how the present legal systems of Muslim countries have been shaped by socio-political developments. It records major changes in governance and law, tracing in particular the role of Islam and sharia in this process. The second part presents the actual legal situation and shows to what extent national legal systems have or have not distanced themselves from the tenets of 'classical sharia' (see 1.2 below); these sections also address the compatibility of these systems with the rule of law and human rights (see 1.4 below). The country studies focus on those areas of national law, where the introduction of sharia has caused most concern, namely constitutional law, family and inheritance law, and criminal law.

Purpose and perspectives

This book does not only offer a wealth of data, it also employs a set of conceptual perspectives, or frames, in order to forge the data into a useful body of knowledge.

Through our first frame, we look at a particular country and its national legal system, for we can only start to understand the relationship between sharia and national law by looking at countries individually. Therefore this book is in the first place a repository of country-based knowledge. In addition, this frame also serves as a tool to gain insight into the broader picture of 'the Muslim world'. The first frame is further explained in 1.3 and 1.4. Preliminary results are presented in the concluding chapter in 14.4.

Our second frame is thematic: the book focuses on what are probably the four main concerns that have arisen and dominated the political debate about sharia-based law over the last few decades. Those concerns are the alleged supremacy of sharia, the status of women, degrading punishments, and human rights. In this aspect, the book differentiates itself from similar collections which usually focus on one single theme, either constitutional law, or women, or criminal law, or human rights. This frame is explained in 1.3, and results can be found in 14.3.

Our third perspective is historical. We look at how the relationship between sharia and national law has evolved since 1800, with a focus on the twentieth century, and following developments until the present day. This is explained below in 1.6; results are summarised in 14.2.

Our fourth perspective is governance. It regards the relationship between sharia and national law essentially as a major challenge for each state, i.e. to form and apply the main rules for a stable, prosperous, and just society, interacting with major political players and social groups. Section 14.5 reflects on governance aspects.

The fifth frame of this book addresses the struggle between 'moderates' and 'puritans' in each country and in the Muslim world at large; this dichotomy plays a crucial role in the discussion on factors that influence the relationship between sharia and national law. The points of departure of both 'camps' are explained in 1.5. Going beyond this dichotomy, the study will show that the ideological-religious spectrum is influenced by a number of other (f)actors adding to the complexity of the picture.

The sixth perspective is normative pluralism. It positions sharia as one of the normative systems that have had an impact on the people and states in the Muslim world. It is a fact that customary law, colonial law, foreign law, and international law, including human rights law, have also exerted significant influence on the development of national law and local legal practices until this very day (see 14.5).

This multiplicity of frames allows the book to be used for several purposes and by various readerships. The study enables country-by-country comparison, whilst at the same time all periods, governance contexts, areas of law, concerns and issues can be compared. In addition, the book may help in developing a realistic overview of the problem as a whole. It strives to appeal to students of law, of history, of governance, and of Islamic studies. It also aims at informing decision-makers and observers in the field of foreign policy and international relations, for whom our assessments of the (in)compatibility of sharia-based law with the rule of law, including human rights, may be useful. And finally, it may serve to counterbalance the image of sharia as depicted by the constant stream of media reports and the alarmist responses which are mentioned in the preface of this book. Perhaps reading this book will help to put things in perspective.

Approaches chosen

The focus of this book lies on the contemporary legal systems of twelve, predominantly *developing* countries with clear Muslim majorities.[2] The book certainly does not pretend to be a major book about sharia as such. There are excellent works by renowned authors such as Hallaq (2009), Vikør (2005), or the earlier generation of Coulson (1964) and Schacht (1964), who focus on sharia – or Islamic law – itself. They do so mostly from a historical perspective, usually dealing with recent developments only briefly at the beginning or end of their studies. They explore the issues of the formation and theory of sharia, its methodologies, and its prescriptions, in great detail. There is also a rich selection of literature about particular aspects of sharia, on Islam and constitutional law, Islam and human rights, the status of women and family law in the Arab world, Islamic criminal law, Islamic courts, etc.

In contrast, this book looks at the processes of incorporation of sharia in national legal systems from a socio-legal perspective. This means that the authors do not only describe the contents of the law, but also try to shed light on the formation and functioning of law in context. One of the strong points of socio-legal scholarship is its capacity to distinguish law from social reality, 'law in the books' from 'law in action', text from context. This is important because it is precisely in this border area that confusion and contestation about sharia have often originated.

As for the historical parts of the respective country chapters, the authors have identified longitudinal and recent trends. In the sections about recent history (1985 to the present) they pay particular attention to governance contexts, facilitating our understanding of why actors made certain decisions. Thus we have looked at law as a reflection of political and social forces and values that have evolved over time in particular societies.

The study's focus on national laws raises questions about its relevance, such as: Do these laws really matter to ordinary people? How do these laws relate to the local social realities of justice seekers? Several of the chapters refer to studies in legal anthropology about the interaction between citizens and legal institutions. I regret that the scope of this project did not allow more space to the authors, some of whom are indeed social and legal anthropologists, to go down to the grassroots level and present local case studies. Still, you may notice that much of their writing is informed by first-hand knowledge of local developments. In this way, the book tries to link law not only to history and governance, but also to society at large.

The term 'Muslim countries' in this book is used merely to describe the setting. It does not imply any social, political, or legal characteristic, and has no explanatory value. The term 'developing countries' is more important in this respect. The countries in this book are often societies that face serious development problems. Not only do many developing countries suffer from insecurity, economic stagnation, poverty, injustice, and a lack of quality education and proper health care, they also see first-hand that their traditional rural societies are falling apart in the face of rapid urbanisation. Breakdown of social control in such transitional societies has led to a rise of social ills common in almost every country in the world – crime, prostitution, drug abuse, drinking. Often socio-political conditions are not conducive for national law and governance to take over the full and effective regulation of society. Corruption, lack of resources, and other inefficiencies appear to be endemic.

The approach taken in this study fits within the academic domain that addresses the formation and functioning of legal systems of developing countries and their contributions to governance and development, which at a number of universities worldwide is now called Law, Governance, and Development (LGD) studies. The impetus for the study at hand stems from that intellectual tradition. LGD studies have their roots partly in the studies of colonial law and postcolonial law. Generally, LGD studies is regarded as part of the broader category of socio-legal studies, which combines the study of law with the legal specialisations of other disciplines.[3]

Many LGD case studies have drawn gloomy conclusions about the effectiveness of national law in Asia, Africa and Latin America, about injustices and the lack of 'real legal certainty'. Explanations often refer to the colonial heritage of legal pluralism, the imbalance of political power, uneven economic conditions, and/or legal and institutional weaknesses. These explanations differ considerably from an approach, which mainly points at the islamisation of law as the root cause of injustice and failing legal systems in the Muslim world. Such approach has become fashionable among some islamologists and philosophers, who consider Koranic verses as the unchangeable, uniform, normative essence of Muslim thought and behaviour. In contrast, socio-legal scholars focusing on the interaction between law and social context, are prepared to observe change, and diversity, both in legal texts as well as in social practices.

1.2 Sharia incorporated

Conceptualisation of sharia and Islamic law

This book will often refer to the term 'sharia'. Like its counterpart 'Islamic law' the term 'sharia' is surrounded with confusion between theory and practice, between theological and legal meanings, between internal and external perspectives, and between past and present manifestations.

According to Islamic jurisprudence, theology and historiography, the rules of sharia are based on the revelation by God of his plan for mankind to the Prophet Muhammad until his death in 632 (Vikør 2005: 20). In order to interpret God's will from the available sources, religious scholars developed Islamic jurisprudence (*fiqh*) from the eighth century onwards. The scholars (*ulama*) put God's revelation into effect, drafting a scientific, legal corpus of behavioural rules. Notably, in the first two centuries numerous scholarly *fiqh*-books were filled with case studies and rules. From the outset, many differences of opinion cropped up, for example disagreements over the sources of sharia, its unchanging character, its scope, and its validity 'as law'. Some of the authors, such as Al-Hanafi, Al-Maliki, Al-Shafi'i and Al-Hanbali gained great influence. Their names were given to different *fiqh*-schools, which came to represent 'the dominant opinions' of what we may call 'classical' sharia, especially since two centuries later Muhammad's 'gate to free interpretation (*ijtihad*) was closed'.[4]

The profession of the Muslim scholars who, thus, studied and developed the sharia, has always been a mixture of what we nowadays would call theologians and jurists. In Arabic those among the *ulama*, who specialise in Islamic jurisprudence are referred to as *faqih* (plur. *fuqaha*, expert of *fiqh*, jurist, or 'legal' scholar). They may work as a scholar and teacher in a seminary, as a *mufti* (the one who issues *fatwas* or legal opinions about what rule of sharia applies to a particular case) or as a judge (*qadi*).[5] The broader category of *ulama*, is usually translated as 'religious scholars', or just 'scholars'. While in this book different authors use all of these terms sometimes in different ways, in the introduction and conclusion of this book I will refer to the *ulama* as 'scholars'. Islamic law has often been said to be a law of scholars, as opposed to civil or continental law, which is often regarded as law-maker's law, and common law, which is supposedly judge-made.

It has been the perennial objective of Islamic scholars to discover and develop 'the sharia' as a concrete body of rules and principles. Common people used to consult the scholars, asking them what 'the sharia' would prescribe in a particular case. Meanwhile, the many differences in interpretation between, for example, Sunnis and Shiis, and between the different schools of law, are obvious. Scholars who studied Islamic jurisprudence have explained the diversity as a result of its open, discursive character, which should help to bridge the gap between the divine abstract source and the variety of human behaviours and contexts to which it should apply. There seems to be agreement among modern scholars about the very diversity of sharia itself. Vikør (2005: 1) states in the introduction to his history of Islamic law:

> There is no such thing as a, that is one, Islamic law, a text that clearly and unequivocally establishes all the rules of a Muslim's behaviour. There is a great divergence of views, not just between opposing currents, but also between individual scholars within the legal currents, of exactly what rules belong to Islamic law. The jurists have had to learn to live with this disagreement on and variety in the contents of the law.

Likewise, another scholar of Islamic law, Peters (1997: 260) wonders if sharia is a legal system at all '[...] because such a diversity of opinions exists next to one another [and] [e]ven within the schools of law there are often differences of opinion'. The rules of sharia are not unambiguously laid down in the law, but rather they are formulated in scholarly explorations or, as Peters states, 'in a continuous debate with their predecessors and colleagues' (ibid: 260, translation by JMO). Fuller (2003: 57), a senior political observer, for instance, states:

> There is no one Sharia but rather many different, even contesting ways to build a legal structure in accordance with God's vision for mankind. A single Sharia doesn't exist. It is not a book that one can purchase. It is shaped, and interpreted by humans' differing understanding of what the Qur'an and the Prophet's life and experience mean.

Yet, we face the problem that many people – from 'puritan' Islamists to their Western critics – continue to assume and propagate that the sharia is a uniform thing, a fixed set of norms that is binding upon all Muslims, regardless of where they live, and which cannot be modernised, because it is 'divine and unchangeable'. Indeed, many nations, groups, and individuals use the term sharia to present *their* interpretation as *the* definitive divine law. How then can this idea of a fixed, unchangeable sharia, deriving from Islamic theology, be consonant with the social reality of widely diverging interpretations of sharia, or, as Fuller and others suggest, of a diversity of 'sharia's'? A realistic solution starts with the acknowledgment that the manifold ways in which law-makers, judges, religious scholars, academics, and others refer to the sharia, should be analysed and categorised. In the course of this project it has proven useful to discern four distinct ways in which the term sharia is used, namely as divine abstract sharia, as classical sharia, as historically transferred sharia, and as contemporary sharia.

First, *divine, abstract sharia*: this is God's plan for mankind and as such contains the rules for good order and human behaviour that should guide his religious community. The existence of this divine, abstract sharia is accepted as a fact by all devout Muslims, 'moderate' or 'puritan' (see 1.5). Before it can be applied in practice it needs explanation and elaboration by scholars. Al-Azmeh (1993: 12) has considered the implications of this abstract meaning of sharia for the debates surrounding islamisation of law, noting that:

> Islamic law is not a code. This is why the frequently heard call for its 'application' is meaningless, most particularly when calls are made for the application of sharia – this last term does not designate law, but is a general term designating good order, much like nomos or dharma [...].

Secondly, *classical sharia*: this is the corpus of rules, principles, and cases that were drawn up by *fiqh*-scholars in the first two centuries after the Prophet Muhammad. Sharia, in this sense, is concrete and refers to the classical writings of leading scholars and the early commentaries on them. As such, classical sharia necessarily bears the traces of how religion, society, and politics were experienced in particular parts of the world more than a millennium ago.

Thirdly, *historically transferred sharia*: this includes the whole body of interpretations developed and transmitted throughout a history of more than a 1,000 years across the Muslim world, from the alleged closure of the gate of free interpretation to its reopening in the nineteenth century, and up to the present day. The notion of historically transferred sharia encompasses an immense, full spectrum of considerations and ideologies – ranging from personal beliefs to state ideology, from living law to formal positive law, from moderate to 'puritan' interpretations. While classical sharia, as taught and interpreted by mainstream, conservative religious scholars, has been the main point of reference in most Muslim countries, certain modernist scholars have seen and seized opportunities for smaller and larger reforms of sharia. Usually, though not always, they did so on the basis of the classical religious sources and commentaries. This was especially so in the nineteenth and twentieth centuries when many interpretations of the classical sharia were introduced as reforms of the national legal systems of Muslim countries, including, for example, throughout the Ottoman Empire and in Egypt, Iran, Afghanistan, and Pakistan.

Lastly, *contemporary sharia*: this concept of sharia refers to the whole of principles, rules, cases, and interpretations that are actually in use at present throughout the Muslim world. Contemporary sharia has become a vast, fragmented, and dispersed mass. Ideas travel ever faster following domestic and international migration, the missionary (*daqwa*) movements since the 1970s, and the use of journals, radio, television, and the Internet. While governments, institutes of higher religious education, and mass movements all promulgate and publish their own versions of sharia, individuals and study groups around the world seek their own preferred scholars to instruct them about the prescriptions of 'the sharia'.

Hopefully this fourfold distinction will help the reader, when coming across the term sharia in this book, to understand from its context which notion of sharia is actually meant. It may also help to recognise those instances in which different meanings of sharia are conflated, such as in the famous phrase 'introducing the sharia'. Some authors, also in this volume, use the term sharia mainly for the divine sharia, which is abstract and general. They call the other three – all results of human activity – *fiqh*.

Sharia incorporated

The title *Sharia incorporated* is meant to catch the essence of the twelve stories that make up this book.[6] In all Muslim countries of old sharia has been regarded as a divine plan. To be applicable and practical, however, the principles and rules of sharia must be interpreted and laid down. This has always raised vital questions, such as: Who will do this? When and where? To what extent? How? And with what purpose? Will there be a check on this power? What if people do not agree? Initially, as indicated above, religious scholars performed this task, and often with a considerable degree of autonomy from the rulers. That situation has changed notably since the early nineteenth century, when the world was gradually divided up into independent states.

States by definition consist of institutions that are supposed to have the authority to make and enforce rules that govern their people. Their internal and external sovereignty is a *conditio sine qua non* of their existence. Therefore, states can in principle not accept the existence of a parallel structure with similar objectives, unless it can be incorporated in the structures and laws of that state itself. This is exactly what we have seen happening with sharia.

Intermediate stages of incorporation occurred as long as Muslim territories formed part of colonial empires – or the Ottoman empire for that matter – during the nineteenth and early twentieth centuries. After independence, which came to the Muslim states in three big waves, in the 1920s, the 1940s, and the 1960s (see 14.2), the new political elites had to decide how religion should be embodied in ideology, policy, and law. Suddenly nationalist leaders and religious leaders, who had fought side by side in the struggle for independence, became opponents. For in all Muslim countries the new political elite of independent states opted for supremacy of their own authority, their own decrees, their own national laws. That was the new rule of the game, and it would not change. All other normative systems and the traditional elite were to be incorporated into the state's legal, political, and administrative systems. As such, state interference with sharia became broad and deep. Political and legal marginalisation became the fate of both sharia as well as of the class of scholar-jurists, who had developed and applied it.

As you will read in the following chapters, the modalities of incorporation differed hugely. The kings of Saudi Arabia, who have always had to rely on support of the powerful religious elite of Wahhabi scholars, proclaimed the Quran and the Sunna to be the country's 'constitution', and as such denied that name to the 'basic law' that spells out the organisation of that state. They gave the Wahhabi scholars important positions and powerful voices within the state legal and political system. To the contrary, the new elite under Atatürk removed sharia from the Turkish legal system and kept tight control on religion through the *Diyanet*, the state office for religious affairs. The King of Morocco became 'commander of the faithful' and had a decisive voice in how sharia-based law would be codified in family legislation. The government of Egypt accepted in its constitution the principles of sharia to be '*the* source of legislation', but ultimately decided not to adopt its substantive criminal law, and to modernise its family law. In Iran, the Shah failed to recognise the political power of the scholars in his country; upon the overthrow of his regime, Khomeini and his clerical associates became the new political elite who could incorporate their views in state policies and national law.

A consistent fact in all twelve national laws except for secular Turkey is that sharia has been incorporated in the state system, often adapting old interpretations of sharia to socio-economic changes. Although criticised and contested by many different – if not all – sides, the incorporation of sharia by the state remains essentially a fact of life. About this incorporation different political camps use different discourses to further their goals. So it is not uncommon to see that certain acts of incorporation are regarded as islamisation of national law by one camp and as annexation of sharia by the state by another (see 1.5).

1.3 Countries, concerns, and contested issues

Selecting twelve Muslim countries

In order to have a fair representation of the Muslim world, twelve Muslim majority countries were selected. These twelve countries represent about two thirds of the world's total Muslim population of 1.5 billion (see table 1 below). Most Muslims live in South and Southeast Asia, and a considerable number live in Sub-Saharan Africa. This study includes countries from those regions, thus avoiding the common tendency of equating the Muslim world with the Arab world or the Middle East. The selected countries include five countries from the Middle East and North Africa (Egypt, Morocco, Saudi Arabia, Sudan, and Turkey), three from Central and South Asia (Afghanistan, Iran, Pakistan), two from Southeast Asia (Malaysia, Indonesia) and two from West Africa (Mali and Nigeria). The politico-legal orientation of the governments of these countries ranges from 'puritan' to 'moderate' to 'secularist'. They vary in size of their population, percentage of Muslims, their social and economic development, their security situation, the degree of democratisation, and their political stability.

Table 1 *Twelve countries by number of inhabitants, % Muslims*

Country	*Inhabitants (Mln.)*	*Muslims (%)*
Egypt	80,3	90
Morocco	33,8	99
Saudi Arabia	28,0	100
Sudan	41,0	70
Turkey	71,2	100
Afghanistan	31,9	99
Iran	70,0	98
Pakistan	174,0	97
Indonesia	234,7	86
Malaysia	24,8	60
Mali	12,6	90
Nigeria	140,0	50

Source: Bartleby: http://www.bartelby.com/151/indexes/countries/1.html, accessed March 2010

For the purposes of this study, a 'Muslim country' is understood to be a country of which at least 55 per cent of the population is Muslim. The international organisation of Muslim countries, the Organisation of the Islamic Conference, has 57 member states. Of these, 41 or roughly three quarters meet the above-mentioned definition. The fourth quarter is made up of member states with Muslim minorities. For a long time Malaysia was considered a borderline case at 55 per cent, but this number is now commonly estimated at 60 per cent. Strictly speaking,

Nigeria, with a Muslim population of only about 50 per cent, does not meet our definition of a Muslim country. However, the size and importance of the country – and the ramifications of the programmes of sharia implementation recently undertaken in twelve of its Northern states – led to the decision to include Nigeria in this study.

Main concerns, contested issues, common assumptions, and questions

There are four main concerns that have arisen as a consequence of the islamisation of law:

(i) Supremacy of sharia
(ii) Legal status of women
(iii) Cruel corporal punishments
(iv) Violations of human rights

The book's preface refers to the post 9/11 context in which these concerns took centre stage, namely heated domestic and international debates and strongly conflicting ideas on Islam, and especially sharia. To Muslim 'puritans', embracing the sharia has always seemed the very best thing that they themselves and their country could do. Muslim 'moderates' have held different views both of the role of sharia in state and society and of how sharia should be interpreted; but being Muslims, they have of course not been opposed to sharia as such. For many people in the West, however, sharia started symbolising the main foreign threat to their society. Among those alarmed, vocal academics, politicians, and other opinion leaders embarked on a more confrontational course.

For years the abovementioned concerns were constantly brought to public attention, and the sensitised media were able to report almost daily on worrisome issues from the Muslim world – topics ranging from the prosecution of Baha'i in Egypt, to the rise of a 'puritan' Muslim party in Morocco, to honour killings in Turkey, to the hanging of young homosexuals in Iran, to violent attacks in Pakistan, or to public flogging in Aceh, Indonesia. Most of the headlines covered a specific issue that seemed to fit well within one of the four main concerns mentioned above. For the purpose of systematic analysis, I have listed those worrisome issues and added the alarmist assumptions that since a few years have become so common in the West.

Supremacy of sharia

Within this first area of concern, the following issues can be distinguished:

- *Scope.* This issue concerns the extent to which sharia influences a national legal system as a whole. Many assume that in Muslim countries sharia has pervaded all areas of public law and private law.

- *Territory.* This issue involves the geographical spread of particular sharia-based laws within a particular country. It is often assumed that islamisation of the law in a specific district or province represents a wider change and spread throughout the whole country.
- *Orientation.* This issue touches on which of the competing views and movements within the Muslim world is actually dominant, especially in interpretations of sharia. Many assume that islamisation of law automatically implies the supremacy of 'puritan' views, rather than 'moderate' perspectives.
- *Basic norm.* This begs the question as to whether the foundational norm of a country's legal system is the constitution itself – as opposed to 'the sharia' or 'Islam' – if particular provisions in the constitution state that sharia is the main source of legislation or that every law should comply with the tenets of Islam. It is often assumed that an increasing number of constitutions have actually introduced sharia as their highest or basic norm.
- *Legal decision makers.* This issue is about who ultimately decides the rules in a legal system: religious scholars, who are experts of the *fiqh*? Or the office holders and officials of the state, such as elected parliamentarians, administrators and bureaucrats, and professional judges trained in national, largely secular, law. Many assume that sharia-based legal systems are theocracies that leave decisions in law-making, interpretation, and adjudication to religious scholars trained in Islamic religious institutions rather than to professional policy-makers and jurists trained in secular universities. Consequently, law enforcement in these systems is assumed to be entrusted to a religion-based sharia police.
- *Islamic codification.* The issue is whether the existing law codes, which were often based on Western models, have been thrown overboard completely and replaced by fully Islamic codes. It is often assumed that Western law codes have indeed been replaced by new Islamic codes that are totally different.
- *Islamic courts.* The issue is whether states have established separate Islamic judiciaries that have taken on the functions of secular state courts. A popular assumption is that Islamic courts have indeed been established or entrusted with increased powers.
- *Islamic ruler.* The issue involves the conception of an Islamic government as essentially authoritarian, without powerful elected parliaments or independent courts capable of maintaining a check on the powers of the ruler or head of state. Many assume that heads of the executive power possess vast legal authority derived from sharia, and without any democratic constraints.

Most of these eight issues are addressed in a country's constitutional law.

Legal status of women

Within this second area of concern we selected the following issues.

- *Repudiation (casting off).* The question is whether a man's right, bestowed upon him by classical sharia, to repudiate his wife at will, unilaterally, and without having to give any reason, is still valid. It is often assumed that husbands can indeed divorce their wives arbitrarily by unilateral declaration without judicial or governmental approval.
- *Polygamy.* This issue involves the right of a man, as provided for by classical sharia, to conclude multiple marriages with up to four wives, as he likes and without the need for permission of the first wife or of state authorities. Many assume that Muslim men can marry up to four wives at will.
- *Divorce.* This issue concerns the possibilities for a woman to obtain a divorce from a court, which according to classical sharia are very limited. A common opinion is that a woman can hardly initiate a divorce.
- *Inheritance.* The issue is that classical sharia provides that in the case of inheritance a female heir inherits half of what a male heir in a similar position would inherit. It is generally assumed that a woman indeed inherits only half of the portion of a man.

These four issues are addressed in a country's personal status, family, and inheritance law.

Cruel corporal punishments

In this third area of concern, cruel corporal punishments, the most prominent issues are threefold:

- *Hadd offences.* This issue involves the enactment of five, and in some countries six, criminal provisions, based on classical sharia, that prescribe heavy corporal punishments for specific crimes, namely extramarital sex (*zina*), accusation of extramarital sex, robbery, theft, consumption of alcohol, and, according to some schools of thought, apostasy. Many assume such provisions have indeed been enacted.
- *Execution of corporal punishments.* The issue is whether it is common practice to actually administer corporal punishments, such as stoning and amputation. It is readily assumed that these barbaric punishments are regularly executed throughout the Muslim world.
- *Retribution and blood money.* This issue involves the enactment of criminal provisions, based on classical sharia, that entail the

retribution (*qisas*) of violent offences, such as murder, manslaughter, and assault, according to the principle of an 'eye for an eye'; and that retribution can also be bought off with 'blood money' (*diyya*). It is generally assumed that retaliation provisions are common and applied in practice.

These three issues are addressed in a country's criminal law.

Violations of human rights

This fourth area of concern is different from those mentioned above in that it departs from established normative standards – those of international human rights treaties with universal objectives –, and refers to institutional mechanisms for identification and condemnation of violations. It includes the abovementioned concern with women's legal status by reference to the right to freedom from discrimination, enacted in the international Convention on the Elimination of All Forms of Discrimination against Women (CEDAW). It also encompasses the right to physical and mental integrity, which is guaranteed by the international Convention against Torture, and Other Cruel, Inhuman or Degrading Treatment or Punishment (CAT). This area of concern is thus broader and addresses all areas of law. For the purpose of this study four issues are selected.

- *Freedom from discrimination.* The issue is that besides the discrimination of women in family and inheritance law, sharia-based law also discriminates against several other groups, including homosexuals, non-Muslims, 'deviant' Muslims, adherents of other religions, and atheists. The assumption is that such discriminatory provisions have indeed been enacted, and as such make life for minority groups difficult, or even impossible.
- *Freedom of religion.* The issue is the Islamic prohibition against leaving one's faith, which constitutes the crime of apostasy and is punishable under classical sharia law with heavy penalties, allegedly even in some circumstances the death penalty. It is commonly assumed that criminalisation of apostasy violates the freedom of religion for Muslims.
- *Other prohibitions of and prescriptions for (un)Islamic behaviour.* This issue relates to the legal obligation to refer to Islam, its prescriptions, and its symbols with deep respect only – for women to wear the veil, for Muslims to refrain from music and dance, and for compulsory education in Islamic scriptures. Many assume that such provisions are often enacted and in practice encroach upon fundamental freedoms.
- *Adherence to international human rights law.* The issue is whether Muslim countries have accessed, ratified, and implemented the

major human rights treaties. It is often assumed that Muslim countries are not bound by such human rights treaties, and that they have not established national human rights laws and institutions to promote human rights domestically.

Economy and finance

Each of the twelve country studies in this book pays attention to most of the abovementioned concerns and issues. In addition, they briefly touch on sharia-based law in the sphere of economy and finance. Such law, it is assumed, includes a ban on Islamic banks to charge interest. Muslims must also pay special religious taxes to religious authorities, symbolising their adherence to religious, rather than worldly, authorities. As there is no direct connection with the violation of any human right, this aspect has led to minimal, if any, Western concerns and criticisms in the international debates on sharia and the rule of law. To the contrary, Western banks, law firms, and governments have taken a keen interest in Islamic banking.

Monitoring the islamisation of law

The abovementioned issues, totalling about twenty, constitute a useful set for monitoring the impact of islamisation on national legal systems. The selection of issues remains contestable, but by and large this set may serve as a fair representation of the issues that have dominated domestic and international debates about Islam and sharia. For the authors of the country studies, each issue was an open question, to which a verifiable answer had to be found. By aggregating the outcomes of the twelve country studies, this research project has obtained a rich set of data that enables a systematic comparative overview of legal provisions. If we also take into account the historical and socio-political background of legal change on these issues, we may begin to grasp a better understanding of the changing relationship between sharia and national law in the Muslim world.

1.4 National legal systems, three delicate areas of law

Composition of national legal systems

At first glance most developing countries seem to have national legal systems set up like that of any more developed country. The term 'national legal system' here refers to the whole body of legal rules, legal institutions, and legal processes. Developing countries have laws on any conceivable topic, many of which closely resemble the laws of developed countries. They also have much the same legal institutions, such as legislatures at central and regional levels, ministries, executive agencies, regional and local governments, supreme courts, appeal courts and courts of first instance, ombudsman institutions, bar associations, law faculties, legal aid institutions, etc. As most Muslim countries fall in the category of developing countries, the main set up of their laws and legal institutions is not different from that of any other country.

A closer look at the structure of legal systems of developing countries, however, reveals layers and fragmentation. Under the surface of the more visible present-day national laws, we find layers of legal provisions and ideologies deriving from, for example, the socialist, authoritarian era of the 1960s and 1970s, of colonial law, of religious law, and of tribal customary law. The 'geo-legal' structure of a country, though, is far from uniform. Customary law, for example, may apply in one place, for one group, or for one particular topic, while elsewhere, for other parties or a different topic, religious law or a national law may apply instead of the customary law applied elsewhere. The layers of law differ in territorial scope, in subject matter, and in institutional set-up.

Customary law is strong in rural areas, and often concerned with dispute settlement, land law, inheritance law, and in many regions with family law. Its key actors are traditional authorities, i.e. chiefs and traditional councils. In most Muslim countries Islamic law has a particularly strong impact on family and inheritance law. Since colonial law used to recognise the indigenous law as 'law of the natives', it gave rise to the formal incorporation of customary and religious courts in the judiciary. After independence, most young states wanted to assert full control over the law of their subjects. Rather than maintaining the colonial legacy they strived for unification of their legal systems. And indeed, most developing countries have developed an impressive amount of national laws and established the relevant national legal institutions to implement these laws. In comparison to the staggering numbers of modern national laws and regulations, the hard kernel of sharia rules over which actual agreement exists, is rather miniscule. Yet, in the same way as customary law, sharia has continued to play a role until today, as we shall see in the country studies.

The inheritance of colonial law also consists of codifications of civil and criminal law, of jurisprudence, of laws of procedure, of types of judicial organisation, of legal styles and ways of legal reasoning, legal education, and legal language adopted primarily from European models. The colonial legal traditions have been carried on in developing countries by legal professions and scholarship. Former British colonies like Nigeria, Pakistan, and Malaysia are now members of the Commonwealth and still exchange legal information with other Commonwealth countries. Former French colonies – e.g. Morocco and Mali – are still oriented towards French legal development and legal information. Remarkably, French law has also been a major reference for the codifications of Egypt, Iran, and Afghanistan, even though they were never colonised. Egyptian law, especially its civil code, has had a major impact throughout the Middle East, from the Gulf States to Afghanistan. In contrast, Turkish civil law has largely been based on the Swiss Civil Code. Thus, different 'centers of radiation', to use the concept of Arminjon's work on comparative law, have influenced the legal systems of developing countries, including those which form part of the Muslim world (Arminjon, Nolde & Wolf: 1952). Table 2 (see below) provides some basic information about the centers of radiation influencing the twelve legal systems under review, such as their constitution, colonial legal tradition, school of Islamic jurisprudence, and the role of customary law.

Today, domestic laws are increasingly influenced by public international law. International organisations like the WTO, ILO, FAO, WHO, IMF, World Bank, and UNDP provide advice on domestic legal drafts. Financial aid is often made conditional upon the adoption of law reform. Human rights conventions and movements have also prompted legal change. Competition between developing countries for foreign direct investment has been another driving force behind emulating the laws of 'successful' countries. While this enumeration of centres of radiation is far from complete, it is clear that law-makers in developing countries have been drawing from various domestic, foreign, international, and transnational sources in their efforts to achieve national policy objectives.

Dysfunctions of legal systems

Whatever sources have been used in the formation of the laws of developing countries, and whether they include versions of sharia or not, it is common knowledge that the actual operation of these legal systems is marked by serious dysfunctions and shortcomings. Many legal systems simply fail to fulfil what is their main task, namely providing justice and legal certainty for all.

Table 2 *Twelve national legal systems with their legal traditions*

Country	*Year of independence*	*Year of present constitution/ last amendments*	*Colony/ Protectorate*	*Legal tradition*		
				Civil law/ Common law	*Fiqh tradition*	*Scope of customary law (1: small; 2: moderate; 3: vast)*
Egypt	1922	1971[1]	Ottoman, Britain	Civil law	Hanafi	1
Morocco	1956	1996	France	Civil law	Maliki	2
Saudi Arabia	1932	-[2]	-	-	Hanbali	1
Sudan	1956	2005[3]	Britain	Civil/ Common law	Hanafi	3
Turkey	1923	1982[4]	-	Civil	-	
Afghanistan	1919	2004	(Britain)	Civil law	Hanafi/Shia	3
Iran	-[5]	1979	-	Civil law	Shia	2
Pakistan	1947	1973[6]	Britain	Common law	Hanafi	3
Indonesia	1945	1945[7]	Netherlands	Civil law	Shafi i	2
Malaysia	1957	1957[8]	Britain	Common law	Shafi i	2
Mali	1960	1992	France	Civil law	Maliki	3
Nigeria	1960	1999	Britain	Common law	Maliki	3

[1] Several important amendments were incorporated, notably in 1980, 2005 and 2007.
[2] According to the Basic Ordinance (1992) the country's divine sources of Islamic law form its constitution.
[3] This is an Interim Constitution for a five years period, after which South Sudan will decide about its future.
[4] The constitution was last amended in 2004
[5] The history of independent Iran goes back thousands of years.
[6] Many amendments were incorporated.
[7] Since 1998 four important amendments have strengthened the rule of law considerably.
[8] Since 1957 hundreds of amendments were enacted.

This lack of justice and legal certainty can in part be attributed to legal causes, such as the inadequacy of laws, restricted or faulty legal mandates of institutions, and incomplete or vaguely construed legal procedures. In addition, the dysfunctions are closely related to other, non-legal problems of development and governance, such as insecurity, poverty, illiteracy, authoritarianism, and corruption. Curing the problems of legal systems, therefore, presupposes progress in other areas. The plurality, fragmentation, and overlapping of normative systems in most developing countries add to the problematic nature of governance and law. It would require much imagination to see how the general Islamist recipe – 'introduction of the sharia' – can provide a practically feasible way out of these complex problems. Meanwhile, the common objective and direction to which most countries have subscribed is the 'rule of law'. This has become an appealing concept because it reflects the ideal of justice, which underlies all ideologies, religions, and nation-states, and it also provides for an elaborate set of legal and institutional standards with practical guidance.

Rule of law and human rights: authoritative standards?

Rule of law has become the most common international umbrella concept prescribing normative standards for legal systems (Tamanaha 2004). International donor policies have made good governance and the rule of law a focal point of their assistance to developing countries (Carothers 2003). Meanwhile, there has been much debate about the clash, as Huntington phrased it, between the 'Western' concept of the rule of law and Islamic concepts of law, or more specifically about the compatibility of sharia with human rights. But what does the rule of law mean, how Western is this concept, and how does it relate to human rights? Bedner (2010) has concluded on the basis of an extensive literature review that the rule of law concept can be best understood by distinguishing two complementary sets of standards, namely procedural and substantive standards, as well as a third set regarding what he calls 'control mechanisms'.

The main procedural standards of the rule of law, as accepted in authoritative documents and academic literature, are that (a) state policies must employ written laws – acts, ordinances, decisions – as major instruments; (b) all state actions must be subject to law; (c) the law must be clear and consistent in substance, accessible and predictable for citizens, and general in its application; and (d) the substance of the law and its effectuation must be influenced by citizen approval.

As for the main substantive standards of the rule of law, there is consensus that all laws and their interpretations must be subject to (a) fundamental principles of justice; and (b) human rights and freedoms of individuals, notably civil and political rights, social and economic rights, and group rights.

In order to control compliance with these procedural and substantive principles, the rule of law, as Bedner has proposed, also requires a third set of elements to be in place, namely of control mechanisms: (a) the executive arm of the state must establish internal correction mechanisms on unlawful administrative actions; (b) an independent judiciary, accessible for every citizen, must be responsible for conflict resolution through interpretation and application of the law; and (c) complementary quasi-judicial institutions, such as an ombudsman, a national human rights-institution, and various tribunals, must be in place to further ensure compliance with the rule of law.

Over the last few decades the legal systems of the world have undoubtedly moved towards this rule of law. Yet, while country A's legal system may have succeeded in complying with most rule of law standards, it can still violate certain human rights. In the case of a Muslim country, such violation may stem from its adherence to certain interpretations of sharia. 'Puritan' regimes will as a matter of principle refuse to formally review provisions of the divine sharia against secular legal standards, but instead prescribe a reverse testing. 'Moderate' regimes rather tend to accept the rule of law to be the dominant standard for most practical purposes. In fact, both camps can agree about most of the abovementioned elements of the rule of law, since there is no conflict with any sharia provision. Yet, certain human rights standards are contested by puritans time and again as being 'Western' and 'un-Islamic'. From a human rights perspective, it is precisely the violation of those standards that has given rise to the concerns and contested issues listed above in 1.3. The recurring conflicts about those issues have made certain parts of national law in the Muslim world rather thorny and delicate, politically speaking. We find those delicate parts mostly in constitutional, family, and criminal law. For this reason, the focus in the legal sections of each country study is on these three areas of law and their relationship to sharia in the country at hand.

1.5 Ideological-religious currents and discourses

The moderate-puritan dichotomy and beyond

Throughout the twentieth century different views were held across the Muslim world about what should be the relationship between sharia and national law. They ranged from Saudi Arabia's preservation of classical sharia to Turkey's strict secularism. Two discourses have fuelled the interpretation and implementation of sharia more than any other, namely those espoused by 'puritans' on the one hand, and by 'moderates' on the other hand. Both believe, as Abou El Fadl explains, 'in the oneness, completion and perfection of God' and in his mercy and compassion (Abou el Fadl 2007: 127-132). They also agree that God should be approached by human beings 'with submission, humility and gratitude'. However, 'puritans' and 'moderates' differ dramatically in their ideas about what God wants from human beings, how mankind should use its ability to reason, and in particular about the role of sharia in that relationship.

Moderate Muslims believe that in the moment of creation God has entrusted humanity with a heavy responsibility, by providing human beings with rationality and the ability to differentiate between right and wrong. They should use this capacity to relentlessly strive to achieve goodness, which includes justice, mercy, and compassion. Those are actually the real objectives of God's law. As Abou El Fadl writes:

> In moderate thought, God is too great to be embodied in a code of law. The law helps Muslims in the *quest* for Godliness, but Godliness cannot be equated to the law. [...] the technicalities of the law cannot be allowed to subvert the objectives of the law. Therefore, if the application of the law produces injustice, suffering, and misery, this means that the law is not serving its purposes [...] then the law must be reinterpreted, suspended, or reconstructed, depending on the law in question (ibid: 130-131).

In contrast, in the 'puritan' conception, good Muslims should be fearful of God and study and obey his rules as strictly as possible. Whatever is in the sacred sharia is thought to reflect God's mercy and compassion. So, what they need is a sharia which prescribes exact rules to which they can submit by strict compliance. Through this only will they obtain salvation:

> Through meticulous obedience, Muslims will avoid punishment in the Hereafter and will enter Heaven. [...] By performing acts of submission, Muslims earn good points, and by disobeying God they earn sins (or bad points). In the Final Day, God will total up the good points and the sins. Heaven or Hell is determined by the balance of points [...] (ibid: 127).

In the 'puritan' paradigm there are no grounds for legal reforms that take contemporary socio-economic changes into account. In the 'puritan' view:

> The actual social impact that the law might have upon people is considered irrelevant. Although people might feel that the law is

harsh or that its application results in social suffering, this perception is considered delusional (ibid: 128-129).

While the opposition between 'moderates' and 'puritans' has been a constant throughout the history of Islam, contemporary politics and societies feature an ideological-religious spectrum which is in fact broader and more complex than this dichotomy. Orientations of strategic Islamic movements and groups range from nationalist, secularist, human rights, feminist, liberal, social services, clean government, modernist, and democratic, to conservative, traditionalist, orthodox, pan-islamist, radical, and ultimately, revolutionary, militant, and terrorist (cf. Fuller 2003; Hallaq 2003). In practice, these orientations often overlap and the meanings and connotations of the labels often differ. Political positioning of such movements on religious issues often intersects with other issues of domestic and foreign policy. Many of these movements and groups are quite pragmatic and versatile, as power configurations surrounding them are in constant flux and choices must be made between competing political discourses.

Major discourses about incorporation of sharia

Different political actors have voiced a variety of discourses on the incorporation of sharia. Governments have done their best to present the incorporation as a deliberate policy that both demonstrates their respect for religious beliefs among the people and provides them with state-guaranteed legal certainty. According to this discourse the government has opted for an incorporation that contributes to nation-building and socio-economic progress, and is thus beneficial. While certain groups may disagree with the outcome, the government has acted as an arbitrator who, standing above the parties, has come up with the best possible and most balanced solution. Often governments have ensured themselves of the support of high-ranking clerics, who have gone along with this state discourse about the beneficial incorporation of sharia.

In contrast, Islamic scholars, who have *not* posited themselves as an extension of the government, have presented the incorporation of sharia as the political elite's erroneous appropriation of the power to interpret God's will, to ascertain the rules of sharia, and to administer justice accordingly. This power used to be theirs. So, for them, the incorporation of sharia constitutes a marginalisation of their profession and the distortion of a good thing that has now fallen into the wrong hands. Academic expositions about the transformations of sharia often concur with this narrative. Hallaq (2009) describes the fate of sharia as the result of a lost battle. He points to the fact that the political elites of the independent Muslim countries have interfered much more broadly and deeper in religion in their societies than their colonial predecessors ever dared. Feldman (2008) similarly depicts the scholars as the good experts of justice who used to exert a necessary and beneficial influence on authoritarian rulers, until modern bureaucratic regimes chose to sideline them and made a mess of what used to be a capable religious administration of justice.

The disappointment of the scholars about their marginalisation by the state is not shared by the 'puritans'. In their discourse, the incorporation of sharia is the product of an essentially impious, amoral, and opportunistic governance. They contend that rulers and scholars have both failed to comply with God's law; they have indulged in luxury and corruption, neglected their real duties, and plunged their country into misery. Incorporation of sharia, as it was conducted by such unfaithful elites – lackeys of the West! – must be brought to an end so that revolutionary Islamist forces can take over and promulgate new laws in full accordance with God's will.

While these are perhaps three of the leading discourses about incorporation of sharia in the Muslim world, the first two make themselves seldom heard in the West, while the third has got through only to some extent. In Europe and North America another discourse about this incorporation dominates all others, namely that which equates incorporation of sharia with islamisation of law, deterioration of human rights, and a threat to both world peace and Western civilisation.

1.6 Towards a realistic history of sharia and national law

Selecting turning points and historical periods

The interaction between sharia and national legal systems has a long history, which has been depicted in the academic literature in different ways. While Hallaq and Feldman have denounced the displacement of sharia in modernising states, others such as Huntington and Marshall have emphasised the islamisation – if not rapid then 'creeping' – or 'shariaisation' of national law. The country studies in this book attempt a balanced interpretation of that history. Normally the history of each country would deserve its own periodisation. However, for the purpose of comparison this study has used a common periodisation for all country studies.

We have used the year 1800, the beginning of the nineteenth century, as a starting point because it marks the start of major modernisations in law and governance, both in the Ottoman Empire and Egypt, as well as in European colonies in Asia. Since Napoleon's 1798 journey to Egypt, the Middle East was suddenly confronted with European progress and modernity. In this period Islamic modernism emerged and Muslim scholars 'reopened the gate of free interpretation'.

The next turning point, 1920, was chosen since it marks the end of the first World War, the subsequent end of the Ottoman Empire, and the rise to independence of most Muslim countries in the Middle East. What followed was a period of nationalism, state-building, and, especially after 1945, a rapid succession of ideologies and foreign influences. Sharia as a normative system continuously had to face new political contexts, from modernisation and liberalism during the interbellum to socialism and authoritarianism in the 1950s and 1960s. Ambitious legal policies of political elites were often informed by an urgent desire for unification, modernisation, and secularisation and aimed for a wholesale transformation of societies. The governments, however, lacked the capacity to implement, and social resistance to the transformations turned out to be considerable (Allott 1980).

We have chosen 1965 as the starting point for the decline of this over-ambitious nationalist, and often socialist and secular-oriented, rule in a major part of the Muslim world. The heroic age of the first generation of national leaders like Nasser and Sukarno was coming to an end. African decolonisation was largely completed, and many of the young Muslim countries in Asia and Africa went searching for their own ideologies and identities. Disappointed by broken promises of development and the failures of governments, several countries experienced ideological and power vacuums, which in countries, such as Iran, Pakistan, and Sudan were filled by coups that brought islamisation of law and governance.

As noted in the book's preface, developments during the twenty-five years after 1985 have been the subject of heated debates and speculations about the islamisation of law. An important objective of the historical part of this study is to provide a balanced assessment of this process in recent decades.

The histories of national legal systems in the chapters ahead start mainly from around 1800. About the long period before 1800, the studies had to be brief. Yet, the preceding millennium was important as an era that saw the growth and flourishing of sharia, as well as emerging tensions with the laws of the state. Therefore, this section ends with a brief introduction to that early period.

The millennium of sharia as the living law (c. 800-c. 1800)

In theory the legal system of the early, burgeoning Muslim state knew only one lawgiver (God), one prevailing legal system (sharia), and one type of judge (the *qadi*, who formed the single-headed sharia court). Since 750, however, a parallel legal system under the Abbassid Caliph developed, serving practical and administrative needs (Esposito 1998: 22; Vikør 2005: 190). As rulers do, the Caliph made rules, issued decrees, and passed judgments himself. Formally, these decisions served to carry out his main task, namely the preservation of sharia. The justification under sharia was that rulers were granted a discretionary power, or *siyasa*. This power was seen as permissible – acknowledged by the *ulama* – in so far as it did not conflict with the sharia (Esposito 1998: 23; Vikør 2005: 192).

A part of this parallel system under the Caliph, a sort of professional administration of justice, was set up with boards of grievances or *mazalim* courts. Initially, these were only intended for complaints against high government officials or judges, but gradually the Caliph broadened the jurisdiction of the *mazalim* courts to include criminal, administrative, and trade cases. In this way, the competence of the sharia courts was reduced to family and inheritance law, religious endowments, and in certain regions, perhaps also contract law. The *mazalim* courts were not the only type of non-sharia courts that existed from the early days of the caliphate. More important for most people were the police courts (*shurta* courts), which operated as a separate system based on police investigations and which were 'unhampered' by the strict rules of evidence prescribed by the sharia (Vikør 2005: 190-195). Thus, a dual system of state law and religious law operated, theoretically unified by the principle of *siyasa*. As most country chapters will reveal, customary law prevailed in most rural areas, as a third important element.

From 1500, after centuries of stagnation, several Muslim princedoms developed into expansive empires with considerable military power: the Ottoman Empire in the Middle East and Southeast Europe, the Mughal Empire on the Indian subcontinent, and the Shiite Safavid Empire in Persia. As cultural capitals, Istanbul, Delhi, and Isfahan became worthy successors to the Baghdad of the Abbasids (Esposito 1998: 26). In addition, the Ottoman sultan bore the religious title of Caliph. Islam provided the legitimation, the political ideology, and the law for the governing of the three large empires. Sharia was the official prevailing law in all three. The actual scope of sharia courts, however, was usually limited to family law and inheritance law. The sultans continued to issue their own decrees and maintained the *mazalim* courts. Sometimes their princely edicts differed from classical sharia. In the fifteenth century, the Ottoman sultan decreed that the strict *hadd* punishments were not to be applied under his rule (see 6.1). In the three empires, the sultans were virtually absolute rulers and were supported by vassals, civil servants, and military forces.

In opposition to this absolutist rule, the *ulama* tried to maintain their own basis of power. In the Ottoman and Mughal empires this was done through an implicit alliance with the ruler. In the Safavid Empire, the *ulama* maintained a more independent position, in accord with Shiite doctrine. Certain *ulama* were active as judges, as state advisors, and for the enforcement of the law. Above them, in addition to a chief judge, was now also a chief religious functionary, known as the chief *mufti*, or the *Shaykh al-Islam* (in the Ottoman Empire) or the *Sadr al-sudir* (in Persia and South Asia). According to Hallaq (2003: 1710), the system of Islamic religious scholars functioned as a counterweight to the state and government, and 'it did so with remarkable independence and success.' However, 'the judge[s] who [were] appointed and paid by the state' were soon suspected of being 'agents of corrupt politics'. Other religious scholars or *ulama* were responsible for an expanded and often flourishing educational system. Finally, they controlled a large number of social services. The *ulama* often used the income from land grants and religious endowments (*waqf*) for mosques, hospitals, schools, and other public services. In this way, they acquired much authority among the people, which strengthened their position *vis-à-vis* the secular authority. Thus, Islam and sharia functioned for about a thousand years in the Muslim world as a system of religion, governance, and law. As Abou El Fadl writes:

> The Shari'a [...] functioned like the symbolic glue that held the diverse Muslim nation together, despite its many different ethnicities, nationalities, and political entities. [...] [T]he Shari'a remained the transcendent symbol of unity, and the jurists [scholars] were the Shari'a's guardians [... and] stayed above the petty political and military conflicts and [...] provided the quintessential source of religious authority in the Muslim world (Abou El Fadl 2007: 34).

Although practice was often different from the sacred doctrine, Islam, nevertheless, furnished the people with a cohesive element and historical continuity. Rule according to sharia was the common element, as it was also the minimum requirement for an Islamic government. The recognition by the ruler that sharia was the official law preserved the unity of the community and its Islamic character. Under the great sultanates, Islamic law was thus 'the criterion for the legitimacy of an Islamic state' (Esposito 1998: 31).

1.7 A voyage around the Muslim world

After this introduction it is now time to proceed to the country chapters, embarking on our voyage around the Muslim world, which starts in Egypt (see chapter 2), the ancient kingdom on the border of the two continents Africa and Asia. Egypt, the largest country in the Arab world, has played a central role in the development of law in the Middle East. During the nineteenth century, Egypt became one of the prime leaders of modernisation in the region. Later, the country was to become the centre of Islamic modernism inspired by Muhammad Abduh. The country was also home to the great legal scholar Sanhuri, who managed to draft a civil code during the interbellum on the basis of French law, Egyptian case law, and sharia, which was to be introduced in over a dozen countries in the region. In 1980 a constitutional amendment declared the principles of sharia to be the main source of legislation, but, as we will see, this would not stop the liberalisation of marriage law.

From Egypt, we will move to the very Western corner of the Muslim world, Morocco (see chapter 3). When the country became a French Protectorate in 1912, the sultan agreed to seek French assistance for the development of its legal system. Soon after independence in 1956, Morocco introduced a codification of sharia, the Personal Status Code of 1958. Having been amended several times, it now contains one of the most progressive family laws in the Islamic world. During this process, the king, who according to the constitution is 'Commander of the Faithful', played an important role.

Like many Muslims do each year, we now set course for Saudi Arabia (see chapter 4), where we find a different set of legal rules altogether. Protecting the Holy Places where Islam originates from and hosting the annual pilgrimage, Saudi Arabia, led by the ruling dynasty of the Sauds, takes centre stage in the Muslim world. Sharia is its national law, and law reform has been slower and more cautious than in any other country. For decades, the powerful clan of the Wahhabi, which sits in the country's most powerful religious seats, has promoted missionaries all over the world to present the Wahhabite puritan model as the only right one. Religious missions in Asia, Europe and Africa were funded by profits made from the rich oil reserves.

Next we cross back over the Red Sea to Africa, to the Sudan (see chapter 5). This state has been devastated by long lasting civil wars arising from the conflicts between the Islamic North, the non-Islamic South, and later with rebel groups in Darfur. When in 1983 general Numeiri had not succeeded in lifting his poor country into a higher stage of socio-economic development, he announced a grand scale islamisation of the law. Since then, the Sudan has tried to 'cleanse' its legal system of all traces of liberal British and Egyptian-French roots. However, as part of the peace negotiations with the South in 1998 and 2005, relatively liberal constitutions were put back in place.

From the Sudan we continue into Turkey (see chapter 6), the country that is considered by some as the bridge between Europe and the Middle East – among the most populous countries in the Middle East, like Egypt and Iran, and a country that has been steering its own ideological course for almost a century. Atatürk turned Turkey into a secular nation after the end of the First World War, and to date it continues to be so. However, the rise of religious parties, such as the AK led by Erdogan, has repeatedly led to tensions involving the army, the police, and the judiciary. Perceived as symbol of religiosity, the issue of the wearing of the veil has been the centre of tense political and legal debate, perhaps more so than in any other country in the world.

Our journey continues into Afghanistan (see chapter 7) in Central Asia. King Amanullah tried to reform this country at the same time when and in the same way as Atatürk was busy reforming Turkey. Yet, nation building in Afghanistan turned out to be a slow and difficult process. Since the late 1970s, a large part of the country became the battle field for tribal warlords, Russian troops, and Islamic resistance fighters. The 1990s saw how the resistance forces were joined and overruled by a new militant movement, established with support from the United States, Saudi Arabia, and Pakistan: the Taliban. During their authoritarian rule, the Taliban gave Osama bin Laden the opportunity to prepare the infamous Twin Towers attack in 2001. After the subsequent American invasion, the Taliban were expelled and foreign troops were deployed to support the government in Kabul in hopes of maintaining the rule of law in this poor and fragmented country.

If one crosses the border into Iran (see chapter 8), one arrives in a relatively organised and developed country. It is here that the Shah launched his greatest modernisation policy, which only partially succeeded. In response to severe political repression, the Iranian people supported the 1979 Islamic Revolution *en masse*. More than thirty years after the Revolution, it may seem that the strong islamisation of the legal system has barely, if at all, been toned down. Iran is the only country of our dozen where religious scholars have seized executive and judicial power and oversee the governance of the state. However, over the last decades, social, intellectual and political movements have vigorously advocated legal change – with some limited successes – and reformers have gained an increasing amount of support. During the 2009 election campaigns, opposition against the present regime and calls for reform became massive.

Pakistan (see chapter 9), a country stricken by poverty and ethnic conflict, had a troublesome start and until the present day is frequently uprooted by violence. As is the case in Afghanistan, customary law is still dominant in the rural areas. Military and civil presidents have upheld a fairly authoritarian regime. In 1979, General Zia ul-Haq overthrew the democratically elected government of Ali Bhutto in a *coup d'état* and tried to legitimise his rule by introducing a strict adherence to Islamic law. Large nationalist parties, as well as the judiciary, which follows the British legal tradition, exert a moderating influence on the extensive power of the presidents as well as on the islamisation of the national law.

Just a few hours by plane one reaches Southeast Asia, an area where Islam has blended in with local custom (*adat*) and the old traditions of Hinduism and Buddhism. Indonesia (see chapter 10) is the largest Muslim country in the world, an enormous archipelago of thousands of islands, and home to hundreds of ethnic groups. While Dutch colonial rule recognised the country's elaborate systems of customary *adat* law, since independence in 1945 the emphasis has been on national law. Islamic law has remained in a secondary position. Consequently, the word Islam does not appear in Indonesia's constitution. But this country, too, has been subject to efforts of islamisation. Yet, the consecutive governments – democratically elected since 1998 – have continued to steer a course with national unity as their overriding objective. Islamisation of law has so far been quite limited, the remote province of Aceh, however, being an exception.

It takes only a short trip overseas to Malaysia (see chapter 11), where almost the same language is spoken. This country provides a home to both the Islamic Malay population as well as a large minority group of Chinese, has, like other Muslim countries, seen a rise of Islamist movements in the last decade. These movements strongly contrast the older, more tolerant and moderate form of Islam that has been the mainstay of Malaysia's history. The judiciary, operating in a British legal tradition, has had to play a crucial role in dissolving conflicts that arise out of the more assertive stance of 'puritan' Muslim movements.

From one region in the 'periphery of the Muslim world' to another: Sub-Saharan Africa. In poverty-stricken Mali (see chapter 12), an ex-French colony, the state is fairly secular by nature, and the predominantly rural population adheres mostly to customary law. Yet, here too, Islamic traditions and Muslim missionaries have left their mark on politico-legal developments. Mali, relying on development aid, is confronted with Western donors who wish to improve the position of women, and with Islamic donors such as Saudi Arabia who wish to increase the influence of classical sharia. To date, the government has been able to preserve stability and steer a course of compromise between the conflicting forces.

The final stage of our journey takes us to Nigeria (see chapter 13), the most populous country in Africa, which is divided into an Islamic North and a Christian South. This federal state, rich in oil, has experienced many violent conflicts, both between tribal as well as between religious groups. Military coups brought the country under army rule for long periods. Only since 1999 civilian rule has been reinstated. The year 2000 marked the significant event of eleven provinces in the

North promulgating Islamic criminal law. Ten years later this book reconstructs the events and takes stock of the results.

After this cursory voyage you have reached the end of the introductory chapter. Hopefully you are now prepared to immerse yourself into the fascinating individual country chapters, and to gain, while reading, an ever more complete overview and deeper insight into how sharia has been incorporated in national legal systems throughout the Muslim world.

Note to Preface

1 Berger 2006; Otto 2006; Otto, Dekker & Van Soest-Zuurdeeg 2006.

Notes to Chapter 1

1 In this chapter in particular and in many parts of the book the term 'sharia' is used instead of 'Islamic law'. For the purpose of this study it was found preferable to differentiate between sharia and law. The term sharia then denotes divine rules that, according to the religion of Islam, emanate from God. The term law, as commonly used, refers to man-made rules and norms, issued by and enforceable by state institutions. Of course we can also define the term law more broadly to encompass systems of religious law and religious authorities, but in the context of this study that could also easily create unnecessary confusion. Readers can especially be confused when in certain literature about sharia (translated from Arabic into English), authors refer to 'sharia' by using the term 'the law', as in the phrase for example '[t]he status of women according to the law is equitable to men'.
2 Except for Nigeria, see 1.3.
3 These specialisations include legal history, sociology of law, legal anthropology, law and development studies, law and economics, comparative law of developing countries, court studies, and the legal dimensions of political and governance studies.
4 This closure of the gate has been an established theory but some authors have contested it, a.o. Hallaq (2009).
5 Dispute resolution according to classical *fiqh* requires parties and/or the judge to consult a *mufti*, whose *fatwa* will then be applied to the case by the judge. Today, this system is still in use in Saudi Arabia.
6 The term 'incorporated' is merely introduced in order to point at the historical process, in which states have appropriated the legal function of sharia. The term does not have the connotation of a business entreprise or a multinational company and should not be understood as such.

Bibliography

Abou El-Fadl, K. (2007), *The Great Theft. Wrestling Islam from the Extremists.* New York: HarperCollins Publishers.

Al-Azmeh, A. (1993), *Islams and modernities.* London: Verso, Phronesis.

Allott, A. (1980), *The limits of law.* London: Butterworth.

Arminjon, P., B. Nolde, & M. Wolff (1952), *Traité de droit comparé.* Paris: Librairie générale de droit et de jurisprudence.

Bedner, A. (2010, forthcoming), 'An Elementary Approach to the Rule of Law', *Hague Journal on the Rule of Law.*

Berger, M.S. (2006), *Klassieke sharia en vernieuwing.* Amsterdam: Amsterdam University Press.

Buruma, I. (2007), *Murder in Amsterdam, The Death of Theo van Gogh and the Limits of Tolerance,* London: Atlantic Books.

Carothers, T. (2006), *Promoting the rule of law abroad: in search of knowledge.* Washington D.C.: Carnegie Endowment for International Peace.

Coulson, N.J. (1964), *A history of Islamic law.* Edinburgh: Edinburgh University Press.

Esposito, J.L. (1998), *Islam and politics.* Syracuse: Syracuse University Press.

Feldman, N. (2008), *The Fall and rise of the Islamic state.* Princeton: Princeton University Press.

Fuller, G.F. (2003), *The future of political Islam.* New York: Palgrave Macmillan.

Hallaq, W.B. (2003), 'Muslim rage and Islamic law', *Hastings Law Journal* 54(6): 1705-1719.

Hallaq, W.B. (2009), *Sharia. Theory, Practice, Transformations.* Cambridge: Cambridge University Press.

Hirsch, S. (2006), 'Islamic Law and Society Post-9/11', *Annual Review of Law & Social Science* Vol.2, December 2006: 165-186.

Huntington, S.P. (1998), *The clash of civilizations and the remaking of world order.* New York: Touchstone.

Ibn Warraq (1995), *Why I am not a Muslim,* see http://www.markhumphreys.com/islam.html, accessed 2 May 2010.

Lewis, B. (2002), *What Went Wrong? Western Impact and Middle Eastern Response,* Oxford: Oxford University Press.

Lewis, B. (2003), *The Crisis of Islam. Holy War and Unholy Terror,* London: Phoenix.

Marshall, P. (2005), *Radical Islam's Rules. The Worldwide Spread of Extreme* Shari'a *Law.* Freedom House's Center for Religious Freedom. Oxford: Rowman & Littlefield Publishers, Inc.

Otto, J.M. (2006), *Nationaal recht en sharia. Rechtssystemen in moslimlanden tussen traditie, politiek en rechtsstaat.* Amsterdam: Amsterdam University Press.

Otto, J.M., A.J. Dekker & L.J. van Soest-Zuurdeeg (eds.) (2006), *Sharia en nationaal recht in twaalf moslimlanden.* Amsterdam: Amsterdam University Press.

Peters, R. (1997), 'De hedendaagse toepassing van het islamitisch recht', in H. Driessen (ed.), *In het huis van de islam: geografie, geschiedenis, geloofsleer, cultuur, economie, politiek,* 259-277. Nijmegen: SUN.

Schacht, J. (1964), *An introduction to Islamic law.* Oxford: Clarendon.

Tamanaha, B.Z. (2004), *On the rule of law: History, politics, theory.* Cambridge: Cambridge University Press.

Vikør, K.S. (2005), *Between God and the Sultan: A history of Islamic Law.* London: Hurst.

2 Sharia and national law in Egypt

Maurits Berger and Nadia Sonneveld[1]

Abstract

An example to many an Arab state, Egypt's contemporary legal system is itself reflective of various foreign, mostly European, influences. Focussing on the relationship between sharia and national law in Egypt, this chapter will show the pervasiveness of this foreign influence and its particular influence during colonial times, when the sharia and the sharia courts were relegated to the realm of personal status law, and under Nasser, when the sharia courts were abolished altogether in the interest of his nationalisation and unification programmes. Even the subsequent upsurge in Islamic religiosity, resulting in a public return to religion from the 1970s onward and the constitutional amendments of 1971 and 1980 declaring the principles of sharia to be the main source of Egyptian legislation, did not lead to a significant return of sharia in Egypt's legal system. In fact, successive reforms of personal status law demonstrate the considerable pressure the government feels to satisfy the needs of the international community. Making use of independent interpretation of the sources of the sharia (*ijtihad*), Egypt has thus far succeeded in introducing reform that is in line with the international agreements it has signed, but that could also be presented as Islamic at home. This duality will be explored in two separate sections of this chapter – an historical overview of developments pre-1920 until present and an analysis and presentation of contemporary Egyptian law.

Table of contents

The advent of Islam in the early seventh century A.D. was followed by a period of rapid expansion that brought Islam and the Arabic language to Egypt. Egypt's strategic location between North Africa and Southwest Asia is exemplified by the completion of the Suez Canal in 1869, turning the country into an important hub of world commerce and geopolitical importance. Egypt gained its independence from Britain in 1922 and became the Arab Republic of Egypt in 1952. With a current population of approximately eighty million people, Egypt is the most populous country in the Middle East. The overriding majority – approximately 90 per cent – are Sunni Muslim. The remaining 10 per cent of the population is predominately Coptic Christian, but other Christian denominations are also represented. The Jewish community emigrated during the late 1950s. Arabic is the official language in Egypt. Most legislation has been based on European and, later, on Anglo-Saxon legal systems. Since 1980, the 'principles of sharia' are the primary source of legislation.

(Source: Bartleby 2010)

2.1 The period until 1920

European influence and sharia reform

During the period from 640 until 642, Egypt – then part of the Byzantine Empire – was conquered by Islamic armies coming from the Arabian Peninsula. Egypt's population was primarily Coptic, but over the course of the next two centuries most Copts converted to Islam. Egypt has played a central role in Islam's history, not least because of its Islamic educational institution, al-Azhar. Founded in 972 A.D. in what is now the medieval quarter of Cairo, al-Azhar quickly became reputed and developed into one of the main centres of Islamic learning in the world. Not surprisingly, the Grand Sheikhs of al-Azhar and its religious scholars (*'ulama'*) have often influenced Egyptian politics. In turn, the Egyptian authorities have attempted to exert influence over the university throughout the centuries and with varying success (see 2.2).

From 1517 onwards, Egypt became a semi-autonomous province of the Ottoman Empire. In response to Napoleon's brief occupation of the country (1798-1801), the sultan of the Ottoman Empire sent a military force under leadership of Muhammad Ali to Egypt to end the French occupation. When the French troops left the country in 1801, Muhammad Ali (1769-1848) declared himself Egypt's legitimate and rightful leader and was able to secure the country an even more autonomous position within the Ottoman Empire. Muhammed Ali established a monarchical dynasty that would remain in power until its overthrow in 1952. Inspired by the French, he implemented a rigorous program of modernisation, which drew heavily on European, particularly French, expertise and ideas; the military, educational system, laws and legal institutions, and the state apparatus (infrastructure and administration) were reformed according to European models.

With the opening of the Suez Canal in 1869, Egypt suddenly became of great geopolitical strategic importance. This was in particular the case for Great Britain whose lifeline to British India went through that canal. In the years to come, Egypt became increasingly afflicted by tremendous debt and financial mismanagement. In order to protect their investments in Egypt, several European countries, led by Great Britain, decided in 1882 to place Egypt under 'guardianship', which in practice meant *de facto* British colonial rule. *De jure*, Egypt remained part of the Ottoman Empire, a situation that continued until 1914 when the Ottoman Empire entered the war on the side of the Germans. As one of the allied countries, Great Britain took the opportunity that year to declare Egypt a British protectorate, a status that lasted until 1922.

Legislative reforms

In the nineteenth century, multiple forms of legislation and jurisdiction operated alongside each other. Muslims, Christians, and Jews maintained their own religious family laws and family courts. Courts with jurisdiction over Muslims – the sharia courts – also applied (uncodified) Islamic jurisprudence to other cases brought to the attention of these courts (e.g. contractual and land disputes). In addition, there were national courts, which applied governmental legislation as its primary source of legal authority. When located in rural areas, these courts often applied customary law as well. Finally, cases involving disputes between foreigners and Egyptians were referred to the so-called Mixed Courts; disputes between foreigners were referred to their respective consulates (based on a certain degree of legal immunity as part of the Capitulations Treaties concluded in the previous centuries between the Ottoman Empire and European states).

Starting in the 1880s, the Egyptian legal system went through a process of unification (Brown 1997; Cannon 1988), and in 1883, national laws were introduced in the fields of civil, commercial, criminal, and procedural law. These laws were adopted from European models, especially the French, German and Italian ones, and contained very little, if any, reference to Islamic law (Najjar 1992). New national courts were created to implement these codes, but the jurisdiction of the Muslim, Christian, and Jewish family courts remained untouched (until 1955), as was the case for the Mixed Courts (until 1949).

The process of legal and social modernisation at the end of the nineteenth century was paralleled by reforms in Islamic thought, in particular regarding the scope of sharia. The movement that initiated these reforms became known as *al-nahda*. Literally translating as 'awakening', the *al-nahda* is a modernisation and reform movement that originated in Egypt in the latter half of the nineteenth century and spread to other Arab countries. It found its expression in the adaptation of Western codes and later in the codification of rules of sharia concerning the family and inheritance (Najjar 1992: 62). Rifa'a Bey al-Tahtawi (1801-1873), scholar of the mentioned al-Azhar, played an important role in this process. He was one of a first group of Egyptians who were sent by the government to study in Europe. Upon return, he became an important religious scholar (*'alim*) and eventually the ideologue behind the reforms Muhammad Ali wanted to introduce. As such, one of the key problems al-Tahtawi found himself faced with was the question of how Egypt could be modernised without losing its Islamic character. According to al-Tahtawi, the solution lay in adapting the sharia to 'modern times' through using a method of selection (*takhayyur*), which, in certain situations, allowed Muslims to follow legal interpretations of Sunni schools of jurisprudence other than their own (Esposito 1982: 50; Öhrnberg 1995: 523-524).[2]

Modernising sharia

A later pioneer in the area of modernisation of the sharia was another Azharite, Muhammad Abduh (1849-1905), who wielded great influence in his capacities as a religious scholar (*'alim*), state mufti,[3] and minister. Although Abduh was a proponent of modernisation, he argued that the process needed to be implemented on the basis of the sharia rather than a blind adoption of the Western model (Haddad 1994: 30-59; Hourani 1970: 130). Upon his visit to France he came to the conclusion that modern European societies had created a social order that was much closer to the Quranic ideals than Muslim societies had achieved thus far. Hence, the famous remark that is attributed to him: 'In France I saw Islam but no Muslims; in Cairo I see Muslims but no Islam.' Along with Jamal al-Din al-Afghani (1838-1897), Abduh tried to develop an Islamic alternative for the swift social and legal changes that were being forced through by Muhammad Ali and later by the British in Egypt. This alternative became known as *al-salafiya*, and has as its most important goals reformation of Islamic education and the perception of Islam so that Islam could find its place within a society undergoing constant change.[4]

Like al-Tahtawi, Abduh considered the four Sunni schools of jurisprudence equal to one another and he therefore rejected the obligation to conform to a single school of jurisprudence (*taqlid*). He also criticised the methods of the traditional Islamic religious scholars and encouraged Muslims to independently interpret sources of sharia such as the Quran and the Sunna (sayings and doings of the Prophet) through a procedure called *ijtihad*. In this sense, Abduh went one step further than al-Tahtawi since the latter, being a proponent of *takhayyur*, still considered himself to be bound to the four schools of jurisprudence.

Abduh was of the opinion that the national development of Egypt was hampered because Muslims were not applying the sharia in a correct manner. Unable to make use of the rights granted to them by Islam, Abduh considered women to be especially subordinated in society. He argued that their position had to be improved, not just by granting them access to education, but by reforming the sharia, in particular the parts related to marriage and divorce.

In 1915, a committee was established with the task of overseeing reform of the sharia in the fields of marriage and divorce. It was comprised of jurists and various religious scholars from the four Sunni schools of jurisprudence (Qassem 2002: 20). In the year 1920, the Islamic reform movement found expression in the first codification of sharia in Egypt: rules of marriage, divorce, and other family matters were codified in Law No. 25/1920 on Muslim personal status. Using the principle of *takhayyur*, this law had incorporated jurisprudence from the Maliki school, which granted women easier grounds on which to apply for divorce through the courts than the Hanafi school, the official school of jurisprudence in Egypt. Despite Abduh's efforts to stimulate independent and more progressive interpretations of the sharia, the drafters of the new legislation did not, however, use the principle of *ijtihad* and instead stayed well within the limits of the doctrines of the four schools of jurisprudence.

These developments took place against the backdrop of continued, and rising, Egyptian nationalism. These nationalist movements were expressed in both religious and secular forms and called with increasing fervour for independence from the British.

2.2 The period from 1920 until 1965

The ousting of the Egyptian royalty and the British – towards formation of a socialist republic

In 1922, the British protectorate ended and Egypt became an independent constitutional monarchy. Its first constitution, modelled after the Belgium constitution, was adopted in 1923. It established a parliamentary democracy with political parties and elections. The ruling dynasty of 'khedives' from the line of modern Egypt's founder, Muhammad Ali, was continued as a royal monarchy. Independence was not, however, complete because the British retained significant responsibilities in the areas of national security, defence, and foreign policy. Great Britain also did not hesitate to use its position to interfere in internal affairs, as it still considered Egypt, and in particular the Suez Canal, a vital part of its sphere of influence in the Middle East. In fact, British troops stationed in Egypt were not even fully withdrawn until 1956, after the Suez crisis.

Moreover, this new political system was largely dominated by the old elite, namely the king and landowners with enormous land holdings and entrepreneurs who collaborated closely with foreign businesses and the British occupying forces. The Egyptian population, mostly rural and poor, continued to be exploited and oppressed, and was unable to use the new democratic system to articulate its interests. However, two new trends developed in these times: secular and Islamic nationalism.

Egyptian secular nationalism originally began as a resistance movement against the British occupation, but in the 1920s and 1930s expanded into an opposition force against the monarchy and ruling elite, who many Egyptians viewed as collaborators with the British. The nationalist movement was furthermore influenced by the developments in neighbouring Palestine, which was also under British (mandate) rule, and where increasing Jewish migration led to armed conflicts between Palestinians and Jews, culminating in Israel's declaration of independence in 1948.

Egyptian nationalism was also expressed religiously with the Muslim Brotherhood as its main proponent. Created in 1928 by Hassan al-Banna, the Brotherhood initially focussed on education and charitable work, but soon became regarded as a political organisation because of its blending of Islamic, nationalist, anti-colonial, and social programs. Its viewpoint was that in order to improve society and adapt it to modern times one needed to look back to the example of early Islam. As such, the call for the (re)introduction of the sharia was also a part of the organisation's ideology, although this particular point was not used as a political slogan until the 1970s. The Muslim Brotherhood was the first mass organisation based on Islam. Within fifteen years, it counted half a million members and had two thousand offices throughout Egypt. The Brotherhood also established offices in Palestine, Jordan, Syria and Sudan. These independent chapters of the Brotherhood began deciding upon their own national advocacy plans and programs from about the 1950s onwards (Mitchell 1969).

Codification of Islamic personal status law

During this period, the codification of national laws, a process that had already started in the previous century, was expanded to the domain of

Islamic personal status law. The first codification of Islamic personal status law took place in 1920, with new legislation issued in 1923, 1929, and 1931. Laws concerning marriage and divorce for Christians and Jews were not, however, affected by these reforms since their legislation remained with the respective religious authorities rather than with the Egyptian parliament.

These legal endeavours resonated both internationally and domestically. On the international front, Egypt became an example to other Arab countries, which would later enact similar legal reforms. Domestically, this codification process greatly influenced the women's movement, culminating in the establishment of the Egyptian Women's Union in 1923. The leader of the movement was Hoda Shaarawi, who had led the first women's demonstration against the British occupation and who, by publicly removing her veil in 1923, had sent shockwaves through Egypt. The union strongly argued for the improvement of the position of women through family law reform and members emphasised that as Islamic feminists they were not fighting against Islam itself, but rather against male-dominated interpretations of Islam (Badran 1995: 135; Shaham 1997: 7). Although the union did not deny the Quranic basis of men's right to polygamy, it pointed to another verse in the Quran that calls for equal treatment of women, a condition which, the union argued, Egyptian men in the present circumstances would not be able to meet. The novelty of this line of reasoning was perhaps not the argument itself, but the fact that by directly going back to one of the main sources of sharia – the Quran – the union in fact practiced *ijtihad*.

The union also fought to limit the right of repudiation (*talaq*, or divorce without having to produce legal reason) by subjecting its practice to stricter provisions (Badran 1995: 127-130; Esposito 1982: 60; Shaham 1997: 9). These efforts produced some effect. In 1923, the minimum age of marriage was raised to sixteen for girls and eighteen for boys. And, nine years later, in 1929, the Islamic (Muslim) personal status law of 1920 was amended. Husbands' rights to repudiation and polygamy were restricted by the introduction of stricter procedural conditions, though not abolished. The amended law also gave women an additional ground for divorce: maltreatment by the husband.

Despite these earlier more progressive changes, however, in 1931 a new decree on personal status was introduced that included, among other things, a new standard marriage contract in which women could no longer insert substantive stipulations, such as the right to automatic divorce in case the husband married a second wife, or stipulations to the effect that a husband would provide for his wife's children from a previous marriage. The only stipulation that was allowed was the permission for the wife to divorce herself (Zulficar forthcoming). These regulations contrasted with the established legal practice of the Ottoman period, which allowed for more flexibility and freedom to include stipulations in the marriage contract (cf. Abdal Rahman Abdal Rehim 1996; Hanna 1996). Only years later, in 1943, 1945, and 1969, did the Ministry for Social Affairs recommend more stringent procedural conditions in favour of women regarding unilateral divorce and polygamy (Esposito & DeLong-Bas 2001: 58). However, such and other recommendations failed time and again in the face of objections by the religious-conservative lobby, both within the Egyptian parliament and outside of it.

In 1943 and 1946 intestate laws and testamentary inheritance laws were issued, respectively. Interestingly, while some of its provisions were the outcome of a selective reading of the rulings of all four schools of jurisprudence on this matter (*takhayyur*), other provisions surpassed the official teachings of the four schools of jurisprudence. For example, where the four schools follow the principle that bequests are restricted to non-heirs, Article 37 of the testamentary inheritance laws of 1946 decrees that under certain conditions bequests to heirs are also valid (Esposito & DeLong-Bas 2001: 64-65).

Where sharia remained the primary source of inspiration for Muslim personal status law, European law kept its primacy in all other legal areas. For instance, the new Penal Code of 1937 was based on Italian criminal law, and the Civil Code of 1949 on the French civil code. In the latter case, however, the framer of the code, the jurist Sanhuri, declared that sharia was a major source of inspiration. The extent to which this was actually the case remains controversial. Most likely, the main foundation was French civil law, to which several Islamic judicial elements were appended (Hill 1987: 71-83). With regards to the administration of justice, the Court of Cassation was created in 1931 and the Council of State in 1946, both based on the French model (Bernard-Maugiron & Dupret 2002: xxiv-li).

The 1952 revolution

In 1952, a group of young army officers calling themselves the 'Free Officers' committed a coup. The King was deposed and Egypt adopted a new constitution, replacing the 1923 version promulgated under colonial rule. The new constitution proclaimed Egypt to be a 'democratic, socialist republic' but, in actual fact, Egypt quickly developed into an authoritarian military regime. Although formally Parliament was not abolished, its authority was severely restricted and political participation was limited such that only one party – the state party – continued to exist. The Free Officers gained momentum under the populist leadership of Abdel Nasser (1956-1970), and a period of far-reaching socialist reforms followed. Nasser nationalised the banking, insurance, and industrial sectors, redistributed agricultural lands, and introduced free education and health care. In 1956, the Suez Canal was also nationalised, and, faced with international pressure, the remaining British troops left Egypt, thereby ending the last remnants of British colonial rule.

Three significant legal developments occurred after the 1952 revolution: the completion of the process of harmonisation of the legal system (which had been started in 1883); the introduction of socialist principles in legislation and the administration of justice; and, finally, the establishment of the foundations of a police state.

The definitive harmonisation of the judicial system took place between 1949 and 1956. In 1949, the Mixed Courts were abolished. As a result, foreigners became subject to Egyptian law and justice, except where Egyptian rules of private international law stipulated otherwise. In 1955, the separate family courts for Jews, Christians, and Muslims (the latter were called 'sharia courts') were also abolished. The abolishment of the courts did not affect the separate religious family laws of these religious communities, however, which remained intact but were from that point forward to be administered by the national courts. This only applied to matters of marriage and divorce, however; in all other fields of personal status (e.g. custody, inheritance, parentage, etc), sharia was applicable. This concurred with the Islamic legal philosophy that sharia is the dominant law in all matters of personal status, merely allowing non-Muslim exemptions with regard to marriage and divorce (Berger 2005). Islamic law and the language of Islam, therefore, remained important in the field of Muslim personal status law, with far reaching consequences, such as in the field of apostasy (see 2.4 and 2.6 below) (Berger 2003; Yüksel 2007).

The Nasser government's lack of initiative in introducing accompanying substantive reform was reflective of its preoccupation with unifying the public administration as well as its desire to subordinate the religious institutions, including al-Azhar, by turning them into agents of state power. But it had no interest in unifying the different religious personal status laws nor an interest in reforming the Muslim personal status law itself (Yüksel 2007: 170-172). Another probable reason behind the abolishment of the sharia courts, and of special interest for the purpose of this chapter, was that the Nasser government saw the existence of the separate family courts as a legacy of Ottoman colonialism that had to be eliminated, just as it had abolished the Mixed Courts a few years earlier (Yüksel 2007: 161; Brown 1997).

The second development – the introduction of socialist principles in legislation and the administration of justice – was evident in areas such as new rent and labour laws, which significantly strengthened the positions of renters and labourers. Similarly, the position of women was strengthened, for example by the constitutional provision of gender equality and the right to vote. The influence of socialism furthermore transpired in the centralised organisation of the state apparatus, the establishment (and forced membership) of state-run labour unions, and the nationalisation of religious institutions (like al-Azhar) and of religious endowments (*awqaf*). The nationalisation of al-Azhar in 1961 came with the expectation that its scholars (*'ulama'*), who were now government employees, would endorse Nasser's ideas of Arab Socialism and thereby attribute religious legitimacy to his policy (Moustafa 2000).

Finally, national security was given a judicial form. This development mainly precipitated from the increasing confrontation between the new regime and the Muslim Brotherhood, culminating in mass arrests in 1954, the promulgation of an Emergency Law in 1956, and the establishment of security courts to apply the new law. In 1966, military tribunals were created. These measures were not a novelty, however, for they were also applied during the monarchy. The Emergency Law has remained in effect ever since, with only briefly interrupted periods between 1964-1967 and 1980-1981. Since that time, state security agencies have been given an active role in repressing political opposition. Because of the mass prosecution, and in some cases execution, of a number of leaders of the Muslim Brotherhood, emphasis on reintroduction of the sharia into law and society was relegated to the background once again (Peters 1988: 233).

2.3 The period from 1965 until 1985

Islamisation and the *Infitah*

This period was characterised by an upsurge in Islamic religiosity that gradually influenced the debates on social, legal, and political reform. Egypt's defeat in the Six-Day War of 1967 contributed to this resurgence of Islamic sentiments, because many Egyptians saw the military defeat as God's punishment of the nation that had betrayed its religious foundations by introducing the principles of socialism, secularism, and nationalism. In an apparent attempt to exploit this upsurge of religiosity, Nasser decided to make religion a national theme (Jansen 1997: 162).

Although Nasser had implemented many socialist reforms, there had been remarkable little change in the field of personal status law during his rule of Egypt. Consequently, the position of women in particular still lagged behind (cf. Bernard-Maugiron & Dupret 2002: 2; El Alami 1994: 116). For example, women could only obtain a divorce with great difficulty, because judges did not easily grant divorce on the grounds provided by the law, not least because of the complicated procedures involved in providing evidence. Consequently, such court cases often took years without guarantee of success for the women who had petitioned for divorce. Furthermore, although women could become lawyers, ministers, and business executives, they still needed the written permission of their husbands if they wished to travel abroad. Strictly legally speaking, as long as a husband was providing for his wife, she was legally obliged to remain obedient to him. In cases where she behaved 'disobediently', (e.g. by leaving the marital home without his permission), the husband was entitled to petition the court with an obedience claim (*ta'a*), which, if granted, would result in an order for her return to the matrimonial home; refusal to do so would result in her loss of the right to be maintained by her husband (*nafaqa*).

Until 1967, the husband was entitled to engage the assistance of the police to return his 'disobedient' wife home by force. This practice was prohibited that year by a ministerial decree. This, then, constituted the only reform in the field of Muslim personal status law under the Nasser government. According to the Ministry of Justice, more fundamental changes in Islamic personal status law had been planned but they were postponed after the defeat in the Six-Day War of 1967 changed the political climate and agenda (Hatem 2000: 52).

Sharia in the constitution

When Nasser died in 1970, he was succeeded by Anwar Sadat (1970-1981), who responded to the heightened sense of religious awareness in several ways. Perhaps most importantly, in 1971, Sadat initiated the adoption of a new constitution in which Islam was established as the state religion of Egypt and in which 'the principles of the sharia' became '*a* major source of legislation'. In a further attempt to offset leftist and Nasserist political trends in the country, Sadat stimulated the establishment of Islamic student associations at the universities and released thousands of arrested Muslim Brothers from prison. In 1980, the constitution was again amended and the principles of the sharia were elevated from *a* major source of legislation to '*the* major source of legislation' (Art. 2). Hence, following on the socialist and secular decades of the 1950s and 1960s, Islam and sharia now regained an official role in Egyptian law and society.

This official role granted to sharia by the constitution prompted the al-Azhar University to look into the codification of certain legal areas of Islamic law, like penal and civil law. Despite these efforts, no real change was brought about. A draft Islamic penal code was presented by the Azhar to parliament in 1978, but did not result in any change of the existing penal law. Similarly, as a result of a study ordered by Sadat in 1978, recommendations to Islamise existing legislation were presented to parliament but not enacted after Mubarak's taking office in 1981 (Botiveau 1994: 124-125). There were several reasons for this reluctance on the part of parliament and the government. Among them, the stance of the government towards the Islamic opposition had hardened. This was the result of Sadat's overtures towards the Western world, resulting in the economic liberalisation policy of 1974 (*infitah*), as well as negotiations with Israel resulting in the 1979 peace treaty. The peace treaty was heavily criticised by the Islamic opposition as well as the rest of the Arab world. The government was also afraid that Islamisation of existing legislation would lead to tensions between Christians – particularly Copts – and Muslims. Moreover, the government was concerned that such a policy would lead to negative reactions abroad, especially in the United States, and that such reactions could potentially have a detrimental impact on the large flow of American financial aid into the country (Peters 1987: 29-30).

The political and legal importance of the constitutional amendments regarding sharia had interesting effects on the legal position of women, as is illustrated by the 1979 reforms to the Islamic personal status law and the signing of the U.N. Convention on the Elimination of All Forms of Discrimination against Women (CEDAW) in 1980. Preparations for reform of Muslim personal status law in favour of women had already been underway since the 1970s, but the recommendations that had been made to this end were all rejected by parliament (Esposito 1982: 60). Hence, when Sadat dissolved parliament in 1979, he used his constitutional right to issue a presidential decree on urgent matters, whenever the parliament is not in session. This enabled him to pass a draft containing amendments to the 1920 and 1929 laws on Muslim personal status. The 1979 decree was known as Jihan's Law, referring to President Sadat's wife Jihan who was said to have played an instrumental role in the passing of the law (al-Ali 2000: 74; El Alami 1994: 116). The content of the law sparked much resistance, both for practical and religious reasons.[5]

Indeed, the law was so controversial that many judges refused to implement it. They claimed that the law violated sharia and was, therefore, unconstitutional (Bernard-Maugiron & Dupret 2002: 16; El Alami 1994: 116-117; Fawzy 2004: 36). In 1985, the newly established Supreme Constitutional Court, declared the law unconstitutional, but not because it violated the principles of the sharia, but because of violations of legislative procedure (the law was pushed through as an 'urgent matter' at a time, when no such urgency existed).[6]

At first sight, the signing of the U.N. Convention on the Elimination of All Forms of Discrimination against Women (CEDAW) in 1980 appears to be a landslide development for the position of Egyptian women, especially given the fact that according to the Egyptian legal system, international treaties can be applied directly by the national courts.

However, Egypt had inserted several reservations in this treaty stating that the particular articles were not applicable when violating 'Islamic sharia'. On this basis, Egypt formally rejected the equality of men and women in matters of personal status law as stipulated in Article 16 of CEDAW.

Democracy and the rule of law

During Sadat's administration, Egypt was, on the one hand, encouraging Islamisation of society and the legal system. On the other hand, however, the noted 1974 *infitah* policy of economic liberalisation stimulated the improvement of the national economy and the political system (e.g. the multi-party system was re-introduced), the position of women, and Egypt's international relations (i.e. Egypt switched political allegiance from the Soviet Union toward the United States and faced political alienation in the Arab world by entering into a Peace agreement with Israel in 1979). This dual approach was indicative of Sadat's rule, which tried to serve two audiences: a liberal and modern image for the international audience, and an authentic and Islamic image to the Egyptian public. These two approaches could easily contradict each other, as was the case with Jihan's Law of 1979 that was ultimately crafted through and by a series of conflicting national and international interests and pressures (cf. Welchman: 2007: 42-43).

By the early 1970s, efforts to firmly establish the rule of law and a viable democracy looked promising with the reinstatement of a multi-party system, the improvement of the judiciary's independence, and the release of large numbers of Islamists from prison. A decade later, however, Sadat started to crack down on the growing opposition movement in general and the Islamists in particular. This was partly related to the fact that many Muslim Brothers had radicalised as a result of the harsh treatment they had suffered during Nasser's reign. Their release from prison had not abated the processes of radicalisation that began during their imprisonment. Several extremist groups had split away from the Muslim Brotherhood at this point. They considered their fellow Egyptians, and in particular members of the government, to be non-believers who must be violently opposed and combatted. Sadat responded to the rise of political opposition by ordering massive arrests in 1981. During the period of one night, 1,600 opponents were detained, among whom many were Islamists. A few months later, in October 1981, Sadat was assassinated by a member of a new militant splinter group called al-Jihad.

Sadat's death marked the end of an era of attempts to simultaneously modernise, reform, and Islamise Egypt and to open the country up to the arena of international law and commerce. His vice-president, Hosni

Mubarak, also a military man, took over and became the next president in the following elections.

2.4 The period from 1985 until the present

Continuation of Islamisation and modernisation

The regime of Hosni Mubarak (1981-present) can be divided into three distinct periods:
- the 1980s – characterised by relative political and social calm but increasing economic activity and a growing absorption of symbols of Islam within daily social life;
- the 1990s – characterised by both political and economic liberalisation as well as the continuing Islamisation of society and increased legal activity related to the sharia on the one hand and harsh reactions to increasing Islamic opposition and violent Muslim extremism, on the other hand; and
- the first decennium of 2000 – characterised by the political struggle for democratic reforms and progressive Islam-motivated reforms in personal status law.

In similar ways to his predecessor Sadat, Mubarak mostly clung to a pragmatic policy, balancing on a tightrope between the socialist legacy of Nasser and economic liberalisation and between Islamic activism and socio-political reform. In both cases, the issue of sharia in law, society, and governance against the backdrop of the demands advanced by the international community have continued to play central roles in the development of Egypt.

The 1980s

From the 1970s onwards, Egyptian society has provided a striking illustration of the religious revival of Islam. Islam has become a primary source of authority or at the very least a standard that must always be taken into account. Movies, literature, and clothing have become more modest and conservative than thirty years ago, and across all academic disciplines, Islamic views on the subject have become relevant foci of study. Reference to Islam in public discourse has come to dominate all facets of daily life and led to a form of Islamic political correctness (Bayat: 2007). This development is not to be interpreted as a reaction against modernity or international standards. To the contrary, during this and the next decades, one witnesses a trend of conforming Islamic concepts to modern standards.[7] This has led to hybrid solutions, such as the concept of 'Islamic human rights', or the 'Islamic state'. This duality is also illustrated by Egypt's ratification (since 1980) of numerous international treaties contingent on their applicability only where these laws and standards are not 'incompatible with the sharia' (for an overview of these treaties, see 2.9 below).

The influence and pressure of the demands advanced by the international community, on the one hand, and the presence of a form of 'Islamic political correctness', on the other hand, have also affected the development of the personal status law, still the only field of law in Egypt that has been based on sharia. Less than two months after the annulment of the 'Jihan' Law, the Egyptian parliament passed new legislation on the Islamic personal status law (Law No. 100/1985). It was probably no coincidence that the introduction of a new Islamic personal status law occurred right before the start of the 1985 U.N. conference on women's rights in Nairobi. The Egyptian government under Mubarak did not wish to be branded with a negative international reputation at this point and tried to improve its image with this new law (Badran 1995: 135; Karam 1997: 146). At the same time, however, the government did not want to confront opponents of Muslim personal status law reform any more than necessary. Consequently, the government made sure that the clauses that had provoked so much controversy in 1979 were removed from the new law.[8] Still, the 1985 law was certainly more progressive and pro-women's rights in comparison to the previous personal status laws from the 1920s, which it sought to amend[9] (see also 2.6 below) (cf. El Alami 1994).

The ambivalence of the Mubarak regime was also evident in the field of political liberalisation. Like his predecessor, Mubarak released the members of the Muslim Brotherhood from prison. Most of them renounced violence and committed themselves to charitable work, including education and health care. Ironically, it was through these non-political activities that the Brotherhood was able to manifest itself as an alternative to the state, in particular in the health care and education sectors, and to gain a large following among the population. The socialist welfare promises that the government still officially acclaimed, but failed to deliver, was now provided by the Islamic organisations.

However, the Muslim Brotherhood was prevented from formally establishing itself as a political party, because the admittance of a party into the political system was made subject to a number of strict conditions: its program had to be substantially different from those of other parties; any criticism of the constitution was prohibited; the party could not campaign at or be involved in public demonstrations; and, most importantly, the party could not be founded on religious principles. This complicated the process of promised political liberalisation as the Egyptian government was now faced with a dilemma: refusing to grant party status to a group such as the Muslim Brotherhood, which enjoyed a significant amount of popularity, would be undemocratic, but granting it official party status would likely result in the group's gaining of even more legitimacy and power. A compromise was eventually found whereby individual Muslim Brothers could participate under the banner of another party or as independent candidates without having to hide their own sympathies. Moreover, in 1984 and 1987, members of the Brotherhood entered into electoral alliances with the liberal Wafd Party and the Islamist Labour Party, respectively.

The 1990s

In the 1990s, the Muslim Brotherhood continued its activities in the areas of health care and education. Their popularity and efficiency became illustrative of the government's dysfunction in these areas. This implicit criticism of the government became painfully clear during the 1992 earthquake, when first aid workers from the Muslim Brotherhood reached the disaster scenes much earlier than those of the government. In response, a law severely restricting such operations was promptly adopted.

After a period of relative calm, Egypt was confronted with other, violent forms of Islamic activism as Muslim extremists committed an unprecedented wave of attacks on ministers, security forces, and later Copts and tourists. These events culminated in 1997, when Muslim extremists massacred 63 tourists in Luxor (Upper Egypt). Mubarak re-instated the state of emergency and Egypt rapidly became a place where anyone displaying Islamic sympathies risked being arrested and tried in a military tribunal. Mubarak created these military courts in the early 1990s after state security courts began to acquit accused on grounds that evidence against them had been obtained through the use of torture and, as such, was inadmissible (Brown 1997). The move to try civilians in courts where the evidentiary standards were far less stringent than civil or even security courts was quite a dramatic break with the previous decades' emphasis on support for democratic institutions and rights-based legislation.

The growing popularity of the Muslim Brotherhood combined with violent attacks by Muslim extremists in Upper Egypt, and the fact that Islam had become a generally accepted part of the social and political discourse did not leave legal development unaffected. Individual claimants began bringing claims before the courts as to the 'un-Islamic' content of books, films, and government decisions (e.g. the prohibition on wearing the *niqab* (veil covering the face) in public schools and the ban on female circumcision in state hospitals) (Bälz 1998, 1999).

In some cases, claimants found a sympathetic ear within the judiciary. This appeared especially to have been the case, when Islamist lawyers brought before the court the case of university professor Nasr Abu

Zayd, whom they accused of apostasy on the basis of his academic writings. While apostasy is not punishable under Egyptian penal law, it does carry certain legal consequences under personal status law such as the interdiction of marriage between a Muslim woman and a non-Muslim man, or intestate inheritance between Muslims and non-Muslim relatives. In the case of Nasr Abu Zayd, it was argued that his writings rendered him an apostate and, consequently, that the marriage with his Muslim wife was void, since he was not a Muslim anymore (Berger & Dupret 1998; Berger 2003). This argument was upheld by the Court of Cassation, which, after lengthy deliberations on the nature of his writings, ruled in 1997 that Nasr Abu Zayd was indeed an apostate. This argument has since then been successfully used against a number of Egyptian intellectuals (Yüksel 2007: 179), although legislative changes have curtailed this practice.[10]

In contrast, the Supreme Constitutional Court, entrusted with the review of legislation on the basis of their constitutionality – including Article 2 declaring sharia to be 'the principal source of legislation' – has adopted a more cautious position with regard to the use of Islamic rules and principles (Bälz 1998, 1999; Bernard-Maugiron 1998, 2003). The Court has laid down a few important ground rules: first, it is the only court allowed to rule on (in)compatibility of Egyptian legislation with the sharia; and, second, only legislation implemented after 1980 must conform to the principles of the sharia. Furthermore, the Constitutional Court holds a restrictive view of what is encompassed by obligatory rules of sharia and, consequently, accords the legislature a wide margin of legislative freedom.

The 1990s were also tumultuous with regard to the subject of human rights. Several Egyptian human rights organisations that adopted an independent and critical stance towards the government were established. Western countries gave considerable financial and moral backing to these groups in an effort to further stimulate a broader agenda for developmental cooperation, which placed a high value on the development of civil society. The Egyptian government tacitly tolerated these organisations; but, in 1999, it amended the law on non-governmental organisations so that human rights organisations came directly under the scrutiny of the Ministry of Social Affairs, causing these organisations to lose their independence. Furthermore, in 2000, several human rights organisations were indicted for accepting Western funds to finance their activities. This action was justified with a dormant decree from 1992 that was based on the Emergency Law.

As for economic liberalisation, the economic crisis of the 1980s necessitated far-reaching economic reforms. Western willingness to waive large parts of Egypt's considerable international debt after its participation in the Gulf War in 1991 was a first step in this process. By 1996, the Egyptian government had embarked on structural measures of privatisation and liberalisation (Dupret 2003). These measures were met with great confidence from national and foreign investors as well as from the World Bank and the IMF. Because the constitution of 1980 required all legislation to be in conformity with the principles of sharia, the new economic and commercial legislation has been scrutinised in this respect. This constitutional requirement has thus far, however, not proven to be an obstacle to the enactment and implementation of laws that complied with the modern financial world, such as the 1999 Code of Commerce.

Islamic finance has gained popularity, but it has manifested itself in the private finance sector rather than within the scope of the above mentioned legislation (al-Ahmad 1996). Its focus on consumer credit in combination with its Islamic credentials have made Islamic banking an attractive alternative to common banks that, due to their socialist heritage, traditionally targeted large industrial and construction projects. Even a major fraud scandal in one of the main Egyptian Islamic finance houses in the early 1980s failed to affect the credibility of Islamic finance. By the late 1990s, Islamic financial services were provided by Egyptian as well as international banks. A matter of debate remains, however, as to what extent 'Islamic finance' is indeed another way of financing or whether it follows established economic and legal principles, but refrains from certain types of activities, thereby rephrasing its financial products in 'Islamic' terms (el-Gamal 2003; Kuran 2004). The fact that Islamic financial institutions were not affected by the financial crisis of 2008 was reason for some to argue the superiority of this kind of financing; others pointed out that Islamic finance takes place in a niche of the financial market, which happened to be outside the scope of activities that were involved in the crisis.

Concluding, we can say that the 1990s saw a mounting legal activity in which the sharia played a pivotal role. From the side of the government, which had committed itself under Sadat to the sharia by means of constitutional reform, most legislation paid lip service to the sharia (mostly with the remark that the law 'is not contradictory to sharia principles'), but actually showed no radical changes in terms of the previous legislation or significant differences with comparable legislation in non-Muslim countries. By contrast, Islamic regulation gained much popularity in the private sector. This was primarily expressed in dress codes and rules of morality and social behaviour, but also in adoption of Islamic financial instruments, whether by private banks or in neighbourhood settings. This private initiative also became manifest in the increase of litigation on Islam-related matters. This is exemplified by the many cases in which intellectuals, academics, and artists have been accused of un-Islamic behaviour or views that, if proven, would render them apostates. Cases brought before the Supreme Constitutional Court on claims that promulgated decrees and laws contradict the sharia, and therefore Article 2 of the Constitution, are also indicative of this trend. The general eagerness to petition the courts since the 1990s has resulted in a growing importance in the role of the judiciary, whereby the lower courts show a tendency to easily accept Islamic rules and legal reasoning, often to be rebuked by higher courts for failing to adhere to the national law of Egypt.

The new millennium

After the relative political calm and economic optimism of the late 1990s, the new millennium brought with it new setbacks as Muslim extremists again committed a series of bloody attacks in 2004 and 2005. While the government reacted harshly and arrested many people, it simultaneously implemented a number of political reforms. Many analysts see this liberalisation and modernisation of policy as a reaction to the 9/11 attacks in the United States, which caused a major change in American policy *vis-à-vis* the Middle East. Where in the previous two decenniums, the U.S. had supported the Egyptian regimes for its stability rather than its democratic credentials, this policy was drastically revised after the 9/11 attacks. The U.S. administration was of the opinion that the lack of democracy in Arab countries was the root cause of Islamic terrorism.

With this change in American policy, the Egyptian government was forced to walk the tightrope between undemocratic measures allegedly needed in the interest of security and stability, and international pressure to democratise. For example, in 2005 and 2007, the government presented constitutional amendments in which the one-candidate presidential elections (i.e. people could vote 'yes' or 'no' for a single presidential candidate nominated by parliament) were changed into multi-candidate elections (2005). At the same time, however, the number of presidential terms was increased, allowing President Mubarak to again run for office. In the presidential elections of September 2005, nine candidates ran alongside President Mubarak. However, in ways similar to the one-candidate elections, the multi-candidate elections were rife with allegations of foul play, violence against the opposition and demonstrators, and coercion and intimidation, causing a number of international players and human rights groups to question Egypt's 'newfound' democracy. In any case, Mubarak won the elections and began his fifth term in office.

Another amendment presented as a democratic reform was the proposition to lift the state of emergency in exchange for more stringent anti-terrorism and anti-opposition regulations. Parliament consented, but allowed for another extension of the state of emergency until mid-2010, during which period it intends to draft new anti-terrorist legislation to replace the Emergency Law.

Other 'democratic' constitutional amendments that were severely criticised include those relating to political participation and the electoral process. Article 5 of the Constitution was amended in order to prohibit not only the formation of a political party on religious grounds (a ban that already existed in the Law on Political Parties of 1977), but also any political activity on a religious basis or within any religious frame of reference. In addition, Article 62 of the Constitution was amended in such a way as to marginalise the participation of independent candidates in elections. Most likely these amendments were motivated by the parliamentary elections of late 2005 in which the independent candidates of the Muslim Brotherhood won a landslide victory.

Finally, amendments to Article 88 of the Constitution minimised judicial supervision over elections through the establishment of an electoral committee that is no longer comprised purely of judges, but now includes additional members to be appointed at the discretion of, and directly by, the President. According to critics, this amendment was a response to the increasing number of judicial decisions following each election, invalidating parliamentarian seats due to irregularities in the electoral process.

In contrast to the 1990s, when no legal initiatives were undertaken in the field of Islamic personal status law, the first years of the new millennium witnessed several substantive reforms. This period of reform is symbolically expressed by one of the most radical reforms also being Egypt's first law of the twenty-first century. Article 20 of Law 1/2000 effectively provides for the right of women to unilaterally divorce their husbands through a court procedure called *khul'* (Sonneveld 2009; see also 2.6). This is exceptional for two reasons. Firstly, while the law was presented as a law of procedure, it, in actual fact, contains rules of substantive law. Secondly, although the article on *khul'* was presented as being in accordance with the sharia, it is not part of the corpus of any of the four Sunni schools of jurisprudence. Sunni jurisprudence is unanimous in accepting a *khul'* divorce *only* upon permission of the husband, but the new Egyptian law deemed the husband's consent to his *khul'* divorce irrelevant. This law therefore brought about an expansion of the authority of the legislature with regard to interpretation of the sharia. In addition to the instruments that had been used by Egyptian legislature until 1985 in pushing for legal reforms, namely *takhayyur* and *talfiq*, the concept of *ijtihad* had now been incorporated in order to reach an interpretation of *khul'* nonexistent in the four Sunni schools of jurisprudence (cf. Arabi 2001). The Supreme Constitutional Court affirmed this interpretation, declaring in December 2002 that the article on *khul'* was in compliance with the sharia.

A number of other reforms in personal status law were enacted quietly during this period in the slipstream of the successful introduction of the *khul'* law (Sonneveld 2009). In August 2000, for instance, after consistent opposition during the 1990s, a new standard marriage contract was introduced and adopted; it gives women the right to insert substantive conditions, such as the right to automatic divorce in case the husband marries a second wife and the right to work and education, in the marriage contract. In November 2000, another controversial issue was tackled, when women were given the option of applying for a passport without the consent of their husbands, which, in turn, gave them the right of travel without spousal consent.

In January 2003, the first female judge was appointed in Egypt. Tehani al-Gebali became a judge on the Supreme Constitutional Court. Together with the coming into force of the new family courts in October 2004, this move was seen by many proponents of women's rights as a first step towards the appointment of female judges in family courts. Indeed, in April 2007, this goal was realised when the Supreme Judicial Council swore in thirty female judges to different courts of first instance in Cairo, Giza, and Alexandria.[11]

In legal terms, the first decade of the millennium was characterised by two developments: political reforms of an allegedly democratic nature; and reforms in the field of personal status laws. Whereas the latter were based on Islamic law, the first were not. Interestingly, the Islamically-motivated reforms of personal status law were more progressive than ever before, while the political reforms largely paid lip service to democracy, imparting little actual change. One of the explanations for the apparent paradox in introducing women's rights by way of reference to sharia is the concerted effort of a number of women activists to base reform in the multiple sources on Islamic thinking and the sharia by exploring ways of *ijtihad*, thus in effect sidestepping the intellectual legacy of classical Islamic legal theory (Arabi 2001; Singerman 2005).[12]

2.5 Constitutional law

Egypt's constitution was adopted in 1971, and amended in 1980, 2005 and 2007. The 1971 constitution replaced Nasser's heritage of one-party socialism with the more democratic system of a parliament with political parties. The amendments of 1980 were concerned with the role of sharia in national legislation (see below) and laid down the powers of the Supreme Constitutional Court, which had been established the year before. Of the 2005 and 2007 amendments, the latter were the most comprehensive (see 2.4). Their main thrust is toward democratic reform and economic liberalisation. New repressive provisions about emergency law have already been contested strongly, and the political debate about the need for another round of reforms is expected to continue.

According to this constitution Egypt is a 'democratic state' based on the separation of the three powers of the government, the People's Assembly and the judiciary. The political system is officially based on the plurality of parties, but at the same time it is forbidden to establish a political party on the basis of religion, race or gender, nor when the new party's programme is similar to that of an existing party. In addition, the constitution lays down the basic rights and freedoms of citizens, which include the freedom of belief and the freedom of practising religious rights, the freedom of expression, as well as press freedom.

The Supreme Constitutional Court was established for the purpose of reviewing compatibility of legislation with the Constitution. In Egypt, legislation is promulgated by the People's Assembly. The 1980 amendment made 'the principles of the sharia' *the* primary legal source for all Egyptian legislation. The Supreme Constitutional Court has ruled that this condition for legislation only applied to laws promulgated after 1980. Although the Supreme Constitutional Court is the only judicial forum with jurisdiction to evaluate the constitutionality of laws, the Supreme Administrative Court (the highest legal organ of the Council of State) has also played a role in assessing legislative compatibility with the sharia. From case law it appears that both Courts interpret 'principles of the sharia' restrictively. According to both courts, these principles are confined to rules that are 'fixed and indisputable', which technically refers to rules explicitly mentioned in the Quran or the Sunna, and that are not open to deviation or interpretation. For all other rules, the Courts have held that the Egyptian legislator is authorised to independently interpret the sharia (*ijtihad*) in a way that respects the goals and intention of the sharia (Arabi 2002; Bälz 1998, 1999; Berger 2003; Dupret 1997).

The Constitution provides for an independent and non-arbitrary judiciary. The Egyptian judiciary is indeed known for that. In section 2.4 we have noted, for example, that the government in its prosecution of alleged terrorists felt compelled to turn to military tribunals because regular as well as security criminal courts began to increasingly acquit suspects due to the unlawful manner in which evidence had been procured. Another example is the nullification of electoral results at various elections, although this form of judicial scrutiny was curbed by the constitutional amendment of 2007.

2.6 Personal status and family law

Egyptian personal status law is based on the Hanafi school of jurisprudence. This law applies to all Egyptians, regardless of their religion. An exception applies to issues of marriage and divorce, where Christians and Jews may apply their own laws.[13] Application of these laws is determined by the religious denomination of the litigants involved, providing that the couples are of the same religion (Islam, Christianity, Judaism), denomination (for the Christians: Catholic, Orthodox, and Protestant), and sect (for the Orthodox: Coptic, Greek, Syrian, Armenian). For marriages between individuals of different religions (e.g. the union between a Jew and a Christian) or between different denominations (e.g. the union between a Catholic and an Orthodox) or between different sects (e.g. the union between a Greek Orthodox and a Coptic Orthodox), the Muslim law of marriage and divorce applies (Berger 2001).

Islamic personal status law, including marriage and divorce, has only been partially codified in Laws No. 25/1920 and No. 25/1929, both amended and augmented by Laws No. 100/1985 and No. 1/2000. Where the codified law is silent on a given matter, the judge must resort to the 'prevalent opinion within the Hanafi school of jurisprudence' (Decree on the Organisation of the Shari'a Courts (1931), Art. 280).

Marriage

A marriage concluded in accordance with the applicable religious law (Islamic, Christian, or Jewish) needs to be registered in order for it to be legally valid. For Muslims, registration must be undertaken with the civil registrar (*ma'dhun*). Non-Muslims and foreigners are required to register their marriage with the Ministry of Justice. Unregistered marriages – *urfi* marriages for Muslims, church/synagogue marriages for non-Muslims – are, in principle, in legal limbo. While they may be considered socially valid, they are not recognised by the courts as per Article 99 on the Law on the Organisation of Sharia Courts. This is especially problematic for women who are, thus, prevented from petitioning the court for enforcement of their marital rights (e.g. maintenance or divorce). However, after the introduction of new procedural law on personal status in 2000, women in *urfi* marriages have been given the possibility to divorce, on the condition that they provide some form of documentation proving their marriage.

One of the formal conditions to an Islamic marriage is the offer and acceptance of the bride and the groom in the presence of two male Muslim witnesses. A religious ceremony or the presence of a cleric is common, but not required under the law. In August 2000, a new marriage contract was introduced which added the possibility of including certain conditions for marriage annulment. Another condition of an Islamic marriage is the dower (*mahr* or *sadaq*), a sum of money to be paid by the groom to the bride.[14] Usually, only a small part is paid upon conclusion of the marriage (*muqaddam al-sadaq*, or prompt dower) and the remaining part (*mu'akhkhar al-sadaq*, or deferred dower) upon divorce or decease of the husband. The dower must be registered in the marriage contract.

Divorce

Under Islamic law, men may end their marriages unilaterally without being required to produce a reason for the divorce. This form of divorce, or end to the marriage, is called repudiation (*talaq*). Under Egyptian law, this right is upheld but can only be enforced once the husband has registered the divorce with the civil registrar (*ma'dhun*) within thirty days after he has pronounced the *talaq*. The registrar is, in turn, required to notify the wife of her divorce. Failure to register the repudiation does not render the divorce invalid, but is punishable by a jail sentence of up to six months and/or a penalty of up to two hundred Egyptian pounds (approximately 25 Euros).

A woman in Egypt can initiate divorce in various ways: in court by judicial divorce (*tatliq*), by means of contractual stipulations, and by way of *khul'* (upon payment of financial compensation and renunciation of financial rights). The latter can also take place outside the court when the husband divorces his wife upon her request (which mostly is granted only upon payment of financial compensation).

In the first type of female-initiated divorce (*tatliq*), the wife may petition the court for divorce on one of the grounds identified in the law. These grounds include: a) the husband's absence of more than one year without an acceptable excuse, or a three-year absence caused by a prison sentence; b) damage or harm caused to the wife, which is defined on the basis of the wife's socio-economic position (and in certain cases including the husband marrying a second wife); c) failure by the husband to fulfil his legal obligation of maintaining his wife; and d) a severe illness of the husband of which the wife was not aware at the time the marriage was concluded.

The second way for women to obtain divorce is through contractual stipulations. Since 2000, a woman has the possibility to include such stipulations in her marriage contract. For instance, she can stipulate that her husband will not marry another wife or that she is allowed to work outside the home. When the husband violates these stipulations, a woman has the right to dissolve the marital bond. Another kind of contractual agreement is that the man cedes his right of *talaq* to his wife, so that she may unilaterally divorce herself (*talaq al-tafwid*). In actuality, however, women in Egypt seem reluctant to make use of this new right (Sonneveld 2009).

In the third form of divorce, a wife may ask her husband to divorce her in exchange for financial compensation. In practice, financial compensation in these cases has meant the waiving of alimony payments or of the remaining portion of the dower. This divorce, concluded by mutual consent, is referred to as *khul'* or *ibra'* and falls under the purview of the civil registrar (*ma'dhun*). A non-consensual form of *khul'* was incorporated into Egyptian law for the first time in 2000, introducing a radical break with the *khul'* as commonly defined by classical Islamic jurisprudence. According to this jurisprudence, a *khul'* divorce requires the husband's consent. The woman's wish for divorce could, therefore, easily be frustrated by the husband, either because he did not want to divorce her or because he found the financial compensation inadequate. Under the new law of 2000, the divorce has to be legally accepted by the judge – without the need for the husband's consent – when the wife has met all of the following conditions: a) she forfeits her financial rights; b) she returns to her husband the prompt dower which her husband gave her when contracting the marriage; c) she goes through a period of reconciliation; and d) she explicitly proclaims in court that she hates living with her husband and, as a result of that, is afraid to cross the limits of God.

Another type of divorce that has gained notoriety is the invocation of nullity of a marriage based on the conversion or apostasy of one of the spouses. This is related to the rule that allows for mixed religious marriages if the husband is Muslim, but declares void a marriage between a Muslim woman and a non-Muslim man. If in a non-Muslim marriage, for instance, the woman converts to Islam, her marriage is rendered void. The same applies to a Muslim couple where one of the two – but especially the husband – renounces Islam or converts to another religion, hence becoming an apostate of Islam. These situations occur in non-Muslim marriages in order to obtain a divorce. Since the 1990s, however, it has also been used as a legal instrument to substantiate the accusation of un-Islamic behaviour: since apostasy as such is not punishable under Egyptian law, a third party may call upon Egyptian marriage law in order to nullify a marriage of a person due to his or her alleged apostasy. The most infamous case was that of the abovementioned Nasr Abu Zayd, a university professor whose work was considered blasphemous, and who in 1996 was divorced from his wife on the basis of apostasy. Consequently, the legal basis upon which a third party could raise such a divorce case (*hisba*) has changed: from 2001 only the public prosecutor may raise divorce cases on the basis of the accusation of apostasy.

Since the establishment of a new Family court system in 2004, all matters pertaining to divorce, such as alimony and custody, are treated by one and the same judge in one court. The new legislation also specifies that husbands in divorce cases initiated by their spouses can appeal only once against the court's decision and this appeal cannot be to the Court of Cassation. In case of a divorce through *khul'*, the husband cannot appeal at all.

Consequences of divorce

After divorce, children are entitled to alimony (*nafaqa*) to be paid by the father. Since 2000, men who do not fulfil their alimony obligations are punishable with jail sentences of up to thirty days.

Egyptian law allows for two kinds of financial compensation for the ex-wife, depending on the type of divorce. In the event of a regular repudiation or judicial divorce, men are required to continue maintaining their ex-wives for a period of three months (the so-called *'iddah* period during which the woman cannot marry another man in order to make sure that she is not pregnant by her ex-husband). In case of repudiation, the man is also obliged to pay financial compensation (*muta'*), if the wife did not play a role in bringing about the repudiation and did not consent to it. This compensation may equal the maintenance for a period of up to at least two years. Women who initiated the divorce through *khul'* or by invoking breach of the marital contract stipulations are not entitled to either *'iddah* or *muta'* compensation.

With regard to the children of divorced parents, a distinction must be made between guardianship (*wilaya*) and fosterage (*hadana*) of the children. Guardianship refers to the overall supervision of the children in financial affairs and matters such as the choice of school. Guardianship lies with the father and remains with him after divorce until the children reach maturity. Fosterage on the other hand is the day-to-day care of children and is the right and duty of divorced mothers. According to Egyptian law, this right applies to daughters until the age of twelve and to the sons until they reach ten years of age. Once the fosterage periods lapses, children are transferred to the care of their father unless a judge determines that it is in their best interest to remain with their mother. In case of the latter, the law allows fosterage of girls to be extended until they marry (or reach the majority age of 21 years before that time) and of boys until they reach the age of fifteen.

Inheritance

Islamic inheritance law has a strong religious foundation due to the many inheritance rules laid down in the Quran and Sunna. Egyptian intestate and testamentary inheritance laws (Law of 1946 and 1943, respectively) are based on the Hanafi school of law, although selective use has been made of rules of the other schools of law (*takhayyur*). In some instances rules have been inserted that have no basis in sharia at all, like the possibility to testate to legal heirs.

Intestate law adheres to the complicated system of fractions and portions of the estate to be divided in a certain order among the heirs specified in the Quran and the male heirs on father's side. By testament, a maximum of one third of the estate may be bequeathed. These laws apply to all Egyptians, regardless of their religion. This means, among other things, that according to intestate inheritance law women are entitled to half the amount men are entitled to if they both occupy the same testamentary inheritance positions (e.g. when they are brother and sister). It also means that Muslims and non-Muslims may not legally inherit from each other; these rules, however, do not apply to testamentary bequests. Therefore, in the case of a marriage between a Muslim man and a non-Muslim woman, the spouses may not inherit from each other; neither may the children in such a marriage, who are legally considered Muslims, inherit from their non-Muslim mother. However, this religious impediment does not apply to the testamentary inheritance, so that Muslims may freely – but up to a maximum of one third of the estate – testate to non-Muslims and vice versa.

2.7 Criminal law

The Egyptian Criminal Penal Code, adopted in 1937, was influenced by the Italian Criminal Code, but does mention in Article 7 that its application should not 'violate a right established by the Sharia', a restriction that was rarely applied (Najjar 1992). Egyptian criminal legislation applies many fundamental rule of law concepts such as the principle of legality of crime and penalty, a presumption of innocence, equality of arms, and the right to a defence (Akida 2002: 39-40).

Under Egyptian criminal law it is possible to criminally prosecute missionary activities conducted by non-Muslims on the basis of Article 98f of the Criminal Code, while missionary activities conducted by Muslims are allowed. Such cases have thus far never led to actual legal prosecution by the public prosecutor. It must be noted, however, that this provision is related to public order rather than to sharia. This is probably due to both a colonial past with strong Christian missionary activities and a pan-Arab past with an emphasis on Arab unity as opposed to religious disunity: this has led up to the general notion that religious disharmony, whether created by incitement or missionary activities, is detrimental to national security.

Overriding the Criminal Code, however, is the Emergency Law, which has been in effect since it was enacted in 1956 (although it actually dates back to the monarchy), with the exception of two short breaks in the periods between 1964-1967 and 1980-1981. The required parliamentary permission for extending the state of emergency is duly given every three years. The main justification for this extension is the fight against terrorism and Islamic extremism. This law authorises the president to enforce measures that are contrary to national laws, such as restricting the freedom of association, assembly, and expression; the searching of people and places; and the arbitrary arrest and extended detention of persons suspected of posing a threat to national security. Presidents Sadat and Mubarak repeatedly used their unbridled rights under the Emergency Law in their alleged fight against terrorism and Islamic extremism.

2.8 Other legal areas, especially economic law

Pursuant to the economic liberalisation policies (*infitah*) started by President Sadat in the 1970s, only in 1996 did Egypt seriously began a process of implementing extensive economic reforms. To this end, legislative changes and legal amendments have been introduced that posed drastic changes of the otherwise socialist-oriented legal structure. For example, in 1999 a new commercial code was promulgated that incorporated the latest legal developments in modern commercial law. Remarkably, this, and other legislation on matters of investment, private enterprise, and the stock market, has until now been found to be in accordance with sharia (as is required by Article 2 of the constitution).

Due to the liberalisation of the economy and its regulations, private commercial and financial initiatives have picked up considerably since the 1980s (Amin 1995; Moore 1997; Oweiss 1990). A special branch that gained popularity within this development was the financial business based on Islamic principles, commonly referred to as 'Islamic banking' or 'Islamic finance'. These principles include the avoidance of usury and the prohibition of interest, and have resulted in the creation of legal constructs for financial contracts that meet the standards of modern financial transactions as well as the tenets of sharia. Contracts for mortgage and insurance, while technically not permitted, are now possible in an alternative form of contract that meets the requirements of sharia. The significance of these Islamic financial instruments is widely debated. While some argue that the newly construed Islamic contracts are not essentially different from common modern contracts, others point at the fact that Islamic finance only covers a limited part of the field of finance and investment (el-Gamal 2003; Kuran 2004).

2.9 International treaty obligations and human rights

Egypt's formal commitment to international human rights is laudable, with numerous treaty and convention ratifications beginning from the early 1980s. Its actual human rights record, on the other hand, is poor. Egypt remains a state ruled by an authoritarian regime where fundamental rights such as the prohibition against torture and ill-treatment, freedom of expression, and due process under the law are regularly denied.

The almost continuous use of the Emergency Law since 1956 makes it easier for the authorities to arrest and detain for extensive periods of time anyone who poses what they consider to be a threat. While its use has been justified by the threat of terrorism and Islamic extremism, in practice it has meant regular crackdowns on the Muslim Brotherhood; unjustified and unchecked arrests and detentions of journalists, bloggers, and human rights defenders; and political harassment and arbitrary detention of opposition leaders and supporters.

Several local and international human rights organisations have for many years criticised Egypt's human rights record, in particular with regard to routine torture, arbitrary detentions, and unfair trials before military and state security courts. In 2005, President Mubarak faced unprecedented public criticism, when he clamped down on pro-democracy activists challenging his rule.

There is quite some legislation that is discriminatory with regard to non-Muslim minorities. Laws dating from Ottoman times that restrict the building of churches and open worship for non-Muslims have recently been eased, but major construction still requires governmental approval. Another issue is that of the religion mentioned on Egyptian identity cards. Because the Egyptian legal system only recognises three religions (Islam, Christianity, and Judaism), members of other religions, such as Baha'ís, cannot obtain identification documents (although an Egyptian court in early 2008 ruled to the contrary). Also, a Muslim who converts to another religion cannot change his identity card, (which, for instance, would be helpful to indicate the applicable family law to the court).

It must be noted that the role of sharia in this respect is limited. An exception is personal status law, which contains quite some gender and religious inequalities that are directly derived from Islamic tenets. It is this aspect that also shows in the reservations made by Egypt in its ratification of international human rights treaties. These reservations generally state that the treaty should not infringe upon principles of the sharia.

For example, when ratifying the International Covenant on Civil and Political Rights (ICCPR) in January 1982, Egypt noted the following: 'taking into consideration the provisions of the Islamic Sharia and the fact that they do not conflict with the text annexed to the instrument, we accept, support and ratify it.' Similar reservations were made to the Convention on the Elimination of All Forms of Discrimination against Women (CEDAW). These reservations are either expressed with regard to entire treaties or with regard to specific articles. In contrast, the June 1986 ratification of the Committee Against Torture (CAT) took place without the specification of any reservations. This can be explained by the fact that the sharia-reservations usually refer to issues of equality, in particular equality based on gender and religion. As demonstrated in section 2.6, such inequalities are widespread in the Egyptian religion-based family laws (both for Muslims and non-Muslims), laws that are often considered sacrosanct.

A complicated case of human rights violations is that of female circumcision, an age old custom that pre-dates Islam and is practised by both Christians and Muslims in Egypt. According to recent estimates, FGM is practiced on more than 95 per cent of girls in Egypt. In the 1990s, the Sheikh of al-Azhar, one of the highest religious authorities in Egypt, declared this practice to be in conformity with Islam. His successor, Sheikh Tantawi, has expressly argued the opposite since 1996. A similar rejection was made by the Coptic pope Shenouda. A 1996 ministerial decision banning female circumcision in hospitals and clinics was brought before court for allegedly conflicting with the sharia, but this case was emphatically rejected by the Supreme Administrative Court (Bälz 1998). The ministerial decree proved ineffective, however, and in 2007 a law made it punishable to perform such circumcision. However, the custom appears hard to eradicate.

The Egyptian state, while often guilty of perpetrating or condoning human rights violations, claims to adhere to human rights. For this purpose, the government in 2003 established the National Council for Human Rights, headquartered in Cairo; its director directly reports to the president. The council has come under heavy criticism by local NGO activists, who contend it undermines human rights work in Egypt by serving as a propaganda tool for the government to excuse its violations and to provide legitimacy to repressive laws such as the renewed Emergency Law (soon to be replaced by counter-terrorism legislation).

2.10 Conclusion

Although brief, the French occupation of Egypt in 1798-1801 inspired Egyptian leaders to modernise the country according to European models. In 1883, comprehensive national legislation of mainly French origin was introduced, as was a new national court system to implement the new laws. As a result, the jurisdiction of existing sharia courts was limited to personal status law. Later, in the 1920s, this personal status law was codified, at the time a unique development in sharia jurisprudence.

While limited in terms of its applicability in national law, sharia remained important as calls for modernisation were paralleled by reforms in Islamic thought. Islamic modernisers were intent on modernising the country, but they did not want Egypt to lose its Islamic character. Thus, rather than blindly adopting Western models, they argued that modernisation needed to be rooted in sharia. In order to adapt sharia to modern times, Islamic reformers such as al-Tahtawi and Abduh argued that the four (Sunni) schools of Islamic Law were equal to each other and that instead of conforming to one school of law (*taqlid*), Muslims needed to follow the legal interpretations of one of the four schools of law that suited the general public interest best (a practice known as *takhayyur*). Abduh went even further, suggesting that Muslims should independently interpret the sources of sharia by a process of free interpretation (*ijtihad*).

However, at the beginning of the twentieth century, both substantive as well as procedural laws were still largely derived from French codes, with the exception of marriage laws. Reform of sharia was thus largely limited to the field of personal status, where the sharia provisions relating to marriage and divorce were codified. Aiming to enhance the position of women, the first codification of Muslim personal status law in 1920 gave women more rights to divorce while simultaneously curbing men's right to polygamy and divorce by introducing procedural constraints. In 1929, this law was amended, further expanding women's grounds for divorce and curtailing men's right to polygamy and divorce.

This period also witnessed Egypt's independence from Great Britain in 1922 and the introduction of its first constitution in 1923. The constitution was modelled after the Belgium constitution and contained no references to sharia. In 1928, the Egyptian Muslim Brotherhood was established. Though the reintroduction of sharia was part of the organisation's ideology, it was not until the 1970s that it was used as a political slogan.

Under the leadership of Nasser (1952-1970) and the prevalent secular and socialist ideology of that time, the introduction of sharia was pushed even more to the background. In 1955, the Religious Courts were abolished and replaced by national courts although religious laws were not abolished and instead remained intact. Many socialist elements were introduced and women were given more constitutional rights. However, as there were no corresponding reforms in personal status law, women could vote, become ministers and work outside the home, but in order to leave the marital home or travel, they still needed the permission of their husbands.

Egypt's defeat in the Six-Day War of 1967 gave impetus to the resurgence of Islam as many Egyptians considered the defeat to be God's punishment for a nation that had deviated from the true path of religion. Political pressure to introduce the sharia increased and Nasser decided to make religion a national theme, something which was continued under Sadat (1970-1981) and is still today under Mubarak (1981-present).

Upon taking office in 1970, Sadat released many members of the Muslim Brotherhood from prison and in 1971 he was behind the adoption of a new constitution that turned the principles of the sharia into 'a' major source of legislation and Islam into the religion of the state. By a constitutional amendment in 1980 the principles of the sharia were elevated to the status of being 'the' major source of legislation. Turning to the West as well, Sadat had to balance the demands of the international community with growing domestic pressure to introduce sharia in other parts of Egypt's legal system. Walking this tight rope, Sadat signed many international treaties, such as CEDAW and ICCPR, but included reservations to ensure that the human rights provisions would not violate the sharia.

Pre-existing legislation was not affected by the prominent place now assigned to sharia, as the Supreme Constitutional Court ruled in 1984 that for the sake of legal certainty only legislation enacted after the 1980 amendment needed to be in accordance with the principles of sharia. All legislation enacted before 1980 was unaffected by the new constitution. This was especially important in the field of civil and commercial law as the widely applied legal provisions on charging rent on loans were not affected by the Islamic prohibition of usury.

The Supreme Constitutional Court has ruled that new legislation cannot contradict those rules of sharia whose origin and interpretation are definitive. Other rules of sharia, however, are open to independent reasoning (*ijtihad*). Through this ruling, the Court has paved the way for innovative legislation that surpasses the doctrines of the four schools of (Sunni) law. An example of such legislative reform based on sharia is the *khul'* law of 2000, which was ruled constitutional by the Supreme Constitutional Court.

The court also ruled that it is the only court allowed to rule on (in) compatibility of Egyptian legislation with the sharia. Interestingly, most cases that are brought to its attention concern matters of personal status. In other fields of law, there is apparently little pressure to introduce sharia. Seemingly, sharia continues to merely apply to personal status issues. The introduction of the principles of the sharia being the most important source of legislation, the growing influence of Islam in Egyptian society, and extremist Muslim violence, particularly in the 1990s, do not seem to have changed this.

On the basis of these developments, one can conclude that in Egypt's legal system a form of compromise has been found between sharia and Western law. This does not mean that a new system of laws has appeared. The critical element appears to be that national law and legislation must be authentic, and in the eyes of many Egyptians this means that it must be Islamic. Until now, one finds introduction of nominal authentic Islamic legal principles only in personal status law; all other legislation is considered Islamic by virtue of not contradicting principles of sharia. Whether authentic or symbolic, Egypt mostly uses sharia for adapting legislation to current and new situations, in part because of international pressure to adhere to international treaties and conventions.

Notes

1 Maurits Berger is a professor of Islam at the Faculty of Humanities, University of Leiden. Nadia Sonneveld is a senior researcher on the implementation of Islamic law in practice affiliated with the School of Oriental and African Studies (SOAS), University of London, and the Van Vollenhoven Institute, University of Leiden. The authors wish to thank Dr Baudouin Dupret of the Centre d'Études et Documentation Economique, Juridique et Sociale (CEDEJ) and the Université Louvain-la-Neuve for his elaborate comments and suggestions.

2 There are four schools of jurisprudence in Sunni Islam: the Hanafi, Hanbali, Maliki, and Shafi'i schools. An example of *takhayyur* in the Egyptian context is as follows. Under Islamic law, a woman may seek divorce if she can demonstrate that actions taken by her husband have resulted in 'harm' (*darar*). Within the Hanafi school, the Islamic school of jurisprudence relied on in Egypt, *darar* includes physical and financial harm, but not psychological distress or harm. The Maliki school of thought, in contrast, interprets *darar* as physical, economic, or mental harm, and as such permits the judge to accept divorce on any of these grounds (cf. Vikør 2005: 314). Were Egyptian Islamic scholars to interpret harm in the latter manner (i.e. along the lines of the Maliki school), this would constitute *takhayyur*, or an incorporation of legal interpretation outside of Egypt's own (Hanafi) school of jurisprudence.

3 The term *mufti* can have multiple meanings. In general, it translates as 'official interpreter of Islamic law', but in the Egyptian context state *mufti* refers to the position held by the highest, or supreme, advisor on Islamic matters to the state, also known as the 'grand mufti'.

4 *Salafiya* or *Salafism* (literally 'predecessors' or 'ancestors') was a very liberal form of Islam that turned into an ultra-conservative movement a century later, among other things because of its connection to Wahhabism.

5 Controversy arose, for example, over an article that deemed polygamy without the first wife's consent as harmful, and which went so far as to provide the first wife with a right to petition the court for divorce upon the second marriage of the husband.

Another article, which gave women with children the right to stay in the matrimonial home after divorce, enraged men, who facing Cairo's difficult housing market, feared that they would be thrown out of their houses. Disagreement also arose over a provision stipulating that women remain entitled to maintenance (*nafaqa*) even if they work without spousal consent (Fawzy 2004: 35-36).

6 The Supreme Constitutional Court's ruling concerning the unconstitutionality of the 1979 Law on personal status should not be interpreted as the court generally taking an anti-women stance. Having created a furore in Egyptian society in January 2000, the same court ruled in November 2000 that women should be given the right to travel without the consent of the husband, and in December 2002, it declared that the highly controversial right of women to unilateral divorce (*khul'*) was in accordance with the constitution. According to Arabi, the commitment of the Supreme Constitutional Court 'to democratic values and constitutional principles ought to be emphasised' (2002: 353).

7 A process that has been labelled 'post-Islamism' (Bayat 2007).

8 For example, in the case where a husband married a second wife against the will of the first wife, the first wife did not have the automatic right of divorce, as was the case in the 1979 Jihan Law. But, under the 1985 law a woman had to apply to the court to determine whether the second marriage had caused the first wife sufficient harm to warrant the dissolution of the marriage.

9 An example is the introduction of payment of compensation (*mut'a*) in cases where a woman has been divorced against her will and without any cause on her part (see also 2.6 below).

10 For instance, individuals no longer have the right to accuse a third party of apostasy in order to have him or her divorced; this has become the prerogative of the public prosecutor. It explains why an Egyptian court rejected such a divorce case, raised against the feminist writer Nawal el Saadawi in 2001 on grounds that the public prosecutor had not filed the case. See Women Living Under Muslim Laws, 'Egypt: Court rejects Saadawi forcible divorce case', http://www.wluml.org/node/638, dated, 31 July 2001.

11 It must be noted that al-Gebali's appointment to the SCC was not without controversy. As a member of the National Council for Women (a 'governmental NGO' headed by the wife of the president, Suzan Mubarak), many have criticised her for being too close to the government.

12 It must be noted that this new way of introducing personal status reform does not tell anything about the acceptance and practice of such reform among the masses. In fact, much personal status reform was still very controversial (Sonneveld 2009).

13 The Christian laws are those of the Coptic-Orthodox, Greek-Orthodox, Syrian-Orthodox, Armenian-Orthodox, Catholic and Protestant denominations. The Jewish laws are those of the Rabbinic and Karaite sects.

14 The dower is to be distinguished from the dowry (money or goods given by the bride and/or her family to the groom and/or his family).

Bibliography

Abdal Rahman Abdal Rehim, A.-R. (1996), 'The family and gender laws in Egypt during the Ottoman period', in A. Sonbol, el-Azhary (ed.), *Women, the family, and divorce laws in Islamic history*, 96-111. Syracuse: Syracuse University Press.

Al-Ahmad, A.Y. (1996), *The Islamic financial instrument utilization*, PhD dissertation. Loughborough: Loughborough University.

Akida, M. (2002), 'Criminal Law', in N. Bernard-Maugiron & B. Dupret (eds.), *Egypt and its Laws*, 37-48. New York: Kluwer Law International.

Al-Ali, N. (2000), *Secularism, gender and the state in the Middle East: The Egyptian women's movement*. Cambridge: Cambridge University Press.

Amin, G. (1995), *Egypt's economic predicament. A study of the interaction of external pressure, political folly and social tension in Egypt, 1960-1990*. Leiden: E.J. Brill.

Arabi, O. (2001), 'The dawning of the third millennium on *Shari'a*: Egypt's Law no. 1 of 2000, or women may divorce at will', *Arab Law Quarterly* 16: 2-21.

Arabi, O. (2002), 'Beyond power: Neo-Shāfi'ism or the Islamic constructive metaphor in Egypt's High Constitutional Court policy', *Arab Law Quarterly* 4: 323-354.

Badran, M. (1995), *Feminists, Islam and nation: Gender and the making of modern Egypt*. Cairo: The American University in Cairo Press.

Bälz, K. (1998), 'Human Rights, the Rule of Law and the Construction of Tradition: The Egyptian Supreme Administrative Court and Female Circumcision', *Égypte Monde Arabe* (No. 34): 141-154, Cairo: CEDEJ.

Bälz, K. (1999), 'The Egyptian Supreme Constitutional Court and the 'battle over the veil' in state-run schools', in B. Dupret (ed.), *Legal pluralism in the Arab world*, 229-243. The Hague: Kluwer Law International.

Bartleby (2010), 'Egypt', in *World Factbook*, see http://www.bartleby.com/151/eg.html (2008 statistics) and https://www.cia.gov/library/publications/the-world-factbook/geos/eg.html (online edition, last accessed February 2010). Washington D.C.: Central Intelligence Agency.

Bayat, A. (2007), *Making Islam democratic: Social movements and the post-Islamist turn*. Stanford: Stanford University Press.

Berger, M. (2003), 'Apostasy and public policy in contemporary Egypt: An evaluation of recent cases of Egypt's highest courts', *Human Rights Quarterly* 25(3): 720-740.

Berger, M. (2002), 'Conflicts law and public policy in Egyptian family law: Islamic law through the backdoor', *American Journal of Comparative Law* 50(3): 555-594.

Berger, M. (2001), 'Public policy and Islamic law: The modern dhimmi in contemporary Egyptian family law', *Islamic Law and Society* 8(1): 88-136.

Berger, M. (2005), *Sharia and public policy in Egyptian family law*. Groningen: Hephaestus Press.

Berger, M. & B. Dupret (1998), 'Jurisprudence Abu Zeid. Extrats des arrets du Tribunal d'Instance de Giza, de la Cour de l'Appel du Caire, traduits vers le francais et de la Cour de la Cassation, traduits vers l'Anglais', *Égypte Monde Arabe* (No. 34): 169-202 Cairo: CEDEJ.

Bernard-Maugiron, N. (1998), 'La Haute Court constitutionnelle Égyptienne en la sharî'a Islamique', *Awrâq* XIX (Dec.): 103-141.

Bernard-Maugiron, N. (2003), *Le Politique à l'épreuve du judiciaire. La justice constitutionnelle en Egypte*. Brussels: Bruylant.

Bernard-Maugiron, N. & B. Dupret (2002), *Egypt and its Laws*. New York: Kluwer Law International.

Botiveau, B. (1994), 'La politique législative à l'égyptienne', in N. 'Abd al-Fattah (ed.), *Politiques législatives: Égypte, Tunésie, Algérie, Maroc*, 121-136, Cairo: Dossiers du CEDEJ.

Brown, N.J. (1997), *The rule of law in the Arab world: Courts in Egypt and the Gulf*. Cambridge: Cambridge Middle East Studies.

Cannon, B. (1988), *Politics of law and the courts in nineteenth century Egypt*. Salt Lake City: University of Utah Press.

Dupret, B. (1997), 'A propos de la Constitutionnalité de la Sharī 'a', *Islamic Law and Society* 4 (1): 91-113.

Dupret, B. (2003), 'A liberal interpretation of a socialist constitution: The Egyptian Supreme Constitutional Court and the privatisation of the public sector', in Eberhard Kienle (ed.),

Politics from above, politics from below: The Middle East in the age of economic reform, 167-190. London: Al-Saqi books.

El Alami, D.S. (1994), 'Law No. 100 of 1985 amending certain provisions of Egypt's personal status laws', *Islamic Law and Society* 1(1): 116-30.

Esposito, J.L. (1982), *Women in Muslim family law.* Syracuse: Syracuse University Press.

Esposito, J.L. & N.J. DeLong-Bas (2001), *Women in Muslim Family Law.* Syracuse: Syracuse University Press.

Fawzy, E. (2004), 'Personal status law in Egypt: An historical overview' in L. Welchmann (ed.), *Women's rights and Islamic family law: Perspectives on reform*, 30-44. London/New York: Zed Books Ltd.

Gamal, M. el- (2003), '"Interest" and the paradox of contemporary Islamic law and finance', *Fordham International Law Journal* 27: 108-149.

Haddad, Y. (1994), 'Muhammad Abduh pioneer of Islamic reform', in A. Rahnema (ed.), *Pioneers of Islamic revival*, 30-63. London: Zed Books.

Hanna, N. (1996), 'Marriage Among Merchant Families in Seventeenth-Century Cairo', in A. Sonbol, el-Azhary (ed.), *Women, the family, and divorce law in Islamic history*, 143-154. Syracuse: Syracuse University Press.

Hatem, M. (2000), 'The pitfalls of the nationalist discourses on citizenship in Egypt', in S. Joseph (ed.), *Gender and citizenship in the Middle East*, 33-57. Syracuse: Syracuse University Press.

Hill, E. (1987), *Al-Sanhuri and Islamic Law.* Cairo: Cairo Papers in Social Science.

Hourani, A. (1970), *Arabic thought in the liberal age 1798-1939.* Oxford: Oxford University Press.

Jansen, J.J.G. (1997), *The dual nature of Islamic fundamentalism.* London: Hurst and Company.

Karam, A.M. (1998), *Women, Islamisms and the state: Contemporary feminisms in Egypt.* New York: St. Martin's Press.

Kuran, T. (2004), *Islam and Mammon: The economic predicaments of Islamism.* Princeton: Princeton University Press.

Lombardi, C.B. (2006), *State Law as Islamic Law in Modern Egypt: The Incorporation of Sharia in Egyptian Constitutional Law.* Leiden: Brill.

Mitchell, R. (1969), *The society of Muslim Brethren.* New York: Oxford University Press.

Moore, P. (1997), *Egypt: Privatisation and beyond. Meeting the challenges of the 21st century.* London: Euromoney Publications.

Moustafa, T. (2000), 'Conflict and cooperation between the state and religious institutions in contemporary Egypt', *International Journal of Middle East Studies* 32(1): 3-22.

Najjar, F. M. (1992), 'The application of sharia law in Egypt', *Middle Eastern Policy* 1: 62-73.

Oweiss, I. (ed.) (1990), '*The political economy of contemporary Egypt*', Center for Contemporary Arab Studies, Georgetown University.

Öhrnberg, K. (1995), 'Al-Tahtawi', in *Encyclopedia of Islam*, 523-524. Leiden: Brill.

Peters, R. (1987), 'Gods wet of 's mensen wet: de Egyptische politiek en de toepassing van het islamitische recht', *Recht van de Islam* 5: 20-49.

Peters, R. (1988), 'Divine Law or Man-Made Law? Egypt and the Application of the Shari'a', *Arab Law Quarterly* 3: 231-253.

Qassem, Y. (2002), 'Law of the Family (Personal Status Law)' in N. Bernard-Maugiron & B. Dupret, *Egypt and its Laws*, 19-36. London/The Hague: Kluwer Law International.

Shaham, R. (1997), *Family and the courts in modern Egypt: A study based on decisions by the Sharî'a Courts, 1900-1955.* Leiden: Brill.

Singerman, D. (2005), 'Rewriting divorce in Egypt: Reclaiming Islam, legal activism and coalition politics' in R.W. Hefner (ed.), *Remaking Muslim politics: Pluralism, contestation, democratization*, 161-188. Princeton: Princeton University Press.

Sonneveld, N. (2009), *Khul' divorce in Egypt: Public debates, judicial practices, and everyday life*, PhD Dissertation. Amsterdam: University of Amsterdam.

Vikør, K.S. (2005), *Between God and the sultan: A history of Islamic law.* New York: Oxford University Press.

Welchman, L. (2007), *Women and Muslim family laws in Arab States: A comparative overview of textual development and advocacy.* Amsterdam: ISIM/Amsterdam University Press.

Yüksel, S. (2007), *The State's response to legal pluralism: The case of Religious Courts law and courts in Israel, Egypt and India*, PhD Dissertation. Seattle: University of Washington.

Zulficar, Mona (forthcoming), 'The Islamic marriage contract in Egypt: An instrument of social change' in possession of Nadia Sonneveld.

3 Sharia and national law in Morocco

Léon Buskens[1]

Abstract

Islamic law has taken a drastically different place in the legal system of Morocco in the course of the twentieth century. The protectorate rule of France and Spain, between 1912 and 1956, was a turning point. Until then, Islamic law was, at least ideally, the law of the state, although in practice the decrees of the sultan and local customs also had considerable importance. Colonialism implied the creation of a dual legal system, formalisation of Islamic and customary law, and large scale import of European legal norms. After independence, this system of legal pluralism was gradually replaced by a unified legal system based on the French legal model. Nowadays, Islamic norms are mainly to be found in the law of family and inheritance, codified in the *Mudawwana*; in limited parts of the law of evidence; and in some areas of the law on immovable property. Although in this process of state formation Islamic norms have been marginalised in substantive terms, they have recently become very important in the political domain. The king uses Islam to legitimise his rule, while islamist opposition movements refer to sharia as a way to criticise the regime in power. In present-day Morocco, opposing groups engage in public debates in which they invoke their particular understandings of Islam, human rights, and civil society.

Table of contents

The Kingdom of Morocco gained independence in 1956. The country counts over 33 million inhabitants and has a surface area of 446,550 square kilometres – roughly the size of California – not including the area mass of the disputed territory of the former Spanish Sahara. A considerable part of the Moroccan population has Berber ancestors with Arabic, sub-Saharan, and European influences. Distinguishing between Arabs and Berbers on a racial basis is impossible, yet the distinction has begun to gain importance as an ethnic phenomenon. The official language is Arabic, but Berber languages are taught at school on a limited scale. Approximately half of the population mainly uses a Berber language in daily life, while the other half speaks variants of Moroccan Arabic. The French language is used in trade and public administration. Almost the entire population is Muslim (98.7%), while there are small Christian (1.1%) and Jewish (0.2%) minorities.

(Source: Bartleby 2010).

Introduction

For more than a thousand years, Morocco has had a central state administration of some form.[2] Many Moroccans consider the origin of the present Islamic nation to lie in the eighth century, with the establishment of the first Muslim dynasty of the Idrisids. The present contribution provides a brief historical overview of the coming into being of the modern Moroccan legal system and an analysis of the role of Islamic norms in the development of this system. This contribution focuses on the substantive law of Morocco rather than actual legal practice.[3] Because the present-day legal system has been so heavily influenced by French law, the author has chosen not to provide information about the legal system of the former Spanish zone.[4]

The division of periods complies with the general analytical framework of this book. For every period the author analyses the continually shifting configuration of three normative domains: state law, Islamic law, and local customs (cf. Buskens 2000). In the period between 1800 and 1920 Moroccan rulers and scholars attempted to reform the state and its law. Meanwhile, Morocco became more entangled in the web of European imperialism, resulting in the establishment of French and Spanish protectorates in 1912. From 1920 until the early 1960s, the character of the state changed fundamentally, with an emphasis on a new, more powerful central authority and demarcated boundaries. The government introduced modern legislation as an instrument with which to rule this state. During the colonial period the authorities stimulated legal pluralism. Subsequently, from 1961 until the late 1980s, King Hassan II developed his own vision of a modern state. His despotism led to a strong centralisation of the administration, denial of legal pluralism, and serious human rights violations. During the last decade of King Hassan II's rule and continuing into the present reign of his son Mohammed VI (from 1999), the government has shown more attention for human rights in combination with neo-liberal politics, but the interpretations of these norms have varied considerably.

3.1 The period until 1920

Attempts at reform and loss of independence

Moroccan society underwent several drastic changes in the nineteenth and the beginning of the twentieth century, which culminated in the formation of a strong central authority. In the decades around 1800, the sultans Sidi Muhammad III (1757-1790) and Mawlay Sulayman (1792-1822) attempted to reform understandings of Islam, law, economy, and the state system. A period followed in which the central authority faced difficulty in maintaining its power, particularly in the face of a declining economy related to growing European imports. Sultan al-Hasan I (1873-1894) succeeded in considerably expanding the territory over which the central authority (the *makhzan*) exercised effective control.

Islamic law as scholars' law

Available literature on Morocco presents the image of a traditional Islamic legal system during the second half of the nineteenth century. The state system was a mixture of administrative centrally-driven law, Islamic law, and customary law. Authoritative legal scholars formulated Islamic legal norms in accordance with their own visions of sharia. Some scholars worked as Islamic judges (*qadis*) in the name of the sultan. Simultaneously, sultans proclaimed legal rules through decrees called '*dahirs*'. Local representatives of the central authority, such as governors, also offered a form of administrative justice.

In areas beyond the control of the central authority (the *makhzan*), areas often referred to as 'the area of rebellion' or 'dissidence' (*bilad al-siba*), the population acknowledged for the most part the leadership of the sultan as '*amir al-mu'minin*', which meant 'the leader of the community of believers'.[5] Recognition of his role as a leader did not, however, result in tax collection or the acceptance of his legal norms. In large parts of Morocco, the population lived according to the norms of local custom, applied by community councils called *jama'as*. In some regions these councils appointed judges, who judged according to Islamic norms. Although scholars criticised these local customs in their writings, they simultaneously searched for practical solutions for the problems of everyday life. The many collections of their legal opinions on particular issues (*fatwas*) offer valuable insight into their attempts to accommodate Islamic law and local practices.

As in most pre-modern Muslim societies, the treatises of the legal scholars (the *fiqh* books), were the main sources for Islamic norms. In Morocco, the legal scholars almost exclusively followed the doctrine of the Maliki school, as formulated by the Egyptian scholar Khalil bin Ishaq al-Jundi (died 1365) in his *Mukhtasar*, a concise overview intended for memorisation. Generation after generation of Moroccan scholars added their explanations to this compendium in order to render it intelligible to their students. Many commentaries circulated in handwriting among scholars and legal practicioners. Furthermore, scholars copied, on a large scale, manuscripts about specialised legal questions, compilations of *fatwas*, and answers from authoritative predecessors to questions on concrete legal issues. This *responsa*-literature fulfilled an important role in the application of Islamic law in practice, and contributed greatly to the further development of the legal doctrine.

In the nineteenth century, the city of Fez was the intellectual and political centre of the country. Many important scholars taught at the mosque university al-Qarawiyyin in Fez (cf. Berque 1949). Despite rivalries among scholars from different regions, the legal scholars (*fuqaha'*) from Fez were in principle considered to be the most authoritative. And, for many students, studying at the Qarawiyyin University was the highest goal. In the works of the school of Fez, many references can be found to the rituals and customs of the bourgeoisie of the city, but scholars also attempted to construct rules that reached beyond these local traditions so as to represent a more abstract, general custom. The scholars of Fez moreover legitimised to a certain degree the sultan's regime. Their recognition was an important condition for the effectiveness of the central authority. Together with treatises of authoritative scholars from other parts of Morocco, the legal treatises of the school of Fez formed a sort of proto-national tradition of the Maliki law.

The traditional form of jurisprudence sanctioned a form of Islamic orthodoxy in which recognition of the special position of descendants of the prophet Mohammed (the *shurafa'*), the veneration of 'saints', and allegiance to mystic orders played an important role. These conceptions contributed to the legitimacy of the political system, in which the sultan as a descendant of the Prophet was imputed with miraculous gifts and blessings, or *baraka* (cf. Munson 1993). Many legal scholars were also members of mystic orders and wrote treatises about the orthodoxy of Sufism. The connection between Maghribi Malikism and traditional orthodoxy was embodied in the work of the nineteenth century scholar Al-Mahdi al-Wazzani, who compiled an authoritative collection of *fatwas*, and also wrote a treatise in which he defended the traditional veneration of the saints against criticism inspired by the Egyptian reformer Muhammad Abduh (cf. Berque 1949). This polemic shows that the Maliki tradition was not static and isolated, but instead dynamic and responsive to foreign developments.

One of the manifestations of these internal dynamics were the attempts of several Moroccan scholars and sultans to reform Islamic thinking from the second half of the eighteenth century onwards. Sultan Mawlay Sulayman, for instance, sent his son Ibrahim to Arabia in 1812 to acquire knowledge about Wahhabism (Abun-Nasr 1963: 94; El Mansour 1990: 137-143). Contact with the Wahhabis contributed to the sultan's disapproval of visiting the graves of saints and other folk practices. His father, Sidi Muhammad II, had already started with attempts to reform the study of Islamic law, for instance by contesting the dominance of Khalil's *Mukhtasar.* He also demonstrated great interest in Hanbalism, the understanding of God's will revived by the Wahhabis. Reformist ideas from Egypt became known among a small circle of students and scholars in Fez in the second half of the nineteenth century (Abun-Nasr 1963). Calls for a puritan interpretation of orthodoxy were also perceived in the works of traditional scholars such as Ma' al-Aynayn. These developments fit within more general tendencies of puritanism and reform that characterised many Muslim societies in the late eighteenth century (cf. Voll 1994; Peters 1980).

European expansion

In economic and political terms, Morocco was increasingly pulled into the European sphere of influence. The country was surrounded by areas controlled by Europeans, such as French Algeria and the Spanish and French territories in the Sahara. From 1830, France protected its interests on the Eastern border with Algeria. Spain occupied the Northern city of Tétouan and enforced an unfavourable peace treaty upon the central authority, or the *makhzan*, in 1860. Likewise, in 1907, France found a pretension to occupy the area surrounding Casablanca. In response to these developments, some Moroccan scholars and political leaders, including Sultan `Abd al-Hafiz, called for a holy war (*jihad*) against the French who threatened the frontiers of Morocco (Burke 1976).

From the second half of the nineteenth century and the early part of the twentieth century, European law began to spread in earnest through European consulates in the form of consular courts. In response to the growing rivalry amongst European countries competing for influence, Morocco and several other European countries and the United States concluded the treaty of Madrid in 1880. Among other things, they reached a consensus about the doctrine of *allégeance perpétuelle*, which formally clarified that in principle, Moroccans would always remain

Moroccan citizens, regardless of which foreign entity ruled them or which other nationality they would acquire (cf. Guiho 1961: 91-97). This notion remains until today one of the foundations of the Moroccan law of nationality, which creates concern for Moroccan immigrants who wish to obtain citizenship of the European countries in which they have settled.

In 1910, attempts at reform resulted in two proposals for a constitution that were influenced by political developments in Iran, the Ottoman Empire, and Egypt. The first proposal advocated, among other things, a legal system in accordance with the sharia. Both proposals contained the institution of a parliament. At that time, few people appeared to be interested in these ideas coming from the East, but later nationalist activists used these documents in their struggle for independence as proof for the Moroccan constitutional tradition (Pennell 2000: 143-145).

Creation of the protectorate

In 1912, France and Spain had won the bid against other contesters such as Germany and Great Britain, obtaining the authority to support the sultan in modernising the country. One of the justifications for creating the protectorate was the necessity to address the vast foreign debts that the Moroccan sultan had accumulated through extensive European loans. The Spanish gained control of the Northern part and an enclave in the South; the rest of the country was placed under the authority of France, with the city of Tangier functioning as an international zone under the joint administration of several foreign nations.

Article 1 of the 1912 Treaty of Fez established that the sultan and the French agreed to legal reform, according to what the French government deemed necessary. With the establishment of the protectorate, the power of the central authority would prove to be greatly strengthened. The character of the legal system would also undergo a fundamental transformation in the decades to come. The French created a dualistic system whereby indigenous law, including Islamic, Jewish, administrative, and customary law functioned in parallel with modern law based on a European model. French scholars and administrators immediately began with legislative activities that resulted in 1913 in a code of contracts (*Dahir formant codes des obligations et des contrats*). This code remains the cornerstone of Moroccan civil law.

The First World War slowed down French reform plans and obstructed military actions to submit the *jihad*-waging rural areas to the new *mahkzan*. The French not only needed their own soldiers to fight the Germans in Europe, but soon began to enlist men from the colonies, among them Moroccans, to join their forces.[6] Only from 1920 onwards were the French able to seriously resume work on establishing a new Moroccan state and a modern legal system. After the newly gained independence in 1956, the protectorate regime created by the French would form the basis of the present Moroccan legal system.

3.2 The period from 1920 until 1965

Colonial rule as the foundation of a modern state

The period between 1920 and 1934 was marked by the establishment of a strong, centrally administered state. The French and Spanish armies used brutal force to pacify the Berber regions in the South, the Middle-Atlas, and the North. The most famous episode from this battle of conquest was the Rif War (1921-1926). The Spanish protectorate government eventually succeeded in subduing the *jihad* of the inhabitants of the Northern mountainous region led by reformist scholar Muhammad bin Abd al-Karim al-Khattabi with significant help from the French army. Both parties suffered great losses and committed atrocities. The Spanish army even resorted to the use of poisonous gas bombs delivered to them by the German government in a desperate attempt to win the war of the guerrillas. Traces of this war can still be found in the Rifian landscape today.

With the gradual pacification of the Moroccan territory, the central government claimed a monopoly in the development and promulgation of legal norms in the new state structure. A norm only had the status of a legal rule when the central government had recognised it as such and formally promulgated it. In this process Islamic law and customs became incorporated into the formal framework of state law.

Colonial legal pluralism

The 'framing' of various normative domains in a state context implied an official recognition of a situation of legal pluralism, which until then the Islamic scholars had only grudgingly accepted through the accommodation of *fiqh* to local customs in areas where they could not do otherwise. Colonial rule divided the national legal system into two large domains, namely the Sharifian and the French or Spanish administration of justice.

The Sharifian administration of justice, as it was coined by the French to set it apart from European-derived law and to connote the law's link to the sultan, himself a descendent of the Prophet Mohammed (a *sharif*), was further subdivided into four areas of law:

- Islamic law administered by Islamic judges according to rules of Maliki *fiqh*;

- *Makhzan*-law as a continuation of the pre-protectorate administration of justice by government officials according to the rules promulgated by the sultan;
- Customary law for the officially recognised Berber regions; and
- Jewish law applied by rabbinical courts.

The competence of the courts depended on the religious and ethnic backgrounds of the parties involved and the nature of the conflict. The Sharifian administration of justice took place under supervision, or *contrôle*, of French and Spanish officials who, depending on the region, had either a civil or a military status.

Europeans in principle fell under the French or Spanish system. The consular administration of justice was abandoned by all countries in the course of the protectorate, with the exception of the United States. The French and Spanish administration of justice was inspired by the legislation in France and Spain. Formally, however, this system was also Moroccan: administration of justice took place in Moroccan courts in the name of the sultan and in accordance with Moroccan law. While colonial authors often spoke of French and Spanish law, Moroccan scholars used the term 'modern' to refer to this part of the law (cf. Essaîd 1992: 271-272).[7]

Islamic law obtained a well-defined place as part of Sharifian law within the protectorate system. Islamic judges took care of administration of justice mainly in family and inheritance matters for Muslims and for immovable property rights that were not registered and with which no French party was involved. French officials supervised the work of the judges, which was formalised according to French 'rational' norms. In practice, this meant that legal procedure was structured according to the French model, which, for example, introduced appeal requirements and the creation of archives to keep court records.

New forms for legal norms

The interference of French control also resulted in changes in the substance of Islamic law. The way in which the French formulated their legal texts created new genres of legal writing, such as codification (Buskens 1993). Since the conquest of Algeria in 1830, French scholars had been studying Maliki law as it had developed in the Maghrib (Henry & Balique 1979). They published important editions and annotated translations of authoritative legal texts and documents recording Moroccan legal practice. These writings, authored by foreign scholars, led to a summarising and restructuring of the legal tradition itself as in their task of compilation and annotation scholars necessarily showed preference for certain writings and views of Moroccan scholars over others, thus creating a colonial vulgate.[8]

In the incorporation of customary law in the protectorate legal system the same tendencies can be discerned as for Islamic law: control, formalisation, and standardisation. In a 1914 *dahir*, the sultan, instigated by the French, had already formulated the principle that Berber population groups should have their own administration of justice based on local customs. This principle was further elaborated in the notorious *dahir berbère* of 1930 (Lafuente 1999). According to this decree, large groups of the Moroccan population no longer fell under Islamic law, but were instead subjected to their 'own' Berber legal norms. Administration of justice took place through local community councils under the supervision of French officers. This control implied that French researchers and administrators described and systematised the legal norms and the judgments of the councils in impressive overviews, such as Aspinion (1946) on the customary law of the Zayyan tribe and Marcy (1949) on the Zemmour. In the Rif region, the Spanish military officer Emilio Blanco Izaga engaged in similar work with his monumental studies about the customs of the Aith Waryaghar (Hart 1995).

French administrators and scholars were led in their formalisation of customs into law by previous experiences in Algeria, notably in the Berber mountains of Kabylia. The preference of customary law over Islamic law was a widespread colonial phenomenon that was also prominent, for instance, in the Dutch legal policies pursued in Indonesia. In the Netherlands during this same period, scholars such as Christiaan Snouck Hurgronje and Cornelis van Vollenhoven were advocating for a transformation from custom (*adat*) to customary law (*adat law*) in order to satisfy the sense of justice of the native population (cf. Burns 2004). Scholars from a number of European nations maintained extensive contact, and as such shared experiences and their visions of colonial rule. Snouck Hurgronje, for example, in addition to being a prominent advisor and scholar in Indonesian affairs, was also appointed as an honorary advisor to the French protectorate administration in Morocco.

Opposing Arabs and Berbers

Some European administrators and scholars viewed colonial legal politics as an instrument of recognition of 'native cultures' and as a means of advancement for the 'natives'. In the eyes of the French, the Berbers were merely superficially islamised and actually possessed European racial and cultural roots. From their perspective, in the distant past, at the time of the church father Augustin (of Berber descent), they had been Christians. Some colonial officials cherished the hope that the Berbers could once again be converted to Catholicism and become allies in the fight against Islamic-Arab invaders, who had occupied their country at a later time.

Many progressive Maghribis considered the confrontation between Islamic law and local custom to be artificial and aimed at creating discord. Laying down both systems of norms in separate and contradictory colonial vulgates and regulations was an expression of a divide-and-rule policy aimed at the continuation of European-Christian dominance. The *dahir berbère* was by far the most important symbol of the colonials' divisive policies, and as such the primary target of opposition for the young, educated middle class. Outside of Morocco, as far as the Dutch Indies, Muslim activists were also protesting on a large scale against what they, too, perceived as an anti-Islamic legal policy being implemented by European rulers.

Islamic reformism and nationalism

These young Moroccan townspeople presented a programme that promoted Islamic reformism and nationalism as an alternative to European dominance. Their reformism implied a rejection of traditional orthodoxy, in which the veneration of saints and a Moroccan form of Malikism, with respect for local customs, were important. The French administrators had canonised this traditional orthodoxy in their endeavours to rule Morocco by means of indirect rule, relying on the elite of *makhzan*-officials and Islamic scholars. For the reformists, the traditional orthodoxy was a form of superstition and control, as they considered many of the loyal scholars to be collaborators.

Moroccan reformism was part of an international revival movement that intended to purify Islam by returning to the original Islam of the pious early Muslims (*salaf*), which in this particular context meant breaking away from many customs introduced in the orthodox Islam in the course of the centuries. For them, thinking in terms of schools of law was less important. The *Salafiyya* movement initially had many supporters in Egypt, Syria, and Lebanon; it later spread throughout the Muslim world. The reform movement of Muhammad bin Abd al-Karim al-Khattabi, the hero of the Rif War, was a precursor to this Moroccan form of puritanism. Reformers felt connected with Muslims all over the world, and were part of the revival movements that developed from the late nineteenth century. Exiled leaders of the Moroccan reformists found shelter in Egypt, where they met activists from other parts of the Muslim world who shared their views as well as their plans for political action. Colonial regimes demonstrated great concern over Pan-Islamism, which they considered to be a possible source of worldwide rebellions and conspiracies of Muslim populations against their Christian rulers.

For Moroccan intellectuals, Islamic reformism and internationalism were inextricably linked with nationalism. They wanted to be free from the reigns of French and Spanish occupiers and to unite the entire region into one nation. Their plan was that this independent state would be ruled by the activists according to the principles of pure Islam as formulated by *salafiyya* thinkers such as the young religious scholar Allal al-Fasi and other prominent members of the independence movement.

Independence and codification

In 1956 resistance against colonial rule led to independence for a reunited Morocco, meaning both the Spanish and the French protectorates fell once again under the same borders and under the control of the *makhzan*. Sultan Muhammad V had played an increasingly important role in the nationalistic movement from the time of the Second World War and came to symbolise national unity for all parties. He adopted the title of 'king' instead of 'sultan' and quickly placed himself at the head of the state. Nationalistic reformers led by Allal al-Fasi hoped for an entirely revised legal system based on a new interpretation of sharia. They were, however, ultimately disappointed as genuine reform remained limited to the abolition of customary law in the Berber regions and a codification of family law in the 1958 'Code of personal status' (the *Mudawwanat al-ahwal al-shakhsiyya)*.

The *Mudawwana* (personal status code) was a symbol of regained national unity: one corpus of legal rules was from now on applicable to all Muslims living in Morocco. In substance the law remained close to the traditional Maliki doctrine, to the extent that Lapanne-Joinville characterised it as 'une sorte de loi-cadre à rebours' (Lapanne-Joinville 1959: 101). In the choices between different legal scholarly opinions, the legislator was guided by reformist ideals, such as the protection of weaker parties, women and children, against possible abuse by men of their God-given privileges. Although the Tunisian family law of 1957, the *Majalla*, had served as a source of inspiration, the Moroccan legislator did not consider radical reforms to be desirable nor possible. For the Jewish minority in Morocco, family law was not codified, but the classical compilations of the Jewish legal scholars remained in force.[9]

The legal system of the new Morocco was in many ways a continuation of the colonial system as developed by the French. The codifications of criminal law and criminal procedure in 1962 and 1959, respectively, contained virtually no references to classical Islamic law, but instead drew inspiration from French law.

The new government continued the formation of a modern nation state through the submission of 'rebellious' regions, the centralisation of the government, and the establishment of a monopoly on the development of legal norms. On this basis, the *makhzan* proceeded with a legal policy that was primarily focussed on unification and modernisation. Islamisation of the law was largely an ideological preoccupation of a group of nationalist reformists. For the actual rulers islamisation of the law was merely a symbol of political legitimacy to which they paid lip service through the codification of the *Mudawwana*. State law was of prime importance, and allowed only very limited space to Islamic norms, while denying or even resisting the existence of local customs.

3.3 The period from 1965 until 1985

Authoritarian rule and the creation of a unified legal system

After the premature death of King Muhammad V in 1961, his son Hassan took over the throne. He considered it his task to transform Morocco into a modern state, which in the first place meant strengthening the central authority of the king. He used the law as one of the instruments at his disposal for control and the continuation of the reigning `Alawi dynasty.

In 1962 King Hassan II invited the Moroccan population to approve of the constitution designed by him by means of a referendum, the first one in Moroccan history. The constitution was strongly inspired by French constitutional law, as King Hassan had studied law in France. At first sight, the constitution formed the basis for a democratic regime: Morocco was set up as a parliamentary democracy with several parties. Islam occupied a limited position as the state religion; there was no further mention of Islamic law in the entire constitution.

The constitution did, however, grant a great deal of power to the king. Article 19, in which the king was given the task of acting as the 'commander of the faithful' (*amir al-mu'minin*) was of particular importance. King Hassan was to shape this institution according to his own particular views during his rule, making it a truly invented tradition. In his opinion, Islamic leadership consisted of having complete authority in all matters relating to Islam, including the interpretation of Islamic law. For Hassan, the constitution was an instrument that allowed him to impose an autocratic regime. He repeatedly dissolved the parliament and proclaimed a state of emergency, and also freely promulgated several new versions of the constitution. In practice, King Hassan replaced the democratic principles embedded in the constitution with an authoritarian rule.

Authoritarian rule and contestation

The first twenty-five years of King Hassan's rule are known as 'the years of lead'. They were characterised by serious violations of human rights and elimination of political adversaries. In the 1960s the progressive elements of the Istiqlal movement, which had formed a political party of their own soon after independence, expressed strong criticism of the king. In 1964, King Hassan reacted by having their exiled leader Mehdi Ben Barka kidnapped in broad daylight in Paris. The former crown prince's teacher of mathematics, Ben Barka, quite literally disappeared without a trace. During the years to come many activists would share this fate. In addition to outright intimidation tactics, Hassan regulated internal politics by controlling the election of members of parliament as he pleased. Resistance against him led members of the army to instigate rebellions in 1971 and 1973, which included assassination attempts on his life. Miraculously, Hassan managed to escape death every time, only serving to strengthen the belief some had that the king possessed God-given power.

At the beginning of the 1970s the kingship was no longer the symbol of national unity it had been during the resistance against the colonials in the 1950s. In an attempt to create a new rallying point of national unity, Hassan called on his subjects to join in a peaceful march in 1975 in order to incorporate the Spanish Sahara in the Moroccan territory. The grand Moroccan ideal had been important for many in the struggle for independence and was still able to enthuse a considerable part of the population in the 1970s.

Moreover, for many rural poor, the march to the Sahara contained a promise of a better future. Prosperity had remained a privilege for a small elite on whom Hassan relied for the enforcement of his regime. The nationalisation of the Moroccan economy at the expense of the interests of the former colonists had been especially advantageous for the king and his clients. The vast majority of the population, both in rapidly growing cities and in the countryside, continued to live in great poverty. For many, emigration to Western Europe was the only way out. Unrest periodically manifested itself in the cities in the form of violent protests against rising food prices, one of the last large-scale outbreaks being 'the bread riots' of January 1984.

From the late 1970s onwards an increasing part of the population turned to political forms of Islam to express its feelings of discontent (Zeghal 2005). King Hassan saw the Iranian Revolution of 1979 as a serious threat to his regime. He harshly persecuted his islamist critics and condemned Imam Khomeini's views in the strongest terms. His Minister of Religious Affairs propagated a moderate form of traditional orthodoxy, which presented Malikism as an age-old tradition in

Morocco and articulated Islam as the way of 'the proper middle'. This policy focus had almost no impact on the development of substantive Islamic law. In fact, since the codification of the *Mudawwana* in the late 1950s, there had been numerous pleas for reform of Islamic family law, all of which remained unheaded, despite ever more vocal demands for reform from the 1980s onwards. The king rightly understood that it would be extremely difficult for him to reform the vulnerable symbol of Islamic identity and national unity to everyone's satisfaction. Modernists, reformists, conservatives, and islamists all held strongly deviating conceptions of the substance of an ideal Islamic family law (cf. Buskens 1999).

Unification of the legal system

Some of the most important events for the development of the Moroccan legal system in this period were the Arabisation, Moroccanisation, and unification of the law. A complete unification of the law was brought about by the law of 26 January 1965, which came into force on 1 January 1966 (Azziman 1986). It ended the division between *Makhzan* and 'modern' (previously French, Spanish, and international/Tangiers) legal rules. The Islamic courts were also integrated into the same unified system. Unification of the law implied the choice for 'modern' law as developed in the former French protectorate. The norms of the Spanish and international zone of Tangiers were abolished. Islamic law and Jewish law only kept their place in family affairs. Islamic norms furthermore regulated the transfer of rights to non-registered immovable property, and the administration of religious institutions (*wafqs* or *habus*).

The law of 26 January 1965 also determined that only persons of Moroccan nationality could act as judges, which meant the end of the work of over one hundred judges of French and Spanish nationality. The administration of justice was from that moment forward to take place entirely in Arabic. A large amount of laws and regulations therefore had to be translated into Arabic. The organisation of the judicial system remained strongly inspired by the 1913 Code of Civil Procedure promulgated by the French.

In practice, the system of 1965 proved to be strenuous and costly. Hence, new laws on the organisation of the courts and legal procedure were introduced in 1974, bringing about a drastic reform of the legal system. These laws still form the basis for the present judicial administration. The judiciary consists of four layers: 'jurisdiction communale et d'arrondissement' (lowest level local courts); first instance courts; Courts of Appeal; and a Supreme Court. Once again the influence of French legal models on these reforms was considerable.

The most important development with regard to Islamic law since the codification of the family law was the promulgation of a new statute governing professional witnesses who write down documents for all matters in which Islamic law applies (the *'udul*, sing. *'adl*). The institution of Islamic witnesses has a history of more than a thousand years in Morocco. Colonial administrators had increased their control over the *'udul* by implementing measures such as the creation of archives and the levying of taxes. The law of 1982 and a ministerial decree of 1983 fully integrated the *'udul*, and thereby also brought this important branch of Islamic evidence law into the new legal order (cf. Buskens 1999, 2008).[10] Through the incorporation of this classical Islamic institution, government control was further strengthened. Thus, the government affirmed once again that in Morocco Islamic law only functioned within the context and by the grace of state law.

3.4 The period from 1985 until the present

Human rights as an instrument of control and criticism

The last fourteen years of King Hassan's 38-year rule were characterised by cautious changes in the political system. Opposition groups increasingly invoked the concepts of human rights and civil society to voice their criticisms of the regime (cf. Hegasy 1997; Rollinde 2002; Sater 2007; Touhtou 2008). The sharp attacks on the political system by various islamist movements were worrisome for the central government because critics used the very Islamic idiom which the king himself used to justify his regime (Tozy 1999; Zeghal 2005). The islamists also increasingly called on human rights standards in order to claim their right to freedom of expression. Pressure from abroad meant that King Hassan could no longer ignore the growing criticism of his human rights record. Extremely critical publications appeared in France and, with the end of the Cold War and less geopolitical interest in Morocco, the United States also began to exert more pressure on Morocco to respect its human rights obligations. Eventually, the king could no longer refuse the visit of representatives of Amnesty International.

From the end of the 1980s the Moroccan government made attempts at solving its economic problems through neo-liberal means, such as large scale privatisation of the public sector and promotion of foreign investments. Through steps toward economic liberalisation the king attempted to increase support for his regime among the urban middle class. Until that point in time, Hassan had largely ruled by relying on his strong patronage relations with the rural elite. The increasing freedom for the media and the intellectual debate stimulated by new policies on public expression were also aimed at creating legitimacy for the regime in the eyes of the urban middle class. In 1990, the *makhzan* formally adopted the discourse of human rights by setting up a national human rights institution ('Conseil consultatif des droits de l'Homme'). Finally, a Minister for Human Rights was appointed in 1993. The fact that the highly respected professor of law Omar Azziman was prepared to fulfil this difficult post was a considerable success for King Hassan II.

The acceptance of the *makhzan* by a considerable part of the middle class was also the result of the widespread horror over the savage civil war in neighbouring Algeria, in which islamist groups played an important role. Many Moroccans preferred Hassan's despotism to the display of bloody chaos being witnessed over the border. The king continued to use the Moroccan tradition of Malikism as a means to counter his islamist critics. As part of this strategy, the Ministry of Religious Affairs published important classics on Islamic law and theology at low prices. The king also demonstrated his religiosity and particular views on Islam by inviting obedient scholars to deliver a series of pious speeches in the palace each year during the fasting month of *Ramadan*.

Though the state from the early 1990s onwards began to permit the establishment of non-governmental organisations, it simultaneously tried to control these initiatives (cf. Hegasy 1997; Sater 2007; Touhtou 2008). Some of these groups specifically targeted the improvement of women and children's rights, while others focussed on regional identity issues, notably in Berber-speaking areas. The *makhzan's* evident increased openness on issues of Berber language and culture indicated that the regime had chosen to no longer associate the Berber issue with colonial policy and collaboration. Instead of repressing these movements, the king attempted to co-opt the Berber activists. In a royal speech in 1994 King Hassan recognised the importance of Moroccan 'dialects' next to 'the language of the Qur'an' (Kratochwil 2002). The king issued a decree permitting the teaching of these Berber 'dialects' at schools (Sater 2007: 141). On a formal political level, the constitutional modifications of 1992 and 1996, which introduced a two-chamber parliamentary system, also suggested new openness and democratisation. King Hassan presented the referenda about these proposed constitutional modifications as *bayas*, collective oaths of loyalty to his person, which would legitimise his rule.

Hesitant family law reforms

King Hassan again granted a symbolic role to Islamic family law in the creation of his new order. In 1992, after many years of debate, the king was finally prepared to consider a reform of the *Mudawwana*. He explicitly stated, however, that an eventual modification of the law should not become a topic of public debate between different political factions. He used the example of the Algerian civil war as a possible consequence of public confrontation on this matter, thus legitimising his firm control over the reforms. As it happened, the parliament had been dissolved due to upcoming elections and the king, according to the constitution, had the power to single-handedly promulgate laws. Hassan explicitly referred in his speeches to his right to use *ijtihad* (free legal interpretation) as commander of the faithful. Ultimately, he claimed to hold the highest authority in the interpretation of Islamic law, and, as such, promised to protect the interests of his female subjects as a real father of the nation.

In the end, the legal reform proposals were the result of consultations of a committee consisting mostly of religious scholars and jurists appointed by the king himself. Participation of women's organisations in these consultations was severely limited. Despite his broad based public statements beforehand, modifications proclaimed by the king in September 1993 were extremely modest. The revised articles had little effect on male privileges concerning marriage, guardianship, polygamy, and repudiation. The main effect was new administrative procedures, supervised by judges and professional Islamic witnesses (the *'udul*), that made it more difficult for men to abuse their privileges. Rather than contribute to more equal and progressive relations between men and women, though, the new more stringent measures seemed to result in men attempting to escape from their obligations through informal ways, for example by simply disappearing when wishing to divorce their wives, instead of repudiating them in an orderly fashion.

In short, the revisions of a limited number of articles of the *Mudawwana* appeared to be largely a gesture by the king towards progressive, and vocal, groups to indicate his political willingness to consider reform. Reform from the king's perspective meant change that would not shock the traditional conceptions of Islam and society held by the majority of the population. A compromise proved to be virtually unreachable: islamists and orthodox were troubled by every reform, while the reformers remained disappointed by the lack of genuine change. In the end, all camps were forced to grudgingly accept the authority of the commander of the faithful.

A new family law code

According to a decision made by King Hassan, the elections of November 1997 were to result in what in French was called *'l'alternance'*: the parties that had until then formed the opposition would now be given the chance to form a government and to rule the country for several years. This particularly concerned the socialist USFP (Union

Socialiste des Forces Populaires) and the centre-right Istiqlal party. Furthermore, in these elections the PJD (Parti de la Justice et du Développement), an islamist party permitted by the king and often referred to as 'the king's islamists' ('les islamistes du roi') obtained twelve seats in parliament. The new government that started in March 1998 aroused hope for social and political change. The government had ambitious ideas for social reforms for women in particular.

Indeed, within a year, in March 1999, the government presented a grand plan to get women more involved in the development of the country. Part of it was a drastic reform of family law to promote the equality between men and women. The expectations increased when King Hassan died in July 1999 and was succeeded by his eldest son Mohammed VI. The young king explicitly presented himself as a social reformer and happily made use of the nickname 'king of the poor', which he quickly acquired after ascending to the throne. He promised his support for reform plans in favour of the poor and the weak, which included women and children. With little ceremony he replaced the loyal collaborators of his father, such as the feared Minister of Interior Driss Basri, in order to symbolise the break with the old regime in a manner that would not directly forsake his father.

Supporters of the drastic reforms of family law hoped that the king would be on their side. They desperately needed his support because the government plans for radical reform of the *Mudawwana* had received a great deal of fierce condemnation from the side of traditional orthodox scholars and islamists. The traditionalists also expected support from the king because of the old ties between the `Alawi dynasty and the Islamic scholars and also because the former Minister of Religious Affairs, a faithful ally of King Hassan II, had expressly chosen their side. The clergy felt threatened in their traditional power concerning the interpretation of Islamic law. Islamists of all sorts, both those loyal to the king and those supporting revolutionary reform, used the debate over family law to find out how much space the young king would allow them to express their views in public. The apogee of the confrontation took place on 12 March 2000 in the form of two protest marches, one in Rabat *for* and one in Casablanca *against* government plans to reform the family law. The number of participants was difficult to estimate, but hundreds of thousands of people were involved. Notably, islamists and traditionalists were able to gather considerably more people in Casablanca than the progressive groups in Rabat.

In the course of the year 2000 tensions between the different factions increased. Each group was convinced of its own interpretation of Islamic law. There were accusations back and forth of heresy and un-Moroccan ideas and conduct. The progressive groups were, in the eyes of the traditionalists and islamists, lackeys of the West. The reformers, in turn, portrayed their opponents as 'Taliban' and representatives of Saudi Wahhabism. Their differences appeared to be irreconcilable. Moroccan migrant communities in Western Europe also engaged in fierce discussions about the family law. In Morocco itself all factions, with the exception of the revolutionary islamists, called on the young king to decide what should happen with the family law. Finally, on 5 March 2001 King Mohammed VI reacted by promising to set up a committee to formulate a draft for the family law. He officially established this committee on 27 April 2001. Among its sixteen members, there were three women. The majority of members were Islamic scholars, jurists, and judges.

For the time being it appeared that the conservatives and the islamists had gained the upper hand. The debate on family law was waged almost entirely in Islamic terms. Progressive groups frequently referenced the applicability of universal human, women's, and children's rights and the importance of international women's conferences and conventions, but they never dared to voice the possibility of viewing Moroccan family law from a secular perspective.[11] By constantly referring to *ijtihad*, the modernists placed themselves within the Islamic tradition. The various islamist groups also succeeded in publicly expressing their views on Islam and its role in politics. The public atmosphere that existed in the newly emerging civil society in the post Hassan II period offered all sides an opportunity to participate in the political arena. This was a big step forward as compared to the repressive regime of Hassan II (cf. Buskens 2003).

On 16 May 2003 the world was shocked by a series of terrorist attacks in Casablanca. When the inconceivable news came that the culprits were Moroccan, king Mohammed VI reacted sharply against those who had abused their newfound freedom of expression. He claimed the right to interpret Islam as commander of the faithful and took strict measures against islamist activists. The repression was so fierce that it immediately provoked protests by human rights activists.

Concomitant to its repression of radical forms of political Islam, the government also offered an alternative view of what it considered 'real' Islam to be. With the appointment of a new Minister of Religious Affairs, historian and novelist Ahmad al-Tawfiq, the king wished to promote a policy concerning Islam in which an individual experience of religion was stressed as an antidote to political activism. As with new policies on Berber language and culture, this signalled that for the government mysticism (Sufism) had lost its association with colonial rule and 'backwardness'. Intellectuals and other members of the urban middle class had already rediscovered Sufism as an authentic Moroccan understanding of a peaceful Islam.

Mohammed VI settled for relatively liberal reforms of the *Mudawwana*, which he announced in a speech at the opening of the new parliamentary year in the fall of 2003. For the first time, an Islamic family law in Morocco became the subject of a parliamentary debate. The representatives of the islamist PJD proposed numerous amendments, but, in the end, both chambers voted unanimously for the new family law. On 3 February 2004 the king proclaimed the new *Mudawwanat al-usra*. With publication in the official government bulletin, the new family law went into effect immediately.

Many reform-minded people were satisfied with the results, although they considered the new law to only be a first step. They felt that they were the victors in the debate. Conservatives and islamists had no choice but to accept the inevitable. The real winner, however, appeared to be King Mohammed VI. Through his manoeuvring and an unexpected course of events he had been able to strengthen his power considerably. He emphasised his right of *ijtihad*, while simultaneously demonstrating himself to be a democrat by allowing a parliamentary debate on the law. He had grounded the contents of the new law in a liberal interpretation of Islam, linked to notions of progress and social justice. He emphasised continuity with the previous family law by presenting the reforms as further elaborations of the reforms granted by his late father in 1993.[12] Although traditional Malikism had lost substantial ground in favour of modernism, the modifications were justifiable within the context of traditional *salafiyya* ideology of the nationalist movement. The new law was, however, an explicit rejection of puritan views as preached by Wahhabis from present-day Saudi Arabia.[13]

As in the first years of the creation of an independent state, during the reign of his grandfather, Islamic family law proved once again to be a powerful symbol: King Mohammed VI showed his subjects at home that he still was in charge of his country and had effectively wielded his power. At the same time, the new family law was a sign to the outside world: the young king presented Morocco as a model for all Islamic countries, a state that wished to propagate a modern moderate Islam. This message was well received by Morocco's traditional Western allies France and the United States. The presidents of both states praised the new law as an important step forward, the king as a wise arbiter, and both as an example to the entire Muslim world.

In actual fact, the reforms were not as drastic as the previous government in 1999 had envisaged. The social meaning of the reforms would depend to a large extent on the ways in which judges would interpret the new law. Until now, our knowledge about actual practice is scant; progressive Moroccan scholars and activists have been very critical of the judges' interpretations of the new law (e.g. Benradi et al. 2007).

Research on judicial practice and everyday understandings of the law is still required.

The extent to which globalisation played a role in the debate over Moroccan family law was remarkable. Modernists as well as conservatives and Islamists defended their positions by referring to universal norms of human rights and international conventions. The different factions thereby propagated their own forms of universalism. Modernists referred to the women's conferences in Cairo (1994) and Beijing (1995), islamists to notions of puritanism, such as Wahhabism. To a certain extent they agreed on the fact that they could disagree with one another in the public sphere of the civil society.

Control of the public sphere

King Mohammed VI succeeded in dominating the debate about family law, just as the *makhzan* has attempted from the early 1990s onwards to control the debate on human rights and non-governmental organisations. In this way the state hoped not only to gain the support of the emerging middle class, but to simultaneously secure continued control of the public sphere. The result was previously unknown freedom for the press, for social movements, and for Berber activists. Mehdi Ben Barka, who had been a symbol for the oppressive rule of King Hassan II, became a symbol for the new democratic system of Mohammed VI after shocking revelations about his disappearance and the relatively open debate about it. Several weeks after his father passed away, the new king established a committee to compensate victims of unjust detention or disappearance (cf. Slyomovics 2005). In January 2004 Mohammed VI installed the '*Instance équité et reconciliation*', a government body whose task it was to investigate the human rights violations in Morocco during the 'years of lead' by convening public meetings throughout Morocco (cf. Vairel 2004). Names of the accused were not allowed to be mentioned.

The dominant political culture has remained rather authoritarian also in other domains. News about the royal family that is considered too outspoken has led, for example, to censorship and even criminal prosecution (cf. Hidass 2003). During the last years, the position of the *makhzan* appears to have hardened. As recently as 2009, there continue to be indications of severe censorship; the judiciary has reacted with high fines for journalists and further limitations on press freedom. It remains to be seen to what extent the *makhzan* will manage to control the discourse of human rights and civil society and to turn it into an instrument to dominate public debate. Many intellectuals and activists do not seem willing to give up the freedom they have tasted during the last years.

Drastic changes have not taken place in the Moroccan legal system in the course of the last twenty-five years concerning the relationships between state law, Islamic norms, and local customs. Since the protectorate period state law has constituted the framework in which other forms of normativity are integrated. Islamic law has remained relatively marginal, although the regime confirmed its symbolic importance through the reforms of the *Mudawwana*. New liberties for Berber movements and non-governmental organisations do not imply renewed recognition of customary norms, although scholars and activists can, after years of denial of the existence of Berber customs, openly publish on the issue (e.g. Arehmouch 2001, 2006; Ouaazzi & Aît Bahcine 2005; Hitous 2007; Belghazi 2008). The most remarkable development is the increased attention of government and social organisations for international legal norms, notably human rights, as laid down in international conventions. While Islamic family law has gained renewed meaning as a political symbol, 'human rights' (*huquq al-insan*) as a concept has become the most important political discourse in present-day Moroccan society, as a means of both legitimising and criticising government policy.

3.5 Constitutional law

Since 1962 Morocco has had a constitution (see 3.3). This constitution has been revised four times, namely in 1970, 1972, 1992, and 1996. The most important reform of the 1996 constitution is the institution of a parliament consisting of two chambers; previously the parliament consisted of a single chamber (cf. Buskens 1999: 51).

The Moroccan constitution does not contain a stipulation regarding the position of Islamic law in the legal system. All versions only speak of Islam in general terms. In the preamble, Morocco is described as an Islamic state; the state motto is: 'God, the fatherland, the king' (Art. 7).

Article 6 stipulates that Islam is the state religion and that the state guarantees religious freedom to all. Government policy is explicitly focussed on the peaceful co-existence of Islam, Christianity, and Judaism. Jews and Christians each have their own institutions, which are recognised by the state and entitled to certain tax benefits. There appears to be less acceptance of 'heretic' Muslims, such as Shi`ites, Ahmadis, and Baha'i, and for revolutionary islamists. The extent to which religions that are not recognised by Islam are accepted is unclear. In the past, members of the Baha'i community were prosecuted and hindered (cf. Buskens 1999: 51-52). It appears as though these prosecutions by the government have ceased (U.S. State Department 2009). The small community of foreign Hindus is also allowed to practice its religion. Each year a festival for sacred music with performances stemming from religious traditions from all over the world is organised in Fez, with the explicit backing of the authorities. The festival fits with the official image of tolerance and religion as a personal experience that the government promotes. The victims of the 9/11 attacks in New York were commemorated in a ceremony in the cathedral of Rabat, whereby representatives of the three main religions came together, as well as important representatives of the *makhzan*. A group of orthodox *'ulama'* expressed fierce criticism of the presence of Muslims at this ceremony in a *fatwa*. The Minister of Religious Affairs responded immediately by refuting the rebellious scholars (cf. Buskens 2003: 114).

In the preamble of the constitution the legislator explicitly refers to human rights as the foundation of the Moroccan system. The constitution guarantees Moroccan citizens their fundamental rights. For example, according to Article 5 all Moroccans are equal before the law. Article 8 grants men and women equal political rights. All citizens have access to public functions on the basis of Article 12. The influence of French public law is also evident in the separation of powers and in the structure of the state and the legal system, as was previously mentioned.

The most peculiar aspect of the Moroccan constitution concerns the position of the king in the state system: he has considerable powers. Article 19 is of particular importance for the relation between Islam and the constitution. It refers to the king as 'the commander of the faithful' (*amir al-mu'minin*), who has responsibility for, among other tasks, ensuring respect for Islam. The king is, therefore, not only head of state, but also leader of his subjects in Islamic matters. King Hassan II, the architect of the Moroccan constitution, regularly referred to this function in order to legitimise his regime. In his vision he held the highest power in Islamic matters and he had the authority to independently interpret Islamic law (*ijtihad*). The king also serves as chairman of the council of Islamic scholars and determines the substance of Islam in Morocco (Buskens 1999: 52-55). The recent debate about reforms of family law affirmed the key role of Muhammad VI in Islamic matters. According to Article 106, the position of the king and Islam are not subject to constitutional revision or review.

Article 20 determines that the eldest son of the king succeeds him. This signifies that the head of state can never be a woman or a non-Muslim. Despite this construction, women have already been holding positions as ministers and as members of parliament for a number of years. Both King Hassan II and his son Muhammad VI have also appointed influential counsellors from the tiny Jewish community, with which the royal family maintains excellent relations.

3.6 Family and inheritance law

The reform of family law in 2004 is the most important event in the area of Islamic law in Morocco since the codification of the *Mudawwana* in 1957-1958. The new law symbolises continuity with tradition, as well as change. This is already implied by its title *Mudawwanat al-usra* ('Code for the Family'). The law, like its predecessor, is named *Mudawwana*, literally 'collection' or 'code of law'. The name is also a reference to the famous overview of Maliki jurisprudence composed by the Maghribi scholar Sahnun in the ninth century. Instead of the factual specification *al-ahwal al-shakhsiyya*, or 'the personal status', added to the 1958 code, the legislator specified the new law as referring to *al-usra*, or 'the family'.

The legislator explicitly focusses on new rules to promote the stability of the nuclear family, within which men and women are to act as equals. Although King Muhammad VI repeatedly positioned himself as a great supporter of the rights of women and children, he ultimately legitimised the reforms by presenting them as measures to promote the effectiveness of the revisions introduced by his late father Hassan II in 1993. In comparison with the old code of law, which contained 298 articles, the new code with its 400 articles is much more extensive. In addition to important innovations, the legislator has also retained much of the material from the old *Mudawwana*, partially rephrased. The new law, like its predecessor, contains a reference in the last article to the Maliki legal tradition. New in this code is the reference to *ijtihad*, which must serve justice, equality, and a harmonious family life, all of which constitute important Islamic values. At the same time the legislator cautions that efforts toward reform through the use of *ijtihad* should not go too far, always keeping in mind fundamental principles of fairness.

Until the reforms of 2004 the patriarchal model of family relations formed the basis for Moroccan family law. Marriage and regulations concerning divorce, descent, custody over children, and inheritance law were structured by intrinsically unequal relations of exchange between a husband and wife. According to this conception of marriage, the man offers a bride price and financial support to the woman in return for her obedience and sexual availability. This patriarchal model is rooted in classical Islamic law and the related world view, as well as in conceptions shared by many Moroccans. In family law this resulted in institutions criticised by reformers, such as obedience of a wife to her husband, polygamy, male marriage guardianship over daughters, and repudiation as a male privilege.

The new *Mudawwanat al-usra* is meant as a break with this model, as the change of its name already indicates. The overriding principle of the new model is contained in Article 4, which states that the goal of marriage is 'the formation of a stable family under supervision of both spouses'. According to Article 1 of the old *Mudawwana*, the husband was considered to be the head of the family. In the stipulations on the legal consequences of marriage, the distinction between rights and duties of husband and wife are replaced with one article that describes their reciprocal duties. The woman is no longer required to be obedient to the man; instead, 'the wife and the husband together are responsible for the administration and the control of the house and the children' (Art. 51(3) Mud). The view of equality between the spouses underlies numerous other reforms in the new family law. However, some traces of the old patriarchal model remain, such as the obligation for the husband to provide his wife with a bride price and maintenance, the possibility for polygyny, the prohibition for Muslim women to marry non-Muslim men, the male privilege of repudiation, the different rights of fathers and mothers over their children, and the inequality in inheritance.

Marriage

One of the most important issues in the reform was the institution of marriage guardianship. According to the Maliki school of law, a woman has to be represented by a male marriage guardian, preferably a close relative such as a son, father, brother, nephew, or grandfather, when contracting a marriage. Some modernists considered this subordination to be outdated. In an opinion poll, however, it appeared that not only conservatives and islamists, but also many reform-minded persons were opposed to abolishing this institution (Buskens 2003: 106-107). The large majority of the respondents considered control by the family over an intended marriage to be a core value in Moroccan culture. Nevertheless, the legislator decided to offer an adult woman the possibility to marry without a marriage guardian (Art.s 25-25 Mud). The new law adopted a view current in the Hanafi school and, thus, remained within the bounds of classical law. In 1993 the legislator had carefully taken a first step in this direction by making marriage guardianship optional for an adult woman whose father had died (Art. 12(4) Mud 1993). At that time, the right of a father to force his daughter into marriage against her will (*jabr*) was also completely abolished (Art. 12(4) Mud 1958; Art.s 5, 12 Mud 1993). According to the new law of 2004, adult Moroccan women can enter into a marriage autonomously, although they may still opt for assistance by a male guardian.

Another issue garnering continued attention has been the minimum age of marriage. In 2004 the minimum marriage age for women was raised from 15 to 18 years, becoming equal to the required age for men (Art. 19 Mud). Islamists fiercely protested against this increase in age, arguing that it would be a source of moral decay. Article 20 offers the judge the possibility to exempt women from this requirement, granting them permission to marry at a younger age. In this case they need a marriage guardian to conclude the contract for them. They would also need the consent of their legal guardian since they have not yet reached the age of legal majority. The reforms of 2004 lowered the age of legal majority for both girls and boys to 18 years (Art. 209 Mud).

It is still not possible for a Muslim woman to marry a non-Muslim man. The Moroccan legislator does, however, permit a Muslim man to marry a Jewish or Christian woman, in accordance with classical sharia rules (Art. 39(4) Mud). Few activists advocate the elimination of this inequality, which is supported by the majority of the population. Some, such as the Moroccan imam El-Moumni in Rotterdam (the Netherlands), argue that it is wrong or even forbidden for Muslim men to marry non-Muslim women in situations where Muslim women have difficulty finding husbands, as seems to be the case in many Muslim immigrant communities in Western Europe (cf. Van Koningsveld & Tahtah 1998: 58-59).

The obligation for the husband to give his wife a bride price (*mahr* or *sadaq*), a clear patriarchal element, has been maintained in the new law. According to Article 13, the bride price is a condition for the legal validity of a marriage contract, in accordance with Maliki rules. The legislator emphasises that the bride price is a woman's exclusive right, and that as such she can dispose of it as she pleases (Art. 29 Mud). The size and manner in which the bride price is handed over are laid down in the marriage contract. Parties can also include other conditions in the contract so long as they are not in conflict with the law (Art.s 47-48 Mud). An important innovation is the possibility to lay down in a separate document that property acquired by both spouses during the marriage is communal property. If such an agreement is lacking, it remains at the discretion of the judge to decide whether he nevertheless wants to divide the property in case of divorce (Art. 49 Mud).

Under the new law, women have the right to set the condition that their husbands may not marry another woman (Art. 40 Mud). In the reforms, extensive attention has been given to measures limiting polygamy by men by introducing a series of administrative restrictions. The man can only marry another woman in case the judge, his current wife, and his future wife give their permission (Art.s 40-46 Mud). If a husband violates his promise not to marry another woman, his wife can apply for a judicial divorce. Polygamy has been an important symbol in the struggle for reform of the family law. For progressives, it has been seen as a sign of inequality, for conservatives and part of the islamists, a God-given privilege for the man. It is remarkable that the Moroccan legislator, like legislators in other Arab countries, did not dare to abolish this practice completely, even though it seldom occurs in practice.

The reforms expressly emphasise the equality of men and women in marriage (Art. 51 Mud). Neglect of reciprocal rights and duties is sanctioned, and marriages can be dissolved by the judge on the basis of enduring discord (*shiqaq*) (Art. 52 Mud). The rights of children have also received a great deal of attention, with reference to international conventions (Art. 54 Mud).

The 2004 law gives rules for the writing down of a marriage contract by professional witnesses (the *ʿudul*) under the supervision of a judge. These representatives of the government are tasked with seeing to the enforcement of legal stipulations that for example define and condition the minimum age of marriage, polygamy, and mutual consent to the marriage contract. The obligation that a marriage must be mentioned as a side note in the birth register is also meant to contribute to increased government control.

Articles 14 and 15 contain an important innovation concerning the acknowledgement of foreign family law in Morocco. Moroccans who reside abroad may conclude a marriage according to the law of the country in which they are residing. This marriage can be recognised in Morocco, if several requirements of Moroccan marriage law are also met, such as the stipulation of a bride price, the presence of two Muslim witnesses, and the absence of marriage impediments. Article 128 contains a similar rule for the recognition of divorce by a foreign judge.

With these reforms the legislator attempts to find solutions for the possible problems faced by the numerous Moroccans who have emigrated to Western Europe (cf. Rutten 1988; Foblets 1994; Foblets & Carlier 2005; Jordens-Cotran 2007). Maintaining ties with European immigrants is of great importance for the Moroccan economy, since they are the main source of foreign currency. At the same time, the recognition of foreign marriages and divorces are also meant as an expression of goodwill toward the European governments with whom Morocco would like to conclude bilateral conventions concerning the application of Moroccan family law, and to whom it wishes to show a positive image of the Moroccan legal system.

Divorce

The forms of divorce stipulated in the new *Mudawwana* are manifold and complex. The original plan to replace all existing possibilities with a judicial divorce accessible to both spouses equally was not adopted. Judicial divorce based on enduring discord between the couple (*shiqaq*) has been added to the law, next to the already existing forms of divorce in the previous *Mudawwana*. The legislator has probably retained the old forms in order to prevent the reforms from appearing too abrupt and to avoid fierce criticism from opponents. The right of repudiation had great symbolic value in the debates about reforms, both for supporters and for opponents. Conservatives and islamists considered it to be a God-given right that could not be abolished. For defenders of women's rights, it was one of the most blatant examples of inequality between the sexes and a threat to children's rights.

Moroccan family law contains, in addition to decease and annulment due to flaws in the contract, the following possibilities for marriage dissolution:

1. *Repudiation (talaq)*

Repudiation is a simple legal procedure that can be performed by the husband, or by the wife if she has been granted this right by her husband (Art.s 78-93 Mud). The law provides extensive rules for the procedure that must be followed. The *'udul* can only draw up a repudiation document after approval from a judge. The judge summons both spouses and attempts to reconcile them before giving his approval. When attempts at reconciliation fail, the law gives detailed rules that aim to ensure that the woman and any children suffer as little damage as possible from the repudiation. The man, for instance, must deposit a certain amount at the court so that financial support can be provided for his ex-wife and their children. Traditional forms of repudiation, such as by oath, linked to fulfilment of certain conditions, and triple *talaq*s, are not valid under current Moroccan law (Art.s 90-93 Mud).

2. *Repudiation by the judge (tatliq)*

There are two forms of judicial dissolution: repudiation by the judge upon the request of one or both spouses due to enduring discord (Art. 94 Mud); and repudiation by the judge upon the request of the wife. The law only recognises six grounds on which a woman can base her request (Art.s 98-113). The legislator in this regard follows a liberal interpretation of classical Maliki law, which allows the judge to dissolve a marriage in case the man does not fulfil his marital duties to the extent that his neglect harms his wife. Continuation of the marriage in that case is considered unreasonable and undesirable according to the Maliki scholars. The six grounds, as enumerated in the new law, are:

- failure of the husband to fulfil the conditions agreed upon in the marriage contract (Art. 99 Mud);
- the woman suffers harm (*darar*) caused by the husband; in case the woman cannot prove the harm but nevertheless persists in her desire for divorce, she can use the procedure for enduring discord between the couple (*shiqaq*) (Art. 100 Mud);
- failure of the husband to fulfil his duty to provide maintenance to his wife (Art. 102 Mud);

- absence of the man for more than one year (Art.s 104-106);
- ailments and defects that hinder the marriage and of which the person requesting the divorce was unaware at the time of the marriage, such as long-term illness; a man can also request divorce on this ground (Art.s 107-111 Mud);
- refusal of the man to engage in sexual relations with his wife, as expressed in a vow (Art. 112 Mud).

3. *Repudiation by mutual agreement*

This form of dissolution can occur with (Art.s 115-120 Mud) or without (Art. 114 Mud) compensation by the husband to the wife. The repudiation of the wife by her husband in lieu of compensation is known as *khul`*. In case where parties cannot agree about the compensation, women may make use of the procedure for enduring discord (Art. 120 Mud).

All forms of divorce are effectuated under the supervision of the judge, and sometimes professional witnesses as well. Both parties are summoned by the judge in the handling of the divorce. In almost all cases, except for repudiation by the judge due to absence of the man with an unknown place of residence (Art. 113 Mud) or repudiation against compensation whereby parties have reached an agreement about the compensation (Art. 120 Mud), the judge attempts to reconcile the parties prior to approving the divorce. In the procedure to be followed, judges and the *`udul* are tasked with ensuring that men fulfil their financial obligations towards their wives and children. The rules for registration have also been made stricter under the new law. As with marriage status, the civil register of births and deaths contains a side note of the divorce, where applicable (Art. 141 Mud).

Article 128 further broadens the possibilities for divorce by recognising decisions by foreign judges, as was previously mentioned. The new *Mudawwana* in principle grants both men and women the opportunity to request the judge to dissolve their marriage. Although not all Moroccan jurists want to acknowledge this, a certain inequality does remain because men automatically have the right of repudiation by entering into a marriage, while women only have this right in case the man grants it to her. The man's right to repudiation is nevertheless subjected to judicial control. For this reason some Moroccan jurists, including representatives of the Ministry of Justice, argue that the term *talaq* should no longer be translated as 'repudiation', but should instead be considered a special form of judicial divorce.

Descent and relations between parents and children

The *Mudawwana* contains several important innovations as compared to classical Islamic law and the previous family law with regard to descent and the relations between parents and children.

Possibilities to establish the descent of a child with regard to a father have been broadened as a reaction to the important social debate about unmarried mothers with illegitimate children (Bargach 2002). The legislator has made it more difficult for men, who get women pregnant and then abandon them, to escape from their responsibilities. The new law provides the judge more discretion in establishing paternity and the existence of a marriage. Article 16 enables the judge to declare the existence of a marriage, even when a marriage contract is lacking: progeny or pregnancy are considered as means of proof of the existence of a marital bond. Articles 155 and 156 further elaborate on this possibility. When persons assume they are maintaining conjugal relations, without formally having entered into a valid marriage, this can be considered as a case of what is called *shubha*, or maintaining relationships in good faith without actually knowing the legal details. Articles 152 and 155 recognise *shubha* as a valid ground to establish descent. Article 156 provides further conditions for establishing descent in case of a marriage without an official marriage document. If the man denies fatherhood, the law allows the use of all legal means of evidence to establish paternity (cf. Al-Kashbur 2007). With these innovations based on the classical concept of *shubha*, the legislator has taken an important step to limit the negative effects – legal, economic, and social – of illegal descent for both mother and child.

With regard to the authority of parents over their children, the legislator has retained the classical distinction between care (*hadana*) and legal guardianship (*wilaya*), while simultaneously strengthening the position of mothers. During the marriage both parents provide care for their children, *hadana* (Art. 164 Mud). After dissolution of marriage, the mother is the first to obtain the right to care, the father being the second in line (Art. 171 Mud). At the age of fifteen children can choose with which parent they wish to stay (Art. 166 Mud). The mother no longer necessarily loses the right to care if she remarries, unlike under classical law (Art. 175 Mud). Another reform allows the mother more flexibility in exercising her right to move within Morocco, even if this move would result in the children living geographically farther away from their father (Art. 178 Mud). The authority over the children or the legal guardianship (*wilaya*) remains the privilege of the father, in accordance with classical views (Art. 236 Mud). The mother can obtain this right if the father is unable to act as a legal guardian (Art. 231 Mud), a reform of the classical law that was already introduced in 1993 (Art. 148 Mud 1993).

Another important institution related to the patriarchal family model is the husband's duty to provide maintenance to his wife and children (*nafaqa*). This duty has not been abolished: the man remains obliged to support his wife and children (Art.s 194, 197, 198 Mud). The woman, in contrast, cannot be obliged to financially support her husband. In case the father is not capable of supporting his children and the mother is capable of doing so, then it becomes her duty to provide for their maintenance (Art. 199 Mud). The new law strengthens the rights of children to maintenance in cases where they are, for example, still studying or are disabled. In Article 202 the *Mudawwana* refers to the possibility of criminal prosecution when the father neglects his duty to support his family for a month or more.

The Moroccan legislator has respected the classical prohibition of adoption in Article 149 of the *Mudawwana*. A testamentary bequest favouring a person whereby he or she receives part of the inheritance as if he or she were a child is possible, but only within the limits that apply for bequest, thus not exceeding one third of the total inheritance. In addition, the *Mudawwana* offers the possibility to contract the duty to financially support a third party (*kafala*) (Art.s 187, 205 Mud). Morocco succeeded in 1996 in receiving recognition from the Hague Convention on Protection of Children for this institution of *kafala* as one of the instruments for the protection of a child. The recognition of this duty as a sort of adoption was a reason for Morocco to give up its objections towards this convention and become a party to the convention (cf. Buskens 1999: 196-198).

Inheritance law

The structural inequality between men and women is sustained in the rules of the *Mudawwana* on inheritance: a woman inherits half of what a man in the same position inherits (cf. Rutten 1997). Reforms in this area are apparently difficult to realise. In debates, women have addressed this inherent inequality, but it has not been given high priority. For many this is an issue that has only relevance for a small group of wealthy women. It is understood that in these circles fathers know how to use the means offered by law to favour their female relatives.

The legislator did remove the inequality between grandchildren who would be excluded from an inheritance of a grandparent because their parent had died. Since 2004 a bequest is not only obligatory for grandparents in favour of their grandchildren via the son, but also via the daughter (Art.s 369-372 Mud). Hereditary succession between a Muslim and a non-Muslim is still impossible, as between a natural parent and an illegitimate child (Art. 332 Mud).

Judicial practice

Not all Moroccans endorse the new vision according to which women and children have increased rights, while men are forced to accept stricter obligations. In fact, the significance of the reforms largely depends on the way in which judges and *'udul* apply the law in practice.

The administration of justice concerning family law takes place in special family law courts that are part of the first instance courts. Both men and women can act as judges. They supervise the *'udul* – male professional witnesses – who write down marriage contracts and repudiation documents and who divide inheritances. The *'udul* have protested because the reforms have limited their tasks in substance and scope, while at the same time making their jobs more complex and cumbersome in practice. Due to their education in classical law, the *'udul* also generally adhere to a more conservative vision of Islam.[14] Likewise, it appears that not all judges of the old guard are prepared to apply the new visions espoused by the most recent version of the *Mudawwana*. For example, a judge in Rabat in November 2004 responded to the question of whether a woman could always obtain a judicial divorce by stating that nobody could force him to pronounce a divorce. The female president of the family court promptly corrected him by explaining that her older colleague did not yet understand the new law. But indeed, a report from a Moroccan women's organisation indicates that judges do frequently give preference to interpretations of the law, which go back to earlier visions of family life (Ligue Démocratique 2005).[15]

The Moroccan government has started a widespread campaign to clarify the vision of the legislator to the judiciary and to thereby promote the application of the law. The Ministry of Justice organises courses and meetings all over the country. It has also published an official manual for the application of the law in practice, which provides for the proper interpretation of articles and further legitimises their existence in Islamic terms. A French version of this guide has also been published, and is available on the website of the ministry as well.

It is evident that the Moroccan government considers it important that a suitable image of the law is presented outside of Morocco. The new family law could apply in several Western European countries via international private law. Through the reforms, the government wishes to promote international cooperation in legal matters and recognition of Moroccan law. The concern about images held by foreign countries partly explains why an official French translation of the *Mudawwanat al-usra* took so long. Moroccan jurists could not agree on the translation of several terms. The jurists of the Ministry of Justice, for example, were of the opinion that the word *talaq* in the new law should no longer be translated as 'repudiation'.

3.7 Criminal law

In Moroccan criminal law, norms that are directly derived from classical sharia play a limited role. There is no mention of corporal punishments for specified crimes mentioned in the Qur'an (*hudud*) or retribution. The criminal law is for an important part inspired by French legislation and codified in the Code of Criminal Law of 1962, most recently revised in 2003, and in the code of criminal procedure of 1959, of which a new version went into effect on 1 October 2003. The reforms are partly related to the war on terrorism that received a great deal of attention in Morocco following the attacks in Casablanca in May 2003. According to human rights organisations, the methods of prosecution used resulted in violations of human rights, even though Morocco is party to the Convention Against Torture.

Article 222 is one of the few stipulations of the criminal code that explicitly refers to a norm derived from Islamic law. The article sets forth that Muslims who publicly disrespect the rules of fasting in a provocative manner during the month of *Ramadan* can be punished with a fine or detention. This article is part of a series of general articles concerning the respect for religious practices that fall under a chapter on civil rights. The maximum punishments are three years imprisonment and a fine of 500 dirham (around 50 euro). Articles 220 and 221 make the obstruction of religious practices also, in principle, punishable. Article 223 concerns damaging, destructing, or staining buildings, places, and/or objects related to religion. Articles 268 to 270 focus on desecration of tombs and Articles 271 and 272 focus on protecting the integrity of mortal remains, all with maximum punishments of five years imprisonment and fines of up to 1000 dirham (around 100 euro).

Article 220 of the criminal code forbids the undermining of the faith of a Muslim or attempts to convert a Muslim to another religion. The article specifies charity and welfare work as punishable methods of converting a person. Christians who limit themselves to charity work can carry out their work unhindered, but missionary work may result in prosecution and expulsion. Distributing Bibles in European languages is permitted, but for the import of Arabic translations the government refuses to give permission, despite the absence of any explicit legal prohibition (U.S. State Department 2004).

Morocco has made a reservation to Article 14 of the Convention for the Rights of the Child (CRC), which grants children freedom of religion, on the basis that Islam is the state religion. In April 2005 a group of members of parliament for the Istiqlal party called on the Minister of Religious Affairs to take measures against evangelists who presumably tried to convert poor youth. Although apostasy is not punishable for Muslims according to the criminal code, persons who converted to

Christianity were until a few years ago questioned by the authorities and sometimes even detained for a short period of time on the basis of Islamic legal norms (U.S. State Department 2004). Furthermore, converting is not socially accepted and can lead to scoffing and expulsion from the community.

A series of articles make the corrupting of Islamic values with regard to family life and honour punishable. This can be conceived as a confirmation of the patriarchal Islamic family model, which is rooted in the Moroccan culture. These stipulations can, however, for the most part be traced back to the French *Code pénal* and are not examples of the influence of classical Islamic criminal law. Penalisation applies to abandoning children (Art.s 459 and further), child abduction (Art. 471 and further), and abortion absent medical grounds (Art. 449). Articles 479 to 482 concern criminal prosecution with regard to the abandonment of household duties by one of the spouses, non-compliance with the obligation to provide maintenance, and neglect of the children.

In Articles 483 to 496 the criminal code sets forth punishments for a number of violations of public morality and virtue, such as rape, indecent assault, incest, sexual contact between unmarried people, adultery, and the abduction of a married woman. Articles 497 to 504 prohibit prostitution and moral corruption, such as pornography, and Article 608 (4) prohibits the public display of offensive images. Article 488 prescribes an increase in the penalty in case indecent assault, rape, or incest has led to the loss of virginity. According to Article 492, adultery is an offence that is only punishable in case a complaint is made.

The penal code prescribes rules for cultural crimes in which generally men use violence against members of their family or household when they consider their honour to have been tarnished. Article 414 of the criminal code prescribes an increase in the penalty if the accused has used violence against relatives with whom he is in a relationship of authority. Articles 418 to 424, in contrast, allow a decrease in penalty in case a family member or a third party has used violence when he is confronted with an act of a sexual offence. Article 418 allows for manslaughter and maltreatment in case a man catches his wife committing adultery. Article 419 allows castration in case of direct confrontation with an immoral offence. Article 420 excuses a family head for maltreatment, even if this unintentionally results in death, when he is confronted with unauthorised sexual acts in his household. Article 422 states that there can never be a decrease in punishment in case of the murder of a parent. Various women's groups have been struggling for years for the abrogation of Article 418 in particular, which they perceive as an approval of violence against women. Until now this combat against what they consider to be the Moroccan patriarchal 'macho' culture has not been successful (Buskens 2003: 109).

Other articles that can be understood as a protection of Islamic norms without being directly founded on classical Islamic law include, for example, Article 377, concerning false oaths and Articles 368-379 on false testimonies and perjury. Article 609(35) of the criminal code states that predicting the future and explaining dreams is punishable.

Numerous other forms of behaviour that are in conflict with Islamic norms are only punishable in case the party involved does not stay within the state legal framework. Licences are required, for example, for operating gambling halls and organising gambling games (Code of Criminal Law, Art.s 282-286). Selling alcoholic beverages is permitted, but also tied to licences. Alcoholics and other addicts can be forcibly admitted to rehabilitation according to Articles 80-85 when they have committed punishable acts as a result of their addiction.

In sum, one can conclude that the Moroccan criminal law contains few traces of classical Islamic criminal law. French criminal law served as a model that reinforced some 'Islamic' norms concerning family life, public morality, property, and violence. Other Islamic norms, such as the prohibition of gambling and alcohol, are not directly enforced by the law.

3.8 Other areas of law, particularly commercial law

Morocco does not have a comprehensive civil code. The relevant legal rules are spread over several codes and laws. French jurists composed the code of contracts in French in 1913, immediately after the establishment of the protectorate (*Dahir formant code des obligations et des contrats*). This code remains the cornerstone of civil law, yet it barely contains any reference to Islamic legal norms. Other areas of civil law, such as trade law (1996 *Code de commerce*), insurance law (2002 *Code des assurances*), and banking law, are also familiar for jurists who have some knowledge of French law.

Since the end of the 1980s the Moroccan government has been trying to promote economic growth by making it easier for foreign investors to do business in Morocco. There is no prohibition on interest; Moroccan banks offer and demand relatively high interest rates. A legal obligation to pay an Islamic tax (*zakat*) to a religious tax office is also absent from the law.

Rights to real estate are modelled after French law in so far as the real estate is registered in public registers. About 90 per cent of immovable property is not registered, in which case Islamic and customary rules apply. These rules are not codified, but partially gathered in classical legal treatises. Religious foundations (*awqaf*, sing. *waqf*) also exist. They are administered by the Ministry of Religious Affairs and

Religious Foundations and form an important source of income (Stöber 1986). Limited reforms have recently been introduced (cf. Benyahya 2007).

As previously mentioned, the Moroccan state structure and the legal system are characterised by a creative and selective usage of elements of Islamic tradition, the most famous being the institution of 'the commander of the faithful'. Another example of this is King Hassan's response to the riots in Casablanca in 1981, where he tried to appease the masses by creating new institutions to oversee the quality and prices of staple food items. He did so by reinventing in 1982 two economic functions to control the market, namely the *muhtasib* (market inspector) and the *amin* (head of corporations). The terms are taken from classical Islamic law, even though their structure is for the most part new. The *muhtasib* controls the price and quality of goods and services as well as respect and good morals in the public space, hence fulfilling the function of *hisba*. He is supported in his function by *umana'* (sing. *amin*), heads of corporations of craftsmen and merchants. The *muhtasib* is appointed by royal decree (*dahir*), and the *amin* is elected by the members whom he leads.

An example of an invented tradition that uses classical Islamic legal terminology to bestow legitimacy on a modern state institution was the establishment by King Mohammed VI of an ombudsman institution by the name of *diwan al-mazalim*, where citizens could submit complaints about the functioning of government services. The institution was created on 1 December 2001 on the occasion of the international day for human rights. The king presented the institution as a strengthening of human rights in conjunction with the principles of Islamic law and his function as commander of the faithful (*amir al-mu'minin*).

3.9 International conventions and human rights obligations

The Moroccan state officially assigns great importance to human rights. At the end of the 1980s King Hassan II began to pay lip service to human rights as part of a new policy aimed at the urban middle class and economic liberalisation (see 3.4). In 1990 he established a Council for Human Rights, and in 1993 he appointed a Minister for Human Rights. His successor Mohammed VI reformed the Council for Human Rights and implemented the above-mentioned ombudsman institution (*diwan al-mazalim*). On numerous occasions he emphasised the compatibility of Islamic norms with human rights. This official ideology can also be found in the preamble of the 1996 constitution, in which human rights play a prominent role.

Morocco became a member of the United Nations on 12 November 1956, several months after independence and the unification of the three zones into one national state. Since that time, the country has ratified a series of important conventions: the Convention on Genocide; the International Covenant on Civil and Political Rights (ICCPR); the Covenant on Economic, Social and Cultural Rights (ICESCR); the International Convention on the Elimination of All Forms of Racial Discrimination (ICERD); the Convention on the Elimination of All Forms of Discrimination against Women (CEDAW); the Convention Against Torture (CAT); the Convention on the Rights of the Child (CRC) and its two optional protocols; and the International Convention on the Rights of All Migrant Workers and Members of Their Families (ICRMW).

Morocco has made reservations and declarations with the signing of some of these conventions. The reservations to the Convention on Genocide, ICERD, CAT, and ICRMW were made for the purpose of limiting the jurisdiction of international judicial bodies with relation to Morocco and its full compliance with the conventions. In terms of conventions specific to the rights of women and children, as set forth by CEDAW and CRC, Morocco made reservations invoking Islam. The reservation made to the CRC concerns Article 14, which offers children freedom of religion. Morocco refers to the freedom of religion in the national constitution, but also to the stipulation that Islam is the state religion. This means that a Muslim child cannot change his or her religion, and thereby does not have absolute freedom of religion.

The declarations made *vis-à-vis* CEDAW primarily concern Article 2. The obligations to lay down the equality between men and women in legislation, and to take measures accordingly, may not restrict the constitutional stipulations that regulate the succession to the crown. This means that Morocco maintains the requirement that the head of state is a man. Article 2 furthermore only applies in so far as it does not conflict with the stipulations of Moroccan family law which grants different rights to men and women based on Islamic law and which are aimed at creating harmonious family relations. The enforcement of Article 15(4) of CEDAW, which grants women freedom of movement and freedom of residence, was limited by Articles 34 and 36 of the 1993 *Mudawwana* as those articles obliged women to obey their husbands and to live with them. The obligation of obedience has been abolished with the family reforms of 2004, but Article 51 of the 2004 *Mudawwana* still mentions co-habitation as a legal consequence of marriage.

The reservation made to Article 9(2) CEDAW concerns the equality between men and women in the possibility to pass on their nationality to their children. Until 2007 the Moroccan legislation on nationality restricted the right of women to obtain Moroccan nationality for their children. Moroccan women's rights movements have long advocated for the abolition of this discriminatory barrier to obtaining nationality. At present, it appears that while Morocco has not formally withdrawn its reservation, Article 6 of the 2007 Nationality Act allows women to transfer their nationality of origin to children born of foreign fathers and could in practice be considered as a withdrawal of the initial reservation to the Convention on this point.[16]

The reservation made to Article 16 CEDAW concerning the equality of men and women in entering into marriage and the possibility to obtain a divorce is aimed at safeguarding the male privilege of repudiation. According to Moroccan family law in force until February 2004, the marital duties of men and women were unequal: a husband had to offer the woman a bride price and maintenance, whereas his wife enjoyed complete control over her own property. For this reason, the man had the right to repudiation, while the woman had to request a judge for a divorce. In the vision of the Moroccan legislator, this inequality no longer exists in the *Mudawwana* of 2004. In the reservation made to Article 29 CEDAW, Morocco does not subject itself unconditionally to mediation in case of a dispute between states about the interpretation or application of this convention.

Morocco ratified CEDAW in 1993, but never published the text of the convention in the official bulletin. In the context of the debate about reforms of family law, Moroccan women's organisations requested King Mohammed VI to withdraw the reservations and to publish the convention. Their actions were only partially successful: on 26 December 2000 the king proclaimed CEDAW by royal decree, but did not at the same time withdraw Morocco's above-mentioned reservations to the Convention (cf. Buskens 2003: 108-110). Indeed, although it would appear based on Morocco's latest report to the Committee in 2006 and a statement by the Ministry of Justice on the occasion of International Women's Day in March 2006, further reiterated in a royal statement on the occasion of International Human Rights Day on 10 December 2008, that Morocco intends to withdraw most of its reservations to the Convention, it has not yet formally done so. During the fortieth session of the Committee in February 2008, the Moroccan representative (the Minister for Social Development, the Family, and Solidarity) made the argument that some reservations, such as to Article 9 as addressed above, have already begun to take place, but that the Committee should bear in mind that Morocco is still a young nation and that 'attitudes [do] not change overnight'.

In the debate about family law, human rights and international conventions have played an important role for activists of different backgrounds as well as for the government. King Mohammed VI repeatedly emphasised his respect for international law and his desire to bring the family law into compliance with both Islamic law and human rights. The Moroccan Ministry of Foreign Affairs published a book in 1997 in which the international conventions for the benefit of women's rights were extensively presented (Ministère des Affaires Etrangères et de la Coopération 1997). The fact that this work was published in French showed that it was also aimed at improving Morocco's international reputation with regard to its treatment of women and respect for human rights standards.

The Moroccan reservations to the conventions partly serve to allow Islamic norms to prevail, mainly concerning the unequal relations between men and women. On the formal level of Moroccan legislation, the possibilities of conflict between Islamic law and human rights norms are indeed mainly in the domains of the relationships between men and women and between parents, especially fathers, and their children, as regulated in family and criminal law. Particularly the reservation made to Article 2 CEDAW, one of the main articles of the convention, permits Morocco to avoid adjusting its legislation to realise more equality between men and women. According to the official Moroccan view, the 2004 reforms in family law satisfy the required equality between men and women.

In accordance with its reporting obligation under CEDAW, the Moroccan government submitted an official report to the U.N. Committee for CEDAW three times, with the latest in August 2006 acting as a combined third and fourth periodic report. The Committee discussed the reports in meetings in January 1997, July 2003, and February 2008. In each session, the Committee urged Morocco to fully enforce the stipulations of the convention and to withdraw its reservations. According to the Committee, a liberal interpretation of Islam, as practiced in some other Islamic countries that have not made any reservations, could offer a solution for the obstacles Morocco has identified. In the first discussion of 1997, however, Morocco argued that the reservations were the result of a consensus in the Moroccan society, and that they would, therefore, be difficult to modify. The Committee responded that educating the population would be a good method to bring about social changes. Members also expressed their concern about the scarce participation of women in the political system and about reports of high rates of violence against women. In the discussions of 2003, the Moroccan representation presented the proposals for reform of the *Mudawwana* as an important instrument in satisfying the requirement of the convention to abolish all forms of discrimination against women. By the time of the discussions in 2008, the new *Mudawwana* had been brought into force and from the Moroccan representation's perspective comprehensively included 'the principles of equality and shared responsibility'. While the Committee applauded Morocco for its steps thus far, it pressed for clarification as to the status of its withdrawal of the reservations and expressed ongoing concern about discrimination against women and girls in practice as well as in accordance with formal legislation.

The official treaty obligations were also the subject of alternative reports and important debates for women's and human rights organisations within Morocco. They have used the findings of the committee in their struggle for reforms of family and criminal law (cf. Buskens 2003: 108-110). These groups also advocated for the abolitions of reservations made to CEDAW, but have not yet proven fully successful.

As part of its official policy to establish the rule of law and to uphold human rights, the Moroccan government formally established bodies such as the Consultative Council for Human Rights ('Conseil consultatif des droits de l'Homme'), the Ministry of Human Rights, and the Equity and Reconciliation Commission ('Instance équité et reconciliation'). According to numerous reports, however, government actions in practice are often not in accordance with the official policy. International organisations such as Human Rights Watch, Amnesty International, and the U.S. State Department's Bureau of Democracy, Human Rights, and Labor have published detailed reports about the enforcement of human rights in Morocco.

Violations of human rights in several areas are revealed in recent reports from these organisations. The Moroccan authorities took strong actions against various islamist groups after the bomb attacks in Casablanca in May 2003. The employed methods of investigation, arrests, and acts of torture have led to fierce domestic and international criticism. This criticism appears to have resulted in improvements. The freedom of press, particularly in matters concerning the royal family and the status of the Sahara provinces, has seriously suffered over the past years. These violations are, however, not related to Islamic legal norms.

Freedom of religion, as guaranteed in the constitution, proves to be relatively effective in practice. Christians and Jews can practice their religions freely, as long as they do not attempt to convert Muslims. As was mentioned previously, Morocco has made a reservation to the Convention on the Rights of the Child that forbids apostasy for Muslim children. There is less tolerance for deviating Islamic ideas than there is for other religions of the Book. This is partly due to cultural factors, such as the stigma of apostasy, and partly because the government considers Shi`ites to be a direct threat to authority. The *makhzan* supports the ideal of the peaceful coexistence of religions, as can be noted from the welcome prepared for the late Pope John Paul II and the close relationships between the royal family and the Jewish community.

Violence against women is also a topic that has received attention in recent human rights reports. The criminal code determines that certain forms of violence are punishable, but for other forms, such as the so-called 'honour related' offences, there is a possibility for a reduced penalty. In practice, domestic violence is prevalent in Morocco, as in many other Mediterranean and Middle-Eastern societies where gender relations are conceptualised in terms of honour and shame. Human rights organisations have repeatedly called upon the government to take measures against this. The underlying reasons for male abuse, however, are more related to general social and cultural issues, than to specific Islamic norms.

The public debate about human rights in Morocco has shown an unprecedented openness in the past years. A delegation of Amnesty International commented on this new openness following an official visit in January 2005 and again as recently as 2009 in the context of Morocco's progress on women's rights laws and its uniqueness within the Arab world in establishing an Equity and Reconciliation Commission.[17] Not only the official views of government organisations have received publicity, but also the voices of numerous non-governmental organisations. This development of the public sphere can also be understood as a struggle of opposition groups to gain access to the political arena (Hegasy 1997; Rollinde 2002; Slyomovics 2005). An important part of the attention is focussed on disappearances, murders, and torture of political adversaries during the regime of Hassan II, but there is concern that the Commission's investigations are limited and that years later its recommendations have still not been implemented.

3.10 Conclusions

The historical overview demonstrates that Islamic law is not a static corpus of rules, but rather a dynamic tradition that has been changing for centuries in conjunction with social and political developments. During the twentieth century in particular, Islamic law was marginalised in the Moroccan legal system. Under the influence of French and Spanish protectorate rule, state law gained primacy, while Islamic norms and customary law were restricted to a subordinate position within state law. Their incorporation into the legal system also resulted in changes in form and content of Islamic law and customary law. Colonial officials concluded that within this wider framework Islamic law and local customs were to a large extent mutually exclusive systems of normativity. After independence the government further limited the influence of Islamic law and virtually denied the existence of customary law by largely excluding it from the official state system (cf. Buskens 2000).

Form and content of the prevailing Moroccan law are strongly influenced by the French model, with limited Islamic elements. According to the constitution, Morocco is an Islamic state in which Islam is the state religion, but the consequences for the legal system are not further elaborated. Article 19 of the constitution determines that the king is 'the commander of the faithful', which according to the official doctrine means that he has the highest authority with regard to Islamic law. In criminal law particularly the articles concerning morality and public order contain Islamic elements, but are not laid down as rules derived from classical Islamic criminal law. The *hudud* punishments described in the Qur'an and the rules for retribution from classical *fiqh* are entirely absent from Moroccan law. There are only marginal traces of Islamic law in commercial law, and the few Islamic norms do not hinder trade based on a Western model. Islamic restrictions concerning banking or contract formation are lacking. Rights to real estate can be established either according to modern law or Islamic law and local customs. Religious foundations (*awqaf*) also exist and are administered by the Ministry of Religious Affairs.

Family and inheritance law is the most important domain of Islamic legal norms. The *Mudawwanat al-usra* of 2004 applies to all Moroccans, except for the small Jewish community. This family law contains important reforms that are justified by the legislator by referring to the principle of *ijtihad*. The underlying model for family relations assumes the equality of both spouses, instead of the patriarchal family model of classical Islamic doctrine. This patriarchal model is widespread in Morocco as a cultural ideal, although it is at present heavily discussed and losing influence. Both parties should contract a marriage out of their own free will and for the most part equal rights are granted.

However, some elements of the Islamic patriarchal model have been kept. The man still has the duty to provide his wife with maintenance. The right of a man to marry multiple women is also maintained, albeit with strict limitations, as under the new law women are not obliged to accept polygamy. Muslim men are permitted to marry non-Muslim women, whereas Muslim women are only allowed to marry Muslim men. The man has the right to break up the marriage by means of a unilateral action (*talaq*), but he can only do so with the judge's permission. The woman, like her husband, has the right to obtain a divorce from the judge when she does not desire to continue the marriage. With regard to the authority over the children after divorce, the woman has the first right to care (*hadana*), and the man, the first right to legal representation (*wilaya*). In inheritance law a woman receives half of what a man in an equal position receives.

The reforms of family law are couched in an Islamic idiom, with explicit attention to international norms concerning human rights, particularly the rights of women and children. The law is an expression of the political will to enforce social change by giving women and children more rights, and of a moderate progressive vision of Islam. The *Mudawwana* is moreover an expression of the power of the king as the highest interpreter of Islamic law, whose will creates law. The meaning of the new stipulations for daily family life depends to a great extent on the way in which judges, both men and women, and professional witnesses apply the law. In addition, the conceptions and the behaviour of ordinary people, for whom the law is merely one of their frameworks for family life, are also of great importance. The state attempts to set a clear course for the practicing of family law, but the extent to which it has succeeded can only be determined through detailed field research.

The inventory of Islamic legal norms as laid down in positive law leads to the conclusion that Moroccan law only contains a very limited amount of legal norms derived from classical legal tradition. In Moroccan law, one finds predominantly politically inspired interpretations of Islamic law, which have been the subject of an intense public debate during the past years. There is no increasing islamisation of the law. On the contrary, the influence of norms derived from classical Islamic law on state law have further diminished with the 2004 reforms.

Since independence in 1956, Morocco is a member of the United Nations and party to several key human rights conventions. Morocco has made reservations to several conventions by invoking Islamic norms. According to official reports, Morocco does not always sufficiently respect its convention obligations. The regime of the late King Hassan II was especially characterised by serious violations of human rights. These were fiercely criticised by foreign organisations – and inside Morocco in a more disguised manner. Under the rule of King Mohammed VI, Morocco attempted to come to terms with the past through public hearings of the Equity and Reconciliation Commission ('Instance équité et reconciliation'). International pressure and the growing domestic discourse on human rights have had important consequences for the legal system, such as reforms of family law. At the same time, the *makhzan* attempts to continue ruling the domestic debate by appropriating the idiom of human rights and civil society.

In this overview I have paid little attention to legal practice, even though this is of great importance in answering question of islamisation of the legal system. On the political level, we can conclude that Morocco has an autocratic system. The constitution prescribes a separation of powers in a constitutional monarchy, with a democracy and a multi-party system. In the past King Hassan ruled Morocco as an absolute ruler who claimed to know what was best for his country. His function as commander of the faithful meant for him that he could determine the scope of Islam and Islamic law. As such, Islam was an instrument to legitimise his regime. At present, King Mohammed VI, political parties, and social movements appear to strive for a break with the despotism of the past. The manner in which the progressive reforms of family law came about is a paradoxical confirmation of the king's omnipotence with regard to Islamic law.

During the past centuries, Islam has been an instrument to legitimise as well as to contest political power in Morocco (cf. Munson 1993). The doctrine of *jihad* served as a means of resistance against European imperialism in the prelude to the protectorate. The struggle for independence was focussed on the spreading of a 'pure' Islam and the correct interpretation of Islamic law. Hassan II legitimised his state structure in Islamic terms, but since the 1980s his most dangerous critics have also utilised Islamic ideas. From the 1990s islamists have combined this jargon with a human rights discourse. Leftist and liberal opponents also refer to human rights in order to defend their views. The attacks committed by a group of radical islamists in Casablanca in May 2003 formed a turning point in the debate about Islam, law, and politics. Until then islamist groups seemed to have profited the most from the new openness. The king seized upon the general concern and fear to strengthen his power as 'commander of the faithful' and to enforce a moderate progressive Islam, focussed on the personal inner experience, instead of political action.

At present, two somewhat related topics dominate the political scene: Islam and human rights. Moroccans, both ordinary citizens as well as representatives of the *makhzan*, use both discourses in order to justify, but also to criticise, the political system and the prevailing law. With the new openness that came about in the 1990s, the Islamic discourse has once again become important for debate in the public sphere. The previously mentioned marginalisation of Islamic law in terms of positive law is paradoxically related to the revival of the political significance of sharia as a means of political opposition. Islamic law is a powerful political symbol. It was able to mobilise large groups of people in the struggle for independence. It turns out to be capable to do so again in the current debate. Islamic law can stand for strongly deviating conceptions about cultural authenticity that are supported, manipulated, and contested by different factions within society.

The impact of politicisation of sharia on positive law has resulted in reform of family law in favour of women and children. This reform took place within an exclusively Islamic framework, in which the term *ijtihad* played a key role. In present-day Morocco, discussion about family law or political legitimacy is not possible outside this Islamic discourse. This predicament is the result of a long historical process. Since the beginning of the twentieth century, Islamic law has been marginalised in Morocco in terms of substance, yet its significance as a political tool has considerably increased during the last three decades. The fact that sharia has nowadays become primarily a political symbol has created new tensions between varying factions holding opposing views of Moroccan society, just rule, and the place Islam should have in it. This development is by no means unique to Morocco, but fits a more general pattern that can be discerned in many contemporary Muslim societies.

Notes

1 Léon Buskens is professor of law and culture in Muslim societies at Leiden University. He thanks the late Mostapha Naji, the late Robert Rutten, Michèle Boin, Birte Kristiansen, and Friso Kulk for their help in collecting material, as well as Baudouin Dupret for his comments on an earlier version. Many thanks to Julie Chadbourne for her editing of the English text.

2 Abun-Nasr 1987 offers a standard history of the Maghrib. Pennell 2000 gives an overview of Moroccan history from 1830 onwards. El Fassi Fihri 1997 provides an overview of the history of the Moroccan legal system as understood by a judge and diplomat. Sater 2010 provides a recent overview of the present state of Moroccan society and politics.

3 Anthropologists who have published on contemporary legal practice in Morocco include, among others, Bouderbala, Daisy Dwyer, Hammoudi, Mir-Hosseini, Pascon, Rosen, and the present author.

4 Rodríguez Aguilera 1954 offers an overview of the legal system of the Spanish protectorate; Zomeño 2002 discusses the views of Spanish colonial scholars on Islamic law.

5 In the rest of this text I use the translation 'commander of the faithful' for this concept, following the title of John Waterbury's famous analysis of the Moroccan political system. In this particular context I adopt a slightly different translation to convey the existence of a notion of religious unity, which was not identical with a territorial entity in which the sultan exercised effective political control.

6 The German orientalists Ubach & Rackow 1923 offer an overview of customary law in Morocco, Algeria, and Tunisia on the basis of interrogations of prisoners of war from the French colonies taken during the First World War.

7 Rabinow 1989 analyses French ideas about 'modernity', also related to colonial policy. Chapter 9 of his book is devoted to the French colonial policy in Morocco.

8 Examples of this colonial scholarship in action include the bilingual (Arabic and French) magazine *Revue maroccaine de législation, doctrine, jurisprudence chérifiennes (Droits musulman, coutumes berbères, lois israélites)*, created in 1935 by Paul Zeys (judge and former colonial civil servant) and the edition of the Arabic text with a French translation of Gannun's (Guennoun) introductory overview of Maliki law as developed in Morocco by Boris de Parfentief (1958).

9 Zagouri 1961 gives a general introduction to Jewish family and inheritance law as it was applicable in Morocco shortly after independence. Chouraqui 1950 offers an extensive overview of the situation during the protectorate. Caillé 1944 (for the French zone) and Ruiz de Cuevas 1950 (for the Spanish zone) also provide short introductions to Jewish law during the protectorate period.

10 Government control was further strengthened by a new law and decree, promulgated in 2006 and 2008, concerning the *ʿudul* (cf. Benyahya 2009). The introduction of these new rules was related to the family law reform of 2004.
11 Wuerth 2005 analyses the role of women's organisations in the law reform process.
12 Mir-Hosseini 2007 offers a comparative analysis of recent family law reforms in Morocco and Iran.
13 Confusingly, present-day currents promoting puritan understandings of Islam are also often referred to as '*salafiyya*'.
14 The rules governing the work of the *ʿudul* have been reformed by a law of 2006 and a ministerial decree of 2008 in accordance with the 2004 reforms of the family law (cf. Benyahya 2009).
15 Cf. Jordens-Cotran 2005: 76-93.
16 See summary record of the fortieth session of the Committee on the Elimination of Discrimination against Women on 24 January 2008, CEDAW/C/SR.824, p. 4, in which Ms. Skalli, Minister for Social Development, the Family, and Solidarity, one of the institutions responsible for guaranteeing women's rights in Morocco, makes this point that in reality certain reservations had been withdrawn, even if not formally.
17 Amnesty International, *Morocco/Western Sahara: Increasing Openness on Human Rights*, press release MDE 29/01/2005 (Public), dated 24 January 2005 and Amnesty International, *Morocco/Western Sahara: Irene Khan acknowledges positive steps and calls for more progress*, statement, dated 23 March 2009 (both last accessed 1 December 2009). For further information on the general human rights situation in Morocco see e.g. Amnesty International Report 2009, Index: POL 10/002/2009: http://thereport.amnesty.org/en/regions/middle-east-north-africa/morocco.

Bibliography

Abun-Nasr, J.M. (1963), 'The Salafiyya movement in Morocco', in A. Hourani (ed.), *The religious bases of the Moroccan nationalist movement*, 90-105. London: Chatto & Windus.

Abun-Nasr, J. M. (1987), *A history of the Maghrib in the Islamic period*. Cambridge: Cambridge University Press.

Al-Kashbur, M. (2007), *Al-bunuwwa wa-l-nasab fi mudawwanat al-usra. Qira'a fi-l-mustajaddat al-biyulujiyya*. Al-Dar al-bayda': Matba'a Al-Najah al-jadida.

Arehmouch, A. (2001), *Les droits coutumiers amazighs: Izerfan imazighen. Tome I*. Rabat: (published by the author).

Arehmouch, A. (2006), *Code des droits positifs amazigh. Tome II*. Rabat: Edition & Impression Bouregreg-Rabat.

Aspinion, R. (1946), *Contribution à l'étude du droit coutumier berbère marocain (Etude sur les coutumes des tribus Zayanes)*. Casablanca, Fès, Meknès: Editions A. Moynier.

Azziman, O. (1986), 'Les institutions judiciaires', in M. Sehimi (ed.), *La grande encyclopédie du Maroc: Les institutions politiques, administratives, judiciaries*, 151-170. Rabat: La Grande Encyclopédie du Maroc.

Bargach, J. (2002), *Orphans of Islam. Family, abandonment, and secret adoption in Morocco*. Lanham: Rowman and Littlefield.

Bartleby (2010), 'Morocco', in *World Factbook*, see http://www.bartleby.com/151/country/mo.html (2008 statistics) and https://www.cia.gov/library/publications/the-world-factbook/geos/mo.html (online edition). Washington D.C.: Central Intelligence Agency.

Belghazi, H. (2008), *Tada chez les Zemmour : Instances, puissance, évanescence*. Rabat : Institut Royal de la Culture Amazighe.

Benradi, M. et al. (2007), *Le code de la famille. Perceptions et pratique judiciaire*. Rabat: Friedrich Ebert Stiftung.

Benyahya, M. (ed.) (2007), *La legislation relative aux habous et affaires islamiques*. Rabat: REMALD, Collection 'Textes et documents', no. 167.

Benyahya, M. (ed.) (2009), *La profession des adouls*. Rabat: REMALD, Collection 'Textes et documents', no. 219.

Berger, M.S. (2004), *Mudawwana: Marokkaanse familiewet (nieuwe wet van 2004)*. Nijmegen: Ars Aequi Libri.

Berque, J. (1949), 'Ville et université: Aperçu sur l'histoire de l'Ecole de Fès', *Revue historique de droit français et étranger* 27 (4): 64-117.

Burke, E. (1976), *Prelude to protectorate in Morocco: Precolonial protest and resistance, 1860-1912*. Chicago/London: The University of Chicago Press.

Burns, P. (2004), *The Leiden legacy: Concepts of law in Indonesia*. Leiden: KITLV Press.

Buskens, L. (1993), 'Islamic commentaries and French codes: The confrontation and accommodation of two forms of textualization of family law in Morocco', in H. Driessen (ed.), *The politics of ethnographic reading and writing: Confrontations of Western and indigenous views*, 65-100. Saarbrücken & Fort Lauderdale: Verlag Breitenbach Publishers.

Buskens, L. (1999), *Islamitisch recht en familiebetrekkingen in Marokko*. Amsterdam: Bulaaq.

Buskens, L. (2000), 'An Islamic triangle. Changing relationships between Shari'a, state law and local customs', *ISIM Newsletter* 5: 8.

Buskens, L. (2003), 'Recent debates on family law reform in Morocco: Islamic law as politics in an emerging public sphere', *Islamic Law and Society* 10(1): 70-131.

Buskens, L. (2008), 'Tales according to the book: Professional witnesses (*'udul*) as cultural brokers in Morocco', in B. Dupret, B. Drieskens, A. Moors (eds.), *Narratives of truth in Islamic law*, 143-170. London/New York: I.B. Tauris.

Caillé, J. (1944), *La justice israélite dans la zône française de l'Empire chérifien*. Casablanca: Imprimeries Réunies (Extrait de la *Gazette des Tribunaux du Maroc*, octobre 1943).

Chouraqui, A. (1950), *La condition juridique de l'Israélite marocain*. Paris: Presses du Livre Français.

El Fassi Fihri, M. E.-H. (1997), *L'itinéraire de la justice marocaine*. Rabat: Association pour la Promotion de la Recherche et des Etudes Judiciaires.

El Mansour, M. (1990), *Morocco in the reign of Mawlay Sulayman*. Wisbech: Middle East & North African Studies Press.

Essaîd, M.J. (1992), *Introduction à l'étude du droit*. Rabat: Collection Connaissances.

Foblets, M.C. (1994), *Les familles maghrébines et la justice en Belgique: Anthropologie juridique et immigration*. Paris: Editions Karthala.

Foblets, M.C. & Carlier, J.Y. (2005), *Le code marocain de la famille: Incidences au regard du droit international privé en Europe*. Brussels: Bruylant.

Gannun, A. (1958) : see Parfentief (1958).

Guiho, P. (1961), *La nationalité marocaine*, Rabat: Editions La Porte; Paris: Librairie de Médicis.

Hart, D.M. (1995), *Emilio Blanca Izaga : Coronel en El Rif. Una selección de su obra, publicada e inédita, sobre la estructura sociopolítica de los rifeños del norte de Marruecos. Estudios introductorios y notas de David Montgomery Hart. Edición de Vicente Moga Romero y Antonio Bravo Nieto*. Melilla: Ayuntamiento de Melilla, Fundación Municipal Sociocultural, Archivo Municipal, UNED – Centro Asociado de Melilla.

Hegasy, S. (1997), *Staat, Öffentlichkeit und Zivilgesellschaft in Marokko: Die potentiale der soziokulturellen Opposition*. Hamburg: Deutsches Orient-Institut.

Henry, J.-R. & F. Balique (1979), *La doctrine coloniale du droit musulman algérien: Bibliographie systématique et introduction critique*. Paris: Editions du CNRS.

Hidass, A. (2003), 'La liberté d'opinion et d'expression au Maroc: Normes, contingentements et transition démocratique', *Annuaire de l'Afrique du Nord* 39: 255-278.

Hitous, A. (ed.) (2007), *Le droit coutumier et les législations au Maroc*. Rabat: Organisation Tamaynut.

Jordens-Cotran, L. (2005), 'Het Marokkaanse familierecht en de Nederlandse rechtspraktijk', *Justitiële verkenningen* 27(5).

Jordens-Cotran, L. (2007), *Nieuw Marokkaans familierecht en Nederlands IPR*. The Hague: SDU Uitgevers.

Koningsveld, P.S. van & M. Tahtah (1998), 'De boodschap van Khalil el-Moumni, imam van de Rotterdamse Nasr-moskee', *Sharqiyyât* 10 (1): 41-67.

Kratochwil, G. (2002), *Die Berberbewegung in Marokko: Zur Geschichte der Konstruktion einer ethnischen Identität (1912-1997)*. Berlin: Klaus Schwarz Verlag.

Lafuente, G. (1999), *La politique berbère de la France et le nationalisme marocain*. Paris: L'Harmattan.

Lapanne-Joinville, J. (1959) 'Le code marocain du statut personnel', *Revue marocaine de droit* 11: 97-125.

Ligue Démocratique pour les Droits des Femmes (mars 2005), *Rapport annuel sur l'application du Code la Famille*.

Marcy, G. (1949), *Le droit coutumier Zemmoûr*. Algiers: La Typo Litho & Jules Carbonel and Paris: Librairie Larose.

Ministère des Affaires Etrangères et de la Coopération (1997), *Le Royaume du Maroc et les instruments internationaux relatifs aux droits de la femme*. Rabat: Ministère des Affaires Etrangères et de la Coopération, Direction de la Coopération Multilatérale.

Mir-Hosseini, Z. (2007), 'How the door of *ijtihad* was opened and closed: A comparative analysis of recent family law reforms in Iran and Morocco', *Washington and Lee Law Review* 64(4): 1499-1511.

Munson Jr., H. (1993), *Religion and power in Morocco*. New Haven/London: Yale University Press.

Obdeijn, H., P. de Mas & P. Hermans (2002), *Geschiedenis van Marokko*, new edition (orig. 1999). Amsterdam: Bulaaq.

Ouaazzi, E. & L. Aît Bahcine (eds.) (2005), *Droit et société au Maroc*. Rabat: Institut Royal de la Culture Amazighe.

Parfentief, B. de (1958), *En suivant la Zaqqâqiyya. Traité de droit de Si Abdallah Guennoun. Texte arabe et traduction française*. Paris: Institut des Hautes Etudes Marocaines.

Pennell, C.R. (2000), *Morocco since 1830: A history*. London: Hurst & Company.

Peters, R. (1980), 'Idjtihād and taqlīd in 18th and 19th century Islam', *Die Welt des Islams* 20 (3-4): 131-145.

Rabinow, P. (1989), *French modern: Norms and forms of the social environment*. Cambridge/London: The MIT Press.

Rodríguez Aguilera, C. (1954), *Manuel de droit marocain (zone espagnole)*. Paris: Librairie Générale de Droit et de Jurisprudence.

Rollinde, M. (2002), *Le mouvement marocain des droits de l'homme: Entre consensus national et engagement citoyen*. Paris: Karthala.

Ruiz de Cuevas, T. (1950), *Jurisprudencia rabinica en Marruecos (La "Hazzaca")*. Tetuan: Editora Marroqui.

Rutten, S. (1988), *Moslims in de Nederlandse rechtspraak: Een inventarisatie van gepubliceerde rechterlijke beslissingen in zaken waar Islamitische rechtsnormen en waarden een rol spelen 1973-1986*. Kampen: Kok.

Rutten, S.W.E. (1997), *Erven naar Marokkaans recht: Aspecten van Nederlands internationaal privaatrecht bij de toepasselijkheid van Marokkaans erfrecht*. Maastricht: Ph.D. dissertation, Maastricht University.

Sater, J.N. (2007), *Civil society and political change in Morocco*. London/New York: Routledge.

Sater, J.N. (2010), *Morocco: Challenges to modernity and tradition*. London/New York: Routledge.

Slyomovics, S. (2005), *The performance of human rights in Morocco*. Philadelphia: The University of Pennsylvania Press.

Stöber, G. (1986), *"Habous Public" in Marokko: Zur wirtschaftlichen Bedeutung religiöser Stiftungen im 20. Jahrhundert*. Marburg/Lahn: Im Selbstverlag der Marburger Geographischen Gesellschaft e.V.

Touhtou, R. (2008), *Debating civil society in Morocco: Dynamics of gender, development and social capital*. Fez: Ph.D. thesis Sidi Mohamed Ben Abdellah University, Faculty of Arts and Humanities Dhar al-Mahraz, Department of English.

Tozy, M. (1999), *Monarchie et islam politique au Maroc*. Paris: Presses des Sciences Po.

Ubach, E. & E. Rackow et al. (1923), *Sitte und Recht in Nordafrika*. Stuttgart: Verlag von Ferdinand Enke.

U.S. State Department (2009), International Religious Freedom Report 2009, see http://www.state.gov/g/drl/rls/irf/2009/127354.htm.

Vairel, F. (2004), 'Le Maroc des années de plomb: Equité et reconciliation?', *Politique africaine* 96: 181-195.

Voll, J.O. (1994), *Islam: Continuity and change in the modern world*, Second edition (orig. 1982). Syracuse: Syracuse University Press.

Wuerth, O. (2005), 'The reform of the Moudawana: The role of women's civil society organizations in changing the personal status code in Morocco', *Hawwa* 3(3): 309-333.

Zagouri, A. (1961), *Généralités sur l'application du droit mosaïque en matière de statut privé des Marocains Israélites*. Tangiers: Editions Marocaines et Internationales.

Zeghal, M. (2005), *Les islamistes marocains: Le défi à la monarchie*. Paris: La Découverte.

Zomeño, A. (2002), 'El derecho islámico a través de su imagen colonial durante el protectorado español en Marruecos', in F. Rodríguez Mediano & H. De Felipe (eds.), *El protectorado español en Marruecos: Gestión colonial e identidades*, 307-337. Madrid: Consejo Superior de Investigaciones Científicas.

4 Sharia and national law in Saudi Arabia

Esther van Eijk[1]

Abstract

Saudi Arabia is an absolute monarchy, ruled by the House of Saud. It is the cradle of Islam and home to the two holy cities Mecca and Medina. The first article of the Basic Ordinance (1992) states that the Holy Qur'an and the Sunna (traditions) of the Prophet Muhammad are the constitution of the kingdom and that Islamic shari'a is the basis of its legal system. The discovery of oil in the 1930s rapidly changed the country and forced the government to adapt and reform, but at the same time it wanted to hold onto its Islamic character and heritage. This created a split that until today the Saudi government struggles to repair – how best to find a balance between adhering to its Islamic principles *vis-à-vis* calls for progress and political and legal reform? The king has made cautious steps toward reform, notably by restructuring the judiciary in 2007, which is still being put into full effect, and by a 2009 cabinet reshuffle with appointments of moderate ministers, including a female deputy minister of education, and new leadership for the justice sector. This chapter provides a select overview of the role of shari'a in the legal system of Saudi Arabia, both historically and in the present. It should be noted here that Saudi Arabia is a closed and complex country, which makes it difficult to gain access to extensive and recent data about the legal system and the Saudi society at large.[2]

Table of contents

Saudi Arabia comprises about 80 per cent of the Arabian peninsula. The kingdom has a population of well over 28 million people, including at least 5.5 million foreign nationals. About 90 per cent of the Saudis are of Arab ethnicity, the rest being Afro-Asian. Traditionally, Saudi Arabia is a tribal, nomadic society. Following the discovery of oil in 1930s, especially over the last fifty years, it has become more urbanised. The migrant workers come from all over the world, with most from South and Southeast Asia, and neighbouring Arab countries. According to statistics, all Saudis are Muslim, of which 90 per cent are Sunni Muslim and around 10 percent are Shi'ite. The official language of Saudi Arabia is Arabic.

(Source: Bartleby 2010)

4.1 The period until 1920

The political-religious Saud-Wahhab alliance

In the centuries before the arrival of Islam, rival tribes, both nomadic and sedentary, dominated the Arabian peninsula, which is predominantly desert and mountainous terrain, with a few important oasis settlements.[3] Caravan routes passed through the more sedentary areas in the North and along the coastal areas, including the Hijaz, the region on the Western coast of Arabia, with Mecca as its main commercial centre. Besides being a prominent trading centre, Mecca housed the Ka'ba sanctuary, a site of pilgrimage since pre-Islamic times.[4] The Hijaz was – literally – the place of birth of Islam: the Prophet Muhammad was born in Mecca around 570 AD, and in 622 he migrated to Yathrib (later Medina),[5] where he died in 632.

Shortly after Muhammad's death, the Islamic faith rapidly expanded as Muslims conquered the rest of Arabia and far beyond. Its political centre, however, quickly moved from the Arabian peninsula to Damascus in 656, and later to Baghdad in 750. It was not until the sixteenth century, when the Ottomans[6] managed to seize control over some parts of the Hijaz, that the Arab tribes were forced to submit to foreign power (Cleveland 2000: 43). Turkish garrisons were stationed in Mecca, Medina, Jeddah, and other cities. However, the power of the Ottoman empire was limited, with local tribal leaders and rulers governing in this region with a great deal of autonomy.

Ibn Saud and Al-Wahhab

In the eighteenth century the situation changed when the political and religious alliance between the religious scholar and jurist Muhammad ibn Abd al-Wahhab (1703-1793) and Muhammad ibn Saud (died in

1765) gradually gained ground on the peninsula. Muhammad ibn Saud was the ruler (*amir*) of Dir'iyya, a city north of Riyadh, situated in the Najd, the central region of the peninsula. Supported by the puritan movement of Shaykh Ibn Abd al-Wahhab, he conquered large parts of the Arabian peninsula starting in 1744. Ibn Abd al-Wahhab, also from the Najd area, advised Ibn Saud on questions regarding religion, law, and political affairs. Both men shared the goal of establishing a new state 'derived from a divine contract based on the Shari'a. The state, thus, formed an integral part of religion which was not separate from politics, nor politics from morals' (Kechichian 1986: 55).

The ideas of Ibn Abd al-Wahhab formed the ideological basis of the Saudi kingdom. He sought to return to the time of the Islamic forefathers (*salaf*), a return to pure Islam.[7] To accomplish this, he advocated the abolition of all innovations that had polluted Islam over the course of the centuries. He strongly opposed animist practices, Shi'a and Sufi practices such as visits to shrines and tombs, and other customs and rituals so common in eighteenth century Arabia. He emphasised the monolithic character of Islam and the oneness of God. In his view, customary law and indigenous customs contradicting shari'a had to be firmly suppressed (Vogel 2000: xvi). Ibn Abd al-Wahhab based his ideas on the works of the Salafi tradition within Islam, particularly as propounded by two legal scholars, namely Ahmad ibn Hanbal (780-855), founder of the Hanbali school of law, and Ahmad ibn Taymiyya (1263-1328), one of the most prominent scholars of that school.

The Hanbali doctrine traditionally distinguished itself from other Sunni schools of law by its strict adherence to the holy sources. Hanbali scholars emphasised a strict dependence on the Qur'an and the Sunna (teachings and traditions of the Prophet Muhammad) as sources of law and, unlike other schools of law, minimised resort to consensus (*ijma'*) and analogical reasoning (*qiyas*) as methods for imparting legal findings. Not only did Ibn Taymiyya seek to revive Ibn Hanbal's stringent reliance on the revealed texts in his time, his teachings were also influential in the relationship between religious and political authority, manifested in the cooperation of Muhammad ibn Saud and Ibn Abd al-Wahhab and their successors all the way up until today. Ibn Taymiyya believed that the ruler and the *'ulama* (religious scholars) should work closely together. The legitimacy of the ruler depended on his adherence to shari'a; the ruler himself is also subject to the sacred law and, therefore, at least in theory, placed on an equal footing with his subjects. The *'ulama*, for their part, have the obligation to advise the ruler and both should collaborate to uphold the shari'a (Vogel 2000: 202-204).

After Muhammad ibn Saud's death in 1765 his son and subsequent successors extended the rule of the House of Saud on the peninsula. In

1803, the governor (*sharif*) of Mecca was defeated and the Saudi-Wahhabist alliance conquered the Hijaz. Between 1803 and 1814, other territories were conquered by the Sauds. Their rule now stretched far beyond the Hijaz and the Najd towards the eastern coast of the peninsula. To administer the newly gained territories, governors and judges were appointed to cities and villages, representing the rulers from Dir'iyya and to implement the basic principles of Islam, including the collection of religious tax (*zakat*) (Kechichian 1986: 56). Disputes were adjudicated by the local ruler or by a single judge (a *qadi*), appointed by the ruler, who himself would be the only instance for appeal against the *qadi*'s decision, and responsible for the implementation of a *qadi*'s ruling.

The Ottomans were alarmed by the Saudi expansion, and, thus, the Ottoman sultan in Istanbul, Mahmud II, ordered his Egyptian viceroy Muhammad Ali Pasha to suppress this rebellion on the Arabian peninsula. In 1811, Muhammad Ali's son Ibrahim led the campaign in Arabia, and Mecca and Medina soon fell into Ottoman hands again. Seven years later, after a two-year siege, Dir'iyya was also conquered. The Ottoman occupation, however, did not last long: in 1824 Muhammad ibn Saud's grandson Turki ibn Abdullah (1755-1834) obtained hegemony over the Arabian peninsula and made Riyadh the new capital city.

Prince Abdulaziz al-Saud: Founder of the Saudi nation-state

After the death of his successor and son Faisal in 1865, the Saudi regime suffered from internal strife and civil war. This situation lasted until the first decades of the twentieth century, when the Saudi prince Abdulaziz al-Saud, commonly referred to as Ibn Saud (1880-1953), was able to reunite the various tribes of the Arabian peninsula under Saudi rule. In 1902, he defeated the rival Al-Rashid clan and in the subsequent years he conquered Najd, and in 1925 the Hijaz.

The expansion of what is today the Saudi kingdom is often merely ascribed to the eighteenth century Wahhab-Saud alliance, but the role of Abdulaziz al-Saud should not be underestimated. Like his forefather Muhammad ibn Saud, he was above all an astute ruler who was able to successfully play out different tribes against each other and increase his power base by forming smart alliances, for example with the British (Kostiner 1993: 6), as will be evident in the following section.

4.2 The period from 1920 until 1965

The formation of the unified Kingdom of Saudi Arabia

After the First World War, the Middle East changed drastically. The Ottoman Empire collapsed and new states under British and French mandates now neighboured Saudi Arabia. Abdulaziz faced the difficult task of maintaining the support of both the more cosmopolitan Hijaz and his own conservative Wahhabist followers in Najd. He also had to convince the Islamic world that his Wahhabist rule would not endanger the holy cities of Mecca and Medina or the tradition of the *hajj* (the annual pilgrimage), whilst on the other hand ensuring that the new nation-state paid respect to the rules of the new international world order (Vogel 2000: 281-282).

On 8 January 1926, Abdulaziz was crowned king (*malik*) of the Hijaz, adding this title to his existing position as 'Sultan of Najd and its Dependencies'. The new king declared that shari'a was the law of the land and that all four Sunni schools of law deserved respect (Vogel 2000: 89). In the same year, he promulgated a 'constitution' for the Hijaz ('the Basic Directives of the Kingdom of Hijaz'), which declared the Hijaz to be a 'consultative Islamic State'. The Basic Directives allowed for the formation of a Consultative Council (*majlis al-shura*) and a Council of Deputies (*majlis al-wukala*)[8] to be involved in state policy making, respectively as representative and administrative bodies (Al-Fahad 2005: 379-380). The Consultative Council was instructed to develop a new judicial organisation for the Hijaz.[9]

When Abdulaziz conquered the Hijaz in 1925, he found a judicial organisation influenced by the Ottomans. The Hanafi school was the official rite of the Ottoman Empire and had, therefore, been established in the Hijaz, although most of the Hijazis followed the Shafi'i school. The Ottomans had implemented a system of shari'a courts, the panels of which were comprised of one Hanafi chief judge and three assistant judges, one from each school of law (Vogel: 88). In 1927, the king issued a decree stating that the rules of the Ottoman laws would remain effective up and until they were replaced by new rules. Many *'ulama*, however, resisted this decision. At a conference held in Mecca that same year, they issued a legal opinion (*fatwa*) in which they demanded the immediate cancellation of any man-made [Ottoman] laws applicable in the Hijaz and contended that only shari'a provisions ought to be applied (Al-Jarbou 2007: 200-201).

Regardless of the reluctant attitude of the *'ulama* towards state-interference in 'their' domain, Abdulaziz adopted a framework for the courts of the Hijaz in 1927. It was a more elaborate judicial organisation with multiple-judge courts, which were, most importantly, summary and general shari'a courts, and instances of appeal (Vogel 2000: 89). This legal system initially only applied to the Hijaz, but between 1957 and 1960 the system was implemented in the rest of the country. Vogel explains that '[i]n this way Abd al-'Azīz was able to introduce new institutions, gain experience with them, and allow his conservative Najdī 'ulamā' a chance to become familiar with them' before the actual transition took place (ibid: 283).

In Najd, the Wahhabi homeland, a different judicial system had continued to exist until the unification in the late 1950s. Traditionally, the ruler appointed single judges to the major towns, who worked closely with the local governor (*amir*). A judge was only involved after the attempts of the governor to resolve a conflict amicably had failed. The governor would then refer cases to the judge for a ruling according to shari'a, and, after judgement, the case would be submitted to the governor for enforcement if the losing party did not willingly accept the outcome. Appeals were only possible through complaint to the local ruler, who would often refer cases to the senior *'ulama* (Vogel 2000: 88)

In the early 1920s all Sunni schools of law resonated in the Arabian peninsula. In Najd, the Hanbali school of law prevailed, whereas in the Hijaz, the Shafi'i and the Hanafi schools of law were both predominant.[10] In 1927, Abdulaziz suggested that a law code based on rulings of all Sunni schools of law be introduced, but he faced strong resistance from the Hanbali religious scholars. In the same year, all Hijazi shari'a judges were ordered to apply the Hanbali *fiqh* (Islamic jurisprudence). Only when this school of law could not provide an answer to a particular question could one refer to the Hanafi, Shafi'i, or Maliki schools of law (Schacht 1982: 87).

The Saudi kingdom promoted itself as the cradle of Islam and, as such, the guardian of the Holy Sites. Likewise, the Saudi legal system claimed an age-old, untainted continuity, without interference from Western rulers. This claim appeared to be justified to a certain extent. Saudi Arabia, after all, had adopted little to no Western legislation, with one exception being the Ottoman Code of Commerce of 1850. The Code, based on the 1807 French Commercial Code, was stripped of all references to interest and implemented in the Hijaz in 1931 in adjusted form.[11] The *'ulama*, however, resisted the implementation of this man-made law and the shari'a courts refused to apply it (Vogel 2000: 285).

In 1932, the Najd region and the Hijaz were joined together and the current kingdom of Saudi Arabia as a modern nation-state came into existence. Abdulaziz concentrated on consolidating his rule and establishing central authority in the kingdom. He proved to be a masterful tribal politician:

> [a]s astute as he was brave, he proved to be a fair and judicious ruler whose piety, dignity, and accessibility won him the allegiance of his subjects [...] ruling less as an absolute monarch than as a first among equals (Cleveland 2000: 227).

The alliance between Ibn Abd al-Wahhab and Muhammad ibn Saud from the eighteenth century in fact continued: the political and economic authority was vested in Abdulaziz and his governors; the religious and, due to the primacy of shari'a, the legal authority was in the hands of the *'ulama*, in particular the descendants of Shaykh Ibn Abd al-Wahhab.[12] The *'ulama* were responsible for Islamic education and the interpretation of shari'a, and they remained qualified, as specialists on the Word of God, to give the ruler advice (*fatwa*) on any relevant topic.

Discovery of oil: Impetus for state-building and modernisation

In 1938, oil was discovered on the peninsula, which had long been a poor region. The young Saudi kingdom thereby obtained a stable source of income and after the Second World War the country rapidly changed into a prosperous nation. In several areas, new legislation was promulgated to keep up with the economic developments and to advance the transformation of Saudi Arabia into a modern nation-state.

According to the Wahhabi doctrine, based on Ibn Taymiyya's theory, rulers were competent to promulgate necessary legislation for government policy (*siyasa shar'iyya*), provided it was complementary to and not in contradiction with shari'a and served public interest. In modernising Saudi Arabia this legislation was often termed 'royal decree' (*marsum*) or 'ordinance' (*nizam*). It should be noted here that the term *nizam* (ordinance or regulation) is used deliberately as distinct from the term *qanun* (law), and is a term commonly used to refer to codified man-made law; many Saudi *'ulama* consider it to be a Western concept and alien to Islamic shari'a. In addition, the term 'regulatory authority' is used in lieu of 'legislative authority' because the latter term can only be used to refer to God, the only legislature (Al-Jarbou 2004: 14 n. 31). This is important to bear in mind when looking at the effects of the new regulations on the judicial structure. From the 1930s onwards, many specialised tribunals or 'committees' to adjudicate matters in certain areas, such as labour law and commercial law, were created to apply the new regulations, under the supervision of a particular ministry. The Tariffs Committee (1953); the Committee for Commercial Paper Disputes (1963); and the Committee for the Settlement of Labour Disputes (1969) are just a few examples. The king was forced to create these special tribunals because the *'ulama* opposed the new man-made legislation and the shari'a judges refused to apply it (Vogel 2000: 286).

The most important new judicial institution – an administrative court called the 'Board of Grievances' – was created in 1955. This Board heard and investigated complaints filed by Saudi citizens against government officials and agencies; it directly reported to and advised the king, who should take the final decision on the complaint. Initially, the Board was also authorised to investigate complaints against shari'a court judges (Al-Jarbou 2004: 25).[13]

King Abdulaziz died in 1953 and left behind a united kingdom with a central government, a set of administrative legislation, and a remodelled judicial system. The Saudi royal family firmly held onto its power: Abdulaziz was succeeded in rule by his sons Saud (1953-1964), Faisal (1964-1975), Khalid (1975-1982), Fahd (1982-2005), and Abdullah (2005-present).

Unlike his father, King Saud was not a competent head of state. His extravagant lifestyle led the kingdom to the brink of bankruptcy. His reign coincided with the emergence of the secular pan-Arab nationalism of the Egyptian president Gamal Abd al-Nasser (1956-1970). Nasser challenged the Islamic Saudi kingdom by calling for a socialist revolution that would shake the 'feudal' monarchy (Niblock 2006: 58). The royal family felt threatened and isolated by Nasser's success, and countered by starting a worldwide campaign to spread Wahhabi Islam. In 1962, for example, the Saud family founded the Muslim World League in Mecca to promote 'Islamic unity' and to further advocate the Wahhabist version of Islam (Kepel 2004: 52). According to the Saud family, the export of Islam is a holy duty: Saudi Arabia is, after all, the birthplace of Islam and remains the guardian of the holy cities. In the 1950s and 1960s, thousands of Egyptian Muslim Brothers fled to Saudi Arabia, where they were offered political asylum. They played an influential role in the rise of radical Islamist thought among a segment of the Saudi population, which became even more evident in the 1970s (ibid: 51).

In November 1953, a month before his death, the then King Abdulaziz had ordered the establishment of a Council of Ministers. However, it took King Saud until 1958 to promulgate a regulation for the Council of Ministers, laying down the regulatory authority of the government. It granted the council authority to formulate policies related to domestic, foreign, financial, economic, and all public affairs. The regulation determined that an ordinance (*nizam*) could only be proclaimed by royal decree when it had been approved by the Council of Ministers, and would only become effective after it had been published in the official government gazette. The *'ulama* had no formal role in this legislative process, but they were usually consulted in order to ensure that a *nizam* was in accordance with shari'a (Vogel 2000: 289).

As of 1957, King Saud embarked on implementing the abovementioned unification of the judiciary throughout the entire kingdom. Three years later both systems were united under the 'Presidency of the Judiciary' located in Riyadh. With some amendments, the Hijazi system was now applicable to the entire kingdom. The 'Presidency of the Judiciary' remained responsible for many religious and legal matters, such as the issuance of *fatwas*, supervision of religious education, and appointment of persons in important religious positions, until it ceased to exist in 1975 (Vogel 2000: 91-93).

In 1964, on the family's initiative, King Saud was replaced by Crown Prince Faisal, who proved himself to be a more capable statesman and politician than his predecessor.

4.3 The period from 1965 until 1985

Struggle for Islamic authority

King Faisal introduced a series of far-reaching reforms, in areas such as finance, education, health care and, last but not least, the legal system. From 1970 to 1975 the national court system was further developed and formalised in the Judiciary Regulation of 1975. The 'Presidency of the Judiciary' ceased to exist; its tasks were assigned to new institutions, among which were: the Supreme Judicial Council, the Council of Senior 'Ulama, and the Ministry of Justice (established in 1970) (Vogel 2000: 92-93, 108). From then on, the courts fell under the administrative competence of the Ministry of Justice. The shari'a judges, however, had long since been very independent and were suspicious of any state interference. Until today, the government has been unable to completely subdue the shari'a scholars' and judges' suspicion and sometimes bold opposition to the state regulations, as will be discussed below.

The Judiciary Regulation (1975) granted general jurisdiction to the shari'a courts to adjudicate in all civil and criminal disputes except in the areas of law where the specialised committees were competent. The law provided a new set-up for the judicial organisation and introduced the Supreme Judicial Council. This council, operating under the direct authority of the king, formed the top of the judicial pyramid, with appellate courts in Riyadh and Mecca, and larger and smaller courts spread all over the country., The specialised committees, however, fell outside the formal judicial system; they fell within the scope of the executive branch. The Supreme Judicial Council was granted judicial, administrative, and regulatory authority. Besides its supervisory role over the shari'a courts, the Council could establish general principles and precedents that had to be followed by the courts. Moreover, the Council could give opinions about issues upon request of the king, the Council of Ministers, or the Minister of Justice (Al-Jarbou 2004: 21 n. 77).

In 1971, King Faisal set up the Council of Senior 'Ulama with the primary task of providing advice to the king and his government. The council has played a crucial role in the development of government policy since that time (Jerichow 1998: 68).

King Faisal instigated the oil embargo in 1973 in reaction to Western support for Israel during the 1973 Yom Kippur War against Egypt and Syria. Oil prices quadrupled as a result of this embargo. Faisal used the abundant oil revenues to finance a broad modernisation programme. He generously invested in education. He founded religious and secular universities, and thousands of Saudis went abroad to study, especially to the United States. Consequently, a new highly-educated elite emerged, bringing with them a great deal of knowledge and expertise from abroad. Members of the extensive royal family, however, retained the important governmental positions, although some commoners were successful in gaining access to the political arena.[14] Save some exceptions, most Saudis outside the royal family had to be satisfied with civil service positions, albeit with generous compensation and status. Several new ministries, such as the Ministries of Commerce and of Industry and Electricity were created to administer the bursting economic and commercial development (Niblock 2006: 48-49).

The House of Saud: The legitimate rulers?

Alongside this modernisation, Saudi Arabia retained its position as the guardian of Islam, with the Saud family as righteous rulers based on the Qur'an and shari'a. King Faisal claimed that a constitution was unnecessary because 'Sa'udi Arabia [...] has the Quran, which is the oldest and most efficient constitution in the world' (Cleveland 2000: 445). Whereas Faisal still made efforts to modernise the country, many *'ulama* frequently opposed these changes. In 1960, for instance, he suggested that public education for girls be introduced, but he faced heavy resistance from the *'ulama* establishment. He eventually succeeded, but only because he allowed the *'ulama* a supervisory role. This enabled the *'ulama* to have a significant influence on the content of the curricula and to ensure the separation of sexes in the classrooms. On a more general note, the *'ulama* also maintained public order in society with the help of the religious police, officially called the 'Committee for the Promotion of Virtue and the Prevention of Vice'. This religious police guaranteed – and still guarantees – the enforcement of Islamic rules of conduct in the public domain, such as dress codes and the closing of restaurants and shops during prayer time, segregation between the sexes, and the non-propagation of religious beliefs by non-Muslims. As such, the Saudi *'ulama* retained an important and influential role in the state in return for their support to the royal family as 'legitimate Islamic rulers' (Cleveland 2000: 446).

King Faisal was murdered by one of his nephews in 1975; he was succeeded by his brother Khalid. King Khalid was an inexperienced ruler and delegated much of his power to Crown Prince Fahd. In the 1970s Saudi Arabia soared to great heights. Modernisation in the areas of education and health care improved the lives of many Saudis. This, however, could not ward off the emergence of young radical Islamists. On 20 November 1979, five hundred dissidents led by Juhayman al-Utaybi attacked the Holy Mosque in Mecca. Al-Utaybi claimed that the Saud family had lost all their legitimacy as a result of widespread corruption, their decadent behaviour, and their imitation of the West. These accusations were similar to those raised successfully by Khomeini against the *shah* of Iran the very same year. The attack was also aimed at the Saudi *'ulama*, who in the eyes of Al-Utaybi let themselves be used for political purposes by the Saud family. The authorities were completely surprised by the attack. Two weeks later, on 5 December 1979, the assailants were finally overpowered and later executed. A *fatwa* from the Council of Senior 'Ulama later justified the use of violence by the authorities (Kechichian 1986: 60).

The Saudi regime eyed the success of the Iranian revolution led by the Shi'ite leader Ayatollah Khomeini with suspicion. Again large sums of money were invested to spread Wahhabi Islam, this time as a counterweight against the Shi'ite revolution. The Saudi regime contributed millions to the building of thousands of mosques, Islamic centres, and schools all over the world (Ottaway 2004).[15]

In June 1982, King Khalid died of a heart attack; he was succeeded by his brother Fahd who later added the title 'Custodian of the Two Holy Mosques' to his name.[16]

4.4 The period from 1985 until the present

A religious-political balancing act – Tensions and reforms

In August 1990, Iraq invaded neighbouring Kuwait. King Fahd, with the support of the Council of Senior 'Ulama, gave permission to the stationing of foreign, mostly American, troops on Saudi territory as part of the military operation 'Desert Storm' in order to liberate Kuwait (Cleveland 2000: 465). Large expenses as a result of the First Gulf War (1990-1991) and a sharp decline in oil revenues following the drop in oil prices in the 1980s had a detrimental impact on the Saudi economy. Social services could no longer be financed and employment opportunities declined. The deteriorating economic situation and the permanent presence of American troops led to a growing dissatisfaction among the population. Vogel writes:

> With the Gulf War, pressure [...] mounted perhaps because Saudis were dismayed to observe that the king and a few of his family made, all alone, the stupendous decision to invite non-Muslim, non-Arab powers into the kingdom to wage war on a sister Arab country (2000: 295).

In 1990, a group of businessmen, academics, and journalists submitted a petition for political reform. They asked for the creation of a new consultative council, equality among all citizens, more freedom of the press, and an improvement in the position of women. Later that year, on the 6th of November, forty women drove in a convoy of cars through the streets of Riyadh in protest against the existing convention that prohibited women from driving cars. This protest, however, had the opposite effect: the government not only punished the women involved, but it also proclaimed a formal law forbidding women to drive cars.

On the other side of the social spectrum, traditionalists called for stricter observance of shari'a and a greater role for the *'ulama* in decision-making processes. More radical Islamists, often young Saudis from an urban middle-class background, claimed that the regime failed to observe Islamic tenets. They blamed the government for being corrupt and incompetent, worsened by the increasing Western influence and Saudi dependence on the West (Cleveland 2000: 477-478).

The 1992 Basic Ordinance of the Kingdom of Saudi Arabia

Faced with domestic pressure for change, King Fahd felt compelled to introduce political reforms. On 1 March 1992 he promulgated the 'Basic Ordinance of the Kingdom of Saudi Arabia', the 'Ordinance of the Consultative Council', and the 'Ordinance of the Provinces'.[17] Together, these three laws formed the first 'codified' constitutional framework for Saudi Arabia.[18] In an interview three weeks after the introduction of the Basic Ordinance, King Fahd clearly stated that it was not Saudi Arabia's intention to transform the country with these ordinances into a Western democracy:

> The democratic system that is dominant in the world is not a suitable system for the people of our region. Our peoples' make-up and unique qualities are different from those of the rest of the world. We cannot import the methods used by people in other countries and apply them to our people. We have our Islamic system, which is based on consultation (*shura*) and the

openness between the ruler and his subjects before whom he is fully responsible.[19]

Article 1 of the Basic Ordinance declares that the Qur'an and the Sunna are the constitution of the country. Al-Fahad, a Saudi lawyer, noted that the Basic Ordinance reflects '[t]he codification of the *status quo* of essentially unbridled executive power' with the Qur'an and the Sunna 'as the only substantial constraint on executive power' (2005: 385-386). The Ordinance appears to separate the executive, regulatory, and judicial authorities (Art. 44), but the same article concludes by declaring that the king 'shall be the final resort of these authorities' (Tarazi 1993: 264).

Nonetheless, the Basic Ordinance met the petitioners' demand for a new consultative council (*majlis al-shura*), replacing the one that was established in 1926. The 1992 Consultative Council was entitled to lay down regulations and bylaws to meet the public interest, in accordance with the principles of the Islamic shari'a. The Council originally consisted of sixty members, all appointed by the king, for a period of four years. Membership of the Council has increased several times: first in 1997 and later in 2005, bringing today's total number of members to 150. Seated in the Council are *'ulama*, academics, businessmen, and diplomats, mostly men who have been educated at universities abroad. In November 2003, the competence of the Council was somewhat expanded; the Council is now permitted to initiate legislation without prior approval from the king. The Council's influence over legislation and policy has steadily increased, as its legislative proposals have been invariably adopted by the King, and they have, on more than one occasion, taken a bold stand against government efforts to impose taxes and fees (Al-Fahad 2005: 392).

Violence and political challenges

King Fahd's attempts to introduce reforms were, however, unsuccessful in quietening the voices of either the Islamists or reform-minded liberals. Young Islamists in particular insisted that the Saudi monarchy should enforce the Islamic norms more strictly. In the 1990s radical Islamists attacked foreign targets within Saudi Arabia. In June 1996, for example, a truck bomb near an American military compound near Dhahran killed nineteen persons and wounded hundreds of people. The government reaction forced radical Islamists to move to other countries, such as Sudan and Afghanistan. The most famous example was the militant political dissident Osama Bin Laden, who was stripped of his Saudi nationality (Al-Rasheed 2007: 114).

The news that fifteen out of the nineteen terrorists of the 11 September 2001 attacks in the United States were Saudi Arabia nationals shocked many in the West as well as at home. Under pressure from the West, King Fahd openly started a war on terrorism and declared that terrorism is prohibited within Islam. Muslim terrorism, however, also continued to hit Saudi Arabia itself. In May 2003, a series of coordinated suicide attacks were carried out on Western residential compounds in Riyadh, killing 35 and wounding another 194 persons. Since then, the number of clashes between security forces and armed militants, as well as attacks on Western targets and oil companies, have increased in frequency and magnitude (Al-Rasheed 2007: 135-136).

In addition to violence and political tensions, the kingdom has also been faced in the last decades with enormous debts, trade deficits, and a massive population growth. Indeed, the population has increased by more than fifty per cent in the last twenty years. While previously the state had been able to use oil revenues to invest in social services, the costs were now becoming too high. The existing gap between rich and poor also continued to grow, and the unemployment rate among Saudi nationals, especially among the younger generation, skyrocketed, with reported estimates as high as 20 to 30 per cent (Raphaeli 2003: 22-23). These enormous unemployment figures were of particular concern given that there were – and still are today – approximately six million migrant workers in Saudi Arabia. The government announced measures to reduce unemployment, for example by making it compulsory for employers to employ Saudi nationals for certain positions (ibid).[20]

In the early 2000s, several demonstrations and other public actions calling for political reform were organised. The authorities usually ended the demonstrations prematurely by arresting the participants. From the year 2000 onwards, Saudi citizens, individually and collectively, began to more frequently express their discontent by way of another tool for participation provided for by the Basic Ordinance law of 1992, namely the right to petition the king or the crown prince on any particular issue of citizen concern (Art. 43). In January 2003, for example, a significant number of Saudi elite submitted a petition called 'A Vision for the Present and Future of the Homeland' to the then Crown Prince Abdullah. The petitioners called for an independent and reformed judiciary, the creation of human rights institutions, improvement of the rights of women, and a popular election of the Consultative Council (Al-Fahad 2005: 392-393). By March 2004, however, several petitioners, political activists and lawyers were arrested and put in prison. Three intellectuals were sentenced to between six and nine years' imprisonment for incitement to sedition, and for disobedience to the ruler.

The petitioners' demands for political participation were partially met. In October 2003, local elections were announced for one-half of the seats in the municipal councils, the other half reserved for appointment by the government. The elections were held in the spring of 2005, resulting in a success for conservative candidates, who were backed by the *'ulama*.[21] The influential *'ulama* obstructed the participation of women in the elections by both banning them from running for election and also preventing them from voting in the actual elections. Various highly placed officials, however, expressed the opinion that, if it were up to them, women should be able to participate in the next elections. The president of the election committee explained in interviews later that the reason for refusing women to vote was that there was insufficient time to make the necessary arrangements to enable them to participate in the elections.[22]

King Abdullah: A cautious reformer

Crown Prince Abdullah, King Fahd's half-brother, owing to the king's bad health, had been the actual ruler of the Saudi monarchy since 1995. When on 1 August 2005 King Fahd finally died, Abdullah formally succeeded him as king.[23] Immediately he pardoned the abovementioned petitioners of 2004, who were released from prison (Amnesty International 2009b: 14). This confirmed his image as the driving force behind the reforms of the last decade. In 2003, for example, he had founded the 'King Abdul Aziz Centre for National Dialogue', an institute tasked with the organisation of national conferences at which religious leaders of the different Muslim sects, academics, and other prominent opinion leaders could discuss various contemporary topics. Within its first two years of operation, the institute organised five national dialogue sessions, where the conferees openly discussed issues related to reform in education, religious pluralism, the role of women in a modern Islamic state, and political participation of citizens. The government-sponsored debates did not turn out to be as fruitful as probably hoped for by many Saudis and were instead seen as being a 'public-relations exercise envisaged to absorb public frustration and anger' (Al-Rasheed 2007: 15).

In line with its reform policies, the government authorised the establishment of two Saudi human rights organisations, in 2004 and 2005, respectively: 1) the National Society for Human Rights (NSHR), a government-funded organisation; and 2) the Human Rights Commission (HRC), an official governmental body. The NSHR has been modestly active in pursuing reports and complaints about human rights abuses, submitting, for instance in 2007, a critical report to the government on prison conditions.[24] According to Amnesty International, both organisations 'have contributed to raising the visibility of human rights within Saudi Arabia and have assisted the government in preparing its reports on human rights to international treaty monitoring bodies' (Amnesty International 2009b: 11).

Earlier, in 2000, the government had enacted a regulation on Shari'a Procedure, applicable to proceedings before all Saudi courts, not just the shari'a courts. A year later, two other regulations were issued, namely the Criminal Procedure Regulation and the Legal Practice Regulation. The 2001 Regulation on Criminal Procedure stipulates that no punishment may be inflicted except for crimes prohibited by shari'a principles and Saudi national regulations. It contains provisions concerning preliminary detention and rules and procedures of evidence. The law also guarantees the right to seek assistance of a lawyer and includes a prohibition on torture, mental coercion, and arbitrary arrest. Responsibility for the investigation and prosecution of alleged crimes was vested in the Bureau of Investigation and Prosecution (Al-Hejailan 2002: 276-277).

Although the Saudi government has been praised for taking the abovementioned steps, which can be considered as steps towards the rule of law, critics do not have high hopes for any significant progress on the human rights situation on the ground. International human rights organisations such as Amnesty International and Human Rights Watch continue to criticise Saudi Arabia's poor human rights record. The list of accusations is long: human rights violations linked to the war on terror; discrimination against foreign workers and Shi'ite minorities; discrimination against women; violation of the freedom of religion and the freedom of expression; unfair trial standards; and the imposition and execution of corporal punishments in violation of international legal standards.

This being said, in December 2005, Saudi Arabia became a fully-fledged member of the World Trade Organisation (WTO), and with this came obligations, expectations and promises of judicial reform. Consequently, two years later, on 2 October 2007, King Abdullah issued two royal decrees announcing reform of the judiciary, a new Judiciary Regulation and a new Board of Grievances Regulation. The regulation on the judiciary, still being fully put into place at the time of writing, announced among others the establishment of a Supreme Court and separate tribunals for personal status, criminal, labour, and commercial cases. In accordance with the reforms, the Supreme Court is to take over the judicial functions of the Supreme Judicial Council. The new Board of Grievances Regulation provides for a further elaboration of the organisation of the Board, including the creation of an Administrative Judicial Council and a Supreme Administrative Court. The new judicial system was to be implemented during a transition period of two to three years (Ansary 2008), supported by a separate budget of 1.87 billion U.S. Dollars allocated for the upgrade of judicial facilities and the provision of training for judges.

In February 2009, King Abdullah issued a number of additional royal decrees that amounted to a reshuffling of the major judicial, religious, and other authorities. Among those appointed were: several moderate ministers, including a new Minister of Justice, a first female deputy Minister, for Education, new chairmen to the Consultative Council, the Council of Senior 'Ulama, the Supreme Judicial Council, the Board of Grievances, and the 'Committee for the Promotion of Virtue and the Prevention of Vice'.[25]

4.5 Constitutional law

According to Article 1 of the Basic Ordinance of the kingdom of Saudi Arabia (1992):

> The Kingdom of Saudi Arabia is a sovereign Arab Islamic state with Islam as its religion; God's Book and the Sunnah of His Prophet, God's prayers and peace be upon him, are its constitution, Arabic is its language and Riyadh is its capital. [26]

The Qur'an and the Sunna have the highest authority and all legislation is subordinate to them, including the Basic Ordinance itself (Art. 7).

The Ordinance consolidates the vast authority of the king, his wide range of functions and privileges, and declares that succession of the king is restricted to the male descendants of the founding king, Abdulaziz al-Saud, but that the king has the authority to choose and relieve his apparent heir (Art. 5).[27] According to Article 44, the legislative, executive, and judicial powers of government are separate, but the king is not subject to this separation of powers. The king is 'their final authority' and, therefore, a constitutional court is considered unnecessary (Al-Fahad 2005: 385). As the legislative authority and in accordance with Article 67 of the Ordinance, the king can promulgate regulations (*nizams*) where shari'a does not provide a direct answer to certain legal questions, but where regulation is nevertheless necessary, such as in commercial matters. This regulatory authority corresponds to Ibn Taymiyya's theory on Islamic leadership: rulers are allowed to issue regulations necessary for government policy (*siyasa shar'iyya*), provided the legislation serves the public good and that it only complements, and certainly does not contradict, shari'a.

The king of Saudi Arabia is also the chairman of the Council of Ministers and the Prime Minister, and as such he is the head of the executive branch of government. He appoints and relieves his ministers and other high-ranking civil servants by royal decree (Art.s 56-58). Decisions taken by the Council of Ministers have to be ratified by the king. He oversees the implementation of shari'a and the general policies of the state (Art. 55). The king appoints and dismisses judges upon recommendation of the Supreme Judicial Council, and he acts as the highest instance of appeal and has the power to pardon (Art.s 50 and 52).

The Consultative Council (*majlis al-shura*), re-established in 1992, confers with and advises the Council of Ministers (Art. 68). It advises on government policy and may submit regulations and bylaws to meet the public interest or to remove what is bad in the affairs of the state, in accordance with the basic principles of the Islamic shari'a (Art. 67). However, the Consultative Council has limited authority and does exert little direct influence on the decision making. Al-Fahad notes that '[l]egislation adopted by the Council is conceived as mere advice that the sovereign is at liberty to accept or disregard' (2005: 388). Schwartz is of the opinion that the creation of the Consultative Council was merely a 'cosmetic reform' (2005: 38).

Sources of law

The Islamic shari'a is the prevailing law in Saudi Arabia; the sacred law is the foundation of the legal system. As such, the Qur'an and the Sunna are the main sources of law. Judges and other legal scholars (*'ulama*), as the lawful interpreters of the two holy sources, apply the Islamic shari'a in rendering a judgement or advice (*fatwa*) on individual cases brought before them. Because shari'a in Saudi Arabia is not codified in statutes or codes, the traditionally trained judges and scholars, therefore, resort to Hanbali *fiqh*-books in particular in their administration of justice.

It is often claimed that Saudi law is nothing but Islamic shari'a. However, supplemented by government-issued regulations concerning labour, commerce, companies, and so forth, the law is more encompassing than at first glance. Also, one cannot rule out the importance of tribal values and customs in Saudi society, like in most Middle Eastern societies. Esmaeili writes: 'Tribal law or custom is significant in Saudi Arabia in relation to the country's political and governmental structure as well as private and personal law areas' (2009: 18). Yet, Islamic shari'a is no doubt the main feature of the Saudi legal system,

In addition to the shari'a and specialised courts, Saudi Arabia's legal system structurally includes a form of court-recognised mediation offered by Islamic scholars who provide advice (*muftis*). The *mufti*[28] has an important role to play in providing Islamic legal interpretation. When a person wants to know which shari'a principles and rules are applicable in a specific situation, he or she can turn to a *mufti* for advice (a *fatwa*). A court trial can be avoided when two parties agree to bring their dispute to a *mufti* they both respect. Opinions of these religious scholars are often considered as authoritative as a ruling of a judge. In fact, when parties, after obtaining a *fatwa*, still decide to refer their case to a judge in the courts, the judge may well attribute legal value to the *fatwa*. Amicable settlement is the preferred solution for any dispute, either with or without interference of a judge. According to Vogel, over 90 per cent of all civil cases that are submitted to the court are resolved by reconciliation or settlement, thereby 'obviating the judge's ruling altogether' (2000: 120).

Fatwas are also issued by the Council of Senior 'Ulama, established in 1971.[29] Next to this official institution, King Fahd appointed the conservative and opinionated Shaykh Abdulaziz ibn Baz (died 1999) as the Grand Mufti of Saudi Arabia in 1993.[30] His opinions often deviated from the prevailing consensus of the religious establishment, particularly on marriage-related matters.[31] The courts consider legal actions based on such *fatwas* to be valid, even if they contradict the courts' own standard rules (Vogel 2000: 8). Yamani writes that *fatwas* issued by influential government-employed *'ulama* have 'a near-legislative effect' and that 'ordinary *qadis* (judges) [are] unwilling to contradict a formal *fatwa*' (2009: 140). The king, for his part, often reinforces these *fatwas* by requesting the courts to observe and comply with the judgment or advice rendered by either the Council or the Grand Mufti (Vogel 2000: 116).

Another source of law for legal judgements is administrative regulations (*nizams*) that have been legitimised through the abovementioned principle of *siyasa shar'iyya*. These regulations have a clear subordinate status as compared to the *fiqh*, even though the *'ulama* are usually extensively consulted and often enjoy a veto power in the drafting process.[32] Thus, the main reference for a judge remains the Islamic jurisprudence: 'Fiqh continues to govern the bulk of cases, covering personal status, civil contract, tort, property, agency, and nearly all crimes apart from those that specifically enforce the niẓāms.'(Vogel 2000: 175).

Judiciary

Article 48 of the Basic Ordinance determines that 'the courts will apply the rules of the Islamic Shari'ah in the cases brought before them, in accordance with what is indicated in the Book, the Sunnah, and the ordinances decreed by the Ruler which do not contradict the Book or the Sunnah.'[33] Article 46 bolsters the authority of judges in its assertion that the judiciary is independent.

The Basic Ordinance confirms the existence of two judicial branches – the general shari'a courts and the Board of Grievances – but is silent on the specialised committee courts. The shari'a courts are granted general jurisdiction, unless these disputes or crimes fall under the jurisdiction of the Board.[34] The special committees created to implement the *nizams* fall outside the judicial branch; they are *ad hoc* administrative entities falling within the executive branch. The *'ulama* have often opposed the creation of these special committees and have frequently called for the incorporation of these jurisdictions into the shari'a courts. However, since the shari'a courts have clearly demonstrated they do not want to apply the *nizams*, the government has until present not considered unification a viable option (Vogel 2000: 176). Not only do the courts disregard the regulations *per se*, they also pay no attention to, and certainly do not respect, the jurisdiction of the committees created to apply these regulations. Indeed, shari'a judges often hear cases outside their competence as they are reluctant to dismiss a case on grounds that it falls within the jurisdiction of a specialised committee (Al-Jarbou 2007: 226).

As mentioned earlier, in October 2007, judicial reforms were announced by King Abdullah (see 4.4). These reforms had been expected since Saudi Arabia joined the World Trade Organisation in 2005. At the time of writing, it cannot yet be indicated when the judicial reforms will be fully implemented and what the impact and consequences will be on the judicial organisation. Questions that still remain are, for example: What will happen to the specialised committees? Will they still exist, albeit in a stripped-down form? If so, will they continue to function in parallel to the new tribunals? Or, alternatively, will they be abolished all together?

Shari'a courts

According to the new Judiciary Regulation (2007), there will be three levels of shari'a courts all operating under the supervision of the Supreme Judicial Council, in ascending order: first instance courts, followed by appellate courts, and finally the new Supreme Court. Since the new system is not yet fully operational, the current system will be described below, with reference to some important changes foreseen in the new judicial organisation.

At present, there are three levels of shari'a courts, all of them falling under the responsibility of the Ministry of Justice, in ascending order: two types of first instance courts (the summary courts and the general courts), followed by appellate courts, and finally the Supreme Judicial Council.

In a summary court, a single judge is competent to rule in both civil and criminal cases. He is, however, not competent to judge in civil cases where the penalty would exceed a certain amount of money (for example in cases of compensation for physical injury) or in criminal cases that involve possible sentences of amputation, execution, or stoning (Judiciary Regulation (1975), Art.s 24-26). Cases that cannot be adjudicated by a summary court are heard by a general court. Criminal cases that could result in a sentence of amputation, execution, or stoning to death are judged by panels of three judges (Judiciary Regulation (1975), Art. 23). According to Article 20 of the new Regulation (2007), all criminal cases will – in principle – be judged by panels of three judges.

Appeals may be made to the appellate courts in Mecca or Riyadh, where – in principle – three-judge panels adjudicate cases.[35] An appeals court may reverse a decision, amend it, order a retrial, or send the case back with instructions on how the lower court should proceed. The appellate courts' primary concern is to establish whether or not a decision is in compliance with shari'a (Al-Ghadyan 1998: 239-240). In principle, appeals are not admissible against a decision of an appellate court, but many cases – and always those involving the death penalty or amputation sentences – are currently referred to the Supreme Judicial Council for review (Judiciary Regulation (1975), Art. 8).

It is anticipated that this judicial function of the Council will be transferred to the Supreme Court (in formation) (Judiciary Regulation (2007), Art. 11). The king, however, retains his placement at the top of the judicial pyramid in that before an execution of a death penalty, stoning, or amputation can be carried out, the punishment has to be ratified by the king (Basic Ordinance, Art. 50; Regulation on Criminal Procedure (2001), Art. 220).

According to the most recent Judiciary Regulation (2007), a new first instance court system will be established, creating separate tribunals for general, criminal, personal status, commercial, and labour cases (Art. 9). These tribunals will replace the current first instance courts – the summary and general courts. The shari'a courts will, thus, lose their general jurisdiction to hear all cases. The new system seems to resemble modern judicial systems of countries like Egypt and Morocco more than the classical Islamic legal system, where a single judge pronounced judgment without appeal, apart from recourse to the ruler.

Another fundamental difference in the new court structure and planned operation is that each province will have at least one appellate court (Art. 15). As the system is currently set up, each appellate court has a criminal chamber, a personal status chamber, and a chamber for 'other' cases (Judiciary Regulation (1975), Art. 10). Once the new judicial system is operational, though, each appellate court will also have a chamber for commercial cases and a distinct chamber for labour cases (Judiciary Regulation (2007), Art. 16). This appeals system corresponds with the new first instance courts system. Jurisdiction over cases that are now heard by the various special committees, for instance in the field of commercial and labour law, will be transferred to the new first instance and appellate courts (Ansary 2008). Once full implementation of the judicial reforms of 2007 takes effect, the Supreme Court will be the highest authority in the outlined judicial organisation, and will also be comprised of specialised chambers headed by three- or five-judge panels, depending on whether the case may result in imposition of the death penalty or other severe punishments (Judiciary Regulation (2007), Art. 10; Ansary 2008).

Board of Grievances

The Board of Grievances constitutes the second judicial branch of the Saudi system. Due to its strong *fiqh* credentials, the Board is largely respected by the *'ulama* (Vogel 2000: 232). This independent organ, which reports directly to the king, functions as an administrative tribunal, hearing complaints against the government. Next to its function in administrative law, it is – currently – also competent to hear commercial cases and criminal cases involving, for example, forgery and bribery.

At present, the Board operates as the court of appeal for decisions of some of the specialised committees, and it has the authority to enforce foreign judgments and arbitration decisions (Board of Grievances Regulation (1982), Art. 8). Until recently, the appeal function of the Board was not clearly defined and, therefore, ambiguous as to how it operated in practice (Tarazi 1993: 266).[36] Once the new Regulation, issued in 2007, is implemented, it is hoped that this situation will change, providing more clarity on this point.

The new Board of Grievances Regulation (2007) will entail the transfer of the Board's commercial and criminal jurisdiction to the general court system, where the new first instance and appellate courts will take over these competences. The new Regulation also announces the creation of an Administrative Judicial Council and a Supreme Administrative Court.[37] In the new judicial system, the Board will continue to hear administrative disputes involving government agencies (Art. 13).

Judges and lawyers

According to classical Islamic doctrine, a judge (*qadi*) has a religious duty to settle a dispute brought before him: in each individual case he is allowed to use independent interpretation (*ijtihad*) in order to find the most desirable solution. He may disregard previous judgments, either his own or those of other judges, in this process.

A single judge in Saudi Arabia has great discretionary authority in adjudicating cases: 'he is empowered to exercise his personal Islamic understanding and interpretation without recourse to previous decisions relating to similar cases' (Yamani 2008: 139). Yamani further explains that, because of the absence of a system of judicial precedent, diverging judgements of otherwise apparently identical cases are the result of 'differences in interpretation and legal orientations of the judges, and geographical variations between the different politically unified regions in the Kingdom' (ibid: 140).

Only graduates of the shari'a colleges can be appointed judges at the shari'a courts and on the Board of Grievances.[38] The traditional shari'a training, with a focus on Hanbali *fiqh*, is provided by several Islamic universities in the kingdom. Because the shari'a colleges have always taken a passive attitude towards teaching the *nizams* enacted by the government, new law departments were recently established. But, graduates from these latter colleges cannot be appointed as shari'a judges. The members of the specialised committees which apply the *nizams* are usually appointed by a minister, for example the Minister of Commerce. Because they are part of the executive branch, they do not enjoy judicial immunity and independence. They are often professional experts appointed by the ministries and regarded as civil servants, not experts in Islamic law (Al-Jarbou 2007: 224).

In the past, lawyers were considered unnecessary, especially because of the active role judges have in the resolution of cases, as compared to other legal systems. Saudi judges wished to directly deal with the accused, since '[t]he truth is brought to light through [the accused], because he is more aware of himself than is any other' (Vogel 2000: 161, quoting a Saudi judge). It was reported that sometimes judges considered lawyers to be an obstacle to truth-finding and a hindrance to reconciliation between the litigants (Commission on Human Rights 2003: 10-11). Moreover, it has often been argued that even though a defendant is not defended by a lawyer, the shari'a itself offers the necessary protection; judges are, after all, morally obliged to find the truth.

Despite these objections, a professional class of lawyers has emerged in Saudi Arabia. There are two sorts of lawyers active at present, namely lawyers admitted to the shari'a courts and appearing on behalf of clients in some civil cases and experts in the field of commercial law, who are very commonly seen appearing in the specialised committees (Vogel 2000: 161). In family matters in particular, individuals are, however, still almost always represented by a (male) family member, in accordance with local traditions.

4.6 Personal status and family law

The Saudi personal and family law is not codified or compiled in a law code.[39] All cases concerning marriage, divorce, inheritance, and the status of children fall under the general jurisdiction of the shari'a courts. For the most part judges of these courts resort to the Hanbali *fiqh* books when adjudicating a case; they can, however, also consult books from the other schools of law.

Marriage and divorce

Although the Hanbali school of law is generally considered the most conservative of the schools of law, this does not hold true for the stipulations concerning the contract of marriage, as for any type of contract. In contrast to the other schools, classical Hanbali *fiqh* gives considerable leeway towards validating and enforcing stipulations that modify the normal marital rights and duties between husband and wife, in particular stipulations that safeguard the wife's position (Coulson 1964: 190).

Marriage in Islamic law is a contract of exchange between a man and a woman, concluded in the presence of two witnesses. A bride and groom have the right to include stipulations in their marriage contract. Non-compliance with a stipulation constitutes a ground for pursuing dissolution of the marriage in court. For example, a clause can be included in the contract that provides that when the man marries a second wife, the first wife has the right to initiate divorce proceedings. In such a case, it is possible that the husband has granted the wife his right of repudiation (*talaq*); she can then repudiate herself because the husband broke the marriage contract.

When a marriage is concluded without such stipulations, the women's possibilities to obtain a divorce are limited. A woman can ask her husband to divorce her in exchange for waiver of her financial rights (divorce by mutual consent, or *khul'*), namely return of any dower and other remaining financial rights. A woman can seek judicial divorce (*tafriq*) when harm (*darar*) is inflicted upon her by her husband, which is interpreted as any harmful conduct of the husband (physical or mental) that makes conjugal life between the couple impossible. For example, if the husband does not fulfil his obligation to support his wife; if he is not capable of conjugal relations due to a physical or mental handicap; or if he is absent for a long period of time.

In practice, however, it is very difficult for a woman to obtain judicial divorce in Saudi Arabia. She has to prove that harm was inflicted upon her by her husband, quite a challenge in the closed patriarchal Saudi society. Moreover, in the event of divorce, the mother will lose her right to care for her children, specifically her son(s) from the age of seven and her daughter(s) from the age of nine, after which time physical custody is automatically transferred to the father[40] (Human Rights Watch 2008: 31).

Men, on the other hand, are in a far better position to end a marriage. Husbands are granted the unilateral right to repudiate their wives (*talaq*), without reason or legal justification; *talaq* divorce is effective immediately. After an irrevocable repudiation, the repudiated wife can claim the full dower (if a portion of it remained unpaid) and maintenance during a period of waiting following the repudiation (four months and ten days).

Related fatwas on marriage

Some startling *fatwa*s on family law topics, issued by members of the established *'ulama*, are worth mentioning here. In April 2005, the Grand Mufti Abdulaziz al-Shaykh stated that forced marriages are against shari'a and that persons who are guilty of this offence must be punished with imprisonment. In his opinion, forced marriages were the reason why the divorce rate in the country continued to rise, a topic that has increasingly gained public attention (as has the issue of early marriages). Media reports suggest that 50 per cent of marriages end in divorce, with rates as high as an estimated 62 per cent in the western region.[41] In July 2008, the chairman of the Committee for Family Affairs of the Consultative Council, Dr Talal Bakri, said the Council is considering implementing a law to halt the rising divorce rates, in particular to curb the practice of husbands arbitrarily divorcing their wives. Yet, the same Grand Mufti was quoted in the Saudi media last year as having said that ten or twelve-year-old girls are marriageable (Human Rights Council 2009: 15). It should be noted here that this statement is all the more problematic given that there is no law in Saudi Arabia that sets a minimum age of marriage for males or females.

In 2006, a *fatwa*, issued by the international Islamic Fiqh Academy[42], stirred public debate about so-called 'ambulant (*misyar*) marriages', both inside and beyond the kingdom. The main feature of a *misyar* marriage is that spouses agree the wife will continue to live with her parents, thus freeing the husband of his obligation to provide marital domicile for her. It may not come as a surprise to learn that *misyar* marriages are often concluded by polygamous men. Women's rights groups oppose these marriage practices because the wife waivers her rights to maintenance and housing, whereas the man's exemption from his responsibilities towards his wife are not replaced by any other contractual consideration or reciprocal duties. In 1996, however, the then Grand Mufti Abdulaziz ibn Baz had already issued a *fatwa* in which he attributed Islamic legality to ambulant marriage practices, provided that the marriage meets the main prerequisites (i.e. presence of the bride's guardian and two witnesses) and the contract is concluded on mutually agreed upon and binding conditions.[43]

Again, this shows the importance of a *fatwa*, which in this case is, according to Arabi, 'a straightforward endorsement of the Muslim polygamous legal tradition', aiding 'Saudi citizens in the search for solutions to their modern sexual and emotional dilemmas, solutions that would be in line with their faith and its legal strictures' (2001: 166). It should be noted here that this 'solution' is not only adopted by men, but also by Saudi women who might prefer being married, so they enjoy a more 'respectable' social status and might have more freedom to pursue their own interests in life, such as studying or working.

Yamani says in a study written exclusively on this topic that the increase in wealth of many Saudis, due to oil revenues, has led to an increase of the practice of polygamy, especially among the educated, urban Hijazi elite (2008: 215). However, the Saudi government has also played a significant role in promoting polygamy. Yamani contends that the promotion of polygamy in Saudi Arabia is part of a public policy programme promoting the return to Islamic values, in reaction to post-revolutionary, pro-polygamy Iranian practices. Iran's reinstatement of Islamic values and traditions induced Saudi *'ulama* to accept novelties such as *misyar* marriages as legally valid (ibid: 47-48).[44] In 2001 the Grand Mufti Abdulaziz al-Shaykh called upon all Saudi women to accept the concept of polygamy as part of the 'Islamic package', further noting that polygamy is a necessity in 'the national fight against the time bomb [...], the growing epidemic of spinsterhood' (ibid: 52).

Inheritance

Islamic shari'a is the only applicable law pertaining to Saudi Muslims in matters of inheritance and bequests. The Islamic inheritance system is based on tribal customary law of pre-Islamic Arabia, which was modified by the Qur'an in considerable detail (Coulson 1964: 15). The Qur'an guarantees fixed portions of the deceased's estate to so-called 'Qur'anic heirs'.[45] Generally speaking, female heirs are entitled to half of the share of male heirs. After the Qur'anic heirs have received their shares, the residue of the estate will be divided among the agnatic[46] heirs of the deceased. Finally, a Saudi Muslim can dispose a maximum of one-third of his property by bequest to non-Qur'anic heirs (Haberbeck 2010: 29).

4.7 Criminal law

The Regulation on Criminal Procedure (2001) governs criminal proceedings and secures and protects the rights of the accused. It is the country's first criminal procedure law and contains provisions borrowed from Egyptian and French law (Ansary 2008). Substantive criminal law, however, remains uncodified; as in family law, judges commonly apply the Hanbali *fiqh*.

Criminal law comprises three categories, namely *hudud* (fixed Qur'anic punishments for specific crimes), *qisas* (retaliation, as in 'an eye for an eye'), and *ta'zir* (discretionary punishment of the judge). The rules of evidence and penalties for *hudud* crimes are laid down in the Qur'an and the Sunna. There are strict requirements for establishing proof for a conviction of a *hadd* offence. For example, if the accused revokes his confession, alleging that he was forced into confession, the case must be dropped. The case can then be tried as a *ta'zir* case, and the accused, if found guilty, will then be given a discretionary sentence instead of the severe *hadd* penalty. Because of the stringent requirements for *hadd* convictions, most cases are tried as *ta'zir* cases (Vogel 2000: 244-247). Unlike in many other Islamic countries, punishments like death by stoning, amputation, and flogging are actually executed; in the case of death penalty or amputation this requires the approval of the king (see 4.5).

The *qisas* claim is technically a civil claim in cases involving murder or the infliction of bodily harm, which may be prosecuted by the victim or the victim's heir. The penalties that may be claimed for a *qisas* crime include retaliation in kind or compensation (*diya*, i.e. blood money). As for the penalties for *ta'zir* offences, the judge has great discretionary power, since there is no substantive penal legislation. The most common *ta'zir* punishment is lashing. Vogel mentions that public humiliation, cuffing, imprisonment, and fines – although the latter is debated – are other possible *ta'zir* penalties. The death penalty, however, can also be inflicted as a *ta'zir* punishment for crimes such as sorcery and propagandising for heresy (Vogel 2000: 248-249).

Nowadays, many *ta'zir* offences are defined by national regulations (*nizams*), including offences of bribery, counterfeiting, drug abuse, trafficking, and crimes committed by officials. These offences are tried before the specialised committees; penalties for such crimes typically include imprisonment and fines (ibid: 232).

The king may exercise his discretion to pronounce a sentence 'in cases where the offender's guilt is beyond doubt and public interest demands execution (normally, when the crime is heinous); or when the offender, usually because he is a confirmed recidivist, can only be prevented by death from further harming society' (Vogel 2000: 250).

These sentences are decreed without any formal trial, although often legitimised by the leading *'ulama*.

Besides the traditional *fiqh*, the opinions of the Council of Senior 'Ulama constitute legal sources on certain matters of criminal law. The *'ulama*, for instance, issued a *fatwa* on 18 February 1987, that states that drug dealers are to be sentenced to death:

> With regard to the narcotic smugglers, the punishment will be the death sentence as a result of his evil work by bringing a great deal of corruption and deterioration to the country. The smuggler and the person who receives narcotics from abroad will be punished in the same way (Jerichow 1998: 74).

The king and the Ministry of Interior have requested that the courts follow this *fatwa*. The Council of Senior 'Ulama also decided that a person should be sentenced to death when he is found guilty of having perpetrated a terrorist act (ibid: 75).

4.8 Commercial law

Business or commerce is another area which in Saudi Arabia is extensively regulated by shari'a. Basic principles of shari'a oppose various forms of interest (*riba*) and of uncertainty in contracts (*gharar*). Saudi commercial law remains at its root Hanbali *fiqh*; jurisdiction in commercial matters rests with the Board of Grievances, whose judges are chiefly or entirely shari'a-trained.[47] Still, with regard to any modern institution of commercial law, such as commercial paper, companies with artificial personality and limited liability, intellectual property, and securities, Saudi law stems entirely from modern regulations,[48] which are often administered by specialised committees.

For foreign investors, uncertainties surrounding the content of Saudi commercial law, especially as to its fundamental shari'a component, causes various problems and insecurities. This situation is, of course, highly disadvantageous for the Saudi economy. Yet, to date, the government has not been able to find a suitable solution for this problem in the face of the unwillingness of the *'ulama* and shari'a judges to cede control over an area where historically shari'a has held sway.

Saudi Arabia is a huge market for Islamic financial products, and some of the biggest Islamic banks are Saudi banks. It does not, however, actively encourage a separate Islamic banking sector. To allow some banks to call themselves 'Islamic' would indicate that the others are not, an unacceptable situation in a state that upholds shari'a as its basic law (Vogel & Hayes 1998: 12). According to Vogel, Saudi Arabia's attitude towards Islamic banking seems to be relenting, since it has authorised a number of banks to operate on Islamic principles without including the descriptor 'Islamic' in their names, and, conversely, allowed conventional banks to also open 'windows' for Islamic products and services. Some government-owned corporations have even begun issuing *sukuk* (Islamic bonds), something that would traditionally not have been permissible as bonds typically involve interest-based constructions.[49]

The religious alms tax (*zakat*) laid down in the Qur'an is enforced by the state on Saudi citizens with regard to several forms of personal wealth such as on livestock, personal and financial properties, as well as, and perhaps more importantly, ownership shares in companies.[50] *Zakat* on company wealth is calculated and paid by each company on behalf of its Saudi shareholders. Companies also pay income tax with respect to the proportion of their non-Saudi ownership.[51]

In 1999, a Supreme Economic Council was established, charged with introducing and overseeing economic reform in the kingdom. Attached to this Council is an Advisory Commission that has a mandate to review economic policies and laws upon government request. It is also authorised to propose legislation and to make policy recommendations (Al-Fahad 2005: 392). In preparation of its membership of the World Trade Organisation, achieved in 2005, Saudi Arabia has further updated and extended its commercial law regulations.[52]

4.9 International treaty obligations and human rights

The Basic Ordinance addresses the protection of human rights in a general manner. Article 26 stipulates: 'The state protects human rights in accordance with the Islamic Shari'ah.'[53] This formulation allows the Saudi government extensive freedom of interpretation and does not safeguard compliance with internationally recognised criteria, even more so because shari'a is uncodified and open to different interpretations.

In 1948 Saudi Arabia was one of the few countries that abstained from voting on the Universal Declaration of Human Rights (UDHR).[54] Saudi Arabia particularly objected to the article concerning freedom of religion and advocated that the safeguard provided by shari'a with regard to human rights has priority over any safeguards for human rights that the UDHR could offer. Saudi Arabia invoked the same arguments in the 1970s, again refusing to sign other important human rights treaties, such as the ICCPR. More recently, however, the government has affirmed its intention to accede to this convention.[55]

Convention Against Torture

On 23 July 1979, Saudi Arabia ratified the Convention Against Torture (CAT). The ratification, however, was accompanied by two significant reservations. The first reservation stated that Saudi Arabia does not recognise the jurisdiction of the CAT Committee with regard to investigation into alleged practices of systematic torture. Secondly, Saudi Arabia refused to refer cases to the International Court of Justice if disputes were to arise out of interpretation of the convention, when said disputes could not be resolved through other negotiation and arbitration channels. Evidently, Saudi Arabia does not wish to open itself up to interference or investigation by foreigners and/or international agencies.

In 2002, the Committee Against Torture commented on the national report submitted by Saudi Arabia. The Committee expressed its concern about the sentencing and execution of corporal punishments, discrimination against foreigners, and the unbridled powers of the religious police. The representative of Saudi Arabia replied to this with the following statement:

> Corporal punishment was intended as a deterrent: under Shariah law, it should not be administered if there was any doubt about the guilt of the individual or the evidence in the case. The aim was not to punish but to rehabilitate and to protect society. [...] The Koran set out specific sanctions such as amputation, flogging (whipping) and stoning for certain crimes. Those sanctions could neither be abrogated nor amended since they emanated from God.

Another member of the Saudi delegation further remarked during the 2002 session that: 'The Committee [...] presumed to impugn 1,400-year-old religious beliefs in Saudi Arabia. It was not within the Committee's mandate to do so.' At the time of writing, Saudi Arabia had still to submit its second and third periodic reports for Committee consideration, due in 2002 and 2006, respectively.[56]

Convention on Discrimination Against Women

On 7 July 2000 Saudi Arabia ratified the Convention on the Elimination of All Forms of Discrimination Against Women (CEDAW), but here too, it made two critical reservations to the convention. The first reservation states that Saudi Arabia is under no obligation to observe the convention when any term of the convention is considered to be in contradiction with the norms of shari'a. The second reservation asserts that the kingdom is not to be bound by Articles 9(1) and 29(1), which means in practical effect that Saudi Arabia does not grant men and women equal rights with regard to the nationality of their children (a child automatically receives the nationality of the father) and that the country is not prepared to refer cases involving a dispute on interpretation of the Convention to the International Court of Justice. Because the first reservation makes *de facto* every treaty obligation subordinate to the Saudi interpretation of shari'a, several European countries made formal objections to the reservations. They questioned Saudi Arabia's commitment to the object and purpose of the Convention and asserted, moreover, that its reservation contributes to undermining the foundation of international treaty law.

The CEDAW Committee examined Saudi Arabia's initial and second periodic report in January 2008. A recurring topic in the discussion between the Committee and the national delegation was the concept of male guardianship over women. The Committee noted with concern that 'the concept of male guardianship over women (*mehrem*), although it may not be legally prescribed, seems to be widely accepted; it severely limits women's exercise of their rights under the Convention [...]'. The Committee further opined in its concluding observations that:

> [the concept of male guardianship] contributes to the prevalence of a patriarchal ideology with stereotypes and the persistence of deep-rooted cultural norms, customs and traditions that discriminate against women and constitute serious obstacles to their enjoyment of their human rights.

Human rights violations

Despite Saudi Arabia's international human rights obligations, the actual human rights situation has remained worrisome on a variety of levels. Political parties and syndicates are prohibited, and the Saudi media are under heavy censorship. Human rights activists and peaceful critics of the government are routinely arrested, many remaining in prison for lengthy time periods without limitation. Moreover, their chances of getting a fair trial are slim.

Corporal punishments, including death by public beheading, hanging or stoning, have been administered regularly; foreign nationals, mostly migrant workers, have been especially vulnerable. Suspects have been convicted for murder, rape, homosexuality, apostasy, sorcery, drug-related charges, and other offences. The number of executions in 2007 increased considerably as compared to previous years. In that year at least 158 persons were executed, compared to the 39 persons executed in 2006, and in 2008 at least 102 persons were put to death (Amnesty International 2009).

Especially, women's behaviour in public is closely monitored and improper behaviour can have severe consequences. In 2007, a court case caused considerable commotion, both inside and outside Saudi Arabia; a rape victim was sentenced upon appeal to 200 lashes and six months imprisonment. The married woman had travelled in a car with an unrelated man when they were attacked by a group of seven men who raped her and her male acquaintance. They were both sentenced for the crime of 'illegal mingling' (*khalwa*).[57] A month after the verdict, however, King Abdullah pardoned the woman. Commenting on the pardon, the then Minister of Justice, Abdullah bin Muhammad al-Shaykh, stated that the king did not question the court's decision, but that he had acted in the interest of the people.[58]

Women face various forms of discrimination; they are barred from voting, driving, and travelling without permission of their male guardian. In addition, Saudi women are severely limited in their ability to exercise their legal capacity in matters pertaining to marriage, divorce, child custody, and property control. In April 2008, Human Rights Watch published a report highlighting the many human rights abuses resulting from male guardianship policies.[59]

Saudi Arabia is known for being a gender-segregated society: women and men are segregated in schools, universities, health care, and at work. This segregation limits women's educational and employment opportunities. While legally women have the right to choose their own education, open a business, perform financial transactions, and inherit without a male guardian's approval, the reality is that they face major obstacles. For instance, women cannot obtain a professional licence to practice as a lawyer, architect, or accountant (Yamani 2008: 152).[60] Nevertheless, there are also some signs of a trend toward more equality – select female entrepreneurs have set up their own businesses; a few women have been elected into chambers of commerce; and, in February 2009 for the first time in history, a woman was appointed Deputy Minister of Education for Girls.

The country also restricts the freedom of religions other than Sunni Islam. Shi'ites have been particular targets of slander campaigns and violence – also at the hands of state actors. In recent years, they have been severely restricted in their religious practices, and there are reported cases of forced conversions of Shi'ites to Sunni Wahhabism. This pertains not only to Saudi Shi'ites, but also to Asian (Islamic) migrant workers.[61]

Apart from the abovementioned human rights violations that have often been justified by reference to 'the shari'a', it must be noted that in recent years, thousands of people have been arrested and detained in the name of security and counter-terrorism. The trials which have apparently begun in spring 2009, are so shrouded in secrecy that it is impossible to follow their progress or know to what extent the accused are able to enjoy a fair trial (Amnesty International 2009b: 5).

Finally, human rights organisations such as Amnesty International have repeatedly been denied access to the country, despite promises on behalf of the government in the media. In response to the accusations of human rights violations, the Saudi regime has continued to stress the special Islamic character of the country, which in their view requires a different social and political order as a result of its special religious position and tradition (Halliday 2003: 138).

4.10 Conclusion

Saudi Arabia not only has a unique legal system, compared to Western systems, but also compared to other Muslim countries. The Saudi model is perhaps closest to the classical form of shari'a adherence and application which developed after the establishment of Islam on the Arabian peninsula in the early seventh century. Today, fourteen centuries later, uncodified shari'a is still the mainstay of the national legal system. The Basic Ordinance of the Kingdom (1992) in its first article stipulates that 'God's Book and the Sunna of the Prophet' are the Saudi constitution.

Saudi Arabia is an absolute monarchy, ruled by the House of Saud. The country is in fact governed by some one hundred princes, all of whom are descendants of King Abdulaziz al-Saud (died 1953). They occupy key positions, including ministerial posts, military, diplomatic, and governor posts in the provinces.

While the revealed law has always been – and remains – the general law of the land, the government also issues important 'regulations'. However, Islamic jurisprudence remains the first point of reference in cases concerning personal status, crime, civil contracts, property, etc. Judges have resorted primarily to the Qur'an, the Sunna, and *fiqh*-books in their quest for justice. A judge – like all religious scholars – must be competent to interpret the Qur'an and the Sunna in rendering a judgment or advice. He enjoys great discretionary power and is not bound by doctrine of precedent. Religious scholars are also permitted to give their opinions on the application of shari'a by giving legal advice (*fatwa*). *Fatwa*s are of legal importance in Saudi Arabia and judges take them into consideration.

To understand the present law and governance situation of Saudi Arabia, we need to go back into the country's history, its key alliance between political and religious leadership, and the genesis of the Wahhabi ideology of the state.

The eighteenth century alliance between the chieftain, Muhammad ibn Saud and the religious scholar, Muhammad ibn Abd al-Wahhab, both from Najd, was the initial impetus for the formation of the state of Saudi Arabia. Ibn Saud won the loyalty of several tribes and united them into a powerful force; he was greatly aided in this endeavour by the religious teachings of Ibn Abd al-Wahhab. Followers of the Wahhabi sect sought to return to the early days of Islam through strict adherence to the letter and spirit of the Qur'an and the Sunna. Backed by the Wahhabi movement, the house of Saud conquered large parts of the peninsula and the Wahhabi doctrine became the ideological foundation of the future state.

The Saud hegemony was firmly established in 1926 when Abdulaziz Al-Saud was crowned king of the Hijaz, the region around Mecca and Medina. In 1932, the Najd and the Hijaz were united into the current kingdom of Saudi Arabia.

The traditional Najd had a judicial system where a single judge applied the rules of Hanbali *fiqh* under supervision of the local ruler. The cosmopolitan Hijaz, where the Shafi'i and the Hanafi schools of law were predominant, had a more modern judicial organisation, which was developed under Ottoman rule. It took until 1960 before a single, unified system of shari'a courts applicable to the entire country could be implemented. The powerful conservative *'ulama*, especially those from Najd, have remained resistant to state interference in religious affairs, and therewith also in legal affairs. This is why Abdulaziz and his successors had to proceed with great caution in centralising and reforming the legal system.

The use of discretionary power by Saudi kings has been particularly important for the enactment of necessary regulations in the commercial sector following the discovery of massive oil reserves in 1938. Technically, under classical shari'a, rulers have the authority to promulgate regulations for government policy (*siyasa shar'iyya*), provided they are complementary to, and not in contradiction with, shari'a and they serve the public interest. Nevertheless, the *'ulama* have also remained reluctant towards the abovementioned regulations, issued by the state to govern, in particular, commercial and labour affairs. As the *'ulama* opposed the regulations and the shari'a judges refused to apply them, the king was forced to created committees in specialised areas to apply the new regulations. Together with the Board of Grievances, (1955) an administrative court which is competent to hear complaints from citizens against the government, in addition to commercial and some specified criminal cases, these committees have in fact become a second branch of the judicial system, even though they are regarded formally as part of the executive.

From 1970 to 1975, the unified court system was further developed. The Judiciary Regulation (1975) granted general jurisdiction to the shari'a courts to decide in all civil and criminal disputes, except in the areas of law where the specialised committees were competent. A Supreme Judicial Council, under the direct authority of the king, took its place at the top of the judicial pyramid, with appellate courts in Riyadh and Mecca, and larger and smaller courts spread all over the country.

Meanwhile the *'ulama*'s position, as advisors on government policies, was further institutionalised in 1971 with the establishment of the Council of Senior 'Ulama. This council has since successfully curbed several reform efforts made by the government and liberal Saudis, for instance in relation to the improvement of the position of women.

Improved living standards for Saudis, due to the abundant oil revenues in the 1970s, were unable to ward off dissident voices that turned against the state, claiming that the Sauds had lost their legitimacy as righteous rulers because of the extravagant lifestyles of some of its princes, corruption, and their alliance with the West. Internal uprisings coincided with the Iranian revolution led by Ayatollah Khomeini in 1979. The Saudi regime eyed the Shi'ite revolution with suspicion and responded in part by intensifying Wahhabi missionary work abroad. After all, Saudi Arabia was the cradle of Islam and the guardian of the two holy places: Mecca and Medina.

In the following decade, the royal family was confronted with another challenge, namely the financial and political consequences of the First Gulf War (1990-1991) and the temporarily decreased oil revenues. Reliance on U.S. political and military support, and the lack of political participation prompted growing criticism within society. From the 1990s onwards, several groups, including reform-minded liberals, but also radical Muslims, submitted petitions to the king asking for political reform.

Under domestic and international pressure, King Fahd implemented several constitutional reforms in 1992. He promulgated the Basic Ordinance of the Kingdom, which stipulates that 'God's Book and the Sunna of the Prophet' are of the highest authority and all legislation is subordinate to it.

Another demand of the petitioners met by King Fahd was the establishment of a new, partly elected, Consultative Council. The council was created in 1992 and now counts 150 members of different social strata, who are empowered to lay down regulations in the public interest and in accordance with shari'a. For the time being, however, the Council has little actual power and it cannot yet be seen as a fully-fledged parliamentary body.

The modest reforms of the government did not silence the voices of the opposition. Young Islamists have committed bloody attacks against foreign targets since the 1990s, and various radicals were banned from the country, including Osama Bin Laden. The government has also had to contend with the fact that the vast majority of the 11 September terrorist attackers (fifteen of the nineteen) were Saudi nationals. Despite the government openly declaring war against terrorism, radical Muslims continue to carry out attacks against Western targets and other 'infidels' – on Saudi soil as well as in occupied Iraq.

Meanwhile, the process of legal reform continued. Since the late 1990s, several new laws were promulgated, including, for example, the Regulation on Criminal Procedure (2001) and the Legal Practice Regulation (2001), both of which aim to regulate criminal proceedings and better safeguarding the procedural rights of the accused. While the 1975 judicial organisation is still in operation, substantial reforms were announced in autumn 2007. The 2007 Judiciary Regulation establishes a Supreme Court and new first instance and appellate courts comprising special chambers for personal status, criminal, labour, and commercial law matters. Once fully functional, the Supreme Court is to take over the judicial functions of the Supreme Judicial Council. A new Board of Grievances Regulation, also promulgated in 2007, announces the establishment of an Administrative Judicial Council and administrative courts of appeal. As of the time of writing, it cannot yet be indicated what the outcome of the announced reforms will be. For now, duality in the Saudi legal system seems to remain a typical feature.

Although the legal reforms have been welcomed by international organisations and human rights groups, the criticism on the human rights situation in Saudi Arabia has not died down. In particular, the following issues have generated vehement criticism both domestically and abroad: the extremely disadvantaged position of women; discrimination against religious minorities and foreigners; a lack of religious freedom and freedom of expression; torture in prisons; intimidation by the religious police; the execution of cruel corporal punishments, such as beheading, stoning, hanging, amputation, and lashing; and increasing frequency of the use of the death sentence; in 2008 at least 102 persons were executed.

The current King Abdullah, like many leaders, seems to be walking a thin line between reform-minded liberals, conservatives, international pressure, civil society groups, and the *'ulama*. He has carefully opened channels for more political participation. Given that he has to reckon with the conservative *'ulama* and traditional forces within his own family, it is anticipated that Saudi Arabia will, in moving forward – within the realm of Islam – do so at a slow pace.

Notes

1 Esther van Eijk is a PhD Candidate at Leiden University in the Netherlands. This study is based on a study first published in Dutch (Barends & van Eijk 2006). The original study, translated into English by A. Saab, has been extensively revised by Esther van Eijk, who assumes full responsibility for the content of this work. The author wishes to thank Prof. Frank Vogel for his many valuable comments and suggestions on earlier drafts of this study. Thanks are also due to Prof. Baudouin Dupret, Prof. Jan Michiel Otto, and Dr. Nadia Sonneveld for their editorial comments.

2 This chapter is for the most part based on secondary sources of information. The scope of the study requested did not allow for a comprehensive analysis or field-based research on the topic.

3 It must be noted here that in the South-Western part of the peninsula early dynasties did exist; the Kingdom of Saba (or 'Sheba') in present-day Yemen is the best known example (930 BC–115 BC).

4 The Ka'ba is the focal point of Islam. Muslims pray in the direction of the Ka'ba in Mecca, and the shrine is one of the most important sites of the yearly pilgrimage (*hajj*). In pre-Islamic times, the Ka'ba served as a temple for the numerous gods who were worshipped by the Arab Bedouins (Cleveland 2000: 7).

5 This event, the *hijra* (emigration), marks the beginning of the Islamic calendar.

6 The Ottoman Empire conquered large parts of the Arab world in the sixteenth century: Damascus in 1516, Cairo in 1517, Algiers in 1520, Baghdad in 1534, Tripoli in 1551, and Tunis in 1574.

7 Wahhabis are, thus, also called puritans or Salafis.

8 In 1953, the Council of Deputies was replaced by the less powerful Council of Ministers (Al-Fahad 2005: 380).

9 This Hijazi Council remained in existence until 1992, when it was replaced by a new Consultative Council, but had little actual power (Vogel 2000: 282-283).

10 Followers of the fourth Sunni school of law, the Malikis, could also be found on the peninsula. Accordingly, Maliki rules can still be found in the current legal systems of Kuwait, Bahrain, and the United Arab Emirates.

11 See Schacht 1982: 87. A new commercial court with jurisdiction over the Hijaz region had been established in 1926. It was abolished in 1955 because of the imminent national process of unification of the legal system (Vogel 2000: 302). Al-Jarbou writes that the commercial court in Jeddah was abolished because of the influence of the traditionalists (*'ulama*) (Al-Jarbou 2007: 219).

12 The descendants of Ibn Abd al-Wahhab (or Ash-Shaykh) have always – and through to the present – occupied the main religious positions in Saudi Arabia.

13 This specific power lasted until 1964 only. A new Board of Grievances Regulation was enacted in 1982, changing considerably the nature of the Board. Article 1 recognises the Board as an independent administrative institution. Since the 1980s the Board has gained more competences, such as criminal jurisdiction for specific cases arising under, for instance, the Forgery Regulation, the Bribery Regulation, and the Post Regulation. And, in 1987, jurisdiction to handle commercial cases was transferred from the commercial disputes committees to the Board (Al-Jarbou 2004: 33). In 2007 a new Board of Grievances Regulation was issued (see 4.5).

14 For example, Abdallah ibn Hammud al-Tariqi became the Minister of Petroleum and Mineral Resources in 1961; he was succeeded by another commoner, namely Shaykh Ahmed Zaki Yamani (until 1986) (Niblock 2006: 44, 66).

15 The Ministry of Islamic Affairs, Endowment, Da'wa, and Guidance, established by King Fahd in 1993, played a major role in these activities.

16 The central figures in the government were, until recently, King Fahd (died in 2005) and his six brothers, who all held high positions. These so-called Sudayri Seven, were named after Abdulaziz al-Saud's favourite wife, Hassa bint Ahmad al-Sudayri.

17 The Ordinance of the Provinces divided the kingdom into thirteen administrative units.

18 See 4.5 on constitutional law.

19 Quoted in *Human Rights Watch* 1992: Intro.

20 In the last decade unemployment rates have gone down, with 11.6 per cent of the population estimated to be unemployed in 2009 (Bartleby 2009).

21 See e.g. BBC News Online: http://news.bbc.co.uk/2/hi/middle_east/4477315.stm, last accessed 14 January 2010.

22 See also MENA Election Guide: http://www.mena-electionguide.org/details.aspx/13/Saudi%20Arabia/article421, last accessed 14 January 2010.

23 Prince Sultan, the Minister of Defence, has become the new Crown Prince.

24 Human Rights Watch: http://hrw.org/english/docs/2007/04/27/saudia15774.htm (last visited 14 January 2010); National Society for Human Rights: http://nshr.org.sa/english/aRightMenuCMS.aspx?mid=30 (last visited 3 February 2010).

25 See *Saudi Arabia: In Focus* (weekly publication of the Saudi Arabian embassy in Washington, D.C.): http://www.saudiembassy.net/files/PDF/Publications/Focus/2009/09-FOCUS-02-17.pdf, last accessed 14 January 2010.

26 For the English translation see the International Constitutional Law (ICL) Project: http://www.servat.unibe.ch/icl/sa00000_.html, last accessed 9 February 2010.

27 In 2006, the Allegiance Committee was established by royal decree; the Committee is composed of male descendants of the founder, King Abdulaziz, who will play a role in choosing future Saudi kings. Future kings (the protocol will not come into effect until after the current Crown Prince Sultan has become king) will have to seek the approval of the committee for their choice of successor (i.e. crown prince). See the Website of the Royal Embassy of Saudi Arabia in London: http://www.mofa.gov.sa/Detail.asp?InNewsItemID=55889, last accessed 14 January 2010.

28 A *mufti* is a member of the community of religious scholars (the *'ulama*), who is competent to give his authoritative legal opinion (*fatwa*) on a particular issue.

29 In 2007, the government launched an official website for *fatwa*s issued by authorised scholars. Visitors can ask questions on various topics and receive a reply from the Council of Senior 'Ulama. See http://www.alifta.com.

30 He was succeeded by the current Grand Mufti, Abdulaziz al-Shaykh.

31 His writings, including *fatwa*s, were – and still are – considered authoritative. Not just in Saudi Arabia, but all over the world, Muslims accepted his opinions as morally valid and practical guidelines.

32 But see e.g. Al-Jarbou 2007: 209, who writes that 'many laws and regulations are enacted every year without being studied by the Board of neither the Senior *'ulamā'* nor the Higher Council of Justice. The reason is that these laws can be implemented without having the traditionalists approve of them or at least participate in their enactment.'

33 English translation taken from the International Constitutional Law (ICL) Project: http://www.servat.unibe.ch/icl/sa00000_.html, last accessed 9 February 2010.

34 Basic Ordinance, Art.s 49, 53. The Board is not allowed to hear any outcome of the shari'a courts, see Board of Grievances Regulation 2007, Art. 14.

35 However, appeals cases that involve amputation, execution, or stoning to death are adjudicated by panels comprised of five judges (Judiciary Regulation (1975), Art. 13; Regulation on Criminal Procedure (2001), Art. 10). There is a similar provision in the 2007 regulation (Art. 15(1)).

36 Some of its decisions were published by the secretariat of the *Diwan* for some years in the late 1970s, but publication of its decisions was discontinued after that period (Mallat 2007: 163-164 n. 70).
37 The Administrative Judicial Council's jurisdiction is similar to that of the Supreme Judicial Council. See Board of Grievances Regulation (2007), Art.s 4, 5. Articles 8 and 10 of the same regulation describe the mechanism of the Supreme Administrative Court.
38 Besides their classical shari'a college training, most Board of Grievances judges also hold a law degree from one of the legal departments offered by various universities in the country (Al-Jarbou 2007: 222).
39 A government delegation member in discussion with the CEDAW Committee in January 2008 informed the Committee that the government 'was in the process of establishing a high-level scholarly panel, including the various schools of jurisprudence, to codify all the provisions of Islamic law relating to personal status' (CEDAW Committee 2008, Summary record of the 815th meeting).
40 It should be noted here that the father is the primary legal guardian of the child from the moment the child is born. After divorce, the mother can become custodian of the child (i.e. physical custody) until a certain age, after which full custody will be automatically transferred to the father.
41 See *BBC News Online*: http://news.bbc.co.uk/1/hi/world/middle_east/4437667.stm, dated 12 April 2005, last accessed 14 January 2010. See also *Gulfnews.com*: http://www.gulfnews.com/News/Gulf/saudi_arabia/10228620.html, dated 14 July 2008, last accessed 14 January 2010.
42 The Islamic Fiqh Academy, established in 1981, is affiliated to the Organisation of the Islamic Conference (OIC) and is based in Jeddah.
43 See Arabi 2001: Chapter 7; Welchman 2007: 102-105.
44 It should be noted here that some *'ulama* have issued *fatwa*s in which they contend that *misyar* is *zina* (fornication) (ibid: 107).
45 Non-Muslim heirs are excluded as heirs in the estate.
46 Male relatives in the male line.
47 The new Judiciary Regulation (2007) and the Board of Grievances Regulation (2007) provide that the commercial jurisdiction from the Board will be transferred to a specialised division within the regular shari'a court system.
48 The most important regulation governing companies is the Saudi Companies Regulation of 1965 (amended in 1967 and 1982). This regulation, for example, is largely taken from Egypt (Vogel 2000: 288).
49 Personal communication with F.E. Vogel, Leiden, March 2008.
50 It should be noted that citizens of the Gulf Cooperation Council who conduct commercial business in the kingdom are also subject to *zakat*. See: http://www.dzit.gov.sa/en/CommerceZakat/commercezakat1.shtml, last accessed 14 January 2010.
51 Personal communication with F.E. Vogel, Leiden, March 2008.
52 Ibid.
53 English translation taken from the International Constitutional Law (ICL) Project: http://www.servat.unibe.ch/icl/sa00000_.html, last accessed 9 February 2010.
54 The other countries abstaining from voting included the Soviet Union, Poland, Yugoslavia, and South Africa.
55 See Human Rights Watch memorandum: http://hrw.org/english/docs/2006/02/07/saudia12622.htm, dated 7 February 2006, last accessed 14 January 2010.
56 For extensive and up-to-date information on state reports, reporting history, and reservations and objections regarding all UN treaties, see http://www.bayefsky.com (The United Nations Human Rights Treaties).

57 The woman and her male companion were initially both sentenced to ninety lashes. Four of the five accused rapists were sentenced to between one and five years imprisonment and received between eighty and one thousand lashes for the offence of kidnapping, as the Public Prosecution could not prove rape had occurred due to the strict shari'a rules of evidence that apply to this *hadd* crime. See *The Independent News Online*: http://news.independent.co.uk/world/middle_east/article3204058.ece, last accessed 14 January 2010.

58 See *Al Jazeera English Online*: http://english.aljazeera.net/NR/exeres/AF444D2D-E666-437A-A441-37EA99C8BE4F.htm, last accessed 14 January 2010.

59 The study notes that 'there appear to be no written legal provisions or official decrees explicitly mandating male guardianship and sex segregation, yet both practices are essentially universal inside Saudi Arabia' (Human Rights Watch 2008: 4)

60 The 2005 Labour Ordinance states that women are permitted to work in 'all fields compatible with their nature' (Art. 149). The Minister of Justice, however, prohibits the issuing of licences to women to practise the legal profession (Yamani 2008: 152).

61 Saudi Arabia feared that Shi'ite ascendance in the region would be strengthened by the 2003 ousting of the old Sunni regime in Iraq and that Iraq would become a Shi'ite state. It appears that in line with these fears, a number of Saudi religious leaders have encouraged young fighters to go to Iraq and fight against the Shi'ites (Schwartz 2005: 29-32).

Bibliography

Amnesty International (2008), *Amnesty International Report 2008 – Saudi Arabia*. London: Amnesty International Publications. See also http://www.amnesty.org

Amnesty International (2009a), *Amnesty International Report 2009 – Saudi Arabia*. London: Amnesty International Publications. See also http://www.amnesty.org.

Amnesty International (2009b), *Saudi Arabia: Assaulting human rights in the name of counter-terrorism*. London: Amnesty International Publications.

Ansary, A.F. (2008), *A brief overview of the Saudi Arabian legal system*. See http://www.nyulawglobal.org/globalex/Saudi_Arabia.htm.

Arabi, O. (2001), *Studies in modern Islamic law and jurisprudence*. The Hague: Kluwer Law International.

Barends, M. & E. van Eijk (2006), 'Sharia en nationaal recht in Saoedi-Arabië', in J.M. Otto et al. (eds.), *Sharia en national recht in twaalf moslimlanden*, 85-111. Amsterdam: Amsterdam University Press.

Bartleby (2010), 'Saudi Arabia', in *The World Fact Book*, see http://www.bartleby.com/151/country/sa.html, last accessed 30 January 2010. Washington D.C.: CIA; New York: Bartleby.com. For the online edition see *The World Factbook* (2009), https://www.cia.gov/library/publications/the-world-factbook/geos/sa.html, last accessed 30 January 2010.

Cleveland, W.L. (2000), *A history of the modern Middle East*. Boulder: Westview Press.

Commission on Human Rights (2003), 'Report of the Special Rapporteur on the independence of judges and lawyers', *Report on the mission to the Kingdom of Saudi Arabia*, E/CN.4/2003/65/Add.3. New York: United Nations.

Committee Against Torture (2002), *Summary record of the first part (public) of the 519th meeting: Denmark, Saudi Arabia* (CAT/C/SR.519). New York: United Nations.

Committee on the Elimination of Discrimination against Women (2008), *Summary record of the 815th meeting* (CEDAW/C/SR.815). New York: United Nations.

Committee on the Elimination of Discrimination against Women (2008), *Concluding Observations of the Committee on the Elimination of Discrimination against Women: Saudi Arabia* (CEDAW/C/SAU/CO/2). New York: United Nations.

Coulson, N.J. (1964), *A history of Islamic Law.* Edinburgh: Edinburgh University Press.
Esmaeili, H. (2009), 'On a slow boat towards the rule of law: The nature of law in the Saudi Arabian legal system', *Arizona Journal of International & Comparative Law* 26(1): 1-47.
Al-Fahad, A.H. (2005), 'Ornamental constitutionalism: The Saudi basic law of governance', *The Yale Journal of International Law* 30: 375-396.
Al-Ghadyan, A.A. (1998), 'The judiciary of Saudi Arabia', *Arab Law Quarterly* 13: 235-251.
Haberbeck, A. (2010), 'Succession in Saudi Arabia', *Trusts & Trustees* 16: 28-30.
Halliday, F. (2003), *Islam and the myth of confrontation: Religion and politics in the Middle East.* London/New York: Tauris.
Al-Hejailan, H.S. (2002), 'Saudi Arabia', in E. Cotran (ed.), *Yearbook of Islamic and Middle Eastern Law* 7: 271-81.
Human Rights Council (2009), 'Mission to Saudi Arabia', *Report of the Special Rapporteur on violence against women, its causes and consequences,* A/HRC/11/6/Add.3. New York: United Nations. See also http://www2.ohchr.org/english/bodies/hrcouncil/11session/reports.htm.
Human Rights Watch (2008), *Perpetual Minors: Human rights abuses stemming from male guardianship and sex segregation in Saudi Arabia.* New York: Human Rights Watch.
Human Rights Watch (1992), *Empty Reforms: Saudi Arabia's new basic laws,* see http://www.hrw.org/reports/1992/saudi/INTROTHR.htm#P27_6020.
Al-Jarbou, A.M. (2007), 'The Role of Traditionalists and Modernists on the Development of the Saudi Legal System', *Arab Law Quarterly* 21: 191-229.
Al-Jarbou, A.M. (2004), 'Judicial independence: Case study of Saudi Arabia', *Arab Law Quarterly* 19: 5-54.
Jerichow, A. (1998), *The Saudi file – People, power, politics.* New York: St. Martin's Press.
Kechichian, J.A. (1986), 'The role of the Ulama in the politics of an Islamic state: The case of Saudi Arabia', *International Journal of Middle East Studies* 18: 53-71.
Kepel, G. (2004), *Jihad: The Trial of Political Islam.* London: I.B. Tauris.
Kostiner, J. (1993), *The making of Saudi Arabia, 1916-1936: From chieftaincy to monarchical state.* New York: Oxford University Press.
Mallat, C. (2007), *Introduction to Middle Eastern Law.* New York: Oxford University Press.
Niblock, T. (2006), *Saudi Arabia: Power, legitimacy and survival.* London: Routledge.
Ottaway, D.B. (2004), 'U.S. eyes money trails of Saudi-Backed charities', in *The Washington Post,* dated 19 August.
Raphaeli, N. (2003), 'Saudi Arabia: A brief guide to its politics and problems', *Middle East Review of International Affairs* 7: 3: 21-33.
Al-Rasheed, M. (2007), *Contesting the Saudi State: Islamic Voices from a New Generation.* New York: Cambridge University Press.
Schacht, J. (1982), *An introduction to Islamic law.* Oxford: Clarendon Press.
Schwartz, S. (2005), '*Shari'a* in Saudi Arabia: Today and tomorrow', in P. Marshall (ed.), *Radical Islam's rules: The worldwide spread of extreme Shari'a law,* 19-40. Lanham: Rowman & Littlefield.
Tarazi, A.M. (1993), 'Saudi Arabia's new basic laws: The struggle for participatory Islamic government', *Harvard International Law Journal* 34(1): 258-275.
Vogel, F.E. (2000), *Islamic law and legal system – Studies of Saudi Arabia.* Leiden: Brill.
Vogel, F.E. & S.L. Hayes (1998), *Islamic law and finance: Religion, risk, and return.* The Hague: Kluwer Law International.
Welchman, L. (2007), *Women and Muslim family laws in Arab States: A comparative overview of textual development and advocacy.* Amsterdam: Amsterdam University Press.
Yamani, M.A.Z (2008), *Polygamy and law in contemporary Saudi Arabia.* Reading: Ithaca Press.

5 Shari'a and national law in the Sudan

Olaf Köndgen[1]

Abstract

This chapter maps the Sudanese experience around the application of elements of the shari'a from early Islamisation in the sixteenth century to early 2010. It shows how the Sudanese legal system has been shaped by a variety of sources – from customary law and shari'a law to Turko-Egyptian law, British colonial law, and modern Egyptian civil law, to name some of the most important sources. In a second part, the chapter offers an analysis of the role of the shari'a in recent Sudanese legislation: in the constitution, in family and inheritance law, and in the fields of criminal law and economic law. A section on human rights and international obligations further demonstrates where Sudanese shari'a-based legislation clashes with the human rights obligations of the Sudan. Taken as a whole, shari'a application has been expanding from 1983-1985 with a new stimulus as of 1989/1991 with the advent of the present military-Islamist regime. At this juncture, after more than twenty years of military-Islamist rule, expansion of shari'a application has clearly come to a standstill for the time being. Given the threat of Southern Sudan breaking away in addition to the Darfur and other conflicts, shari'a application is not a top priority for the Sudanese regime in 2010.

Table of contents

The Republic of the Sudan came into being on 1 January 1956, when it gained its independence from Great Britain and Egypt. As of mid 2009, an estimated 41 million people live in the Sudan, of whom 70 per cent are Sunni Muslim. They live mainly in the North. An estimated 5-20 per cent of the population is Christian and lives in the South and in and around the capital Khartoum.[2] Another 10-25 per cent of the population professes native religions. Sudan has nineteen important ethnic groups and 597 subgroups. More than a hundred languages and dialects are spoken in the Sudan. Arabic and English are the official languages of the country, for about half of the population Arabic is the mother tongue. The Southern part of the country chiefly consists of a black African population, composed of the Nilotic, Nilo-Hamitic, and Sudanic groups. While the majority of the population is of African descent (52%), many Sudanese are of Arabic descent (39%). Around 9% are Beja.

(Sources: Beck 2001; Bartleby 2010)

5.1 The period until 1920

The rising prominence of Islamic law under Ottoman-Egyptian, Mahdi, and British rule

From the Funj-Sultanate to Ottoman-Egyptian rule

In 1800 the area, which is today the Sudan was largely dominated by the Funj-Sultanate in North and Central Sudan with its capital Sinnar (1504-1820) and the Sultanate of Dar Fur (1640-1916) in the West (Holt 1997: 943-945, 121-125). Early jurisdiction under the Funj – who had adopted Islam under their first king `Amara Dunqas (1504-1534) – was marked by only limited knowledge of the shari´a and the dominance of customary law. By the time of the Ottoman-Egyptian conquest, Islamic law and its institutions had made headway against the king's absolute judicial authority, not the least due to enhanced commercial activities and the presence of a large number of foreign Muslim traders (Spaulding 1977). In Dar Fur Islamic law equally coexisted with customary law, with the former gaining importance in the higher echelons of Fur society. Penal law seems to have been entirely a domain of customary law, '[...] there is no evidence that the shari´a punishments were ever imposed' (O´Fahey & Abu Salim 1983: 9).

It was under Ottoman-Egyptian rule (1820-1881) that, for the first time in their history, the North and the South of the Sudan gradually became united. This process was largely completed with the 1874 conquest of the Sultanate of Dar Fur. In harmony with the new administrative centralism a centralised judiciary was created for the first time with a hierarchical system of local and provincial courts and an appeals court in Khartoum (*majlis 'umum al-Sudan*). Any decision of the appeals court had to be endorsed by the highest mufti and the Governor-General and was sent for final approval to the highest judicial body in Egypt, the *majlis al-ahkam* in Cairo. Which laws were actually applied by the Egyptian administration remains to a certain degree unclear, as relevant archives were later destroyed by the Mahdi's army (see below).[3] In some instances shari'a was applied, in other cases Egyptian military and civil codes appear to have been implemented. In more remote areas, justice was administered according to customary law (Mustafa 1971: 37). As of 1850, a new penal code was introduced as part of the *tanzimat* reforms (see 6.1) and implemented through a newly created system of secular courts (*Nizamiyye*) (Fluehr-Lobban 1987: 30). As a consequence of this, the competence of the shari'a courts was limited to personal status law and matters concerning land rights. Egyptian dominance and the introduction of a unified court system also meant the introduction of Hanafite law.[4]

Shari'a of its own kind: Islamic legislation under the Mahdi

Ottoman-Egyptian rule came to an end when the Mahdi's army conquered Khartoum in 1885. Muhammad Ahmad al-Mahdi, a religious renovator, had set out to liberate the Sudan from its 'infidel' oppressors by means of a holy war (*jihad*). Consequently, after the conquest all verdicts of the judges of the Turco-Egyptian rule were declared void. Using the early community of Muslims as a model, he aspired to restore the religious purity of the Prophet Muhammad's time. The only sources of the Mahdi's legislation were thus the Qur'an and Sunna in his – often idiosyncratic – interpretation. His large number of legal circulars was frequently in conflict with the traditional Sunni schools of law. Thus, for example, the payment of blood money (*diya*) was abolished, retaliation (*qisas*) became compulsory, and more severe punishments were imposed on smoking than on drinking alcohol. Throughout the Mahdi's rule, recourse to the *fiqh* (Islamic jurisprudence) was largely excluded and the position of the traditional religious scholars (*ulama'*) was weakened (Köndgen 1992: 16-18).

Between 1896 and 1899 a joint Anglo-Egyptian army conquered the Sudan and the Anglo-Egyptian condominium was established, which made the Sudan effectively another British colony. The judicial structures of the Mahdi state had been centred largely around the Mahdi. Their collapse, thus, meant that the British 'had to start from scratch' (Salman 1983: 66). The first Penal Code and the Criminal Procedure Act were promulgated in 1899. The former was based on Anglo-Indian colonial legislation, the latter on Egyptian military law, which, in turn, had its origins in British military law. Both had been adapted to Sudanese conditions and the penal code had already been applied in the East African protectorates and Zanzibar. The penal code was re-enacted in 1925.

Serving the Condominium: Shari´a after the British-Egyptian conquest

Lord Cromer, British consul general in Cairo, travelled to Khartoum immediately after the conquest and promised British respect for the application of Islamic law (Salman 1983: 66). Shortly thereafter, the colonial administration was to – at least partially – fulfil his promises. The Mohammedan Law Courts Ordinance of 1902 and the Mohammedan Law Courts Procedure Act of 1915 provided the basis for the creation and procedures of the 'Mohammedan Law Courts'. These courts administered the shari´a in personal status cases and in litigation regarding pious foundations (*awqaf*). The Mohammedan Law Courts Ordinance provided for the Grand Qadis to issue legal circulars (*manshurat*) functioning as provisions and regulating the interpretation of the shari´a. Being published regularly, as they were, these circulars constituted a precursor to codification, an innovation 'the Egyptian ´ulama appear not to have opposed' (Jeppie 2003: 2).

Within the framework of the condominium, the Egyptians were generally kept at bay and only filled the lower ranks in the colonial administration. An exception, however, were the shari´a courts, which were operated almost exclusively by Egyptian judges. Until independence, the Grand Qadi was always an Egyptian (Jeppie 2003: 2). Native or tribal courts dispensing justice in the South and among Muslim nomads in the North received recognition only twenty years after the conquest (Jeppie 2003: 2). Under Reginald Wingate, the Sudan's second Governor-General, fear of a regenerated Mahdism led to a resolute suppression of what was perceived as heterodoxy. As such, Sufi orders were denied legality and surviving Mahdist leaders subdued. Concurrently, the *ulama*, who had never been very important in the Sudan, were granted pensions and status. In 1912, an institute to train *ulama*, emulating al-Azhar in Cairo, was opened in Omdurman. In addition, mosques were built and repaired and the pilgrimage to Mecca (*hajj*) was promoted in order to pre-empt 'fanaticism' (Daly 1997: 746).

5.2 The period from 1920 until 1965

From colonial shari'a to the quest for a constitution

Refining the system

From 1920 native courts were given official recognition and effectively used to gradually supplant the shari'a courts. In order to diminish the status of the shari'a courts, native courts were now given jurisdiction on personal status issues. By 1929, a good number of shari'a courts had been suppressed and native courts set up instead. However, even though reduced in number, shari'a courts continued to exist throughout the era of the condominium (Jeppie 2003: 3).

Throughout the time of the condominium, the shari'a co-existed with British common law and local customary law administered by tribal leaders. As to penal law, provincial administrators and governors were allowed great leeway. The same crime could be punished differently, depending on whether the culprit was a nomad, a Southerner, or an Arab (Köndgen 1992: 19).

The path to independence and beyond

The Sudan's path to independence accelerated with a Self-Government Statute passed in April 1952. In January 1954 it was decided that within a period of three years the Sudanese had to reach a decision between independence and union with Egypt. Immediately after, a Sudanisation committee was established and British officials started leaving the Sudan. In December 1955 the Sudanese parliament unanimously voted for independence.

The Sudan's first constitution a month after the country achieved independence, in January 1956, guaranteed parliamentary rule, the existence of a multi-party system, and free elections. It was intended to be a transitional constitution, later to be replaced by a permanent one. Instead, however, it survived three military takeovers and was revitalised whenever the military had to step down (Warburg 2003: 144).

Three distinct tendencies dominated the discussion about the future constitution and legislation between the years before independence and on into the seventies. Firstly, proponents of an Islamic constitution and legislation were represented above all by the Umma party, the Democratic Unionist Party, the Muslim Brothers (originating from Egypt), and some members of Sufi sects (Kok 1991: 240). Secondly, the camp of the Nasserites, Ba'athists, and Arab nationalists advocated the Egyptianisation of the Sudanese legal system, thus harmonising it with the majority of socialist Arab states and dispensing with the British colonial heritage. Thirdly, a pragmatic camp endorsed the reform of the existing legal system, but rejected its complete replacement by either Islamic or Egyptian legislation. Most of the secular *intelligentia* and graduates of the Law Faculty of the University of Khartoum belonged to this camp (Köndgen 1992: 19-21; Kok 1991: 237-243).

As early as September 1956 a committee began to draft a 'permanent' constitution. Sectarian leaders such as Sayyid Abd al-Rahman al-Mahdi and Sayyid Ali al-Mirghani, joined by the Muslim Brotherhood, advocated an Islamic parliamentary republic with the shari´a as the main source of legislation. Khartoum was to be the capital of a centralised system of government with Arabic as the official language and Islam as the religion unifying the nation (Kok 1989: 439). Non-Muslims were to be granted all rights envisaged by the shari´a. Racial or religious discrimination was to be excluded. Within a period of five years the Sudan was to be fully Islamised. Southern objections against Islamisation and demands for a federal system were dismissed. Thus, when in November 1958 the military took over under General Ibrahim `Abbud, a national consensus on the permanent constitution had not been reached and the draft constitution had not yet been promulgated.

5.3 The period from 1965 until 1985

From democratic interlude to Numeiri's Islamisation programme

Sudan´s second democratic experience

After the downfall of Abbud's military dictatorship in 1964, the Sudan lived through its second democratic stage. A slightly amended version of the transitional constitution of 1956 was reenacted. However, solutions for the constitutional impasse proposed by the different parties concerned had not materially changed. Southern claims to self-determination and demands for a referendum on their future rapport with the Muslim North continued to fall on deaf ears, even with moderate parties in the North (Warburg 2003: 146). As of December 1967 a constitutional committee debated anew a future 'permanent constitution' and in early 1969 presented a draft defining the Sudan as a 'democratic socialist republic under the protection of Islam' (Art. 1). This formulation was meant to placate the left as well as the traditional Islamic right. Falling short of full recognition of the Sudan's religious plurality, Article 3 stipulated Islam as the state religion. The shari´a was meant to be the main source of legislation and all existing laws were to be reviewed in order to bring them into conformity with the shari´a (Kok 1989: 443-444). The draft also set forth that the presidency would be reserved for Muslims only, thus – in constitutional terms – turning Southerners into second-class citizens.[5]

At the beginning of 1969, the Sudan's two largest Sufi orders, Ansar and Khatmiyya, agreed upon a common platform; thus, the creation of a presidential republic with an Islamist constitution was imminent. However, Numeiri's *coup d'état* in May 1969 averted the ratification of this second constitutional draft. Backed by a coalition of Nasserites, communists and Ba´athists, Numeiri immediately outlawed all political parties and revoked the transitional constitution (An-Na´im 1985: 332) in its 1964 version. In March 1970, the new regime bombarded the Ansar in their stronghold on the Nile island of Aba during a head-on confrontation. Their Imam al-Hadi al-Mahdi was killed when trying to take refuge in Ethiopia so his nephew Sadiq al-Mahdi fled to Libya, where he, together with Hasan al-Turabi and Sharif al-Hindi (Democratic Unionist Party leaders), founded the anti-Numeiri-coalition 'National Front'.

Numeiri's honeymoon with the Sudan Communist Party (SCP) did not last long. Disagreements between Numeiri and the SCP on the creation of a single-party system and the ensuing power struggle came to a head when a communist coup attempt in July 1971 fell short of sweeping the Numeiri regime away. However, with concerted Egyptian and Libyan help, a counter-coup brought Numeiri back to the helm. The general secretary of the SCP and hundreds of its members were executed. In the course of the ensuing political reorientation, the United States, Egypt, and Saudi-Arabia became the Sudan's key allies.

Numeiri´s early law reforms: an attempt to break free from the colonial heritage

Soon after Numeiri's takeover, a good part of the legal system came under scrutiny, resulting in the enactment of a succession of new laws. A Law Reform Commission was appointed in 1970; it composed a Civil Code written in Arabic. The code, hastily drafted, was mainly inspired by the Egyptian Civil Code of 1949 and, thus, meant a radical shift from common law to continental (French) European law (Amin 1985: 334). In the description of a Sudanese jurist,

> [...] the commission proceeded to copy with impunity, and with trivial and sometimes absolutely meaningless amendments, section after section and chapter after chapter from the Egyptian Civil Code of 1949, flavouring it here and there with a slightly modified or differently phrased version from the Iraqi, Syrian, or Libyan Civil Codes (Kok 1991: 238).

In the same assembly-line fashion, a Civil Evidence Code (1971), Civil Procedure Code (1972), and draft penal and commercial codes (1972) were expeditiously produced. But Numeiri's 'legal revolution' was not to last. The new codes were revoked in 1974, and the common law was restored once the regime's preoccupation with Arab unity had subsided and given way to other priorities (Kok 1991: 238).

Meanwhile, in February 1972, Numeiri's government and the Southern Sudan Liberation Movement (SSLM) had concluded a peace treaty in Addis Ababa to end the rebellion that started in August 1955 and had continued as a large scale insurgency. The peace agreement, which provided for an autonomous regional government in the South, addressed, among other things, developmental, economic, and human rights questions and was promulgated as the Southern Provinces Self-Government Act in 1972.

In September of the same year, the People's Assembly was convened to hammer out a new constitution. After seven months of deliberations, in May 1973, a 'permanent' constitution was promulgated. Several factors contributed to this success, seventeen years after reaching independence. For one, the non-participation of the sectarian parties and the Muslim Brothers allowed for an official recognition of the Christian and all other Southern religions. Also, important contentious issues, such as the status of the South and the nature of the executive, had been solved beforehand and the ban on political parties had paved the way for the Sudan Socialist Union (SSU) to operate as the sole remaining party in a single-party system. Article 9 of the permanent constitution stipulated that Islamic law and customary law were main sources of legislation. While non-Muslims and secularists in 1973 understood the two to be on an equal footing, Article 9 would later be invoked (in September 1983) to justify the introduction of the shari´a.

In 1974 the Sudan saw yet another wave of new legislation. With the defeat of the pan-Arabist trend, the pragmatist school this time had its way and neither the shari´a nor Egyptian law played a significant role in the drafting process. A Sales of Goods Act, a Contracts Act, a new Civil Procedure Act, an Agency Act, a Penal Code, and a Criminal Procedure Act were promulgated (Köndgen 1992: 22). While the Civil Procedure Act simply repealed the Civil Justice Ordinance of 1929, the Contracts Act, the Sales Act and the Agency Act were for the most part codifications of the pertinent concepts of English law and the Sudanese precedents. As to the 1974 Penal Code, it was an adaptation of the penal code from 1925 and, likewise, free of shari´a elements.

'The Islamic path' – Numeiri finds new allies

Meanwhile Numeiri himself increasingly advocated 'the Islamic path'. During the seventies new Islamic institutions and events were founded such as the 'African Islamic Center', an educational centre for African Muslims (1972) and the 'Festival of the Holy Qur'an' (1973). After forcing his government and high-ranking civil servants to abstain from alcohol (1976), Numeiri gave the 'Islamic path' an important role in his 1977 electoral programme. The same year saw the establishment of a committee for the revision of Sudanese legislation and the first bank working according to Islamic principles.

In the meantime, domestic opposition to the Numeiri regime did not diminish. After several failed attempts to overthrow Numeiri's regime between 1970 and 1975, the abovementioned National Front came very close to toppling Numeiri in 1976. This failed coup attempt was followed by a historical compromise with the leading opposition parties. Its leaders, Sadiq al-Mahdi and Hasan al-Turabi, were co-opted into the Sudanese Socialist Union (SSU). In turn, the National Front agreed to cease its military resistance. However, the Front proved unable to overcome internal divisions. In October 1978, Sadiq al-Mahdi withdrew from the SSU in protest against Numeiri's support of the Camp David agreement.

The majority of Muslim Brothers nevertheless concluded that backing the Numeiri regime was their best option.[6] Al-Turabi and fellow Muslim brethren began to fill government, SSU and other official positions. In August 1977 al-Turabi took over the chairmanship of a committee reviewing Sudanese laws for their compliance with the shari'a; a month later he joined another committee reviewing the constitution (Köndgen 1992: 35-36). The former worked out draft laws banning alcohol, the charging of interest, and on gambling as well as draft laws on alms tax (*zakat*), *hadd* punishments, and a law on the sources of legislation. The *zakat* draft law was ratified by parliament, but repealed due to difficulties with its application. Further, some specialised banks were established to give interest-free loans. In 1979 the position of the Muslim Brothers improved noticeably when al-Turabi was appointed Minister of Justice. While the Muslim Brothers widened their influence within the regime, the political and economic situation deteriorated further in the late seventies and early eighties. The credibility of the Numeiri regime was seriously undermined by drought, the influx of some two million refugees from neighbouring countries,[7] high inflation rates, cutbacks of food subsidies, and inadequate supplies.

Regarding his Southern policy, Numeiri in 1979 began to gradually dismantle the 1972 Addis Ababa agreement. He suggested to the National Congress of the SSU that they restructure the South into three, instead of one, autonomous regions, each with its own regional parliament and government. When in March 1981 the Southern Regional Assembly rejected the motion, he dissolved the Southern Regional Assembly and installed an interim government. Southerners had economic grievances too. Government investment in the South promised under the Addis Ababa agreement had hardly materialised and hopes for oil revenues had been foiled. Thus, in early 1983, the Sudan People's Liberation Army (SPLA) was founded and a civil war broke out, which by June 1983, when Numeiri decided by presidential decree to restructure the South, was already in full swing.

Shari'a as a last resort: Numeiri islamises the legal system

On the domestic front, the situation proved to be little better. A full-scale confrontation between Numeiri and the judiciary had led to a strike between June and September 1983 and a complete collapse of the judicial system. In July 1983, while the confrontation between the regime and the judiciary persisted, Numeiri appointed a three-member committee to islamise the Sudanese legislation. The delicate question of an Islamic constitution was excluded from the agenda. Al-Turabi, whom Numeiri wanted to keep away from the process, had been ousted as Minister of Justice shortly before the committee began its deliberations.[8]

In September 1983, the first new Islamist laws were enacted as presidential decrees. The Sudanese parliament ratified the 'September laws' without further discussion in November 1983. The most important of these statutes were: the Civil Procedure Act (1983), the Civil Transactions Act (1984), the Penal Code (1983), the Criminal Procedure Act (1983), the Evidence Act (1983), the Judgements Acts (1983), the Propagation of Virtue and the Prevention of Vice Act (1983), and the Zakat Act (1984) (Layish & Warburg 2002). It is worth noting that although parliament had the right to introduce a bill, none of the more significant laws enacted before the downfall of Numeiri in 1985 were initiated by parliament. Rather, they were initiated by the Sudanese president himself who was the driving force of the Islamisation process.

Churned out in very much the same fashion as the Egyptianised legislation of the early seventies, certain provisions of the September laws were in conflict with traditional Islamic jurisprudence (*fiqh*). For instance, the Evidence Act required the testimony of four adult men to establish unlawful sexual intercourse (*zina*), but it was in contradiction to the *fiqh* in allowing that 'when it is necessary, the testimony of others may be taken'. The 1983 Penal Code drew heavily on its 1974 predecessor, summary punishments such as flogging, fines or prison no longer corresponded to the gravity of the offence (Köndgen 1992: 42). As to *hadd* punishments, the 1983 Penal Code eclectically took its inspiration from different schools so as to aggravate possible punishments. Simultaneously, the use of 'legal doubts' (*shubha*), used in the *fiqh* to restrict the execution of *hadd* punishments, was rather limited. In combination with the admission of witnesses not approved by the *fiqh*, the application of *hadd* punishments was thereby considerably facilitated.[9] Furthermore, by adding more severe punishments for political offences, the new penal code provided a suitable instrument for the oppression of political opposition.

The September laws were rejected by many Sudanese. In the South, demonstrators protested against their second-class status within the new shari'a system. Not surprisingly, the Sudan Council of Churches also rejected the presidential decrees. In the North, a broad alliance of secular parties, labour unions and liberal Muslims denounced the new laws as un-Islamic, anti-women, generally repressive, and destructive to the unity of the country. According to the Umma party, the September laws represented a distortion of true Islam; Sadiq al-Mahdi suggested that corporal punishment was inadmissible in a society that had not yet attained a fair level of social and economic equality. One of the most outspoken critics of the introduction of the shari'a was Mahmud Muhammad Taha, spiritual leader of the reformist 'Republican Brothers'. For his opposition he would have to pay with his life in 1985 (see discussion below).[10]

After some discussion, al-Turabi and the Muslim Brothers decided to back Numeiri, despite their exclusion from the process of codification. In his earlier writings, al-Turabi had advocated a rather modernist approach towards the shari'a, arguing against a blind imitation of the traditional Muslim jurists (*fuqaha'*) and for an adaptation of Islamic law to the needs of today. However, as the last remaining allies of a discredited regime, the Muslim Brothers themselves had come under pressure. The introduction of the shari'a retrospectively justified their close cooperation with the regime and 'what mattered was that the Islamic laws were in place and that a new atmosphere had been created which the movement [had to] exploit to the full' (Osman 1989: 267).

Theoretically, the shari'a was meant to be applied nationwide, but this proved impossible. The scheduled establishment of a shari'a court in the Southern city of Juba in 1984 had to be cancelled due to strong local resistance. Southerners living in the North, however, were subjected to floggings and amputations (MERIP 1985: 12). For the SPLA, the September laws were yet another important reason, if not the only one, to continue the war that had broken out in the spring of 1983.

In April 1984 the deteriorating economic situation led to a wave of strikes, including by the judiciary. The judges voiced grievances directly connected with the September laws. In order to be able to continue within the new system, some of the most prominent judges saw themselves forced to undergo further training, while others were summarily discharged (Osman 1989: 294). To cope with the crisis, on 29 April 1984 Numeiri declared a state of emergency, which he would use in the remaining year of his rule before his downfall to quell any resistance to the shari'a. For this purpose, a competing body of emergency courts was created. While the regular courts had to deal with proceedings that had been pending for some time, the emergency courts had jurisdiction over all recent and new court cases, thus over all cases to be judged in accordance with the September laws. The judges manning the emergency courts often had no legal training. Furthermore, Numeiri made the presidents of the new courts accountable to him, thus disempowering the Chief Justice and taking formal control of an important part of the judiciary.

Already in June 1984 Numeiri had suggested a long list of constitutional amendments to the People's Assembly. The Islamisation of the legal system under a secular constitution had led to a number of laws becoming unconstitutional. However, with the Supreme Court filled with supporters of the September laws, no judicial review of such laws ever took place (Kok 1991: 242). Now Numeiri suggested the Islamisation of the constitution to bring it into line with the shari'a-based legislation and, above all, his political interests. Islamic terminology was to replace the secular wording of the 1973 constitution. While the president would have become a leader of the faithful (*qa'id al-mu'minin*) for life, the parliament was to mutate into a consultative council (*majlis al-shura*), swearing an oath of allegiance (*bai'a*) to whoever the leader of the faithful determined to be his successor. Thus, the president would not be accountable to parliament, but the new consultative council would owe their allegiance to him.

According to the draft reforms, Article 1 now declared the shari'a to be the sole source of legislation, in contrast to its equal footing to customary law as per the 1973 constitution. The South was to lose its autonomy; all reference to the 'Southern Provinces Regional Self-Government Act' of 1972 had been dropped. Not surprisingly, Numeiri's draft of constitutional amendments met with fierce resistance from national as well as regional parliaments in the South. The September laws had been approved by the parliament in order to avoid its dissolution and, to be sure, due to some genuine sympathy for Islamisation of the legal system. Accepting Numeiri's constitutional amendments, however, would have amounted to a near total (self)-disempowerment of parliament. Once Numeiri had realised that despite some suggestions for corrections parliament was not to be subdued, he adjourned the discussion (Köndgen 1992: 54-55).

From the trial and execution of Muhammad Taha to the end of Numeiri's regime

Probably the most blatant abuse of the implementation of Numeiri's version of the shari'a was the trial and subsequent execution of Mahmud Muhammad Taha, the leader of the 'Republican Brothers' mentioned above. While the Republican Brothers had backed Numeiri during his secular beginnings, they opposed the September laws and Numeiri's divisive Islamisation policies. In May 1983 the confrontation escalated and Taha and fifty of his followers were arrested. In 1984, the Republican Brothers launched a campaign against the September laws, criticising their unconstitutionality and multiple points of contradictions with the *fiqh*. Moreover, several constitutional complaints were deposited on grounds that the new laws discriminated against women and non-Muslims. Numeiri would not tolerate any further criticism of his shari'a: the 76-year old Taha was arrested again, sentenced to death, and hanged for apostasy on 18 January 1985 (Rogalski 1990: 39-51).

While the indictment was initially construed as a state security offence, subsequently Article 458(3) of the Penal Code was invoked. Article 458(3) stipulated that even uncodified *hadd* offences could be punished. During the appellate proceedings Taha was declared an apostate, based on the 1968 decision of a shari'a court, which, at the time, had not had jurisdiction in cases of apostasy. Apart from the highly flawed underpinning of the judgment, the sentence contravened Article 247 of the Criminal Procedure Act exempting persons over 70 years of age from the death penalty. In 1986, posthumously, the death sentence for Taha was eventually declared to be null and void.[11] The execution, highly controversial in the Sudan and strongly criticised in the Western press, was only one more step toward the downfall of the Numeiri regime.

In September 1984 a power struggle broke out between Numeiri and al-Turabi. In spring 1985 all Muslim Brothers were dismissed from their government and SSU positions. Al-Turabi and 200 Muslim Brothers were imprisoned, among them the president of the People's Assembly and one of the judges who had helped to sentence Mahmud Taha. For the Muslim Brothers, this last-minute wave of arrests came as a blessing in disguise. Instead of being drawn into the abyss, they could now portray themselves as victims of the very regime they had helped to stabilise for so long.

When at the end of March 1985 Numeiri abolished the subsidies for bread and fuel, political parties, labour unions, and professional associations formed a broad coalition demanding his resignation. Numeiri, who underestimated the imminent threat to his rule, flew to the U.S. for talks with U.S. president Ronald Reagan. In his absence, bread riots broke out, which escalated to a general strike. On the 6th of April, while Numeiri was already on his way back from the U.S., the Sudanese military assumed power.

5.4 The period from 1985 until the present

Whither shari´a?

Frozen shari´a under Siwar al-Dhahab

The new Transitional Military Council (TMC) under Siwar al-Dhahab (April 1985 – April 1986) abrogated the 1973 constitution, abolished Numeiri's singular political party, the Sudan Socialist Union (SSU), and reinstated the 'transitional' constitution of 1956, thus guaranteeing religious freedom, political pluralism, and separation of powers once again. The execution of *hadd* punishments was suspended as far as amputations were concerned, but floggings were still to be administered. Those convicted under the September laws stayed in prison, joined by others likewise sentenced to single or cross-amputation (see 5.7).[12]

The political forces rejecting the Numeiri-style shari´a legislation proved too weak to have a decisive influence on its abolition during the one-year reign of the TMC. Moreover, key ministers in the new cabinet, such as the Prime Minister al-Djizuli Daf´allah, were either Muslim Brothers or sympathetic to their cause. Hasan al-Turabi, who had been released from prison immediately after the coup, did not lose time in organising a demonstration demanding the retention of the shari´a. Using the newly attained political freedoms – more than forty political parties had been founded or resurrected after the TMC takeover – al-Turabi established the National Islamic Front (NIF), an alliance of Muslim Brothers, Sufis, tribal leaders, *ulama*, and former military officers. The NIF portrayed itself as hard-core defender of the shari´a in their political programme, claiming that Islamic law also best protected the culture and identity of non-Muslims. Resistance to Islamisation, according to the NIF's view, is either 'a Western plot' or emanates from 'Southern Marxists' such as the SPLA-leader John Garang. It is worth mentioning that an important motive for the NIF's enthusiasm for the retention of the shari´a was economic. The banks controlled by the Muslim Brothers had made considerable profits under its Islamic provisions.

Indecision and procrastination under Sadiq al-Mahdi

When the military ceded power to a civilian government in 1986, none of the Sudan's urgent problems had been tackled. The economy continued to be in a precarious situation. No peace treaty with the SPLA had been negotiated. And, even though protest against Numeiri's abuse of Islamic law had been a driving force behind the 1985 demonstrations, the shari'a was still in place.

Unsurprisingly, the first free elections in May 1986 resulted in a majority of the two largest sectarian parties, the Umma and the Democratic Unionist Party (DUP), who together attained an absolute majority.[13] The NIF, with 28 out of 232 possible seats,[14] proved successful, but was excluded from participation in the new coalition government at this time, because it was held partially responsible for the oppression of the Numeiri regime. Sadiq al-Mahdi, as the new prime minister, immediately resumed the quest for an Islamic alternative to the existing shari'a laws. The renewed discussion provoked fierce criticism from the Bar Association and the Sudan Council of Churches.[15] Despite al-Mahdi's repeated promises to revoke the September laws and replace them by completely overhauled legislation, only a few minor corrections were ever effectuated.[16]

In May 1988 the NIF joined the second coalition government of the Umma and the DUP parties, making it a precondition that new Islamic legislation would be enacted within two months. Under Hasan al-Turabi, who became minister of justice and chief public prosecutor, the Ministry of Justice finally submitted a draft penal code in September 1988. Hammered out by a group of jurists led most likely by the NIF, the draft suppressed to a large degree the politically-motivated stipulations of the 1983 Penal Code. The South was to be exempted from *hadd* punishments. The location of the commission of the crime (e.g. North or South), rather than the identity of the perpetrator (e.g. Southerner, non-Muslim, Muslim, etc.), was to be decisive in determining penalties. Highway robbery, thus, was to be punished with cross-amputation in the North and a maximum prison sentence of ten years in the South. On the other hand, non-Muslim Southerners living in Khartoum were subject to the shari'a, while Muslims living in the South could enjoy alcoholic drinks or even become apostates, at least according to a literal interpretation of the letter of the law (Köndgen 1992: 70-71). In parliament, the draft met with resistance from the Southern deputies, who demanded that Khartoum be exempted from any Islamic legislation. The Umma and DUP, even though some of their members had been part of the drafting committee, called for a revision of the draft.

In the meantime, negotiations with the SPLA conducted by Muhammad Uthman al-Mirghani in Addis Ababa had gained momentum, leading in November 1988 to a cease-fire. Al-Mirghani had, unlike Sadiq al-Mahdi in earlier negotiations, agreed to suspend the shari'a and to exclude any call for its implementation from the government's agenda (Warburg 1990: 635). Placated, the SPLA agreed to the convocation of a 'national constitutional conference' that was to deliberate on a new constitution and a new penal code that would be considered acceptable to the non-Muslim Southern minority. Prime Minister Sadiq al-Mahdi did not want to give the credit for having ended the civil war to his political rivals. Siding with the NIF, he deliberately wrecked the DUP/SPLA peace initiative. In protest against his tactics, the DUP left the government coalition.

In the new government, formed in January 1989 with the Umma party and the NIF as the sole remaining coalition partners, al-Turabi became foreign minister, with another NIF member heading the crucial Ministry of Justice. Before the government could decide on a new Islamic penal code, an alliance of labour unions, professional associations, and army officers issued an ultimatum, demanding the ratification of the DUP/SPLA peace agreement and the formation of a new government of national unity. Only after Sadiq al-Mahdi had formed a new cabinet, replacing the NIF with the DUP and representatives of the labour unions and professional associations, the peace agreement with the SPLA was ratified in April 1989. Now the tides had turned in favour of a revocation of the shari´a laws. In mid-June, the al-Mahdi government announced that the shari´a laws would be at last be nullified by the 1st of July and that a government delegation was to meet SPLA representatives to discuss a permanent end to the civil war. However, one day before the cancellation of the shari´a laws, the military intervened once more and ended another – rather short – era of civilian rule.

A regime with an agenda: Bashir and Turabi take over

After the bloodless *coup d'état*, led by Brigadier Umar al-Bashir, the Revolutionary Command Council for National Salvation (RCC) was formed. In addition, the National Assembly was dissolved, all political parties outlawed, the constitution revoked, and a state of emergency declared. Even though al-Turabi, like other religious leaders and members of the former government, was detained after the coup, it later became clear that the coup was in fact staged with the active support of the National Islamic Front.[17] Once firmly entrenched, the Bashir/NIF regime followed a systematic approach toward the transformation of all relevant Sudanese institutions, turning them into NIF bastions. Thousands of civil servants – 14,000 in 1989 alone – were sacked. More than a hundred career diplomats were dismissed; others resigned in protest and were replaced by NIF loyalists (Lesch 1998: 134).

A takeover of educational facilities and the underlying bureaucratic infrastructure was effectuated. The Ministry of Education was purged, teachers and faculty members replaced by NIF members, and the elected faculty unions dissolved. Furthermore, the regime islamised the curricula, and Arabic became the language of instruction in all public universities. The Arabic language excluded many Southern students who often had insufficient knowledge of Arabic to pass the compulsory entry exams (Lesch 1998: 143-145). To enhance its influence, the NIF founded several new universities and doubled numbers in the existing ones. This was important because NIF understood that a higher percentage of university graduates close to the NIF would ensure greater influence in professional associations in the future. By 1996, hundreds of faculty members had been dismissed or left the country. In fact, the brain drain had been so dramatic that a review by the Ministry of Higher Education found a shortage of teaching staff as high as 80 per cent in some universities (Lesch 1998:144).

Judiciary and legislation as cornerstones of the NIF's Islamisation agenda

Not surprisingly, the judiciary was a prime target for the realisation of the NIF's Islamisation programme. According to estimates, 'over sixty percent of all judges have been replaced by appointees of the new regime' (Lauro & Samuelson 1996: 9). Between 300 and 400 judges were dismissed or resigned between 1989 and 1991 alone (Amnesty International 1995: 20). Their replacements often lacked proper training in shari'a beyond personal status matters or were not qualified at all. While purging the traditional judiciary, the Bashir/NIF regime simultaneously built up a parallel system of courts that consisted of Security of the Revolution Courts (later to be re-baptised 'Emergency Courts') and Public Order Courts. One observer came to the conclusion that '[t]he parallel judicial institutions created by the NIF now handle more than 95% of the caseload of the Sudan, and are under the absolute control of the executive branch' (Abdelmoula 1996: 17). This estimate obviously does not take into account the high number of cases tried in customary courts.

While Southern law students, not trained in Arabic, were excluded in practise from access to the legal professions, those who did enter were often trained in newly founded law schools, concentrating on the shari'a and neglecting the Sudanese common law traditions. Many Southern judges were transferred to the North to hold minor positions or left the judiciary to pre-empt dismissal. NIF adherents were appointed in their place to guarantee the application of Islamic law wherever non-military courts in the South were allowed to function (Lauro & Samuelson 1996: 37-38).

According to some observers, many of the female judges who held positions in the civil and in the shari'a-governed personal status courts were dismissed by the new regime or relegated to insignificant assignments (Lauro & Samuelson 1996: 10). A 1996 report from the Lawyers

Committee for Human Rights indicates that neither Southern nor female judges were appointed by the Bashir/NIF regime until the mid-nineties.[18] The regime also made sure that any opposition from the legal profession was muted. Thus, the Sudanese Bar Association was first dissolved after the coup and later 'downgraded to a trade union subject to the controls of the Registrar of Trade Unions and the Minister of Labor' (Lawyers Committee for Human Rights 1996: 37-38). Concomitantly, the Bar Association lost some of its traditional immunities, such as the inviolability of a lawyer's files in his/her chambers.

Not surprisingly, the Bashir/NIF regime also promulgated important legislation to further its strategic goal of an in-depth Islamisation of the Sudanese society. As of early 1991, an overhauled, Islamised penal code was implemented (Bleuchot 1994: 423-427; see also 5.7 below). The new code contained the full range of *hudud* (sing. *hadd*) offences and punishments and included, for the first time in the history of Sudanese law, apostasy. In the same year, for the first time, a Muslim Personal Law Act codified personal status law (Ali 2001: 29; An-Na´im 2002: 83). Other important legislative initiatives include the Public Order Act of 1996 (now the Security of the Society Law), the 1998 Constitution, and the Political Associations Act of 1998.

A cornerstone of the NIF's claim to power was the establishment of parallel military and security forces, meant to gradually replace the existing ones. Accordingly, al-Turabi openly stated that the Popular Defense Forces (PDF) were meant to absorb the regular army and 'mobilise the public behind the jihad' (Lesch 1998: 135), as the war against the Southern forces was now baptised. To al-Turabi, at least according to his public statements, the PDF was a means for the Muslim collective to fulfil its obligation to contribute to *jihad*, implicitly portraying the non-Muslim soldiers of the South as an infidel enemy (Abdelmoula 1996: 20). Thus, while thousands of officers critical of the coup were fired despite the ongoing war in the South, the Popular Defence Forces were built up, from Arab tribal militias, NIF volunteers, drafted students and civil servants, and forcibly recruited teenagers (Lesch 1998: 135). In the meantime, the regime had made sure that most pro-government fighters were Southerners, either rounded up in Khartoum and sent to fight for the Sudanese army in the South or belonging to Southern pro-goverment militias (Martin 2002: 3).

In May 1999 al-Turabi negotiated a secret alliance with Sadiq al-Mahdi in Geneva in order to prepare a regime change towards an NIF/Ansar coalition, whilst simultaneously engaging in plans to get rid of Bashir and the military. To this end, al-Turabi, as speaker of parliament, contrived a motion suggesting the creation of the position of Prime Minister, thus effectively reducing Bashir to a mere figurehead stripped of any real power. When Bashir asked the parliament to postpone the discussion of the motion, he was harshly rebuffed by al-Turabi. Being in no doubt about the imminent threat to his regime, Bashir swiftly dissolved parliament and imposed a state of emergency, which also served as a cover for the regime's human rights violations. Al-Turabi, however, did not easily accept defeat and in February 2001 hammered out a memorandum of understanding between his new party, the Popular National Congress (PNC), and John Garang's SPLA. The bypassed President Bashir forestalled the scheme, had al-Turabi arrested and held him in detention for two-and-a-half years, until his release in October 2003.[19] At the end of March 2004, Hasan al-Turabi was arrested anew and remained in prison until June 2005.

Elimination of the architect of the Sudan's Islamisation programme of the nineties did not, however, lead to a political realignment. Bashir soon made clear that adherence to the shari´a was still a pivotal element of the regime's ideology. At the time of writing, the Islamist statutes are still in force and applied. The statement that the 'Islamic experiment' has come to an end seems therefore premature (Burr & Collins 2003: 253-280).

Peace at last?

In May 2004, a protocol on power sharing between the Bashir government and the SPLA's political wing, the SPLM, was signed in Naivasha, Kenya. In this 'Protocol between the Government of Sudan and the Sudan People's Liberation Movement (SPLM)', the latter agreed to the application of the shari´a in the capital Khartoum; other provisions of the agreement gave guarantees as to the protection of non-Muslims. In principle, the wording of these provisions was meant to safeguard the rights of non-Muslims in the capital, while simultaneously allowing for the continued application of the shari´a in Khartoum as the government saw fit.

In July 2005, the Interim National Constitution of Sudan was adopted after the National Congress Party, representing the central government and the SPLM, had reached a peace agreement (Comprehensive Peace Agreement – CPA) in January 2005. According to this agreement, the Sudan is to be governed by an interim constitution during the six-year transitional period. At the end of this period, in January 2011, a referendum will take place in Southern Sudan to determine whether the South will remain part of the Sudan or whether it will become an independent state. In all likelihood a majority of voters will opt for the latter.

In early 2010 it has become clear that the spirit of reconciliation as reflected in the protocol, the CPA, and in the interim constitution has not been translated into a stable legal and political reality since the signing of the CPA in 2005. Without cooperation of the international community to support CPA implementation and post-2011 arrangements as well as a lasting solution to the conflict in Darfur, the Sudan is risking a return to war.

5.5 Constitutional law

The 2005 Interim National Constitution (INC)[20] largely draws on its 1998 predecessor, but also contains provisions for power-sharing on a 70-30 basis with Southern Sudan; establishment of an upper house representing the states; and creation of a first and a second vice-president, with one of the two from Southern Sudan. Article 218 makes it obligatory for any person running in elections to respect the Comprehensive Peace Agreement and to enforce its main clauses.[21] The INC, not changing the territorial principle applicable before, maintains that the shari´a is to be effective in the North only, thus posing the problem of the status of non-Muslims living in the North. Article 160 calls for an Interim Constitution for 'Southern Sudan', which was promulgated in September 2005.[22]

Islam not the state religion

Only a few of the INC's articles make direct reference to Islam. Most importantly, the Sudan is not defined as an Islamic republic, nor is Islam the religion of the state (Böckenförde 2008: 85). Article 1 of the 1998 constitution set forth that '[t]he State of Sudan is an embracing homeland, wherein races and cultures coalesce and religions conciliate. Islam is the religion of the majority of the population. Christianity and customary creeds have considerable followers.' In comparison, in the INC references to Islam with respect to the nature of the state have been omitted. Instead, Article 1 (INC) states that the Sudan is a multi-racial, multi-ethnic, multi-religious, and multi-lingual state. Thus, *de jure* Islam is not the state religion.

Sources of legislation

Under the 1998 constitution, pivotal regulations, such as those concerning the sources of legislation, contained ambiguous language. Article 65, for instance, read as follows:

> Islamic law and the consensus of the nation, by referendum, Constitution and custom shall be the sources of legislation; and no legislation in contravention with these fundamentals shall be made; however, the legislation shall be guided by the nation's

public opinion, the learned opinion of scholars and thinkers, and then by the decision of those in charge of public affairs.

While Islamic law was named first in this list of sources of legislation, even for the South, it remained unclear what role the other sources were to play in relation to shari'a. In contrast, in the 2005 INC version of the constitution, it is clearly stated that the shari'a is not to play a role in Southern Sudan: 'Nationally enacted legislation having effect only in respect of the Northern states of the Sudan shall have as its sources of legislation Shari'a and the consensus of the people' (Art. 5 (1)). While Southern Sudan is to have its own non-shari'a-based legislation (Art. 5 (2)), the shari'a-clause for the North would leave non-Muslim Southerners in the North to be subject to Islamic law.[23] This situation has been addressed in part by certain safeguards that protect non-Muslims in Khartoum from being subjected to shari'a punishments. No similar provision exists, however, for non-Muslims living outside the capital.

Status of non-Muslims in the capital Khartoum

A fundamental difference with the 1998 constitution is a group of five provisions (Art.s 154-158) protecting the rights of non-Muslims in the capital Khartoum. Next to pledging respect for all religions in the capital (Art. 154), Article 156 outlines the principles that are to guide the dispensation of justice in Khartoum. Apart from the application of tolerance with respect to different cultures, religions, and traditions, Article 156 affirms that: 'The judicial discretion of courts to impose penalties on non-Muslims shall observe the long-established shari'a principle that non-Muslims are not subject to prescribed penalties, and therefore remitted penalties shall apply.' Article 157, finally, calls for the establishment of a special commission 'to ensure that the rights of non-Muslims are protected and respected [...] and not adversely affected by the application of Shari'a law in the National Capital'. It must be mentioned here that Article 156 contradicts the position of non-Muslims in the Criminal Act (1991) in many ways and that a faithful application of the INC would require a substantial reform of the Sudan's penal laws.

Eligibility of non-Muslims to become president of the Sudan

In 1998, Muslim dominance was further ensured by legislators who made Arabic the official language of the Sudan (Art. 3) and also bestowed supremacy (*hakimiyya*) in the state upon *Allah* (God), the creator of mankind (Art. 4). Governance (*al-siyada*) was bestowed upon the people of the Sudan, who practise it as worship of Allah. Thus, governance was exercised by the faithful worshippers of Allah, acting as his trustees. This wording essentially excluded secular Muslims and non-Muslims. These articles, however, have been omitted in the INC. According to the INC a non-Muslim could, theoretically, become president of the whole of the Sudan (Art. 53).

Omission of Islamic precepts

Equally omitted from the INC are most other articles from the 1998 constitution relating to Islamic precepts and notions, such as alms tax (*zakat*), state-based support for martyrs (*shuhada*), the purging of society from Muslims drinking alcohol, and so forth. It goes without saying that the 1991 Criminal Act and other existing laws (e.g. the Public Order Laws) on the different levels (e.g. state, governorate) still give the Northern Islamists enough leverage to pursue its policy of Islamisation and enforcement of Islamic law, at least as long as no substantial legal reforms are undertaken.

The INC expressly makes reference to and confirms the death penalty for *hadd* and retribution-related offences (*qisas*). It also confirms applicability of the death penalty for underage (below 18) and elderly (above 69) offenders in *hadd* or *qisas* cases (Art. 36).

Religious freedom

Concerning religious freedom, Articles 6 and 38 of the INC commit the state to all precepts of religious freedom normally associated therewith. Article 38 stipulates: 'Every one shall have the right to [...] declare his/her religion or creed and manifest the same [...]'. It should be noted here that this right must be seen in the light of the pertinent sections of the Criminal Act (1991), which make apostasy of Muslims punishable by death (Art. 126). Non-Muslims are, thus, free to convert to Islam, but not vice versa. In practise, however, death penalties have not been imposed in cases against converts since the promulgation of the Criminal Act in 1991.[24] But, discrimination against Christians and adherents of native religions was and is still commonplace,[25] irrespective of Article 31, which sets forth that '[a]ll persons are equal before the law and are entitled without any discrimination as to race, colour, sex, religious creed [...] to the equal protection of the law.'

(Un)Equal rights of women

The INC also guarantees men and women equal rights in the areas of civil, political, social, cultural, and economic rights (Art. 32). These guarantees, however, contradict to some degree other Sudanese legislation. Equal rights for men and women are especially relevant with regard to shari'a-based parts of the Criminal Act (1991) and in consideration of family and inheritance laws, which are known to be disfavourable to women in a variety of ways (see below). Article 15 of chapter II on the 'guiding principles and directives' of the INC guarantees that: 'No marriage shall be entered into without the free and full consent of its parties.' In the second section of the same article, the state is called upon to 'protect motherhood and women from injustice, promote gender equality and the role of women in family, and empower them in public life.' Article 22 of the same chapter, however, clarifies that these provisions 'are not by themselves enforceable in a court of law'.

The Constitutional Court

In 1998 a Constitutional Court was established, with jurisdiction over all issues related to the constitution. It can be appealed to by 'any aggrieved persons for the protection of freedoms, sanctities and rights' guaranteed in the constitution (Bantekas & Abu-Sabeib 2000: 543). The INC maintains the Constitutional Court whose president, a deputy, and five members are appointed by the president of the republic with the approval of two-thirds of the Council of States.[26] The president can, thus, ensure a composition of the court favourable to his interests.

5.6 Family and inheritance law

The relevant Muslim Personal Law Act (MPLA) of 1991 is predominantly based on the Hanafite school. However, in order to introduce reforms, particular solutions from the other three Sunni schools, especially the Malikite school, have been introduced (Ruiz-Almodovar 2000: 180; Ali 2001: 30). It is applicable, if both parties or only the husband are Muslim. Christians and Jews may use their respective laws with regard to personal status, marriage and divorce, if both partners belong to the same religious community. Members of Southern Sudanese tribes are subject to customary law. Customary laws with regard to marriage have been codified only for the Dinkas, Luos and Fertit in the Re-statement of the Bahr El Ghazal Customary Law Act (1984).[27] Customary law, however, remains to a large extent uncodified and unpublished. If both partners belong to the (small) community of Hindus, Hindu law is applicable (Ali 2001: 30).

Marriage

Mixed marriages and customary marriages

Even though a Muslim man can marry a non-Muslim woman as long as she belongs to 'a heavenly religion' (i.e. Christianity or Judaism), a Muslim woman cannot marry a non-Muslim man, unless the non-Muslim man converts to Islam (Art. 19 MPLA). In Southern areas not controlled by the government, this regulation is not enforced. In the case of mixed marriages between a Sudanese and a foreign citizen, the effects of such a marriage, such as property rights and child custody, are adjudicated in accordance with the laws of the husband's country.

Unregistered, customary (*´urfi*) marriages are considered valid, but do not result in the same legal rights for women. Under an *´urfi* marriage, for example, a woman is not entitled to alimony.

Dower

The marriage contract obliges the husband to pay a sum of money as a dower (*mahr*) to the wife (Art.s 27-31 MPLA). The dower can also take the form of services or other assets. The full dower gift, which becomes the property of the wife (Art.s 28-29), is due with the conclusion of a valid marriage contract confirmed by the consummation of the marriage. The two spouses can either agree on the dower before the marriage or, if no agreement has taken place, the 'fair *mahr*' (*mahr al-mithl*), based on the social status of the bride, is due at the time of marriage in accordance with Article 29(5) (Ali 2001: 75).

Maintenance during marriage

The wife is entitled to receive maintenance from her husband from the time of conclusion of a valid marriage contract (Art. 69 MPLA). Maintenance includes food, clothing, dwelling, medical treatment, and everything else required in order to live according to custom (*´urf*, Art. 65). In determining the maintenance due, the economic situation of the husband must be taken into consideration. If these circumstances change, the maintenance due changes with it (Art.s 66-67). Maintenance of the wife is due irrespective of whether the wife is well-to-do or has an income of her own. The MPLA (1991) does not recognise any obligation of the wife to contribute to the family income (Ali 2001: 83). In case the husband does not pay maintenance, or only pays part of it, the wife can claim up to three years of arrears, unless the spouses have come to a different agreement (Art. 70(1)).

The wife loses her right to maintenance, if she refuses to move to the common home without legally valid grounds, if she leaves the common home without legally valid grounds, if she prohibits the husband to enter the common home without legally valid grounds, if she works outside the home without the consent of the husband, or if she refuses to travel with her husband without legally valid grounds (Art. 75(a-e)).

Rights of wife and husband

Next to maintenance, the wife has the right to visit and to receive visits from her parents and close family (*maharim*) Wives, however, cannot travel abroad without the consent of their husband or male guardian. (Art. 51(a-b)). She is further entitled to protection with regard to her personal property (*'adam ta'arrud amwalha al-khassa*) and protection from material or mental harm. She also has the right to fair treatment *vis-à-vis* other wives, if the husband has more than one wife (Art. 51(a-d)).

The husband, in turn, has the right to be attended to and the right to obedience from his wife. She also has the duty to guard and defend him, his honour, and his property (Art. 52(a-b)).

Consent to marriage and guardianship

Both parties willing to marry must be past the age of puberty and must consent to marriage out of their own free will. The law does not stipulate a minimum age at which puberty can be considered to have been reached. Both the man and the woman have the right to call off the marriage (Art. 9(a)).

The male guardian (*wali*) marries adult women with their consent (Art. 34). If he refuses to consent to the marriage without justification, however, a judge can replace him and provide legal consent to the marriage in his stead. If the guardian refuses to consent to the marriage of his ward she can demand to be married by a judge (Art. 37(1)). The judge can authorise the marriage of whoever demands it, if it is proven that the guardian refuses to give his consent without legal justification (Art. 37(2)).

In meeting legal requirements for the witnessing of a marriage contract either the testimony of two men is permissible, or of one man and two women (Art. 26).

Divorce

A divorce can be realised in the following ways (Art. 127 MPLA): a) on the (formal) initiative of the husband (*talaq*); b) by initiative of both spouses (the so-called *khul'*), or repudiation against compensation (*talaq 'ala mal*); c) divorce on the initiative of the wife by court decision (*tatliq* or *faskh*); and d) death of one of the spouses.

Divorce initiated by the husband (talaq)

A marriage can be dissolved at any time by the unilateral repudiation by the husband or his representative (*talaq*) (Art.s 128-141); marriage dissolution initiated by the wife using the *talaq* procedure is also valid, if the husband has invested his wife with such authority (Art. 132). The husband does not need to give reasons for the repudiation, and it is not necessary that a court intervenes (Ali 2001: 100). There are two kinds of repudiations, revocable and irrevocable.

Revocable repudiation terminates the marriage contract only at the end of the waiting period (*'idda,*[28] see Art. 136(a)). The husband has the right to return to his wife during the *'idda* period, even against her will (Art.s 139-141). However, for the revocation of the repudiation to be valid, the repudiated wife must be informed of the repudiation within the *'idda* period (Art. 141). Irrevocable repudation terminates the marriage in two ways: 1) after a simple irrevocable repudiation (*talaq ba'in bainuna sughra*) the marriage can only be restored by concluding a new marriage contract and again paying the dower; and 2) after an absolutely irrevocable repudation (*talaq ba'in bainuna kubra*) the former marriage can only be restored by way of a new marriage (as in 1), if the divorced wife is first married to another man and this marriage is consummated and subsequently dissolved (Art. 136(b)).

Divorce initiated by both spouses (khul')

An alternative method of divorce is called *khul'* (Art.s 142-150). In this case both parties agree to dissolve a marriage without court intervention by means of a financial compensation to be paid to the husband by the wife. The financial settlement consists of the wife either returning the dower or giving up her rights to financial compensation, such as renouncing the payment of the parts of the dower not yet payed in exchange for a divorce. The financial settlement cannot be replaced by compensation of a non-monetary form, such as by the wife giving up custody rights to their common children (Ali 2001: 105). *Khul'* divorce is irrevocable.

Divorce initiated by the wife in court (tatliq)

In the framework of the *tatliq* (divorce) procedure, which recognises various valid grounds for divorce, the court intervenes. Grounds for divorce that may be invoked by the wife include, for example, situations such as the husband suffering from an incurable physical defect (Art.s 151-152) or impotence (Art.s 153-161); cruelty of the husband or discord between the spouses (Art.s 162-169); divorce by redemption (Art.s 170-173); failure of the husband to pay maintenance to the wife (Art.s 174-184); absence or imprisonment of the husband (Art.s 185-191); and refusal of the husband to have sexual intercourse with his wife (Art.s 192-195).

Maintenance and financial compensation after a divorce

Following divorce, the wife is entitled to maintenance during the *'idda* period (mentioned above), unless the divorce is the consequence of an illegal act on the part of the wife (Art. 72). A woman in the state of *'idda* who is not breastfeeding has the right to receive maintenance after the divorce for a maximum of up to one year (Art. 73(a)). A woman in the state of *'idda* who is breastfeeding receives maintenance for up to three months after the end of lactation. If she swears that her menstruation fails to appear due to breastfeeding, the period of maintenance will be prolonged to two years and three months after the birth of the child (Art. 73(b)).

In addition to the alimony described above, the divorced woman is entitled to a financial compensation (*mut'a*) equivalent to the maintenance of the *'idda*, not exceeding six months and according to the solvency of the ex-husband (Art. 138, Ali 2001: 110). However, in the following cases, the *mut'a* is not due: a) if the reason for the divorce is the non-payment of maintenance due to the lacking solvency of the husband; b) if the divorce has been caused by a fault (*'aib*) of the wife; and c) if the divorce has been reached by mutual consent against a payment by the wife (Art.s 138 and 2(a-c)).

Custody

After divorce the mother is entitled to custody of boys until they are seven years old and of girls until they are nine years old (Art. 115(1) MPLA). A judge can authorise the custody of divorced mothers for boys between seven years of age until they reach puberty and for girls between nine until the consummation of marriage if it is in the interest of the ward (Art. 115(2)). If the woman who has custody has a different religion than the Muslim father of the ward, she loses custody when the child reaches the age of five or at any time it is feared that she is raising the child in a different religion than that of the father (Art. 114(2)). The father or another male guardian is to supervise all affairs of the ward in the custody of the mother, such as education, guidance, and instruction (Art. 118). The custodial parent may not travel within the country except with the permission of the guardian of the child (Art. 119). On the other hand, the guardian (i.e. the father or another person) also cannot travel with the ward without the permission of the woman who has custody (Art. 120). Financial support of the child is the father's responsibility for girls until the daughter is married and for boys until the son is old enough to earn his own living (An-Na'im 2002: 85).

Polygamy and special clauses

Sudanese personal status law allows for polygamy (Art. 19(b) MPLA). However, the wife has the right to insert a clause in the marriage contract prohibiting the husband from taking additional wives. When there is a violation of this clause, the first wife can obtain a divorce without having to prove damage (*darar*). In general, any clause in the marriage contract is permitted, unless it 'allows for something prohibited or prohibits something permitted' (Art.s 42(1-3)). The husband cannot live with his second wife in the same house where he lives with his first wife, unless the first wife has agreed to such an arrangement. In the latter case, the first wife maintains the right to terminate cohabitation at any moment (Art. 79).

Inheritance

The inheritance laws discriminate against women. Male heirs receive twice the share given to females possessing the same degree of relation to the deceased. Daughters inherit half the share of sons in cases of the death of a parent. A widow inherits a smaller percentage than do her children. Heirs must also be adherents of the same religion. Thus, a non-Muslim widow cannot inherit from her Muslim husband except as a legatee in his will, which amounts to a maximum of one-third of his assets. Of the other two-thirds, distributed according to shari´a principles, she receives nothing (Art.s 344-400 MPLA).

5.7 Criminal law

The Sudan Criminal Act (CA) was promulgated in 1991. Its text is identical to that of a 1988 draft criminal code with the exception of a handful of amendments.[29] Related laws are the Criminal Procedure Act of 1991, and the Evidence Act of 1993.

Hudud offences

The Criminal Act of 1991 (CA), which is based on the pertinent qur´anic prescriptions, defines six offences as '*hudud* offences': drinking alcohol, unlawful sexual intercourse, unproven accusation of unlawful sexual intercourse, banditry, theft, and apostasy.[30]

Only Muslims are to be punished with forty lashes for the drinking of wine (*shurb al-khamr*), and, in extrapolation, for the consumption of any other intoxicating drink (Art.s 3 and 78(1) CA). Exceeding traditional Islamic jurisprudence, Sudanese criminal law also stipulates the same *hadd* punishment for individuals found guilty of the offence of production and/or possession of intoxicating beverages. Non-Muslims, though not subject to the above provisions, face the same punishment – whipping of up to forty lashes – for alcohol consumption in conjunction with causing public nuisance (Art. 78(2)). Recidivists who commit one of the above crimes or anyone found guilty of dealing in alcohol and indicted for the third time is liable to a prison term of up to three years or a whipping of up to eighty lashes; in other words, twice the amount of lashes stipulated for the *hadd* crime may be inflicted on the non-Muslim recidivist alcohol 'dealer'[31] (Art. 81). Non-Muslim women have been particular targets for indictments made in relation to alcohol-related offences.

Unlawful sexual intercourse (*zina*) is punishable by stoning for the *muhsan* and by one hundred lashes for the non-*muhsan*, with *muhsan* being defined as the legal status of an individual who, at the time of the commission of adultery, is in a valid and ongoing marriage that has been consummated (Art.s 145 and 146). Widowers, widows, and divorcees do not therefore fall under the definiton of *muhsan*, different from traditional Islamic jurisprudence (Scholz 2000: 445).

Female victims of rape have, in some instances, suffered grave injustices from Sudanese courts when the rape resulted in pregnancy. Since pregnancy out of wedlock is recognised as proof of unlawful sexual intercourse, in some cases pregnancy was taken for implicit proof of *zina*. In other words, rape can be proven either, rather unlikely, by four male witnesses to the crime or by a confession of the rapist, equally unlikely (Sidahmed 2001: 197-200). If neither the witnesses nor the confession could be produced, a conviction for unlawful sexual intercourse, proven by the fact of pregnancy, was permissible in court.[32] In other more recent cases, however, alleged rape has been recognised as legal doubt, the effect of which is to avert the *hadd* punishment.[33] In all of the cases referenced here, the (alleged) rapist was released for lack of evidence.

Offenders committing *zina* in the Southern states are not subject to the *hadd* punishments, but do face a prison term of up to one year for the non-*muhsan* and up to three years for the *muhsan*, in combination with a possible fine.[34] Non-Muslims in the North, however, are not exempted from the *hadd* punishments and are not treated differently from Muslims, according to the Criminal Act (1991).[35] Hetero- or homosexual anal intercourse (*liwat*) is not subsumed under the article on unlawful sexual intercourse (*zina*). In fact, it is not part of the *hudud* and consequently the prescribed punishment is equally applicable in the Southern states as it is to offenders in the North. Nevertheless, punishment is severe. First and second time offenders are sentenced to one hundred lashes and a prison term of up to five years; the third-time recidivist faces execution or life imprisonment (Art. 148).

Unproven accusation of unlawful sexual intercourse (*qadhf*) is punishable by eighty lashes under the condition that the victim of *qadhf* has not been previously convicted for unlawful sexual intercourse (*zina*), anal intercourse (*liwat*), rape, incest, or practising prostitution (Art. 157). While *liwat* has been defined separately from the *hadd* offence of unlawful sexual intercourse, it is now, inconsistently, subsumed under *qadhf* (Scholz 2000: 447). Among other reasons, the punishment for unproven accusation of unlawful sexual intercourse can be remitted if the offender is an ascendant of the victim or when the defamed person pardons the defamer before the execution of the punishment.

The *hadd* offence of banditry (*hiraba*) is a 'composite crime' and thereby punished according to the gravity of the crime(s) committed. As the smallest common denominator, the crime of *hiraba* is committed by whoever 'intimidates the public or hinders the users of a highway with the intention of committing an offence against the body, or honour, or property' (Art. 167). Thus, if murder or rape are committed in the context of *hiraba*, the punishment will be severe: execution or execution with subsequent crucifixion. If grievous hurt was committed or the property stolen reaches the minimum value required in cases of *hadd* theft, the punishment is cross-amputation, that is the amputation of the right hand and the left foot. All other cases of *hiraba* are punishable by a prison term of up to seven years in exile (*taghrib*). If the offender voluntarily abandons the commission of *hiraba* and declares his repentance before his arrest, the *hadd* penalty will be remitted. However, a prison term of up to five years may imposed and the rights of the victim with regard to *diya* (blood money) and/or compensation must be respected (Art. 169).

Hadd theft (*sariqa haddiyya*) is punishable by amputation of the right hand (and with a prison term of up to seven years for second time recidivists) (Art.s 171 (1) and 171(2)). In comparison to non-*hadd* theft, theft punishable by the *hadd* penalty must fulfil certain conditions. If one of these conditions is not met, the *hadd* penalty will not be due. Among these conditions are that the stolen property must reach a certain value (*nisab*); it must be taken from a safe place where moveable property is kept (*hirz*); and the property must be moveable, belong to another person, and must be taken covertly with the intention of appropriation (Scholz 2000: 449-451). A number of reasons can lead to the remittance of the punishment of amputation for theft (e.g. when the offender has or believes to have a share in the stolen property or when the theft takes place between ascendants and descendants or between spouses). The punishment is also remitted if the offender either restores the stolen property before being brought to trial or becomes the owner of it, or if he retracts his confession and the theft was proven by conviction only.

Apostasy (*ridda*), punishable by death, was codified for the first time in Sudanese history in 1991 (Art. 126 CA). Every Muslim who renounces the creed of Islam either by an express statement or by a conclusive act commits the crime of apostasy (Art. 126 (1)). The law, however, does not specify further which form such a statement or act must take to fall under this definition. Thus, this wording leaves a lot of room for interpretation and, therefore, abuse. However, apart from the notorious Muhammad Taha case (1985), no other execution for apostasy has been reported. Irrespective of the sex, the apostate is given a chance to repent during a period to be determined by the court. If the apostate recants before execution, the punishment will be remitted (Art.s 126(2) and 126(3)). Recent converts are exempted from the death penalty for apostasy (Art. 126 (2)).

Blood money and retribution

Other pertinent concepts of Islamic criminal law, such as blood money (*diya*) and retribution, have also been codified. Blood money has been enacted as possible compensation for crimes such as intentional homicide, semi-intentional homicide, and homicide by negligence (Art.s 130-132 MPLA); abortion (Art. 135); and the infliction of intentional and semi-intential wounds and wounds by mistake (Art.s 139-141).

Retribution (*qisas*, or literally 'an eye for an eye') is the penalty stipulated for causing intentional wounds. Article 29, however, sets forth precise conditions for retribution, namely that the two organs must be similar in type, soundness, and size. There will be no retribution except for a counterpart of the injured organ, and a sound organ cannot be taken for a defective one. Likewise, a whole organ can only be taken as retribution for the loss of a whole organ, and part of an organ only for the loss of a part.[36]

No Islamic criminal law in the South

The provisions of the Criminal Act (1991) on *hudud* offences – drinking alcohol and causing nuisance, dealing in alcohol, sale of carcasses, apostasy (*ridda*), for causing intentional wounds (*qisas*), unlawful sexual intercourse (*zina*), false accusation of unlawful sexual intercourse (*qadhf*), armed robbery (*hiraba*), and theft (*sariqa*) – are not applicable in the Southern states of the Sudan.[37]

Public Order Act

A more tangible enforcement of the regime's view of Islamic values than the Criminal Act of 1991 was, and still is, for many citizens the public order acts of individual governorates. The governorate of Khartoum's 'Khartoum Public Order Act' of 1996, which was 'introduced to storm against society's 'immorality' [...], to organise market places and to control public appearances' is particularly illustrative.[38] In addition to the relevant articles of the Criminal Act of 1991 on alcohol consumption, prostitution, obscene acts, and public morality, all of which were enforced from the time of their promulgation, Bashir issued complementary directives in November 1991 imposing Islamic dress in all government offices, schools, and universities (Sudanow 1992: 26-27). The Khartoum Public Order Act of 1996 went even further in controlling public space, adding new offences such as 'dancing between men and women', 'private parties' without permission, or 'singing of trivial songs' during a party. It further mandated gender separation in public transportation[39] and banned men from working in the hairdressing business. Contraventions against the Public Order Act and relevant articles under the Criminal Act (especially alcohol offences) are tried by Public Order Courts. Their rulings are carried out on the spot. To allow the accused to prepare a defence is not a requirement in Public Order Courts, neither is the right to legal assistance provided for (SIHA 2009: 14). In 2002, the Public Order Act was repealed and supplanted by a 'Security of the Society Law'. In 2009, this Security of the Society Law continued to be applied in Khartoum State.[40]

5.8 Economic law

Islamic finance

Islamic finance, closely linked to the establishment of Islamic banks, did not make its appearance in the Sudan before the late seventies. The first bank to apply Islamic principles was the Faisal Islamic Bank of Sudan (FIBS), which was established by a special act of parliament in 1977 granting it extensive tax concessions and freedom to transfer foreign currency. It began operating in 1978 and proved to be a considerable success. A net profit of 1 million Sudanese Pounds in 1979 rose to 21 million Sudanese Pounds in 1982, enabling the bank to pay to their shareholders 25 per cent return on their investment. Next to practising interest-free banking, the FIBS statutes stipulated that 10 per cent of net profits were to be distributed to the poor as *zakat* (Stiansen 2004a: 156-159).

The unprecedented success of the FIBS led to the establishment of other Islamic banks, some of which had close links with the main political groups.[41] Only the Umma Party did not run its own bank. The Muslim Brotherhood, who already had close links to the Tadamon Islamic Bank, managed in the early eighties to take over all important management positions of the FIBS. Audits of the Bank of Sudan disclosed that loans in many Islamic banks were given preferentially to members of the respective political group to which the bank had links. This had led to a very high default rate on such loans (Stiansen 2004a: 159).

In 1983 and 1984, the Civil Procedure Act, the Civil Transaction Act, and circulars from the Bank of Sudan gradually abolished interest-based bank lending and as of December 1984, Islamic forms of contracts such as *musharaka*, *murabaha*, and *mudaraba*[42] were introduced. Interest-bearing accounts were changed to comply with the new rules. Enforcement of the ban on interest, however, was lax, and in 1986 the new democratic government under Sadiq al-Mahdi re-introduced a choice between banking based on interest and non-interest banking by allowing compensatory rates on loans and the payment of compensatory rates on deposits (Stiansen 2002: 43, 53). The government led by Sadiq al-Mahdi did not, however, change the existing legislation on interest.

After the 1989 Islamist coup these compensatory rates were abolished and the streamlining of Islamic financial contracts gained momentum. Special attention was given to *murabaha* contracts, which until at least the late nineties were the dominant financial contract, used in as much as possibly 80 per cent of all financial transactions (Stiansen 2004b: 83). *Murabaha* contracts in theory consist of a sale agreement in which the bank buys a commodity on behalf of a customer. The latter pays when the good is delivered or after delivery on the basis of an agreed schedule. The profit margin charged by the bank is not considered to be interest because it cannot be changed, i.e. increased, even if the customer fails to pay after having received the commodity. The bank necessarily has to take physical possession of the commodity before it is handed out to the customer. Until the mid-nineties, however, *murabaha* contracts were little more than camouflaged interest-based transactions that minimised the risks for the banks. Thus, banks asked for down-payments, letters of guarantee, liens on real estate, or mortgage loans equivalent to the amount of the *murabaha* contract. The banks normally did not see the commodities bought for clients (Stiansen 2004b: 83). In 1993, a *fatwa* issued by the Bank of Sudan's Shari'a Council established criteria for *murabaha* contracts that would ensure their legality and also bring them closer to the spirit of the shari'a. But it took until 1995 before a tighter supervision by the Bank of Sudan led to an enforcement of the new rules.

The Sudan's experience with Islamic finance is paradoxical. Economically speaking, the experiment has been a failure; the financial sector is extremely weak. The IMF estimated in 1998/1999 that 18-19 per cent of bank loans had to be categorised as 'non-performing'.

Reasons for this weakness include factors external to Islamic finance such as high inflation rates, worsening terms of trade due to declining agricultural production, and the war in the South. Yet, factors inherent to the experience of Islamic finance in the Sudan, often in conjunction with a lack of political control, also contributed to the low performance of Islamic finance. Thus, the Bank of Sudan did little to supervise banks and curb fraud and corruption in connection with lending practises. Only in the late nineties did it introduce restrictions on loans to the higher management of banks and a ban on additional loans to already indebted customers (Stiansen 2004a: 164). Further, banks suffered from high default rates in agricultural finance, especially with regard to advance contracts (*salam*). In years of bad harvest, farmers saw themselves incapable of delivering what they had sold to the bank through such contracts. If no agreement with the bank could be reached, many farmers resorted to not harvesting at all. A breach of contract by farmers under such circumstances was accepted by the Sudanese government, but led to losses for banks of up to 50 per cent in agricultural investments (ibid).

In political terms, however, the introduction, application, and further development of a wide range of tools of Islamic finance has been a success. Sudanese banking laws until 2005 were based entirely on the Qur´an and Sunna, with convential, interest-based financial tools eliminated from the system. Despite these precautions, strong vestiges of interest-based financial techniques survived at least until the mid-nineties.[43] A further advantage for the regime, and closely connected to the application of Islamic finance, is the transfer of wealth to groups closely associated with the regime (Stiansen 2004a: 165).

The Comprehensive Peace Agreement 2005 alongside the Interim National Constitution, however, has changed the legal framework and context of finance in the Sudan. In fact Article 201(2) of the Interim Constitution provides for the establishment of a dual banking system consisting of an Islamic banking system in the North and a conventional banking system in Southern Sudan. The Central Bank shall be responsible for the use and development of both sets of banking instruments, the Islamic one and the conventional one (Art. 202(1)). The Bank of Southern Sudan, as a branch of the Central Bank of Sudan, provides, *inter alia*, conventional banking services (Art. 201(3)) to Southern Sudan. Likewise, the Central Bank of Sudan implements its monetary policy through an Islamic financing window in Northern Sudan and, managed by the Bank of Southern Sudan, through a conventional window in Southern Sudan (Art. 202(1)(a-b)).

Zakat

A national system of voluntary donations of wealthy Sudanese and companies was first institutionalised in 1980. With the application of the Zakat and Taxation Act in September 1984, however, *zakat* lost its character as a religious alms tax and took on instead the form of another tax within the existing taxation system. A Chamber of Zakat (*diwan al-zakat*) under the supervision of the president was created, but the collected sums were not managed on separate *zakat* accounts. Rather, they entered the very state budget they were intended to support. After the downfall of Numeiri in 1986, a new law on *zakat* made the *zakat* administration autonomous. From now on the collected sums were managed separately from the public treasury. The state, however, continued to supervise the use of *zakat* through the Ministry of Social Affairs. The last legislation on *zakat* was a presidential decree in 2001 which reorganised its collection on the national and regional levels (Converset & Binois 2006: 41-44).

Originally *zakat* was also levied on the salaries of all Sudanese citizens. However, due to a large amount of unregistered employment and a lack of control, this system became unmanageable. Today, unofficial *zakat*, i.e. voluntary *zakat* given by individuals, is not paid to the state, but is normally distributed within the families and relatives of the donators (Converset & Binois 2006: 45). In contrast, official *zakat* is levied on all commercial companies, farms, cattle-breeding and dairy operations, poultry farms, fisheries, and more. The proceeds are distributed in kind (cereals, flour, sugar, dates, lentils, etc.) to local institutions, such as hospitals, orphanages or qur'anic schools or in cash in the form of subventions or salaries paid especially to social or health institutions (Converset & Binois 2006: 53).

Some authors claimed in the mid-nineties that the funds levied were being partially re-funnelled into the Islamisation programme, the war in the South, efforts to proselytise prisoners of war, and possibly even used to the personal benefit of high-ranking government supporters (Lauro & Samuelson 1996: 9). Criticism has not fallen silent in more recent times. In particular, critics express concern with maladministration of the collected money, lavish spending on cars and buildings, and the sumptuous lifestyle of parts of the *zakat* management and personnel (Converset & Binois 2006: 42).

5.9 Human rights obligations

The Sudan is party to a number of international human rights treaties, including the International Covenant on Economic, Social, and Cultural

Rights (ICESCR), the Covenant on Civil and Political Rights (ICCPR), the Convention on the Elimination of All Forms of Racial Discrimination (ICERD), and the Convention on the Rights of the Child (CRC). Further, the Sudan is party to the Convention on the Prevention and Punishment of the Crime of Genocide, the Slavery Convention, and the Convention relating to the Status of Refugees. The Sudan is also party to the International Convention on the Suppression and Punishment of the Crime of Apartheid and the African Charter on Human and Peoples' Rights. The Sudan has signed, but not yet ratified, the Convention against Torture and other Cruel, Inhuman or Degrading Treatment or Punishment (CAT). The Sudan is not a party to the Convention on the Elimination of All Forms of Discrimination against Women (CEDAW). With regard to the CAT and CEDAW, the government argues that some of the articles in the two conventions do not comply with the principles of shari´a. In January 2001, President Bashir reportedly said that the Sudan would not sign CEDAW because it was held to contradict Sudanese family values. As of early 2010, the Sudan still had not become party to the two conventions.[44]

Immediately after the 1989 coup, the Bashir regime suspended the 1985 Transitional Constitution and ruled by constitutional decrees enacted by the Revolutionary Command Council (RCC). In relation to this, the Sudan's initial report (1991) to the U.N. Human Rights Committee lodged a derogation concerning its obligations under the ICCPR:

> It became expedient to proclaim a state of emergency with the inevitable derogation from Sudan's obligations under the Covenant on Civil and Political Rights [...] With the achievement of more progress in the peace process and the establishment of the political system, that state of emergency will be naturally lifted and the derogation from Sudan's obligations under the Covenant will be terminated forthwith.

Since that 1991 report, first in 1998, and then in 2005, new constitutions have been enacted, the first of which, in turn, has been partially suspended due to the imposition of emergency law in 1999. It is unclear whether with the lifting of the state of emergency in 2005 in most of the Sudan the above derogations have become groundless.

Legal contradictions between the shari´a and human rights in national and international law

The INC of 2005 (see 5.5) does not mention international human rights as a source of legislation. Article 27 states that 'all rights and freedoms enshrined in international human rights treaties, covenants and instruments ratified by the Republic of the Sudan shall be an integral part of the Bill of Rights (i.e. the INC). It is, however, not clear that these international human rights treaties and conventions enjoy the same legal recognition as other articles of the constitution, nor does the INC explicitly mention that these treaties and conventions are enforcable in Sudanese courts.[45]

In fact, in many instances the INC subjects itself to 'prescribed laws', thus inverting the usual practise of the hierarchy of norms.[46] To date, little progress has been made concerning the adjustment of statutory laws in order to make them compliant with the Interim National Constitution and international human rights conventions to which the Sudan is party.[47]

Thus, Sudanese criminal legislation is clearly in conflict with the country's commitments under Article 7 of the ICCPR, banning torture, cruel, inhuman, and degrading treatment. Especially shari'a-based punishments such as flogging, stoning, crucifixion, and amputation as stipulated in the 1991 Penal Code plainly contradict the ICCPR. While I could not find any trace of an execution of stoning, the punishment of flogging is imposed and executed on a regular basis. While Article 14(5) of the ICCPR guarantees the right of appeal, sentences to flogging in accordance with the Security of the Society Law are in practice carried out instantaneously, and without counsel. The Criminal Act (CA) 1991 allows in cases concerning the *hudud* and *qisas* the death penalty for individuals below the age of 18, while the ICCPR and the CRC both prohibit death sentences against offenders who have not yet reached the legal age of maturity. The *hadd* offence of apostasy and its respective punishment constitute a violation of Article 18(1) of the ICCPR, which guarantees freedom of thought, conscience, and religion. It is also discriminatory in its differential treatment of adherents of the different faiths.

Important shari'a-based stipulations of the CA do not exempt non-Muslims in the northern governorates. Thus, Article 168(1) on armed robbery (*hiraba*) provides for the death penalty and/or crucifixion for Muslims and non-Muslims alike. Similarly, Article 171(1) punishes capital theft (*sariqa*) with amputation of the right hand, irrespective of the faith of the offender. It goes without saying that cruel corporal punishments as such constitute a human rights violation, no matter whether the person sentenced is Muslim or not. In practice non-Muslims in the North are frequently victims of shari'a-based legislation on alcohol-related offences. Thus, the majority of prisoners in the Omdurman Women's Prison were imprisoned for alcohol-related offences. More recently, the Sudanese government seems to have taken measures to rectify this situation.[48]

While the Sudan has not yet signed CEDAW, it is important to mention that the Muslim Personal Law Act 1991 is in contradiction with Article 16 of CEDAW, which calls for equal rights of men and women with regard to their rights to enter a marriage out of their free will and equal rights with regard to its dissolution, and with regard to equal rights and responsibilities as parents and concerning guardianship (Tønnessen & Roald 2007: 27-29). CEDAW also calls on state parties to accord women equality with men before the law (Art. 15). This provision is in clear contradiction with the reduced status of female witnesses in the Sudanese Evidence Act 1993.

Apart from contradictions between the Sudan's obligations under the ICCPR and other human rights covenants and its shari´a-based national legislation, there are many examples of violations of the Sudan's international obligations at a *de facto* level. In addition to the well-known mass killings and mass rape in Dar Fur, one of the most blatant human rights violations that has long persisted throughout the country is the recurrent scourge of slavery. Banned by both the ICCPR (Art. 8) and the Slavery Convention, it has nevertheless continued to be practised with impunity (Lobban 2001 and Darfur Consortium 2009).

5.10 Conclusions

Diversity of legal systems that influenced the Sudan

As this study demonstrates, the Sudanese legal system has been shaped and influenced by a variety of sources since the nineteenth century: by Ottoman-Egyptian law in the nineteenth century, by common law from the beginning of the condominium rule in 1898, by jurisdiction and laws either influenced by or based on the shari´a throughout the history of Islamic Sudan, by modern Egyptian civil law since the early 1970s, by customary law during the entire history of the Sudan, and by the diverse family laws of different denominations. While the different ingredients have occupied different spaces at different times, certain tendencies can be filtered out for the post-colonial period.

The camp advocating for Egyptianisation of the legal system can claim victory for the important field of civil law. After the failed introduction of a slightly modified version of Egyptian civil law in 1971, a second attempt in 1984 was successful. The Sudan has, thus, joined the large group of Arab states that have adopted Egyptian civil law.[49]

Further, the Sudanese legislation has to some extent since 1983 gone through an accelerated process of Islamisation. For more than twenty years, two autocratic regimes have expanded the influence of the shari´a to the detriment of Sudanese legal tradition and customary law. The shari´a has importantly influenced criminal legislation, banking laws, taxation laws (*zakat*), the 1998 and 2005 constitutions, and, as in most Muslim countries, family and inheritance laws for Muslims.[50]

However, with regard to the actual implementation of the *hudud* it has been noted that 'the new legislators seemed rather keen to give an impression of moderate and considerate application as opposed to the cavalier deployment that characterised the 1983 experiment' (Sidahmed 1997: 220). Even though no precise statistics for the number of stonings, crucifixions, floggings, and limb amputations inflicted between 1989 and 2008 is available, a synopsis of the relevant human rights reports since 1989 corroborates Sidahmed's assumption. Enhancing the regime's legitimacy and drawing a boundary 'within which the regime accommodates or excludes other political forces' (Sidahmed 1997: 222), the shari'a – well embedded in a multitude of Islamisation measures – has ostensibly fulfilled the regime's need for Islamic symbolism.

At present, the Sudan possesses a legal system that is characterised by a high degree of legal pluralism. The heritage of the common law is, despite the ups and downs of twenty years of Islamisation efforts, still clearly visible in two important aspects: first of all, certain laws of the time of the condominium are still valid, and, secondly, more recent legislation can be traced back to the condominium in terms of organisation and wording. Most significantly, despite efforts of the Bashir government to marginalise it, customary law is still of major importance in the rural areas of the Sudan. It is estimated that as much as 80 per cent of all cases in the Sudan are judged in accordance with customary law.[51]

Resistance in the North and in the South

The Islamised legislation, introduced by former President Numeiri and reinforced by the current President Umar al-Bashir continues to be objected to by the non-Muslim minority living predominantly in Southern Sudan and in and around the capital Khartoum. Fears of further Islamisation and deep disagreement concerning the Sudanese religio-political identity fuelled the armed rebellion in the South from 1983 to 2005. Compromises over shari'a legislation as negotiated in the 2004 Naivasha peace protocol and stipulated in the Interim National Constitution are a step in the right direction. However, underlying, more complex questions such as the nature of a future constitution, which must include acceptable formulas on democracy, the rule of law, and Sudanese identity, will have to be tackled first.

It can be safely assumed that there is important opposition to the current variant of Islamised legislation in the North as well. It was not without reason that the major thrust for the Islamisation of the legal system came from rather unpopular autocratic regimes. However, during the short-lived democratic interludes (1964-1969 and 1985-1989), the traditional sectarian parties have neither managed to present a viable constitution nor have they translated their own calls for a shari´a-based legislation into lasting concepts, simultaneously acceptable to the Muslim majority and reassuring the non-Muslim minority at the same time.

Contradictions with human rights conventions

The Islamisation programme has also led to serious contradictions between the Sudan's obligations under international human rights covenants and its national shari´a-based legislation. Sudanese government officials have forwarded arguments to counter criticism. At a base level, they maintain that international human rights legislation, such as the ICCPR, forms an integral part of the Sudan's national legislation and can be invoked before national courts within the Sudan.[52] Another popular argument is that 'the rights of the individual [i.e. in an Islamic society] should not prejudice the rights of the community or its public interest'. In other words, the rights of the Muslim community supersede the rights of the individual, irrespective of international treaties. Further to this point, President Bashir has excluded the Sudan's future adherence to CEDAW, claiming that it contradicts Sudanese family values.

It is indeed the case that the Sudan's Islamisation programme, facilitated by emergency laws, has led to a multitude of human rights violations, stemming, among other motives, from a profound disregard of the Bashir regime for the rights of religious minorities, women, non-Arab Muslims, and those professing views of Islam differing from the official Sudanese regime position. Many of the Sudan's human rights violations, however, have no relation whatsoever to shari´a. They must, rather, be attributed to the regime's efforts to stay in power at all costs. Islam, in this context, only serves as one instrument among many others, to attain this goal (Böckenförde 2008: 88).

Perspectives for the future

The January 2005 Comprehensive Peace Agreement (CPA) between the Sudanese government and the SPLM was supposed to lead to important reforms of the legal system. A new constitution is a key issue on the agenda. Apart from some limited changes, the CPA has, however, not yet led to a substantial revision of criminal legislation. Rather, the government stalled any legal reform that could be construed either by its opponents or by its followers as a gradual retreat from its pro-shari´a positions. The CPA, as much as it has been welcomed by the international community, represents a piecemeal approach. In order to achieve a lasting peace in the whole of the Sudan, the regime needs to come to terms with its opponents in Dar Fur, in Eastern Sudan and abroad as well. Only then can legal reforms be expected that take into account the interests of secular Muslims and non-Muslim minorities.

For the time being, several committees concerned with elaborating legal reforms have been set up. Thus, the National Constitutional Review Commission (NCRC), provided for by the CPA and composed of members from several political parties, has identified over sixty laws in contradiction with international human rights standards. It is currently working on certain priority areas such as arrest procedures, rape legislation, evidence laws, and immunity.[53] In 2006 already, the Legislative Standing Committee of the National Assembly (Majlis Watani) had singled out twelve laws for priority areas of reform, including among others the Criminal Act, the Criminal Procedure Act, and the Evidence Act. Other steps were the adoption of a National Action Plan on Combating Violence against Women in 2005 and a new Armed Forces Act (2007), which recognises rape committed in war as an international crime. In 2009 international crimes, such as crimes against humanity, genocide and war crimes, were incorporated in the Criminal Code. Observers, however, are doubting 'whether these changes can result in effective application' (REDRESS 2009: 37-38). The same observers have pointed out that the law reform process since the signing of the CPA has been hampered by a lack of transparency, delays, and 'the lack of mechanisms that ensure the conformity of reformed legislation with the provisions of the INC and the CPA' (REDRESS 2009: V).

In a nutshell, in the beginning of 2010 the Sudan's outlook is rather bleak. The implementation of the Comprehensive Peace Agreement has been obstructed by the North from the beginning. But not only the CPA, also the Darfur Peace Agreement and the East Sudan Peace Agreement lack proper implementation. With less than a year to go until the referendum on the South's self-determination, the referendum will most likely end in a decision in favour of the South's separation. Given the profound lack of trust between both sides a return to the North-South war is looming (International Crisis Group 2009: 1). What these developments will mean for the space the shari'a occupies in the legal system of the Sudan remains to be seen. If indeed a new civil war between the North and the South breaks out, guarantees for non-Muslims given under the INC will become meaningless. Should both sides manage to disentangle peacefully, an important source of pressure against shari'a application would disappear. In either case, the shari'a is likely to hold its ground in the legal system of the Sudan.

Notes

1 The author wishes to thank Prof. Abdullahi Ahmad An-Na'im, Dr Hamouda Fathelrahman, and Noah Salomon for reading and commenting on this article. He also thanks Julie Chadbourne for her meticulous proofreading. Olaf Köndgen holds an M.A. in Islamic Studies from the Free University of Berlin and is currently preparing a Ph.D. dissertation on Islamic criminal law in the Sudan (University of Amsterdam).

2 Estimates of the number of Christians vary widely. Some sources claim that very successful missionary activities have increased the percentage of Christians up to 20% of the overall population.

3 As to the paucity of studies of this era, see Bleuchot 1994: 161-185 and Köndgen 1992: 15.

4 The Malikite *madhhab* was the traditional school in the Sudan until the introduction of the Hanafite school.

5 See also the revealing dialogue between Hasan al-Turabi and Phillip Abbas Gobosh in An-Na'im 1985: 329.

6 A small minority, however, preferred to break off and establish their own organisation. This splinter group called itself 'the Muslim Brotherhood', while the majority faction was organised as the National Islamic Front under their political leader Hasan al-Turabi.

7 In 1983 alone, around 640,000 refugees from Ethiopia, Uganda, and Chad entered the Sudan. See also Abd al-Rahim 1989: 284.

8 Warburg 2003: 187 maintains that Numeiri dismissed al-Turabi 'so that he would not claim the credit for the Islamic laws'.

9 The 1983 Penal Code stipulated *hadd* punishments for crimes similar to *hadd* offences, but not covered by traditional definitions (Köndgen 1992: 42-44).

10 During a prison term in 1946-1948, Taha had developed his own legal theory, propagating a liberal version of the shari'a, adapted to the needs of modern society. Based on his teachings, the Republican Brothers, who had never participated in elections as a political party, called for a democratic state with equal rights for Muslims and non-Muslims and for both men and women. On the juridical aspects of the Taha case see An-Na'im 1986. On Taha and his weltanschauung see Rogalski 1990: 59-121.

11 See discussion in e.g. 'Mahmoud Taha – Sudan's new martyr?', *Middle East*, February 1987.

12 See *Sudan Monitor*, December 1990, Vol. 1, issue 6.

13 However, the elections were a setback for the DUP who gained only 63 seats instead of the 101 seats it had won in 1968. The Umma, in contrast, went up from 72 seats (1968) to 100 seats. See also Kok 1995: 43-49.

14 Altogether, 48 seats remained unoccupied as a result of the war (Kok 1991: 45).

15 See e.g the 1989 article 'Les Chrétiens et la Législation sur la Shari'a au Soudan', in *Islam et Societés au Sud du Sahara* 3.

16 Flogging, used rather summarily under the September laws, had been limited to *hadd* offences.

17 In an interview with al-Turabi's son Sadiq Hasan al-Turabi, it was confirmed that the imprisonment of his father was meant to cover up his involvement in the coup. Personal communication with Sadiq Hasan al-Turabi, dated 10 June 2004.

18 This information was confirmed in an interview with a lawyer at the Institute of Training and Legal Reform in Khartoum on 8 June 2004. However, according to the same source, three women were shortlisted for positions as judges in June 2004.

19 See BBC News online, 'Sudan strongman Turabi arrested', dated 21 February 2001; See BBC News online, 'Sudan Islamist leader released', dated 13 October 2003.

20 See http://www.reliefweb.int/library/documents/2005/govsud-sud-16mar.pdf.

21 The Heidelberg-based Max Planck Institute for Comparative Public Law and International Law (MPI) originally helped to prepare a constitutional framework for the content of the six separate peace protocols. However, the MPI 'Draft Constitutional Framework for the Interim Period' was not adopted by the Sudanese government. Subsequently, the Sudanese government, against the wishes of the SPLM, excluded the MPI from the process and instead relied on their own legal experts. See http://www.qantara.de/webcom/show_article.php/_c-476/_nr-593/i.html. The MPI's draft is downloadable on its website.

22 See http://www.cushcommunity.org/constitution.pdf.

23 For the full text of the Interim Constitution 2005 see the website of the Max Planck Institute: http://www.mpil.de/shared/data/pdf/inc_official_electronic_version.pdf.

24 The hanging of Taha in 1985 is to my knowledge until today the only known execution in the Sudan on the grounds of apostasy.

25 Non-Muslim university graduates have difficulty finding government jobs. There is an undeclared policy of Islamisation of public services in place, leading to non-Muslims losing their jobs in the civil service, the judiciary, and other professions. Christian secondary school students have not been allowed to finish their obligatory military service because they attended church (U.S. Department of State 2003). This is critical because students who do not complete their military service are not permitted to study at universities. There are also recurrent reports of *hadd* punishments being inflicted on Christians. Furthermore, while Muslims may proselytise among non-Muslims, proselytisation among Muslims is *de facto* excluded, since apostasy of Muslims is punishable by death.

26 The newly formed National Legislature, whose members were chosen in mid-2005, has two chambers: the National Assembly (Majlis Watani), i.e. the Lower House and the Council of States (Majlis Wilayat), the Upper House. The National Assembly consists of 450 appointed members, representing the government, former rebels and other oppositional political parties. The Council of States consists of 50 members. These are indirectly elected by state legislatures.

27 For details on Dinka law see e.g. Makec 1986.

28 *ʹidda*: period after a divorce during which remarriage is prohibited in order to guarantee that the wife is not pregnant by her ex-husband.

29 After the downfall of Numeiri in 1985, none of the subsequent military and civilian governments abolished the Islamised penal code, which was introduced in September 1983. After long discussions and some cosmetic modifications (Köndgen 1992: 61-72), the Ministry of Justice, with Hasan al-Turabi as minister and chief public prosecutor at the time, finally submitted a new draft penal code in September 1988. The draft did not have majority support in parliament. However, the new Bashir military Islamist regime that came to power a year later in 1989 drew significantly from the 1988 draft law when it promulgated the Sudan Criminal Act in 1991.

30 For an in-depth comparison between *hadd* offences as defined in the Criminal Act (1991) and traditional Islamic jurisprudence (*fiqh*) see Scholz 2000.

31 'Dealing in alcohol' in the definition of Article 79, CA91 includes storing, selling, purchasing, transporting, and possessing with the intention of dealing therein with others.

32 See cases of Mariam Muhammad 'Abdallah (1985) and Amina Babikr Ahmad (1985), published in *Sudan Law Journal and Reports* (SLJR) of the same year.

33 See e.g. cases of Mariam Muhammad Sulaiman (1989) and Kalthum ʹAjabna (1992), published in *Sudan Law Journal and Reports* of the same years. Compare analysis in Sidahmed 2001.

34 Interestingly, the concept of *muhsan*/non-*muhsan*, which is derived from Islamic criminal law, is applied here to Sudanese citizens who live in areas exempted from the application of the shari´a.

35 For the somewhat contradictory legal situation as of 2005, see chapter 5.5 'Constitutional Law'.

36 Compare also Articles 30-32: on multiple retribution; reasons for the remittance of retribution; and on the relatives of the victim who are entitled to retribution.

37 These provisions, however, become applicable if the accused himself requests their application or the legislative body concerned decides to the contrary. Compare Criminal Act (1991), Art. 5(3).

38 Ratified in October 1996 by the Khartoum State Council as the Khartoum State Public Order Act 1996 in its original form. The Khartoum State Public Order Act was valid only in the Governorate of Khartoum. Similar laws were promulgated in other governorates of the Sudan. See also SIHA (2009): 9-10.

39 During my visits in 2004 and 2009 I observed that this provision was not enforced in Khartoum.

40 A case that found a lot of attention from Western media was the arrest of Lubna Hussein, a well-known Sudanese journalist. She had been arrested in a restaurant for wearing trousers, together with twelve other women. Hussein, however, was indicted under Article 152 of the Criminal Code (1991), not under the Security of the Society Law. See SIHA 2009: 5-6.

41 In this formative phase of Islamic banking in the Sudan, before 1983, some of the newly established banks called themselves 'Islamic' without offering interest-free banking (Stiansen 2004a: 157).

42 For a discussion of Islamic financial contracts as applied in Sudan see Stiansen 2004b: 80-89.

43 It should be noted that the Sudanese government accepts interest-based foreign loans.

44 For CEDAW see http://www.un.org/womenwatch/daw/cedaw/reports.htm#s, for CAT see http://treaties.un.org/Pages/ViewDetails.aspx?src=TREATY&mtdsg_no=IV-9&chapter=4&lang=en.

45 The INC explicitly states that rights described in its Chapter II ("Guiding Principles and Directives") are "not by themselves enforceable in a court of law (art.22)." For a detailed critique of the 2005 Interim National Constitution see 'Observations on the Transitional Constitution', *The Sudanese Human Rights Quarterly* 20 (January 2006).

46 See for example the freedom of beliefs (Art. 38), the right to vote (Art. 41), and the right to own property (Art. 42).

47 On the conflict between Sudanese criminal law and human rights see e.g. REDRESS 2008.

48 According to a government statement, around 800 individuals convicted for alcohol-related offences were released. See REDRESS 2008: 11.

49 For example, Jordan, Iraq, Syria, Algeria, Yemen, Kuwait, and others. See Krüger 1997. Witness to the importance of Egyptian civil law for Sudanese jurists are Khartoum's book shops. Wherever legal literature is available, Egyptian commentaries abound.

50 This is to name the most important legislation of the present regime. It should be noted that systematic research on the influence of Islamic law on the Sudanese legislation from 1989 until present is lacking.

51 Interview with Supreme Court judge, Khartoum, on 6 June 2004.

52 International human rights law is indeed invoked by Sudanese attorneys before Sudanese courts. See personal communication with Noah Salomon, University of

Chicago, on 30 April 2004. I am, however, not aware whether these attempts were successful.

53 For an assessment of current legal reform projects see REDRESS 2009.

Bibliography

Abd al-Rahim, M. (1989), 'Le Soudan indépendant: Gouvernements militaires et coups d'états civils (1956-1985)', in M. Lavergne (ed.), *Le Soudan contemporain*. Paris: Karthala.

Abdelmoula, A.M. (1996), 'The "fundamentalist" agenda for human rights: The Sudan and Algeria', *Arab Studies Quarterly* 18(1): 1-28.

Ali, M.H.F. (2001), *Das islamische Ehe- und Kindschaftsrecht im Sudan: Mit Hinweisen zu den Lehren der Islamischen Rechtsschulen, der anwendbaren Familienrechtsvorschriften für Nichtmuslime im Sudan und im deutschen Familienrecht*. Frankfurt a.M.: Peter Lang.

Amin, S.H. (1985), *Middle East legal systems*. Glasgow: Royston.

Amnesty International (1995), *The tears of orphans*. London: Amnesty International.

An-Na'im, A.A. (1985), 'The elusive Islamic constitution: The Sudanese experience', *Orient* 26: 329-340, 468.

An-Na'im, A.A. (1986), 'The Islamic law of Apostasy and its modern applicability: A case from The Sudan,' *Religion* 16: 197-223.

An-Na'im, A.A. (ed.) (2002), *Islamic family law in a changing world*, 82-85. London/New York: Zed Books.

Bantekas, I. & H. Abu-Sabeib (2000), 'Reconciliation of Islamic law with constitutionalism: The protection of human rights in Sudan's new constitution', *African Journal of International and Comparative Law* 12(3): 531-553.

Bartleby (2010), 'Sudan', in *World Factbook*, see http://www.bartleby.com (2008 statistics) and https://www.cia.gov/library/publications/the-world-factbook/geos/su.html (online edition, last accessed Feb. 2010). Washington D.C.: Central intelligence Agency.

Beck, K. (2001), 'Sudan', in J.E. Mabe (ed.), *Afrika-Lexikon*. Stuttgart: J.B. Metzler.

Bleuchot, H. (1994), *Les cultures contre l'homme? Essai d'anthropologie historique du droit pénal soudanais*. Aix-en-Provence: Presse universitaire d'Aix Marseille.

Böckenförde, Markus (2008), 'The Sudanese interim constitution of 2005', in B. Krawietz & H. Reifeld (eds.), Islam and the Rule of Law: Between Shari'a and Secularization. St. Augustin and Berlin: Konrad-Adenauer-Foundation.

Burr, J.M. & R.O. Collins (2003), *Revolutionary Sudan: Hasan al-Turabi and the Islamist state, 1989-2000*. Leiden: Brill.

Converset, E. & J.-M. Binois (2006), 'La zakat au Soudan: Une alternative islamique à l'aide humanitaire internationale?', independent study published by Institut Univ. D'Etudes du Développement, Genève.

Daly, M.W. (1997), 'Sudan', in *Encyclopaedia of Islam*, New Edition, Volume IX, 746-751. Leiden: Brill.

Darfur Consortium (2009), Darfur. Abductions, sexual slavery and forced labor. Online edition: http://www.antislavery.org/includes/documents/cm_docs/2009/d/darfur.pdf

El-Affendi, A. (1991), *Turabi's revolution: Islam and power in the Sudan*. London: Grey Seal.

Elliesie, H. (2005), 'Friedensprozeß und Verfassungsentwicklung im Sudan', *Verfassung und Recht in Übersee*, 38 Jahrgang, Heft 3: 276-307.

Fluehr-Lobban, C. (1987), *Islamic law and society in the Sudan*. London: Frank Cass.

Gallab, A. (2008), *The first Islamist republic: Development and disintegration of Islamism in the Sudan*. Aldershot: Ashgate.

WLUML, no authors (1997), 'Legal Aid, New Laws & Violence Against Women in Sudan' in *Women living under Muslim laws*, dossier 18 (Oct.), 81, published by International Solidarity Network of Women Living Under Muslim Laws (WLUML), see http://www.

wluml.org/sites/wluml.org/files/import/english/pubs/rtf/dossiers/dossier18/D18-09-vaw-sudan.rtf.
Holt, P.M. (1997), 'Fundj', in *Encyclopaedia of Islam*, New Edition, Vol. II, 943-945. Leiden: Brill.
Ibrahim, N. (2007), 'Post CPA (2007): Restructuring and enhancing the Sudanese judiciary as a means of preserving peace', *Verfassung und Recht in Übersee*, 40 Jahrgang, Heft 4: 471494.
International Crisis Group (2005), 'Sudan's Partial Peace', press release, dated 7 January, see http://www.crisisgroup.org/home/index.cfm?id=3207&l=1&m=1.
International Crisis Group (2009), 'Sudan: Preventing implosion', Africa Briefing No. 68, Nairobi/Brussels, dated 17 December, see http://www.crisisgroup.org/library/documents/africa/horn_of_africa/b68_sudan___preventing_implosion.pdf.
Jeppie, S. (2003), *The making and unmaking of colonial Shari'ah in the Sudan*, unpublished paper read at 46th annual meeting of the African Studies Association, Boston, 30 October – 2 November 2003.
Khalid, M. (2003), *War and peace in the Sudan: A tale of two countries*. London: Kegan Paul.
Kok, P.N. (1989), 'La transition permanente (analyse des constitutions et du système juridique soudanais de 1956 à 1988)', in M. Lavergne, *Le Soudan Contemporain*, 435-467. Paris: Khartala.
Kok, P.N. (1991), 'Conflict over laws in the Sudan: From pluralism to monolithicism', in H. Bleuchot, C. Delmet & D. Hopwood (eds.), *Sudan: History, identity, ideology*, 235-252. Reading: Ithaca Press.
Köndgen, O. (1992), *Das islamisierte Strafrecht des Sudan: Von seiner Einführung 1983 bis Juli 1992*. Hamburg: Deutsches Orient-Institut.
Krüger, H. (1997), 'Überblick über das Zivilrecht der Staaten des ägyptischen Rechtskreises', *Recht van de Islam* 14: 67-131.
Lauro, L.J.& P.A. Samuelson (1996), 'Toward pluralism in Sudan: A traditionalist approach', *Harvard International Law Journal* 37(1): 65-138.
Lawyers Committee for Human Rights (1996), *Beset by contradictions: Islamization, legal reform, and human rights in Sudan*. New York.
Layish, A. (1998), 'The legal methodology of the Mahdi in the Sudan, 1881-1885: Issues in marriage and divorce', *Sudanic Africa* 8: 37-66.
Layish, A. (2000), 'The Mahdi's legal methodology as a mechanism for adapting the Shari'a in the Sudan to political and social purposes', *Revue des Mondes Musulmans et de la Méditerranée* 91-94: 221-237.
Layish, A. and G.R. Warburg (2003), *The Reinstatement of Islamic law in Sudan under Numayri*. Leiden: Brill.
Lesch, A.M. (1998), *The Sudan: Contested national identities*. Bloomington/Indianapolis: Indiana University Press.
Lobban, R. (2001), 'Slavery in the Sudan since 1989', *Arab Studies Quarterly* 23(2): 31-39.
Makec, J.W. (1986), *The customary law of the Dinka*. Khartoum: St. George Printing Press.
Martin, R. (2002), 'Sudan's Perfect War', *Foreign Affairs* March/April: Online edition: http://www.foreignaffairs.com/articles/57818/randolph-martin/sudans-perfect-war.
Mennen, T. (2007), 'Legal pluralism in Southern Sudan: Can the rest of Africa show the way?', *Africa Policy Journal* Vol. 3 (Spring). Online edition: http://www.hksafricapolicyjournal.com/sites/default/files/Legal_Pluralism_in_Southern_Sudan_-_Can_the_Rest_of_Africa_Show_the_Way.pdf.
Merheb, N. (1995), 'Sudan', in P. Behr et al., *Human rights in developing countries, Yearbook 1995*, 325-366. The Hague: Kluwer Law International.
MERIP (1985), 'Report from the South: Khartoum's greatest challenge', Middle East Research and Information Project 135 (Sept.): 11.

Mustafa, Z. (1971), *The common law in the Sudan: An account of the 'justice, equity and good conscience' provision*. Oxford: Clarendon Press.

Natsios, A. (2008), 'Beyond Darfur: Sudan's slide toward civil war', *Foreign Affairs* May/June: http://www.foreignaffairs.com/articles/63399/andrew-natsios/beyond-darfur.

O'Fahey, R.S. & M.I. Abu Salim (1983), *Land in Dar Fur*. Cambridge: Cambridge University Press.

Osman, A.A.M. (1989), *The political and ideological development of the Muslim Brotherhood in Sudan, 1945-1986*. PhD dissertation: University of Reading.

Peters, R. (2005), *Crime and punishment in Islamic Law*. Cambridge: Cambridge University Press.

REDRESS (2008), 'Criminal law and human rights in Sudan: A baseline study', report of REDRESS (London), March.

REDRESS (2009), 'Implementing the Comprehensive Peace Agreement and the National Interim Constitution? An empirical assessment of the law reform process in Sudan: Challenges and prospects', report of REDRESS (London), December.

Rogalski, J. (1990), Die Republikanischen Brüder im Sudan: Ein Beitrag zur Ideologiegeschichte *des Islam in der Gegenwart*. Berlin: Freie Universität Berlin, M.A. Thesis.

Ruiz-Almodovar, C. (2000), El Codigo Sudanes del Estatuto Personal. *Miscelanea de Estudios Arabes y Hebraicos: Seccion Arabe-Islam* 49: 179-224.

Salman, S.M.A. (1983), 'Lay tribunals in the Sudan: An historical and socio-legal analysis', *Journal of Legal Pluralism* 21: 61-128.

Scholz, Peter (2000), 'Die koranischen Delikte (hudud) im sudanesischen Strafrecht', *Zeitschrift für die gesamte Strafrechtswissenschaft* 112 Heft 2: 431-460.

Seesemann, R. (1999), 'Der Sudan und die islamistische Verfassung', INAMO 5(17): 4245.

Sidahmed, A.-S. (2001), 'Problems in contemporary applications of Islamic criminal sanctions: The penalty for adultery in relation to women', *British Journal of Middle Eastern Studies* 28(1/2): 187204.

Sidahmed, A.S. (1997), *Politics and Islam in contemporary Sudan*. New York: St. Martin's Press.

Strategic Initiative on Women in the Horn of Africa (SIHA) (2009), 'Beyond trousers: The Public Order Regime and the human rights of women and girls in Sudan', Discussion Paper, submission to the 46th Ordinary Session of the African Commission on Human and People's Rights, Banjul, the Gambia. See online edition: http://www.pclrs.org/resources/Public%20Order%20Submission%20Paper.pdf.

Spaulding, J. (1977), 'The evolution of Islamic judiciary in Sinnar', *International Journal of African Historical Studies* 10: 408-426.

Stiansen, Endre (2002), 'Is there room for non-Muslims in the Sudan's Islamic economy?', in H. Weiss (ed.), *Social welfare in Muslim societies in Africa*, 39-65. Uppsala: Nordiska Afrikainstitutet.

Stiansen, E. (2004a), 'Interest politics: Islamic finance in the Sudan, 1977-2001', in H. Clement & R. Wilson (eds.), *The Politics of of Islamic Finance*, 155-167. Edinburgh: Edinburgh University Press.

Stiansen, E. (2004b), 'Al-Islam huwa al-hal: The Koran and contemporary Islamic finance', in N. Kastfelt (ed.), *Scriptual Politics: The Bible and Koran as political models in the Middle East and Africa*. London: Hurst.

Sudanow (1992), 'Keeping up appearances', February: 26-27.

Tønnessen, L. & A.S. Roald (2007), 'Discrimination in the name of religious freedom: The rights of women and non-Muslims after the comprehensive peace agreement in Sudan', study published by Chr. Michelsen Institute, Bergen.

U.S. Department of State (2003), 'Sudan', Country Reports on Human Rights Practices 2002, see http://www.state.gov/g/drl/rls/hrrpt/2002/18228.htm.

Warburg, G.R. (1990), 'The Shari'a in Sudan: Implementation and repercussions, 1983-1989', *Middle East Journal* 44: 624-637.
Warburg, Gabriel (2003), *Islam, sectarianism and politics in Sudan since the Mahdiyya*. London: Hurst.
Zysow, A. (2002), 'Zakat', in *Encyclopaedia of Islam*, New Edition, 420. Leiden: Brill.

6 Islam and national law in Turkey[1]

Mustafa Koçak[2]

Abstract

This study examines the effect of religion on the national law in Turkey from the time of the nineteenth century Ottoman State until the present. The period of secularisation of the law, which began with the 1839 *Tanzimat* (Reorganisation), was largely complete after the declaration of the Republic, at which time Atatürk initiated a course of staunchly secular reforms, including the abolishment of the constitutional clause that had previously identified the state's religion as Islam. After the transition to a multiparty regime in 1945 more liberal policies in the field of freedom of religion and conscience were explored. Within the freer environment introduced by the Constitution of 1961, new opportunities for the organisation and expression of Marxist and social democratic party ideologies emerged, along with efforts of groups to expand upon religious freedom. A loosening on the tight state control of the strictly secular operations within the country has been greatly facilitated by the E.U. membership negotiations and the adoption of the E.U. *acquis communautaire*. Even in light of what appears to be increased calls for religiosity over the last decades, however, Islam has had no effect on law, no religious reference has been made in legal texts, and a secular understanding of the organisation of the state has consistently been executed since 1928. The main debate in Turkey is not about Islamisation of the law, but rather about the expansion of freedom of religion and conscience.

Table of contents

The Republic of Turkey was created in 1923 out of the remnants of the Ottoman Empire. According to the 2007 census Turkey's population is close to 71 million and is almost completely Muslim (99.8%). The remaining 0.2 per cent is mostly made up of Christian and Jewish communities. Turks are by far the largest ethnic group in the country, with Kurds forming the most significant community alongside Arab, Armenian, and Greek communities. While Turkish is the official language of the country, Arabic, Kurdish, Armenian, and Greek are also spoken.[3]

(Source: Bartleby 2010)

6.1 The period until 1920

The Ottoman Empire and its modernisation

Throughout the eighteenth century there had been protracted debate between the Ottoman governing class and the religious scholars (*ulama*) on how to make the Ottoman regime more effective. Since the reign of Selim I between 1512 and 1520, the Ottoman sultans had been without doubt the most powerful Muslim rulers in the world. They ruled over large parts of the Middle East, North Africa, and the Balkans and were also the guardians of the three holiest cities of Islam, Mecca, Medina, and Jerusalem. As a result 'Sunnite orthodoxy and the shari'a (*şeriat*),[4] expounded by the *ulama* (learned men) of the Arab world, had become important at the Ottoman court' (Davison 1990: 9).

Confronted with the expansion of the European economic and military spheres of influence in the seventeenth and eighteenth centuries, the Ottoman leaders were divided into two camps. The conservatives favoured a return to the laws of Süleyman (Sulaiman) I (1520-1566) and resisted any reformist movement towards embracing the Judeo-Christian European laws, concepts, and techniques. In contrast, reformists called for the adoption of Western methods of military training, organisation, and administration and for civil, economic, and educational changes as part of the necessary requirements of a modern state. The conservatives pointed to the prescripts of orthodox Islam, stating that state and religion are inseparable. The ruling elite, for its part, attributed the weakening of the Empire to religious bigotry (Toprak 2003: 120-121).

It would, however, be overly simplistic to claim that one camp advocated the shari'a and the other the Western legal tradition. In fact, the Ottoman legal system had already consisted of two different laws for centuries:

> According to Tursun Bey, writing in the late fifteenth century, the sultan could make regulations and enact laws entirely on his own initiative (*siyasa*). These laws, independent of the *şeriat* and known as *kanun*, were based on rational and not religious principles and were enacted primarily in the spheres of public and administrative law (İnalcık 1989: 70).

The area left to the will (*irade*) of the Ottoman sultan was free from the limitations of the shari'a. He could enact laws (*kanun*) in various forms in accordance with – but outside the realm of – the shari'a on the basis of his right to discretion and censure (*takdir* and *tazir*), as recognised by the shari'a (Berkes 1998: 14). As İnalcık writes, '[w]ith the spread of Turkish rule in the mid-eleventh century, the principle of *kanun* became firmly established in Islamic legal practice, since, in Turkish tradition, sovereignty and the establishment of a royal code of laws and *töre* were intimately related. Furthermore, rulers did not wish to recognise any limitation to their political authority' (1989: 70). Schacht further expands on this notion, explaining that:

> In fact the very first of these Ottoman *kanun-names*, that of Sultan Mehmed II (1451-1481), repeatedly refers to Islamic law and freely uses its concepts. It treats, among other matters (Office of the Grand Vizier, court, ceremonial, financial ordinances) penal law; it presupposes that *hadd* punishments are obsolete and replaces them by *ta'zir*, i.e. beating, and/or monetary fines which are graded according to the economic position of the culprit. In fact, these provisions go beyond merely supplementing the *sharia* by the *siyasa* of the ruler, and amount to superseding it. The so-called *kanun-name* of Süleyman I, which in its major parts seems to have been compiled previously under Bayezid II (1481-1512), shows a considerable development along these lines (1964: 91).

In line with these developments, the punishment of *rejm* (killing by stoning of an adulterous woman) was first and last seen in the Ottoman State in 1680 (Öztuna 1978: 200; Akyavaş 1950). Sultan Mehmet IV, who watched the execution of this punishment in Sultanahmet Square (Gökçen 1989: 68), put an end to this punishment, stating, '[f]rom now on, I do not want such disgrace in the Ottoman lands' (Toprak 2003: 118).

After 1800, the reform-minded, who were in favour of modernisation based on European models, began gaining ground relative to the conservatives. The Ottoman Empire could no longer defend itself against the growing military power of Europe, nor ward off European commercial penetration. The realisation of this led Selim III (1789-1807) to introduce the first programme of reforms, increase taxation, establish the so-called New Order (*Nizam-i Jedid*), and establish a modern army and modern technical schools to train cadres for the new regime. Selim's reorganisation sparked protests from a conservative coalition of certain military elites, religious leaders, and others who felt adversely affected by the reforms. Selim was eventually deposed by auxiliary conscripts in 1807. His successor, Mahmud II (1807-1839), nevertheless continued the process of modernisation. He was helped in this by the Grand Vizier Mustafa Reshit Pasha. For all reforms in the aforementioned areas, an educational system was required to furnish young Ottomans with the necessary knowledge. To this end, 'liberal schools' were established based on educational principles different from those prevailing in the rest of the Empire. From these schools there emerged a new generation of reformers with a critical stance towards the traditional (religious) institutions (Berkes 1998: 400-401).

In 1839, the regime proclaimed the 'Noble Rescript', a drastic programme of reforms (the *Hattı Şerif of Gülhane*) developed by Reshit Pasha; this programme also became known as the 'Reorganisation' (*Tanzimat*). The year 1839 was therefore crucial in the process of modernisation and Westernisation of the Ottoman Empire. It marked the start of four decades of major changes throughout the Empire. These changes encompassed the reorganisation of the Ottoman state structure, of civil, territorial, and trade laws, and of the judiciary. The Constitution of 1876 completed this reform process.

Several important steps had, however, already been taken prior to 1839. Mahmud II had already enacted a number of administrative reforms, and in 1838 he promulgated two criminal laws for civil servants. In addition, towards the end of his reign, Mahmud II changed the organisation of the state by establishing a semi-legislative institution which was called the 'Supreme Council for Justice Regulations' (*Meclis-i Valay-i Ahkam-i Adliye*). This advisory organ had the task of preparing laws to carry out proposed reforms. The council worked on the basis of procedures adopted from Western parliamentary democracies. Twenty years later, in 1858, a new advisory organ independent of the Supreme Council was created; the Supreme Council of Reformation (*Meclis-i Ali-i Tanzimat*), whose membership included ministers, *ulama*, and high-level civil servants. Its main function was to prepare legislative designs and regulations, and it generally concerned itself with the principles of the reform policy, while the Supreme Council from then on exclusively focused on matters of administrative adjudication (Bozkurt 1996: 134-137).

In 1861, the two organisations were united into one body called the Council for Judicial Ordinances (Cevdet Paşa 1986 I: 36; II: 153). This council was, in turn, divided into three departments, according to the principles of the separation of powers. The first department focused on administrative matters, the second on the preparation of laws and regulations, and the third on administrative adjudication (Üçok et al. 2002: 284). In 1868 the council was reorganised yet again. This time two judicial authorities were created, a Supreme Civil Court and a Supreme Administrative Court (the so-called Council of State). The former department functioned as the highest body of appeal for civil cases, and the second became the first independent high administrative court (Üçok et al. 2002: 284).

As a result of the 1839 *Tanzimat* (Reorganisation), several important changes had already occurred in the field of criminal law. In 1840, a new penal code was promulgated (Akagündüz 1986: 809). Because it was already commonplace in the Ottoman state to punish offences that were not recognised in Islamic law by using the sultan's right as a pre-Islamic ruler to promulgate laws (*örf* powers), there was little resistance to this promulgation. It was the first criminal law in the Ottoman Empire that applied equally to everyone. Article 1 of the first section of the code formulated this principle as follows: 'a shepherd in the mountains and a vizier will be equal.' In this way, the Ottoman law put an end to the traditional practice in which Muslims received only half the punishment non-Muslims received for the commission of the same offence. The principle of equality and the formulation of this article illustrated the influence of Western law (Bozkurt 1996: 98). In 1851, another new secular penal code was introduced, which recognised for the first time the possibility of bringing a public suit against an accused. The new code created in 1858, which in actual fact was a translation of the 1810 French Penal Code, abolished the traditional *hadd* crimes, for which punishments are ordained by the Holy Qur'an or Sunnah (shari'a), with the exception of the death penalty for apostasy. This code remained in force until 1926.

Changes took place across a whole range of legal areas. For example, in 1858 a Land Code was introduced (Cevdet Paşa 1986 iv: 73-74), which incorporated a number of Islamic laws into a national codification. In addition, closer ties with the West necessitated the introduction of commercial legislation. The first law in this area came in 1850 in the form of a commercial code (Örücü 1992: 45). This legal code was partially a direct translation of the 1807 French Commercial Code (Velidoğlu 1999: 196-197). It included provisions concerning the payment of interest, despite the fact that the payment and collection of interest were prohibited by the shari'a. As such, this legislation constituted a radical step that was then left to the newly-established (1840) commercial courts to implement (Shaw & Shaw 1977: 118).

In 1861, a Code of Commercial Procedure was introduced based on the French model; in 1863 the Maritime Commercial Code, which incorporated parts of French, Belgian, and Prussian law, was created; and, in 1879, a Code of Criminal Procedure followed, the latter essentially being a copy of the French Criminal Procedure Code of 1807.

Probably the most important legal reform of the nineteenth century was the promulgation of a new civil code, the *Mecelle*. The first section of the *Mecelle* was promulgated in 1868, and the code was completed in 1876. Ahmet Cevdet Paşa, a historian and jurist who lived from 1822 until 1895, wrote the biggest part of this grand piece of legislation. Ali Paşa, the Grand Vizier, was an advocate of adopting parts of the French Civil Code and making them the civil laws of the Ottoman Empire, as had been done earlier in the case of the commercial code. Ahmet Cevdet Paşa, however, insisted on following the Islamic tradition and as such prepared a legal code firmly based on the shari'a (Lewis 1968: 122-123). Although the *Mecelle* only remained in force in Turkey until 1926, in other parts of the former Ottoman Empire it remained in use for much longer. This codification proved also to have a significant influence on the Islamic world more generally, remaining in existence until long after the code had been officially abolished following the establishment of the Turkish Republic.[5]

With regard to the Ottoman court system, a reform edict had come into force in 1856 promising equality for all subjects. In order to live up to the promises made to the Western powers, independent mixed courts had already been established to hear civil and criminal cases involving both Muslims and non-Muslim foreigners. In 1847, mixed courts were established for criminal matters and in 1848 for commercial matters. In 1856, a four-level secular court system was designed (Belgesay 1999: 215; Düstur 1872: 445) that culminated in the establishment of a secular jurisdiction in 1869.

Two years later, in 1871, this new system came into force alongside the shari'a courts and, in fact, reduced the authority and jurisdiction of those shari'a courts (Shaw & Shaw 1977: 119). All matters except shari'a were now within the competence of the secular (*Nizamiye*) courts.

The jurisdiction of the shari'a courts was limited to conflicts relating to questions of personal status, family, and succession, subjects that the courts had already handled prior to 1839 and 1871. There were, however, frequent conflicts about jurisdiction between the two sets of courts that ultimately led the Minister of Justice to declare a division of labour between the courts in a circular in 1877. Accordingly, marriage, divorce, alimony, emancipation of slaves, analogy, blood-money (*diyet*), wills, and succession were to be in the domain of the shari'a courts. Commercial matters, penal matters, damages, and contract were to be dealt with by the secular *Nizamiye* courts. Legal suits outside these areas were covered by shari'a jurisdiction, if the parties involved consented to this; they were otherwise subject to *Nizamiye* jurisdiction. Whereas conflicts between the competing courts continued for decades (Bozkurt 1996: 124-125), the national court system was further consolidated by the coming into force of a Code of Civil Procedure in 1879, which created civil as well as commercial courts established on a secular basis.

During the process of codification that followed the establishment of the Supreme Council of Reformation (*Meclis-i Ali-i Tanzimat*), no legal provisions for marriage were enacted. There were also no provisions in the *Mecelle* concerning family law. According to the 1881 Population Regulation, Muslims wishing to marry required permission from the Islamic judge (*kadı*), and non-Muslims had to obtain permission from their own religious heads. The first Ottoman regulation of family matters came in the form of the Family Code of 1917, which will be explained later in detail.

Thus, over the course of about 35 years, the complete modernisation of the Ottoman law was realised. The ideology underlying this change was based on nationalism and modernisation, and later also on constitutionalism. Lapidus comments on this period as follows: 'The modernist point of view was first espoused by the Young Ottomans in the 1860s and 1870s. While committed to the principles of Islam, they called upon the endangered Ottoman regime to transform itself into a constitutional government' (2002: 460). Through this transformation they also promoted a new social morality and revived national culture.

A process of constitutional change was initiated by the issuance of the Ottoman Code of Public Laws, a series started in 1865 (Shaw & Shaw 1977: 119). In 1876, taking advantage of the Ottoman defeat by Russia, the constitutionalists staged a coup that brought Abdul Hamid II to power (1876-1908). Under the pressure of the constitutionalists, Abdul Hamid accepted a new constitution. This first Ottoman constitution (of 1876) was inspired by the Belgian Constitution of 1832 and the Prussian Constitution of 1850 and established a democratic structure in which the role of religious authorities was restricted. It also limited the powers of the sultan, established a representative and decentralised administration, and mandated equality for all religious groups.

The 1876 Constitution still declared Islam as the state religion and set up the caliphate as a constitutional institution. As the Muslim Caliph, the sultan was given the duty to protect and apply the rules of the shari'a and to swear a religious oath accepting this responsibility. The *Sheikh ul-Islam* ('Şeyhülislam' in Turkish), who was the dignitary responsible for all matters related to religious law, religious schools, etc. and next in line after the Grand Vizier, was appointed by the sultan as a member of the Council of Ministers. The *Sheikh ul-Islam* was charged with ensuring harmony between the laws and the shari'a. To this end, he examined whether the laws conformed to Islamic jurisprudence (*fiqh*) and the shari'a. But because the *Sheikh ul-Islam* belonged to the Council of Ministers, he lost his power to issue authoritative legal decisions (*fatwas*) independently. Likewise, his position within the Council of Ministers gradually became less significant. The religious scholars (*ulama*), who were incorporated into the civilian bureaucracy, also lost their independence over time. As such, the bureaucratisation of the *ulama*, a process that began under Mahmud II, had now reached its logical conclusion (Tanör 2002: 267).

The Constitution of 1876 furthermore established a Parliament consisting of two chambers: an elected Chamber of Deputies and a Senate consisting of members of both Muslim and non-Muslim communities, nominated by the sultan. On the various regional and local levels, administrative councils were created consisting of the chief judge, the chief finance officer, and the chief secretary; these functionaries were joined by Muslim and non-Muslim representatives and religious leaders from both the Muslim and non-Muslim communities (Lewis 1968: 388). These representative institutions restricted the monarchical and theocratic character of the Ottoman system.

Neither the Constitution of 1876 nor the new parliament proved durable; before long, the sultan suspended parliament and set up an authoritarian and religiously conservative regime. As head of Islam, Abdul Hamid claimed global authority over all Muslims (Lapidus 2002: 496-497). His regime would be the last of the centuries-old Ottoman Empire.

In 1907, a Congress of the Young Turks established the Committee for Union and Progress (CUP). Following a military coup, the CUP and the army came into power together (Lapidus 2002: 497). They created a parliamentary government and forced the sultan to reintroduce the Constitution of 1876. This constitution, with the inclusion of a few amendments, was then put into effect for the second time. As a reaction to the pan-Islamic policies of Sultan Abdul Hamid II (1876-1908), the Young Turks went from being Islamic modernists to being champions of secular constitutionalism (Lapidus 2002: 460).

Between 1913 and 1918, the CUP carried out a broad programme of secularisation of schools, courts, and legislation. The government also took its first steps towards the emancipation of women. In 1916, the CUP government reduced the powers of the *Sheikh ul-Islam* by transferring jurisdiction over Muslim courts to the Ministry of Justice and the control over Muslim colleges to the Ministry of Education.

In 1917, a new family code based on European principles was promulgated (Lapidus 2002: 498) in the form of a decree, but it remained in force in the Ottoman Empire for only a year and a half, though elsewhere its lifespan proved longer.[6] Because all reforms in the Ottoman Empire were decreed by the sultan, they had a substantial influence and a modernising effect on other Muslim societies. Since the sultan was also the Muslim Caliph, his edicts were accepted even if they deviated from orthodox Islamic practice.

The new family law also established unity in the court structure as competences in the field of family law were removed from the Religious Courts. In the drafting of the family code, the views of all shari'a schools were taken into consideration, rather than just the Hanafi School which was followed by the majority of Ottoman Muslims. The code included separate provisions for Muslims, Christians, and Jews. With the new code, marriage was accepted as a contractual legal act that had to be registered by an authority appointed by the state even though the contracting parties were left free to practise whatever ritual or sacramental forms of marriage they wished (Berkes 1998: 417). Section 38 of the code was aimed at ending the practice of polygamy, relying on a view held by the Hanbali School. According to this section, a marriage contract contained a vow to the effect that the man would not take a second wife and that if he were to do so the first marriage would be deemed to have ended in divorce. As such, it effectively introduced an indirect prohibition on 'second' (polygamous) marriages (Aydın 1998: 314-318).

It was only with the 1926 Turkish Civil Code that unity was created in this field, including for succession, which had until then been subject to shari'a rules. Even today there are separate shari'a succession provisions that apply to individuals who died prior to 4 October 1926 and whose succession issues have not yet been settled.

6.2 The period from 1920 until 1965

The move toward a fully secular republic

The First World War ended in 1918, and on the 30th of October of that same year, a Turkish delegation signed an armistice with the Allies on behalf of the Ottoman Empire. Allied troops occupied various districts in Istanbul, as well as a number of Turkish provinces, strategic roads, and railroads. The various Arab lands that had belonged to the Ottoman Empire were already controlled by the Allied forces, and their imminent independence was assured to them. On 21 December 1918, the Ottoman Sultan Mehmet VI dismissed Parliament. Under the protection of British, French, and American warships, the Greeks invaded Izmir by sea on 15 May 1919, after which they pushed eastwards into the interior (Lewis 1968: 239-242).

Four days after the Greek landing in İzmir, Mustafa Kemal Paşa, Inspector-General of the Ninth Army, landed in Samsun, on the coast of the Black Sea, with orders from Istanbul to supervise the disbanding of the remaining Ottoman forces. Instead, he immediately began organising a nationalist movement and raising an army (Lewis 1968: 242-243). On 23 July 1919, a congress of delegates from the eastern provinces assembled in Erzurum and on 4 September an even more important congress was held in Sivas. The main political goals of these nationalists were preserving the territorial integrity and national independence of Turkey. Meanwhile, under the authority of the sultan new elections were held in December 1919.

In 1920, a power struggle took place between the nationalist movement led by Mustafa Kemal (later to be known as Atatürk) and the followers of the Sultan-Caliph's forces. This conflict threatened to divide the country: 'It was unfortunate for Islam in Turkey that it came to be intimately identified with the forces more concerned to retain their own power, even by collaborating with Great Britain, the supporter of the Greek invasion, than to save the country from partition' (Lewis 1968: 234-274)[7]. The last Ottoman Parliament convened on 12 January 1920; it adjourned its own sessions until 18 March, and on the 11th of April the sultan dissolved it entirely. That same day, *Sheikh ul-Islam* Durrizade Abdullah Efendi, '[...] issued a fetva [*fatwa*] declaring that the killing of rebels, on the orders of the Caliph, was a religious duty [...] (Lewis 1968: 252). Subsequently, the nationalist movement obtained a counter-*fatwa* from the pro-nationalist *müftü* of Ankara aimed at mitigating the effects of the earlier *fatwa*.

Law reforms in the Turkish Republic

On 23 April 1920, the Turkish Grand National Assembly (*Türkiye Büyük Millet Meclisi*, TBBM) held its opening session in Ankara. This occasion marked the beginning of a new era for the Turkish state, namely the era of the secular republic. The basis of the policy of the new Turkish state became laicism, not irreligion: the new regime was not out to destroy Islam, but rather aimed at abrogating its political authority. The power of religion and its exponents in political, social, and cultural affairs would be put to an end and a limit would be set to matters of worship and belief (Lewis 1968: 412). To set an example, the TBBM, in the same year, enacted a Law against High Treason aimed at preventing the misuse of religion for political ends.

The Kemalist period of governance began with the 1921 Constitution, which stipulated that ultimate sovereignty belonged to the Turkish people. On 1 November 1922 the national assembly abolished the sultanate (Decree No. 308/1922, dated 1-2 November).[8] In 1923, the Republican

People's Party (Cumhuriyet Halk Partisi, CHP) was created, with Mustafa Kemal as its first president. Shortly afterwards, he was elected President of the Turkish state. In 1924 the abolition of the caliphate was implemented (see Law No. 431/1924)[9]. The Sultan-Caliph was sent into exile. 'Sovereignty belongs to the nation' became the new slogan of the Republic. The abolition of the sultanate and the caliphate ended a period where a religious institution sat at the apex of the state and was, therefore, a significant step on the path to secularism. The concept of loyalty to the nation replaced the concept of submission to God, and thus secularised the people's identity and sense of belonging. Now that the concept of national sovereignty had been incorporated into the constitution and had moreover been implemented in practice, a new era in which the position of the bourgeois class was significantly strengthened dawned on the Turkish Republic.

Another law, also promulgated in 1924 (Law (*Kanun*) No. 429/1924), abolished the position and office of the *Sheikh ul-Islam*, as well as the Ministry of Religious Foundations. The latter was replaced by a small Office of Religious Affairs. Religious foundations (*Evkaf Müdürlüğü*) came under the direct authority of the Prime Minister. A large number of the religious scholars (*ulama*) were sent into retirement and the remaining religious clerics became minor civil servants. The entire system of religious schools was also dismantled, the *mektep* (school) and the *medrese* (the special high school) being incorporated into a unified system of national education under the direction of the Ministry of Education (Shaw & Shaw 1977: 384-385).

The influence of Islam on the legal system, however, did not disappear entirely. According to Law No. 364/1923 (dated 29 October), which amended the 1921 Constitution, Islam was still recognised as the state religion. In addition, the age-old duty of the ruler to carry out the application of shari'a laws was initially formally upheld by the TBBM.[10] And, when delivering the oath of office, the president and the members of Parliament still accepted the religious formula, the *vallahi* (oath in the name of Allah (God)). Despite these formalities and official recognition of a continued role for Islam, in 1924 shari'a courts were abolished.

In 1925, representatives of the three separate non-Muslim communities (Jews, Armenians, and Greeks) declared to the government in Ankara that they were prepared to give up their rights to their own community laws. This was a very significant development (Tanör 2002: 225-226). In addition to this, the Sufi-orders were declared illegal and closed on the grounds of Law No. 677/1925.[11] Another example of the secularisation of social life was the ban on the wearing of the *fez* and other religious garments. The wearing of the *fez* was prohibited through a separate law (Law No. 671/1925), and regulations were inserted into the penal code making the wearing of religious attributes in public punishable acts (Law No. 676/1925). Another law further specified that certain garments, such as robes and *türban* of an imam or robes and *kippah* of a rabbi, could not be worn (law of 13 December 1934). In addition, certain titles such as *efendi, bey,* and *Paşa*, could no longer be used, and religious titles, such as *hacı, hafiz, hoca,* and *molla*, were also abolished. And finally, calendar and national holidays were revised to remove any connotations of non-secular association.

The principle of separation of religion from politics was further affirmed in the Penal Code of 1926, which laid down penalties for those 'who, by misuse of religion, religious sentiments, or things that are religiously considered as holy, in any way incite the people to action prejudicial to the security of the state, or form associations for this purpose [...] Political associations on the basis of religion or religious sentiments may not be formed' (Art. 163). The same code also prescribed punishments for religious leaders and preachers, who, in the course of their functions, bring the administration, the laws, or executive action into discredit (Art. 241), incite disobedience (Art. 242), or who conduct religious celebrations and processions outside recognised places of worship (Art. 529).

On 4 October 1926, a new civil code, which also incorporated family law based on the Swiss civil code, was enacted. This civil code replaced the *Mecelle*, which was essentially based on the shari'a. The new law abolished polygamy, made the sexes substantially equal in rights to divorce, and required that divorce be subject to court rulings on specified grounds rather than acting as a male prerogative. The regulation of births, upbringing and custody of children, cultural education, marriage, death, and inheritance were no longer the domain of the *ulama* (Örücü 1992: 51-52; Tanör 2002: 276): a marriage contract now had to be concluded before an official marriage registrar; parents were responsible for the religious education of children; and upon reaching majority one had the freedom to choose one's religion.

The influence of European law increased, as witnessed by the foundations of many laws. The 1926 Law of Obligations was for example based upon the Swiss Code, and the Turkish Commercial Law was predominantly German, but eclectically also based upon the French, Belgium, and Swiss Commercial Codes. The Turkish Code of Civil Procedure was adopted from the canton of Neuchatel (Örücü 1992: 52).

The date 14 April 1928 is a significant moment in the process of Turkish laicism. Section 2 of the 1924 Constitution, which said that '[t]he religion of the Turkish State is Islam' and Section 16, citing 'to apply the Shari'a Law' among the duties of the Parliament, were removed from the Constitution, and the oaths in parliament were secularised. The reason given for this was that in the contemporary civilised world it is generally accepted that the most progressive and developed type of state enabling the realisation of the national sovereignty is a laic and democratic republic. Also in 1928, a new Latin alphabet was introduced to replace Arabic. The next measure was the purification of the Turkish language, which was achieved through the removal of all Arabic and Persian influences. And, in 1929, both Arabic and Persian were eliminated from the school curricula.

This was a firm departure from the Arab culture and its religious source. Religious teaching was removed from the curriculum of urban primary schools in 1930 and from that of rural schools in 1939. In addition, foreign school programmes were no longer allowed to contain any religious elements. The Constitution guaranteed women the right to equality in education and employment, and in 1934 they were accorded the right to vote in national elections. In 1935, the first female deputies were elected to the Turkish Parliament.

In 1929, a new Turkish Penal Code was enacted based on the German Penal Code, and in the same year the new Maritime Commercial Code, also inspired by a German code, was accepted. The Code of Bankruptcy was adopted from the Swiss Federal Code. In 1935, all Turks were required to take surnames in the Western fashion. In the 1940s, 'Village Institutes' (*Köy Enstitüleri*) carried the laicist world view to rural areas.

While the Kemalist reforms did indeed restrict the public role of religion, they did not try to change the content of religion except for the call to prayer (*ezan*), which as from January 1932 sounded from the minarets in Turkish. A purely Turkish version of the call was prepared by the Linguistics Society and published by the Office of Religious Affairs (Lewis 1968: 416; Tanör 2002: 276-277). Some reforms, however, did have a clear role in constraining the freedom of religion. Examples of this include: the Law of 1935, which classified mosques and mescit (*masjids)* and allowed some of them to be used for non-religious purposes[12]; restrictive regulations on pilgrimages; and the dissolution of religious Sufi associations (*tarikat*, pl. *tariqas*), the impounding of their assets, the closing of their convents and sanctuaries, and prohibition on their prayer meetings and ceremonies. At times, Article 163 of the Penal Code was used in order to ban and disperse religious meetings (Tanör 2002: 276-277).

Thus, in the 1920s and 1930s Islam was 'de-established' and deprived of its role in public life. The ordinary symbols of Turkish attachment to traditional culture were replaced by new legal, linguistic, and other signs of modern identity (Lapidus 2002: 502-503). Nonetheless, Islam remained 'deeply rooted in the minds and hearts of the people' (Rosenthal 1965: 61).

On 10 November 1938, Mustafa Kemal Atatürk, the founder of modern Turkey, died. İsmet İnönü was elected as the second President of the Turkish Republic. From 1938 to 1945, the Republican People's Party (CHP) was the only political party. It acted in a rather totalitarian manner and maintained its strict laicist policies towards religion. There was no democratic opposition. However, the CHP-run government permitted the reintroduction of military imams into the army as early as 1941 (Ahmad 1977: 364). In 1949, religious education was reintroduced into schools. This consisted of two hours of instruction on Saturday afternoons, but was restricted to those children whose parents had explicitly requested such education. In this way, the state retained control over religion and religious institutions.

Transition to a multi-party regime

In 1945, Turkey introduced a multi-party regime. The Democratic Party was established from within the CHP in 1946. The new democratic dispensation gave much more freedom of expression to various groups, including religious leaders. At this time, the competition for votes forced the CHP and the opposition parties to reconsider their policies concerning Islam. The first thing the Democratic Party did after coming to power (1950-1960) was to amend the Penal Code (§ 526), which from 1932 onwards had forbidden the call to prayer in any language other than Turkish. On 5 July, the ban on religious radio programmes was abolished, and radio stations immediately resumed broadcasting readings from the Qur'an. In October 1950, religious lessons in schools became compulsory for the fourth and fifth grades of primary school, unless parents indicated that they did not desire such education for their children. For the other grades and levels of schools, religious instruction remained optional (Lewis 1968: 418; Ahmad 1977: 365).

In 1951, however, a series of court cases were brought against Islamic reactionaries and against Islamic publications. On 25 July 1951, a bill on Atatürk came into force, giving the government powers to deal with those who challenged the Atatürk reforms. In July 1953, the Law to Protect the Freedom of Conscience was passed to prevent religion from being used for political purposes (Ahmad 1977: 369). This law corresponds to the provisions of the Penal Code of 1926 whereby it was considered a crime to 'establish, organise or administer associations with the aim of adapting the fundamentals of state order to religious rules and beliefs, contrary to secularism, or to affiliate with or encourage others to affiliate with these type of associations' (Art.163). Both laws aimed to protect secularism in the country and the Law to Protect the Freedom of Conscience reinforced Article 163 of the Penal Code. After 1952, a number of political parties were banned. The authorities dissolved the Islamic Democratic Party (IDP) and subjected the party's founders to criminal investigation (Tunaya 1995: 742-744). In 1953, the

Nation Party was temporarily closed on grounds that it was engaging in subversive activities under the cloak of religion; on 27 January 1954, the party was dissolved by court order.

The first military coup and a new constitution

In 1960, the Democratic Party government was overthrown by a military coup. The army, which took control, represented the Westernised elite and was aligned to bureaucrats and students, all of whom defended the laic Kemalist policies. Their opponents were largely rural, small-town business owners and Islamic interest groups. A major reason for the coup was the dire economic situation. There was no question of an Islamic resurgence threatening the reforms. In fact, Kemalism had now brought about a generation of socio-economic changes that had positively influenced a significant minority in Turkey (Ahmad 1977: 373).

The army promulgated a new constitution, a parliamentary regime, and a new economic policy (Lapidus 2002: 506). The Constitution of 1961, which was adopted by the Constituent Assembly, confirmed the laic character of the democratic, social Republic. This constitution forbade the use of religion for political purposes[13], left all decisions regarding the religious education of children to parental discretion[14], and left the Office of Religious Affairs intact. In addition, the Constitution formulated a special article designed to '[s]afeguard [...] the Reform Laws which aim at raising Turkish society to the level of contemporary civilization and at safeguarding the secular character of the Republic and which were in effect on the date this constitution was adopted by popular vote [...]' (Art. 153). The laws in question were then enumerated. Article 154 safeguarded the Office of Religious Affairs, stating that that office 'incorporated in the general administration, discharges the function prescribed by a special law'.

6.3 The period from 1965 until 1985

Grappling with the division between religious identity and political influence

In the period between 1965 and 1985, Turkey maintained its secular character and strengthened its image as a moderate alternative to Islamising countries such as Iran, Pakistan, and Sudan. Nonetheless, in Turkey, emotions frequently ran high when religious matters were at stake.

In the 1965 elections, nearly all Turkish political parties exploited religion. The Justice Party (JP), established in 1961, won the elections. Led by Süleyman Demirel, the JP used the slogan 'we are right of centre and on the path to God'. The CHP, as usual more ambivalent about exploiting Islam, used the old tactics of denouncing the JP and Demirel, for example with the laic retort 'We elected him as a political leader, not as the imam of a mosque' (Ahmad 1977: 378). The JP formed the government and pledged that graduates of the Islamic *İmam Hatip* schools, secondary schools for the training of Islamic religious personnel in Turkey, would be admitted to universities. During this political period, a number of *İmam Hatip* schools were opened in nearly every Turkish province.

The effects of the 1968 student revolution in Paris were also noticeable on Turkish campuses. The first student boycott took place in April 1968 at the Faculty of Divinity at the University of Ankara. This protest was prompted by an incident in which a female student had insisted on wearing her headscarf in class.

On the political front, several revolutionary developments also took place during this turbulent period. In 1969, the National Order Party (Milli Nizam Partisi, MNP), with an Islamic inclination, was established under the leadership of Necmettin Erbakan. In 1971, the army temporarily took control of the state, but quickly restored a civilian administration. Nonetheless, the Constitutional Court closed down Erbakan's MNP in 1972 for having used religion for political gain (Shankland 1999: 87-131).

In 1973, the new Islamic National Salvation Party (Milli Selamet Partisi, MSP) was established; it formed a coalition government under CHP leader Bülent Ecevit. However, the tensions between leftist and rightist parties increased dramatically in the 1970s, leading to violence and bloody clashes that claimed many lives.

The second military coup and the Constitution of 1982

In 1980, yet another military coup took place. The National Security Council banned all parties, outlawed strikes, and abrogated the legislature by forbidding its members from participating in politics for the next ten years. The Consultative Council, comprised of civilians, and the National Security Council together formed the Constitutive Council. This council prepared a new constitution as well as a law regulating the referendum on the Constitution. The Constitution was adopted after the 7 November 1982 referendum yielded a 91.37 per cent yes-vote.[15] Subsequently the 1983 general elections were held in November, and a new democratic period began with the meeting of the new Parliament (Özbudun 1993: 32-33).

In 1983, the Islamic Welfare Party (Refah Partisi, RP) was founded, consisting almost entirely of former members of the MSP (Turan 1994:

31-55). Initially, the party was only able to participate in local government elections; the military authorities of the period prohibited the RP from participating in general elections..

In December 1982, the Higher Education Council issued a regulation banning the wearing of head covers (*türban*). In a 1984 case, the Council of State upheld this prohibition and declared that 'the *türban* is no longer an innocent tradition, but has become a symbol of a world view against the freedom of women and against the fundamental principles of the Republic'.[16]

Before we continue with the events of the 1985 to the present period, we should say a few words about the conflicts inherent in the 1982 Constitution. Three main conflicts can be identified in the Constitution. The first paragraphs of Article 24, which concern freedom of religion and conscience, state that:

> Everyone has the right to freedom of conscience, religious belief and conviction.
>
> Acts of worship, religious services, and ceremonies shall be conducted freely, provided that they do not violate the provisions of Article 14.
>
> No one shall be compelled to worship, or to participate in religious ceremonies and rites, to reveal religious beliefs and convictions, or be blamed or accused because of his religious beliefs and convictions.

First, in distinction from the 1961 Constitution, the 1982 Constitution places education and instruction of religion and ethics under state supervision and control. Article 24 states further that instruction in religious culture and moral education shall be compulsory in the curricula of primary and secondary schools. Since obligatory religious lessons were taught according to the Sunni interpretation of Islam, they came under criticism from other religious groups, especially from the Alevis. The subject was taken to court, as will be explained in the following section, but could not be challenged at the European Human Rights Court since at that time Turkey had not yet accepted the jurisdiction of this court.

The second conflict is stated in Article 136 of the 1982 Constitution. This article ensured the continuity of the Office of Religious Affairs as a part of the general administration, similar to the 1961 Constitution. It is generally accepted in Western democracies that the separation of religion and state affairs is essential in a secular state. Yet, Article 2 of the Constitution firstly identifies the Turkish Republic as a secular state, whilst simultaneously creating an agency to manage religious affairs within the general administration by way of Article 136. Further, Article 89 of the Political Parties Act forbids political parties to aim to abolish or to change the status of the Office of Religious Affairs as an agency of the general administration. Indeed, a number of parties have been closed on grounds that their party programmes were contrary to Article 89 (see 5.4 below).

Thirdly, contrary to Article 24 of the 1982 Constitution, which states that 'no one shall be compelled to reveal religious beliefs and convictions', Article 7 of the Civil Registration Services Act (Law No. 5480/2006) provided that the religion to which people belonged had to be shown in the state register and on identity cards. This issue has been challenged on grounds that it is contrary to secularism, as will also be explained in the following section.

6.4 The period from 1985 until the present

Defending the laic order – The battle against visible signs of Islamism

The period starting with 1985 did not open a new leaf for the state-religion relations in Turkey.[17]. Thus, the events described and analysed in this section should be seen as a natural extension of the previous section. Within the liberal environment introduced by the Constitution of 1961 different thoughts and ideologies found a chance to flourish and to become more organised. During the period of 1960-1980 a young generation had begun to develop under the influence of Marxism, while on the other hand there had been clear signs of development of a group with growing Islamic inclinations. As a result, ideological conflicts and violence followed.

Thus, after the military coup of 1980, the military government was careful to create an environment in which ideological conflicts could not exist, limiting freedoms and eliminating differences. The new generation would, according to their plan, be close to the Turkish-Islam synthesis, being Turkish, Sunni, and secular. Yet, under this authoritarian and nationalist constitutional order, movements demanding the expansion of liberal freedoms in the field of religion and conscience, especially from Muslims of Sunni and Alevi sects, became increasingly organised and vocal from 1985 onwards.

Turkey's acceptance of the jurisdiction of the European Court of Human Rights in 1987 paved the way for many applications for review of the conflicts between the constitution and other regulations outlined above. As will become evident in the discussion below, the issue of religious dress was particularly symbolic and vital in the government's resistance to perceived threats from non-secular groups and their ideas of political and formal social expression.

Legislation banning the Turban

In 1987, yet another legislative prohibition on the wearing of head covers was upheld by the Council of State. Two years later, in 1989, a law from 1988[18] removing the restrictions was annulled by the Constitutional Court in a decision holding as follows:

> A legal regulation cannot take into consideration religious rules, religious beliefs and religious requirements; the regulation related to covering the neck and hair because of religious beliefs is contrary to the principles in the Preamble of the Constitution and specifically to secularism.[19]

In 1992, the government removed a number of religiously-grounded articles from the Penal Code, in order to prohibit the exploitation of religious feelings and propaganda for a state based on religion. Shortly afterwards, in 1993, tensions mounted when several intellectuals were assassinated and allegations that their murders had been carried out by terrorist organisations with Islamic connections surfaced. It was also claimed that there was foreign involvement in these assassinations (Kongar 1998: 225, 261). Around this same time, a hotel in Sivas where 33 writers and artists were staying was burnt down; thirty-seven people were killed, including locals. Various interpretations of this incident see it as a Sunni-Alevi conflict, a clash of secular and religious forces, the use of religion for political ends, or a battle for power between the two camps.

In the local elections of 27 March 1994, the Islamic Welfare Party (Refah Partisi) won more than 19 per cent of the votes. The party gained the mayorships in Istanbul and Ankara; Recep Tayyip Erdoğan became mayor of Istanbul. In March 1995, an Istanbul coffee shop located in a neighbourhood primarily popular with Alevis was attacked, leaving two people dead and fifteen wounded. The military had to be called upon to ease the popular tension following the attack. In the elections of 24 December 1995 the RP even became the biggest party, gaining 21.4 per cent of the votes. Its chairman, Necmettin Erbakan, became Prime Minister of the coalition government.

Banning parties in the name of democracy

In 1996 and 1997, *Refah* politicians gave the impression on several occasions that they no longer supported the secular approach advocated by Kemalism.[20] Consequently, in 1997 the National Security Council acted against the anti-laic activities of the party and forced the RP to give up their participation in the coalition government. The military forces briefed the public prosecutor, the judicial authorities, academics, and the press on the situation, sending the clear message that religious bigotry had become the prime factor threatening national security and that it would no longer be tolerated. A special unit was set up in the General Staff to monitor Islamic activities. The Public Prosecutor of the Republic took further steps, requesting the Constitutional Court to permanently dissolve the RP on the basis that it had become a centre for anti-laic activities. Faced with strong pressure from public opinion, Erbakan handed in his resignation from the chairmanship of the RP and his post as Prime Minister to the President in June 1997.

In January 1998, the Constitutional Court dissolved the RP. However, by February, a new party – the Virtue Party (Fazilet Partisi, FP) – had already been created; all RP mayors joined this new party. In April, the Diyarbakir State Security Court decided that Erdoğan, who was still serving as mayor of Greater İstanbul, had 'sown seeds of hatred among the people' in a speech in Siirt in late 1997. For this offence, the court sentenced him to ten months in prison on the basis of Article 312 of the Penal Code. In addition, he was prohibited henceforth from taking public office and participating in elections.

At this time, some preventive measures were taken to reduce the number of graduates of *İmam-Hatip* schools working in the public sector. Obligatory state education was extended from five to eight years. The university entrance system was also changed so as not to allow graduates from vocational schools to attend any other faculty department except those in their own fields. Many army officers who had come from *İmam Hatip* schools of higher education or who had connections with religious Sufi organisations were dismissed.

The Higher Education Council imposed a new dress code, banning the wearing of head covers and of beards on university campuses. As a result of the legal obligation to have photographs without headcovers on school documents, hundreds of female students could not attend school, which led to protests in October 1998. In May 1998, the president of the Islamic business association 'MÜSİAD' was tried by the Ankara State Security Court because of a speech he made in October 1997, in which he too had allegedly 'sowed seeds of hatred among the people'. In 1999, he was sentenced to sixteen months imprisonment, but the sentence was suspended on the condition of non-recidivism.

Also, in 1998 the building and running of mosques was placed under the supervision of a state organisation. The aim of this was to prevent Islamic communities from having their own mosques and also to reduce their sphere of influence (Kramer 2001: 121-122). At the same time, the High Council for Radio and Television warned Islamic radio and television stations against exploiting religious sentiments. Technical measures to be used as possible measures against the stations if they did not abide by the rules were outlined and discussed. It has been said that these developments were part of a comprehensive campaign begun by the General Staff against 'the spread of Islamic fundamentalism' (Kramer 2001: 122).

In the 1999 elections, the Virtue Party's votes were reduced to 15.41 per cent. A few weeks before the election, the Public Prosecutor had requested the Constitutional Court to ban the party completely. Another law suit related to the dissolution of this party was heard after a female Member of Parliament of the party had taken her oath of office while wearing a headscarf, causing turmoil among Members of Parliament. The Court subsequently dissolved the party, in whose place the Justice and Development Party (Adalet ve Kalkınma Partisi, AK Party) was swiftly created.

The period of the Justice and Development Party and the decision of the European Court of Human Rights concerning the Turban

The elections of 2002 brought the AK Party into power. They emerged the outright winner in the elections, despite having garnered only 34 per cent of the votes. In the local elections of 2004, the party increased in popularity, winning 44 per cent of the vote. Despite its Islamic roots, the party projects the image of a centre-right conservative party that aims for economic development and respects the basic principles of a secular constitutional order. The AK Party has also supported Turkey's efforts towards attaining full membership status in the European Union, and as such considerable progress has been made in the area of human rights, including the rights of suspects and prisoners.

The '*türban* question', a chronic problem in Turkey, reached the European Court of Human Rights (EctHR) in 1998. The applicant, a female student named Leyla Şahin, alleged that a ban on wearing the Islamic headscarf (*türban*) in higher-education institutions violated her rights and freedoms under Articles 8, 9, 10 and 14 of the Convention and Article 2 of Protocol No. 1. (Case of *Leyla Şahin vs. Turkey*, Application No. 44774/98). The judgment of 29 June 2004 referred to the historical and sociological circumstances in Turkey, and appeared to be influenced by the previous *Refah* case:

> The Court does not lose sight of the fact that there are extremist political movements in Turkey which seek to impose on society as a whole their religious symbols and conception of a society founded on religious precepts (see para.s 32, 33) [...] Each Contracting State may, in accordance with the Convention provisions, take a stance against such political movements, based on its historical experience (*Refah Partisi and Others*, cited above, § 124). The regulations concerned have to be viewed in that context and constitute a measure intended to achieve the legitimate aims referred to above and thereby to preserve pluralism in the university (para. 109).

The Court went on to say:

> A margin of appreciation is particularly appropriate when it comes to the regulation by the Contracting States of the wearing of religious symbols in teaching institutions, since rules on the subject vary from one country to another depending on national traditions [...] and there is no uniform European conception of the requirements of 'the protection of the rights of others' and of 'public order' [...]. It should be noted in this connection that the very nature of education makes regulatory powers necessary (para. 102).

In so holding, the court granted Turkey the discretion to preserve the laic life-style, women's rights and public order in the face of religious movements seen to be attempting to impose their world-views.

This judgment was assessed differently by different sectors of the Turkish community. The general consensus was that this was more a political decision than a legal one. For instance, Nuray Mert of the *Radikal* newspaper, critical of the judgment, wrote: 'European democracies have not yet gone beyond their preconceptions and assumptions about Islam, Moslems and their social demands. Therefore, the decisions reached reflect these views.'[21] Another journalist, Gündüz Aktan, also of *Radikal*, drew attention to the inconsistencies in the judgment:

> The inconsistencies can be explained thus: Even though those that wear the *türban* are in the minority, in a country where there are extreme trends, they can become the majority, in which case equality will be violated for those who do not wear the *türban*. Those who now benefit from Article 9 by following their beliefs in a pluralist society, except being able to wear the *türban*, may not respect this principle then. Authorities must remain 'neutral' regarding religious beliefs. Allowing the wearing

of the *türban* would create a privilege for those who wear it and constitute a discrimination against those who do not.[22]

From time to time, the Head of the Office of Religious Affairs (*Diyanet*), Ali Bardakoğlu, has taken up the discussion on the '*türban* question,' once expressing the view that 'the wearing of the headscarf has never been a condition of either being a Moslem or being considered one.'[23]

A recent development is a draft bill on the organisation of the *Diyanet* (*Diyanet İşleri Başkanlığı Teşkilat Kanunu Tasarısı*) prepared by the Council of Ministers.[24] According to this bill, the usage and administration of all mosques in Turkey will belong to the *Diyanet*. At present, of approximately 80,000 mosques in Turkey, only 4,000 belong to the *Diyanet*, the rest belong to associations (7,076), private persons (3,379), and private foundations (936). The *Diyanet* states that they only hear of a newly constructed mosque when asked to allocate religious posts and that this situation leads to a gap in supervision.[25] If the draft becomes law, all new mosques and their annexes, such as gardens, courtyards, lodgings for the *imams*, will be transferred to the *Diyanet*.[26] The aim of this significant development is to have the administration and control by the state in all areas pertaining to mosques and to prevent their use for purposes other than for religious services.

Regime discussions and the search for a new constitution

In May 2007, the AK Party proceeded to elect the President of the Republic by insistence rather than by reaching consensus, which led to a strong reaction in some quarters of the society. The Constitutional Court annulled the first round of the elections for lack of the necessary quorum of two-thirds of the full membership of the Assembly. On the evening of the same day that the opposition party took the elections to the Court for annulment, the Chief of General Staff drew attention on the army web page to the fact that attempts by those who want to erode the foundations of the Republic have become denser and that the reactionary sectors of society have taken courage from recent developments.[27] This has been interpreted in the media as a 'warning'.[28]

The army accused the government of tolerating radical Islam and vowed to defend laicism. It must be remembered that Turkey's army has toppled three governments since 1960, and analysts said there were fears that it could intervene again. In 1997, it had been army pressure that led to the ousting of Turkey's first Islamist Prime Minister Necmettin Erbakan.[29]

In demonstrations throughout April and May of 2007 in Ankara, İstanbul, İzmir and Samsun, the message was 'the laic order of Turkey is in danger'. Many have been complaining that religious sentiments were becoming more prominent in daily life, children were being harassed, alcoholic drinks had become expensive, religion had become a criterion of promotions in public sector jobs, and many areas of İstanbul looked more and more like the Middle East, with girls and boys sitting separately in many places and an increasing number of covered women.

However, the surveys carried out in 1999 and 2006 by the Turkish Economic and Social Studies Foundation (TESEV) showed a different analysis of the picture than the generally accepted views or preconceptions in Turkish society. In November 2006, the Foundation published the results of their survey *Değişen Türkiye'de Din, Toplum ve Siyaset* ('Religion, society, and politics in a changing Turkey'). The aim of the survey was to provide a rational basis for discussion as the foundation believed that misinformation and manipulation of the public opinion were causing conflict between various sectors of society in the public sphere. The report (hereinafter 'TESEV Report') is the first serious study conducted on the much debated Islam factor and its threat to the secular order of the state and deserves to be examined in more detail in order to show the changes in the sociological nature of the Turkish society.

The respondents of the survey identified the five most important problems in Turkey as follows: (1) unemployment (38.2%); (2) terrorism/national security/Southeast problem/the Kurdish problem (13.8%); (3) the high cost of living/inflation (12.1%); (4) education (10.2%); and (5) economic instability (6.5%). Interestingly, only 3.7 per cent of those polled saw the *türban* issue as an important problem (TESEV Report: 23, 45). Contrary to general belief, findings revealed that there had been a decrease in the number of 'covered' women in 2006, as compared to 1999. The percentage of women who said they did not 'cover up' in public was 27.3 per cent in 1999, versus 36.5 per cent in 2006. The percentage of those wearing a headscarf, stole or head-handkerchief (*yemeni*) went from 53.4 per cent in 1999 to 48.8 per cent in 2006; the percentage of those wearing the over-garment (*çarşaf*) was 3.4 per cent in 1999, but only 1.1 per cent in 2006; and the percentage of women wearing the *türban* went down from 15.7 per cent in 1999 to 11.4 per cent in 2006. Thus, the conclusions of the survey indicate that contrary to the claims of both the 'laic' and the 'Islamist' sectors, the '*türban* question' is not on the agenda of Turkish people (TESEV Report: 23).

Yet, the survey also simultaneously indicated an overall increase in pietism in Turkey. The percentage of those who answered the question about how they would define themselves with 'Turkish' remained fairly constant at 19-20 per cent in the intervening seven years. But the percentage of those who answered 'Moslem' went from 36 per cent in

1999 up to 45 per cent in 2006, while the percentage of those who defined themselves as 'a citizen of the Turkish Republic' fell from 34 per cent to 30 per cent. However, while 73 per cent of those surveyed said that laicism was not under threat, when asked whether they would like to see a *shari'a state*, 21 per cent in 1999 and 8.9 per cent in 2006 answered in the positive (ibid: 30).

According to the journalist-author Taha Akyol:

> If further questions had been put to those who answered in the positive in order to find out what people meant by the word *shari'a* which they regarded as sacred, this percentage would have fallen to 7-8% even in 1999, and in 2006 this percentage would have been 4-5%.[30]

Also, according to the survey, as the social status of the individual moved higher, religious tendencies were replaced by liberalism and laic law was preferred (TESEV Report: 39-43). Akyol said that in the end, difficulties in this area would be overcome if Turkey could sustain stability in democracy, market economy, urbanisation and education (ibid).

Results also highlighted that the vast majority of the Turkish population did not see a connection between terrorism and Islam. Moreover, respondents expressed their belief that even if a country were to be occupied, its people should not resort to terrorism and generally rejected any support for such action against a civilian population (TESEV Report: 30).

On 22 July 2007, an early general election took place. Immediately after the elections, in spite of the results indicated in the TESEV Report above, discussions about the secular regime and the constitution surged anew. The AK Party asked Professor Özbudun to head a commission to prepare a draft of a new constitution. However, commission deliberations on the feasibility of lifting the ban on head covering, which was preventing female students from attending university, were perceived as damaging to the secular nature of the state.

The first signs of a new legal regulation relating to the *türban* were evident in Prime Minister Recep Tayyip Erdoğan's statement at a press conference on 14 January 2008 on the occasion of an official visit to Spain. In his statement Erdoğan expressed that even if it is used as a political symbol, it is not a crime to wear a headscarf and that symbols cannot be banned. He further stated that it was sad that while students in Europe and America could freely attend university wearing the *türban* that in the so-called age of freedom such a problem should exist in a country where 99 per cent of the population is Muslim. He said that this problem would be resolved in a short time.

As a result of this speech, the ensuing debate on the *türban* occupied Turkey's agenda, causing lawyers, a number of organisations such as the main opposition party, the Court of Cassation, the Council of State, universities, and so forth to make consecutive statements on the matter. While some legal experts argued that – being contrary to the decisions of the Constitutional Court, the Council of State, and the European Court of Human Rights – Erdoğan's consideration of the *türban* as a political symbol was unconstitutional, others asserted that it should be considered an expression of freedom of speech.

Without waiting until the draft constitution was presented to the parliament, in 2008 a bill was prepared reforming Articles 10 and 42 of the current Constitution (1982) to allow female students to attend university while wearing a scarf or other head covering. AK Party in coalition with MHP was able to pass the bill, thus amending the constitution. The opposition parties, namely deputies from the CHP and DSP, brought these changes to the Constitutional Court on the basis that such changes were unconstitutional because they damaged the secular foundation of the state. The Constitutional Court annulled the constitutional changes on the grounds that it was contrary to the irrevocable provisions of the constitution. According to the Court,

> Covering for the sake of religious belief and the freedom to wear clothing symbolising one's accepted religion may cause conflict in society by the use of pressure on individuals whom they understand do not share the same belief as themselves. This may induce them to perform preventive and harmful acts against one another's freedom of religion and belief and even to exclude those who are not of their own beliefs.[31]

While the Court deliberations continued, on 14 March 2008 the Chief Prosecutor filed a brief before the Constitutional Court requesting the dissolution of AK Party on the basis of its activities, deemed to constitute 'anti-secularism.' The Chief Prosecutor claimed that the AK Party has become the focus of acts contrary to secularism and also requested that 71 persons be prohibited from politics, among these being President Gül and Prime Minister Erdoğan.

The case concerning AK Party's closure was decided on 30 July 2008. The qualified majority needed for the closure could not be achieved, so the request for closure was denied by the Constitutional Court with six acceptances to five rejections. The court held that the evidence did not prove that the aim of the defendant political party was to eliminate the democratic and secular order of the state or to destroy the general principles of the constitutional order by intolerance or by use of force. The court further found that the defendant party had not used the political power available to it for the purpose of inciting violence and that as such the actions of the AK Party were not seen to be serious enough for the dissolution of the party. The court concluded, however, that the actions in question did violate the principle of a democratic and secular republic and that the aggravating nature of these actions warranted penalisation of the defendant party in the form of a reduction of one-half the amount of state financial assistance received by AK Party.

6.5 Constitutional law

Turkey is a constitutional parliamentary democracy with a wide range of human rights enshrined in the present Constitution of 1982. The first three articles formulate a number of fundamental principles described as 'immutable provisions' in Article 4. Articles 1, 2, and 3 stipulate that the form of government is a republic and outline the constituent characteristics of the system which include it being a democratic, laic, constitutional state that respects human rights. The Constitution further sets forth that the state is an indivisible whole. The republic remains loyal to Atatürk's nationalism and the fundamental tenets set forth in the preamble, which reads in part as follows:

> In line with the concept of nationalism and the reforms and principles introduced by the founder of the Republic of Turkey, Atatürk [...] The understanding of absolute supremacy of the will of the nation [...] the recognition that [...] reforms and modernism of Atatürk and that, as required by the principle of laicism, there shall be no interference whatsoever by sacred religious feelings in state affairs and politics [...] thus commanding respect for, and absolute loyalty to its letter and spirit.

In addition to these limitations, Article 174 of the Constitution affords protection to certain laws, namely the Laws of the Radical Reform, which were passed at the time of the formation of the republic, and which still are regarded as a *sine qua non* of modernisation and secularisation – the major aims of the republic. Örücü points out that:

> [t]he aim was to import "modernity" on a major scale. Important consequences arising out of the above are the strict control on political parties and the use of freedoms such as those of expression, the press, association and religion, and a self-referential legal system (Örücü 2003: 133).

The Office of Religious Affairs (Diyanet)

The Office of Religious Affairs was created in the Republican period and was given a structure that complied with the secular structure of the state; it was given the mandate to carry out religious affairs pertaining to faith, worship, and moral principles; to inform society on religion; and to administer places of worship.[32] As indicated above, the Constitution of 1982 places the Office of Religious Affairs within the administrative structure of the state. Article 136 reads as follows:

> The Office of Religious Affairs, which is within the general administration, shall exercise its duties prescribed in its particular law, in accordance with the principles of secularism, removed from all political views and ideas, and aiming at national solidarity and integrity.

In terms of its structure, the Office of Religious Affairs is a public institution placed within the state organisation. This fact has been seen as a contradiction to the secular nature of the state. It can be observed that within this context, there are three views regarding the functioning of the *Diyanet*. The first view is that the *Diyanet* should be totally abolished and that religious matters should be dealt with solely by the religious communities. The second view is that the *Diyanet* should not provide services for different religious communities, that it should be above religious conflicts, and that it should only serve to protect religion at large. The third is the majority view, which protects the present position of the *Diyanet*. This reflects the official position. The cases that signify these views are discussed in the following subsection.

Banning of parties

Constitutional Court cases concerning the banning of parties on the grounds of preserving either the secular nature of the state or the position of the *Diyanet* within the central government can be seen throughout the 1980s to the present day, the most recent case being the abovementioned dissolution of AK Party in 2008.

The Law on Political Parties sanctions in its Article 89 advocating changes in the position of the Office of Religious Affairs within the framework of the Constitution with dissolution of the political parties involved. The decisions of the Turkish Constitutional Court have drawn on this regulation a number of times. For example, the Freedom and Democracy Party (Özgürlük ve Demokrasi Partisi, ÖZDEP) stated in its party programme that the state should not interfere in religious affairs; this should remain within the realm of the religious communities. On this point, the party pledged to grant national and religious minorities the means to develop their communities, language, culture, traditions, philosophy, and religious convictions and practices in an atmosphere of democracy and freedom. The Constitutional Court decided, on the basis of this, to dissolve the party for its promotion of ideas contrary to Section 89 of the Law on Political Parties,[33] among other reasons: 'ÖZDEP interpreted secularism in its modern shape and defined secularism as the separation of state and religion. ÖZDEP believed that the *Diyanet* (Office of Religious Affairs) should not be situated in the general administration of the state.'[34] The Court said that advocating the abolition of the Office of Religion Affairs amounted to undermining the principle of secularism.[35]

The second political party brought before the Constitutional Court was the Democratic Peace Movement Party (Demokratik Barış Hareketi Partisi, DBHP). In its preliminary defence the party relied on criticism voiced by lawyers and said: 'Since the *Diyanet* only deals with the religious affairs of Muslims, this creates inequality between them and members of other religions.' Although the party foresaw some changes in the organisation of the *Diyanet*, it did not want to abolish it and accordingly proposed that 'the *Diyanet* should be above all religions and protect them all rather than being involved in the conflict between religious sects.'[36]

A third party, the Democratic Mass Party (Demokratik Kitle Partisi, DKP) stated in its programme that '[r]eligious affairs and education should not be undertaken by the State but be left to the community at large and religious communities.[37] They further voiced their opinion that '[t]he running of religious centres and the education and training of religious personnel, their appointment, pay and related matters should be the concern of only religious communities.'[38]

Only one party which suggested the abolition of the *Diyanet* was dissolved;[39] the others, which wished to change the status and function of the *Diyanet*, were not dissolved (Koçak 2002: 146-147).

Another important judgment in this connection was the dissolution of the *Refah Partisi*, a case which was also dealt with by the European Court of Human Rights (EctHR).[40] The EctHR agreed with the interpretation of the Turkish Constitutional Court that the RP was dissolved on grounds that it had become 'a centre of activities inimical to the principle of secularism' and that 'the rules of the sharia are deemed to be incompatible with democracy, and the intervention of the State to preserve the secular nature of the political regime is considered "necessary in a democratic society."'[41] As such, dissolution of the party was not found to be in violation of Article 11 of the European Convention on Human Rights (ECHR). The EctHR worded its decision as follows:

> Refah's infringements of the principle of secularism can be classified in three main categories: (i) those which tended to show that the Refah intended to set up a plurality of legal systems, introducing discrimination on the grounds of belief; (ii) those based on references made by Refah members to jihad (holy war) as a political method; (iii) those which tended to show that Refah wanted to apply the shari'a to the Moslem community.[42]

This ruling is still under discussion in Turkey. Many agree with the joint *dissenting opinion* of the European Court that the evidence was not compelling. The *dissenting opinion* declared that the dissolution of the party was based exclusively on the public statements and actions of leaders and members of the party, but not on the statutes or political programme of the party, nor the election manifesto or other public statements issued by the party. No provision was found that served to undermine the secular character of the state as embodied in the constitution and the party programme rather explicitly recognised the fundamental principle of secularism.[43]

The majority of judges on the European Court, like the Constitutional Court, determined that a system of legal pluralism would lead to discrimination between individuals on the basis of their religion and that such a societal model would be incompatible with the values and principles outlined in the ECHR. But according to the *dissenting opinion*, there was no evidence in the material presented to the court that the party, once in government, had undertaken steps to actually introduce legal pluralism as described above.

Later the decision was reaffirmed by the Grand Chamber stating that 'the constitution and programme of a political party could not be taken into account as the sole criterion for determining its objectives and intentions'. The Court further concluded that:

> There were thus convincing and compelling reasons justifying Refah's dissolution and the temporary forfeiture of certain political rights imposed on the other applicants. It followed that Refah's dissolution might be regarded as "necessary in a democratic society" within the meaning of Article 11 § 2 and there had accordingly been no violation of Article 11.

Mandatory religious education

Article 24 of the 1982 Constitution introduced a new course on religious culture and morality into all primary and secondary schools as a compulsory subject.[44] Since 1980, the national curriculum presents both Atatürk and the Prophet Mohammad, showing them in some way as objects related to religion (Kaplan 2003: 113). Such courses thus promote identification with the Turkish nation and its impressive history, reaching contemporary levels of economy and technology and obedience to State authority (Kaplan 2003: 114).

However, the ECtHR, and subsequently the decisions of the Turkish Council of State, found the content of the obligatory nature of religious and ethical studies to be unacceptable. In brief, the Court decision in the case of *Hasan and Eylem Zengin vs. Turkey* reads as follows:

> [...] the Court concludes that the instruction provided in the school subject "religious culture and ethics" cannot be considered to meet the criteria of objectivity and pluralism [...] to respect the religious and philosophical convictions [...] of the Alevi faith, on the subject of which the syllabus is clearly lacking.[45]

Currently, the course on religious studies and ethics is still part of the educational programme and all students of primary and secondary schools are obliged to take this course. However, following the two judgments of the Turkish Council of State (*Danıştay*) corroborating the decision of the ECtHR[46], the syllabus, which was initially in accordance to Sunni principles, was changed incorporating ethics studies and the philosophy of all religions.

6.6 Personal status, family, and inheritance law

Concerning personal status, family, and inheritance law, at present, there is no place within the laws of the Turkish Republic for religious rules or the shari'a. The Swiss civil code concerning persons, family, and succession was promulgated with modifications on 4 October 1926. The Swiss Law of Obligations was translated from its French text and promulgated on 22 April 1926. The current Turkish Civil Code of 2001 is an updated version of the earlier code. In 2001, a first paragraph was added to Article 41 of the Constitution, which states that the family is the basis of the society and relies on equality between the spouses.

Although polygamy was legally banned with the acceptance of the Swiss civil code in 1926, it is still possible to find polygamous unions in some regions, particularly in rural areas in the south-eastern part of the country; however, it is rare and was not very common even before 1926, when the Swiss civil code came into force (Kağıtçıbaşı: 6). A survey by Remzi Oto and Mustafa Ozkan indicated that nearly a third of polygamist men married for the second time after falling in love with another woman. Some were forced into marriage at an early age and wanted a second wife, while others viewed a second marriage as a form of self-assertion and proof of their manhood.[47]

With respect to inheritance, although the civil code gives the same inheritance rights to women as it does to men, it is not unknown that in some traditional and isolated areas a woman inherits either nothing or one-half of what a man receives. However, the disputes are solved within the family or within the village context and have little or nothing to do with the state legal or administrative structures (Kağıtçıbaşı 1982: 7).

Personal disclosure of religious information

As explained in the previous section, Article 7 of the Civil Registration Services Act is in conflict with Article 24 of the Constitition of 1982, and as such the issue of disclosure of one's religious affilitation remains a concern. This issue had been taken to the Constitutional Court, which decided the case in 1995, stating that the requirement to fill in the information box on one's religion was not contrary to the principle of secularism.[48]

The issue was later challenged again by Mr Işık after his request to change his religious affiliation on his identity card from 'Islam' to 'Alevi' was denied by the administration. On 7 September 2004 the District Court dismissed the applicant's request, basing its decision on the opinion it had sought from the legal advisor to the Office of Religious Affairs. In brief, the court held that the term 'Alevi' referred to a sub-group of Islam and that the indication 'Islam' on the identity card was correct. The applicant appealed against this decision, but the Court of Cassation upheld the judgment of the District Court.

The issue then was taken to the ECtHR, which addressed in its holding the legality of including religious information (or including a 'religion' box) on identification cards as follows:

> The Government further contended that since the law of 2006 the applicant, in any event, could no longer claim that he was a victim of a violation of Article 9, because since then all Turkish citizens had been entitled to request that the information about religion on their identity cards be changed or that the appropriate entry be left blank. On this point the Court found that the law had not affected its assessment of the situation. The fact of having to apply to the authorities in writing for the deletion of the religion in civil registers and on identity cards, and similarly, the mere fact of having an identity card with the "religion" box left blank, obliged the individual to disclose, against his or her will, information concerning an aspect of his or her religion or

most personal convictions. That was undoubtedly at odds with the principle of freedom not to manifest one's religion or belief.[49]

6.7 Criminal law

The Penal Code of 1926 was updated and promulgated on 9 September 2004 in the framework of harmonisation with the laws of the European Union. There have been no direct or indirect references to shari'a law in Turkish criminal legislation since the 1930s.

6.8 Commercial law and banking

In the area of banking, banking with no interest is at times discussed and is not considered to indicate a diversion from laicism. In any event, if there were to be such legislative moves, the Constitutional Court would likely annul these as contravening the constitutional principle of secularism. Moreover, Turkey has met the Copenhagen criteria and obtained on 17 December 2004 a date for negotiations with the European Union for full membership, discussions which began on 3 October 2005 and are ongoing. The Turkish legal system and Western laws are in harmony in this field.

6.9 International agreements concerning human rights

Turkey signed the European Convention on Human Rights in 1950 and ratified it in 1954. It signed the Convention on the Elimination of All Forms of Discrimination against Women in 1979, ratifying it in 1985; it came into force in Turkey on 19 January 1986. On 7 May 2004, a new paragraph on equality was appended to Article 10 of the Constitution, which reads as follows: 'Women and men have equal rights. The State is under an obligation to ensure that this right operates in everyday life.'

Turkey also signed the 1966 International Covenant on Civil and Political Rights in 1970. This covenant was ratified in 2003. The country accepted individual application to the European Commission of Human Rights in 1987, individual application to the European Court of Human Rights in 1989, and compulsory jurisdiction of the European Court of Human Rights in 1990.

Turkey ratified the European Convention for the Prevention of Torture and Inhuman or Degrading Treatment or Punishment in 1987 and signed the Convention Against Torture in 1984, ratifying it in 1988. In 1990, a 'Human Rights Investigation Commission' was set up under the auspices of the Turkish Parliament. Turkey also ratified Protocol 6 of the ECHR concerning the prohibition of the death penalty, as amended by protocol 11 on 17 September 2003, and removed the death penalty from Turkish law.

In June 1997, Turkey ratified the Eleventh Protocol of the European Convention on Human Rights and Fundamental Freedoms, which restructured the machinery for enforcement of rights and liberties guaranteed by the Convention. In the process of harmonisation with the E.U., the country has accepted a number of laws, the so-called 'harmonisation packages,' to adapt the Turkish legal system to the legal systems of European states.

6.10 Conclusion

The dualistic law of the Ottoman Empire, with its division between custom (*örf*) and shari'a law, has to some extent paved the way for the adoption of Western legal codes long before the foundation of the secular Republic (Rosenthal 1965: 313). The large-scale legislation of the Ottoman state, by so-called *kanun*-laws, was based on the sultans' *örf* powers (Rahman 1966: 80), which gave the Ottoman sultan the means to respond to the pressure of events and to promulgate new laws and institutions based on Western laws and Western institutions as he saw fit (Akyol 1999: 143-158).

Although the Ottoman sultans fulfilled the dual functions of head of the sultanate and of the caliphate, they effectively only operated as sultans. It is important to note that European law was not imposed upon the Ottoman Empire; there were rather voluntary borrowings, imitations, and adaptations. No part of the Empire had ever been a European colony (Örücü 1992: 40), though certain parts, such as Egypt, did have a semi-colonial status during the final decades of the Empire. Lapidus also emphasises this point: 'Unlike other Muslim empires, the Ottomans maintained their sovereignty and were able to implement their own program of modernisation and reform' (Lapidus 2002: 493).

Therefore, the modernisation movement hailing from the 1839 Reorganisation (*Tanzimat*) was the result of the will and desire of the Ottoman-Turkish ruling class and elite. The 1839 movement started a transition from religion-based law to national Western-inspired law. Through the increase of Western influences, a cultural and legal dualism was created. The legal system became a 'mixed jurisdiction': two bodies of law of different origin, reflecting the rules and principles of two of the major legal families in the world. The civilian tradition and

Islam were in effect operative together. However, the secular legal system gradually narrowed the scope of religious laws and widened its own area of application: '[T]he nineteenth century surely opened the way for the twentieth century reforms as well as creating that important element, an educated, enlightened elite' (Örücü 1992: 51).

The second extremely important period for the Turkish legal system began in 1920, when the Ottoman Empire collapsed and the Turkish Republic rose from its ashes. The founder of the Republic, Kemal Atatürk, tolerated the continued existence of Islamic law in the Republic for only a very short period of time. Especially during the period 1924-1929, a number of voluntary receptions of codes of law from Western countries gave Turkey its civilian, secular character. The Constitution of 1924 confirmed the principle of laicism as a key foundational principle of the Republic. After the 1930s, the influence of the shari'a on national law evaporated. However, although Islam no longer exercises a direct influence over the political, economic, and legal life of the nation, it does exert an indirect influence on public life through its effect on the social behaviour of the individual and communities.

After 1945, tendencies towards more democracy and Islamisation have alternated with periods of military rule and enforced secularisation. Since the introduction of the multi-party system, religion has become a political tool used for propaganda by most of the political parties. From the establishment of the Republic until today, many political parties have indeed been dissolved on the basis that they were involved in anti-laic activities. In 1960, there was a military *coup d'état*, which resulted in the appending of a bill of fundamental and social rights into the constitutional framework, rather than implementation of a policy of repression, as might have been expected. There was another military coup in 1980, which resulted in a change of attitude both toward rights and liberalism, and which led to the 1982 Constitution.

After the general election of 2002, the AK Party came to power. This party was positioned right-of-centre in the political spectrum and exhibited certain Islamic tendencies. One of the reasons for this politicisation of religion was 'the fact that the State has interfered with religion, and that it has tried to decide what people should believe in and how they should live' (Bulaç 2003: 133). An alternative interpretation is offered by Yavuz (2003), who claims that the AK Party symbolised the 'democratisation of Islam.' According to the second analysis there is no actual difference between any given European Christian democratic party and the AK Party. In fact, it is said that the priority of this party, whose membership is largely drawn from the dissolved Islamic Welfare Party (Refah Partisi), is integration with the European Union. Following a problematic period in the 1980s and 1990s, in which the country was a frequent target of foreign criticism, Turkey has endeavoured to stay within the limits set by international law and to show its concern for international legitimacy, as evidenced by the role it played in the 1991 Gulf War, in the aftermath of the 11 September 2001 disaster, during the Afghan War, and recently in the 2003 Iraq intervention.

With regards to the relationship between state and religion, it seems that the state is in charge of religious affairs. There are no Religious Courts, only secular national courts. The Office of Religious Affairs is directly responsible for the supervision of all aspects of religious life. There are compulsory courses on religion and ethics, but no religious garments may be worn in schools, including head covers. The country plays an important role in the prevention of a possible clash of civilisations. Turkey has consistently sided with the Western world during the international conflicts listed above. Turkey has also embraced the *acquis communautaire* of the European Union in the legal, political, and economic areas. Despite difficulties, it appears that the country is on its way to becoming a full member of the E.U.

Nonetheless, not all Turks – not even those who insist on the separation of Islam from politics – agree on the current character of Islam and its role in the state. The population can be divided between traditionalists and modernists who continue to debate these issues. Both religious and secular groups express their dissatisfaction with the Republic's understanding of laicism and the way in which this principle is implemented.

There are two different perceptions of secularism which are at the centre of the religious conflict in Turkey. The first of these perceptions is passive secularism, which does not require the state to act. The second is assertive secularism, which differs from passive secularism in that it gives the state a duty to transform the society and the individual in a rational way. This understanding of secularism does not attribute a social role to religion in the lives of individuals except in their own conscience and in places of worship. The fact that the general staff and the judges of the High Courts[50] have accepted the perception of assertive secularism has caused the demands for the expansion of the freedom of religion and conscience to be seen as a threat directed against the Republic. The reason for the conflict over the issue of the *türban* has arisen from these two different and opposing views of secularism. Other concerns are largely in relation to the position of the Office of Religious Affairs within the state's administrative structure and the implementation of compulsory religion and ethics courses in schools. An author reflecting the views of the Islamist circles sums up the situation as follows:

> Religious circles do not oppose "laicism as a natural attitude of the State". The State should guarantee freedom of conscience

> and religion; must be equidistant to all religions and beliefs; prevent the domination of one belief group and system over others; but should not prevent the living together overtly of all beliefs in the public domain according to the principle of "unity within plurality". Religious people in Turkey wish to see laicism understood in this manner (Bulaç 2003: 133 ; Kaplan 2003: 107-116).

On these issues there is a wide variety of opinion and a constant pluralist discussion in Turkey (Kara 2003: 87-106; Kaplan 2003: 107-116). At the root of these debates we find a power struggle between CHP, which is the founder party of the Turkish Republic and the main opposition in the present parliament, the bureaucracy, the military and the judiciary on the one hand and the political power of the government led by the AK Party, backed by the votes of the people, on the other. Although the judgments of the ECtHR have made a certain impact on the Turkish political and constitutional culture, the solution to this conflict is closely related to the historical and political baggage that Turkey carries[51] and depends on leaving the power struggle aside, reaching a compromise, and achieving a political consensus on the issues discussed.

Notes

1 The author has purposefully chosen for a different title for his chapter. The main reason is that the secularisation of the law was largely complete after the declaration of the Republic and the abolishment of the constitutional clause that identified the state's religion as Islam. The rules of sharī'a have not played any role since this process was completed about ninety years ago.

2 Professor of Public Law at Okan University Faculty of Law, Istanbul, Turkey. The author wishes to thank Prof. Dr Esin Örücü for her suggestions and comments and also his colleagues Assist. Prof. Dr Sevinc Aydar and Research Assistant Bilgehan Savascı for their assistance and support.

3 For statistics and up-to-date information from the Turkish government, see http://tuik.gov.tr. Note that due to the paucity of objective empirical research done on ethnic groups in Turkey the author has chosen not to provide exact numbers of communities in this chapter. To give a general idea, however, the Turks are thought to form more than three-quarters of the total population.

4 The Turkish word for sharia (sharī'a) is *şeriat*. Throughout the text the author will use the term sharī'a.

5 Among the countries where the *Mecelle* was in use we can cite Egypt, Hijaz (Saudi Arabia), Iraq, Syria, Jordan, Lebanon, Cyprus, Palestine and Israel. The *Mecelle* was in force in Albania and Bosnia Herzegovina until 1928 and in Kuwait until 1984. Until quite recently, it was also still in force in Israel (Kaşikçi 1997: 33; Karçiç 1994: 46).

6 This law was in force in Syria until 1953 and in Jordan until 1951; it was also used as a reference for decision-making in Israel/West Bank and is still in use in Lebanon. Though this decree was not directly in use in Iraq, two edicts by the sultan on related matters were implemented in that country (Aydın 1998: 318). It has been utilised as

a non-binding, persuasive source of law in family matters in Bosnia Herzegovina (Karçiç 1994: 46).

7 See also Ahmad 1977: 363-364; Berkes 1998: 431-460.

8 Düstur 1872: vol 3, 152.

9 Official Gazette No. 63, dated 6 March 1924.

10 Sections 2 and 16 of the Constitution of 1924 cite the application of the Shari'a Law among the duties of the Parliament.

11 The law is dated 13 December 1925. It has been said that the role of the Nakşibendi Sect in the Seyh Sait uprising was an important factor in taking such a radical decision (Tanör 2002: 276).

12 For example as stables, lofts for the storage of hay or wheat, etc.

13 Article 19 of Part 2, § 2, states: 'No person shall be allowed to exploit and abuse religion or religious feelings or things considered sacred by religion in any manner whatsoever for the purpose of political or personal benefit, or for gaining power, or for even partially basing the fundamental social, economic, political and legal order of the State on religious dogmas. [...]'

14 Article 19 of Part 2, § 2, states: 'Religious education and teaching shall be subject to the individual's own will and volition, and in the case of minors, to that of their legally appointed guardians.'

15 For more discussion and analysis about the 1982 Constitution, see 5.5.

16 See Danıştay 8. Daire (Council of State, 8th Division) E. 1984/636.K.1984/1574, dated 13 December 1984.

17 As we have stated in the beginning, the sections as constructed for this study this chapter were formed by taking into account the history and key developments of other Islamic countries. For Turkey, the 1980 military coup would have been a more natural time to start a new section.

18 This law made amendments to the Law on Higher Education. It added a provision stating that it is compulsory to be dressed in modern clothes in higher education institutions, but it is free to wear a headscarf or turban to cover one's head and neck for religious beliefs. This law was made to enable access to university education to female students who covered their heads because of their religious beliefs.

19 The judgment of the Constitutional Court, E. 1989/1, K. 1989/12, in *Resmi Gazete* (Official Gazette) No. 20216, dated 7 March 1989.

20 For instance, in January 1997 Prime Minister Erbakan invited some leaders of Sufi paths and dervish orders (*tariqas*) to the Office of the Prime Minister for dinner during Ramadan. The Iranian Ambassador who was invited to a 'Kudüs evening' and the Mayor of the Sincan region of Ankara made speeches on 2 February 1997, understood by some to be calls for the overthrow of the republican regime. The following day military tanks drove through the streets of Sincan, the Mayor was apprehended and Iran had to call back its Ambassador.

21 See Mert, N. (2005), 'AIHM'nin Türban Kararı', in *Radikal*, dated 15 November.

22 See Aktan, G. (2004), 'AIHM Türban Kararı (1)', in *Radikal*, dated 7 July.

23 See Report: http://www.internethaber.com, dated 14 September 2006.

24 For the full text of the Bill see www.basbakanlik.gov.tr/docs/kkgm/kanuntasarilari/101-1262.doc.

25 See http://www.webhatti.com/wh-haber-bulteni/23938-turkiye-de-3-bin-379-kisinin-tapulu-camisi-var.html, 15 May 2007.

26 See http://www.haber3.com/haber.php?haber_id=222515, dated 29 March 2007.

27 See http://www.tsk.mil.tr/, dated 27 April 2007.

28 For analysis and related discussion, see Turkish newspapers from 28 April 2007 (e.g. http://www.radikal.com.tr/index.php?tarih=27/04/2007 and http://hurarsiv.hurriyet.com.tr/goster/haberler.aspx?id=2065&tarih=2007-04-27).

29 See e.g. http://news.bbc.co.uk/2/hi/business/6606723.stm, dated 1 May 2007.
30 See Akyol, T. (2006), 'Dindarlık, Laiklik, Kimlik', in *Milliyet*, dated 22 November.
31 Judgment of Constitutional Court of 5 June 2008, E. 2008/16, K. 2008/116.
32 See http://www.diyanet.gov.tr/english/default.asp,
33 Section 89: 'Political parties shall not have an aim that runs counter to Article 136 of the Constitution, which provides that the Office of Religious Affairs is bound to carry out the duties assigned to it in accordance with the principle of laicism.' It is anticipated that this article will soon be abolished. Discussions surrounding this issue will not, however, be further addressed in this chapter.
34 Judgment of the Constitutional Court of 23 November 1993, E. 1993/1, K.1993/2, AMKD (Journal of Constitutional Court Decisions), No. 30, Vol. II, pp. 845-935, in particular pp. 879, 906.
35 Compare dissenting opinions in E.1993/1 (Siyasi Parti Kapatma), K.1993/2, dated 23 November 1993, AMKD (Journal of Constitutional Court Decisions), No. 30, Vol. II: 841-935.
36 Compare Judgment of the Constitutional Court of 22 May 1997, E.1996/3 (Siyasi Parti Kapatma), K.1997/3, *Resmi Gazete*, No: 24067, dated 2 June 2006, p. 21.
37 Compare E.1997/2 (Siyasi Parti Kapatma), K.1999/1, KT. 26 February 1999, *Resmi Gazete*, No. 24591, dated 22 November 200, p. 63.
38 *Resmi Gazete* (Official Gazette: 131), No. 24591, dated 22 November 2001.
39 See note 32. This was one of the judgments of the Court that led to the decision to revoke Article 89 of the Constitution.
40 Judgment of the Constitutional Court of 16 January 1998: E.1997/1, K.1998/1, dated 16 January 1998, AMKD (Journal of Constitutional Court Decisions), No. 34, Vol. II, pp. 762-1145.
41 See *Refah Partisi Erbakan, Kazan and Tekdal and Others vs. Turkey*, Judgment No.s 41340/98, 41342/98, 41343/98, 41344/98, Decision of 3 October 2000, para. 59. For further analysis, see Koçak & Örücü 2003: 399-423.
42 See ibid, para. 68.
43 The topic of Islamic marriage, for example, was not discussed in the party programme or in speeches made by party functionaries, nor did it play a role in the case against the party.
44 The Turkish Constitution of 1982, § 24(4): 'Education and instruction in religion and ethics shall be conducted under state supervision and control. Instruction in religious, cultural and moral education shall be compulsory in the curricula of primary and secondary schools. Other religious education and instruction shall be subject to the individual's own desire, and in the case of minors, to the request of their legal representatives.'
45 See the case *Hasan and Eylem Zengin vs. Turkey*, Judgement (Application No. 1448/04), dated 9 October 2007, para. 70.
46 See Danıştay 8. Daire (Council of State 8th Division), E. 2006/4107, K. 2007/7481, dated 28 December 2007; and E. 2007/679, K. 2008/1461, dated 29 February 2008; E. 2006/4107, K. 2007/7481, dated 28 December 2007.
47 See Report (2005): 'Too much of a good thing; Turkey and polygamy', *The Economist* 377, Issue 8458: 71, dated 24 December.
48 See Judgment of Constitutional Court of 21 June 1995, E.1995/17, K. 1995/16.
49 See Judgment of ECtHR, *Sinan Işık vs. Turkey*, Application No. 21924/05, dated 2 February 2010.
50 According to Articles 146-158 of the 1982 Constitution, the High Courts in Turkey are the Constitutional Court, the Court of Cassation, the Council of State, the Military Court of Cassation, the High Military Administrative Court and the Court of Conflicts.
51 Koçak & Örücü 2003: 407-408.

Bibliography

Ahmad, F. (1977), *The Turkish experiment in democracy 1950-1975*. London: C. Hurst & Company.

Akagündüz, A. (1986), *Mukayeseli İslam ve Osmanlı Hukuku Külliyatı*. Diyarbakır: Dicle Üniversitesi Hukuk Fakültesi Yay.

Aktan, G. (2004), 'AİHM Türban Kararı (1)', in *Radikal*, dated 7 July.

Akyavaş, R. (1950), *Resimli Tarih Mecmuası*. İstanbul.

Akyol, T. (1999), *Osmanlı'da ve İran'da Mezhep ve Devlet*. İstanbul: Milliyet Yay.

Aydın, M.A. (1998), 'Hukuk-u aile Kararnamesi', in *Türk Diyanet Vakfı İslam Ansiklopedisi*, 314-318. İstanbul: Türk Diyanet Vakfı Yayınları.

Bartleby (2009), 'Turkey', in *World factbook*, see http://www.bartleby.com/151/country/tu.html (2008 statistics) and https://www.cia.gov/library/publications/the-world-factbook/geos/tu.html (online version). Washington D.C.: Central Intelligence Agency.

Belgesay, M.R. (1999), '*Tanzimat ve Adliye Teşkilatı*', in C.I. Tanzimat, İstanbul: Milli Eğitim Bakanlığı Yay.

Berkes, N. (1998), *The development of secularism in Turkey*. London: Hurst & Company.

Bozkurt, G. (1996), *Batı Hukukunun Türkiye'de Benimsenmesi*. Ankara: Türk Tarih Kurumu Yay.

Bulaç, A. (2003), 'Türk Modeli Laikliğin 21. Yüzyılda Geleceği', in, *Devlet ve Din İlişkileri-Farklı Modeller, Konseptler ve Tecrübeler*. Ankara: Konrad Adenauer Vakfı Yay.

Çarkoğlu, A. & B. Toprak (2006), *Değişen Türkiye'de Din, Toplum, Siyaset*. İstanbul: TESEV Yay.

Cevdet Paşa, A. (1986a), *Tezakir, I*, (C. Baysun, ed.). Ankara: Türk Tarih Kurumu Yay.

Cevdet Paşa, A. (1986b), *Tezakir, II*, (C. Baysun, ed.). Ankara: Türk Tarih Kurumu Yay.

Cevdet Paşa, A. (1986c), *Tezakir, IV* (C. Baysun, ed.).Ankara: Türk Tarih Kurumu Yay.

Davison, R.H. (1990), *Essays in Ottoman and Turkish history, 1774-1923*.London: Saqi Books.

Düstur (1872), *Birinci Tertip*. İstanbul: Matbaa-i Amire.

Gökçen, A. (1989), *Tanzimat Dönemi Osmanlı Ceza Kanunları ve Bu Kanunlardaki Ceza Müeyyideleri*, İstanbul: Ahmet Gökçen Yayını.

İnalcık, H. (1989), *The Ottoman Empire: The classical age, 1300-1600*. New York: Orpheus Publishing Inc.

İnalcik, H. (1994), *An economic and social history of the Ottoman Empire*, Vol. i, 1300-1600. Cambridge: Cambridge University Press (paperback edition 1997).

Kağıtçıbaşı, Ç. (1982), 'Introduction', in Ç. Kağıtçıbaşı (ed.), *Sex roles, family and community in Turkey*. Bloomington: Indiana University Turkish Studies Press.

Kaplan, S. (2003), '1980 Sonrası Türkiye'de Devlet ve Din' in *Devlet ve Din İlişkileri-Farklı Modeller, Konseptler ve Tecrübeler*, 107-116. Ankara: Konrad Adenauer Vakfı Yay.

Kara, İ. (2003), 'Türkiye'de Laiklik Uygulamaları Açısından Diyanet İşleri Başkanlığı', in *Devlet ve Din İlişkileri-Farklı Modeller, Konseptler ve Tecrübeler*, 87-106. Ankara: Konrad Adenauer Vakfı Yay.

Karçiç, F. (1994), *Bosna-Hersek İslam Hukuku*. İstanbul: Balkan İlmi Araştırma Merkezi.

Kaşıkçı, O. (1997), *İslam ve Osmanlı Hukukunda Mecelle*. İstanbul: Osmanlı Araş. Vakfı.

Koçak, M. (2002), *Siyasal Partiler ve Türkiye'de Parti Yasakları*. Ankara: Turhan Kitabevi.

Koçak, M. & E. Örücü (2003), 'Dissolution of Political Parties in the Name of Democracy: Cases from Turkey and the European Court of Human Rights', *European Public Law* 9: 399- 423.

Kongar, E. (1998), *21. Yüzyılda Türkiye*, 14th edition. İstanbul: Remzi Kitabevi.

Kramer, H. (2001), *Avrupa ve Amerika Karşısında Değişen Türkiye* (Translation, A. Çimen). İstanbul: Timaş Yayınları.

Lapidus, I.M. (2002), *A history of Islamic societies*. Cambridge: Cambridge University Press.

Lewis, B. (1968), *The emergence of modern Turkey*. London: Oxford University Press.

Mert, N. (2005), 'AİHM'nin Türban Kararı', in *Radikal*, dated 15 November.
Örücü, E. (2003), 'The Turkish experience with judicial comparativism in human rights cases', in E. Örücü (ed.), *Judicial comparativism in human rights cases*,131-154. London: ukncd /biicl.
Örücü, E. (1992), 'The impact of European law on the Ottoman Empire and Turkey', in W.J. Mommsen & J.A. de Moor (eds.), *European expansion and law*, 39-58. Oxford/New York: Berg Publishers.
Özbudun, E. (1993), *Türk Anayasa Hukuku*. Ankara: Yetkin Yay.
Öztuna, Y. (1978), *Büyük Türkiye Tarihi*. İstanbul: Ötüken Yay.
Rahman, F. (1966), *Islam*. London: Weidenfelt and Nicolson.
Rosenthal, E.I.J. (1965), *Islam in the modern national state*. Cambridge: Cambridge University Press.
Schacht, J. (1964), *An introduction to Islamic law*. Oxford: Clarendon Press.
Shankland, D. (1999), *Islam and society in Turkey*. London: The Eothen Press.
Shaw, S.J. & E.K. Shaw (1977), *History of the Ottoman Empire and modern Turkey*, Vol. ii, London: Cambridge University Press.
Tanör, B. (2002), *Kurtuluş Kuruluş, Dördüncü Bası*, İstanbul: Cumhuriyet Kitapları.
Toprak, B. (2003), 'Türk Modeli Laikliğin 21. Yüzyılda Geleceği' in *Devlet ve Din İlişkileri-Farklı Modeller, Konseptler ve Tecrübeler*. Ankara: Konrad Adenauer Vakfı Yay.
Tunaya, T.Z. (1995), Türkiye'de Siyasi Partiler 1859-1952, Tıpkı Basım, İkinci Baskı, İstanbul: Arba Yay.
Üçok, C., A. Mumcu & N. Bozkurt (2002), *Türk Hukuk Tarihi*. Ankara: Savaş Yayınları.
Velidedeoğlu, H.V. (1999), *Kanunlaştırma Hareketleri ve Tanzimat*. İstanbul: Milli Eğitim Bakanlığı Yay.
Yavuz, M.H. (2003), *Islamic political identity in Turkey*. New York: Oxford University Press.

7 Sharia and national law in Afghanistan

Nadjma Yassari and Mohammad Hamid Saboory[1]

Abstract

Legal pluralism is the hallmark of Afghan legal reality. Afghan law is a combination of Islamic law, state legislation, and local customary law. This chapter traces the origins of that plurality and shows that the lack of clarity regarding the relationship between these different sources of law and the absence of guidelines as how to resolve conflicts between them is still causing many problems in Afghanistan today. Despite the existence of official law, i.e. the formal legal system established under the provisions of a constitution, the socio-legal reality is not reflected by it, and the law in the books does not represent the norms that actually govern the lives of the majority of the population. For ordinary people and villagers, who form the majority of the populace, tribal/customary and Islamic law are more significant and actually better known than any state legislation. As a result, in Afghanistan it is not the implications of sharia or sharia-based law that, at least for the moment, prevents the application and implementation of international legal and human rights standards, but the lack of a system by which the rule of law may be established so that the legal system is capable – practically, socially, politically – of guaranteeing and enforcing laws effectively. Although the Government of Afghanistan is committed to carrying out its duties imposed not only by Afghanistan's domestic laws but also by the country's international obligations, the greatest challenge to action is the lack of security and the fragile peace balance in the country.

Table of contents

With an estimated population of more than 30 million inhabitants, Afghanistan is composed of more than ten ethnic and tribal groups, most of whom have lived together in the country for centuries. These include the majority Pashtuns, who constitute almost one half of the population, followed by a quarter of the population of Tajiks (27%), and sizeable communities of Uzbecs (9%) and Hazara (9%). Turkmen (3%), Aimaq (4%), Baluch (2%), and small communities of Brahui, Nuristani, Pashaie, Pamiri, Khirgiz, and Qizilbash are also represented. Each of these groups has had its own forms of languages, culture, and religious beliefs over the course of Afghanistan's history. However, the centuries-long interaction between all these groups, although distinguishable by accent and clothing for example, has resulted in a cultural blending of various Afghan ethnic and tribal traditions (Wardak 2005: 63). The country is almost exclusively Muslim with a majority Sunni population (80%) and an estimated 19 per cent Shi'i population. Afghan Persian or Dari is the official language, spoken by about one half of the population, with Pashtu, also an official language, spoken by some 35 per cent of people. Turkic languages are also spoken by some groups (11%), as well as another thirty minor languages that have been identified (e.g. Baluchi and Pashai). Many individuals speak more than one language.

(Source: Bartleby 2010)

7.1 The period until 1920

The struggle for an independent and unified nation

Afghanistan's geographic placement at the crossroads of civilisations determined its fate as early as the fourth century B.C. when Alexander the Great defeated the Persian invaders who had been the first to achieve domination. A series of conquests followed with particularly devastating invasions by the Mongol leaders Genghis Khan and Tamerlane. Two thousand years of ravage and invasions stalled the establishment of a unified state, which did not come about until the eighteenth century. The first Afghan kingdom, more a confederation of tribes then, was established by Ahmad Shah Durrani in 1747. He was approved as the first Afghan king in Kandahar in a mass gathering of the Afghan people referred to as the 'Great Assembly' (*Loya Jirga*), which was only later again taken up when it was reactivated as the National Assembly in the early twentieth century (see 7.3). Afghanistan ultimately emerged as a nation in the mid-nineteenth century, by which time the new rulers had to cope with the colonial ambitions of the British and the Russians (Reynolds & Flores 2005: 1-3).

The Second Anglo-Afghan War of 1878-1880 resulted in the creation of an independent Afghan kingdom within the British sphere of influence, serving as a buffer zone between Russia and India. Its present boundaries were fixed during the reign of King Amir Abdul Rahman (1880-1901), who aimed to bring the region's tribes and ethnic groups under centralised control, unify the country politically, and establish a central government with a certain degree of standardised administration. Amir Abdul Rahman held the position of King and Chief Justice, issuing verdicts in accordance with the principles of Islamic law and traditions.

In 1896 a compilation of criminal rules based on Hanafi law was proclaimed (Vafai 1988: 24). The king was vested with the authority to preside cases dealing with rebellion, embezzlement, forgery and bribery by government officials, treason, and crimes against the state and members of the royal family. In all other cases, law was dispensed by Religious Courts and religious judges. Statutory enactments of this area were basically designed to reiterate Islamic law. For example a guide called 'the judges principles' (*asās ol-qod,āt*) that drew from the classical Hanafi law was issued by Amir Abdul Rahman in the late 1880s and was designed to control the activities of the judges (Kamali 1985: 35; Vafai 1988: 24). Additionally, judges had to comply with an elementary court procedure outlined in a guideline for civil and criminal matters called 'book of governance' (*ketābče-ye h,okūmatī*). Amir Abdul Rahman divided the existing laws of his kingdom into three groups: sharia law, administrative laws (*qānūn*), and tribal laws. Likewise, he established three kinds of courts: the Religious Courts, which in fact already existed, that dealt with religious and civil matters; criminal courts administered by chiefs of police (*kotwals*) or by judges; and a board of commerce consisting of merchants, who settled business disputes (Vafai 1988: 11-12). Tribal groups had always had their own ways of dispute settlement. This was done in particular through the local assemblies (*jirgas*) following a specific procedure (see 7.10).

Amir Abdul Rahman reigned with an iron fist. The country was stable with little or no internal unrest. Afghanistan remained, however, a fragmented country with local governors acting with virtual autonomy. In addition, the country was held in a stranglehold by a corrupt and fanatic system of Islamic clerics (*mullahs*), absolutely opposed to any advancement that could potentially weaken their power. This held especially true in the tribal hinterlands of Afghanistan.

After Amir Abdul Rahman's death, his son Habibullah succeeded him. Habibullah (1901-1919) eased the system of compulsory conscription, dismantled his father's secret intelligence service, and put an end to some of the most brutal forms of corporal punishment. At the same time, religious organisations regained some of their former influence

(Ewans 2001: 80). The new king also founded a state council for tribal affairs and gave the tribal chiefs more autonomy in the administration of regional affairs. He ensured that the quality of education was improved by setting up schools of higher education based on the French model as well as military academies and teacher training institutes. The first hydroelectric power plant was also built during his reign. Under Habibullah a four-part compilation of Islamic law encompassing the civil and criminal principles of the sharia was made, the so-called 'Supreme Commandments' (*sirāj ol-aḥkām*), to be used as a framework of reference by judges (Kamali 1985: 35).

During World War I, Habibullah aligned himself with the British. This was a dangerous decision because the population was strongly opposed to the British and their domination of their country. Many Muslims were reticent about supporting an 'infidel empire' against the former seat of the Caliphate, the Ottoman Empire. Habibullah was accused by his people for having failed to achieve full independence from all foreign powers and was assassinated on 20 February 1919 in a hunting resort far from Kabul. When Amanullah, Habibullah's son, succeeded to the Afghan throne in 1919, the country was plagued with ethnic divisions, tribal conflict, and corrupt religious fanaticism.

7.2 The period from 1920 until 1965

The struggle between modernity and traditionalism

1919-1933: The first Afghan constitutions

Amanullah's first act as a king was to declare war on the British to end their domination in Afghanistan. On 3 May 1919, the third and last Anglo-Afghan war started and ended with the Treaty of Rawalpindi signed on 8 July 1919. Amanullah (1919-1929) was determined to reform Afghan society. From 1919 to 1923, a series of political, legal, and judicial initiatives were taken at his instigation with the aim of resolving the fractures of Afghan society (Kohlmann 1999). Slavery was formally abolished; campaigns of reconciliation against the violent divisions between Sunni and Shi'i were undertaken; and the status of the non-Muslim minorities was improved by abolishing their *jezye* tax (a poll tax levied from non-Muslims in Islamic societies).

Amanullah sought to bring Western secular law to his homeland. He was looking in particular at Kemal Atatürk in Turkey and Reza Shah in Iran. In April 1923, he enacted Afghanistan's first formal written constitution, the constitution of the government of Afghanistan, the *neẓāmnāme-ye asāsī-ye dūlat-e ᶜālīe-ye afghānestān* (Vafai 2001: 93).[2] This first legal text, consisting of 73 articles, included a list of basic freedoms that the Afghan people had never been awarded, such as freedom from torture, freedom from unlawful search and seizure, personal freedoms, and guarantees of justice from government officials. Islam was inscribed as the official religion of the state, but the constitution also granted protection to the followers of other religions. The equality of all Afghan citizens, access to political rights, personal freedom, freedom of the press, and the right to education were guaranteed. The Constitution of 1923 prohibited extra-judicial or extra-legal punishment; courts were to be the only legitimate institutions to deal with all disputes within society. The independence of the judiciary and the courts was recognised, and any kind of intervention in court procedure was prohibited. A special High Court was established temporarily to deal with crimes committed by members of government and ministers. Elementary education was declared compulsory for all Afghan citizens. Amanullah also introduced the right of women to education, permission for female students to travel abroad for higher education purposes, abolished child marriage, and put restrictions on polygamy. He furthermore issued a new administrative regulation, transferring jurisdiction of family matters from the Religious Courts to civil courts (Vafai 1988: 12).

Afghanistan's first constitution triggered the enactment of a plethora of other legislation (*neẓām-nāme*) related to administration, education, social institutions, trade, and industry. More than 51 *neẓām-nāme* were published between 1919 and 1927,[3] including the Law on Marriage, Wedding and Circumcision (*neẓām-nāme-ye nikāh,, ᶜarūsī, khatneh sūrī*) in 1921, as amended in 1926. This statute and all its successors (the Marriage Laws of 1934, 1949, 1960 and 1971) were a piecemeal legislation, enacted to address very specific questions on particular, mostly economic issues revolving around marriage, such as the expenses for weddings and other family ceremonies.[4]

In 1925, a penal code (*neẓām-nāme-ye ᶜomūmī-ye jazā*) was published (Vafai 1988: 25). It contained 308 articles and was primarily based on sharia principles, with some influence from the French penal code of the time. Article 1 of the Afghan Penal Code (1925) categorised crimes into three categories, as is done in the classical sharia: *ḥodūd* (class of punishments that are fixed for certain crimes, including theft, fornication, consumption of alcohol, and apostasy); *qes,ās,* (retaliation); and *taᶜzīr* (punishments that are administered at the discretion of the judge). The law concerning the court procedure (*neẓām-nāme-ye tashkīlāt-e asāsī*) required judges and the sharia courts to issue decisions in accordance with the provisions of the penal code. A group of religious scholars (*ulama*) also compiled a guide for judges (*tamassok al-qod,āt-e amāniye*). It consisted of two parts, a civil and a criminal part (Kamali 1985: 37). The first enactment of a military penal code (*neẓām-nāme-ye jazā-ye ᶜaskarī*) was another major step towards more legal certainty, especially considering that the Constitution of 1923 embraced the principle of the rule of law in criminal matters (Art. 21).

Amanullah's reforms were, however, responded to with hostility. The advent of civil, secular law was not accepted by Amanullah's assorted enemies among the *mullahs*, who saw their power fading in a more educated society. They accused the *neẓām-nāme* of being un-Islamic and in violation of God's laws. When Amanullah attempted to change the free day of the week from Friday to Thursday and ordered the unveiling of women and the compulsory wearing of European dress, the enraged *mullahs* joined forces with the tribesmen, who resented Amanullah's meddling in their affairs, and gradually began to destabilise his government. Amanullah had to make concessions. In the late 1920s, he agreed to end female education by the age of twelve, to rescind the prohibition on child marriages, to allow polygamy, and to strike down the freedom of religion as set forth in the *neẓām-nāme* (Kohlmann 1999). His efforts to provide Afghanistan with a modern legal framework were perceived as too radical by his fellow countrymen. His constitution and the changes he endeavoured to introduce underestimated the strength of traditionalism and conservative opinion.

Despite his many attempts to unify the country and help it overcome its ethnic and religious fractures, these grew only worse as the country became subject to fanatically competing leaders with extremist ideologies. In early 1929, Amanullah abdicated and went into temporary exile in India. His attempt to return to Afghanistan failed, as he could not secure the support from his people. From India, the ex-king travelled to Europe and settled in Switzerland, where he died in Zurich in 1960.

In contrast to Amanullah, his successor Nadir Shah (1930-1933), a military general in Amanullah's reign, adopted a more conservative path. His policies are reflected in the Constitution of 1931, which overruled many of the Amanullah reforms and numerous *neẓām-nāmes*. Against the backdrop of near anarchy in the country following Amanullah's abdication, a new constitution (*oṣūl-e asāsī-ye dūlat-e ʿālīe-ye afghānestān*) was promulgated on 31 October 1931 (Ewans 2001: 101). It contained 110 articles and clearly endorsed the traditional supremacy of sharia in Afghanistan. This is manifested in the numerous references to the sharia, which essentially amounted to proclaiming sharia as the law of the country. Islamic law continued to dominate judicial practice, and the limited number of statutes that still existed was mainly concerned with procedural and administrative matters. The Constitution of 1931 was not only in clear contrast with its predecessor in its emphasis on adherence to Islam in legislation and government affairs but also clearly more conciliatory towards the tribal establishment.

The progressive views of Amanullah and the conservative approach of Nadir Shah created discontinuity in the legal and social order; the contradictory objectives of the constitutions of 1923 and 1931 gave further rise to disorientation and dissatisfaction. The need for corrective measures to bring about a balance between the expressions of the modernist and conservative ideological currents in the country was strongly felt.

1933-1964: Modernity and traditionalism revisited

In 1933 Nadir Shah was assassinated. His son Zahir Shah succeeded him at the age of 18. While officially Zahir Shah was proclaimed king, from 1933 onwards Afghanistan was effectively ruled by his uncle Hashim, who took the position of royal prime minister (1933-1946). Hashim was keen to implement the strict rule of the sharia (Ewans 2001: 104). Nonetheless, the proliferation of newspapers and journals, although under strict censorship, allowed for the exchange of ideas among the Afghan elite regarding the interactions between modernity and the rule of Islam in society and the life of the individual. Archaeological excavations conducted by the French fostered some ideas of a glorious pre-Islamic past, and encouraged secular ideas among Afghan intellectuals. The Afghan economy advanced with the introduction of Western banking institutions, the enhancement of exports of agricultural products, and transit trade through Russia. External relations expanded with other countries such as Japan, Germany, Italy, and the United States. In 1946, Hashim retired following the wish of the royal family and was replaced by Sardar Shah Mahmoud Khan, another uncle of Zahir Shah, as prime minister (Ewans 2001: 105).

Sardar Shah Mahmoud Khan (1946-1953) was a more tolerant and liberal ruler. He had political prisoners released and allowed a certain degree of freedom of the press. Relations with the United States improved, many projects were undertaken in construction, and the educational system started to develop once again. Despite all his efforts, however, the country was moving toward destabilisation once again. In 1953, Sardar Shah Mahmoud Khan was replaced by his cousin, Mohammad Daoud Khan, who took over the position of prime minister. Through cooperation with the Soviet Union and the United States, the economy was further developed. While the American influence was visible at the University of Kabul, the Russians pressed for another institute of higher education and established the Kabul Polytechnic. The Afghan army was reformed and modernised with Russian weapons after America twice refused the proposal made by Afghan authorities to supply the Afghan military with arms (Magnus & Naby 2002: 47).

The Constitution of 1931 remained in force, ensuring the prominent position of the sharia. From 1933 until the promulgation of a new constitution in 1964, a mixed pattern in legislation developed, leading to confusion over the relationship of state law to sharia, especially in cases of ambiguity and conflict between them. The courts generally applied the Arabic manuals of the Hanafi school of law and the Ottoman *Mejelle*, i.e. the codified version of the Hanafi school for civil transactions, excluding family law (Kamali 1985: 36). An early departure from this pattern came about with the promulgation of the Commercial Code of 1955 and the Commercial Procedure Code of 1963, both of which were not based on the sharia but on Western models (see 7.8).

This period can be seen as a time in which attempts were made to bring together the modern and conservative elements in Afghanistan. When members of the royal family appeared unveiled at the annual ceremony marking Afghanistan's independence, for instance, the religious establishment protested seriously. Daoud, who was well versed in matters of theology, though, insisted that veiling was not required in Islam. When the mullahs persisted with their campaign, they were thrown into jail without getting any public support. This was an altogether different outcome of events than had been the case with the fiasco of Amanullah's attempted reforms thirty years earlier.

7.3 The period from 1965 until 1985

Communism and the Republic of Afghanistan

1964-1973: Zahir Shah and tentative constitutionalism

Daoud was forced to resign in 1963. Shortly thereafter, Zahir Shah promulgated Afghanistan's third constitution, which was approved by the *Loya Jirga* (the National Assembly) on the 1st of October 1964.[5] This constitution was conceived over a period of eighteen months and reflects to a certain degree public consultations and debates from this period in its contents. The 1964 Constitution paid attention to issues of institution-building and democratic structures, namely the role and structure of a parliamentary democracy and the independence of the judiciary. Indeed, this constitution introduced for the first time, at least on paper, the separation of powers to the Afghan legal system.

The constitution excluded members of the royal family from political offices, but retained considerable powers for the king (Amin 1993: 17). As head of the state, he embodied national sovereignty and was the guarantor of the basic precepts of Islam and of the country's independence. The king was supposed to be a follower of the Hanafi doctrine

(Art.s 6-8). According to Article 15 of the Constitution of 1964, the king was accountable to no one and had to be respected by everyone.

Article 2 of the constitution declared 'the sacred religion of Islam' as the religion of Afghanistan. Equality of all human beings (Art. 25), secrecy of people's communication (Art. 30), and freedom of expression (Art. 31) were declared to be fundamental rights. A fundamental step towards more political participation was taken in Article 32 of the constitution; it allowed for the first time the formation of political parties. The aims and activities of a party, as well as its ideology, had to be in accordance with the values embodied in the constitution. Financial resources should be available to create a political party, and a party formed in accordance with the provisions of the law could not be dissolved without judicial proceedings and the decision of a competent court.

Article 103 of the constitution introduced a new institution, that of the Attorney General. Its duty was to investigate criminal activities as an independent body of the executive power of the government. The judicial branch was not to interfere in its activities. The office of the Attorney General was similar to the American institution of Attorney General, indicating that to a certain extent the Constitution of 1964 was influenced by the U.S. Constitution.

Although the Constitution of 1964 concentrated most state authorities in the person of the king, it was still the most liberal constitutional document ever in Afghanistan. Parliament was to consist of two houses; the House of the People (*Wolesi Jirga*), elected by the people of Afghanistan in free, general, secret, and direct elections in accordance with the provisions of the law for a period of four years; and the House of the Elders (*Meshrano Jirga*), one-third of its members to be appointed by the king and the remaining two-thirds to be elected in free, general, secret, and direct elections (Art. 43). The government was required to publish all legislation in the Afghan Official Gazette (*jarīde rasmī*) which was to be distributed to the courts and other legal institutions.[6]

The judiciary was to consist of a Supreme Court and other courts, with the task of adjudicating all litigation brought before them (Art. 98). The judges, who could be held accountable by the newly founded Supreme Court, were appointed by the king (Art. 99). The Supreme Court was established, with branches for civil, commercial, criminal, military, and national security cases. For the first time, a juvenile court was established in Kabul to adjudicate in cases where the defendant had not yet reached the age of fifteen (Lau 2003: 52).

The 1964 constitution was the first to provide a clear definition of 'law' and to establish a formal order of priority in favour of statutory law. Article 69 provided:

> Law is a resolution passed by both Houses, and signed by the king. In areas where no such law exists, the provisions of the Hanafi jurisprudence of the sharia of Islam shall be considered as law.

Although the rights and duties given to the Houses of Parliament by the 1964 Constitution were important and could have been the basis for people's participation in politics, in reality, the Houses remained largely ineffective, and no significant body of statutory law emerged. The Constitution of 1964 had established a powerful parliament and, thus, reversed the hitherto prevailing role of a more powerful executive. Consequently, the two engaged in a power struggle, both failing to adjust to their new roles under the constitution. Thus, like its predecessors, the third Afghan constitution was not implemented. No law for the formation and organisation of political parties was drafted, nor did any independent political party emerge, much less gain permission to be registered in Afghanistan (Rubin 2002: 73). The king's democratic experiment failed because he did not allow the constitutionally-mandated liberties to take root, as is evidenced by the fact that there was no law on political parties or on provincial councils and municipalities and by the fact that no attention was paid to the judicial reforms required by the 1964 Constitution. The conflict between the legislative and executive powers further exacerbated the instability and problems plaguing the Afghan political scene.

On 1 January 1965, Noor Mohammad Taraki formed the People's Democratic Party of Afghanistan (PDPA), which became known as the 'Khalq' party. Like all other parties in Afghanistan, the PDPA was an unofficial, clandestine party that was not registered with the government. The PDPA soon split into two parties because of disagreements between its leaders Taraki and Babrak Kamal. Whereas Taraki remained head of the 'Khalq' party, Karmal established the 'Parcham' party in 1967.[7] Most of the supporters of Khalq were Pashtuns from the rural areas in the country. The Parcham supporters came mostly from urban citizens and supported social-economic reforms in the country. The Khalqs accused the Parchams of being under the allegiance of Zahir Shah.[8] Meanwhile, the influence of communism began to become ever more visible, both groups being consistently pro-Soviet, and being strongly supported by the Russian embassy and Soviet advisors in Kabul.

A Criminal Procedure Code was enacted in 1965; it consisted of 500 articles addressing in particular the arrest, detention, interrogation, and trial of the accused. The code also covered the implementation of punishments, the temporary duration of imprisonment, and the differentiation between the role of the police and prosecutors and the supervision of their duties and responsibilities. It is not entirely clear whether this new code was inspired by Soviet law. In any case, it signified the introduction of a secular piece of legislation, which brought the Afghan legal system closer to Western legal traditions.

1973-1978: The creation of the Republic of Afghanistan

On 17 July 1973, Mohammad Daoud Khan – the cousin of Zahir Shah and his prime minister until 1963 – carried out a military coup with the support of a small number of troops and a handful of military officers associated with the PDPA while Zahir Shah was in Europe. For the first time in its history, Afghanistan was proclaimed a republic. Meanwhile, the communist party was increasingly influencing various parts of Daoud's government by pushing its own allies and supporters into key administrative positions. This triggered opposition by the religious establishment and fostered the emergence of Islamic groups. Daoud clamped down on these Islamist groups. In 1974, the leader of the Muslim Brotherhood, Mohammad Niazai, was arrested along with some 200 followers (Ewans 2001: 131). Determined to get public support for his government, Daoud decided to crack down on the communist parties as well.

Had Afghanistan's ruler legalised the functioning of political parties and political parties been institutionalised through periodic elections, competition for power and influence could have taken place through the ballot box. In the absence of institutionalised and democratic mechanisms for political change, however, the competition between leftist and Islamic groups soon assumed the shape of armed conflict.

In 1976 a new penal code was enacted based primarily on Islamic principles, but drawing also on European criminal codes.[9] Article 1 of the Penal Code of 1976 defines the scope of application and sets forth as follows:

> This law regulates offences that call for discretionary (*ta*ᶜ*zīr*) penalties. Any person who commits a crime calling for fixed punishment (*h,add*, pl. *h,odūd*) or retaliation (*qes,ās,*) or the payment of blood money (*diyat*), will be punished according to the principles of the Hanafi school of law.

That meant that the *h,odūd* crimes were not within the scope of application of the penal code. However, whenever a *h,add* crime could not be established by Hanafi evidence law, the punishment for that crime would fall within the scope of the 1976 Penal Code, if evidence was sufficient *vis-à-vis* the standards set by the code. The penal code, thus, provided for an alternative procedure, making *h,odūd* crimes punishable under the principle of *ta^czīr*, with prison sentences of various durations.

The unstable legal situation led to the enactment of yet another constitution on 24 February 1977.[10] Daoud was elected president for a period of six years. The new constitution transferred all authorities of the king under the 1964 Constitution to the president of the state. Daoud also occupied the position of prime minister, foreign minister, and minister of defence. The power over the judiciary, which until then had been vested in the person of the king, was also transferred to the president, and the position of Chief Justice granted to the Minister of Justice.

The Constitution of 1977 differs considerably from the previous three constitutions. Alongside the emphasis on Islam, the 1977 Constitution introduced for the first time the notions of nationalism and socialism. Article 22 of the 1977 Constitution designated Islam as the religion of the state without reference to the prominence of the Hanafi school of law, as had the previous constitution (1964). Article 64 went further than the previous constitution, however, as it contains a repugnancy clause, subjecting all laws to a process of assessment on their compatibility with the basic principles of the sacred Islamic religion. Yet, in other respects the law was more liberal. For instance, Article 28 repeated the principle of equality of gender, stating that: '[T]he entire people of Afghanistan, both men and women without discrimination and privileges, have equal rights and obligations before the law.' The addition of the passage 'both men and women' was completely new and had never been in any Afghan legal document so far. Articles 39 and 40 of the 1977 Constitution granted freedom of assembly for all citizens of Afghanistan provided the assemblies are unarmed. A one-party system led by Daoud's party (the National Revolutionary Party) was created by Article 40 of the 1977 Constitution. A national assembly called the *melli jirga* replaced the former Parliament of the 1964 Constitution by substituting the two houses (House of People and House of Elders) with only one assembly (Art. 48 et seq.).

Also in 1977, the Afghan Civil Code (CC), modelled on the Egyptian Civil Code of 1949, was enacted as a further piece of legislation aimed at modernising the legal system.[11] The code encompasses 2,416 articles that regulate all aspects of civil law, including family and inheritance law. The code blends sharia-based law (mainly in the field of family and inheritance law) and modern secular law to solve the existing problems and thereby secure social stability in society. The code was in particular influenced by the French civil code, for example in matters regarding the age of capacity for transactions and the requirement for registration of documents concerning marriage, divorce, parentage, and kinship

(Art. 48 CC). To clarify the relationship between different sources of law, Article 1 of the code provides that in cases where there is an explicit regulation in the law, independent interpretation of the court (*ejtehād*) is not allowed. However, if no such explicit rule exists, the court may fill the gaps with the rules of the Hanafi school of law. Finally, the Civil Code of 1977 did not allocate any role to customary law, despite its prominent role in Afghanistan.

1978-1985: The Saur-Revolution, the mojāhedīn, and Soviet invasion

In April 1978, yet another coup, the so-called Saur-, or April-Revolution (*thavr*), was staged by parts of the PDPA. Daoud and his family were killed and power was handed over to a joint military-civilian Revolutionary Council, with Taraki serving as its head, president, and prime minister. The constitution was amended by a declaration the following day on 28 April 1978. All governmental affairs had to be executed through decrees and procedures of the Revolutionary Council. Decree No. 8/1978[12] implemented a stringent land reform, redistributing the land and severely limited the ownership of land. Any land considered as surplus was confiscated without compensation and redistributed to landless peasants and farmers. Modern Soviet type cooperatives were designed to replace the traditional rural economic relationships. In the field of civil law, on 17 September 1978 Decree No. 7 was promulgated. It abolished the bride price, or transfer of money from the groom to the bride's family, called *walwar* in Afghanistan (see 7.6); set the minimum age for marriage at 15 and 18 for girls and boys, respectively; and prohibited child and forced marriages.[13]

Meanwhile, Islamic resistance groups (the *mojāhedīn* movements) had started to form themselves outside Afghanistan. After the arrest of Niazai in 1974, some of his supporters, such as Hikmatyar and Rabbani, had fled to Pakistan. In 1974, they had split away from the main party, with Hikmatyar establishing the Islamic Party and Rabbani, the Islamic Society party. Besides these two groups, numerous other *mojāhedīn* movements were formed. These groups would later play a central role in the resistance against the communist rule and against the Russian military invasion (Magnus & Naby 2002: 151).

In 1979, internal conflicts within the PDPA escalated. Factional conflicts and the strong presence of the *mojāhedīn* movements in Pakistan and inside Afghanistan persuaded the Russians to act. Basing themselves on the Soviet-Afghan Treaty of Friendship of 5 December 1978, which allowed for military intervention by the Russians in the event of any threat to their interests in the area, Russian troops invaded Afghanistan on 27 December 1979. Karmal, the leader of the Parcham party, mentioned above, was installed as head of the Democratic Republic of Afghanistan.

Some 850,000 Afghan refugees had fled the country by May 1980, with an estimated 750,000 Afghans applying for asylum in Pakistan and an additional 100,000 in Iran (Ewans 2001: 158). The Russian invasion was strongly condemned by the international community. Member states of the Organisation of the Islamic Conference gathered in Saudi Arabia and declared the invasion to be a threat to international peace and stability. The U.N. General Assembly passed seven resolutions condemning the invasion, all without practical effect. In the meantime, however, seven *mojāhedīn* opposition groups had come together in Peshawar in Pakistan and merged into the so-called Afghanistan's Islamic Union of Mujāhedīn on 16 September 1981 (Ekhwan 2002: 15).

Meanwhile, in Kabul, Karmal was concerned with gaining internal legitimacy among the Afghan people. He promised a government in which all factions and parties would be embraced and represented; a new constitution with provisions for elections and a multi-party system; land reform; amnesty for returning refugees and political prisoners; freedom of religion; and the establishment of Islamic institutions that could act as advisory bodies to the government. To appease public opinion, he restored the old black, red, and green national flag that was replaced after the Saur-Revolution by a flag without the green colour representing Islam.

On 21 April 1980, the fifth Afghan constitution was promulgated.[14] It contained 68 articles. In order to avoid a direct clash with public opinion, the Constitution of 1980 did not explicitly mention communism or Marxism in its provisions. Instead, it just pointed to the objectives, views, policies, organisation, and responsibilities of various administrative institutions in the government according to the PDPA program. Article 54 of the 1980 Constitution upheld the institution of the Supreme Court and reorganised the court system by providing for provincial and city courts, as well as special courts to try specific cases such as military cases. In March 1980, the Law on the Organization and Jurisdiction of the Courts was passed; it was amended less than two years later on 22 December 1981.[15] This law specified the court procedure and set out the hierarchy of the courts. Articles 12 and 13 of this law mandated the establishment of a bar association to 'provide legal assistance for the defence of accused persons'. Karmal also created a Department for Islamic Affairs, which was to act as an advisory body for the government on Islamic affairs.[16]

Despite these initiatives, the government continued to lose credibility. This was particularly so given its rampant disregard of national and international legal and human rights standards it purported to support (e.g. ICCPR, CESCR, CERD, and CAT; see 7.9). During this period, there were frequent human rights violations at the highest levels of power, ongoing illegal detentions of political activists and religious leaders, and the well-publicised executions of members of opposition groups, in the absence of any trial or pretence of justice. In consequence, Afghanistan became an area of instability in the region, ravaged by internal conflict and foreign intervention. A March 1985 human rights report prepared for UNCHR details accounts of deliberate bombing of villages, massacres of civilians, and execution of prisoners of war belonging to resistance groups (Ermacora 1985: 12)

In the mid-eighties the war was particularly intense. The Afghan government, supported by Soviet troops, was involved in major combat all around the country, with the government focusing all its attention on its military campaigns rather than anything else. On 26 September 1982, the heads of the Islamic states conferring in Nigeria suspended the membership of Afghanistan from the Organisation of the Islamic Conference.

Foreign countries such as China, the U.S., Saudi Arabia, and Iran considerably helped the resistance groups within and outside Afghanistan. The alliance of the seven *mojāhedīn* groups, however, revolved only around their common struggle against the Russians and the Kabul regime. Besides this, the resistance groups had little in common and were involved in persistent factional disputes. From the very beginning, they were as much prepared to cooperate with each other as to fight each other. Neither their shared Muslim faith nor the concept of the need for a holy war (*jihād*) to oust the Russians was strong enough to outweigh their personal, tribal, and ethnic interests. All efforts to foster their commonness and bind them together into a unified movement failed. This lack of unity meant that the *mojāhedīn* were unable to coordinate their activities inside Afghanistan or carry out a unified strategy for their common objectives. In fact, this was one of the main reasons behind the unsuccessful attempts of the *mojāhedīn* to overthrow the communist regime in Kabul.

In April 1985, Karmal held a *Loya Jirga* in Kabul, inviting 1,800 representatives from around the country. With only 600 members attending, the assembly failed to garner much legitimacy as a genuinely representative body. The elections of August 1985 were yet another unsuccessful attempt by Karmal to legitimise his government (Ewans 2001: 165), as was the creation of a National Reconciliation Commission that was to design a new constitution. All his attempts to incorporate a broader participation of the non-communist groups into his government failed.

7.4 The period from 1985 until the present

From civil war to democracy

1985-1992: Afghan civil war

In autumn 1985, the Russians replaced Karmal with Najibullah, who was the head of the secret service department of the communist regime. His instalment to power was a political decision aimed at creating a stronger and more decisive government able to protect the continuity and power of the communist regime, even after the eventual military withdrawal of the Russians (Ewans 2001: 168). The international community's efforts to put an end to the Russian occupation moved very slowly, and no agreement had been reached so far. It was not until 28 July 1986 that the Soviet leader at the time, Gorbachev, facing heavy international pressure, announced that the Russian troops would be withdrawn, and that this withdrawal would be completed by October 1986.

In fact, Soviet troops only left Afghanistan on 15 February 1989. This represented a great challenge for the communist regime in Kabul. Najibullah had to stay in power without the support of the Soviet troops. Towards the end of 1987 the government of Najibullah, in an effort to reconcile the conflicting parties, drafted a new constitution, which was adopted on 29 November 1987 by the *Loya Jirga*.[17] The new constitution was similar to the Constitution of 1964 in its reference to the sacred religion of Islam (Art. 2). According to Article 94 of the 1987 Constitution, eight different governmental institutions were given the power to propose, introduce, amend, or repeal laws. The constitution also introduced the Constitutional Council of Afghanistan as a supreme institution for the interpretation of laws and international treaties in accordance with the constitution of the country. It was also to act as a consultative body for the president in legislative matters.

In 1990, Najibullah called upon the *Loya Jirga* to ratify a new constitution. In comparison to the two previous constitutions of 1980 and 1987, the 1990 Constitution did not make use of communist terminology. Islam and nationalism were back on the front page.[18] Article 1 proclaimed Afghanistan to be an 'independent, unitary and Islamic state'. Article 5 set forth provisions for a multi-party system. Article 25 gave due attention to the private sector for the establishment of private enterprises, and Article 20 encouraged foreign private investment.

The PDPA was reformed and renamed the Homeland Party. In November, Najibullah met with leaders of the *mojāhedīn* and representatives of the former king Zahir Shah to seek a political solution to the ongoing conflict. U.N. Secretary General Perez de Cuellar proposed plans for an international consensus on a peaceful settlement in

Afghanistan in May 1991. It aimed at Afghanistan's independence and self-determination, a cease-fire, halting the flow of weapons into the country, and a transitional mechanism leading to free and fair elections. The Kabul regime, Iran, and Pakistan accepted the resolution. The alliance of the seven *mojāhedīn* groups in Peshawar was, however, unable to consent on the composition of the future government in Afghanistan.

In this situation of negotiations, one of the strongest allies of the Kabul regime, Dostum, an Uzbek who had control of some of the northern provinces, seized the opportunity and joined forces with the resistance militias of Ahmad Shah Massoud, a Tajik to take Mazaar-e Sharif, the capital of one of the key provinces in the North of Afghanistan. This move was the death warrant for the peace plan of the United Nations and Najibullah's regime. Some parts of the Kabul regime joined ranks with the *mojāhedīn*. The advantage shifted decisively in their favour. They believed that victory was theirs and saw no need to stick to any U.N. peace plan that would include a role for Najibullah and his supporters (Ewans 2001: 177).

On 18 March 1992, Najibullah resigned and accepted the formation of a transitional government led by the *mojāhedīn* in close cooperation with the United Nations, despite the fact that the resistance groups were still struggling over power-sharing arrangements. Until then, the civil war that was waged in fact between the different *mojāhedīn* groups, rather than against communists, had been limited to some parts of the country. After the collapse of the Kabul communist regime the armed conflict spread into Kabul and the rest of the country. Government administration, legal institutions, universities, schools, and all other educational and social institutions did not function any longer and were simply closed down.

1992-2001: The Taliban and the rise of fundamentalism

The collapse of the Najibullah regime and the seizure of power by the *mojāhedīn* symbolised the end of a functional state structure in Afghanistan. A 51-member council called the Islamic Jihad Council (*shūrā-ye jihādī-ye eslāmī*), consisting of thirty field commanders, ten *mullahs*, and ten intellectuals, was established to rule the country for a period of two months. The Council was succeeded by an interim government that held power for four months. The problems were enormous: on the one hand, the new government had to deal with a state apparatus that lacked legitimacy; on the other hand, the resistance parties were not able to establish a functioning government. In the course of the civil war almost all the state institutions had been looted or destroyed (Ewans 2001: 181). The Ministry of Justice was used as a military base, and all legal documents and laws stored at the ministry were destroyed during the five years of *mojāhedīn* domination.[19]

No new constitution was drafted, nor had the constitution of the previous regime been repealed; not a single decree was issued during the *mojāhedīn* rule to identify the sources of law for the judiciary and other legal organs; no central legislative activities took place during this period of time; and there was uncertainty as to the applicable laws in all fields (Lau 2003: 5). The difficulties were exacerbated by the ongoing civil war. This enhanced the rule of traditional law, i.e. classical Islamic and customary law (especially the *Pashtunwali*, an ethical customary code of the Pashtuns), since they represented the only continuity in the country. In more remote areas, where statutory laws had never arrived, the principles of Islamic and customary law had always been the primary sources for the resolution of legal and social conflicts (Lau 2003: 4).

Afghanistan was more fragmented than ever when the Taliban, a movement of indoctrinated students of Islam from the refugee camps in Pakistan, emerged in 1994. As head of the government, Rabbani controlled Kabul, its outskirts, and the North-East of Afghanistan. The West (the province of Herat) was controlled by Ismael Khan. The East (the Pashtun provinces) was under the leadership of an independent group of *mojāhedīn* commanders in Jalalabad, who occasionally fought against each other. A small region south and east of Kabul was controlled by Hekmatyar. The northern six provinces were under Dostum's command. And, finally, the Hazaras controlled the province of Bamian. Furthermore, dozens of warlords and leaders of militia groups exercised their control and harassed the population throughout the country (Rashid 2000: 21). Even international aid organisations feared entering Afghanistan, as the country was drowning in a savage civil war.

The successful expansion of the Taliban movement saw them control almost ninety per cent of the country by 1998. This, however, did not lead to the reestablishment of a strong state. The government activities of the Taliban were limited to the provision of security by incorporating local combatants into their own military structure and to the introduction of a bizarre and harsh version of Islamic law, with implications in all areas of law, such as public executions and a vigorous application of the *h,odūd* punishments (Schetter 2002: 113).

An announcement on Radio Kabul on 28 September 1996 stated that 'thieves will have their hands and feet amputated, adulterers will be stoned to death and those drinking alcohol will be lashed'. TV, video, satellite dishes, music, and games, including chess and football, were pronounced un-Islamic (Rashid 2000: 50). The Taliban also established a Department for the Promotion of Virtue and Prevention of Vice (*amr bi-l-ma^{c}rūf va nahī-ye an-al-monkar*) that was given unlimited authority for the enforcement of all the decrees issued by the Taliban government.[20] A decree issued in 1997 by Mullah Omar, the founder of the Taliban movement, declared that all the laws against the principles of Hanafi Islamic jurisprudence were not applicable.[21] The Taliban announced via the radio that after the seizure of Kabul, they would abolish all the laws and regulations of the communist regime and reintroduce the system of law that was in place during Zahir Shah's reign (1964-1973), with the exception of the provisions related to the king and the monarchy.

They also claimed to support the principles of representative, non-discriminatory government based on the principles of the sharia (Ewans 2001: 205). That never happened; the Taliban regime violated all principles of the Constitution of 1964. Throughout their rule, the Taliban executed *ḥ,add* and *qeṣāṣ* punishments that had not been applied in the recent legal history of Afghanistan. The option of paying blood money to the victim's family in lieu of corporal punishment was not used very often. Amputation of hands and feet for theft and stoning of adulterer and adulteress were executed. The Taliban meant to deter people from committing crime and, therefore, ordered executions and amputations to be held in public in the sports stadium of Kabul.

One of the Taliban's first acts was the execution of former president Najibullah who had been living on U.N. premises since 1992. There was no trial, and the public display of Najibullah's dead body revolted many people outside and within the country.

Under the Taliban, discrimination against women peaked. They issued numerous edicts to control literally every aspect of women's behaviour, in both the public and private spheres. They were forbidden to take employment, to appear in public without a male relative, to participate in government or public debate, and to receive secondary or higher education. As a result, women were deprived of the means to support themselves and their children. Only female doctors and nurses were allowed – under strict observation of the religious police – to work in hospitals or private clinics. These edicts were issued by the abovementioned Department for the Promotion of Virtue and the Prevention of Vice and enforced through summary and arbitrary punishment of women by the religious police.

The Taliban claimed that they were prepared to provide for education and employment opportunities for women as soon as the social and financial circumstances were convenient. Unfortunately, such conditions for a sound Islamic program for women were never ascertained, with some subsequently claiming that such program had never existed in the first place.

The Taliban received support in the form of donations from foreign sponsors, located mostly in Saudi Arabia, Pakistan, and the United

States. New recruits from the religious schools (*madāres*) located in Pakistan were urged to join the Taliban movement to fight against the *mojāhedīn* groups in the North of the country. On 20 March 1996, more than 1,000 religious scholars and tribal leaders gathered in Kandahar to discuss the policies and platforms of the Taliban regime for the future. On the 4th of April, the assembly ended with the announcement of a *jihād* against the Kabul government still run by the *mojāhedīn* groups. Mullah Omar was named 'Commander of the Faithful', a title once abolished by the reformer-king Amanullah (Ewans 2001: 195).

In May 1996 Osama bin Laden, whose Saudi Arabian citizenship had been revoked in 1994, arrived in Jalalabad. He had been travelling to the Pashtun border areas between Pakistan and Afghanistan since the early eighties, where he had established training camps for the resistance forces against the communist regime. He cooperated with the Taliban who offered him their protection. Bin Laden provided the Taliban with extensive financial and human resources. After the bombing of the U.S. embassies in Kenya and Tanzania in 1998, Bin Laden became the world's most wanted terrorist. The Clinton Administration responded to the bombings of their embassies with cruise missiles directed against training camps that had been run by Bin Laden in Afghanistan since 1981. Ironically, these camps had at an earlier point in their history been supported by the U.S., Saudi Arabia, and Pakistan for training Afghan opposition soldiers to fight the Soviet occupiers.

With the assassination of Massoud on 9 September 2001 and the attacks of 9/11 in the U.S., the situation changed dramatically. The Bush Administration held Bin Laden responsible for the terrorist attacks of 9/11 and accused the Taliban of sheltering him. Consequently, starting on 7 October 2001, the United States began air strikes against the Taliban as part of a campaign aimed at putting an end to the rule of the Taliban regime, an objective that was soon achieved. This was done ostensibly in support of the so-called Northern Alliance of the *mojāhedīn* groups, since the Taliban regime had only been internationally recognised by Pakistan, Saudi Arabia, and the United Arab Emirates.

2001-present: Democracy and the future of Afghanistan

On 27 November 2001, a conference was held in Bonn, Germany, which brought together representatives of the resistance groups, consisting of the main civil war parties and warlords, pro-Zahir Shah technocrats and intellectuals, and two other small Afghan groups based in Pakistan and Iran (Wardak 2005: 65). Although the present anti-Taliban groups could not be considered to represent the Afghan people, the 'Agreement on Provisional Arrangements in Afghanistan pending the Re-Establishment of Permanent Government Institutions', also known as the 'Bonn Agreement', provided a framework for the process of state formation to create a broad-based, multi-ethnic, and representative government in Afghanistan. Executive powers were vested in Hamid Karzai, a Pashtun, as head of the Interim Administration of Afghanistan on 22 December 2001. Karzai was reconfirmed as the head of the Interim Administration by the 1,550 members of an Emergency *Loya Jirga* held in Kabul on 10 June 2002.

On 14 December 2003, a nine-member commission presented a new draft constitution to the Constitutional Loya Jirga, the constitutional assembly, for the new Afghan Republic. The text of the constitution had been drafted following public consultations that took place over a period of several months. After almost three weeks of heated debates, the *Loya Jirga* approved the new constitution; it was signed on 26 January 2004 by Karzai. This cleared the way for the restoration and implementation of the rule of law, and hopes were expressed for an imminent end to the power of the warlords and the anarchy gripping the country (see 7.5).

The Bonn Agreement set June 2004 as the target date for the formation of a fully representative and elected Afghan government. However, that timeframe was repeatedly changed. When on 31 March 2004, the second international conference on Afghanistan's future took place in Berlin ('the Berlin Conference'), a work plan was issued for the Afghan government to hold free and fair elections in autumn 2004. Prior to the elections, the full exercise by citizens, candidates, and political parties of their political rights under the 2004 Constitution was to be ensured. These rights included, among others, freedom of organisation, freedom of expression, and the principle of non-discrimination, as well as paying particular attention to the participation of women as both voters and candidates. In the end, the decision was taken to hold presidential elections in October 2004, delaying parliamentary, provincial, and district voting until April 2005 (International Crisis Group 2005).

Thus, the first presidential elections in Afghanistan were held on 9 October 2004. According to U.N. officials, nearly 10 million voters were registered in the country. Since no census of Afghanistan has ever been taken, it is not possible to know how many eligible voters there actually were. Nearly 42 per cent of the registered voters were women, but it should be noted that that figure dropped to less than ten per cent in some provinces in the southeast. In addition, over one million Afghan refugees in Pakistan and Iran were registered to vote in the elections. Amongst seventeen challengers (including a female physician), the interim president Karzai was elected and sworn in as first elected Afghan president on 8 December 2004.

The first parliamentary elections in 36 years in Afghanistan, scheduled for April 2005, were finally held on 18 September 2005, with 2,800 candidates running for the 249 seats of the Lower House, among whom were 344 women. In contrast to the 80 per cent turn out rate for registered voters during the presidential elections, reports indicate that only about 50 per cent of the 12.4 million registered voters cast their vote during the parliamentary elections.[22]

A new Electoral Law with 57 articles, adopted on 27 May 2004, regulated the conduct of elections. Article 20 of the law provides for a single, non-transferable vote (SNTV) system under which candidates may run either individually or be nominated by a party. Under this system, party lists are not admitted.[23] Political parties may endorse or nominate candidates, but they are not allowed to use party symbols on the ballot, making it difficult for voters who wish to vote along party lines to identify their chosen candidates on Election Day. It must be noted that political parties have a serious credibility problem in Afghanistan. They are often associated, on the one hand, with the Communist Party and the Soviet invasion and, on the other hand, with the Islamist military groupings who formed to fight the Soviets and whose infighting produced much of the instability and bloodshed of the 1990s. Consequently, many Afghans do not trust political parties and see them as pursuing self-interested policies for their particular ethnic group, clan, or tribe. This is one of the primary reasons the SNTV system, which allows for a focus on individuals rather than parties *per se*, was chosen for use in the first elections in Afghanistan after so many decades of strife (Reynolds & Wilder 2005: 9).

The SNTV has, however, been criticised as being ill-suited for a country like Afghanistan. According to international observers, to be successful under this type of voting structure, a party must have sufficient control over its support base in each contested district to instruct it how to allocate votes among the party's candidates. Otherwise, the party risks having too many votes cast for one candidate, beyond the minimum needed for election, and too few for others. A system that encourages party development and participation in the political process would have been more desirable given Afghanistan's nascent democracy (International Crisis Group 2004).

As in the past, the 2004 Constitution provides for two houses in the *Loya Jirga*. The Lower House (the *Wolesi Jirga*) has 249 seats, with members directly elected by the people. Each of the 34 provinces is a single constituency in the *Wolesi Jirga*. Ten seats are reserved for the *Kuchi* (nomads) community (Electoral Law, §2, Art. 20), with the remaining 239 seats distributed among provinces in proportion to their population, with each province having at least two seats. Each member of the *Wolesi Jirga* enjoys a five-year term expiring on the 22nd of June of the fifth year (2004 Constitution, Art. 83). Mohammad Yunos Qanuni, the former Minister of Interior and Education, was elected head of the Lower House.

The Upper House (the *Meshrano Jirga*) consists of a mixture of appointed and elected members (total 102 members). Sixty-eight members were selected by the 34 directly elected provincial councils, and another 34 were appointed by President Karzai (Art. 84, 2004 Constitution). President Karzai's appointments were vetted by an independent U.N.-sponsored election board and included seventeen women (50%), as required by the constitution. Sebghatulla Mojadeddi was appointed President of the *Meshrano Jirga* by President Karzai.

The new National Assembly has the potential to play a vital role in stabilising Afghanistan, institutionalising political competition and giving voice to the country's diverse population. By being accountable to the Afghan people, it can demand accountability of the presidential government. However, the success of this institution remains delicately poised, particularly because of the absence of a formal role for political parties, essential for mediating internal tensions.

Meanwhile, at the London Conference on 31 January–1 February 2006, donor nations pledged to help rebuild Afghanistan over the next five years with a sum of 10.5 billion dollars (equivalent at the time to 8.7 billion Euros). Some 80 per cent of this amount represents new money, with the remainder made up of outstanding portions of earlier pledges.[24] The key elements of the so-called Afghanistan Compact set out specific targets for improving security, governance, the rule of law and human rights and for enhancing economic and social development. A further vital and cross-cutting area of work is eliminating the narcotics industry, which remains a formidable threat to the people and state of Afghanistan, the region, and beyond.

At the Afghanistan Conference in Rome in July 2007 international donors pledged to support the training of judges, the building of new prisons, and the enactment of other measures to strengthen Afghanistan's judicial system with an additional 360 million dollars. President Karzai told the conference that urgent priorities included low salaries, poor infrastructure, and the training of personnel.

However, the security situation has deteriorated in the past several years. According to a report by the United States Institute of Peace, the year 2009 was the most violent on record for Afghans and international forces since 2001, and Afghan and international public confidence is diminishing.[25] Contrary to their pledge in 2007, the Afghan government and its international allies are mainly focused on two issues, namely combating corruption within the Afghan government and resolving the ongoing conflict with the Taliban. All other issues have become secondary. The lack of security, economic development, effective rule of law, and coordination of efforts will, however, always stand in the way of sustainable progress in the country. As these problems are interrelated, none of them can be tackled without simultaneously addressing the others.

On 1 December 2009 the Obama administration announced that the U.S. would send another 30,000 troops to Afghanistan, but also start withdrawing troops as per July 2011. It is unclear whether such an increase in troop presence will boost security in Afghanistan, if no serious attention is given to the promotion of the rule of law, development, institution-building, and economic growth.

The presidential election of 20 August 2009 is another illustration of the growing instability in Afghanistan. With more than 40 presidential nominees, about 5 million people cast their votes.[26] The outcome of the election was marked with fraud and voting irregularities; no single candidate managed to obtain 51 per cent of the total votes. As the allegations of widespread fraud gained ground, a runoff election was scheduled to take place on 7 November 2009. On 1 November 2009, Karzai's main challenger Abdullah pulled out of the runoff election. Karzai, who won 49 per cent of the total votes in the first round of the election, was thus announced the elected president by the Independent Election Commission of Afghanistan. Although the election was over, the irregularities and fraud connected to the election process raised doubts about the legitimacy of the government. The reappointments of Dostum as Army Chief of Staff and Qahim as First Vice President, two prominent warlords accused of human rights violations and war crimes, further increased concerns about Karzai's government and his leadership.

On 28 January 2010 the latest Afghanistan Conference took place in London. The conference was meant to bring together the international community to 'fully align military and civilian resources behind an Afghan-led political strategy'.[27] A radical increase of civilian and military security forces is planned with the aim of reaching 171,000 members in the Afghan Army and 134,000 Afghan policemen by the end of 2011, bringing thus the total security force numbers to over 300,000. Furthermore, measures were announced to tackle corruption, including the establishment of an independent Office of High Oversight and an independent Monitoring and Evaluation Mission. According to agreements made at the conference, development assistance shall be better coordinated in the future, with the aim of increasingly channelling funds through the Government of Afghanistan. Interestingly, the strategy of the international community on Afghanistan embraces also the policy of the Afghan Government to integrate ex-warlords by offering economic incentives to those who 'renounce violence, cut links to terrorism and agree to work within the democratic process'.

Meanwhile, the parliamentary elections planned for May have been postponed until September 2010. The election commission cited several reasons for its decision: security concerns, logistical challenges, and a budget shortfall, to name a few. The postponement of elections was hailed by Western donors, as it allows more time to put election reforms in place in order to avoid the repeat of the widespread fraud that marred the 2009 presidential elections. The postponement may also give the electoral institutions additional time to carry out the necessary preparations for the elections and to make improvements to the electoral process based on lessons learned during the 2009 elections.

7.5 Constitutional law

The Constitution of 2004[28] proclaims in its very first article that 'Afghanistan is an independent, unitary, and indivisible Islamic republican state'. Article 3 contains a repugnancy clause stating that 'In Afghanistan, no law may be contrary to the beliefs and provisions of the sacred religion of Islam. ('*mokhālef-e moᶜtaqedāt va aḥkām-e dīn-e moqaddas-e eslām*'). This is not new, since all Afghan constitutions, except for the 1980 Constitution, contained such a clause. This version of the constitution, however, fails to define what is to be understood as the 'beliefs and provisions of the sacred religion of Islam' or what the expression 'Islamic republican state' encompasses.

Article 130 of the constitution in fact stipulates the priority of statutory law over Islamic law, noting that 'The courts shall apply this Constitution and other laws when adjudicating cases'. The article further reads:

> When no provision exists in the constitution or the law for a case under consideration, the court shall, by following the principles of the Hanafi School of law and within the limitations set forth in this constitution, render a decision that secures justice in the best possible way.

It is, however, not clear whether these constitutional postulates imply that the ethical values of Islam govern the interpretation of the laws, or that the constitution and state-enacted law set the framework within which Islamic law must operate (Yassari 2005: 48).

Closely linked to these questions is the question as to who is to interpret the constitution. The proposal to establish a genuine 'Supreme Constitutional Court' was rejected in the drafting process of the 2004

Constitution. Consequently, the constitution, as it is currently formulated, foresees two distinct institutions with competence in interpretation matters. In the first place, Article 157 sets forth that an 'Independent Commission for the Supervision of the Implementation of the Constitution' should be created. Yet, according to Article 121, it is the Supreme Court that has the competence to 'review laws, legislative decrees, international treaties and conventions on their compliance with the Constitution and to interpret them, in accordance with the law [...]'. This constitutionally instituted dichotomy may cause serious problems in the future (Yassari 2005: 49). However, as an Independent Commission for the Supervision of the Implementation of the Constitution was never established, this problem is not acute and the task of interpreting and supervising the implementation of the constitution is conducted by the Supreme Court.

While articulating that 'Islam is the sacred religion of Afghanistan', Article 2 of the 2004 Constitution also asserts that followers of other religions are free to exercise their faith and perform their religious rites within the limits of the law. Furthermore, Article 130 sets forth that with reference to cases under court consideration, if no relevant statute is found the Hanafi school of law is to be utilised to the exclusion of all the other schools of Islamic jurisprudence. However, a new development in this constitution is the recognition, for the first time, of Shi'i law as a source of law to be used in cases where Afghan Shi'i are involved. Article 131 of the Constitution provides:

> In cases involving the Shi'i followers, the court shall, in disputes concerning personal status matters, apply the Shi'i school of law in accordance with (statutory) law. In other disputes, where no provision can be found in this Constitution and other laws, the courts shall adjudicate the case in accordance with the rulings of the Shi'i school of law.

It should be noted that in the first part of the article, the constitution makes explicit reference to matters of personal status, as opposed to other areas of the law, such as criminal and constitutional law. The latter portion of the same article, however, offers some freedom of interpretation, as it provides that whenever both parties to a legal dispute (other than in matters of personal status) are Shi'i followers and no ruling can be found on the basis of legal standards articulated in the constitution or other statutes and acts, the judge may apply the rules of the Shi'i school of law. Thus, whenever existing statutes, such as the civil code, do apply the scope of application, Shi'i law is excluded (Kamali 2005: 30).

In response to Article 131 of the 2004 Constitution a Code of Personal Status of Shi'i Afghans was promulgated in July 2009.[29] This law had been quietly making its way through Afghanistan's parliamentary system since 2007, when President Karzai finally signed the bill in March 2009, with the intention to gain the support of the Shi'i minority for the August 2009 election, without however paying attention to its content and potential backlash. Whereas there was generally a consensus among Afghans that the law as such was a positive development, giving rights and recognition to a historically excluded and persecuted minority, the content of some provisions of the bill that included several restrictions on the rights of Shi'i women caught the attention of national Afghan and international human right groups and the international media, causing the law to soon be dubbed the 'rape law' by Western journalists. Although the law had been circulated and shared with some local authorities and members of the civil society, it had received minimal public debate. According to a report of the Afghanistan Research and Evaluation Unit, the process of law making had lacked any public participation; this has revealed the weak links between policymakers and their constituents. It also showed a continued emphasis on ethnicity, sect, and faction as a basis for political alliances and organisation, rather than on partisan platforms that speak of issues of public interest (Oates 2009: viii). After strong public reactions, the bill was amended and some of the contested provisions, such as the rules on temporary marriage, were omitted; the amended Code of Personal Status with its 236 articles came into force on 27 July 2009 (see 7.6).

The 2004 Constitution requires the head of state to be a Muslim. He is the patron of the religion of Islam and, as such, must protect the 'basic principles of the sacred religion of Islam, and the constitution and other laws' of Afghanistan (Art. 63). The constitution has, however, omitted in this regard a reference to the Hanafi school of law, meaning then that there is no requirement that the president be a follower of the Hanafi doctrine. The article further prescribes that the president, unlike the construction of the king under Article 15 of the 1964 Constitution, is not beyond accountability. Article 69 expands upon this principle in its articulation of the impeachment procedure and removal from office of the president when he is charged with treason, crimes against humanity, or any other serious crime.

Article 116 foresees a three-tier court system with a Supreme Court, appeals courts, and district courts. The constitution does not, however, give detailed rules on the structure of the courts. According to Article 123, the rules related to the structure, authority, and performance of the courts and the duties of judges shall be regulated by statutes.

In January 2005, a temporary Supreme Court of Afghanistan was established. President Karzai appointed nine judges to the court, all of them Islamic scholars, including one Shi'i scholar. Fazl Hadi Shinwari, an Islamic scholar known particularly as being ultra-conservative was appointed as Chief Justice. The temporary Supreme Court operated until the parliamentary election in September 2005 and the formation of a new *Loya Jirga*. In summer 2006, President Karzai appointed several new, more moderate members to the Supreme Court. However, he also chose to re-nominate Shinwari as Chief Justice. Despite controversy surrounding the validity of Shinwari's legal credentials, his nomination was allowed to continue, but ultimately failed when voted on in Parliament. Karzai then chose his legal council, Abdul Salam Azimi, to succeed Shinwari. Azimi's nomination passed, and the new court was sworn in on 5 August 2006.

With regard to women's rights, the Constitution of 2004 contains an equality clause. According to Article 22,

> [a]ny kind of discrimination and privilege between the citizens of Afghanistan is prohibited. The citizens of Afghanistan – whether man or woman – have equal rights and duties before the law.

While the express wording of this article forbids discrimination between men and women, legal rules contained in the Civil Code 1977 and the Penal Code 1976 (see 7.6 and 7.7) as well as actual social practice, in particular in accordance with customary law, do. The equality clause must, thus, be seen as an article that had to be included in any modern constitution, but one that does not reflect the way women and their position in society are conceived in male-dominated and war-ravaged Afghanistan. It remains highly doubtful that women will be able to successfully rely on this article for the protection of their rights in the foreseeable future.

7.6 Family and inheritance law

The current Afghan Civil Code dates back to 1977; it contains provisions on family and inheritance law that are essentially a codification of the Hanafi school of law, with inclusion of some provisions of the Maliki school of law. Family law provisions cover matrimonial law, polygamy, child custody, and divorce. The enactment of the Civil Code constituted a step forward from its antecedent, the Marriage Law of 1971, which was silent on polygamy. Moreover, its provisions on child marriage and divorce did not match any of the family law reforms that had taken place elsewhere in the Middle East, the Maghreb, and Pakistan in the 1950s and 1960s. In contrast, the Civil Code of 1977 introduced reforms on child marriage, polygamy, and divorce. These amendments (see discussion below) do not, however, sufficiently address the social need for more effective measures, and they do not further either the equality clause contained in Article 22 of the 2004 Constitution or the principles outlined in the CEDAW to which Afghanistan is a signatory.

An enormous gap exists between the professed support for the principle of equality and the reality of tribalism in Afghanistan's traditional society. The importance and prominence of customary law, and especially the customs and principles that are known collectively as the *Pashtunwali*, which enjoy quasi-legality and apply to virtually every aspect of daily life, should not be underestimated. These rules pertain mostly, but not exclusively, to the commission of crimes, especially those committed against persons and/or property (International Legal Foundation 2004: 7). Such conflicts are primarily resolved by an exchange of women from the family of the perpetrator of the crime to the family of the victim. Women involved in this exchange (*bad* or *badal*) do not have any say.

Custom-based and traditional attitudes towards women are difficult to change. Many women in Afghanistan cannot even hope to dream of enjoying something even resembling equal rights, despite the fact that the twentieth-century constitutions all boldly proclaim the opposite.

Marriage

The Civil Code of 1977 accords women the right to choose a husband without the prior consent of their guardian, in accordance with the Hanafi school of law. With reference to child marriage, Articles 70 and 71 of the Civil Code specify a marriageable age of eighteen for boys and sixteen for girls, but dilutes in the meantime the effect of its own provision by providing that a 'valid marriage contract may be concluded by the contracting parties themselves, or by their guardians and representatives' (Art. 77 CC). The law, thus, falls short of addressing abusive exercise of the power of guardianship whereby parents, brothers, and uncles often impose their will on minor, and even adult, boys and girls. More recently, the Supreme Court has approved of a new standardised marriage contract (*nekāḥ-nāme*), with the explicit aim of curbing forced and child marriages. It remains to be seen whether in absence of any sanction people will abide by it. This will also depend on the observance of the requirement of registration.

The 1977 Civil Code introduced a registration requirement for all marriages. According to Article 61 every marriage has to be registered. The competent body for the registration of marriages is currently the district court of the area where the parties reside.[30] However, according to Afghan officials and current reports, in most parts of the country, marriages are neither certified nor registered. Only 5 per cent of the marriages have been registered (Ertürk 2006: 8). This means that the vast majority of Afghans are not officially registering their marriages. The registration of births, marriages, divorces and deaths are indispensable for determining the population number and ensuring legal security in a modern state. Due to the lack of reliable registration, it is not possible to collect statistics with regard to the marriage of minors for example. Likewise, in marital disputes, due to the lack of official documents, it is hard to prove the existence of a marriage.

The lack of registration is partly explained by the fact that non-registration does not affect the validity of the marriage: a marriage is considered religiously valid without registration. The participants of a workshop on family law, conducted by the Hamburg Max Planck Institute for Private Law (MPI) in 2006 in Kabul,[31] argued that a further reason why people do not register their marriages is their distrust in courts. Accordingly, it is against the Afghans' way of thinking, habits, and traditions to begin their marital life by going to a court, even if it is only in order to register the marriage. The other reason for not registering marriages is the fact that there is no need for it in daily life. Presenting certified documents is rarely necessary in Afghanistan. Thus, a simple but effective method for promoting registration would be a compulsory presentation of the marriage certificate to employers and landlords. For this purpose, trustworthy, extrajudicial registration authorities should be set up all over Afghanistan.

A further important issue in marriage law is the so-called bride price (*walwar*)[32], which has to be differentiated from the Islamic dower (*mahr*).[33] *Walwar* is a customary tradition whereby the groom or his family has to pay to the head of the bride's household a sum of money (or commodity) supposedly to reimburse the parents of the bride for the financial loss they suffered while raising their daughter. *Walwar* originates in the tribal tradition of Afghanistan, and viewed from the Pashtun perspective, it is a matter of honour: the higher the *walwar*, the higher the esteem of the husband's family for the bride. Some have argued that the concept of *walwar* is wrongly considered as 'selling girls', since this view ignores the socio-cultural background of the institution. The idea underlying *walwar* is to provide some financial relief to the girl's parents who purchase gold and silver ornaments, clothes, household utensils, etc. as dowry for their daughters. However, even if the dowry may be paid for out of the *walwar*, this is not a legal or customary obligation; *walwar* very often does not benefit the girl's family nor does it flow into the expenses for the wedding ceremony, also paid for by the family of the groom (Kamali 1985: 85).

The amount of commodities or money acceptable as *walwar* differs from province to province, as do the social attitudes with regard to this practice. In the 1980s, Kamali recorded amounts varying between 20,000 and 200,000 Afghanis depending on the geographic areas; a uniform figure could not be given. Likewise, a report conducted by the abovementioned Hamburg MPI in 2005[34] revealed equally variable amounts of payment of *walwar*. Data revealed, for instance, that the *walwar* for a virgin girl ranged from 2,000 U.S. dollars (about 85,000 Afghani) to 40,000 U.S. dollars (1,700,000 Afghani) for the first marriage of a girl. This amount might be even higher if the man was already married; it would double for the third marriage and increase further for the fourth marriage. It is important to add that the amount of *walwar* can also vary according to chastity, beauty, education, and the social class or economic standard of the girl and her family.

The need to purge the Afghan way of life of this tradition detrimental to society at large has been strongly felt. Accordingly, *walwar* has been prohibited in all family law legislation prior to the Civil Code of 1977. The Marriage Law (1921) explicitly forbade the practice of *walwar*, as did its successor, the Marriage Law of 1926. Both statutes failed, however, to specify any means of enforcement or sanction in case of infringement. The Marriage Law of 1949 contains similar provisions. According to its Article 5, the bride is denied any further gift (including *walwar*) in addition to her dower. Article 6 provides the groom with some means of action and stipulates that the government is authorised to take action in a situation where, after the completion of a valid marriage, the guardian of the bride refuses to allow the bride to join her husband because of his refusal to pay extra money. This provision, however, had hardly a scope of application since normally the bride price is to be paid before the conclusion of the marriage (Kamali 1985: 87; Tapper 1991: 144).

Subsequent legislation repeated the prohibition of *walwar* (so Art. 15 of the Marriage Law 1971), but as its predecessors, the Marriage Act 1971 failed to specify the competent court to hear cases on the matter, the penalties involved, or the way the violator should be prosecuted. The absence of sanctions made Article 15 inapplicable in practice. The intention of the legislator to eliminate *walwar* did not include any effective measure for the enforcement of the prohibition or sanctions for violation. The civil code also does not address the issue, thus failing to tackle one of the most burning issues in Afghan legal reality. With no effective measure to sanction its breach, the practise is still widespread in Afghanistan today.

In a country suffering from widespread poverty and unemployment this institution must be reconsidered in view of the fact that many men cannot afford it and are forced to sell their land or travel abroad to earn money for it (Yassari 2005: 58-59). Ironically, economic reasons also play a significant role in the persistence of *walwar*. The girl child can become an asset exchangeable for money or goods. Families see committing a young daughter (or sister) to a family that is able to pay a high price for the bride as a viable solution to their poverty and indebtedness. The custom of *walwar* may motivate families that face indebtedness and economic crisis to 'cash in' the 'asset' as young as six or seven, with the understanding that the actual marriage is delayed until the child reaches puberty. However, there is no guarantee that this is really observed and some reports indicate the danger of little girls being sexually abused not only by the groom but also by older men in the family, particularly if the groom is also a child (Ertürk 2006: 8).

Polygamy

The civil code confirms the validity of polygamy, but makes it contingent on conditions such as just character of the husband, his financial ability to maintain more than one wife, existence of a lawful reason, and consent of the new wife (Art.s 86, 89 CC). Polygamy remains permissible under the requirements of Article 86 of the Civil Code, which reads as follows:

> Polygamy can take place when the following conditions are fulfilled: 1) when there is no fear of unequal treatment as between the wives; 2) when the husband has sufficient financial means to maintain his wives. This includes food, clothing, housing and adequate medical care; 3) lawful reason, such as the first wife remaining childless or her suffering from diseases that are difficult to cure.

Since judicial permission prior to a polygamous marriage is not required to certify that the husband has indeed fulfilled these requirements, these provisions are not likely to be very effective. Judicial intervention is only possible after the polygamous marriage has been concluded. Consequently, when an Afghan man enters a polygamous marriage, violating any of the legally prescribed conditions, the second marriage will be valid (Ertürk 2006: 11). It will only give the wife (be it the first or the second) a right to judicial divorce on the basis of harm (*ḍarar*, see below) in cases where the husband failed to fulfil the stipulated conditions (Art.s 87, 183 CC).

These rules, once again, fail to address the social realities of Afghanistan, placing the burden of proof entirely on the wife. It is extremely difficult for an Afghan woman to prove that her husband is unjust and has inflicted injury on her. The current legislation cannot, therefore, be considered a real remedy for the difficulties Afghan women face. Since polygamy in the Afghan society is considered to be less of a social stigma than divorce, divorce is very rare and discouraged by social pressure. Moreover, it is questionable whether the entitlement to divorce is a real option to many Afghan women. In many cases, a woman may prefer putting up with the polygamous marriage of her husband, rather than to petition for a divorce that would likely leave her without financial means.

Divorce

Until the introduction of the Civil Code in 1977, divorce was exclusively governed by Hanafi law. Any legislation that addressed the subject prior to this time was of a piecemeal nature and essentially left the sharia law intact. The civil code, thus, represents the first attempt to comprehensively codify the sharia law of divorce. It provides for four types of marriage dissolution:

- First, there is the repudiation of the wife by the husband (*t,alāq*). The provisions of *t,alāq* are codified in Articles 135-155 of the civil code and reflect the Hanafi rules. Under the code the husband's unilateral right to divorce, without giving any reasons and without recourse to the courts, has been retained. The husband's may pronounce the *t,alāq* verbally, in writing, or even by gesture (Art.s 139, 135 CC). Witnesses are not required and the repudiation does not need to be registered. The code is completely silent on that matter. The possibility of the husband to divorce his wife with no further formalities causes a permanent legal insecurity for the women as to their marital status.
- The second form of divorce is the judicial divorce initiated by the wife (*tafrīq*) (Art.s 176-197). This kind of divorce must be based on specific grounds that are borrowed from the Maliki school of law. The grounds for judicial divorce include: the husband suffering from an incurable disease; his failure or his inability to maintain his wife; absence/desertion for three years without a lawful excuse; the husband's imprisonment for ten years or more, in which event she can ask for a divorce after the first five years of imprisonment; and harm (*ḍarar*) which can denote both physical and psychological injury (Art.s 89, 176, 191, 194).
- Thirdly there is the divorce against payment (*kholᶜ*) (Art.s 156-176). This kind of divorce is initiated by the wife whereby she provides

financial consideration in exchange for her divorce. *Khol*ᶜ represents the only form of dissolution whereby the wife has the right to initiate divorce proceedings without pleading a special reason such as harm or injury as grounds for divorce. Under Hanafi law, however, it can only be effectuated with the husband's consent, severely limiting the scope of this right. The rules on *khol*ᶜ in the Afghan code fail to take note of the family law reform measures that other Muslim countries have introduced. An Afghan woman's attempt to utilise *khol*ᶜ under the Civil Code can, therefore, be frustrated simply by the husband's refusal to agree to her proposal.

Finally, there is the annulment of the marriage (*faskh*) (Art.s 132-134), the legal dissolution of the marriage contract on the basis of an absence of a key requirement for the legality of the contract. This can be the case when one of the two parties has not consented to entering into the marriage, when psychological illnesses (such as insanity) are detected, or when the dower is inadequate (Kamali 1985: 184).

It is clear that the Afghan Civil Code does not meet the standards envisaged in the Bonn Agreement or the equality clause of the 2004 constitution. Therefore, in order for the civil code to reflect these standards, it needs to be revised, not only with reference to polygamy and divorce, but also with regard to all of its provisions that do not comply with these standards.

Code of Personal Status of Shi'i Afghans

The Code of Personal Status of Shi'i Afghans (CPS) is composed of 236 articles. Article 1 states that the code was drafted in response to Articles 131 and 54 of the Constitution of 2004 to regulate the personal status of Shi'i Afghans. Accordingly, the Supreme Court must appoint eligible Shi'i judges to implement the code (Art. 2). Whenever issues arise that are not addressed by the provisions of the CPS, the court shall decide in accordance with the Shi'i Ja'fari school of law as espoused in the writings (*fatwas*) of its most renowned and recognised religious authority the so-called 'source of imitation' (*marja*ᶜ*-e taqlīd*) (Art. 3).

According to Article 123 of the CPS, the husband is the head of the family. This kind of regulation is found in almost all family codes in Islamic countries. However, Article 123 further provides that the court may appoint the wife as head of the household, if it is established that the husband is intellectually unable to assume this position. The much contested Article 132(4) of the first draft of the code, which provided that the wife had to be sexual available whenever the man so wished, was omitted in the final version, as was the chapter on temporary marriage, which is recognised under Shi'i law, but prohibited under all

Sunni schools of law. Furthermore, Article 94 CPS stipulates that the marriageable age for women is 16 and for men 18, which is remarkable considering the Shi'i rules allowing for marriage from the age of puberty, i.e. 9 for girls and 15 for boys.

7.7 Criminal law

As mentioned earlier, according to the Bonn Agreement, all legislation that does not conflict with the regulations stipulated in the existing legal codes or with the international legal obligations to which Afghanistan has committed itself shall remain in place. Thus, to this extent, the Penal Code of 1976 is still applicable. Furthermore, the Law on Detection and Investigation of Crimes of 1978 (LDIC), the Counter Narcotics Code of 2005, the Juvenile Code of 2005, and the Police Law of 2005 are applicable. The Criminal Procedure Code of 1965 (CPC), as amended in 1974, has been replaced by a new Interim Criminal Procedure Code (ICPC) that was ratified by the Ministry of Justice on 25 February 2004. The Code has 98 articles and was prepared by the Italian Justice Project Office, an Italian organisation responsible for oversight and implementation of legal reform projects funded by the Italian government in Afghanistan. Regrettably, these sets of laws do not always operate well together. For example, Article 98(3) of the ICPC states:

> Upon promulgation of this law, any existing laws and decrees contrary to the provisions of this code are abrogated.

This article has been causing confusion and various problems for legal practitioners in the executive and the judiciary. For a police officer, a prosecutor, or a judge, it is extremely difficult to know which article(s) of the LDIC or CPC is contrary to the provisions of the ICPC and which is not (Gholami 2007: v).

Furthermore, according to some reports, substantive criminal law in Afghanistan continues to be governed in large part by Islamic law (Danish Immigration Service 2000: 35; Lau 2003: 21) and in certain areas by customary law (International Legal Foundation 2004: 14). Some of the punishments awarded for *h,add* offences, such as, for instance, the stoning to death of an adulterer if certain evidential requirements are met, do conflict with both the 2004 constitution, which prohibits the imposition of punishments 'incompatible with human dignity' (Art. 29), and Afghanistan's international legal obligations. This is also true for the *Pashtunwali* justice system, which is based on the principle of *bad*, or the exchange of women between families when a crime is committed as compensation for the crime (Lau 2003: 22). However, it is not known whether the present administration intends to modify these aspects of Islamic and customary criminal law. It is in these areas that the most flagrant conflicts with international human rights standards still exist, and this is, together with family law, the two areas of law likely to be the most sensitive to reform.

7.8 Other legal areas, especially economic law

The first Afghan Commercial Code was enacted in 1955. It contained 945 articles encompassing regulations on the merchant, (Art.s 1-115), commercial companies (Art.s 116-470), commercial documents (Art.s 471-588), and commercial transactions including commercial agency and insurance (Art.s 589-945). Islamic law did not influence Afghan commercial legislation, as this legislation was based on the Turkish Commercial Code, which was, in turn, based on Western secular legislation, especially on German and Swiss law.

Traditional Afghan society with its tribal structures found it hard to adapt to the provisions of the code, as it did not match people's needs, nor could they fulfil the requirements of the code. Article 117 of the Commercial Code (1955) defined, for example, various kinds of companies that had to be registered at the High Court of Appeal in Kabul, with the Ministry of Justice publishing all relevant information (e.g. trade mark, name of the company, and other specifications) in the Official Gazette.

The areas of intellectual property, banking, money exchange, and industrial property had never been codified and also required urgent regulation in order to attract foreign investors and industries. Accordingly, several statutes were published to cover these areas of commercial activities. The following statutes still exist and are applicable according to the Bonn Agreement: the Commercial Code of 1955; the Commercial Procedure Code of 1963; the Law of the Chamber of Commerce of 1951; and the Law for the Registration of Trade Marks of 1960. Since twenty-five years of civil war have turned the economy into a war economy (Schetter 2002: 109), it is difficult to assess the effectiveness of statutory commercial law in Afghanistan today.[35]

In 2002, a new Investment Law was enacted. [36] It aims to attract and secure foreign investment in Afghanistan. It was amended in December 5, 2005. According to Article 2, the State is committed to maximising private, both domestic and foreign, investment and to creating a legal regime and administrative structure that will encourage and protect foreign and domestic private investment in the Afghan economy in order to promote economic development, expand the labour market, increase production and export earnings, promote technology transfer, improve national prosperity, and advance the people's standard of living. The only requirement to invest in Afghanistan is to maintain a valid bank account and to pass a criminal background check. Investments in Afghanistan can be 100 per cent foreign-owned (Art. 10).

In September 2003, a new Banking Law was passed by Presidential Decree.[37] It contains 101 articles and is clearly investor-friendly as long as contracts are followed. There are, however, scant provisions for enforcement in case of any default. Afghanistan lacks special courts for banking matters, and there is no recognition of foreign judgments. Interestingly, the law makes no reference to the principles of Islamic Banking. Islamic banking and interest-free banking are still in their infancy in Afghanistan. The civil war has played its part in bringing about this situation. There are currently no Islamic banks in the country, and there is no legislation covering the institutional and procedural aspects of this kind of banking. The war and the period following it have brought even the regular banking system to the brink of collapse (Kamali 2005:26).

7.9 International treaty obligations and human rights

The Constitution of 2004 contains a long list of guaranteed basic human rights of the citizens of Afghanistan. Afghanistan has also ratified the following international treaties: CEDAW, CRC, CAT, CERD, CESCR, and the ICCPR.

During the past twenty-five years, though, Afghan society has been through an extraordinary amount of violence. Throughout this period, serious abuses of human rights and war crimes by all sides in the conflict have taken place, including massacres, looting of houses and property, rapes, revenge killings, illegal imprisonment, the torture and murder of prisoners, and assassinations of political opponents (Amnesty International 2002). The legacy of war, poverty, and religious fanaticism has particularly affected Afghan women, who have suffered from both cultural and structural inequalities and violence in Afghan society for centuries. The persistence of this situation over the past quarter of a century has produced what Wardak calls a 'culture of human rights abuses' that is justified, and even positively sanctioned, in the shadow of warlordism in Afghanistan (Wardak 2005: 73).

After the fall of the Taliban regime, the Afghan Independent Human Rights Commission (AIHRC) was established on 2 June 2002 in response to Article 58 of the 2004 Constitution.[38] The AIHRC is the product of a national consultative process between Afghan human rights activists, the Interim Administration at the time, and the United

Nations. Creation of the Commission was also encouraged and supported by Resolution 134/48 of the U.N. General Assembly in 1993, and the Paris principles. The Commission, with its eight branch offices throughout the country, aims to protect and promote human rights across Afghanistan. In accordance with the 2004 Constitution, the AIHRC functions as a permanent institution for the monitoring and, where necessary, investigation of the human rights situation in Afghanistan. AIHRC is funded by donor countries assisting Afghanistan, and, as such, forms an important part of national income for the country. The AIHRC is currently chaired by Sima Samar, a well-known women and human rights advocate and activist within national and international forums. Before chairing the Commission, she was elected as the Vice-Chair of the emergency *Loya Jirga*.

Since its establishment, the AIHRC has regularly reported on violation of human rights, related in particular to women, children, and civilian casualties and death as a result of ongoing clashes between the NATO and Taliban and perpetrators of war crimes in Afghanistan. Their latest report, the Report on the Situation of Economic and Social Rights in Afghanistan of November/December 2009 aims to assess the status of economic and social rights in Afghanistan in the year 1387 (2009) against the national and international obligations of the government with respect to these rights. The report highlights that one of the most significant challenges in Afghanistan is still the worrying security situation. Despite existing commitments, strategies, and policies developed to improve the socio-economic situation of Afghans, many men, women, and children continue to suffer from extreme poverty, high unemployment, systemic discrimination, and a lack of access to healthcare, schools, and adequate housing. Implementation and enforcement of legislation to protect social and economic rights also remains limited due to weak judicial institutions.[39]

The social reality of human rights protection in Afghanistan thus reveals a depressing picture of almost complete legal impunity. Not only do grave past violations of human rights remain unpunished, but abuses continue without any immediate prospect of bringing the perpetrators to justice. Any reform of the legal system to bring it in line with international human rights standards or with the provisions of the new constitution will require as an essential prerequisite the existence of a stable, functioning, and capable state, both able and willing to enforce laws (Lau 2003: 4). At present, this is sadly not the situation in Afghanistan.

7.10 Conclusion

The Afghan legal system and its evolution throughout the last hundred years have been coloured by three factors: its traditional and tribal government and local customary laws; Islamic law; and the development of statutory laws by the central state authorities.

The relationship between Islamic law and customary law is complex. Local customs and customary law continue to have a very prominent role. Despite official statements to the contrary, people usually resort to the chiefs and eldest of their communities, whom they frequently refer to as the 'white beards' (*rīsh-e sefīd*), for dispute resolution. Generally, when a dispute arises, the parties agree on whether the dispute is to be resolved 'sharia-wise' or in accordance with customary law, e.g. mainly the *Pashtunwali* (International Legal Foundation 2004: 7). There are very few reports and data on the application of customary law in Afghanistan. Decisions of the *jirgas* are conveyed orally, and there are no written reports. In many cases, customary law strictly contradicts Islamic law. This is especially so in cases where women, without their consent, are given into marriage to settle disputes between families. In these circumstances, and as is often the practical reality, the status of Afghan women under customary law is worse than the status afforded to them under the most conservative interpretation of Islamic law.

Historically, there has been simultaneous coexistence and competition between sharia and customary law. While Islamic law, namely the Hanafi school of law, substantially controls matters of personal relationship and most aspects of inheritance, local custom prevails in land tenure. In criminal matters, both sources of law can govern the case.

All Afghan constitutions, except the Constitution of 1980, endorsed the traditional supremacy of sharia in Afghanistan. This is manifested in the numerous references made to the sharia, proclaiming it as the law of the nation. This can be explained by the fact that Afghans have always had recourse to Islamic law. It has been the single constant to have steadily survived a century of law reform and legal insecurity. Note, for instance, a reminder of Afghan's political and legal history: the burst of modern legislation under Amanullah between 1919-1929 was abrogated by the succeeding regime; the Western-oriented reforms of the 1970s were eventually completely undone in the communist era; and the attempts to turn the legal system of the country from its religious tribal and customary basis to an imposed emphasis on a general Sovietisation of the legal system after 1978 failed.

Since the latter half of the nineteenth century, a number of efforts have been made to modernise and secularise the existing legal system, or at least specific areas of the law. Statutory legislation is a latecomer on the scene, meant to supplement the sharia especially in areas that were not covered by the latter. Legislation in traditionally sharia-dominated fields such as family law, law of property, contracts, and evidence mainly sought to codify the substantive sharia rules for purposes of easy reference by judges and lawyers. In this respect, they are seen as merely a restatement of Islamic law (e.g., Art.s 497-750 CC, reflecting Hanafi contract law). Other pieces of legislation, such as the Commercial Code on the other hand, are genuinely secular codifications.

These legislative initiatives have frequently been accomplished only through the employment of drastic, even violent, measures (Reynolds & Flores 1993: 1). Ironically, the general effect has been to generate strengthened support for Islamic and customary law at the local level. Furthermore, Afghan legislation (secular and otherwise) has been limited both in its quantity and quality. The result is disjointed legislation, with many gaps and unregulated areas of law. Röder calls the legal landscape 'a patchwork' of various norms (Röder 2009: 257). While the nation may be a unified state in a strict sense, the law is in practice a fragmented *mélange* of secular, customary, and religious law variously applied according to local acceptance of central legislation and modified by shifting conditions of governmental authority. Legal pluralism is the hallmark of legal reality in Afghanistan.

Without exception, all surveys of the Afghan legal system have made note of the fact that Afghanistan's statutory laws and regulations exist solely on paper (Weinbaum 1980: 51). Most of the literature also points to the fact that for ordinary people and villagers, who form the vast majority of the population, tribal/customary and Islamic law are far more significant and actually better known than state legislation (Amin 1993: 66). The limited practical value of Afghanistan's statutory laws has to be attributed to the decline and demise of central political authority in Afghanistan as a result of the civil war, but also to the lack of training of legal professionals and the inability to adapt statutory law to Afghanistan's particular circumstances. This means for instance that judges either do not know the law well, or know it, but are reluctant to apply it. The *de facto* subdivision of the legal system into official statutory law and unofficial mainly unwritten law is characteristic of the Afghan legal history ever since attempts were made to introduce statutory laws. The difficulty of implementing statutory laws also has very practical considerations: many of the statutes have for a long time been unavailable, due to the destruction of archives and the complete breakdown of administrative order during the years of civil war.

Hence, in Afghanistan it is not the implications of sharia or sharia-based law which, at least for the moment, prevent the application and implementation of international legal and human rights standards, but the lack of a system by which the rule of law may be established so that the legal system is capable of – practically, socially, politically –

guaranteeing and enforcing laws effectively. Although the Government is committed to carrying out its duties imposed not only by Afghanistan's domestic laws but also by the country's international obligations, the greatest challenge to action is the lack of security and the fragile peace balance in the country.

A functional legal system in Afghanistan, which is applied by legal professionals and accepted by the population, requires incorporation of certain aspects of Islamic and customary law, within the limits imposed by human rights considerations. It is impossible to reject the existing body of tribal laws in its entirety, as this will damage the legal reform process; but at the same time, discriminatory practices, especially those against women, must be abolished. This, in turn, means bringing about a gradual change of popular attitudes on part of the population at large concerning the application of those rules that infringe upon basic human as well as basic Islamic rights. This is the *conditio sine qua non* for change. As long as practices such as *bad* and *walwar* are not seen as disgraceful and against human dignity, imposing a system from above will not be successful in Afghanistan. In changing these practices, history, traditional structures, and the failures of the past must be taken into consideration.

Notes

1 Nadjma Yassari is a senior fellow at the Max-Planck Institute for Comparative and International Private Law in Hamburg, where she heads the Department for the laws of Islamic countries. Hamid M. Saboory is an independent consultant, providing services to several NGOs in Europe and North America on legal reform and development issues related to Afghanistan. He holds an M.A. in International Relations from Syracuse University and an M.A. in Middle/Near Eastern Studies from New York University. The authors wish to thank Prof. Mohammad Hashim Kamali from the Islamic University of Malaysia for his great help in collecting the necessary materials for this report.

2 *Nezām-nāme* is the Dari expression for legal enactment. They are the first legal documents representing statutory law in Afghanistan, with the first being the 1923 Constitution. The expression was later changed to *os,ūl-nāme.*

3 According to the latest report of the Ministry of Justice in Afghanistan, the total number of *nezām-nāmes* ('laws') enacted is 75. A list of these laws, acts, decrees, etc. is available in the Library of the International Development Law Organization (IDLO) in Rome and online at: http://www.idlo.int/afghanlaws/index.htm. See also Kamali 1985: 36.

4 There is unfortunately very little research and analysis on the actual effect of these statutes. It may be presumed that they did not really have much impact on behaviour and traditions, since one of the economically most devastating traditions of Afghan society, the *walwar* (as will be exemplified under 7.6) not only survived but is still practiced widely in Afghanistan today. See Kamali 1985: 83-105.

5 Afghan Official Gazette No. 12/1964, dated 1 October.

6 The Official Gazette was first published in 1963. Publication was irregular and stopped temporary due to civil wars and foreign invasion. It resumed its regular publication in 2001, after the fall of the Taliban regime.
7 *Khalq* literally means 'masses' or 'people'. *Parčam* literally means 'banner' or 'flag'. The names are derived from newspapers each party published. Khalq, edited by Taraki, was published only six times before the government banned it. After the split, Karmal and his supporters published the Parcham newspaper. Khalq's membership was primarily Pashtun and rural, while Parcham was predominately urban, middle-class Tajiks.
8 This was said because the Parcham newspaper '*Parcham*' was tolerated by the king himself and its publication permitted from March 1968–July 1969.
9 Afghan Official Gazette No. 347/1976, dated 7 October.
10 Afghan Official Gazette No. 360/1977, dated 24 February.
11 Afghan Official Gazette No. 353/1977, dated 5 January.
12 Decree No. 8/1978 was already brought into effect in September, Afghan Official Gazette No. 412/1978.
13 Afghan Official Gazette No. 409/1978, dated 17 September.
14 The constitution of the democratic government of Afghanistan (*oṣūl-e as,ās,ī-ye jomhūrī-ye demūkrātīke afghānestān*)[o], Afghan Official Gazette No. 450/1980, dated 21 April.
15 Afghan Official Gazette No. 479/1981, dated 22 December.
16 Afghan Official Gazette No. 471/1981, dated 5 January.
17 Afghan Official Gazette No. 660/1987, dated 29 November.
18 Afghan Official Gazette No. 728/1990, dated 29 May.
19 This is based on eye-witness accounts and interviews with members of the Ministry of Justice conducted by Hamid Saboory in Kabul during 2003.
20 Afghan Official Gazette No. 788/1999.
21 Afghan Official Gazette No. 783/1997, dated 12 May.
22 Some sources reported participation as high as 62 per cent, but this is unverified
23 According to the Afghanistan Research and Evaluation Unit (AREU), this kind of election system is nowadays only used in Jordan, Vanuatu, the Pitcairn Islands, and partially in Taiwan (Reynolds & Wilder 2004: 12).
24 The United States pledged an additional 1.1 billion dollars in financial aid for the coming U.S. fiscal year from October, slightly less than the 1.2 billion dollars from the World Bank. One billion dollars were also pledged by the Asian Development Bank; 855 million dollars by Britain; 480 million dollars by Germany; and 450 million dollars by Japan. Additionally, the European Union pledged 268 million dollars; Spain 182 million dollars; India 181 million dollars; the Netherlands 179 million dollars; Saudi Arabia 153 million dollars; Pakistan 150 million dollars; and Norway 144 million dollars. France trailed well behind with 55 million dollars.
25 See http://www.usip.org/node/5023.
26 See http://www.iec.org.af/results/index.html.
27 See http://afghanistan.hmg.gov.uk/en/conference/.
28 For an English translation of the Afghan Constitution of 2004, see 'Annex C, Constitution of Afghanistan 2004', in Yassari 2005: 271-329.
29 Afghan Official Gazette No. 988/2009, dated 27 July.
30 Global Rights, Afghan Family Law, Book 2: 16. Global Rights is a group of human rights activists formed in 2002 for the rule of law, access to justice, ensuring and publicising human rights.
31 See http://www.mpipriv.de/ww/de/pub/mitarbeiter/yassari_nadjma.cfm.
32 The equivalent Dari terms are *toyāna, pīsh-kash* and *shīr-bahā*; *qalīn* is the Uzbek equivalent and the Nuristani used the term *malpreg* (Kamali 1985: 84).

33 The expression 'dower' is used here to denote the Islamic institution of *mahr.* It should not be confused with the expression of 'dowry', which denotes the girl's trousseau, i.e. the (household) items that she brings into marriage.
34 See http://www.mpipriv.de/shared/data/pdf/mpi-report_on_family_structures_and_-family_law_in_afghanistan.pdf.
35 According to Asifa Kakar, a judge at the Supreme Court, commercial division, the Commercial Code is being applied in the court. There are, however, no publications of court decisions. There are also no private compilations accessible for reference.
36 Afghan Official Gazette No. 803/2002, dated 11 September.
37 Presidential Decree No. 63/2003, dated 18 September.
38 See 'Decree of the Chairman of the Interim Administration', http://www.aihrc.org.af, dated 6 June 2002.
39 See http://www.aihrc.org.af/English.

Bibliography

Amin, S.H. (1993), *Law, reform and revolution in Afghanistan.* Glasgow: Royston.

Bartleby (2008), 'Afghanistan', in *World Factbook,* see http://www.bartleby.com/151/af.html. Washington, D.C.: Central Intelligence Agency.

Commission on Human Rights (for Resolution 1985/38 of 13 March 1985 No E/CN.4/1986/24) (1986), 'Report on the situation of human rights in Afghanistan prepared by the Special Rapporteur, Mr. Felix Ermacora, in accordance with Commission on Human Rights resolution 1985/38' see http://www.unhcr.org/refworld/pdfid/482996d02.pdf.

Danish Immigration Service (2002), 'The political, security and human rights situation in Afghanistan', *Report on fact-finding mission to Kabul and Maza-i-Sharif, Afghanistan and Islamabad, Pakistan,* published 7 March 2003, see http://www.unhcr.org/refworld/docid/3ef7f0c84.html.

Ekhwan, S. (2002), *Oral history of Afghanistan from 1900-1992.* Teheran: Center of Historic and Diplomatic Documentation (in Farsi).

Ertürk, Y. (2006), 'Integration of the human rights of women and a gender perspective: Violence against Women, its causes and consequences', *Report of the Special Rapporteur on Violence against Women* E/CN.4/2006/61/Add.5 Mission to Afghanistan, dated 15 February 2006. New York: Commission on Human Rights of the United Nation.

Ewans, M. (2001), *Afghanistan – A new history.* Richmond Place: Curzon Press.

Gholami, H. (2007), Basics of Afghan law and criminal justice - A manual for the Afghan police and legal professionals, see http://www.auswaertiges-amt.de/diplo/de/Aussenpolitik/. RegionaleSchwerpunkte/AfghanistanZentralasien/Downloads/Polizei-Legal-Manual.pdf.

Global Rights (2006), 'h,oqūq-e fāmīl (Afghan Family Law)', *Legal Aid Guidelines,* Vol. 2. Kabul: Global Rights.

International Crisis Group (2004), *Asia Report* No. 88, dated 23 November 2004, see http://www.crisisgroup.org.

International Crisis Group (2005), *Asia Briefing* No. 39, dated 2 June 2005, see http://www.crisgroup.org.

International Legal Foundation (2004), 'The customary laws of Afghanistan', Report (September), see http://www.theILF.org.

Kamali, H. (2005), 'Islam and its Sharia in the Afghan Constitution 2004, with special reference to personal law', in N. Yassari (ed.), *The Sharīʿa in the constitutions of Afghanistan, Iran and Egypt – Implications for private law,* 23-44. Tübingen: Mohr Siebeck Verlag.

Kamali, H. (1985), *Law in Afghanistan: A study of the constitutions, matrimonial law and the judiciary.* Leiden: Brill.

Kohlmann, E. (1999), '*An Afghan Ghazi: The modernization and reforms of Amir Amanullah Khan*', Washington D.C., 9 December, see http://law.upenn.edu/~ekohlman/amanullah.pdf.

Lau, M. (2003), '*Afghanistan's legal system and its compatibility with international human rights standards*', *Report of the International Commission of Jurists*, see http://www.icj.org/IMG/pdf/doc-46.pdf.

Lau, M. (2002), '*An introduction to Afghanistan's legal system*', *Yearbook of Islamic and Middle Eastern Law* 8: 27-44. Den Haag: Kluwer Academic Publishers.

Magnus, R. & E. Naby (2002), *Mullah, Marx, and Mujahid*. Colorado: Westview Press.

Oates, L. (2009) 'A closer look - The policy and law-making process behind the Shiite Personal Status Law', *Afghanistan Research and Evaluation Unit* (Sept.): Issues Paper Series.

Rashid, A. (2000), *Taliban: Militant Islam, oil and fundamentalism in Central Asia*. London: I. B. Tauris.

Reynolds, A. & A. Wilder (2005), 'A guide to parliamentary elections in Afghanistan', *Afghanistan Research and Evaluation Unit (AREU)*, August, see http://www.areu.org.af/.

Reynolds, A. & A. Wilder (2004), 'Free, fair or flawed: Challenges for legitimate elections in Afghanistan', *AREU*, Sept., see http://www.areu.org.af/.

Reynolds, T. & A. Flores (2005), 'Afghanistan', in T. Reynolds & A. Flores (ed.), *Foreign law, current sources of codes and legislation in jurisdictions of the world, Vol. III: Afghanistan, Africa, Asia and Australasia* (updated Dec. 2005). Littleton: Rothman.

Röder, T. (2009), 'Kollisionen zwischen Sharīʿa, Gesetz und Stammestradition in Afghanistan', in M. Kötter & G.F. Schuppert (ed.), *Normative Pluralität Ordnen*, 257-30. Baden-Baden: Nomos Verlag.

Rubin, B.R. (2002), *The fragmentation of Afghanistan: State formation and collapse in the international system*. New Haven: Yale University Press.

Schetter, C. (2004), *Kleine Geschichte Afghanistans*. München: C.H. Beck.

Schetter, C. (2002), 'The "bazaar economy" of Afghanistan – A comprehensive approach', in Noelle-Karimi (ed.), *Afghanistan – A country without state*, 109-128. Frankfurt am Main: IKO-Verlag.

Tapper, N. (1991), *Bartered brides – Politics, gender and marriage in an Afghan tribal society*. Cambridge University Press: Cambridge.

Vafai, G. (1988), *Afghanistan: A Country Law Study*. Washington, D.C.: Library of Congress.

Wardak, A. (2005), 'Building a post war justice system in Afghanistan', in N. Yassari (ed.), *The Sharīʿa in the Constitutions of Afghanistan, Iran and Egypt Implications for Private Law*, 61-82. Tübingen: Mohr Siebeck Verlag.

Weinbaum, M. (1980), 'Legal elites in Afghan Society', *International Journal of Middle East Studies* 12: 39-57.

Yassari, N. (2005), 'Legal pluralism and family law: An assessment of the current situation in Afghanistan', in N. Yassari (ed.), *The Sharīʿa in the constitutions of Afghanistan, Iran and Egypt: Implications for private law*, 45-60. Tübingen: Mohr Siebeck Verlag.

8 Sharia and national law in Iran[1]

Ziba Mir-Hosseini[2]

Abstract

In the nineteenth century, the last of a series of tribal dynasties ruled Iran, and the Shia religious establishment had a monopoly of law, which was based on their interpretations of sharia. The twentieth century opened with the first of two successful revolutions. In the Constitutional Revolution of 1905-1911, democratic nationalists sought an end to absolute monarchy, a constitution, and the rule of law. They succeeded in laying the foundations of an independent judiciary and a parliament with legislative powers. The despotic, but modernising Pahlavi shahs (1925-1979) maintained (though largely ignored) both the constitution and parliament, curtailed the power of the Shia clergy, and put aside sharia in all areas of law apart from family law, in favour of a secular legal system inspired by European codes.

The secularisation of society and legal reforms in the absence of democracy were major factors in the convergence of popular, nationalist, leftist, and Islamist opposition to Pahlavi rule, which led to the 1978-1979 Iranian Revolution under Ayatollah Khomeini. Islamist elements gained the upper hand in the new Islamic Republic. Determined to reestablish sharia as the source of law and the clergy as its official interpreters, they set about undoing the secularisation of the legal system. The new constitution attempted an unusual and contradictory combination of democracy and theocracy; for three decades Iran has experienced fluctuations, sometimes violent, between emerging democratic and pluralistic popular movements and the dominance of theocratic despotism. The legal system is often the arena for confrontation between more conservative and patriarchal interpretations of the sharia and the more liberal and pragmatic interpretations that see no contradictions between sharia and democracy and human rights.

Table of contents

The Islamic Republic of Iran was born in 1979 after a popular revolution that ended more than 2,500 years of monarchy. Iran was never colonised, but for much of the nineteenth and early twentieth century it was a major arena for Great-Power rivalry between Russia and Britain. Iran has a population of over 70 million, of which 89 per cent are Shiite, 9 per cent Sunni and the remaining 1-2 per cent Christians, Jews, Zoroastrians, and Baha'is. Persian-speakers are the dominant and largest ethno-linguistic group (51%), followed by the Azarbayjani Turks (24%), Gilaki and Mazandarani (8%), Kurds (7%), Arabs (3%), Lurs (2%), Baluches (2%), and Turkmen (2%). Seventy per cent of the population speaks Persian or related languages, with 26 per cent speaking Turkish or related languages. More than half the population lives in towns and cities. Eighty per cent of the population are literate; there are 22 million students, including three million enrolled in universities, of whom well over 50 per cent are female. The legal voting age is 16 and approximately 50 per cent of the electorate are under the age of 30.

(Source: Bartleby 2010)

8.1 The period until 1920

Monarchy versus religious authority

Islam came to Iran, then known abroad as Persia, in the seventh century when the Ummayad Arabs brought an end to the Zoroastrian Persian Sasanid Empire, though mass conversion to Islam did not occur for some time. After centuries of foreign occupation and short-lived native dynasties, the country was unified in 1501 by Isma'il, sheikh of the Safavi Sufi order, when he became the first ruler of the Safavid dynasty. Shah Isma'il declared the state religion to be Twelver Shiism; Iran remains the only country where the official religion is Shia Islam (adherents number 10 per cent of Muslims worldwide). Distinguishing features of this faith relevant to law are the recognition of twelve Imams as legitimate successors of the prophet (the imamate), the occultation (*gheibat*) of the last Imam, the possibility of reinterpretation (*ejtehad*) by qualified scholars, and emulation (*taqlid*) of supreme religious authority (*marja'iyat*).[3]

For Shia, leadership of the Muslims passed after the Prophet to his descendants, the Imams, rather than to the (elected) Caliphs, as is believed by Sunni Muslims. Each Imam was designated by the previous one, starting with the Prophet's cousin and son-in-law 'Ali and ending with the twelfth Imam, Mohammad Mahdi, the 'Imam of Time', who went into occultation; his return will mark the end of time, but in his absence, the religious scholars (the ulama[4]) assume the guidance of the Shia. Among the Shia, qualified scholars are known as *mojtahed*, indicating that they are able to exercise judgment, or independent interpretation of the law from the sources (*ejtehad*). According to the Shia theory of *taqlid*[5] any man or woman who has not reached the stage of *ejtehad* is an emulator (*moqalled*) and, as such, must choose a leading *mojtahed* to be their own spiritual guide (*marja'-e taqlid*, 'model/source of emulation'), whose opinions in matters of religious law are binding on those who follow him.[6] A *marja'* (pl. *maraje'*) becomes recognised after a long process of acquiring respect for his teaching and scholarship, especially after qualifying as an ayatollah by writing a legal treatise or manual (*resaleh*) for those who have chosen to follow him in religious matters. One class of treatise is 'Explanation of problems' (*towzih al-masa'el*), a compendium of legal opinions, in a fixed format, starting with rulings about ritual acts such as prayers and fasting, and proceeding to chapters about contracts, such as marriage and divorce. Before the Iranian revolution, no scholar would publish his treatise, or be recognised as an ayatollah, while his own *marja'* was alive.

Annual religious taxes for the Shia include *zakat* (alms for the poor and needy) and *khoms* (one-fifth of income), payable to the *marja'*. Half of the *khoms* goes to Seyyeds, descendants of the Prophet; the other half, the 'Imam's share' (*sahm-e imam*), is considered to be the Imams' inheritance from the Prophet. A *marja'* receives it in his capacity as representative of the Imam of Time; he is free to spend it as he deems suitable. The *sahm-e imam* is, thus, a major source of wealth and power for the religious leaders. The *maraje'* live and teach in seminaries, known collectively as *howzeh* (short for *howzeh 'elmiyeh*, 'Scientific circle/milieu'). The two most important seminaries are in Najaf in Iraq and Qom in Iran; each city has a number of theological colleges, and both have become widely known as centres of not only religious learning but also political Islam.

The relation between religious and worldly power has always been a major source of dispute and difference among the Shia. In theory, in the absence of the Imams, no worldly power is legitimate. The earlier Safavid Shahs, as Sufi sheikhs, enjoyed unchallenged spiritual authority with which to bolster their political power. Since the seventeenth century, however, the relation between the Shahs and the Shia clerics has been complex and difficult.[7] In practice, most leading scholars have been quietist, keeping themselves apart from the world of politics and government, advising the ruler but refraining from action, at least so long as he was felt to be preserving Islam. But other clerics, especially since the nineteenth century, have played an active political role, taking different positions on crucial issues such as the scope of their independent judgement *(ejtehad)* and religious authority *(marja'iyat)*, how injustice and oppression should be opposed, and whether the Shia faith can accommodate man-made laws.

The Safavid dynasty fell in 1722, to be replaced eventually by the Qajars, who ruled from 1779 to 1925. During the nineteenth century, the institution of *marja'iyat* emerged separately from the state, and came to encapsulate the notion of supreme religious authority. The birth of 'modern' Iran is often dated to the early nineteenth century. After two disastrous wars with Russia, Qajar Iran was exposed to a wide range of new ideas, thanks to the increasing presence of European diplomats, merchants, and military advisors, the despatch of elite young men to be educated in France, and not least the translation and publication of European literary and political materials. At the same time, Iran found itself the object of imperial rivalry between Russia and Britain. The Qajar rulers, especially Naser ad-din Shah (1848-1896) and his son Mozaffar ad-din Shah (1896-1907), came under severe pressure and ultimately undertook policies that would compromise the country's integrity. In constant debt, they raised money from foreigners by selling concessions; this was widely interpreted, especially by the religious classes, as selling the country and Islam. One such example, the Tobacco Concession of 1891, led to a massive and successful popular protest, orchestrated by the leading cleric Mirza-ye Shirazi. This was the start of the movement that culminated in the Constitutional Revolution of 1905-1911.

1906-1911: The Constitutional Revolution

Until the Constitutional Revolution, the source of law in Iran was the sharia as interpreted by the senior clerics. The Shahs had installed a dual court structure. In addition to a system of state (*orfi*) courts supervised by a secular minister of justice, a system of religious sharia courts also functioned. The Shah appointed the head of the justice department and the religious judges, though in many places judges remained self-appointed. In this way, he sought firm control over the entire administration of justice. The sharia courts, presided over by clerics, had jurisdiction over all matters relating to family, inheritance, and civil law; the *orfi* or state courts had jurisdiction over matters involving the state. However, in practice the sharia courts enjoyed almost all judicial power and dealt with cases in accordance with well-developed Shia rules of jurisprudence (*feqh*) (Banani 1961: 68; Amin 1985: 52-60). At the local level, the clergy, together with tribal chiefs, big landowners and merchants, controlled the urban and rural population. Clerics supervised land transactions and provided for both education and social care.

The constitutional movement brought together a wide range of different elements: merchants and clerics, Muslim reformist intellectuals, secular liberals and nationalists. The common aim, if on differing grounds, was to limit the absolutism of the Shah through a constitution, an elected legislature, and an independent judiciary. Many supporters of the movement did not, however, appreciate the implications of its secularist, liberal, and democratic nature. The leading Shia clerics were ambivalent and took different positions. Mirza Mohammad Hossein Na'ini (1860-1936), the most high-ranking cleric to support the movement, provided for instance religious arguments for the rejection of absolutism and a defence of constitutionalism.[8] In contrast, the main clerical opponent of the constitution, Sheikh Fazlollah Nuri, argued that ideas of democracy and freedom, the reforms advocated by the constitutionalists, and the establishment of a parliament to enact legislation, were in contradiction with Islam. He further maintained that men and women, Muslims and non-Muslims have different status and rights under the sharia, and as such cannot be treated on an equal basis. Nuri was opposed to the establishment of parliament on the grounds that any man-made law would necessarily clash with religious law. In his view, religious scholars must control the process of law-making as well as the judiciary.

In August 1906, Mozaffar ad-din Shah was forced to grant a parliament (National Consultative Assembly, *Majles-e Shura-ye Melli*), and at the end of December, shortly before his death, he signed the first constitution (*Qanun-e Asasi*, 'Fundamental Law'). The constitution, which was largely secular, with an emphasis on popular sovereignty, codified several constitutional rights, such as freedom of expression and equality before the law. Following objections by religious scholars, a Supplement to the Constitution was drafted to include more references to Islam and to the necessity for the scholars to approve all laws. The new Shah, Mohammad 'Ali, signed the Supplement in October 1907; but the following year, with Russian help, he staged a successful coup against the constitutionalists. In 1909, constitutionalist forces advanced on Tehran, deposed the Shah, and executed Sheikh Fazlollah Nuri. Parliament was restored, along with the constitution.

One of the main demands of the constitutionalists was the creation of a House of Justice (*edalatkhaneh*). This was reflected in the 1907 Supplement, nineteen articles of which (Art.s 71-89) define the power, nature, and organisation of the courts, and lay the basis for an independent judiciary and a unified legal system (Amanat 1992). At the same time, the clergy were given a concession in the form of Article 2, which required that parliament's enactments must never be at variance with the sacred precepts of Islam, and established a body of five clerics with veto power over bills deemed to be in contradiction with the sharia. In the same year (1907), a four-tier civil court system was created in Tehran: the Court of Property and Financial Claims, the Criminal Court, the Court of Appeals, and the Supreme Court of Appeals. In

1908, a Dispute Court was created to deal with disagreements between civil and sharia courts. In 1911, parliament set up a temporary committee to consider 'transitional laws', and the French jurist Pierny was charged with designing codes of criminal, trade, and civil law. To contain the opposition of the clerical establishment to these measures, their temporary and experimental nature was stressed (Banani 1961: 69).

But the process of law reform soon ground to a halt, due to skirmishes between parliament and the clergy, who were adamant about retaining the sharia as the only source of law and their power as its sole interpreters. In short, the creation of a new judiciary became entangled in the ideological struggles that remained unresolved in the Constitutional Revolution. The new parliament survived, the foundations of a secular democracy had been laid, and there was evidence of the beginnings of a lively, independent press, but religious elements were still strong factors in governance and daily life, and the potential for monarchical despotism remained.

8.2 The period from 1920 until 1965

Modernisation and authoritarian rule

1920-1926: The rise of Reza Shah Pahlavi

The early 1920s saw the end of the Qajars and a return to despotism under the new Pahlavi dynasty. During the World War, Russian, Turkish, and British forces occupied much of Iran. Reza Khan, a Cossack officer, rose to prominence while dealing with the disorders that pervaded the provinces in the aftermath of the war. Following a coup d'état in 1921, he became War Minister, then Prime Minister, and in 1925 parliament proclaimed him Shah. The clergy, deeply shaken by developments in neighbouring Turkey and fiercely opposed to his original plan to establish a republic, watched from the sidelines in dismay.

A westernising secular nationalist, Reza Shah formed a strong military and a centralised bureaucracy. He also established both the secular judiciary and the greatly expanded secular educational system that the constitutionalists had wanted. In these and other ways he deprived the clerics of their former monopolies and resources, though he did not go as far as his model Kemal Atatürk in Turkey. Though many of his reforms were popular, he ignored or manipulated the constitution and ruthlessly suppressed dissent. The clerics, labelled fanatical reactionaries in this modernising milieu, were reduced to silence. Upon assuming the throne, Reza Shah amended the 1906 Constitution to ensure that his male descendants would succeed him. Further amendments in 1949, 1957, and 1967 increased the monarch's powers. Although

Article 2 of the Supplement, regarding the primacy of sharia, was retained, the Shah's modernising zeal and the authoritarian nature of the Pahlavi monarchy rendered it irrelevant.

Reform of the legal system, halted a decade earlier, could now be pursued in earnest. A number of measures between 1926 and 1936 led to the establishment of a predominantly secular legal system. Its conceptual and organisational inspiration was the French system, and its architect, 'Ali Akbar Davar, a graduate of law from the University of Geneva. As the new Minister of Justice, Davar dissolved the old judiciary with parliament's approval in 1926. With the aid of French legal experts, he began a radical restructuring and reform of the system, which ultimately resulted in the complete exclusion of the clergy. In 1927 a new Ministry of Justice was created. Consequently, some six hundred newly appointed judges, many with European education, replaced the clerical officials in Tehran.

1926-1941: Reza Shah and the creation of a modern legal system

In most areas of law, sharia concepts were put aside and European-inspired codes were enacted, including codes of Commercial Law (1932) and Civil Procedure (1939), Criminal Law and Criminal Procedure (1912, 1926, 1940 and 1911, 1932, respectively). Only the new Civil Code retained the sharia. Many of its 1,335 articles are in effect a simplification and codification of majority opinion within Shia jurisprudence. Although the clergy had lost their role in defining and administering family law, as in other areas of the law, the commission appointed by the Ministry of Justice in 1927 to draft the code used the three most authoritative Shia legal texts (namely, Najm ad-din Mohaqqeq Helli's *Sharaye' al-eslam*, Zein ad-din Shahed Sani's *Sharh-e lom'eh*, and Mortaza Khorasani's *Makaseb*) as sources, and the Belgian, French and Swiss codes as models (Mehrpoor 2001: 6).

Parliament approved the civil code in two phases, in 1928 and 1935. Volume 2, dealing with personal status and the family, retained the patriarchal notion of family as constructed in classical Shia jurisprudence. In 1931 a separate marriage law required that all marriages and divorces be registered in civil bureaus to be set up in accordance with the regulations of the Ministry of Justice. In the same year, parliament passed a law defining sharia courts as 'special courts', which not only reduced their jurisdiction to disputes involving the essential validity of marriage and divorce but also placed them under the authority of state courts (Banani 1961: 78-79). In 1932 another law deprived the clerics of one of their main sources of income by relegating to secular courts the registration of legal documents, of ownership, and of other transactions concerning property. The secularisation of the judiciary culminated in 1936 when the employment of clerical judges was terminated, almost overnight, through a law that required serving judges to have a law degree from either Tehran Faculty of Law or a foreign university. It was also in 1936 that Reza Shah's policy of unveiling (*kashf-e hejab*), begun a decade before, reached its zenith with a law prohibiting women's appearance in public wearing a traditional Iranian chador or scarf. This ultimate secularising measure was to send the public a strong message about the emasculation of religious-based law and practice.

Reza Shah's legal reforms, in the words of one of his admirers, 'achieved no less than the Westernisation of the judicial concepts, institutions, and practices of Iran' (Banani 1961: 76). But the authoritarian way in which they were implemented led to further polarisation between sharia and state law; the deliberate exclusion of the clergy alienated them and put them on the defensive. The reforms were not accompanied by the promotion of independent decision-making, democracy, or democratic institutions. Further, Reza Shah's adoption of European legal systems and codes bypassed the philosophy that informed them, as his autocratic rule would not tolerate the impartial operation of the new judiciary.

1941-1965: Muhammad Reza Shah, Mohammad Mosaddeq, and the rise of Ayatollah Khomeini

At the start of World War II, Reza Shah clearly favoured Germany, and his reign came to an abrupt end in 1941 when British and Soviet forces occupied Iran and forced him to abdicate in favour of his son Mohammad Reza. Over the next decade renewed political debate and activity, dominated by the communist Tudeh party and the secular National Front, culminated in Mosaddeq's nationalist government of 1951-1953, which initiated grand economic and political reforms and led to the temporary exile of the Shah and the nationalisation of the oil industry. Mosaddeq's secularism antagonised the clerical establishment, while Britain and the USA were frightened by his nationalism and the rise of the Tudeh. In 1953, after a CIA-engineered coup, Mohammad Reza Shah resumed his reign as a U.S.-supported autocrat. During the following years, he alienated much of the country by allowing a massive increase of U.S. influence, and by suppressing further dissent and indeed parliamentary activity.

Following the death of Ayatollah Seyyed Aqa Hossein Qommi in 1947, Ayatollah Hossein bin 'Ali Tabataba'i Borujerdi emerged as the highest religious authority – the sole *marja'* of the Shia. Though opposed to the Tudeh and Mosaddeq, Borujerdi was a political quietist and remained in the Qom seminary, which he is credited with reorganising. Meanwhile, other clergy were planning to resume a more active political role in opposition to the Shah's policies. Their plans escalated rapidly after Borujerdi's death in 1961, which itself precipitated a crisis in the supreme religious authority (*marja'iyat*) as there was no single scholar prominent enough to succeed him in this capacity. In 1962, in an effort to gain popular support, the Shah instituted his 'White Revolution' or 'Revolution of the Shah and People', including land reform and votes for women. Soon after, Ayatollah Khomeini came to prominence, publicly denouncing the Shah for his attacks on the clergy and his increasing dependence on foreigners. On 5 June 1963, Khomeini was arrested. The authorities violently put down large protest demonstrations in Tehran, Qom, and other cities. Khomeini was released in April 1964, but rearrested in October after a fiery sermon against the Shah. This time, he was exiled to Turkey; in October 1965 he was allowed to change his place of exile to Najaf, where he stayed until 1978 (Martin 2000: 62-64).

8.3 The period from 1965 until 1985

From autocratic monarchy to Islamic Republic

1965-1978: The Family Protection Law, and the revolutionary movement

Under Mohammad Reza Shah there were few adjustments to the legal system, which was still based on the 1906 Constitution and on the hierarchical French model of the legal system implemented by his father. In 1963, as part of the 'White Revolution', in order to provide accessible and simpler administration of justice, rural tribunals (*khaneh-ye ensaf*) were set up, consisting of five members appointed from among local villagers. They were competent to handle land and water disputes and low-value civil suits. Many thousands of these tribunals were created by 1979; though they further secularised the administration of justice in the villages, there is evidence that they were controlled by the richer peasants (Hooglund 1982: 128).

The major legal reform under Mohammad Reza Shah was the Family Protection Law (FPL) of 1967, which put men and women on the same footing in terms of access to divorce and child custody. Though the initiative for the reform came from the nascent women's movement, by the time it became law it had already been co-opted by the official Women's Organisation of Iran under the patronage of Princess Ashraf, the Shah's twin sister. This compromised the legitimacy and significance of the reforms. The left and the secular opposition identified the FPL with the despotic Pahlavi regime, which had already appropriated the women's movement. The clerical establishment, for its part, was united and vocal in denouncing the reforms; Ayatollah Khomeini issued a fatwa that any divorce under the FPL was invalid under the sharia (Algar 1980: 441).

The events that led to Ayatollah Khomeini's exile in 1964 marked the start of the revolutionary movement. The independence of the judiciary was further undermined after 1965. Politically significant legal cases were given to government-oriented judges and special tribunals were introduced, weakening the regular administration of justice. Military tribunals, for instance, had jurisdiction in cases of state security and in narcotics cases (Amin 1985: 55-63). Numerous violations of civil and political human rights took place. Meanwhile, the Shah's 'White Revolution' and his ambitious plans for socio-economic development and modernisation focussed on increasing production, land reform, providing credits in the countryside and housing in the rapidly growing cities. Much land was transferred from big landowners and religious endowments (*waqf*) to small farmers, but the agrarian sector barely progressed, and promises to fight poverty and provide social services were not fulfilled. Bad governance, corruption, and extravagance were accompanied by widening wealth and income gaps. By the mid-1970s Iran was in an economic crisis.

1978-1982: The revolution and the establishment of an Islamic Republic

Opposition to the Shah came from many directions. Among leftist groups, the Tudeh, discredited by their links to the USSR, lost support to the Marxist Fedayin-e Khalq and the Islamist-socialist Mojahedin-e Khalq, whose guerrilla activities against the regime escalated in the early 1970s as the Shah's excesses further alienated the intellectuals and the people. Among the religious opposition, Ayatollahs Mahmud Taleqani, Morteza Motahhari, and Allameh Tabataba'i contributed greatly to the creation of a modernist Islamic political discourse, along with religious intellectuals like Jalal Al-e Ahmad, Mehdi Bazargan, and 'Ali Shariati (Dabashi 1993). A number of Islamic associations of professionals, students, and intellectuals became fora for revolutionary ideas and sought to counter secular or non-Muslim groups. One of the most important religious intellectuals was Mehdi Bazargan, who (with Yadollah Sahabi and Ayatollah Taleqani) in 1961 founded the Liberation Movement (Chehabi 1990). From 1966 until its closure in 1972, the Hosseiniyeh Ershad (a religious meeting-place in north Tehran) was the main forum for the new Islamic discourse. Key Muslim intellectuals lectured there, including Shariati, the most popular and influential Islamic ideologue of the revolution (Rahnema 1998).

By the mid-1970s the opposition came under the leadership of Ayatollah Khomeini from his exile in Iraq and later (in 1978) in Paris. The revolutionary forces were united in their main aim: to reject the autocratic, unjust, and unaccountable Pahlavi monarchy, the inequalities in society, and the overwhelming influence of the USA. But the alternatives they sought were as multiple and varied (and often contradictory) as they were themselves: a popular democracy; a classless society; a socialist state; national autonomy; an Islamic government, with rulers guided by the ulama and the sharia.

The success of the revolution was assured when on 16 January 1979 the Shah left Iran for good, and on 1 February Ayatollah Khomeini returned in triumph. The first decade after the revolution was a period of establishment of the Islamic Republic, marked by the war with Iraq (1980-1988) and by bitter struggles, first between the different elements that had contributed to the revolution, and then between the proponents of liberal-democratic and theocratic Islam, whose values became jointly enshrined in the constitution.

The Revolutionary Council immediately appointed Mehdi Bazargan to form a provisional government, composed mainly of National Front and Liberation Movement members, moderate non-clerical Islamists, and nationalists, all of whom wanted a secular democratic republic. Khomeini's clerical followers had different ideas. Inspired by Ayatollah Motahhari (Dabashi 1993: 147-215), they soon formed the Islamic Republican Party (IRP), led by Ayatollah Mohammad Beheshti together with Akbar Hashemi Rafsanjani and 'Ali Khamene'i, both of whom were later to be president. These were populist Islamic radicals intent on establishing an Islamic state governed by Islamic law. They were opposed by quietists in the seminaries who wanted the clerics to abstain from government, and who were represented by Ayatollah Kazem Shariat-madari, whose supporters formed the Islamic People's Republican Party. Also contending for power and popular support were the Islamic-socialist Mojahedin-e Khalq (MEK) and leftist groups, such as the communist Tudeh and the Fedayan, who wanted a socialist state and some autonomy for ethnic minorities.

The early months of 1979 were marked by the first 'Reign of Terror', as religious extremists implemented hard-line interpretations of Islamic law. Members of the previous regime (military officers, members of the Shah's court, capitalists), as well as prostitutes, adulterers, and homosexuals, were summarily executed. In May, Ayatollah Motahhari, a leading moderate political cleric close to Khomeini, was assassinated, and in September the death of Ayatollah Taleqani, another influential moderate, was another blow to the progressive and moderate faction in the revolutionary leadership. Amid this violence, the new order took shape. On 30 March a referendum had overwhelmingly approved the formation of an Islamic Republic. Many of the early leaders such as Bazargan wanted it to be called 'Democratic Islamic Republic'; but at Khomeini's insistence the version put to the referendum did not include the term 'democratic'. During the spring, Bazargan's government and the Revolutionary Council prepared a draft constitution, which was approved by Khomeini; at this stage, there was no mention of clerical rule. In August, an assembly of experts – dominated by the IRP – began to produce a final draft that included the notion of 'guardianship of the jurist' (*velayat-e faqih*).[9] A further referendum approved this constitution on 2 December.

On 4 November, radical student 'Followers of the Imam's Line' occupied the U.S. Embassy and took hostages. Bazargan resigned in protest, and the religious hardliners took control of government. They had already begun their offensive against democrats, liberals, secularists, and leftists as well as regional insurgents from the mainly Sunni ethnic minorities (that is, Kurds, Khuzistan Arabs, Turkmen, Baluch). Members of Bazargan's Liberation Movement were removed from the structures of power, though they remained the only tolerated opposition party; they were dismissed as 'liberals', implying they were not Islamic enough. In the 1990s, they would become known as the Nationalist-Religious Alliance.

In January 1980, Abol-Hasan Bani-Sadr, an Islamic modernist who had been among Khomeini's advisors in Paris but was opposed to clerical rule, was elected president; but in March, elections to the new parliament brought the radical IRP to power. The struggle intensified between the main Islamist factions (IRP and the Followers of the Imam's Line), Bani-Sadr's followers, and the MEK, the most prominent and popular Islamic leftist organisation. Then in September, Iraqi forces invaded, starting a war that was to last eight years.

In June 1981 parliament impeached Bani-Sadr and, with Khomeini's agreement, he was dismissed. The MEK were banned, and clashes with them grew more violent. Also in June, a powerful bomb exploded at the IRP headquarters while a meeting of party leaders was in progress, killing a large number of senior government officials. The MEK were blamed for these and other political assassinations, notably, in August, those of newly elected president 'Ali Reja'i and Prime Minister Mohammad Javad Bahonar. In July both former president Bani-Sadr and MEK leader Massoud Rajavi fled to France. Between June 1981 and May 1982, in a second Reign of Terror, most of the MEK were executed or imprisoned; those who survived went into exile (Abrahamian 1989). The Islamic state and clerical government were secured. In a violent return swing of the pendulum, religious despotism had ousted both secularism and democracy.

The unresolved tensions that brought about the revolution were in effect written into the 1979 Constitution, a compromise document with an uneven fusion of democratic and theocratic principles and institutions (Arjomand 1992; Schirazi 1997). On the one hand, it recognises the people's right to choose who will govern them, establishing democratic and legislative institutions such as the parliament and the presidency, both elected by direct popular vote. On the other hand, it subordinates the people's will to that of the clerical establishment through the institutions of guardianship of the jurist (*velayat-e faqih*) or Leadership (*rahbari*)[10] and the Guardian Council (*shura-ye negahban*), composed of twelve members, six of whom are jurists (*foqaha*; pl. of *faqih*) appointed by the Leader, the other six being laymen nominated by the head of the judiciary and approved by parliament, with a tenure of six years.[11] It grants the Leader a wide mandate and a final say in running the state and charges the Guardian Council, acting as an 'Upper House' with veto powers, with deciding whether laws passed by parliament conform to the sharia and the constitution. In effect, they are the official interpreters of the constitution and sharia.

The constitution names Khomeini as Leader for life, and creates an Assembly of Experts (*Majles-e Khebregan-e Rahbari*) to choose his eventual successor and supervise his activities, to ensure that he complies with his religious and constitutional duties. The 86 members of this Assembly are elected every eight years; only *mojtaheds* are eligible to stand, and from the outset conservative clerics have dominated the Assembly. From its inauguration in 1983 until his death in 2007, the Assembly was headed by Ayatollah 'Ali Meshkini, a powerful conservative who often acted as Friday Prayer Leader in Qom. In practice so far, the Assembly has merely endorsed the actions of the Leader. The constitution allows the Guardian Council to supervise all elections, which they have interpreted as the right to vet candidates' eligibility to stand. This means that, in effect, the Assembly of Experts and the Guardian Council form a closed system that allows the Leader unlimited power. Through his appointees to the Guardian Council, he can control both the legislative and the executive powers (Schirazi 1997; Buchta 2000).

With the merger of religious and political power, the state embarked on a fierce process of islamising law and society that continues today. The ultimate aim has been to return both law-making and the administration of justice to the clerics and to get rid of what they see as the pernicious secularisation of the Pahlavi era. In measures mirroring those of Reza Shah, the courts have been restructured and civil judges gradually purged and replaced by clerical judges. New codes based on *feqh* have been enacted to enable the judiciary to conform to Shia legal norms, replacing codes inspired by European laws. Articles of the civil code that deviated from *feqh* were amended and a High Judicial School was created in Qom to train clerics to serve in the judiciary.[12] The numbers of clerics swelled rapidly, and by the late 1980s hundreds of them had been recognised as ayatollahs; the highest rank was now Grand Ayatollah.

1982-1985: The Islamisation of the legal system

From the outset, attention has been focussed on two areas of law – family and criminal laws – where the sharia courts' jurisdiction was terminated in the 1930s. In February 1979, barely two weeks after the collapse of the Pahlavi monarchy, a directive from Ayatollah Khomeini's office declared the Family Protection Law 'non-Islamic' and announced its suspension and the reinstitution of the sharia, that is, articles of the 1935 Civil Code dealing with family. There followed a period of uncertainty until new Special Civil Courts were created by a law with the same name, ratified by the Revolutionary Council in September 1979. These courts were to be presided over by clerical judges free from the provisions of the Civil Procedure Code, hence the term 'Special'. Their establishment was seen as a first step towards the application of sharia in its most important sphere: the family. It was the outcome of a compromise between those who urged the immediate restoration of sharia and those who argued for a gradual approach (Mohaqqeq-Damad 1986: 513-522; Amin 1984: 132-133). It also set the trend for subsequent changes.

'Return to sharia' has not been a return to the classical *feqh* notion of plural and uncodified laws; the judiciary has retained not only many of the legal concepts and laws of the Pahlavi era, but also the notion of a centralised and unified legal system. The most drastic changes, as we shall see, took place in the area of criminal law, where Islamic legal concepts were entirely put aside in the 1920s. The wearing of hijab became compulsory for women. The education system was segregated, and though universities remained mixed, regulations were introduced to separate the sexes in class and on campus. State censorship of the media (familiar under the Pahlavis) intensified. Places of recreation were closed, alcohol, prostitution, and homosexuality were forbidden. The combination of Islamic doctrine, sharia, legislation based on sharia, fatwas, and pre-revolutionary legislation often resulted in confusion. Courts were forced to choose among available legal sources in an eclectic manner (Zubaida 2003: 200).

Alongside the general courts, Islamic Revolutionary Courts also entered the scene, under Khomeini's supervision and with his silent approval. Local *komitehs* (supporters of the Islamic revolution) acted as informal police and took opponents of sharia to court. Government authority was unpredictable and normal procedures were not followed. Closed hearings, secret verdicts, and mass executions resulted. The human rights situation, deplorable under the Shah, did not improve. Khomeini's regime was intolerant of those with different beliefs, and was supported by a callous police force and numerous vigilante groups.

Victims included citizens who did not agree with the new religious ideology, Baha'is, and members of MEK.

Human rights violations by the regime took many forms. Political parties were prohibited, demonstrations were violently broken up, reform-oriented media shut down, and political adversaries locked up indefinitely. Political executions by shooting or hanging also occurred regularly, most often within prisons such as the notorious Evin in Tehran. The right to a fair and open trial was violated by torture, forced confession, denial of legal assistance, and closed proceedings in revolutionary and Islamic courts. The government was also active outside Iran in prosecuting and liquidating adversaries of the regime.[13] Iran did not take a defensive stance in international human rights fora. In 1982 Iran was asked about the role of Islamic law in relation to compliance with the ICCPR, in particular about Articles 20, 21, and 26 of the Constitution, which assimilated human rights. The Iranian representative gave a simple answer: 'In case of conflict between a law and the scope of Islam, priority goes to Islam.'[14]

In order to facilitate legislation considered to be socially necessary, even if it was in conflict with sharia, Khomeini gave a fatwa in 1981 granting parliament the authority to proclaim such legislation with absolute majority votes. Subsequently, the Guardian Council ignored this fatwa and refused to approve much legislation promulgated on the basis of it. Khomeini responded in 1984 with another fatwa authorising parliament to create legislation based on the Islamic principles of social necessity (*zarurat*) and expediency (*maslahat*) with a two-thirds majority. Even this strengthening of parliament's position did not bring the desired changes in the Guardian Council's behaviour (Schirazi 1997: 63-64).

8.4 The period from 1985 until the present

Growing tensions between theocracy and democracy

1985-1989: Khomeini's last years and the constitutional crisis

In the aftermath of the revolution, the inherent tensions between theocratic and democratic elements in the state, and between the two competing notions of sovereignty embodied in the concepts of *eslamiyat* and *jomhuriyat* (roughly, 'Islamism' and 'republicanism'), had been the main sites of confrontation among the Islamist, nationalist, and leftist forces whose alliance had led to the revolution's success. With secularists and 'liberal' Islamists like Bani-Sadr, the MEK and Bazargan, and the Liberation Movement defeated and excluded from the structures of power, argument was confined to religious terms and focussed on the issue of the religious legitimacy of political authority.

As long as Ayatollah Khomeini was alive, the basic tensions were managed and did not confront the Islamic Republic with a crisis of legitimacy. There were several reasons for this. First, apart from Khomeini's personal charisma as Leader, and his religious standing as supreme religious authority (*marja'*), his style of leadership helped to bridge the gap between the two sides. Not only was he mindful of – and responsive to – the popular will, he managed to rise above factional politics and to avoid being claimed by any faction. Perhaps the most important reasons were the freshness of the revolutionary momentum and the fact that the politics of the period were preoccupied with the Iran-Iraq war, a unifying force that provided the mechanisms for suppressing dissent.

As the Islamic Republic consolidated itself, a structural contradiction between the two notions of supreme authority – the *marja'iyat* and the *velayat-e faqih* – became increasingly evident. The first has no overt political claims, having evolved through a tacit consensus between Shia masses and clerics; it is democratic in nature in that a *marja'* derives his position from personal recognition by individual followers. The guardianship of the jurist (*velayat-e faqih*), on the other hand, relies on the apparatus of state and demands allegiance from every citizen. In so doing, it not only establishes the authority of one single jurist over all others but also breaks away from orthodox Shia political theory, which denies legitimacy to any form of government in the absence of the twelfth Imam. It invests the Leader with the kind of powers and mandate that Shia theology recognises only for the Prophet and the twelve Infallible Imams (Arjomand 1988; Sachedina 1988; Akhavi 1996), and as Zubaida observes, it is closer to the Sunni political theory of Caliphate than the Shia theory of Imamate (Zubaida 1993).

By 1988, the tension between the two notions of authority intensified and brought about a constitutional crisis. There was conflict not only between the clerical supporters and opponents of *velayat-e faqih*, but also between the factions within the ruling elite, who held differing views of authority and the way the country should be run. In March 1989, Khomeini's dismissal of his designated successor, Grand Ayatollah Hossein 'Ali Montazeri, added a new edge to the tension. Montazeri was the only recognised *marja'* who supported the theory of *velayat-e faqih*. He had impeccable revolutionary credentials: he had spent years in the previous regime's prisons, played an instrumental role in inserting the *velayat-e faqih* into the constitution, and published discussions on the subject from both theoretical and theological angles (Montazeri 1988-1990). But he was also a vocal critic of government policies and practices, unwilling to keep silent in the face of what he saw to be contrary to his religious beliefs. His dismissal, the outcome of an acrimonious struggle for the succession, was in effect a proof of the impossibility of combining the traditional (*marja'iyat*) and new (*velayat-e faqih*) notions of religious authority.

The crisis was resolved when Ayatollah Khomeini himself gave his blessing to the separation of the two institutions (*velayat-e faqih* and *marja'iyat)* and authorised a committee to revise the constitution. Following his death in June 1989, the Assembly of Experts chose the incumbent president, Seyyed 'Ali Khamene'i, as the new Leader of the Revolution. As a middle-ranking cleric, Khamene'i had no possible claim to spiritual leadership, and he lacked Khomeini's religious authority and charisma. The concept of *velayat-e faqih*, and the legitimacy of its mandate, had to be revised. The committee duly produced a revised constitution, which no longer specifies that the Leader must be a recognised *marja'*, but merely able to issue opinions (fatwas) in all fields of Islamic law (Arjomand 1992).

1989-1997: Consolidation of the power of the Supreme Leader and growing dissent

In July 1989, parliament speaker 'Ali Akbar Hashemi Rafsanjani was elected president. A popular referendum ratified the revised constitution, which abolished the office of prime minister (filled since 1981 by Mir-Hossein Mousavi) and transferred its executive powers to the presidency. With Khamene'i as the new Leader and Rafsanjani as president, the Islamic Republic entered a second phase, named 'Reconstruction' by its supporters, 'Mercantile Bourgeois Republic' by others (Ehteshami 1995; Ansari 2000). Rafsanjani's priorities and his pragmatic approach reversed some of the earlier policies, notably in the areas of economy and foreign affairs. The welfare policies of the wartime government under Prime Minister Mousavi were replaced by measures that encouraged the growth of the mercantile bourgeoisie and state-connected entrepreneurs (Ansari 2000: 52-81).

The new phase saw important changes, notably some tactical ideological shifts that accompanied the breakdown of the delicate balance of power and the working relationship that had developed between the two ruling 'factions', the so-called 'Rightists' and 'Leftists'. Although often spoken of as polarised factions, these terms are relative, the Rightists being more conservative and theocratic, the Leftists more progressive and democratic; they were all, of course, Islamists and supporters of Khomeini. Indeed, differences among them are best seen as positions around which people gathered in relation to specific issues, many in the centre shifting position according to the issue (Moslem 2002).

The Leftists, who had dominated the state under Khomeini (Mousavi was one of them) and enjoyed his implicit sanction, were now gradually ousted from the structures of power. Their 'radical' elements – including those who had engineered the seizure of the U.S. Embassy in 1979 – were purged from key positions. A new configuration of 'Islamic republicanism' was forged, facilitated by the revised constitution and the consolidation of the Rightist faction.

The constitutional amendments may have settled the crisis over legitimate authority, but they led to a renewed tension between the two competing notions of sovereignty, which dominated Rafsanjani's presidency (1989-1997) and forced a redefinition of the relationship between religious authority and the state. To resolve the constitutional conflict between *velayat-e faqih* and *marja'iyat*, to defuse the discord between the Guardian Council and parliament, to ensure a more pragmatic approach to the application of Islamic law, and to compensate for the loss of Khomeini's charisma, the revised 1989 Constitution extended the mandate of the Leader. This extension drew sanction from a letter by Khomeini in 1988 in response to a question by Khamene'i, then president, who wanted his consent to oppose the Leftist-dominated policies of parliament and government. Khomeini had written that the Leader's mandate is absolute, that he can even order the suspension of the primary rules of Islam (for example regarding prayer or pilgrimage) if the interests of the Islamic state (*maslahat-e nezam*) demand it. Clearly, when Khomeini had to choose between the sharia and the survival of the state, he chose the latter (Arjomand 1992: 156-158).

This letter revealed the tension between the application of juristic rulings and the demands of running a state. At the time, the Leftists had welcomed it, as they saw the empowerment of the state through a strengthened Leadership as a way of defusing legalistic objections and obstacles coming from the seminaries. Now it was the Rightists, with Khomeini dead and one of their number as Leader, who argued – in an ideological U-turn – for further expansion of the Leader's power (Moslem 2002: 74).

The revised constitution gave the Leader not only the power to determine the general policies of the state and to oversee their implementation, but also control over more institutions, notably Television and Radio (IRIB): compare the revised version of Article 110 with the original. A new body, the Assembly to Discern the Best Interest of the System (*Majma'-e Tashkhis-e Maslehat-e Nezam*), known as the Expediency Council, created by Khomeini in February 1988, was now constitutionally sanctioned (Art.s 110, 112; see Schirazi 1997: 233-247). The Leader appoints the thirty-one members of this council from various ideological factions loyal to the regime. Its mandate is to vet laws passed by parliament (now renamed 'Islamic Consultative Assembly',

Majles-e Shura-ye Eslami) but found by the Guardian Council to be in contradiction with the sharia; in other words, to mediate conflict between popular sovereignty (as represented in parliament) and clerical sovereignty (as represented by the Guardian Council). The Expediency Council also has the task of advising the Leader on important issues of national concern (Buchta 2000: 61-63).

The 1989 Constitution increased the power of the non-elected institutions at the expense of the elected ones, and thus came to reflect the views of those who reject the restrictions imposed on *velayat-e faqih* by the 1979 Constitution (Schirazi 1997: 52-55). The Leadership, emptied of the aura of sanctity that believing Shia traditionally associate with the person of the *marja'*, and with its democratic credentials seriously dented, now had to serve the interests of the Rightist faction and to rely more and more on the consensus of the clerical establishment. This, in practice, made Khamene'i, the new Leader, a hostage to the seminary politics in which the most traditional Rightist elements – those connected to the bazaar – had the upper hand.

Rightists came to dominate all those institutions that represented the theocratic side of power in the Islamic Republic, notably the judiciary, whose head is appointed by the Leader, and the Guardian Council. During the first phase of the Islamic Republic when Khomeini was Leader, this council had included both Leftists and Rightists; it had used its constitutional mandate of supervision (*nezarat*) of all elections in the Islamic Republic to allow only insiders ('our people', *khodi*) to run for elected office, excluding secularists, religious liberals, the 'uncommitted', and outsiders ('not our people', *gheyr-e khodi*) generally. In the second phase, the council contained solely Rightists, and during the 1992 parliamentary elections it started to use its power – now reinterpreted as a duty of 'approbatory supervision' (*nezarat-e estesvabi*) – to disqualify candidates from the Left so as effectively to ensure that the Right had a majority in the new parliament (Menashri 1992; Baktiari 1996).

By the mid-1990s the Leftist faction also lost all their influence in the judiciary, and while they kept their middle-rank officials in government, they no longer had ministers. One of the last was Mohammad Khatami, Minister of Culture and Islamic Guidance; he resigned in 1992 under pressure from the Rightist faction, who saw his liberal policies as allowing a form of 'cultural invasion'. But the honeymoon between President Rafsanjani's government and the traditional Right was soon over; and by the time of the fifth parliamentary elections in 1996, a modernist Rightist group, known as Servants of Construction, emerged under Rafsanjani's patronage (Ansari 2000: 82-109; Moslem 2002: 180-251). Meanwhile, set aside from decision-making bodies, some of the senior Leftist clerics retired from politics and returned to the seminaries;

others formed political groups and bodies in the seminaries, or set up research and study groups in Tehran and devoted themselves to 'cultural activities', which in post-revolutionary Iran signifies the independent study of society and politics (Jalaeipour 2003). The Leftists generally entered a period of political retreat and reflection, during which some of them broke away from theocratic and absolutist ideology and started to argue for democratic principles and the rule of law (Ashraf & Banuazizi 2001b). In so doing, they joined the increasing numbers of ordinary citizens disillusioned by the increasing rift between the ideals of the revolution they had supported and the realities of the Islamic state.

Women, more than any other sector, had reasons to be disaffected. They felt the harsh reality of subjection to a patriarchal interpretation of Islamic law when applied by the legal machinery of a modern state. They kept their suffrage rights, but most of the pre-revolutionary legal reforms were abolished. Men regained their rights to unilateral divorce and polygamy, while women's rights to divorce and child custody were limited and they were forbidden to study mining and agriculture, to serve as judges, and to appear in public without hijab. Many Islamist women, who had genuinely, if naively, believed that women's position would automatically improve under an Islamic state, were increasingly disappointed. They included some early activists, who had played instrumental roles in discrediting secular feminists and destroying the pre-revolutionary women's press and organisations, as well as many ordinary women for whom Islam meant justice and fairness (Mir-Hosseini 1996).

Debates about gender issues, harshly suppressed after the revolution, started to resurface. By the early 1990s, there were clear signs of the emergence of an 'Islamic feminism': a new gender consciousness and a critique of the gender biases in Islamic law. Some of the earlier restrictions on subjects women could study were removed (1986); family planning and contraception became freely available (1988); divorce laws were amended so as to curtail men's right to divorce and to compensate women in the face of it (1992); and women were appointed as advisory judges (1992) (Ramazani 1993; Mir-Hosseini 1996). It is certainly true that the Islamic Republic's rhetoric and policies in the 1980s marginalised and excluded so-called 'Westernised' women, but it is also true that they empowered many other women, who came to see themselves as citizens entitled to equal rights. It was becoming increasingly apparent to them that they could not become full citizens unless a modern, democratic reading of Islamic law was accepted.

This reading was what a group of Muslim intellectuals, advocates of what came to be known as 'New Religious Thinking' (*now-andishi-ye dini)*, were trying to achieve. The adverse impact of the implementation of Islamic law, as defined in classical texts of traditional jurisprudence (*feqh-e sonnati*), had already produced a kind of rethinking and reworking among the clerics. A new school of 'Dynamic Jurisprudence' (*feqh-e puya*) tried to arrive at a new interpretation of Islamic law by taking into account the factors of time and place. This school emerged in the late 1980s, following two rulings by Ayatollah Khomeini making chess games and music permissible (*halal*). It has supporters among the younger generation of clerics, and its senior advocates, such as Ayatollahs Ebrahim Janati, Mousavi-Bojnurdi and Yousef Sane'i, have issued a number of progressive fatwas with regard to women's rights and other social issues. Members of the school have attempted to rethink the assumptions behind the jurisprudential theories that inform classical interpretations of sharia. They have, however, met opposition and sometimes persecution by conservative clerics.

The New Religious Thinkers included laymen and women as well as clerics, all of whom now saw a widening gap between the ideals of the revolution and the realities and policies of the Islamic state in which they lived. Representing various strands of modernist Shia thought that had remained dormant during the war with Iraq, they offered new interpretations of Islam and began to articulate a theoretical critique of the Islamic state from an Islamic perspective (Sadri 2001; Jahanbakhsh 2001). Most prominent was Abdolkarim Soroush, who published a series of controversial articles between 1988 and 1990 on the historicity and relativity of religious knowledge, later developed as a book on 'The Theoretical Contraction and Expansion of Sharia'. In a direct challenge to the religious authority of the clerical establishment, Soroush sought to separate religion from religious knowledge, arguing that, while the first was sacred and immutable, the second was human and evolved over time as a result of forces external to religion itself (Kurzman 1998; Soroush 2000).

Thus, after over a decade of the experience of Islam in power, Islamic dissent began to be voiced among 'insiders' and became a magnet for intellectuals whose ideas and writings now formed the backbone of the New Religious Thinking. Whereas in the 1980s these men and women had seen their role as consolidating the Islamic Republic, in the 1990s, armed with Soroush's theory of the relativity of religious knowledge, they wanted to create a worldview reconciling Islam and modernity, and argued for a demarcation between state and religion. They argued that the human understanding of Islam is flexible, that Islam's tenets can be interpreted to encourage both pluralism and democracy and to allow change according to time, place, and experience. For them, the question was no longer who should rule, but how they should rule, and what mechanisms there should be to curb the excesses of power. In this way, they began to cross the red lines that had previously circumscribed any critical discussion of the political dogma that sanctioned the concentration of power in the institution of Leadership.

Soroush and his co-thinkers tried to redefine and rework Islamic concepts and succeeded in producing discourses that were to become highly attractive to youth and women. Like 'Ali Shariati, Soroush was immensely popular while being criticised and disdained by secular intellectuals. But there were fundamental differences in their visions and conceptions of Islam, which were undoubtedly shaped by the politics of their own times. Shariati turned Islam into an ideology to challenge the Pahlavi monarchy. For Soroush, Islam is 'richer than ideology', and all his thinking and writing are aimed at separating the two (Cooper 1998; Kurzman 2001; Ghamari-Tabrizi 2004). But he has himself become the ideologue of a reformist, democratic Islam, by his critique of '*feqh*-based Islam', widely read as an attack on the rule of the jurist (*velayat-e faqih*).

The New Religious Thinkers have revived classical debates on the nature of the divine law, which in turn reactivated a crucial distinction that the early wave of Islamic activists distorted and obscured: this is the distinction between the sharia and the science of *feqh*, which lies at the root of the emergence of the various 'orthodox' schools of Islamic law. They contend that, while the sharia is sacred, universal, and eternal, *feqh*, like any other system of jurisprudence, is local, multiple and subject to change in its doctrines and premises.

1997-2005: Reformist governments and the dual state

In the 1997 presidential elections, a last-minute political alliance between Rafsanjani's pragmatic modernist right and the Islamic left put forward former culture minister Mohammad Khatami to oppose Akbar Nateq-Nuri, the candidate of the traditionalist right. The people voted *en masse* for Khatami, who stood for 'democracy' and 'rule of law', and whose ideas and language were drawn largely from Soroush and his co-thinkers. Once again the popular will began to assert itself, expressing resentment of the injustices brought by the application of pre-modern interpretations of the sharia, and of the undemocratic nature of the current Leadership.

The reformist movement that emerged in the aftermath of this election was the logical and inevitable outcome of the spread of the New Religious Thinking at both popular and political levels (Wells 1999; Moslem 2002). Almost overnight, cleavages shifted and new political alliances were forged. Those who had campaigned for Nateq-Nuri, mainly of the traditionalist right, were labelled 'conservatives'. Those who voted for Khatami and supported his vision called themselves 'reformists', but came to be known as the 'Second Khordad Front' (after the date of

Khatami's election). The reformists were a loose coalition with a wide range of views and little consensus on aims and directions of reform.

The victories of reformist candidates in the municipal and parliamentary elections of 1999 and 2000, and Khatami's re-election in June 2001 with over 77 per cent of the vote, showed the strength of the mass support for the advocates of the new discourse and their vision of Islam. One of Khatami's main supporters, Mehdi Karroubi, head of the main clerical organisation of the Leftist faction, the Society for Militant Clerics (*majma'-e rowhaniyun-e mobarez*)[15], was elected to the important role of speaker of parliament. But despite these electoral gains, which put them in charge of both executive and legislative powers, the reformists were unable to fulfil their electoral promises. Instead, they became both internally divided and locked in a fierce political battle with their opponents, who now were identified and aligned with the theocratic and unelected side of the Islamic Republic. The unelected bodies succeeded in frustrating most of the government's initiatives and the legislative moves of the reformist parliament (2000-2004). They also silenced key reformist personalities, by assassination, by prosecution and imprisonment, and by closing down the vibrant free press that was one of their main early achievements and platforms.

Bodies under the Leader's control, namely the Guardian Council, the Expediency Council, and the judiciary played the central role in containing and frustrating reformist efforts to translate their vision and programmes into policies. The first two either rejected almost all the bills introduced by reformist members of parliament, or allowed their enactment only after changing them so much that they were emptied of progressive elements. At the same time, the judiciary assigned certain branches of the Press Court and the Revolutionary Courts to restrict the scope of debates by prosecuting reformist intellectuals, journalists, and even members of parliament. The non-constitutional Special Clerical Court, which since 1997 has acted like an inquisition, performed the task of containing clerical proponents of reform.[16]

The resultant situation was a stalemate, a 'dual state' that lasted until the next parliamentary elections in 2004. Divided and unable to deliver on their electoral promises or to bring change in the structure of power, the reformists started to lose popular support. By the time of the February 2003 council elections, the stalemate produced what the reformists had feared most: voter apathy. Conservatives won the major cities by default – in Tehran, the turnout was a mere 14 per cent –, though not the villages and small towns.

For the parliamentary elections the following year, the Guardian Council disqualified a large number of reformist candidates, including eighty sitting members. The reformists protested, members organised a sit-in, and there was talk of President Khatami's resignation, but to no avail. The election went ahead without the participation of the largest reformist parties. The conservatives won the election, but victory came at a price: in order to appeal to the popular legitimacy on which the Islamic Republic was founded, they had to appropriate the reformist platform, at least its rhetoric. Running under the banner of 'Renovators' (*abadgaran*), they now promised to implement 'religious democracy', economic reforms and prosperity, and to respect the rule of law and young people's desire for change, diversity, and fun. They even refrained from putting the names of their better-known personalities on their lists of candidates, so as not to evoke sour memories. The turnout of around 42 per cent was the lowest for any parliamentary election in the Islamic Republic, though not as low as the reformists had warned. In some constituencies there was no competition, as all reformist candidates were disqualified. Radical elements among the Conservatives, some from the ranks of the Revolutionary Guards, now calling themselves Principlists (*osulgara'ian*) won the majority of seats.

2005-2009: The dual state ends, theocratic forces predominate

In June 2005 the theocratic forces brought the 'dual state' to an end, when one of their candidates, the hardliner and former Revolutionary Guard Mahmoud Ahmadinejad, won the presidential election – a victory that astounded both insiders and outsiders. But to achieve this, they had to show their hand. The Guardian Council's disqualification of reformist candidates could not eliminate centrists like Hashemi Rafsanjani and Mehdi Karroubi. To ensure a reasonable turnout, the Leader had to intervene at the last minute to undo the disqualification of Akbar Mo'in, who represented progressive reformists. The means by which the theocratic forces regained the presidency – rigged ballot boxes, interference with the electoral process by organising mass votes for their candidate – further undermined the popular legitimacy and mandate on which the Islamic Republic had rested.

The failure of the reformists in the 2005 election was also one of the unintended consequences of U.S. policy in the Middle East. Despite Iran's assistance in dislodging the Taliban in Afghanistan in 2001, U.S. President Bush included Iran in his 'Axis of Evil' in early 2002. Despite Iran's help in stabilising Iraq following the U.S. invasion in 2003, the Bush administration refused to talk to Iran about nuclear and other issues and appeared determined on regime change in Iran. These rebuffs all had a decisive impact on Iranian internal politics. The conservative and theocratic forces in Iran were able to point to the reformists' foreign policy failures, and to use the threat of invasion to silence voices of dissent and to derail the democratic process. The hardliners had what they needed internally as well as the opportunity to aim for regional influence and popularity in the Muslim world.

The structural tensions in the Islamic Republic persisted, however, and broke down the conservative alliance behind Ahmadinejad, just as they had divided the coalition that brought Khatami into office. In the December 2006 elections for local councils and the Assembly of Experts, and in the March 2008 parliamentary elections, the hardliners led by Ahmadinejad himself and his mentor, Ayatollah Mohammad Taqi Mesbah-Yazdi, failed to gain any ground; a new alliance of moderate reformists and conservatives won a majority in the Assembly of Experts. The key figures in this alliance were former president Khatami, former speaker of parliament Karroubi, and former president Rafsanjani, now head of the Expediency Council and increasingly leaning towards the reformists. Both Karroubi and Rafsanjani had been defeated by Ahmadinejad in the June 2005 presidential elections. The death in July 2007 of Ayatollah Meshkini, head of the Assembly of Experts since its inception, led to intense competition between hardliners and moderate clerics to replace him. In September the Assembly elected Rafsanjani as their head.

The most – perhaps the only – lasting achievement of the Khatami's two terms of presidency (1997-2005) was to have nurtured and protected a new public sphere, which survived after reformists were ousted from government. It comprised a vocal and dynamic press and virtual media (websites and weblogs), the universities, the seminaries, and parliament, where the ambiguities and contradictions in the original idea of the Islamic state, its translation into law and policy, and the role of Islamic jurisprudence (*feqh*) in everyday life were all candidly debated. The conservatives closed many reformist publications and prosecuted numerous prominent and outspoken reformists, many of them being jailed for several years; nevertheless, these measures failed to silence the debates and to circumscribe the public sphere, but rather highlighted the urgency of the debates and the necessity for such a sphere.

Indeed, the very fact that the scope of debate is limited to Islam, sharia, and the constitution has resulted in sharpening the contrast between two visions of Islam and the two modes of governance. One is an absolutist and legalistic Islam, premised on a notion of 'duty' that tolerates no dissent and makes little concession to the people's will and contemporary realities. The other is a pluralistic and tolerant Islam, based on human rights and democratic values. The first vision, advocated by hardliners, has an undemocratic reading of the constitution, in which guardianship of the jurist (*velayat-e faqih*) is an element of faith. According to them, the Leader, as ruling jurist, derives his mandate from God and his post through designation (*nasb*); the role of the

Assembly of Experts is confined to 'discovering the will of God'; the Assembly, like other bodies including Parliament, is at the disposal of the Leader, whose powers are not to be limited by human laws but by divine law – the sharia. This view is aired in the sermons and publications of the most radical ideologues among the supporters of the Islamic State, such as Ahmadinejad's mentor Ayatollah Mesbah-Yazdi and his students in Qom; and it is defended by the increasingly powerful Revolutionary Guards.

The second vision, advocated by reformists and, increasingly since 2005, by moderate conservatives, has a more democratic reading of the constitution, in which *velayat-e faqih* is a religio-political theory. According to them, the Leader derives his mandate from the people, who elect him indirectly through the Assembly of Experts and can depose him if he fails to fulfil his constitutional duties or abuses his constitutional powers. They argue that not only does the hardliners' reading of the constitution negate its clear and definite republicanism (*jomhuriyat*), it is a travesty of the ideals and achievements of the 1979 revolution, perpetrated by those who want to reproduce monarchical relations in an Islamic format.

The 2009 presidential election campaign took shape against the background of these debates and developments. Various reformist groups and individuals formed a coalition to mobilise people to vote, and persuaded former President Khatami to run again. Karroubi, who lost the 2005 election to Ahmadinejad, also announced his candidacy; he ran on behalf of the Etemad-e Melli Party, which he had formed in 2005, shortly after resigning from all his governmental posts in protest against what he described, in an open letter, as interference by one of Khamene'i's sons and the Revolutionary Guards in getting Ahmadinejad elected. Then in March, after twenty years of political silence, Mir-Hosseini Mousavi entered the presidential race, and before long Khatami withdrew in his favour. As the last prime minister, who had had both Ayatollah Khomeini's backing and a popular base due to his welfare polices, Mousavi had been urged by the Left/Reformist faction to run for president in both 1997 and 2005, but he had refused. Now, as an independent centrist candidate, his campaign was reminiscent in many ways of Khatami's in 1997. It was run by a group of young activists, who, lacking access to the state-controlled media – in particular TV that was heavily biased toward Ahmadinejad – skilfully used digital media to reach large numbers of people. The polls were ambiguous – and notoriously unreliable – but it was widely expected that either Mousavi would win or the election would go to a second round. Even the conservatives were anxious that Ahmadinejad might not win his second term, and made preparations to ensure that he did.

On election day, 12 June, the turnout throughout the country was high. But it was followed by what many have interpreted as a military coup d'état. From the beginning, numerous serious irregularities were reported: Revolutionary Guards and the Interior Ministry clamped down on Ahmadinejad's opponents; in many cases, they kept their representatives out of both polling booths and counting stations; they attacked Mousavi's campaign headquarters and arrested his aides and other prominent reformists and journalists. The official result was announced on TV only two hours after polling ended, declaring Ahmadinejad the winner with 63 per cent of the votes, Mousavi second with less than half that, and the other two candidates (Karroubi and Mohsen Reza'i, a former head of the Revolutionary Guards) with single figures. There were indications that these proportions had been decided in advance of the polling. Mousavi and Karroubi refused to accept the results, and asked for a recount. On 13 June, Ahmadinejad celebrated his victory, and in a provocative speech referred to those objecting to the poll as 'dirt and dust' that would be soon washed away. On 15 June, an estimated 2 million protesters marched through Tehran with the single slogan, 'Where is my vote?' This was the biggest protest march since the 1979 revolution, and a direct challenge to the theocratic forces. It was followed by more protests, which the government met with violence. In a much-awaited Friday prayer speech on 19 June, Khamene'i, instead of finding a healing formula, threw oil on the fire. He blamed foreign media for 'doubts over election results', dismissed the protesters and warned them of further government violence if they persisted. But the protests continued, leading to the formation of the popular movement for change, which came to be known as the Green Movement, under the joint – but very diffuse – leadership of Mousavi, Karroubi, and Khatami, with Rafsanjani attempting to mediate reconciliation with the Leadership.

8.5 Constitutional law

Iran's first constitution was ratified in 1906 following a revolution that ended the absolute monarchy. In 1979, after another popular revolution, a new constitution was adopted, which abolished the monarchy and established an Islamic Republic; it was amended in 1989. As the background and political features of each constitution have been already discussed, this section outlines articles in the current constitution relating to legislative and judicial powers.[17]

The constitution combines religious, ideological, and democratic elements. It consists of 177 articles, divided into fourteen chapters, each on a specific theme. The lengthy preamble tells the story of the 1978-

1979 revolution, stressing the religious and ideological rationale for the merger of religious and political power. The following extract gives a flavour of the document's ideological vision and the primacy it gives to Islam and the clergy, seen as saviours of Islam and the people:

> The unique characteristic of this Revolution, as compared with other Iranian movements of the last century, is that it is religious and Islamic. The Muslim people of Iran, after living through an anti-despotic movement for constitutional government, and anti-colonialist movement for the nationalization of petroleum, gained precious experience in that they realized that the basic and specific reason for the failure of those movements was that that they were not religious ones. Although in those movements Islamic thinking and the guidance of a militant clergy played a basic and prominent part, yet they swiftly trailed off into stagnation, because the struggle deviated from the true Islam. But now the nation's conscience has awakened to the leadership of an exalted Authority, His Eminence Ayatollah Imam Khomeini, and has grasped the necessity of following the line of the true religious and Islamic movement. This time the country's militant clergy, which has always been in the front lines of the people's movement, together with writers and committed intellectuals, has gained new strength (lit: impetus) under his leadership.

Chapter I (Art.s 1-14), 'General Principles', continues in the same vein. It outlines the principles of popular and religious sovereignty, Shia doctrines, the form of government, separation of powers, the state goals, the legislature, the judiciary, the source and scope of laws, official religion and language, culture, family, religious minorities, and in short the aims of the revolution. Religious and popular sovereignty are stressed in two contradictory articles. Article 4 states:

> All civil, penal, financial, economic, administrative, cultural, military, political, and other laws and regulations must be based on Islamic criteria. This principle applies absolutely and generally to all articles of the Constitution as well as to all other laws and regulations, and the fuqaha' of the Guardian Council are judges in this matter.

Article 6 declares, however:

> In the Islamic Republic of Iran, the affairs of the country must be administered on the basis of public opinion expressed by the means of elections, including the election of the President, the

> representatives of the Islamic Consultative Assembly, and the members of councils, or by means of referenda in matters specified in other articles of this Constitution.

Chapter 6 (Art.s 62-99) concerns legislative powers. Articles 62-90 provide for a unicameral parliament, the Islamic Consultative Assembly, consisting of 290 members elected by direct and secret ballot for four years; its consultations must be open and full minutes of them made available to the public by radio and the official gazette. Parliament drafts legislation, ratifies international treaties, approves the country's budget, and has the power to impeach the president and government ministers. It also possesses the right to investigate and oversee all affairs in the country. In terms of legislative authority, Parliament may legislate on all matters within the bounds of Islam and the constitution, but all its legislation must be evaluated and approved by the Guardian Council (Art.s 71, 72).

Articles 91-99 of Chapter 6 provide for the Guardian Council. It consists of twelve members (six clerical and six non-clerical jurists) who serve for six years. The Leader appoints the six clerical jurists, the other six being nominated by the Head of Judiciary and elected by Parliament. The council's role is to ensure that all laws in the country are in line with Islam and the constitution, and it has the authority to interpret the constitution and to supervise all elections – an authority which, as already discussed, ensures the concentration of power in the hands of clerics.

Chapter 8 of the amended constitution states that, following Khomeini's death, the Leader should be chosen by experts, that is an Assembly of clerics, themselves elected by the people but subject to the approval of the Guardian Council (Art.s 107 and 108). The conduct of the Assembly and the mode of popular election are to be determined by the Assembly itself, which also has the duty of reviewing the performance of the Leader, and dismissing him if necessary (Article 111).

The amended version of Article 112 provides for an additional legislative body, the Expediency Council, created by Ayatollah Khomeini in 1988 to resolve disputes between Parliament and the Guardian Council. The Leader appoints members of the Expediency Council; they convene at his orders, and also act as his advisory body. The council's members propose its regulations, which are then ratified by the Leader.

Chapter 11 (Art.s 156-174) provides for an independent judiciary. In the 1979 version, the judiciary was to be run by a High Judicial Council; in the 1989 version, it is to be headed by a senior *feqh*-expert (*mojtahed-e 'adel*), appointed by the Leader for five years. The Minister of Justice, chosen by the president from among candidates recommended by the Head of Judiciary, is responsible for liaising between the executive and judicial powers. The Supreme Court, formed according to regulations drafted by the Head of Judiciary, is charged with supervising decisions of the lower courts to ensure both conformity with the laws of the country and uniformity in judicial policy. Article 162 requires that the chief of the Supreme Court be a senior *feqh*-expert, appointed by the Head of Judiciary in consultation with the Supreme Court judges for a term of five years.

8.6 Personal status and family law

As noted earlier, these laws were codified as part of the legal reforms during the reign of Reza Shah, the first Pahlavi monarch. Until then the clergy had the monopoly of defining and administering family law; they performed marriages and divorces and dealt with disputes relating to marriage and inheritance in sharia courts, in accordance with the principles and procedures of Shia law.

Inheritance

Inheritance law was codified in 1928 as part of the Iranian Civil Code. Part 4 of Book 1 of the Code ('On Wills and Inheritance') sets out various aspects of inheritance law in 124 articles (Art.s 825-949), which remain faithful to Ja'fari or Ithna 'Ashari (Twelver) Shia jurisprudence. Like Sunni law, the Shia law of inheritance is based on a system of rights that grant the legal heirs of the deceased a share of his estate. Its salient features are as follows:

- Surviving relatives of the deceased are grouped in order of precedence, based on class (*tabaqeh*) and degree (*darajeh*) of closeness of blood relationship. As a class, descendants precede antecedents. Within the class, relatives nearer in degree to the deceased exclude more remote ones. In all classes, a male's share is double of that of a female.
- The chief difference between Shia inheritance law and Sunni law is that the former grants a higher status to females as legal heirs. If a deceased person is survived only by daughters (no sons), in Shia law daughters inherit the whole estate, whereas in Sunni law they inherit half the estate and the other half goes to the nearest agnate (s) of the deceased.
- A man or woman can make a will but testamentary power is curtailed in two respects. First, a legal heir cannot be excluded nor can the share to which he or she is entitled be reduced. Secondly, no

more than one-third of the amount of one's net estate can be willed away without the consent of the legal heirs.

In 2007, the Zainab Society, a conservative women's association that supported Ahmadinejad in the 2005 election (several members were elected to Parliament in 2004) presented a bill to Parliament amending Civil Code Article 946; this article, reflecting the majority Shia position, states that a man inherits a share of the entire estate of his wife, but a widow cannot inherit land, only 'moveable property' and a share of the value of any buildings or trees. The amendment proposed to enable a widow, like a widower, to inherit a share of the entire property of her spouse. The bill was ratified by Parliament in 2009, and approved by the Guardian Council in February 2010. This – a small but progressive step by a conservative government – remains the only reform in the area of inheritance law.[18]

Marriage and the Civil Code

Family law, however, has an uneven history of reform. It was codified in 1935 as part of the civil code. Articles 1031-1206 of Volume Two deal with kinship, marriage, termination of marriage, family relations, and children. They retain the patriarchal bias of the sharia. Limited reforms were introduced, adopting principles from other schools of Islamic law so as to extend the grounds upon which a woman could obtain a judicial divorce to include the husband's refusal or inability to provide for her (Art. 1129), his refusal to perform his marital (sexual) duties, his maltreatment of her and his affliction with a disease that could endanger her life (Art. 1130). Otherwise, the only departure from classical Shia law is Article 1041, prohibiting the marriage of girls under thirteen (Banani 1961: 69-84).

Meanwhile, in 1931 a marriage law had been enacted, consisting of 20 articles and 2 notes setting out procedural rules for implementation of the civil code concerning matrimonial transactions. Articles 1 and 2 required that marriages and divorces be registered in civil bureaus set up in accordance with the regulations of the Ministry of Justice. Failure to do so did not affect the validity of the marriage or the divorce, but incurred penalties and the loss of legal recognition by the state, thus reflecting a dual notion of legality: legal/official (*qanuni/rasmi*) as opposed to religious (*shar'i*). Article 3 set financial penalties and prison terms for all those involved in the marriage of girls under thirteen years of age. Articles 4 and 8-17 – all incorporated, in slightly different wording, into the 1935 Civil Code – deal with a wife's right to maintenance and her right to initiate divorce proceedings, requiring that such actions be brought initially to civil courts. In the same year, the jurisdiction of sharia courts was reduced to disputes involving the essential validity (*asl*) of marriage and divorce (Banani 1961: 78).

The 1967 and 1975 Family Protection Laws

A major change in the sphere of family law occurred in 1967 with the enactment of the Family Protection Law (FPL), which curtailed men's rights to arbitrary divorce and polygamy. The civil code was left intact and reforms were achieved through procedural devices (Hinchcliffe 1968). Comprising 23 articles and 1 note, the FPL introduced new rules for registration of marriage and divorce and set up new courts for dealing with all kinds of familial disputes. All divorcing couples were required to appear in these courts, which had their own procedural rules and were presided over by civil judges, some of them women. In the absence of spouses' mutual consent to divorce, and upon the establishment of certain grounds, the court would issue a certificate referred to as 'Impossibility of Reconciliation'. Grounds available to men were parallel to those available to women; both could apply to the court to appoint arbiters to try to bring about reconciliation, although the final decision on divorce and child custody arrangements rested with the court (Art.s 6-13). Registration of a divorce without a court certificate was made an offence, subject to the penalty of six month's to one year's imprisonment for all parties involved, including the registrar (Art.s 14, 16). To avoid a clash with sharia provisions that recognise divorce as the exclusive right of a man (reflected in Art. 1133 of the 1935 Civil Code: 'A man can divorce his wife whenever he wishes'), the FPL resorted to a legal device: it required that conditions in which a divorce certificate could be requested from the court be included as stipulations in all marriage contracts (Art. 17). Article 4 of the 1931 Marriage Law, repeated in Article 1119 of the Civil Code, also recognises stipulations in marriage contacts, giving a wife, in certain conditions, the right to divorce herself on behalf of her husband after establishing in court the existence of a stipulated condition. Before the FPL, it was up to the woman, in effect her family, to negotiate such a right for her, which seldom happened. The FPL made these stipulations an integral part of every marriage contract. In large urban centres, courts that dealt with family disputes and were regulated by FPL procedural rules became known as 'FPL Courts'.

In 1975, the FPL was replaced by another law with the same title, comprising 28 articles and 19 notes, which extended the reforms of the FPL and formally repealed any prior laws conflicting with its mandate. It increased the minimum age at marriage from 15 to 18 for females and from 18 to 20 for males, placed women on a more equal footing with men with respect to divorce and child custody, and provided the courts with discretionary powers to grant or withhold divorces and to decide on child custody arrangements.

Marriage, divorce and polygamy in the Islamic Republic

In the Islamic Republic, two parallel and opposing developments with respect to family law can be detected: the validation of the patriarchal mandates of classical jurisprudence, and attempts to protect and compensate women in the face of them. The first began with the Special Civil Courts Legislation (SCCL) in September 1979, which created courts by the same name to replace the Family Protection Courts that had been suspended shortly after the victory of the Revolution in February. The SCCL contained twenty articles and three notes, all but one concerned with defining the structure and jurisdiction of its courts, which are invested with the same degree of discretionary power as enjoyed by the FPL courts (Mir-Hosseini 1993: 55-56). It allowed the registration of divorce by mutual consent, but retained an element of the FPL reform: Article 3, Note 2 required that, if a husband wished a divorce, the court must first refer the case to arbitration; if reconciliation proved impossible, the husband should be given 'permission to divorce'. This note was in evident contradiction with the classical Shia position that grants men the right to unilateral and extra-judicial divorce (codified as Art. 1133 of the 1935 Civil Code). The contradiction was resolved by reference to a Koranic verse that speaks of the appointment of arbiters in the event of marital discord.[19]

The FPL was never formally repealed, however, and elements of it have been retained in other areas of family law, although in an *ad hoc* and inconsistent manner. The Guardian Council and the High Judicial Council (until its abolition under the 1989 amended constitution) undertook the revision of laws found to be in contradiction with sharia provisions. In 1982 and 1991, they deleted, amended, or replaced fifty articles of the 1935 Civil Code (Mehrpoor 2001: 8-16). Article 1041, which set a minimum age at marriage (thirteen for females and fifteen for males), was amended in 1982 to prohibit marriage prior to puberty (defined in the amended Article 1210 as nine lunar years for girls and fifteen for boys). The Special Civil Courts can give permission to marry a girl under thirteen; yet Article 3 of the 1931 Marriage Law, which sentences those involved in a marriage of a girl under thirteen to from six months' to two years' imprisonment, has been left intact.

A similar ambiguity informs the law on polygamy. In 1984, the penalty introduced by the 1975 FPL (Art. 17) for registering a polygamous marriage without court permission was declared to be inconsistent with sharia (Guardian Council, Opinion No. 1488, dated 9 Mordad 1363/31 July 1984). Yet Articles 5-7 of the 1931 Marriage Law, requiring a man to declare his marital status at the time of marriage and fixing a sentence of six months' to two years' imprisonment if the second wife brings a legal action for deception, have not been repealed.

The situation over polygamy becomes more complicated if temporary marriage (commonly known as *mut'a* or *sigheh*; see Haeri 1989) is also taken into consideration. Although the civil code recognises this as a valid marriage, the 1931 marriage law and all subsequent legislation – even after the Revolution – are silent about the formalities of registration. The FPL, by both omission and commission, excluded disputes involving *mut'a* from adjudication on the basis that, not being registered, they were devoid of legal validity. The aim was to discourage, and even to prevent, this type of marriage without directly banning it. After 1979, however, the Special Civil Courts not only heard disputes involving temporary unions but could authorise their registration, thus giving them 'legal' (*qanuni*) status (Mir-Hosseini 1993: 162-171).

With respect to a mother's custody rights and control over her children after divorce or the death of the father, the FPL reforms were severely curtailed. Article 15 of the 1975 FPL, placing a mother on the same level as a paternal grandfather in terms of natural guardianship (*velayat-e qahri*) of her children, was among the first to be repealed in October 1979 (Safa'i & Emami 1995: 164-168). In the event of divorce, the Civil Code gives a mother the right to custody of a daughter until the age of seven and of a son until two (Art. 1169). Although a woman acquires custody of her children if her husband dies (Art. 1170), she loses it if she remarries (Art. 1171) and she must submit to the authority of their paternal grandfather (Art. 1180). A single-article law passed in July 1985 gives the widow of a 'martyr' (killed in the war with Iraq) the right to receive her dead husband's salary and to keep custody of their children even if she remarries.

With the relaxation of restrictions on men's rights to polygamy and unilateral (but not extra-judicial) divorce, attempts were made to compensate and protect women. In 1982, new marriage contracts were issued, carrying two stipulations that marriage notaries are required to read out to couples. The first stipulation entitles a woman to claim half the wealth that her husband acquires during marriage, provided that the divorce is neither initiated by her nor caused by any fault of her own. The second enables women to obtain a judicial divorce on more or less the same grounds available to them under the FPL; the only difference is that, in conformity with the sharia mandate on divorce, the husband can now refrain from signing any of these stipulations. In practice, however, the presence or absence of his signature under each clause has no effect on the woman's right to obtain a divorce, as the decision lies with the judge. Civil Code Article 1130 was amended in 1982 to empower the judge to grant or withhold a divorce requested by a woman, if he considers that the continuation of marriage would entail 'hardship and harm' (*'osr va haraj*) (Mir-Hosseini 1993: 65-70, 1996, 1997).

In December 1991, following pressure by women and the rising divorce rate, a more radical step was taken with the introduction of the Amendment to Divorce Regulations (ADR), which reinstates the rejected elements of the FPL divorce provisions, but under a different legal logic. ADR, a single-article law with 7 notes, was approved by Parliament in March 1992, but disputed by the Guardian Council. It was eventually ratified in November 1992 by the intervention of the Expediency Council. ADR outlaws the registration of any divorce without a court certificate, requiring all divorcing couples, even those who have reached an agreement, to go through a process of arbitration. If the arbiters, one chosen by each side, fail to reconcile them, the court allows the man to effect and register a divorce only after he has paid his wife all her dues, unless he convinces the court of his inability to pay (Notes 1, 2, and 3). The wife's dues consist of her marriage gift (*mahr*, promised to her on marriage, but normally never given except in case of divorce) and maintenance during the waiting period (*'edda*, a period after divorce or widowhood during which a woman cannot remarry, lasting three menses or, in case of case of pregnancy, until delivery). Note 5 allows for the appointment of women as advisory judges to work in co-operation with the main judge. Note 6 – disputed by the Guardian Council – enables the court to force the husband to pay her 'exemplary wages' (*ojrat al-methl*), monetary compensation for the work she has done during marriage (i.e. raising children and housework, which she is not obliged to do by classical jurisprudence), provided that the divorce is not initiated by her and is not caused by any fault of her own.

In 1994 the Special Civil Courts disappeared, with the enactment of the Law of Formation of General Courts. Until 1999 family disputes were heard in these General Courts, which were presided over by either a senior cleric or a civil judge, with jurisdiction over all types of cases, from criminal to familial. Cases involving a dispute over the essential legality of marriage and divorce were referred to courts whose presiding judge was authorised by the Head of the Judiciary.

In 1996, a bill signed by 150 deputies was presented to Parliament demanding the formation of Family Courts on the basis of Article 21 of the Constitution. These Family Courts were duly formed, and began work in 1999. Following Khatami's 1997 election and the emergence of the reformist movement, family law reform became a major arena of confrontation between Khatami's reformist government and the conservative-controlled Parliament. Then in the 2000 parliamentary election, women's rights and the reform of family law were central to the successful campaign that led to the reformist domination of the new Parliament. To fulfil their electoral promises, the reformists presented 41 bills that aimed to modify in various ways the inequalities that women face in law. But the Guardian Council rejected almost all of them, including the proposal to join the Convention on the Elimination of all forms of Discrimination Against Women (CEDAW). Eventually, however, after mediation by the Expediency Council, 21 of the 41 bills were passed into law, albeit in some cases with their gender-egalitarian tone and intent weakened or nullified. The bills passed included amendments to the 1935 Civil Code raising the minimum age of marriage and expanding women's grounds for divorce and custody rights.

Family law and women's activism in Ahmadinejad's presidency

The conservatives regained control of Parliament in 2004, and reform of family laws entered a lull. Meanwhile, women's activism became more radical and daring. In September 2006, following attacks on a peaceful women's gathering in a central Tehran square, a group of activists launched the 'One Million Signatures' campaign to change all laws discriminating against women. Patterned after Moroccan women's activism in the 1990s, this campaign is largely conducted by the activism of young women, and through the internet.[20]

In July 2007 Ahmadinejad's government presented a bill to Parliament that has not yet become law. Entitled 'Protection of the Family', it aims to do away with not only the pre-revolutionary reforms that have been retained in practice, but also the protective measures introduced in the 1980s and 1990s. The bill was originally prepared by the Judiciary to set up procedural rules for the Family Courts, but the government altered some of its articles. Four articles in particular alarmed women's groups and became the focus of protest; they make it easier for men to be polygamous and restrict women's ability to gain compensation. Article 22 relaxes the regulations for the registration of temporary marriages. Article 23 allows a man to contract a second marriage without the consent of his first wife, if the court decides that he can afford it. Article 25 requires the Ministry of Finance to demand tax payments from women at the time of marriage, if they stipulate a marriage gift (*mahr*) that exceeds a certain limit. Above all, Article 52, by repealing all previous laws and acts, in effect dismantles not only the reforms introduced under the FPL that have continued to ban the registration of polygamous marriages without a court order, but also the 1992 Amendment to Divorce Regulations that requires a man to pay compensation to his wife in the form of 'exemplary wages' before he can exercise his unilateral right to divorce.

Women's rights activists, including some conservative groups, joined forces in opposing the 'Protection of the Family' bill. Calling it 'Destruction of the Family', they succeeded in getting the support of progressive and reformist clerics. Grand Ayatollah Sane'i declared that taking another wife without the true consent of the first wife was prohibited (*haram*) according to Islamic law, since polygamy in modern contexts entails 'harm and hardship' for the majority of women. In September 2008, a group of women's rights activists went to Parliament to lobby against the bill, as it was about to be debated. They succeeded in persuading members of Parliament to withdraw the bill, and to send it to the parliamentary commission for legal affairs. It was announced that Article 23, inserted by Ahmadinejad's government, would be removed.

But then, in the heat of the unrest that followed the June 2009 election, Article 23 was reintroduced in modified form: the court may allow a man to register further marriages, if he can establish certain conditions, which are more or less those specified by the 1975 FPL.[21] In January 2010, Parliament ratified the bill, taking advantage of the closure of the reformist press and the arrest of a number of women's rights activists. The fate of the bill remains uncertain, however, as the Guardian Council has returned it to Parliament for revision. A member of the Judicial Commission in Parliament observed that it is unlikely to be debated again soon, as the council considers restrictions on men's right to polygamy to be in contradiction with sharia.[22] Meanwhile, women's rights activists have started a new campaign, 'NO to Anti-Family Bill'.[23]

8.7 Criminal law

The first steps at reforming and codifying criminal law in Iran came with the success of the constitutional revolution. The constitutionalists sought an end to the dual sharia and state jurisdictions and the creation of a systematic and secular criminal justice system, inspired by European criminal law. In order to preempt or at least to defuse clerical concerns as to whether the sharia courts would continue to implement Islamic criminal law, they began in 1911 with a Code of Criminal Procedure, approved tentatively by the first Parliament. Then in 1912, Parliament approved a complete Criminal Code, drafted by the French jurist Adolph Pierny, which contained no element of Islamic jurisprudential concepts. This, the first major legal reform in Iran, had a limited impact, since the sharia courts continued to operate until the rise of Reza Shah. The 1912 code was repealed by the 1926 Criminal Code, amended in 1940; the Code of Criminal Procedure was amended in

1932; both then remained in force until the 1979 revolution. Although Islamic concepts were retained intact in the area of family law in the form of substantive law, when it came to criminal law Reza Shah abandoned them, in both substance and procedure (Banani 1961: 69-70; Amin 1985: 113; Faghfouri 1993: 284).

A major priority of the clerics who took power after the Revolution was to replace the 1926 Criminal Code by one based on Islamic legal concepts. In 1983, the High Judicial Council codified traditional juristic concepts of crime and punishment in the form of an experimental bill entitled 'Islamic Punishment: Fixed Punishments (*hodud*), Retaliation (*qesas*), Blood Money (*diyeh*) and Discretionary Punishments (*ta'zirat*)'. The Guardian Council rejected the bill, however, finding it to be inconsistent with sharia; but after Ayatollah Khomeini's intervention, the bill was ratified for an interim period of five years (Mehrpoor 1995: 99-136; Rahami 2005: 593-594). The sections on Discretionary Punishments retained many elements of the Criminal Code but introduced a number of new offences, for instance those related to women's dress and to moral behaviour.

In 1991, a new criminal code was approved by Parliament on an experimental basis for five years (it was renewed twice, in 1996 and 2001). It consists of five Books. Book One is on Generalities (Art.s 1-62). Book Two (Art.s 63-199) concerns *hodud*, crimes considered as violations of God's limits, with mandatory and fixed punishments derived from textual sources (Koran or Sunnah). It contains 8 chapters, each dealing with one class of offence. Chapter One defines the crime of illicit sex (*zena*) and specifies the punishment as 100 lashes, but stoning to death for married offenders. Chapter Two prescribes death as the punishment for sodomy (*lawat*), while Chapter Three lays down 100 lashes as punishment for lesbianism (*mosahaqa*), or death if the offence is repeated after three convictions. Pimping (*qavadi*), defined as bringing two or more persons together for the purpose of *zena* or *lawat*, is punished, according to Chapter Four, by 75 lashes and (for a man) expulsion from his place of residence for three months to one year. A slanderous accusation (*qazf*) of illicit sex (Chapter Five) will be punished by 80 lashes. Chapter Six specifies 80 lashes for a Muslim caught drinking alcohol (*mosker*), and for non-Muslims if they drink in public. Chapter Eight gives amputation as the punishment for theft (*serqat*) but under conditions that are hard to establish.

But the most politically controversial offences, dealt with in Chapter Seven, are waging war against God (*moharebeh*) and corruption on earth (*efsad fi'l-arz*). These are defined together as resorting to arms to create fear and terror among the people, a notion derived from Koran 5: 33; the judge will decide between the following punishments: hanging, severance of the right hand and the left foot, or banishment. Since the beginning the Islamic regime has used accusations of these offences extensively to justify eliminating adversaries (Zubaida 2003: 194). Disapproved political behaviour, such as membership in a forbidden organisation or activities aimed at overthrowing the regime, are also liable to these charges. And in the aftermath of the disputed June 2009 election, they have been once again widely levelled at members of the opposition who do not accept the election results.

Books Three and Four of the 1991 Code concern crimes against the person, such as bodily harm and homicide. In such cases, the victim or the victim's family can demand either retaliation or blood money. Book Three, on Retaliation, contains two chapters: the first (Art.s 204-268) deals with Retaliation for Life and the second (Art.s 269-293) with Retaliation for Bodily Harm. Book Four is on Blood Money (Art.s 269-497), defined as monetary compensation paid to the injured party or the relatives in case of murder or manslaughter or bodily harm. The sums of compensation that can be demanded are not equal for Muslim and non-Muslim victims.

Book Five, on Discretionary Punishments, reproduces the 1983 law on offences other than those named under 'Hodud, Retaliation and Blood Money'. These constitute the majority of all criminal offences, and include most offences named in the pre-revolutionary criminal code.

From the outset the international human rights community condemned the codification of Islamic criminal justice concepts, in particular stoning as punishment for adultery, and the unequal legal treatment of women and non-Muslims. After Khatami's 1997 election, the reformist press began to air an internal critique too. Though this critique met fierce conservative reaction, leading to the prosecution of its advocates, it has continued unabated and has, in fact, intensified. In 2002, in the course of 'constructive dialogue' with the European Union, Iran issued a kind of moratorium on stoning; the head of the judiciary issued a directive to judges to that effect, while keeping the laws on illicit sex unchanged. The moratorium continued until the hardliners regained control of government under Ahmadinejad.

In May 2006, the execution of a woman by stoning led a group of women and men activists to form the Network of Volunteer Lawyers, who launched a campaign to remove stoning as punishment for adultery from the Criminal Code (Terman 2007). They started to take up and publicise cases of those sentenced to stoning, mainly women from deprived backgrounds and victims of familial disputes. The campaign brought further international and domestic attention to the issue, and succeeded in reversing many convictions and freezing others, as well as engaging the authorities in a dialogue on the need to rethink pre-modern concepts of crime and punishment. In 2007 they became part of a larger international campaign launched by Women Living Under

Muslim Laws.[24] However, as Iran's confrontation with the international community over their 'nuclear ambitions' intensified, hardliners in the judiciary have managed to carry out further stonings, and numerous women remain under sentence.[25]

In 2007, the provisional 1991 Criminal Code had already been renewed twice, and the government published a draft replacement. The new Code became the subject of a great deal of criticism inside and outside Iran for its non-adherence to human rights law. While the bill no longer mentions stoning as a punishment for adultery, it has added apostasy to the Hadd crimes. In 2008, the bill was debated in Parliament, which modified several articles; it was ratified in September, but at the time of writing (February 2010) the Guardian Council had still not approved it.

8.8 Other areas of law[26]

Money loans

Since 1979 it has been forbidden for private individuals as well as banks and insurance companies to charge or pay interest on loans. This prohibition is contained in the constitution. Article 49 of the Constitution furthermore states that interest or unjust enrichment (*riba*) is punishable and adds that the government is competent to confiscate property acquired through *riba* and to return this property to the rightful owners, or, in case this is impossible, to add this property to the public goods.

Stipulating interest in money loans is unlawful and punishable. Every agreement, including buying and loaning, whereby an additional favour is stipulated to the advantage of one of the parties, is considered to contain *riba*. The Criminal Code summarises this in Article 595 as a punishable act. The parties in a contract can in this case be punished by imprisonment for six months to three years, or by 74 lashes. Those convicted, moreover, must pay a fine of the same amount as the stipulated *riba*. If it cannot be determined to whom the *riba* is due, then the amount goes to the state. If the payer of *riba* can prove that this was done out of necessity, then punishment will not be imposed.

In the world of banking, charging premiums proportionate to the supplied services is legally permissible. It is also permissible for banks to give a voluntary reward to customers who put their money in the bank. With regard to money loans this is also permissible provided no interest is stipulated. The levels of compensation conform to the percentages of interest that apply for short-term credit in other countries.

There are no legal regulations for exceptions that exist with regard to *riba*; these are determined based on jurisprudence. If *riba* is stipulated in a loan, then the clause is null but the agreement remains intact. It is permissible for the debtor to give the creditor an addition, as long as this happens voluntarily. Banks make use of this possibility to accommodate their clients with their deposits. Everything takes place voluntarily, and thus nobody suffers loss. Muslims are furthermore allowed to stipulate *riba* in contracts with non-Muslims (Ansari-Pour 1995: 165-191).

Tax law

The most important taxes in Iran are profit taxes paid by companies and income taxes for private persons, which are subject to the regime of corporate income tax and the Direct Taxes Law, respectively. These laws have no relation to sharia.[27] *Zakat*, the religious tax on all Muslims, and the special Shia tax (*khoms*), continue to be paid voluntarily on a private and individual basis; while the organisation and finances of the seminaries (which used to be paid for by the *khoms* tax) have come increasingly under control of the state since Khamene'i became Leader in 1989.

8.9 International treaty obligations and human rights

Article 4 of the 1979 Constitution sets forth that sharia not only dominates positive law in Iran, but also prevails over every form of customary law and international law, including in the domain of human rights (see 8.5). Consequently, the unequal treatment of men and women and of Muslims and non-Muslims, have been the focus of international criticism, especially regarding the treatment of Baha'is, stoning, and juvenile executions. In the 1980s, during Khomeini's leadership and the war with Iraq (1980-1988), Western governments directly or indirectly supported Saddam Hossein, and Iran took a rejectionist stance towards international human rights treaties. Iranian representatives adopted a confident tone, claiming that since the sharia is the essence of justice, commitment to the sharia and its rules must take precedence over all others. For instance, in July 1982, the leader of the Iranian delegation to the United Nations Human Rights Committee in Geneva said that 'Iran believes in the supremacy of Islamic laws, which are universal.' He went on to clarify that 'Iran would choose the divine laws' in cases where human rights treaties are irreconcilable with sharia on some point (Amin 1985: 106). However, Iran remained a party to the ICCPR, which they joined in 1967; but like the previous regime, the Islamic

Republic did not sign the optional protocols 1 and 2 concerning the individual right of Iranian citizens to complain and the prohibition on the death penalty.

After the end of the war with Iraq and during Rafsanjani's presidency (1989-1997), Iran began to have a more positive attitude towards international human rights law, and pursued a policy of engagement. It joined the Convention on the Rights of the Child (CRC), which went into effect in August 1994, but, like many other Muslim countries, with a general reservation: 'The government of the Islamic Republic of Iran reserves the right not to apply any provisions or articles of the Convention that are incompatible with Islamic laws.' In 1997, with the election of Khatami and the emergence of the reform movement, a lively debate emerged on the notion of Islamic human rights, and the government's policy of supporting civil society by allowing the creation of NGOs helped improve the human rights situation to some extent (Mayer 2000; Mokhtari 2004). Nevertheless, there are some important human rights treaties that have still not been ratified, notably the Convention Against Torture (CAT) and the Convention Against Elimination of All Forms of Discrimination against Women (CEDAW). Efforts by Khatami's government and the reformist Parliament (2000-2004) to ratify these conventions were frustrated by the Guardian Council. In 2002, the government presented a bill to Parliament for Iran to join CEDAW; Parliament ratified it, but the Guardian Council rejected it, so it went to the Expediency Council, which still has to issue a decision.

After Ahmadinejad's election in 2005, when the theocratic forces took control over all three branches of government, they embarked on systematic efforts to curb civil society and muzzle the press. They closed down many NGOs and reformist publications, yet debates over human rights have intensified, and many high-ranking clerics and reformists started to publish their views on Islam and human rights. The most significant is a 2007 book by Grand Ayatollah Montazeri, in which, in response to questions posed by senior religious scholars, he makes a juristic case for the compatibility of sharia and international human rights law, arguing that dignity is the entitlement of every human being, because it is part of their humanity, and so the Islamic state must honour and protect it.[28] This is the first time that a Shia supreme religious authority (*marja'*) has argued for human rights from a religious perspective. More significantly, perhaps, Montazeri, who had devoted his scholarship in the 1980s to justifying the rule of the jurist (*velayat-e faqih*), by 2000 had became an advocate of human rights.

The sharia as interpreted by the Guardian Council, and as reflected in the laws of the Islamic Republic of Iran, continues to be in conflict with international human rights law. As evident from the sections on family and criminal laws, they contain a number of provisions that are in contradiction with customary international human rights law. In addition, many of the numerous human rights provisions in the constitution of the Islamic Republic have never been translated into law. For instance, 'due process' is regulated perfectly on paper. Articles 32 and 34-39 of the constitution specify conditions by which the legal system in Iran must abide: the regulation of prosecution, appearing before the judge, the right to legal assistance, the right to cross-examination of witnesses, and the right of appeal. The Islamic Republic has systematically violated all these conditions from the outset, and violations have multiplied since the disputed 2009 election attracted further international attention.

On 15 February 2010, the Universal Periodic Review, to which all U.N. Members are subjected, severely criticised Iran's human rights record during the past four years.[29] The Iranian delegation, led by Mohammed Larijani, Secretary-General of Iran's High Council for Human Rights, rejected the criticisms and spoke of the 'biting language' of 'Western delegations'; he cited articles of the Iranian Constitution that protect human rights and stated, '[n]o Baha'i is prosecuted because he is a Baha'i' and that prosecuted and jailed demonstrators were guilty of 'terrorist activities'.[30]

8.10 Conclusion

Sharia and national laws in Iran: An unfinished project

Twentieth-century developments in Iran, as elsewhere in the Muslim world, intensified two deep-rooted oppositions in politics and society: between despotism and democracy and between sharia and secular national law. Secular democrats gained the upper hand initially, in the 1905-1911 constitutional revolution, yet the promised democracy and rule of law failed to take root, for a combination of internal and external reasons; the resultant impasse was resolved by the despotic but modernising and secularising Pahlavi monarchy. A brief resurgence of democracy in the late 1940s was again brought to an end by a foreign intervention in 1953; over the next 25 years, both democratic and theocratic opposition to Pahlavi rule grew until the eruption of the 1978-1979 revolution.[31]

The victory of the revolution, and foundation of the Islamic Republic that followed, marked the acme of political Islam, with its slogan of 'return to sharia'. For some it was the beginning of a new dawn, when God's law – the sharia – would bring Muslims the justice and prosperity that secular nation-states failed to deliver. For others, including many of those who had originally participated in the revolution, it was the undoing of over half a century of state modernisation, and the return of religious fanaticism. Whatever its nature, and however it was perceived, the Iranian Revolution changed the landscape of the Muslim world. It inspired Muslim masses and reinvigorated intellectual debates over the nature and possibilities of the sharia.

Since its birth, the new Islamic Republic has confronted the challenges of all twentieth-century states, yet evolved in ways that inside and outside observers did not predict. Ruled by clerics, it combined not just religion and the state, but also theocracy and democracy. The founders made two broad assumptions: first, that what makes a state 'Islamic' is adherence to and implementation of the sharia; secondly that, given free choice, people will choose 'Islam' and will, thus, vote for clerics as the interpreters and custodians of the sharia. When they framed the constitution, the founders included both theocratic and democratic principles and institutions. The constitution clearly recognises the people's right to choose who will govern them. But some institutions, including Parliament and the presidency, though elected by direct popular vote, are nevertheless subordinated to clerical oversight and veto. This contradiction remained unresolved but unproblematic while Ayatollah Khomeini was alive and able to mediate it.

In practice, as the revolutionary fervour subsided, neither of the initial assumptions proved as valid or as clear-cut as the early revolutionaries and the framers of the constitution had hoped, and soon cracks in the system began to appear. Khomeini's death in 1989 forced a redefinition of the relationship between religious authority and the state. His successor as ruling jurist and Leader, Ali Khamene'i, lacked his religious authority and charisma. There were increasing signs of popular dissatisfaction with state policies. Either the notion of 'Islamic', as defined by the ruling clerics, had to adapt to the political exigencies of a modern democracy, or the people's choice must be restricted or bypassed, which would mean betraying the revolution's democratic ideals and losing the popular support from which the Islamic Republic drew its legitimacy. The Islamic Republic entered a new phase in which the tension between theocracy and democracy intensified. Khamene'i increased the power of the non-elected bodies, which now came to be identified with the theocratic side of the state, at the expense of the elected bodies, representing the democratic side, the republic. Using the institutions at his disposal, Khamene'i expanded his power base and narrowed the scope of democracy, especially by introducing a more stringent vetting of candidates for elected office. This tactic misfired in the 1997 presidential elections, when people rejected the candidate endorsed and supported by the regime, and voted for Mohammad Khatami, the candidate who promised to promote civil society and rule of law.

Khatami's election inaugurated a new round of debates and struggles and a realignment of forces and factions. His government's relatively liberal policies allowed the voices of dissident intellectuals, both lay and clerical, to be aired in the press and reach the public. Prominent among these were the 'New Religious Thinkers', who displayed a refreshingly pragmatic vigour and a willingness to engage with non-religious perspectives. They forced a rethinking and reworking of the founding concepts of the Islamic Republic, and of the stormy and unequal marriage it had made between theocracy and democracy.

Developing a critique of the despotic Islamic state from within an Islamic framework, the 'New Religious Thinkers' sought a rights-based political order that could open Muslim polities to dissent, tolerance, pluralism, and women's rights and civil liberties. They argued – like the great Muslim jurist and philosopher al-Ghazali in the eleventh century – that Islamic jurisprudence (*feqh*) is temporal and changeable; and – like all Muslim reformers since the late nineteenth century – they sought to establish conceptions of Islam and modernity as compatible. But they made and shaped these ideas in a different political context. In the Islamic Republic, as elsewhere when Islamists gained power in the late twentieth century, 'return to sharia' in practice entailed legislating and enforcing rules devised by pre-modern Muslim jurists, i.e. classical *feqh*. The results have been so out of touch with social realities, with the current sense of justice and with people's aspirations, that ordinary people and religious intellectuals alike came to rethink and redefine their notions of sacred and mundane in the sharia. It is not that the sharia has lost its sanctity; rather, the state's ideological use of the sharia and its penetration into the private lives of individuals have brought home the urgent need for legal reform and for the withdrawal of the state from the religious domain.

The 2005 presidential election marked another turning point. Having lost the popular argument to the reformists, but buoyed by the Khatami government's failures in both domestic policy and foreign relations, Khamene'i relied on the Revolutionary Guards to ensure the election of Ahmadinejad and the consolidation of the Leader's control of all the institutions of state. But the demand, particularly by women and the youth, for legal and social reform and restoration of the freedoms they had tasted could not be suppressed, and it erupted in the 2009 presidential election campaign. The Green Movement that emerged after the much-disputed re-election of Ahmadinejad, and the violent attempts by the 'Security Forces' to suppress it, showed clearly the extreme polarisation that has developed, no longer between Islam and secularism, but between despotism and democracy. Before his death in December 2009, Grand Ayatollah Montazeri, one of the founders of the Islamic

Republic, and now the Green Movement's spiritual leader, denounced the state as a religious dictatorship and declared that it was now neither Islamic nor a republic (Torfeh 2009).

Khatami and the reformists failed to bring tangible changes in the structure of power; they lost many battles, and they faced many political setbacks, but they had one major and lasting success: they demystified the power games, which until then had been conducted in a religious language, and the instrumental use of sharia to justify autocratic rule. Now the notion of sharia as an ideal enabled the reformists in Iran to argue for democracy and the rule of law and to challenge patriarchal and despotic laws enacted in the name of Islam. They did so by appealing to Islam's higher values and principles, and by invoking concepts from within Islamic legal theory, notably the distinction between sharia as 'divine law' and jurisprudence (*feqh*) as the human understanding of the requirements of the divine law.

The reformists' successor, the broad-based Green Movement, is still young; at the time of writing (February 2010), it is only eight months old, and its fortunes depend on both internal and global political developments. Some commentators are predicting the imminent collapse of the theocratic regime, others insist that the struggle will be long and painful. The leaders of the Movement, Mousavi, Karroubi and Khatami, as well as different groups of supporters, have issued numerous manifestos and lists of demands. All of them insist on an end to theocratic despotism, free elections, the accountability of those in power, and the abolition of legal and extra-legal discrimination between men and women and between Muslims and non-Muslims; it is too early to expect a detailed programme for legal reform. It remains to be seen whether this latest confrontation, the most violent in the history of the Islamic Republic, can be resolved by a new accommodation between the opposing and contradictory elements in the constitution.

Notes

1 Parts of this chapter (as acknowledged in footnotes) are drawn from an early draft by Albert Dekker and Maarten Barends, to whom I am most grateful. My warmest thanks go to Richard Tapper for his support, comments, and suggestions. I am also indebted to Jan Michiel Otto and Julie Chadbourne for valuable editorial help. Remaining errors are mine.

2 Ziba Mir-Hosseini is an independent consultant, researcher, and writer on Middle Eastern issues, based at the London Middle East Institute and the Centre for Middle Eastern and Islamic Law, both at SOAS, University of London; since 2002 she has been Hauser Global Law Visiting Professor at New York University.

3 *Taqiyeh* (dissimulation of belief), often identified as a Shia distinguishing feature, is not relevant to the legal system.

4 In this chapter, terms of Arabic or Persian origin that are commonly found in English dictionaries, such as ulama, sharia, hijab, Koran, are given as English words.
5 *Taqlid*: emulation, accepting the views of previous scholars as authoritative.
6 This is one aspect in which Shiism has been linked to Sufism, with its core spiritual relationship of teacher-disciple (*pir-morid*).
7 See Lambton 1964; Algar 1969; Akhavi 1980; Keddie 1983; Momen 1985; Arjomand 1988; Bayat 1991.
8 In his book *Tanbih al-ummah wa tanzih al-millah* (Admonition of the public and refinement of the people), published in 1909.
9 A *faqih* is an expert in *feqh*, jurisprudence.
10 Art. 110. *Rahbar*, or *rahbar-e enqelab* (Leader of the Revolution), is the term commonly used, both in the constitution and in everyday political discourse in Iran, for the leading jurist (*faqih*).
11 Articles 91-99 set out the role, composition, and scope of activity of this council.
12 For an analytical and critical account of these processes, see Mohammadi (2008).
13 See http://www.hrw.org/reports/1990/WR90/MIDEAST.BOU-02.htm#P106_25125, accessed 14 August 2008. For an analysis see Mayer (2000).
14 See summary of records of meetings issued under CCPR A/37/40/1982/no.324, http://www.bayefsky.com/./html/iran_t4_ccpr.php.
15 The society was formed in 1988, when a group of clerics clustered around Karroubi and Khatami separated from the Association of Militant Clergy (*jame'eh-ye rowhaniyat-e mobarez*), with Khomeini's blessing. This separation was the result of the debates and disagreements among the clerical ruling elite over approaches to politics, pragmatism, ideological purity, and Iran's relation with the world.
16 This court was formed at Ayatollah Khomeini's order in the aftermath of the Revolution in order to try the clerics associated with the previous regime. It was revived in 1987 to try a close associate of Ayatollah Montazeri. Its formation then was disputed as unconstitutional; and in 1988, in a letter to Parliament, Khomeini suggested that the court should be aligned with the mandates of the constitution, but only after the Iraq war ended. After Khomeini's death (and the end of the war) the court continued to function, coming under the control of the conservatives (Baqi 2001; Mir-Hosseini 2002).
17 For the text in English, see http://www.iranchamber.com/government/laws/constitution.php and for the text before the 1989 amendments, see http://www.servat.unibe.ch/icl/ir00000_.html.
18 See http://zeinab.ir/index.php?option=com_content&view=frontp; see also http://www.iranzanan.com/point_of_view/cat_6/000659.php.
19 Surat al-Nisa, verse 35, reads: 'If ye fear a breach between them twain, appoint (two) arbiters, one from his family, and the other from hers; If they wish for peace, Allah will cause their reconciliation' (Yusuf Ali translation). See Mir-Hosseini 1993, 2007 for discussion.
20 For the campaign, see http://www.we-change.org/spip.php?article19 and also http://www.feministschool.com/english/spip.php?rubrique3.
21 See Change for Equality (2010), 'Women fight polygamy proposal', http://www.forequality.info/english/spip.php?article645, dated 8 February; Feminist School (2009), 'Last change on the Family Protection Bill', http://www.feministschool.com/english/spip.php?article344, dated 26 November.
22 See http://www.feministschool.com/spip.php?article4148.
23 S. Moqadam (2010), 'No to Anti-Family Bill' (in Persian), http://www.roozonline.com/persian/news/newsitem/article/2010/february/17//-3d95903e6a.html, dated 26 February [Bahman 1388].
24 For the launch of the campaign, see http://www.wluml.org/node/5621.

25 See Amnesty International (2008), '*Iran: End executions by stoning*' http://www.amnesty.org/library/info/MDE13/001/2008/en.
26 This section was drafted by Albert Dekker.
27 See http://www.iranworld.com/Laws/ltr-r096.htm.
28 The book was published by Montzeri's office in Qom and also made available on his website: http://www.amontazeri.com/farsi/frame4.asp.
29 See http://www.hrw.org/en/news/2010/02/16/un-council-review-highlights-irans-poor-record; see Amnesty International's comments, http://www.amnesty.org/en/library/info/MDE13/021/2010/en.
30 See 'UN review affirms need for more pressure to improve human rights': http://www.iranhumanrights.org/2010/02/un-review/ and 'Ebadi appeals to international community to counter Iran's tragedy': http://www.rferl.org/content/Ebadi_Appeals_For_Help_To_Counter_Iran_Crackdown/1956527.html.
31 For further analysis, see e.g. Farhi 2003; Mir-Hosseini & Tapper 2006.

Bibliography

Abrahamian, E. (1989), *Radical Islam: The Iranian Mojahedin*. London: I. B. Tauris.

Akhavi, S. (1980), *Religion and politics in contemporary Iran: Clergy-State relations in the Pahlavi Period*. Albany: SUNY Press.

Akhavi, S. (1996), 'Contending discourses in Shi'a law on the doctrine of *wilayat al-faqih*', *Iranian Studies* 29(3/4): 229-268.

Algar, H. (1969), *Religion and state in Iran 1785-1906: The role of the ulama in the Qajar period*. Berkeley: University of California Press.

Amanat, A. (1992), 'Constitutional revolution: Intellectual background', *Encyclopedia Iranica* 6: 163-176.

Amin, S. H. (1985), *Middle East legal systems*. Glasgow: Royston.

Ansari, A. (2000), *Iran, Islam and democracy: The politics of managing change*. London: Royal Institute of International Affairs.

Ansari-Pour, M. A. (1995), 'Prohibition of interest under the Iranian legal system since the Revolution', in H. L. Ruttley & C. Mallat (eds.), *Commercial law in the Middle East*, 165-191. London: Kluwer Law International.

Ansari-Pour, M. A. (1996), 'Country surveys: Iran', *Yearbook of Islamic and Middle Eastern Law* 3: 342-51.

Arjomand, S. A. (1988), *The turban for the crown: The Islamic Revolution in Iran*. Oxford: Oxford University Press.

Arjomand, S. A. (1992), 'The Constitution of the Islamic Republic', *Encyclopaedia Iranica* 6: 151-158.

Arjomand, S. A. (2002), 'The reform movement and the debate on modernity and tradition in contemporary Iran', *Int. J. Middle East Stud.* 34: 719-731.

Algar, H. (1981), *Islam and revolution: Writings and declarations of Imam Khomeini* (translation). Berkeley: Mizan Press.

Ashraf, A. & A. Banuazizi (eds.) (2001a), 'Intellectuals in post-revolutionary Iran', special issue of *International Journal of Politics, Culture and Society* 15(2) (Winter).

Ashraf, A. & A. Banuazizi (2001b) 'Iran's tortuous path toward "Islamic Liberalism"', *International Journal of Politics, Culture and Society* 15(2) (Winter): 237-256.

Baqi [Baghi], E. (2001), '*Dadgah-e vizheh-ye rowhaniyat, Didgah-e mo'afeqan va mokhalefan*' ('The Special Clergy Court: Perspective of supporters and opponents'), *Aftab* 10: 40-47 [Azar 1380].

Bakhash, S. (1985), *The reign of the ayatollahs: Iran and the Islamic Revolution*. London: I. B. Tauris.

Baktiari, B. (1996), *Parliamentary politics in revolutionary Iran: The institutionalization of factional politics.* Gainesville: University Press of Florida.

Banani, A. (1961), *The modernization of Iran (1921-1941).* Stanford: Stanford University Press.

Bartleby (2010), 'Iran', in *World Factbook,* see http://www.bartleby.com/151/country/ir.html (2008 statistics) and https://www.cia.gov/library/publications/the-world-factbook/geos/ir.html (online edition, last accessed February 2010). Washington, D.C.: Central Intelligence Agency.

Bayat, M. (1991), *Iran's first revolution: Shi'ism and the constitutional revolution of 1905-1909.* New York/Oxford: Oxford University Press.

Boroujerdi, M. (1996), *Iranian intellectuals and the West: The tormented triumph of nativism.* Syracuse: Syracuse University Press.

Buchta, W. (2000), *Who rules Iran? The structure of power in the Islamic Republic.* Washington DC: Washington Institute for Near East Policy & Berlin: Konrad Adenauer Stiftung.

Chehabi, H. (1990), *Iranian politics and religious modernism: The liberation movement of Iran under the Shah and Khomeini.* London: I. B. Tauris.

Cooper, J. (1998), 'The limits of the sacred: The epistemology of 'Abd al-Karim Soroush', in J. Cooper, R. Nettler & M. Mahmoud (eds.), *Islam and modernity: Muslim intellectuals respond,* 38-56. London/New York: I. B. Tauris.

Dabashi, H. (1993), *Theology of discontent: The ideological foundation of the Islamic Revolution in Iran.* New York: New York University Press.

Ehteshami, A. (1995), *After Khomeini: The Iranian Second Republic.* London: Routledge.

Farhi, F. (2003), 'The politics of reform in the Islamic Republic of Iran', in S. Akbarzadeh & A. Saeed (eds.), *Islam and political legitimacy,* 50-69. London: Routledge Curzon.

Faghfoory, M. H. (1993), 'The impact of modernization on the Ulama in Iran: 1925-1941', *Iranian Studies* 26(3/4): 276-312.

Ghamari-Tabrizi, B. (2004), 'Contentious public religion: Two conceptions of Islam in Revolutionary Iran. Ali Shari'ati and Abdolkarim Soroush', *International Sociology* 19(4): 504-523.

Haeri, S. (1989), *Law of desire: Temporary marriage in Iran.* London: I. B. Tauris.

Hinchcliffe, D. (1968), 'The Iranian Family Protection Act', *International and Comparative Law Quarterly* 17: 516-521.

Hooglund, E. (1982), *Land and revolution in Iran 1960-1980.* Austin: University of Texas Press.

Jahanbakhsh, F. (2001), *Islam, democracy and religious modernism (1953-2000), from Bazargan to Sorush.* Leiden: Brill.

Jalaiepour, H. (2003), 'Religious intellectuals and political action in the reform movement', in Negin Nabavi (ed.), *Intellectual trends in twentieth century Iran: A critical survey,* 136-146. Gainesville: University of Florida Press. See also http://www.drsoroush.com.

Kamali, M. H. (1989), 'Sources, nature and objectives of Shari'ah', *Islamic Quarterly* 33: 215-235.

Keddie, N. (ed.) (1983), *Religion and politics in Iran: Shi'ism from quietism to revolution.* New Haven: Yale University Press.

Kurzman, C. (ed.) (1998), *Liberal Islam: A sourcebook.* New York: Oxford University Press.

Kurzman, C. (2001), 'Critics within: Islamic scholars protest against the Islamic state in Iran', *International Journal of Politics, Culture and Society* 15: 341-359.

Lambton, A. K. S. (1964), 'A reconsideration of the position of the marja' al-taqlid and the religious institution', *Studia Islamica* 20: 115-135.

Martin, V. (2000), *Creating an Islamic state: Khomeini and the making of the new Iran.* London: Tauris.

Mayer, A.E. (2000), 'The universality of human rights: Lessons from the Republic of Iran', *Social Research* 67(2): 519-536.

Mehrpoor, H. (1995), *Didgah-haye jadid dar masa'el-e hoquqi* (New perspectives in legal issues). Tehran: Ettela'at (1374).

Mehrpoor, H. (2001), *The Civil Code of Iran.* Tehran: Daneshvar.

Menashri, D. (1992), 'The domestic power struggle and the fourth Iranian majles elections', *Orient* 33(3): 387-408.

Mir-Hosseini, Z. (1993), *Marriage on trial: A study of Islamic law, Iran and Morocco compared.* London: I. B. Tauris (2nd edition 2000).

Mir-Hosseini, Z. (1996), 'Divorce, veiling and feminism in post-Khomeini Iran', in H. Afshar (ed.), *Women and politics in the Third World*, 142-170. London: Routledge.

Mir-Hosseini, Z. (1999), 'Family law iii. In modern Persia', *Encyclopedia Iranica* 9: 192-196.

Mir-Hosseini, Z. (2002), 'The conservative-reformist conflict over women's rights in Iran', *International Journal of Politics, Culture and Society* 16(1): 37-53.

Mir-Hosseini, Z. (2007a), 'When a woman's hurt becomes an injury: "Hardship" as grounds for divorce in Iran', *Hawwa: Journal of Women in the Middle East and the Islamic World* 5 (1): 111-126.

Mir-Hosseini, Z. (2007b), 'How the door of ijtihad was opened and closed: A comparative analysis of recent family law reform in Iran and Morocco', *Washington & Lee Law Review* 64(4): 1499-1511.

Mir-Hosseini, Z. & R. Tapper (2006), *Islam and democracy in Iran: Eshkevari and the quest for reform.* London: I. B. Tauris.

Mohammadi, M. (2008), *Judicial reform and reorganization in 20th century Iran: State-building, modernization and islamicization.* London: Routledge.

Mohaqqeq-Damad, S. M. (1986), *Barrasi-ye feqhi-ye hoquq-e khanevadeh* (Jurisprudential investigation of family law). Tehran: Nashr-e Olum-e Ensani [1365].

Mokhtari, S. (2004), 'The search for human rights within an Islamic framework in Iran', *The Muslim World* 94: 469-479.

Momen, M. (1985), *An introduction to Shi'i Islam: The history and doctrines of Twelver Shi'is.* New Haven: Yale University Press.

Montazeri, H. 'A. (1988-1990), *Dirasat fi wilayat al-faqih wa-fiqh al-dawlat al-islamiyah* (four volumes). Qom: Dar al-Fikr [1367-1369]; Persian edition, *Mabani-ye feqhi-e hokumat-e eslami* (Jurisprudential bases of Islamic government) (three volumes). Tehran: Keyhan [1368-1370].

Moslem, M. (2002), *Factional politics in post-Khomeini Iran.* Syracuse: Syracuse University Press.

Mottahedeh, R. (1985), *The mantle of the Prophet: Religion and politics in Iran.* London: Chatto & Windus.

Rahami, M. (2005), 'Development of criminal justice in the Iranian post revolutionary Penal Code', *European Journal of Criminal Justice* 13-14: 585-602.

Rahnema, A. (1998), *An Islamic utopian: A political biography of Ali Shari'ati.* London: I. B. Tauris.

Ramazani, N. (1993), 'Women in Iran: The revolutionary ebb and flow', *Middle East Journal* 47: 409-428.

Sachedina, A. (1988), *The just ruler in Shi'ite Islam: The comprehensive authority of the jurist in Imamite jurisprudence.* Oxford: Oxford University Press.

Sadri, M. (2001), 'Sacral defense of secularism: The political theologies of Soroush, Shabestari, and Kadivar', *International Journal of Politics, Culture and Society* 15(2): 257-270.

Safa'i, S. H. & A. Emami (1995), *Hoquq-e khanevadeh, Vol 2: Qarabat va nasab va asar-e an* (Family Law, vol. 2: Kinship and paternity and their effects). Tehran: Tehran University Press [1374].

Schirazi, A. (1997), *The constitution of Iran: Politics and the state in the Islamic Republic.* London: I. B. Tauris.

Sial, O. (2006), 'A guide to the legal system of the Islamic Republic of Iran', see http://www.nyulawglobal.org/globalex/iran.htm.

Soroush, A. (2000), *Reason, freedom and democracy in Islam: Essential writings of 'Abdolkarim Soroush*, translated and edited by M. Sadri & A. Sadri. Oxford: Oxford University Press.

Terman, R. (2007), *Stop stoning forever campaign: A report*, see http://www.stop-killing.org.

Torfeh, M. (2009), 'Neither Islamic nor a republic', see http://www.guardian.co.uk/commentisfree/belief/2009/aug/29/iran-clergy-infighting-ayatollah.

Wells, M.C. (1999), 'Thermidor in the Islamic Republic of Iran: The rise of Muhammad Khatami', *British Journal of Middle Eastern Studies* 26(1): 27-39.

Zubaida, S. (1993), 'The ideological preconditions for Khomeini's doctrine of government', in his *Islam, the people and the state: Political ideas and movements in the Middle East*. London: I. B. Tauris.

Zubaida, S. (2003), *Law and power in the Islamic world*. London/New York: I. B. Tauris.

9 Sharia and national law in Pakistan[1]

Martin Lau[2]

Abstract

The creation of Pakistan in 1947 satisfied the demand of British India's Muslims for a homeland at the end of colonial rule but left unresolved the nature of the newly founded state: had it been founded to enable India's Muslims to live in accordance with Islamic law or was its primary purpose to protect them against the fate of living as a religious minority in a Hindu majority state? Until the mid 1970s, Pakistan's political elites fudged the issue by allocating a largely symbolic role to Islam in the constitutions of 1956, 1962 and 1973 but retaining the colonial legacy of Islamic family law. It was only in 1979 that the military dictator Zia ul-Haq purported to turn Pakistan into an Islamic state by imposing Islamic criminal laws and creating specialist Islamic courts empowered to strike down laws deemed contrary to Islam.

The impact of Zia's measures has been profound: despite the opposition of many of the mainstream political parties to the Zia era Islamic laws and institutions, any proposal for reform triggers popular protests, instigated by small, conservative, Islamic parties. It is mainly the country's higher judiciary which, together with the government, holds attempts at further Islamisation measures in check, and which reforms those areas of law that continue to be governed by Islamic law. The judiciary's ability to counter the forces of Islamisation reflects its growing importance as a check on governmental lawlessness and protector of human rights.

Table of contents

The independence of British India in 1947, and its subsequent partition, led to the founding of the Islamic Republic of Pakistan, a state which was itself partitioned into two parts, namely West Pakistan and East Pakistan. Following a civil war, East Pakistan declared independence and became Bangladesh in 1971. It is the former western half which retained the name Pakistan and which is the subject of this chapter. Its current population numbers close to 174 million people and is comprised of multiple ethnic groups, the main ones being Pashtun, Punjabi, Sindhi, Baloch, and Muhajir. Pakistanis are nearly all Muslim (97%), the vast majority of which are Sunni (77%) and the remainder Shia (20%). Christians, Hindus, and Parsees belong to religious minority groups (3%). Under the laws of Pakistan, members of the Ahmadiyya community are also considered to be a non-Muslim religious minority. While Urdu is the official language of Pakistan, only eight percent of the population actually speaks it as their first language. In contrast, the Punjabi (44%) and Sindhi (14%) languages are much more widely spoken. The lingua franca of the Pakistani elite and the state apparatus is English.

(Source: Bartleby 2010)

9.1 The period until 1920

From diversity to uniformity

Early history

Pakistan came into existence in 1947 but its laws and legal traditions form part of the wider history of South Asian civilisations and cultures. This history began about 40,000 years ago, when humans migrated from East Africa to North India, expanding their presence gradually to the South (Talbot 1998, Wolpert 2009). The transition from hunter-gatherers to settled communities who relied on farming, growing wheat and barley and keeping goats and sheep, occurred in the hills of Baluchistan, now part of Pakistan, around 8000 BC. Some of the symbols associated with Hinduism can be traced back to these early communities. Clay figurines of mother goddesses and humped bulls as well as phallic symbols made of stone are reminders of the ancient roots of the Hindu religion. Close to these hills, along the fertile valley of the Indus river, emerged the ancient civilisation of Harappa and Mohenjo-daru, which lasted from about 2500 to 1600 BC. Covering an area of some five million square miles, with urban centres housing up to 35,000 inhabitants, the Indus valley civilisation was based on irrigated agriculture and a commercial economy, which was interwoven with regional trade stretching as far as Sumeria (Wolpert 2009: 19).

Changes of the ecology and of the course of the Indus river lead to the decline and eventual disappearance of the Indus valley civilisation. The migration of the Aryan Indo-European people from areas around the Caspian and the Black Sea between 1500 and 1000 BC marks the beginning of the Hindu religion and ancient Hindu law. The Aryans brought to India herds of cattle and domesticated horses, as well as their own language, Sanskrit. The early Aryans did not use bricks, knew no system of writing, and the physical traces they left behind consist mainly of bronze weapons, bows and arrows. Their enduring legacy to Indian culture is their religion. An orally transmitted body of texts, known as the Rig Vedas, the books of knowledge, consisting of Sanskrit hymns, which are addressed to the Aryan gods to solicit their favours, are the oldest ingredients of Hindu religion. The texts, written down for the first time around 600 BC, also testify to the ancient origins of the Hindu caste system and the myths of epic battles, such as the Mahabharata, which continue to be prominent elements of modern Hindu and South Asian culture.

Buddhism and Jainism emerged as religious reforms of Hinduism in the fifth century BC but it took another 1200 years before Islam, South Asia's second most important religion, arrived on the Indian sub-continent. Muslim traders made contact with communities along the West Indian Malabar coast in the early seventh century CE (Engineer, 2006). The first territorial presence of Muslims was established through the conquest of Sindh by Muhammad bin Qasim, who claimed the province of Sindh in present-day Pakistan for the Umayyad Caliphate. In the tenth century Mahmud of Ghazni, in present-day Afghanistan, conquered Punjab and made it part of the Ghaznavid Empire. Another successful invasion from the North, lead by Muhammad of Ghor, lead to the formation of the Delhi Sultanate in the twelfth century. The emergence of Islamic dynasties in the northern parts of India culminated in the establishment of the Mughal empire in the sixteenth century. In the course of two centuries the Mughals created an empire which encompassed most of the northern parts of India and whose administrative structures proved so efficient that many of them were adopted by the East India Company, when in the course of the seventeenth century it displaced, and eventually, in 1857, removed the Mughal dynasty from power.

The impact of colonialism

The arrival of the British, in the shape of the East India Company, in the seventeenth century forms the starting point of any discussion of modern Indian and Pakistani law. The origins of the system of courts, legal procedures and much of the substantive law of both India and Pakistan can be traced back to British rule. The lasting influence of the legacy of colonialism on the legal systems of India and Pakistan can, however, not obscure the fact, that the colonial legal system emerged in a process of interaction with indigenous laws and cultures. This interaction becomes most visible in Pakistan's family laws, which originated from a colonial attempt to apply Islamic law to its Muslim subjects (Kolff 1992, Menski 1997).

Prior to the arrival of the British, South Asian laws reflected the political, economic, religious and cultural diversity of the Indian sub-continent. The spectrum of political organisations ranged from the centralised system of administration of the Moghul empire, powerful Hindu and Sikh kingdoms and small princely states ruled by Hindu and Muslim dynasties, to small, self-governing communities of hunter-gatherers in India's mountains and jungles. The mainstay of the pre-industrial economies of India was agricultural, carried out under diverse systems of land tenures and holdings and as a result the main revenue of most Indian rulers was derived from imposing tax on land ownership. Regional trade, the production of goods such as cotton, and the presence of highly skilled craftsmen and artisans in India's busy cities meant that in the seventeenth century, India's economies and wealth were on par with that of many European countries.

The legal cultures of pre-colonial India matched the diversity found in all other areas of life. Despite this diversity, it is possible to identify religion as an important element of India's legal traditions. Both Islam and Hinduism contained within themselves a rich body of legal precepts and prescriptions, and equally many rulers defined and legitimised their power with reference to religion. Religion also played an important part in creating and maintaining social order, for instance in the form of the Hindu caste system, or in guiding the conduct of individual believers. Legal culture was also greatly influenced by locality: the further a community was removed from a centre of political power, the weaker the writ of the ruler. The absence of centralised political power or its inability or unwillingness to impose a unified legal system on the populace meant that in many areas, from rural areas to urban communities, localised forms of dispute resolution were the norm rather than the exception. These local fora for dispute resolution could coalesce around religious elements, as for instance in the case of Hindu caste councils and *panchayats*, or around tribal allegiance, such as the *jirgas*, i.e. councils of elders of some of North India's Muslim communities. The rules applied by this diverse mix of legal institutions was equally diverse. Whilst religious norms were important, they were often supplemented by local customs. As a result, the notion of parts of India governed by Hindu or Islamic law was a colonial invention, never matched by legal reality. Diversity and fluidity were the hallmarks of pre-colonial legal cultures, with religion playing an important but not overriding role (Menski 1997).

The East India Company (EIC) added another element to this rich mix of legal traditions, but in no way displaced them. The persistence of India's legal traditions in the face of conquest was a result of a combination of reasons. First and foremost was the way in which India was conquered: the EIC had began its presence in India as a trading company, establishing trading posts, the so-called 'factories', along India's coastline. Whilst its Charter of 1600 allowed it to make and administer laws in its 'territories', this power was confined to the areas directly controlled and administered by the EIC itself (Ali 2000: 141).[3] As a result, the EIC applied its own laws only to the trading posts themselves, but recognised local laws and cultures outside the so-called presidency towns of Madras, Bombay and Calcutta. The confinement of English and EIC-made laws to these presidencies also had practical reasons. Whilst the EIC was able to establish political control over an ever increasing portion of India's population, it lacked the means to impose its own legal system on them. Indeed, attempting to do so could have endangered its hold over a growing number of subjects as well its ability to generate a profit for its shareholders and employees.

By the beginning of the nineteenth century the EIC controlled about two thirds of India. A trading company had become India's most powerful ruler, administering and governing a vast territory populated by an equally vast diversity of people, cultures, and religions. In this period of conquest, Indian laws had not remained untouched. The EIC primary purpose and function, namely to make money, had a direct impact on two distinct areas of law. Firstly, there was the need to maintain law and order. This was achieved by creating a body of criminal laws, often modelled on English precedents, designed to contain any challenges to its rule (Fisch 1983). Secondly, there was the need to make money. The acquisition of large tracts of land and people changed the economic character of the EIC. No longer was it merely a trading company but also a collector of land revenue, having assumed this power from the rulers it had displaced. The collection of land revenue made it imperative to identify in a legally enforceable manner an individual who was liable to pay tax for a particular piece of land. Equally, the legal system had to be able to adjudicate disputes over the ownership of land. The colonial legal system thus emerged in a piecemeal and disjointed fashion, being propelled by the economic and political concerns of the EIC.

Religion, law and Anglo-Mohammadan law

At least in theory, the EIC left undisturbed the laws and legal institutions which were not of direct interest to its rule. This is reflected in the declaration of Warren Hastings, the first Governor-General of the Bengal Presidency, in 1772, according to which in the courts of the EIC 'in all suits regarding inheritance, marriage, caste and other religious usages and institutions, the laws of the Koran with respect to the Mohammedans and those of the shasters with respect to the Gentoos [Hindus] shall invariably adhered to; on all such occasions the Moulvies or Brahmins shall respectively attend to expound the law, and they shall sign the report and assist in passing the decree' (Rudolph, S. and Rudolph, L. 2001). The notion of a mixed legal system, consisting of a unified hierarchy of colonial courts that administered a diverse system of substantive laws, depending on the area of law and the religion of the parties at issue, would, at first glance, suggest that at least in the area of family law, the indigenous laws of India's population would survive the impact of colonialism intact.

In practice, however, the arrival of colonial courts, staffed by British judges and administered by a colonial government, left a deep impact on the many manifestations of India's indigenous family laws. The courts of the EIC were popular with the Indian population, so much so that in the course of the first half of the nineteenth century many were over-burdened with the number of suits filed by the colonial subjects and a system of court fees was introduced to stem the flood of litigation. The popularity of colonial courts for the adjudication of a wide range of disputes, including those concerned with areas of law to be decided in accordance with Hindu or Islamic law, posed a challenge to judges who had no knowledge of either Hindu or Islamic laws and jurisprudence. Until 1864, judges of the EIC courts were assisted by 'experts' in Hindu and Islamic law; invariably locally prominent Hindu priests and Muslims learned in classical Islamic law would render opinions on the applicable religious law. As a result, elements of local, customary law were gradually replaced with a more rigid, orthodox, text-based interpretation of Hindu and Islamic law. This process of replacement was aided by the common law background of the colonial judiciary who were used to a system of binding precedence and as a result relied on previously decided cases whenever questions of indigenous law came before them.

In addition, there was a growing number of translations of treatises on both Hindu and Islamic law, which were increasingly used by judges to determine the 'personal law' applicable to a dispute. By 1864, the availability of a body of case-law and textbooks was judged sufficient to be able to dispense with the services of the indigenous experts of

Hindu and Islamic law: since then judges themselves determined, interpreted and applied the religiously based system of personal laws.

By the middle of the nineteenth century the colonial legal system, which had emerged more by accident than long-term planning, was marked by three distinctive features. Firstly, it was built on a hierarchy of colonial, 'modern', courts, whose judgements were enforced by a powerful state. Secondly, it incorporated two sets of laws, namely religiously based family laws and uniform civil and criminal laws. Lastly, the legal system was overseen by a colonial government, that assumed 'a superior reformist posture within the framework of a "holding operation" to keep the peace' (Dhavan 2001: 308.). The reformist stance of the colonial government was a cautious one, with some practices, such as *sati*[4] and child marriage, being outlawed (Ferguson 2003: 134). The reluctance to interfere with religious beliefs of the indigenous population, and hence with their religiously based family laws, was re-enforced by the uprising of 1857.

The so-called 'mutiny' of 1857 had been preceded by the gradual infusion of Christian missionary zeal in the policies of the EIC. Whilst the eighteenth century had been one of unashamed lust for profit, the first decades of the nineteenth century witnessed the rise of the Evangelical movement in Britain, which would also make its presence felt in the India of the EIC. The policy of non-interference with indigenous religions softened and the ban on Christian missionaries working in India was lifted in 1813. The missionaries's success in converting Indians was limited, but their impact on EIC policy was very visible. Laws were enacted to promote conversions, such as the Caste Disabilities Removal Act 1850, which preserved the rights of inheritance under the personal law that a convert had held prior to conversion, and campaigns against 'barbaric' practices, for instance female infanticide, were prominently pursued. The 1857 uprising, triggered by the refusal of Indian soldiers to bite off the ends of newly introduced cartridges that had been treated with animal fat, was interpreted as a reaction against a British plan to Christianise India.

The end of the 1857 uprising not only spelt the end of the Mughal empire but also that of EIC rule: in 1858 India became a crown colony of British India. The mutineers had proclaimed that they were motivated by a desire to protect Islam and to rid India of infidels. In order to prevent another mutiny, Queen Victoria publicly proclaimed that the crown would 'abstain from all interference with the religious belief or worship of any of our subjects, on pain of our highest displeasure' and 'that generally, in framing and administering the law, due regard be paid to the ancient rights, usages, and customs of India'.[5]

Islamic law and political identity

The official policy of non-interference with the religions and customs of the colonial subjects was accompanied by conscious efforts to modernise the laws of British India. Over the next four decades an all-encompassing codification of all areas of law, except those concerned with the personal laws of the native population, resulted in a set of statutory laws which to this day apply in an almost unchanged form in the successor nations of British India, i.e. Pakistan, India and Bangladesh. First came the Indian Penal Code 1860, followed by the Contract Act 1872 and the Evidence Act 1872. Around the turn of the nineteenth century two acts were enacted governing the procedures to be applied in criminal and civil trials.[6]

The continuation of the system of personal laws, in line with Queen Victoria's proclamation, created not only distinct bodies of Hindu and Islamic law but also contributed to the emergence of distinct Hindu and Muslim political communities. The latter was not just the outcome of unequal legal treatment, but also of a conscious colonial policy of 'divide and rule', meant to prevent a repeat of the rebellion of 1857. Hindus were favoured when it came to employment in the Indian civil service, being regarded as better educated and more willing to cooperate with the colonial state. Muslims, on the other hand, faced a crisis of self-confidence. The defeat of 1857 had resulted in the dismantling of the Mughal empire, the execution or banishment of many prominent members of the *ulama*, and the relegation of Muslims to a community distrusted by its colonial rulers. In its reaction to this crisis, the Muslim community was divided in outlook but united in method: both conservative and progressive saw education as the key to regaining their pre-1857 status. Conservative Muslims founded religious seminaries, chief among them the Deobandi school near Delhi, which used British educational methods, such as a sequential curriculum, organised classes and paid teaching staff, in order to reform the Muslim community. Their objective was not participation in the colonial enterprise but the moral reform of Muslims, encouraging them to shed un-Islamic practices and to adhere to a literal interpretation of the Koran. The liberal elements amongst the Muslim community also addressed the issue of education, but aimed at equipping young Muslims with the means to compete with their Hindu counterparts by acquiring Western knowledge and skills. Sir Sayyid Ahmed Khan's Islamic University in Aligarh, founded in 1874, became the focal point for the modernisation of Islamic thought, educating a generation of young Muslims, who would, in the twentieth century, become ardent supporters of the Indian national movement.

The British policy of divide and rule became most visible in the system of separate electorates for Muslims and Hindus, which was a feature of all forms of representative self-government conceded by the colonial government. The policy fostered the conviction of Muslim political elites that they were different and separate from the Hindu subjects of the colony. By the late 1930s, this conviction matured into the belief that the Muslims of British India were not just in terms of religion different from Hindus, but constituted a distinct nation, entitled to establish a country of their own as and when the British granted independence to India.

The grant of very limited rights of self-governance at the local level at the end of the nineteenth century was not sufficient to stem the rising tide of the Indian national movement. From its inception, the movement was divided along religious lines, albeit that the two communities initially joined hands in their campaign for self-government. The Indian National Congress, founded in 1885, was in theory a secular body and open to all of India's creeds and religions. Nevertheless, Hindus formed the vast majority of its members. Founded by intellectuals, lawyers and social reformers, it was transformed into a mass movement under the leadership of Mahatma Gandhi, who joined the Indian National Congress upon his return from South Africa in 1916. In 1906, Muslims followed suit, founding a representative body of their own, the All India Muslim League. Many of the founding members were inspired by the modernistic outlook of Sir Sayyed Ahmed Khan, the founder of the Aligarh Islamic University. Its initial aims were modest: rather than asking for self-government the Muslim League resolved to further 'the protection and advancement of our political rights and interests, but without prejudice to the traditional loyalty of Musalmans to the Government, and goodwill to our Hindu neighbours'. The Muslim League soon became an important mouthpiece of the Muslim community, albeit that it never appealed to British India's conservative *ulama*, who regarded it as a secular organisation, unlikely to promote the cause of Islam.

The first two decades of the Indian national movement were marked by a substantial degree of collaboration between the Muslim League and the Indian National Congress. The two organisations represented different constituencies, with the Indian National Congress managing to transform itself into mass movement representing not only intellectuals but also the largely Hindu peasantry. The Muslim League attracted in the main Muslim professionals, especially those who lived in Hindu majority provinces. The early affinities of the two organisations is best exemplified in the person of Muhammad Ali Jinnah, the founder of Pakistan. Jinnah had started his political career as a member of the Indian National Congress, which he joined in 1886, becoming a member of the Muslim League only in 1913. Until 1920 he was simultaneously a member of Congress, and, from 1916 onwards, the leader of the Muslim League. Both organisations stood united in their goal of 'home rule' and despite representing different communities, they entered into express alliances to further the cause of self-government. In 1916, the Muslim League and the Indian National Congress entered into the 'Congress-League Joint Scheme of Reforms', better known as the Lucknow Pact and issued a joint statement calling on the British to respect the right to self-determination of the Indian population. Congress and Muslim League agreed to share power in the executive and legislative assemblies according to a formula which gave Hindus two-third and Muslims one-third representation in these bodies. On religious measures, the Lucknow Pact stipulated that they could only be undertaken if they had the support of at least three-fourth of the members of the concerned community. In response, the British conceded some reforms, for instance extending employment opportunities in its civil service and allowing for limited forms of self-government at the local and provincial level. But these initiatives did little to mitigate popular grievances. The basis of the discontent – the colonial domination – remained unchanged.

Political violence in the form of terrorism in the 1910s and 1920s was met by ever harsher measures adopted by the colonial authorities to restore and maintain law and order. The most infamous of these measures was the draconian Rowlatt Act in 1919 which dispensed with many of the procedural safeguards of the criminal law in the case of terror related offences. Muhammad Ali Jinnah resigned from the Imperial Legislative Assembly when the Rowlatt Act was passed by the government majority in the face of the united opposition of its Indian members, who had voted against it.[7] The First World War, in which the British fought against Turkish Muslims, produced the last occasion for Muslim-Hindu unity. Under Gandhi's leadership the Indian National Congress supported the Khilafat (Caliphate) Movement (1919-1925), which campaigned for the protection of the Ottoman empire. The Khilafat movement, concerned with an Islamic cause, also marked the first active participation of the traditional *ulama* in the independence movement, which, for the first time, used Islam as a symbol of political mass communication (Esposito 1998: 93). The Muslim-Hindu entente gave rise to unprecedented manifestations of communal harmony and unity, perhaps best illustrated by an event which occurred on 4 April 1919, when a Hindu, Swami Shraddhanand, was asked by a delegation of Muslims to address about 30,000 Muslim worshippers, who had assembled in the grounds of Delhi's main mosque, the Jama Masjid. He accepted the invitation, recited from the Vedas and received thunderous applause (Singh 2009: 110). The defeat of the Ottoman empire in 1924 and the subsequent abolition of the Caliphate brought the Hindu-Muslim entente to an end.

9.2 The period from 1920 until 1965

The realisation of Islamic nationalism

The demand for Pakistan

The 1920s were marked by an increase of communal tension as well as distrust between the leadership of Congress and Muslim League. In 1920, Jinnah resigned as a member of Congress in protest against Gandhi's civil disobedience movement, which he regarded as a dangerously populist and illegal campaign, likely to lead to anarchy and a breakdown of law and order. Under Jinnah's leadership the Muslim League assumed the role as the sole representative of British India's Muslims in opposition to Congress, which relentlessly pursued the ultimate goal of home rule and independence on the platform of mass action and agitation. The colonial government reacted with a combination of repressive measures, including attempts to silence Congress by imprisoning its leadership, and political concessions, such as the Government of India Act 1935, which granted self-government at provincial level, albeit under the supervision of the central government.

Provincial elections under the 1935 Act spelt the end of any hope for a resumption of the Hindu-Muslim entente: Congress won a resounding victory in the Hindu majority provinces but refused to share power with the Muslim League. To Jinnah, this stance amounted to proof that Congress could not be trusted to share power with Muslims as and when British India was granted independence. From then onwards, the Muslim League's demand for independence was a qualified one: if there was to be self-government, it had to take shape in a form which would protect Muslims against a Hindu majority. By 1940 this objective had matured into the two nation-theory: Hindus and Muslims were so different in character that they could never form one nation. According to Jinnah, the creation of an independent state, to be called Pakistan, was the only way to protect Muslims against the prospect of living under Hindu rule.

The claim that Muslims constituted a separate nation made it imperative for Muslim politicians to create a distinct Muslim political and also legal identity. The latter was threatened by the recognition and application of local customs by British Indian courts in the area of family law. Whilst in principle the large corpus of reported decisions dealing with Islamic family law was based on the application of Quran and Sunnah – in line with the resolutions of Warren Hastings in 1772 and Queen

Victoria in 1858 – in practice the Islamic family law produced by colonial courts was far more amorphous. In many cases, especially those concerned with disputes over land, colonial courts had also recognised local customs as the applicable law. This posed a challenge to the Muslim League: if Muslims were to be governed by local customs, which were by definition determined and proven by reference to the customary usages prevalent in a locality, how could they be distinguished from the non-Muslims of the same area? Did a Muslim loose his identity as a Muslim by ordering his life in accordance with laws which were not in any way connected to his religious identity as Muslim but were frequently based on Hindu legal traditions, such as the exclusion of females from the right to inherit from the estate of the deceased?

Muslim personal law

The demands for an Islamisation of British India's family laws provided the answer to these questions: Muslims had to be governed by Islamic law if they were to form a community which was distinct and separate from their Hindu counterparts (Williams 2006: 83-91). Success came in 1937, when the Muslim members of the Imperial Legislative Assembly passed the Muslim Personal Law (Shariat) Application Act 1937. Section 2 of the Act provides that:

> Notwithstanding any customs or usage to the contrary, in all questions (save questions relating to agricultural land) regarding intestate succession, special property of females, including personal property inherited or obtained under contract or gift or any other provision of Personal Law, marriage, dissolution of marriage, including talaq, ila, zihar, lian, khula and mubaraat, maintenance, dower, guardianship, gifts, trusts and trust properties, and wakfs (other than charities and charitable institutions and charitable and religion endowments) the rule of decision in cases where the parties are Muslims shall be the Muslim Personal Law (Shariat).

The 1937 Act satisfied the aspiration of British India's Muslims to be governed by a body of family laws which was distinctly and recognisably Islamic. However, it was not an unqualified success: any question pertaining to agricultural law was excluded from the application of the Act and hence could, if the parties so desired, be governed by local customs. In practice, this often involved the application of rules of inheritance which departed from the Islamic law of succession in that they excluded females from the inheritance.[8]

A second measure to foster a distinct legal identity of British India's Muslims was the passage of the Dissolution of Muslim Marriages Act 1939. The 1939 Act enumerates the grounds on which a Muslim woman can obtain a decree for the dissolution of her marriage. Viewed from a gender perspective the 1939 Act can be regarded as a measure to improve the legal position of Muslim wives. However, the main purpose of the 1939 Act was a political one, namely to prevent Muslim wives from dissolving their marriage by converting to Hinduism. Section 4 of the 1939 Act provides that 'The renunciation of Islam by a married Muslim woman on her conversion to a faith other than Islam shall not by itself operate to dissolve her marriage'.[9]

The purification of Islamic family law and the creation of a distinct legal identity of Muslims in the closing years of colonial India can be regarded as the first phase of the Islamisation of laws in Pakistan. In 1947, when Pakistan came into existence, the country inherited a body of Muslim personal laws, commonly referred to as Anglo-Mohammadan law, which was in the process of being returned to the principles of classical Islamic law. The birth of Pakistan in 1947 was not the outcome of demand for the creation of an Islamic state, but implicit in the demand for a homeland for British India's Muslims was a promise that Muslims would be governed by Islamic family laws not based on local, and potentially un-Islamic, customs and usages, but the principles of sharia.

From today's perspective somewhat counter-intuitively, the majority of conservative and orthodox Islamic parties and movements refused to join Jinnah's call for the creation of Pakistan, instead aligning themselves with the Indian National Congress or staying out of politics altogether. Although Jinnah himself avoided any firm promise to create an Islamic state, the Muslim League regularly used religious appeals in its provincial elections campaigns during the 1940s, and it also endeavored to bring Islamic scholars into its ranks. However, these attempts were only partially successful. In October 1945 the Muslim League managed to convene a conference in Calcutta of several prominent members of the *ulama*. The outcome of this conference was the founding of the All-India Jamiaat-i Ulema-i Islam, which organised party conferences in support of Pakistan (Pirzada 2000: 10). Its president, Allama Uthmani, later became a member of the Pakistan Constituent Assembly, having run on the Muslim League ticket in the elections of 1946.

1947: The creation of Pakistan

Pakistan emerged as an independent state on 15 August 1947, the same day as its neighbour India.[10] As a matter of law, the new state owed its existence to the provisions of a British act of parliament, the Indian

Independence Act of 1947. This act not only granted independence, but also determined the shape of the new nation's legal system immediately following independence, providing in section 18(3) for the continued validity of all colonial laws. For a British parliament to make provisions for the content of a legal system of an independent state would seem to run counter to the very notion of sovereignty, were it not for section 6 of the same act, which provided in clear terms that 'The legislature of each of the new Dominions shall have full power to make laws for that Dominion, including laws having extra-territorial operation'.

Having been granted full powers to pass any law, Pakistan – at least as a matter of law – was a fully independent and sovereign state at the stroke of midnight of 15 August 1947. In actual practice, however, it was section 18(3), rather than section 6, of the Indian Independence Act that would occupy the more prominent role in the development of Pakistan's legal system. For almost ten years, until the adoption of the Constitution of 1956, the country was governed by the provisions of the 1935 Government of India Act, as modified by the Indian Independence Act, and any law passed by the Constituent Assembly,[11] which also acted as the country's legislature during this long period of transition. The odd result was that Pakistan, having come into existence after a long and hard struggle to establish a homeland for India's Muslims, continued to be governed by a legal system that had been adopted with hardly any modifications from its colonial past. There was no *tabula rasa*, with the slate being wiped clean of the vestiges of colonialism at the earliest opportunity following independence, to be replaced by Islamic law, or an Islamic form of government, in whatever shape.

Was the decision to continue to be governed by colonial laws made by default, or had this result been planned by the founders of Pakistan? This question may seem academic, given that Pakistan has been independent for over sixty years, were it not for the fact that there is still no political consensus on the role of Islam in the legal system. The lack of consensus becomes visible in the frictions and controversies that accompany any measure designed to introduce even minor changes to the Islamic criminal laws promulgated in 1979, or in the debates over the introduction of an Islamic banking and finance system. On one side of the spectrum are those who argue that Pakistan had been founded as an 'ideological state', to be governed by Islamic law. From this perspective, any attempt to change this legacy would amount to a denial of the legitimacy of the state itself, a betrayal of those Muslims who had been willing to sacrifice their lives for the creation of an Islamic state. Conversely, there are those who argue that although Pakistan was founded as a homeland for the Muslims of British India, it was conceived as a secular rather than a religious state (Metcalf 2004: 21). Writing in 1955, some eight years after Pakistan gained independence,

G.W. Choudhury observed that the failure to adopt a constitution was due to the fact that 'the framers of the constitution were faced with the problem of producing a document that would be satisfactory to secularists and sectarians alike' (Choudhury 1955: 591).

The framing of Pakistan's constitution: the Objectives Resolution

The Objectives Resolution was the first product of the Constituent Assembly of Pakistan and was meant to guide the drafting of Pakistan's first constitution. In structure and tone it mirrored that of India's Objectives Resolution,[12] but its references to Islam were regarded controversial, especially amongst the non-Muslim members of the Constituent Assembly.[13] From today's perspective, the discussions surrounding the adoption of Objectives Resolution have a certain air of *déjà vu*, given that the principle arguments, and tensions, have remained the same over the past 60 years: is Pakistan's legal order a secular one, with the state taking no interest in the religions of its citizens apart from allowing them to practice them? Or is Pakistan an Islamic state, which gives preferential treatment to its Muslim citizens?

The main concern for non-Muslims was not the promise that Muslims should be enabled to order their lives in accordance with Islam – after all this had been the colonial practice as visible in the system of personal laws for both Muslims and Hindus – but the Objectives Resolution's opening sentence which provided that: 'Whereas sovereignty over the entire universe belongs to God Almighty alone and the authority which He has delegated to the State of Pakistan through its people for being exercised within the limits prescribed by Him is a sacred trust; This Constituent Assembly representing the people of Pakistan resolves to frame a constitution for the sovereign independent State of Pakistan.' The non-Muslim members of the Constituent Assembly claimed that the Objectives Resolution envisaged the creation of an Islam state and was in breach of the promises made by the founder of Pakistan, Mohammed Ali Jinnah, who had died prematurely on 11 September 1948 and who had taken no part in the drafting of the Resolution. His vision, they charged, had been to create a secular state in which religion was to be regarded as an entirely private matter. The leader of Pakistan's Congress Party, Chattopadhaya, referred to his heritage as follows:

> Now what will be the result of this Resolution? I sadly remind myself of the great words of the Quaid-i-Azam that in state affairs the Hindu will cease to be a Hindu; the Muslim shall cease to be a Muslim. But alas, so soon after his demise what you do is that you virtually declare a State religion! You are determined

> to create a *Herrenvolk*. It was perhaps bound to be so, when unlike the Quaid-i-Azam—with whom I was privileged to be associated for a great many years in the Indian National Congress—you felt your incapacity to separate politics from religion, which the modern world so universally does. You could not get over the old world way of thinking. What I hear in this Resolution is not the voice of the great creator of Pakistan, the Quaid-i-Azam (may his soul rest in peace), nor even that of the Prime Minister of Pakistan, the Honourable Mr. Liaquat Ali Khan, but of the *Ulemas* of the land.[14]

The concerns of the Hindu members of the Constituent Assembly were to prove entirely correct, albeit that the erosion of the rights of minorities and the creation of an Islamic state took place over a long period of time. Pakistan's first constitution was only completed and adopted in 1956. Until then, the laws inherited from British India served as a temporary constitution and constituted the bulk of the new country's substantive laws.[15]

The Constitution of 1956

Having adopted the Objectives Resolution against the wishes of its minority members, the Constituent Assembly embarked on the task of drafting the constitution. It turned out to be an arduous and controversial undertaking. In the period from 1949 and 1956 no less than three draft constitutions were prepared and the Constituent Assembly itself was dismissed and re-constituted on a different basis in 1954. The demarcation of the role of Islam in the new constitutional order was one reason for the slowness, but a more important cause of the delay was the difficulty to unite West and East Pakistan. The two units of Pakistan were separated by more than one thousand miles – by ship it was quicker to get from Karachi to Marseille than to Chittagong – and the physical divide was matched by differences in culture, language, customs, and economic conditions.

A first draft constitution was produced in September 1950. Its Islamic provisions were purely symbolic: the Objectives Resolution was to serve as a preamble, and there was to be 'compulsory teaching of the Holy Quran to the Muslims' (Choudhury 1967: 34). Under pressure from an increasingly vociferous Islamic opposition the subsequent drafts of the constitution incorporated the principle that the laws of Pakistan should be in accordance with Islam. Two possible models emerged to fulfill this requirement. Firstly, the creation of a mechanism of judicial review which would allow the higher courts to strike down laws deemed not to be in accordance with Islam. In the alternative, the obligation to make the body of substantive laws conform with Islam could be imposed on the law-makers themselves, i.e. parliament.[16]

The second draft constitution, presented to the Pakistani public in December 1952 adopted the latter approach. Its Islamic provisions were elaborate: a chapter on 'Directive Principles of State Policy' enjoined the state to eliminate *riba*,[17] to prohibit 'drinking, gambling and prostitution in all their various forms', to promote and maintain Islamic moral standards, to promote the understanding of Islam, and to bring 'the existing laws into conformity with the Islamic principles' (Choudhry 1967: 27). None of these directives could be enforced in a court of law, but the draft constitution provided in a separate chapter, headed 'Procedure for Preventing Legislation Repugnant to the Quran and the Sunnah', a mechanism to ensure that all legislation was in accordance with Islam. This mechanism envisaged the setting up of a 'Board consisting of not more than five persons well versed in Islamic Laws' (Choudhry 1967: 27), which would examine a law on the basis of Islam. Its recommendations could be overturned by a simple majority of a joint sitting of the two houses of parliament. Thus, the Islamic repugnancy clause only applied to prospective laws but left the legacy of colonial laws undisturbed.

While these provisions satisfied the Islamists, the second draft constitution sparked protests from West Pakistan, which took objection to the parity envisaged by the draft. The controversies and disputes surrounding the delicate matter of the Islamic character of the newly founded state were matched by an equally serious disagreement about the relations between East and West Pakistan. The former was the more populous of the two units, and if ever there were national elections based on an adult franchise, East Pakistan's politicians would in all likelihood be in control of the government of Pakistan.[18] The attempts to reconcile the conflicting interests and jealousies between East and West Pakistan in a constitutional document proved to be a major stumbling block on the road towards a constitution. A third draft constitution was framed by the Constituent Assembly in the course of 1953 and 1954. Intensely watched by the world press, the Constituent Assembly reconvened on 7 October 1953, and a month later, on 7 November 1953, the first legally binding decision was taken, though in the absence of the Hindu members, who had walked out in protest: Pakistan became an 'Islamic Republic'. A year later, on 6 October 1954, the Constituent Assembly adopted the third draft constitution. It retained the requirement that the legislature should not 'enact any law which is repugnant to the Holy Quran and the Sunnah' (Choudhury 1967: 199) but provided that 'the Supreme Court alone should have jurisdiction for determining whether or not a particular law is repugnant to the Holy Quran and the Sunnah'. The third draft constitution was favourably received by the

Pakistani press, and even the Jamaat-i Islami, the main Islamic party, approved of it as being in accordance with Islam. On 24 October 1954, just days before the Constituent Assembly was to reconvene, Governor General Ghulam Muhammad announced its dissolution, stating that 'the Constituent Assembly as at present constituted had lost the confidence of the people and could no longer function' (Binder 1961: 361).

A second Constituent Assembly, whose members were elected from the existing provincial legislative assemblies, approved a fourth draft constitution on 8 January 1956. This constitution was promulgated on 23 March 1956. The 1956 Constitution adopted some of the Islamic features of the first draft constitution. The Objectives Resolution became the preamble, and the Islamic provisions contained in the Directive Principles of State Policy remained largely unchanged. The same applied to the qualifications of the head of state, who had to be a Muslim, and to the repugnancy clause. The latter, however, had become wider, providing that no law should be enacted that was contrary to Islam, but also that existing legislation should be brought into conformity with the injunctions of Islam. This seemingly stringent provision was, however, rendered legally ineffective because it could not be enforced by a court. Instead, it was to be implemented by a board of experts who would report their recommendations to the National Assembly within five years. There was no obligation on the National Assembly to adopt these recommendations. This rather tame Islamisation measure, rather oddly, was approved by the religious parties, including the Jamaat-i Islami, which had by then become wary of the Supreme Court being given jurisdiction to carry out this exercise (Binder 1961: 372). Chief Justice Muhammad Munir had shown his secular credentials in his Report on the Punjab Disturbances, issued in 1954, which had roundly condemned Islamic extremism.[19]

The Constitution of 1962

The life of the 1956 Constitution ended abruptly on 7 October 1958, following a *coup d'état* instigated by General Ayub Khan, who was declared chief martial law administrator by President Iskander Mirza. None of its Islamic provisions had been implemented. The 1956 Constitution was replaced by a Laws (Continuance in Force) Order, 1958, which in turn was replaced by the Basic Democracies Order, promulgated on 27 October 1959. After four years of martial law a new constitution came into force on 1 March 1962.

The Islamic provisions of the 1962 Constitution were largely modeled on the pattern of its 1956 predecessor, but there were important differences in that many references to Islam had been omitted. Most glaring was the change in the official name of the country: Pakistan had become simply the Republic of Pakistan.[20] In the text of the Objectives Resolution as incorporated in the 1962 Constitution, the original provision that 'the authority exercisable by the people within the limits prescribed by Him is a sacred trust', was shortened to 'the authority exercisable by the people is a sacred trust', thereby removing any limitation on the legislative powers of the people. Pressure from Islamists, represented by the Jaamat-i-Islami and the Jamiat Ulema-i-Islam, forced Ayub Khan's government to pass the Constitution (First Amendment) Act 1963 which restored the original wording of the Objectives Resolution and renamed the country as 'Islamic Republic of Pakistan'.[21] Like its 1956 predecessor the 1962 Constitution made the constitutional provision that all laws should be in accordance with Islam unenforceable. Along with other Islamic provisions, it was contained in a chapter on 'Principles of Policy' and thus unenforceable. An Advisory Council of Islamic Ideology was to prepare annual reports on the Islamic legitimacy of new and existing laws, but such advice was not binding on parliament.[22] In addition, the 1962 Constitution provided for the setting up of an Islamic Research Institute,[23] which was to 'undertake Islamic research and instruction in Islam for the purpose of assisting in the reconstruction of Muslim society on a truly Islamic basis'.[24] The establishment of the Islamic Research Institute was part of a deliberate attempt to wrestle from the Islamists, chiefly Mawlana Mawdudi's Jamaat-i-Islami, the monopoly over the interpretation of Islam. Headed by Fazlur Rahman, an internationally known and respected scholar of Islam, the Islamic Research Institute propagated a modernist, rational interpretation of Islam (Rahman 1970). Ayub Khan's attempt to inculcate a modern vision of Islam was accompanied by reforms of Muslim personal law[25] and the imposition of government control over Islamic charitable trusts (Malik 1990). Throughout his tenure, Ayub Khan was locked in battle with the Jamaat-i-Islami, imprisoning its leader Mawdudi several times and attempting to dissolve the party altogether.

The period of 1962 until 1971 was marked by the war with India in 1965 over the disputed territory of Kashmir and the secession of East Pakistan. As anticipated in the purely advisory provisions of the 1962 Constitution, there was no serious attempt to implement the constitutional requirement to make all laws conform with Islam. In contrast , the 1962 Constitution protected against judicial review the most significant reform of Islamic family law ever witnessed in the Indian sub-continent, namely the Muslim Family Laws Ordinance 1961 (MFLO) (see 9.6).

The MFLO has its origins in the recommendations of the Commission on Marriage and Reform, established in 1955, which contained wide-ranging proposals to reform Muslim personal law. The MFLO reformed the law governing divorce, marriage and inheritance.

Under section 7 of the MFLO a divorce is only valid if the husband notifies both his wife and the Union Council, a local government body, of the divorce and if at the expiration of 90 days after receipt of the divorce the couple has not been reconciled. The Union Council is asked to constitute an arbitration council to assist with the efforts to prevent the dissolution of the marriage. Non-compliance with these requirements renders a divorce invalid. In respect of polygamous marriages, the MFLO requires a husband who wants to marry a second wife to obtain the permission of his first wife as well as that of the Union Council. Failure to do so does not render the polygamous marriage invalid but exposes the offender to penal sanctions and allows his first wife to obtain a divorce. In respect of inheritance law, section 4 of the MFLO allows an orphaned grandchild to inherit from his or her grandfather. All three reform measures were opposed by Islamists but given that the MFLO was promulgated in the form of an ordinance during the period of martial law, their protests were futile.

The Muslim Personal Law (Shariat) Act 1962 was the only other law passed during the Ayub Khan era which concerned Islamic law. As discussed above, this Act extended the application of the 1937 Act to agricultural land. Legislation reforming the management of Islamic trust properties in the form of the West Pakistan Auqaf Properties Ordinance 1959 was meant to weaken the influence of traditional elites and the *ulama* (Braibanti 1965: 87).

The period occupied by the 1962 Constitution also witnessed the emergence of an increasingly assertive judiciary, which insisted on its right to review the constitutional validity of all laws. However, this emphasis on the power of judicial review was not as yet linked with any programme of Islamisation but concerned the rights of the judiciary to enforce fundamental rights.[26]

9.3 The period from 1965 until 1985

The birth of Bangladesh and the Islamisation of Pakistan

The partition of Pakistan

While managing to keep the upper hand against the Islamists, Ayub Khan was not so successful in the conflict with India over the disputed territory of Kashmir. Pakistan's attempt to gain control over the Indian state of Jammu and Kashmir in the summer of 1965 quickly escalated into a full-blown war with India, which saw both countries' forces entering each other's territory. The short war, which started on 6 September 1965, and ended about two weeks later with a ceasefire, marked the beginning of the end of Ayub Khan's regime. His opponents saw in the ceasefire a humiliating defeat for Pakistan, and long-held grievances erupted in civil unrest, especially in East Pakistan. The founding of the Pakistan People's Party in 1967 served to unite popular opposition to the regime in West Pakistan, but failed to unite the country. In East Pakistan, Mujibur Rahman's Awami League dominated the political landscape with an increasingly insistent demand for provincial autonomy. On 25 March 1969, Ayub Khan resigned from office and handed over power to the army chief of staff, General Yahya Khan. The handover was in direct violation of Ayub Khan's 1962 Constitution. Yahya Khan was to rule Pakistan until December 1971. By then, East Pakistan had seceded from Pakistan in a bloody civil war to become the independent nation of Bangladesh, and Zulfikar Ali Bhutto and his Pakistan People's Party had emerged as the main political force in West Pakistan.

The Constitution 1973

Because of his party's success in West Pakistan in the 1970 elections, Zulfikar Ali was able to build political consensus for the drafting of a new constitution. In April 1972 an interim constitution was introduced, and on 14 August 1973, following an occasionally acrimonious debate, the National Assembly in its capacity as Constituent Assembly adopted a new constitution - hence referred to as 'Constitution 1973' - for what remained of Pakistan. The Jaamat-i-Islami reluctantly approved the new constitution, conceding that they did not have the means to stop its passage (Pirzada 2000: 79). At first glance the Constitution 1973 replicated the approach taken by its predecessors. The basic structure of non-justiciable constitutional provisions urging the state to bring all laws into conformity with Islam and a provision for the setting up of an advisory body on Islamic law was retained and like its predecessors the new constitution contained a separate chapter headed 'Islamic Provisions' that provided for the setting up of a Council of Islamic Ideology.[27] In line with constitutional precedent, the council had an advisory role and enjoyed no inherent jurisdiction to ensure that its recommendations were acted upon by parliament. Similarly, no law could be challenged by way of judicial review on the ground that it had been found to be repugnant to Islam by the Council of Islamic Ideology. However, the increasing influence of Islamic parties is visible in the constitution's additional references to Islam, which had been missing from the previous constitutions. Both the Prime Minister and the President had to be Muslims but the oath to be taken by them included a statement to the effect that they believed in 'the Prophethood of Muhammad (peace be upon him) as the last of the Prophets and that there can be no Prophet after him, ...'.[28] This provision was intended to prevent Ahmadis from assuming these offices. In a further affirmation of the religious foundation of the constitutional order Islam was declared the state religion.[29]

Using Islam: The Ahmadis

The Constitution 1973 shared the fate of the Constitution of 1962 in that shortly after coming into force it was amended as a result of pressure from Islamic parties. This time, however, the amendments were more than just symbolic measures of appeasement but involved the declaration of the members of the Ahmadiyya community as non-Muslims. Under the Constitution (Second Amendment) Act 1974 Ahmadis were included in the list of non-minorities for the purposes of representation in the provincial assemblies[30] and an amendment to Article 260 of the Constitution 1973 defined a Muslim as:

> A person who does not believe in the absolute and unqualified finality of the Prophethood of Muhammad (peace be upon Him), the last of the Prophets or claims to be a prophet, in any sense of the word or of any description whatsoever, after Muhammad (peace be upon Him), or recognises such a claimant as a prophet or a religious reformer, is not a Muslim for the purposes of the Constitution or Law.[31]

This constitutional amendment relegating the members of the Ahmadi community to the status of non-Muslims is evidence of two connected developments: firstly, the increasing strength of conservative Islamic parties which enabled them to control the streets under the banner of Islam and instigate large scale disturbances whenever they declared Islam to be under threat. Secondly, they reveal the growing influence of international Islamic movements in Pakistan. Additionally, the amendment also gives credence to the claim that Bhutto and his PPP exploited appeals to Islam to bolster flagging support whenever it was expedient to do so (Nasr 1994: 181-182). At first glance, the re-definition of Ahmadis as non-Muslims brought to a conclusion a demand made by Islamic parties since before independence. The use of the phrase 'finality of the Prophethood' in the new article 260 (3) was of significance, since it mirrored the name of the Council for Protecting the Finality of Prophethood (*Tahaffuz-i-Khtam-i-Nabuwawat Tehrik*), formed as early as 1952 to demand the removal of Ahmadis from the fold of Islam (Pirzada 2000: 21). Viewed from this perspective the amendment in 1974 marked the destination of a development which had been pushed by Islamic parties for two decades.

However, a closer look reveals that the country-wide agitation and disturbances of early 1974 had a new quality. The Ahmadi issue had been dormant and sitting in 'cold storage' ever since 1954 and for the preceding twenty years there had been no agitation for the exclusion of Ahmadis from the pale of Islam (Kaushik 1996: 37). However, the return of democracy in the early 1970s gave fresh impetus to Islamic parties, who were by now receiving buoyancy from the emergence of the international Islamic 'awakening'. The agitation to declare Ahmadis non-Muslims which gripped Pakistan in the first half of 1974 had been preceded by the Islamic Summit, held in Lahore in February 1974, in the course of which King Faisal promised Bhutto economic aid in return for resolving the Ahmadiyya issue. Leaders of the Jaamat-i-Islami and the Majlis-i-Ahrar had called on Saudi Arabia to put pressure on the Bhutto government to address the Ahmadi issue (Kaushik 1996: 43). A new round of disturbances erupted in 1974, leading to the formation of the 'All Parties Khatm-i-Nubuwwat Action Committee', which represented not only Islamic parties but also other opposition parties, and a country-wide strike on 14 June 1974. Bhutto initially rejected the demands of the Action Committee but on 30 June 1974 agreed to form a Special Committee of parliament to discuss the issue and allowed PPP members a free vote on the issue. On 7 September 1974 the bill to amend the Constitution 1973 was unanimously passed by the National Assembly, with Bhutto declaring that 'the first principle of the PPP was "Islam is our Faith"' (Pirzada 2000: 124). The internationalisation of the Islamic movement during the Bhutto era continued with the holding of the International Seerat Conference in March 1976, sponsored by the Pakistani government. In his opening address, Bhutto stressed the importance of the concept of the finality of Prophethood (Kaushik 1996: 53). The banning of the drinking of alcohol and the declaration of Friday as a holiday instead of Sunday followed in 1977.

Despite his promises to improve the conditions of Pakistan's poor, Bhutto had disappointed them. There were no meaningful land reforms and Bhutto was unable to reduce the power of the military, the bureaucracy and the landed oligarchy, which had dominated Pakistani politics ever since independence. His appeals to religion were therefore part of a 'balancing act between various interest groups' which left the state paralysed and enabled religious parties, which had done badly in the 1970 elections, to gain greater visibility and importance (Nasr 1994: 76). In preparation for the 1977 elections opposition parties formed the Pakistan National Alliance, which included also Islamic parties such as the Jamaat-i-Islami, and which campaigned against Bhutto using appeals to Islam and blaming the loss of East Pakistan on Bhutto's secularism and his personal moral turpitude.

Bhutto's PPP won the elections but the victory was short-lived. Allegations of vote-rigging ended in popular unrest and riots. Negotiations between Bhutto and the Pakistan National Alliance, mediated by Saudi Arabia, were however cut short. On 5 July 1977, Bhutto was removed from power by a *coup d'état* led by General Zia ul-Haq.

Islam and martial law: the Zia era

Zia's declaration of martial law and the subsequent introduction of a wide range of legal measures marked the beginning of the first serious attempt by a government to Islamise the legal system of Pakistan. The motivation behind Zia's relentless drive to make Pakistan an Islamic state, were two-fold. Firstly, it provided a justification for his coup and his failure to hold elections: according to Zia, successive governments had failed to make Pakistan an Islamic state. Assuming the role as the saviour of Pakistan's destiny, Zia resolved to return the country to democracy only as and when it had been turned into a truly Islamic state. Secondly, by taking command of the Islamisation project, Zia was able to sideline Islamic parties and take control of the Islamic discourse. By adopting the agenda of the Islamists, Zia effectively silenced them.

Islamisation became the primary instrument of state formation and a means to destroy the popular appeal of the PPP, whose leader Zulfikar Ali Bhutto was executed in 1979, following a murder conviction. International isolation turned into support for Zia's regime when the Soviet Union invaded neighbouring Afghanistan in 1979, turning Zia's regime into an important ally of the United States. Zia's Islamisation project, in the first two years used for purely domestic purposes, now became a potent weapon in the fight against communism in neighbouring Afghanistan. Pakistan not only provided shelter to millions of Afghan refugees, but also a staging ground for the Mujahedin, who, secretly financed and armed by the United States, fought the communist enemy in the name of Islam.

Initially, Islamisation proceeded tentatively. The first concrete measure was the creation of separate electorates for non-Muslims in September 1978. This was followed by the promulgation of the Hudood Ordinances in 1979 and the Zakat and Ushr Ordinance in 1980. The promulgation of the Hudood Ordinances introduced Islamic criminal law for the first time since it had been gradually displaced during British colonial rule in favour of English criminal law. The Islamisation of the legal system was accompanied by a concerted effort to Islamise Pakistani society, culture and economy. Islamic symbolism, public floggings, the enforcement of fasting and prayer, the building of mosques and financial support for private, religious schools, known as *madrasas*, were some of the many measures taken by Zia's regime to control the minds and hearts of the people.

Challenges to Zia's regime emerged in the early 1980s when the theme of Islamic solidarity showed the first strains. With its foundations firmly in Sunni Islam, the Islamisation measures strained the relationship between Sunni and Shias, contributing to sectarian strive between the two communities which continues to the present. Ethnic divisions, especially those between Punjab and Sindh, fuelled the Movement for the Restoration of Democracy, founded in 1983 by Benazir Bhutto, who while in exile had succeeded her father Zulfikar Ali Bhutto as the leader of the PPP. In 1984 Zia held a referendum to show public support for his Islamisation measures and to confirm him as President. Elections on a non-party basis followed in 1985, with the new parliament protecting his position by passing the Constitution (Eighth) Amendment Act 1985. The constitutional amendment protected all Islamisation measures introduced by Zia against judicial review and secured his position as President by introducing a constitutional provision which allowed the President to dismiss a government.[32] The elections were won by the Pakistan Muslim League (PML), a party with a strong basis amongst the landholding classes of Punjab. In 1988, Zia dismissed the PML government, following disagreement over the introduction of further Islamisation measures. Shortly after the promulgation of the Shariat Ordinance 1988, Zia died in an aircrash in August 1988. The Zia era had ended, but the effects of his Islamisation measures continue to be felt today.

The period of 1977 to 1988 is most visibly associated with the suppression of the rights of women, in particular in the form of the Zina (Enforcement of Hudood) Ordinance 1979, and of religious minorities. Ahmadis, who had already been declared non-Muslims in 1974, were now made subject to an Ahmadi specific criminal law, which made it a criminal offence for Ahmadis to 'pose' as Muslims.[33] Less visible, but equally important, was the Islamisation of the judiciary and the legal discourse.

Islam and Pakistan's judiciary

Until Zia's coup in 1977 a self-contained, professional and socially conservative judiciary with deep educational roots in the English common law had administered a legal system that despite frequent constitutional breakdowns and political upheavals had retained its colonial shape. At the time of independence the entire colonial legal system had been adopted by Pakistan and its main elements, the Anglo-Indian codes, had continued in force with hardly any changes. Constitutional provisions asking the state to bring all laws into conformity with Islam had been unenforceable and the judiciary itself only rarely left the safety of the colonial legacy to explore the landscape of Islamic law. On the few occasions when they did, judges engaged in the reform of family law, for instance by extending the right of Muslim women to seek a judicial divorce of their marriage,[34] or referred to Islam in order to assert democracy and constitutionalism[35] or applied Islamic law to areas of law not covered by statutory laws.[36] Neither the use of Islam in support of state building in the 1950s nor Bhutto's Islamic populism in the 1970s had affected the basic structure of the legal system or the composition of its higher judiciary.

The year 1977, however, also constitutes a watershed for Pakistan's judiciary. Implementing his totalitarian enterprise of Islamisation Zia endeavoured to bring the judiciary in line with his policies. Judges reluctant to endorse his rule were removed from the benches of the four high courts and the Supreme Court in 1977 and in 1981 and their power of judicial review curtailed. The weakening of the power of the higher judiciary was compounded by the creation of the Federal Shariat Court in 1980.[37] The new court was given the jurisdiction to review the validity of laws, either on its own motion or by being petitioned to do so by a member of the general public, on the basis of Islam. Excluded from its jurisdiction were the constitution, Muslim personal law and any law relating to the procedure of any court or tribunal.[38]

9.4 The period from 1985 until the present

The rise and fall of democracy

New orientations of judicial Islamisation

The Federal Shariat Court proceeded to review the Islamic vires of the entire body of Pakistan's codified law. Whilst the vast majority of laws survived the examination intact, there were nevertheless important exceptions. The most important relate to criminal law and banking law. In respect of the former, the Federal Shariat Court held that provisions covering the offences of murder and assault were contrary to Islam, forcing the government to base this area of law on Islamic principles.[39] The charging of interest was declared repugnant to Islam in 1992.[40] In addition, the FSC formulated several Islamic fundamental rights, amongst them 'the right to justice' and 'the right to be heard', which were used as a basis for the judicial review of laws.

In a parallel development, some judges in the 'secular' high courts also began to engage in an Islamisation drive of their own and began to review laws on the basis of Islam. Chief among them was Justice Tanzil-ur-Rahman, a justice of the Karachi High Court and former chairman of the Council of Islamic Ideology, who in a series of decisions invalidated parts of the MFLO[41] and declared the charging of interest un-Islamic.[42] The basis for these decisions was article 2A of the Constitution 1973. Introduced as part of the Eighth Amendment in 1985, article 2A incorporated the provisions of the Objectives Resolution into the main body of the constitution. According to Justice Tanzil-ur-Rahman:

> [....] the Courts in Pakistan are bound by the Constitution, and any law repugnant to the Constitution is void. The principles and provisions of the Objectives Resolution, by virtue of Article 2-A, are now part of the Constitution and justiciable. Any provision of the Constitution or law, found repugnant to them, may be declared by a superior Court as void [...].[43]

If allowed to continue, the newly found jurisdiction could have fundamentally changed the legal system of Pakistan because unlike the FSC there were no limitations imposed on the self-arrogated powers of judicial review. By the early 1990s there were serious concerns that the legal system might unravel if judges like Justice Tanzil-ur-Rahman were allowed to continue to invalidate laws on the basis of Islam. The Supreme Court decided to intervene, observing that the unrestrained judicial review in the name of Islam could lead to a situation where 'the very basis on which the Constitution is founded [...] could be challenged'.[44] In 1992, the Supreme Court ruled that apart from the FSC no other court had the power to invalidate laws, or indeed the Constitution 1973 on the basis of Islam.[45]

References to Islam nevertheless began to permeate the judgements of Pakistan's higher courts in relation to the emergence of public interest litigation. The term 'public interest litigation' denotes human rights cases which are brought in the public interest and not by a petitioner asking for the adjudication of a personal claim. Public interest litigation first started in India in the mid-1980s, but by the early 1990s it was being adopted by Pakistan's higher judiciary. What makes Pakistani public interest litigation cases unique is their frequent reliance on Islamic law, principally to widen the scope of constitutionally guaranteed fundamental rights. There is hardly any case concerned with the enforcement of fundamental rights in the 1990s which does not refer to Islam in some way. Justice Afazal Zullah can be singled out as one of the most outspoken and active proponents of this 'indigenisation' of Pakistan's constitutional law. In 1990 he introduced the higher judiciary's 'Scheme for the Protection of Human Rights of All Classes of Society in the Country', declaring that

> [the] Superior Judiciary has clearly emphasised the need for a genuine effort for the reconstruction of the Islamic concepts in

> this field [ie protection of human rights] and for evolving steps in an indigenous manner for guiding and motivating the citizens and the State for asserting, promoting and enforcing the legal rights of citizens guaranteed by Islam, the Constitution and the Law.[46]

On the whole the infusion of Islam into the human rights' jurisprudence was beneficial, but there was one important exception. In a case concerning the constitutional validity of the criminal law which made it an offence for members of Ahmadi to 'pose' as Muslims, the Supreme Court declared that the constitutionally guaranteed right to freedom of religion could be restricted in order to protect Islam.[47]

Islam and democracy

The death of Zia in 1988 ushered in a period of democracy which was to last until 1999, when General Pervaiz Musharraf staged a *coup d'état*. The decade of democracy was marked by the inability of the two main political parties, Benazir Bhutto's PPP and Nawaz Sharif's PML, to create stable and lasting governments. The PPP won the elections in 1988 but a dismissal of Benazir Bhutto's government by the President in 1990 enabled the PML to return to power. In 1993, it was the Nawaz Sharif's government's turn to be dismissed. In subsequent elections the PPP emerged with a slim majority. Benazir Bhutto's government lasted until 1996, when following another dismissal, Nawaz Sharif formed a government, albeit it for the last time. Perhaps unsurprisingly, Musharraf's coup in 1999 was largely unopposed by a population which had become disillusioned with the realties of a fragile democracy.

Of the two parties, it was only Nawaz Sharif's PML which sought to continue Zia's Islamisation policies. However, in practical terms the only legal change his regime brought about was in the form of section 4 of the Enforcement of Shari'ah Act 1991, which mandated judges to apply Islamic law to those areas not covered by statute (see 9.5). The other Islamisation measure, namely the introduction of Islamic criminal law relating to murder, in the form of the Criminal Law (Amendment) Act, 1997, constituted a significant change in the criminal law, but was not a result of any policy of Nawaz Sharif's government (see 9.7). The amendment had been required as a result of a decision of the Federal Shariat Court.

Whilst Nawaz Sharif was not able to follow with actions his repeated promises to make further progress with Islamisation, Benazir Bhutto was unable to fulfil her promise to remove some of these measures. Neither the laws discriminating against religious minorities nor the controversial Hudood Ordinances were in any way amended, leave alone repealed, under her two governments.

The end of democracy: Musharraf's rule

In October 1999, the army deposed Nawaz Sharif through a *coup d'état* and General Pervez Musharraf, the then Chief of Army Staff, took over power. He immediately suspended the Constitution 1973 and through a decree made all existing legislation 'subject to the Orders of the Chief Executive'. As was the case with previous coups, the constitutional validity of Musharraf's actions was immediately challenged before the Supreme Court. Anticipating defeat, Musharraf promulgated the Oath of Judges Order 2000, requiring all judges of superior courts to take a fresh oath of office thereby swearing allegiance to the military and vowing not to challenge decisions taken under the military rule.[48] Those who refused to take the new oath were dismissed, leaving behind a judiciary that was purged of any dissent. The newly constituted Supreme Court duly endorsed the constitutional validity of Musharraf's coup, granting him three years before holding fresh national elections and allowing him to amend the constitution.[49] Until 2002, the provincial assemblies and the National Assembly were dissolved and Musharraf ruled through executive order. On 20 June 2001, Musharraf assumed the position of President of Pakistan. A year later, on 30 April 2002, he held and won a referendum, thus legitimising and extending his presidency for five years.

Suspended from the Commonwealth and internationally isolated, Musharraf's fortunes improved with the terrorist attacks in the United States on 11 September 2001: he immediately declared his support for the U.S. in its fight against global terrorism, pledging Pakistani support for the fight against the Taliban and Al Qaeda.

Musharraf's next hurdle appeared when in 2002 the three year period granted to him by the Supreme Court came to an end and he faced the prospect of having to hold elections. In order to remain in office, wide-ranging amendments to the Constitution 1973 were required, especially in respect of the powers of the President to dismiss an unruly parliament. On 21 August 2002, Musharraf promulgated the Legal Framework Order 2002 (LFO). The LFO contained numerous amendments to the Constitution 1973, widely regarded as 'undermining the parliamentary system of government and provincial autonomy' (Khan 2009: 660). The LFO revived the controversial Article 58(2)(b) of the Constitution 1973, allowing the President to dissolve the National Assembly at his discretion, introduced a National Security Council consisting of members of the armed forces,[50] and validated all laws made by the Musharraf regime.[51]

National Assembly elections followed in October 2002, resulting in a thin victory of a splinter party of the Muslim League, the PML-Quaid-e-Azam (PML-Q), which was supporting Musharraf. Pakistan's two leading politicians, Nawaz Sharif of the PML, now called the PML-Nawaz, and Benazir Bhutto of the PPP, were prevented from contesting the elections. Following a criminal conviction for the attempted hijacking of Musharraf's plane, Sharif was allowed to escape imprisonment and to settle in Saudi Arabia, on the condition that he would not return to the country for a period of ten years and would not participate in Pakistani politics. By this time, Benazir Bhutto had left Pakistan in order to avoid having to answer charges of corruption. Despite Bhutto's absence, the PPP came second. A new alliance of religious parties, which had united under the name of Muttahidda Majlis-e-Amal (MMA), came in third. Whilst trailing in the national elections, the MMA scored resounding victories in the relatively sparsely populated province of Baluchistan and in the North-West Frontier Province (NWFP). This victory was attributed to the anger in the tribal areas over Pakistani aid to the American-led operation against the Taliban in Afghanistan, as well as to resistance against the autocratic rule of Musharraf and the often harsh methods employed by the Pakistani army in fighting Islamist insurgents (Hilton 2002). The MMA won an absolute majority in the NWFP and immediately attempted to introduce provincial legislation to locally implement the sharia.

The unexpectedly strong showing of the parties opposed to Musharraf led to an impasse in the National Assembly, because they refused to take an oath under the provisions of the LFO. For over a year no business could be conducted, until December 2003 when an alliance of the MMA and the PML-Q passed the Constitution (Seventeenth) Amendment Act 2003. This amendment incorporated the provisions of the LFO into the Constitution 1973.

However, the support of the MMA in getting the Seventeenth Amendment passed had been made conditional on General Musharraf resigning as Chief of Army Staff at the end of 2004, thereby honouring the constitutional prohibition on the President holding any other office of profit.[52] Musharraf reneged on his promise, with political parties close to him passing the President to Hold Another Office Act 2004 on 14 October 2004.

The decline of President Musharraf's fortunes began in 2005 when the government's attempt to privatise one of the largest nationalised industrial enterprises, the Pakistan Steel Mills Corporation, was declared unconstitutional by the Supreme Court.[53] This was the first time in seven years that the Supreme Court had taken a stance against an action of the government. The case was heard by a nine-member bench of the Supreme Court, which included the Chief Justice Ifthikar Chaudhry, who had assumed this position on 30 June 2005. Other cases followed, with the Supreme Court and some of the high courts taking up cases of alleged human rights violation *suo moto*, i.e. on their own motion.

The ebbing away of judicial support for his regime posed a problem for Musharraf whose tenure as President was coming to an end in 2007. He needed the Supreme Court's support if he was to be allowed to seek re-election whilst retaining the position of Chief of Army Staff. Musharraf decided to act against the Chief Justice on 9 March 2007, when he ordered him to resign or face proceedings for misconduct. When the Chief Justice refused to resign, the government commenced proceedings against Chaudhry before the Supreme Judicial Council. Musharraf had, however, underestimated the public reaction against the suspension of the Chief Justice. Nationwide protests and a sustained media campaign for his reinstatement commenced. Meanwhile, the Supreme Court stayed the proceedings of the Supreme Judicial Council on 7 May 2007. Two months later, on 20 July 2007, the Supreme Court issued an order setting aside the reference against Chaudhry and restoring him to the position of Chief Justice.[54]

Musharraf's position had been weakened by the reinstatement of the Chief Justice and during the summer of 2007 Pakistan saw the first stirrings of political change. By the end of 2007 both Musharraf's term as President would come to an end, and national and provincial assembly elections were due to be held. There were indications that the two politicians who had dominated Pakistani politics in the 1990s, former Prime Ministers Benazir Bhutto and Nawaz Sharif, were preparing themselves to return to Pakistan in order to participate in the parliamentary elections scheduled for January 2008. In August 2007, Musharraf began secret consultations with Benazir Bhutto on a possible power-sharing deal. In the meantime, Nawaz Sharif began to prepare the ground for his return to Pakistan by challenging the legality of his exile.[55] The Supreme Court allowed his petition, holding that 'no constraint can be placed on a Pakistani citizen to return to his country under Article 15 of the Constitution'.[56]

Towards the end of 2007, Musharraf's position seemed to improve. On 28 September 2007, the Supreme Court dismissed a petition that had challenged the legality of Musharraf running for re-election as President whilst retaining his post as head of the armed forces. The path was now clear for him to seek re-election. On 6 October 2007, he won the vote of the country's legislators with an overwhelming majority and commenced his second term as President.

However, the victory was flawed by the fact that the two main opposition parties had boycotted his re-election. Furthermore, on 17 October 2007 the Supreme Court began hearings on the constitutionality of Musharraf's re-election. The political uncertainty was compounded by the return of Benazir Bhutto from exile on 19 October 2007. Her return had been made possible by the promulgation of the National Reconciliation Ordinance 2007 on 5 October 2007, which provided her, and other politicians, with immunity from prosecution for corruption-related offences between 1986 and 1999 (Lau 2009).

On 3 November 2007 President Musharraf, faced with the real possibility that the Supreme Court might block his attempt to assume office as re-elected President, staged a second *coup d'état*, this time directed not against a democratically-elected government but against the country's higher judiciary.[57] With three short orders he imposed a state of emergency, suspended the constitution, and removed a large number of judges from the benches of the four high courts and the Supreme Court. On the same day, Musharraf issued the Provisional Constitution Order No. 1/ 2007, which resurrected the Constitution 1973 in a modified form. The Oath of Office (Judges) Order 2007 dismissed the entire higher judiciary but allowed those judges who, after having been invited to do so, agreed to take the new oath contained in a schedule of the Order to resume their functions. The new oath enjoined a judge to perform his or her functions in accordance with the Proclamation of Emergency and the Provisional Constitutional Order 2007. Of the judges of the Supreme Court, only five took the new oath. Chief Justice Chaudhry was not among them. An attempt to declare the Proclamation of Emergency unconstitutional in the form of a short order passed towards the end of the day on 3 November by a seven-member bench of the Supreme Court ended with the storming of the Supreme Court by armed forces and Chaudhry being placed under house arrest. Out of 95 judges of superior courts, only 32 took the new oath.[58] Musharraf's actions were challenged before the Supreme Court, but predictably, given that its members had taken the new oath, none of the claims was successful.

On 18 November 2007, President Musharraf resigned as Chief of Army Staff. The emergency was lifted on 15 December 2007[59] and with both Benazir Bhutto and Nawaz Sharif having returned to the country the election campaign for the parliamentary elections, scheduled for 8 January 2008, began. The impression of a return to normality was brutally shattered on 27 December 2007, when Benazir Bhutto was killed in a suicide bomb attack.

Postponed to 18 February 2008, the elections resulted in a clear victory of the two opposition parties, the PPP and the PML(N), with the PPP now being headed by Asif Zardari, the widower of Benazir Bhutto. The two parties entered into a power-sharing agreement and formed a coalition government. An agreed goal of the coalition was the restoration of the judiciary to its state before the proclamation of the November 2007 emergency. This agreement was, however, not adhered to, and on 12 May 2008, the PML(N) left the coalition government. Three months later, on 18 August 2008, Musharraf, faced with impeachment proceedings, resigned as President. Presidential elections, held on 6 September 2008, resulted in a comfortable victory of Asif Zardari of the PPP.

The beginning of 2009 saw more political drama. Pakistan's legal profession had launched a national Lawyer's Movement, demanding the reinstatement of Chief Justice Chaudhry. Demonstrations at the end of February 2009 forced the PPP government to issue an executive order allowing Chief Justice Chaudhry to resume his office on 23 March 2009.

The gradual normalisation of public life is, however, far from complete. Attempts to broker a peace deal with the Taliban in the Swat valley broke down at the end of April 2009, prompting the government to attempt to dislodge them from Swat with military force.[60] Operations began in the beginning of May 2009, with an estimated 15,000 Pakistani troops deployed in the Swat valley. Military operations in Swat have been followed by an on-going military campaign against the Taliban to regain control of the tribal areas bordering Afghanistan.

In sharp contrast to the rise of the Taliban in remote areas of the country, in the first decade of 2000 Pakistan's elites have increasingly turned against the wave of Islamisation measures of both the 1980s and 1990s. An attempt by the MMA to introduce an Islamic ombudsman system in the North West Frontier Province was stopped in its tracks by the Supreme Court, who declared the bill to be unconstitutional.[61] The infamous Zina Ordinance 1979 was reformed in 2006 when the Protection of Women's Rights Act came into force. At the beginning of 2010 neither the government nor the main opposition party has expressed any desire to initiate measures to resume the Islamisation of the legal system. Instead, private media channels and national newspapers have began to engage with the topic of secularism, inspired by the decision of the Bangladeshi government to remove references to Islam from the Constitution of Bangladesh at the end of February 2010.[62]

9.5 Constitutional law

State ideology and constitution

The current constitution dates back to 1973. It has since been amended so many times that one can hardly refer to it as still being the same constitution as it was at its inception (Mehdi 1994: 71). However, despite many changes,[63] it has retained some of the basic features shared by all of Pakistan's constitutions. Most importantly, the Constitution

1973 is evidence of the partial success, and survival, of Jinnah's two nation-theory. The success must be described as partial since the Constitution 1973 marks the beginning of a re-constituted, smaller Pakistan, following the creation of Bangladesh in 1971. Nevertheless, it reflects the state ideology of Pakistan, denoting it as an Islamic republic and naming Islam as the state religion. At the root of the Constitution 1973 is, in the official terminology, Islam as the state ideology, which is founded on the historic wish of the Muslims of British India to form their own nation.

While having been created in the name of Islam, Pakistan has found it difficult to define the precise of role of Islam in the life of the nation. Was Pakistan a state created to enable Muslims to live in accordance with Islamic law, or was it to be a state which enabled Muslims not to live in a Hindu theocracy? In the case of the former, Pakistan's legal system would have to become an Islamic one. In case of the latter, no particular prescriptions or conditions for the role of Islam in the newly-founded state existed. Since the statements of Jinnah, the 'sole spokesman' of India's Muslims, on this issue were ambiguous, it is the country's own historical experience that has determined which role Islam was to play in the project of nation building.

Like any other state, Pakistan calls in its constitution for obedience to its laws. Throughout its history Pakistan has been facing challenges to its legitimacy from Islamic groups who have claimed that the principle duty of a Muslim is not to the state, or a constitution, but his religion. The difficulties and problems inherent in the attempts to demarcate and define of the role of Islam in Pakistan have led to a balancing act, with the state and its elites trying to control the Islamic discourse and to use it to their own advantage.

Controlling Islam and harnessing the forces of Islam for their own purpose has been problematic. In respect of law, the first of these problems concerns the normative foundation of the legal system. Should this foundation be based on the principles of Islam even if the constitution itself limits the role of Islam? Or is the fundamental norm located in the constitution itself, which provides for the basic powers of the state and primary rights of the citizens? The Pakistani state and its citizens have not been able to build a sustainable consensus about a formula which reconciles the secular and the religious elements within its constitutional order. Throughout the nation's history, appeals to Islam have been used to foster state formation and national unity. At the same time, the forces of Islamic radicalism, be it in the shape of Islamic parties or of Islamic insurgents like the Taliban, have been able to take advantage of the state's reliance on Islam: if Pakistan was founded in the name of Islam, then how could Pakistan's largely secular legal order be justified?

At present, it can be stated that the pendulum has swung decisively towards a more secular definition of the state. Gone are calls for Islamisation, and instead there is debate about human rights, the powers of the president and the future of the state itself, which is being destabilised by almost daily terrorist attacks, all committed in the name of Islam.

In 2010 it is the Constitution 1973 and not an ambiguous reliance on an Islamic state which holds the nation together. But it cannot be forgotten that within the Constitution 1973 there are numerous references to Islam, many of them constituting possible avenues for another wave of Islamisation, should the state and its leaders decide that that Islam needs to be resurrected for the survival of the nation.

The constitution and the rule of law

According to article 5(1) of the Constitution 1973, loyalty to the state is the basic duty of every citizen, article 5(2) stipulates that 'Obedience to the Constitution and the law is the inviolable obligation of every citizen. [...]', and article 6(1) provides that 'Any person who abrogates or attempts or conspires to abrogate, subverts or attempts or conspires to subvert the Constitution by use of force or show of force or by any other unconstitutional means shall be guilty of high treason.' This set of provisions is concluded with article 6(2) which provides that 'Any person aiding or abetting acts mentioned in clause 1 shall likewise be guilty of high treason.'

The provisions calling for constitutional obedience are accompanied by Part II of the Constitution 1973, which contains constitutionally guaranteed fundamental rights. The most basic and important of these fundamental rights of the citizens are the ones to life and liberty (article 9), to equality before the law (article 25), to freedom of expression (article 19) and to freedom of religion (article 20). Importantly, the Constitution 1973 contains express provisions for the enforcement of these rights. Article 8(1) provides that 'Any law, or any custom or usage having the force of law, in so far as it is inconsistent with the rights conferred by this Chapter, shall, to the extent of such inconsistency, be void.' Articles 184 and 199 respectively grant the Supreme Court and the provincial high courts the jurisdiction to declare laws and decisions null and void if they are judged to violate fundamental rights. The importance and reality of these two provisions is evidenced in the large number of public interest cases for the enforcement of these rights which have been brought before the higher courts. Interestingly, while these cases are based on fundamental rights, which appear in the Constitution 1973 without any reference to Islam, they often 'endorse Islamic principles of justice' (Lau 2006: 95-119). In many of these public interest litigation cases, references to Islam and Islamic principles of justice fulfil the role that was previously played by 'principles of natural justice'. References to Islam have even been used to create new fundamental rights, such as the right of justice and an absolute right to be heard. The jurisprudence of Pakistan's higher judiciary demonstrates that a harmonic interplay between Islamic principles and human rights is possible, and that references to Islam do not as of necessity result in a violation of basic freedoms.

Islamic precepts as a basic norm

The dual character of the Constitution 1973 is revealed in its Islamic provisions, which establish the Islamic foundation of the nation and suggest that the precepts of Islam constitute the basic norm of the Constitution. Article 1, stating that Pakistan is an Islamic republic and that Islam is the state religion, is of a declaratory nature and has had little legal effect in the development of Pakistan's legal system. However, as could be seen further above, Article 2A, added to the Constitution in 1985, has been used extensively by Pakistan courts in the context of constitutional cases. Article 2A stipulates that '[t]he principles and provisions set out in the Objectives Resolution are reproduced in the Annex and hereby made substantial part of the Constitution and to have effect accordingly.' The Objectives Resolution 1949 was the first constitutional document passed by Pakistan's Constituent Assembly (see 9.2). Once incorporated into the main body of the Constitution 1973 the Objectives Resolution's provision that 'Muslims shall be enabled to order their lives in the individual and collective spheres in accordance with the teachings and requirements of Islam as set out in the Holy Quran and Sunnah' was taken up by judges in order to review the validity of laws on the basis of Islam, and, throughout the 1990s, to justify an expansive interpretation of the constitutionally guaranteed fundamental rights.

In addition to Article 2A, references to Islam also appear in Chapter 2, entitled 'Principles of Policy'. Article 29 provides that these principles cannot be enforced in any court, unlike the fundamental rights, but that it is the responsibility of the state 'to act in accordance with those Principles in so far as they relate to the functions of the [state]'. Article 31 of Chapter 2 repeats the duty of the state to enable Muslims to order their lives in accordance with Islam, but adds more detail to this duty: the state is asked to encourage Quranic studies and the teaching of the Arabic language. Article 37 (h) enjoins the state to prohibit the drinking of alcohol, with non-Muslims being exempted from this provision as long as they consume alcohol for religious purposes. Article 40 requires the state to 'endeavour to preserve and strengthen fraternal relations' with other Muslim countries. Article 41(2)(a) specifies that the president must be a Muslim.

Finally, Part 9 of the Constitution 1973, entitled 'Islamic Provisions', contains Article 227(1), the famed 'repugnancy' article, which provides that 'All existing laws shall be brought in conformity with the Injunctions of Islam as laid down in the Holy Quran and Sunna [...] and no law shall be enacted which is repugnant to such Injunctions.' Similar to the approach adopted in the Constitutions of 1956 and 1962, Article 227(1) could initially not be enforced in any court when the Constitution 1973 was adopted. This changed in 1980 when the Federal Shariat Court was created by Zia ul-Haq in order to review existing and new legislation on the basis of Islam.

The Federal Shariat Court and the Council of Islamic Ideology

According to Article 203C, the Federal Shariat Court (FSC) consists of not more than eight members, including a Chief Justice, not more than four judges who should have the same qualification as a high court judge, and a maximum of three religious scholars (*ulama*). Article 203D(1) provides that:

> The Court may, either of its own motion or on the petition of a citizen of Pakistan or the Federal Government or a Provincial Government, examine and decide the question whether or not any law or provision of law is repugnant to the Injunctions of Islam, as laid down in the Holy Quran and Sunnah of the Holy Prophet.

In addition, Article 203DD, establishes the FSC as the court of appeal in all cases involving the Hudood Ordinances 1979. The seemingly sweeping powers of the FSC are restricted by Articles 203B-C, which exclude several important areas of law from the power of judicial review by the FSC, in particular, the constitution, procedural law, and Islamic personal status and family law. Its decisions are appealable to the Shariat Appellate Bench of the Supreme Court. The Shariat Appellate Bench of the Supreme Court is the highest and final court of appeal and consists of five members: three Supreme Court judges and two *ulama* appointed by the president (Art. 203F(3)). It must be emphasised that the *ulama* constitute a numerical minority in both courts, and legally qualified judges the majority.

Article 228 deals with the Council of Islamic Ideology (CII). Its members, whose number may not exceed twenty, are appointed on the basis of their 'knowledge of [...] Islam, or their understanding of the economic, political, legal or administrative problems of Pakistan'. The CII has an advisory function, namely to make recommendations to the legislative and the executive on the manner in which the Islamisation of social life may be realised. It can also advise on whether or not a law conflicts with the injunctions of Islam and propose ways to restore conformity. Finally, the Council is meant to identify those injunctions of Islam that can be enacted as official legislation.

The position of the Council was strengthened by the establishment of the FSC (Lau 2006: 32). Whenever the FSC declared a law to be in conflict with the injunctions of Islam, the Council assumed the task of drafting an Islamic alternative, which in turn could be used by the legislature. This was, for example, the case with the drafting and eventual implementation of the Islamic criminal law on murder and assault in the form of the Criminal Law (Amendment) Act, 1997. In the 1980s and 1990s the CII was an important driver in the Islamisation of the legal system, but with the appointment of Mohammad Khalid Masud in June 2004, the CII, which used to have a reputation of being rather conservative, has developed a more moderate and progressive character. Following amendments to the Zina Ordinance in 2006, the Jamaat-e-Islami accused the Masud's CII as being a 'rubber stamp' for the abolition of *hadd* punishments and other Islamic laws. (Imran 2006).

The judiciary and the Islamisation of laws

The FSC and the Supreme Court have ensured that stonings and amputations, punishments authorised under the Hudood Ordinances 1979, have never been executed in Pakistan. After 1985, Islamists attempted to use Article 2A in order to review the Islamic *vires* of laws and of the constitution itself, not just before the FSC, whose jurisdiction was limited to certain areas of law, but also before the country's high courts, whose jurisdiction was, as they argued, unlimited in scope. Some high court judges responded positively to these suits, invalidating even laws that were expressly protected against amendment or judicial review by the constitution itself, like the Muslim Family Laws Ordinance 1961. Other judges refused, arguing that it was only the FSC that had the power to review laws on the basis of Islam.

However, judicial activism in the name of Islam was considered controversial within Pakistan's higher judiciary. As discussed in section 9.4, between 1985 and 1992 judges like Justice Tanzil-ur-Rahman invalidated a number of laws on the basis of Islam. In the process, they often embarked on personal campaigns to purify the legal system from un-Islamic elements (Lau 2003: 200). This 'golden period' of unfettered Islamisation lasted until 1992 when the Supreme Court intervened, declaring that article 2A could not be used as the basis for a review of legislation.[64] In the cases of *Kaneez Fatima vs. Wali Muhammad* (Lau

2002: 205) and *Hakim Khan vs. Government of Pakistan* (Lau 2003: 197-202) the Supreme Court ruled that Article 2A may only be used in order to interpret legislation and the Constitution but that the Islamisation of the legal system itself was the duty of the legislature, and not that of the courts. As a result of these decisions, a judicial review of existing laws on the basis of Islam can only be undertaken by the FSC. With these precedents, the period of judicial experimentation with regards to the Islamisation of laws on the basis of Article 2A came to an unambiguous end (Lau 2003: 202).

The politics of Islamisation

Since the late 1990s, legislators, judges, the FSC, and the Council of Islamic Ideology have reached a common understanding as to the pace and the direction of Islamisation: without exception, all efforts in this regard have aimed at making existing Islamic laws more gender-sensitive by reducing their negative impact on the position of women and to produce interpretations of Islam that are in harmony with constitutionally-guaranteed fundamental rights. Many human rights violations were committed during the reign of Musharraf from 1999 until August 2008. However, on the whole, they were perpetrated not in the name of Islam, but rather in the fight against Islamic extremism, regional separatist movements and political opponents. This does not make these rights violations any less serious, but the change is nevertheless significant because it signals the end of the period of radical Islamisation that marked the Zia years and also parts of the 1990s.

The Enforcement of Shari'ah Act 1991, which was passed under Nawaz Sharif's government, bears the traces of a fundamental political compromise. The 1991 Act has a primarily declaratory character, restating provisions from the constitution and its preamble. The seemingly stringent provision contained in section 3(1) that 'The Shari'ah, that is to say the injunctions of Islam, as laid down in the Holy Quran and Sunnah, shall be the supreme Law of Pakistan' is followed by section 3 (2) which stipulates that the legal position of the current political system, including the national parliament and the provincial parliaments and the existing administrative system, may not become the subject of review by any judicial body. In other words, rather than promoting Islamisation through the courts, section 3(2) essentially protects the political system from potential judicial interference in the name of Islamisation.

Other political compromises were needed with respect to the attempt at Islamisation undertaken by the MMA government of the NWFP (see 9.4). Its Hisba Bill, which sought to set up an Islamic ombudsman system, was not even allowed to make an appearance on the statute book, the bill itself having been declared unconstitutional before the provincial governor could give his assent.[65]

Despite the overall slowing of the pace of Islamisation, there remain in Pakistan significant areas that are governed by a mixture of customary and Islamic law, occasionally supplemented by Pakistani statutes extended to these areas. Entitled the Federally Administered Tribal Areas (FATA), a belt of territories straddling the land along the Afghan and Pakistani border, these areas have never been fully included in the law of the land but instead have been governed directly by Islamabad under special laws and constitutional provisions, such as the Frontier Crimes Regulation 1901. The FATAs are directly ruled by a representative of the government, the so-called 'political agent', who, in the manner of a quasi-colonial 'indirect rule regime', leaves matters of local administration and conflict resolution to traditional councils. Important aspects of national and provincial legislation thus do not apply here.

A surge of Taliban activities in the tribal areas of Pakistan in 2008 and the beginning of 2009, with several areas, such as the Swat valley near Islamabad, falling effectively under the control of the Taliban, has left the government of Pakistan in a difficult position. Should the armed forces fight the insurgents or should they be appeased, primarily by giving in to the Taliban's main demand, namely the introduction of Islamic law and courts? In April 2009, the government chose the former, issuing the Sharia Nizam-e-Adl Regulation 2009 (SNA)[66] as part of a peace deal with the Taliban. In return, the Taliban promised to stop all fighting, though they were not asked to disarm or disband.

At least on paper, the SNA aims to address the Taliban's two main criticisms of Swat's legal system, namely the absence of Islamic law and institutions and the long delays experienced by litigants and complainants in the disposal of cases. With respect to the former, the SNA provides for two measures. Firstly, it re-establishes the existing court structures by providing for three tiers of courts, with *Qazi* courts at the trial level, followed by an appeal court called a *Zillah* court, and an apex court by the name of *Dar-ul-Qaza*. Secondly, the SNA provides that the judges of these courts have to be judicial officers of the NWFP, but as an additional qualification they also need to have completed a sharia course from a recognised institution, defined as 'the Shariah Academy established under the International Islamic University Ordinance 1985 or any other institution imparting training in Uloom-e-Sharia and recognised as such by the government' (Section 2(e) of the SNA).

The government is also empowered to appoint executive magistrates who enjoy exclusive jurisdiction over the trial of criminal offences contained in the Pakistan Penal Code (1860) and carrying a punishment of up to three years. However, in practice their jurisdiction goes well beyond the offences contained in the Pakistan Penal Code because they can also try an individual for any offence under the established principles of sharia. What these offences are remains unspecified in the SNA and seems to rest on the individual interpretation of the executive magistrate. Is the flying of kites or the shaving of beards against the established principles of the sharia? In a similar vein, the SNA introduces Islamic law as new substantive law for the area, providing in Section 19 (2) that:

> Notwithstanding anything contained in any law for the time being in force all cases [...] shall be decided by the courts concerned in accordance with Sharia'h: provided that cases of non-Muslims in matters of adoption, divorce, dower, inheritance, marriage, usages and wills shall be conducted and decided in accordance with their respective personal laws.

The SNA also lists a number of laws which continue to apply to the Swat region, but even these laws can be ignored by a judge if in his opinion they are not in accordance with the 'Sharia'h'. The SNA also aims to tackle delays by imposing strict time limits on the hearing and disposition of cases as well as encouraging out-of-court settlements. With the Pakistani army having stepped up military operations against the Taliban in Swat, on the ground that the peace deal had been breached by them, there must be doubts about the future of the SNA, which has also been criticised by the media and human rights organisations as well as the international community. In addition, it appears that the Taliban themselves have circumvented the system of official courts and is at present enforcing their own interpretation of Islamic law through commanders on the ground.

9.6 Family and inheritance law

The Muslim Family Laws Ordinance 1961

The main legislation in the area of family law is the Muslim Family Laws Ordinance 1961 (MFLO). It represents a moderate interpretation of Muslim family law, most importantly, restricting the rights of men in the area of divorce and polygamy. Section 6 of the MFLO provides that a husband who wants to marry a second wife needs to obtain the permission of the Union Council, which then assesses whether the proposed extra marriage is 'necessary and just' (MFLO, section 6(3)). Valid reasons for a second wife include 'sterility, physical infirmity, physical unfitness for conjugal relations, wilful avoidance of a decree for restitution of conjugal rights, or insanity on the part of the existing wife' (Mehdi 1994: 164). If the husband enters into a polygamous marriage without the permission of the Union Council, the first wife can seek a divorce and the husband is liable to be punished with a fine or prison sentence (MFLO, sections 5(a), 5(b)).

The MFLO also restricts the right of a Muslim husband to repudiate his wife. Section 7(1) MFLO recognises the traditional unilateral repudiation (*talaq*) by the husband, but subjects a man using this kind of divorce to a compulsory procedure which, if not followed strictly, will invalidate his *talaq*. The repudiation only becomes legally valid ninety days after the mandatory notification thereof to the Union Council, or similar body of the local government, and to his wife. Failure to abide by this obligation is punishable by a prison sentence of up to one year or a fine of 5,000 rupees (approximately 44 Euros). After notification of the divorce, the Union Council forms a mediation commission that is tasked with attempting to bring about reconciliation between the husband and his wife. The divorce only becomes valid after the expiry of the ninety days, if no reconciliation of husband and wife is possible within this period. In the absence of notification of the divorce to the Union Council or the wife, the divorce is regarded as invalid.

Section 8 of the MFLO confirms that the husband can, at the time of the marriage, delegate the right of divorce by repudiation to his wife.[67] In addition to section 8 of the MFLO, there is also recent case law which has extended the right of Muslim women to seek a judicial dissolution of their marriage. Women are now able to procure a divorce solely on the basis of their own testimony to the effect that their marriage has broken down and that they can no longer live with their husbands 'within the limits of Allah'.

The criminalisation of adultery and fornication as a result of the Zina Ordinance 1979, however, had an unintended effect on the umbrella of procedures initially designed to offer some protection of women's rights. After the passing of the law, abandoned wives who had since remarried were unexpectedly accused of adultery by their former husbands, the latter claiming that because they had not followed the procedures contained in Section 7 of the MFLO, they had never validly been divorced, and hence were guilty of adultery. In order to protect the women involved, judges dealing with these cases often decided that the divorce had been valid, despite non-compliance with the MFLO, thereby weakening the obligatory character of the mandatory notification. Consequently, some have claimed that men's right to repudiation is once again governed by the classical sharia rather than the MFLO (Menski 1997: 30-31), but an analysis of recent legal rulings shows that Section 7 is being upheld in cases concerning purely family, not criminal law, matters. The Protection of Women Act 2006 has finally put the matter to rest by providing that it is sufficient for a woman to believe herself to be validly married to avoid a charge of adultery. Thus, even if the divorce preceding her re-marriage turns out to be invalid, she will not face charges as long as she can convince the court that she had reasons to believe that the divorce and her subsequent marriage were valid (Lau 2007).

Inheritance law

Save for one reform brought about by the MFLO, which introduces into Pakistani law a rule of Maliki law,[68] inheritance law remains governed by classical sharia regulations on this subject, although these norms have never actually been codified into legislation or legal codes. Whilst being discriminatory towards women, who as a general rule inherit only half of what is due to a man, the Islamic law of inheritance was nevertheless a significant improvement on pre-Islamic tribal customs, under which women inherited little or nothing at all. To this day, many women in Pakistan are deprived of their inheritance rights under Islamic law because families prefer to follow customary laws, which often exclude women from inheriting. In many regions of Pakistan, women are still completely excluded from the inheritance.[69]

In 2003, the Justice and Law Commission of Pakistan argued for a better monitoring of the implementation of Islamic inheritance law. In its report, the commission observed that women and children were often robbed of the inheritance to which they were entitled under Quranic law by a multitude of tricks and false promises. Islamic inheritance law, the commission claimed, was a command coming directly from God and a legal obligation that had to be abided by in letter and in spirit. It, therefore, asked its secretary to devise an effective plan of action aimed at achieving compliance with inheritance law, especially regarding the rights of women and children.[70] To date, no such action plan has been launched.

9.7 Criminal law

The legal codes introduced by the British form the basis of Pakistani criminal law. The codes in question are the Pakistan Penal Code 1860, the Code of Criminal Procedure 1898, and the Evidence Act 1872. These laws were substantially amended as a result of Islamisation measures. This applies to the area of blasphemy, where amendments to the Pakistan Penal Code took place in 1980, 1982, and 1986, the Ahmadiyya-specific amendments in the Pakistan Penal Code (1984), and the incorporation of Islamic law on murder and assault in 1997. With the exception of the Zina Ordinance 1979, which was substantially amended by the Protection of Women Act 2006, the Hudood Ordinances of 1979 remain in force.

The Hudood Ordinances and the Women's Protection Bill

The socalled Hudood Ordinances, promulgated by Zia ul-Haq in 1979, actually consist of four separate ordinances, namely the Offences against Property (Enforcement of Hudood) Ordinance 1979, the Offence of Zina (Enforcement of Hudood) Ordinance 1979, the Offence of Qazf (Enforcement of Hadd) Ordinance 1979, and the Prohibition (Enforcement of Hadd) Order 1979. Collectively known as the 'Hudood Ordinances', they were meant to Islamise Pakistan's corpus of criminal law. The Hudood Ordinances 1979 provide for corporal punishments for offences falling under the five *hadd* crimes. These punishments include the amputation of limbs, death by stoning, and flogging; the most severe of these *hadd* punishments, namely death by stoning, has never actually been executed in Pakistan. Higher judicial authorities have blocked executions by stoning (see below) as they have also consistently prevented amputations from being executed. Flogging, either in public or inside prisons, however, was executed on a regular basis during the 1980s. Corporal punishments can also be imposed for the *hadd* offences of drinking of alcohol and false accusations of illegal sexual relations, which are punishable by eighty lashes.

About half of the criminal cases brought before the courts under the Hudood Ordinances were concerned with the Zina Ordinance (Chadbourne 1999: 3). Prior to its amendment in 2006, the Zina Ordiance made any sexual intercourse outside a valid marriage a criminal offence. If the guilty party was married at the time of the offence or had been married previously, the punishment was death by stoning, as long as four male, adult, Muslim witnesses of the highest moral standing had witnessed the illicit congress. In all other cases, *zina* was punishable by lashes or imprisonment, or both.

In many cases, the punishments awarded by trial courts were reduced on appeal, or the accused acquitted. The Zina Ordinance itself was reviewed on the basis of Islam by the Federal Shariat Court in 1981. In its decision, the Federal Shariat Court ruled 4 to 1 that death by stoning was against the principles of Islam and that hundred lashes was the correct punishment for the offence of adultery (Khan 2001: 641). Zia managed to get the decision overturned after replacing the judges of the FSC with more compliant ones. In 1982, a newly constituted Federal Shariat Court overruled its own previous decision, finding punishment of stoning to death in accordance with Islam. Despite this decision, both the Supreme Court and the Federal Shariat Court have maintained their overall reticent attitude with regard to severe corporal punishments.

With the amendment of the Zina Ordinance in 2006, its adverse impact on women's rights is much reduced. As a result of the Protection of Women Act 2006 rape and fornication are no longer treated as Islamic *hadd* crimes, but are governed by the Pakistan Penal Code, thus removing them from the jurisdiction of the Federal Shariat Court. The Zina Ordinance as it currently stands only deals with the *hadd* offence of adultery, but the procedural and evidential hurdles to be surmounted before a woman can even be charged with the crime are such that it is unlikely that there will be many, if any, convictions. The passing of the bill led to much political upheaval and clearly illustrated the profound dichotomy permeating the Pakistani political scene. The bill was supported in the National Assembly by Benazir Bhutto's opposition party PPP as well as President Musharraf's party and the other parties in his governing coalition. In fact, the PPP, along with other liberal-minded parties and individuals, continues to call for a complete repeal of all Hudood Ordinances. In contrast, the MMA and other Islamic parties voiced their strong criticism of the bill, calling it un-Islamic. MMA's general secretary Maulana Fazlur Rehman, for example, warned that the bill would 'make Pakistan a free sex zone'.[71]

The blasphemy laws

Since 1980, Section 298A of the Pakistan Penal Code stipulates that:

> Whoever by words, either spoken or written, or by visible representation, or by any imputation, innuendo or insinuation, directly or indirectly, defiles the sacred name of any wife (Ummul Mumineen), or members of the family (Ahle-bait), of the Holy Prophet (peace be upon him), or any of the righteous Caliphs (Khulafa-e-Rashideen) or companions (Sahaaba) of the Holy Prophet (peace be upon him) shall be punished with imprisonment of either description for a term which may extend to three years, or with fine, or with both.[72]

Blasphemous words, spoken or written, and visual representations are punishable.[73] Since 1982, imprisonment for life has been stipulated for the wilful damaging, defaming, abusing, denunciation, and improper use of a copy of the Quran (S. 295B). In 1991, the punishment for blasphemy was enhanced to the death sentence as a result of a ruling of the Federal Shariat Court, which held that the alternative punishment of imprisonment for life was contrary to Islam[74]. An appeal against the decision was rejected by the Shariat Appellate Bench of the Supreme Court in 2009[75]. Following the religiously motivated murder of eight Christians in the Punjabi village of Gojra in July 2009, Pakistan Minister for Minorities announced that the government would review the blasphemy laws because "This law is being misused. People have been extrajudicially killed and falsely implicated and are now behind bars."[76]

The Ahmadi-specific criminal laws of 1984

Under these laws, members of the Ahmadiyya community face a prison sentence of up to three years when they refer to themselves as Muslims or attempt to propagate their faith (PPC, S. 298B). The same punishment is applicable whenever they undertake any public act that may 'outrage' the religious beliefs of Muslims in any possible way (PPC, S. 298C).

Islamic criminal law of murder and assault

Starting in 1980, Pakistan's Federal Shariat Court decided in a number of cases that the law on murder and bodily harm, as contained in the Pakistan Penal Code, was un-Islamic because it did not allow the victim of an assault, or, in the case of murder, his heir, to determine how the offender should be treated. Classical Islamic law allows the victim or his heirs three options: firstly, they can demand monetary compensation from the perpetrator of the crime; secondly, they can insist on him being punished; and lastly, they can pardon him. As a result, the degree of punishment – retribution, financial compensation ('blood money'), or pardon – is in principle decided upon by the victim or the victim's family. When and if the victim dies, the family can demand the death penalty. In cases of physical injury the victim may also demand retribution. This could mean that the perpetrator of the crime has to face a mutilating punishment in accordance with the principle of 'an eye for an eye, a tooth for a tooth'. In 1997 this Islamic criminal law of murder and assault was incorporated into the Pakistan Penal Code under the provisions of the Criminal Law (Amendment) Act (1997). In recent years, complaints have been raised against the practice of 'buying off' punishments for murder through the payment of blood money, but as yet the law has not been amended in response to these criticisms, save for the area of honour crimes, which are now punishable by twenty years' imprisonment, irrespective of any compromise with the family of the victim or pardon by them (Wasti 2009).

9.8 Other areas of law

A number of laws are aimed at the creation of an Islamic economy and social welfare system. The Constitution of 1973 contains directives that enjoin the state to abolish interest (*riba*), to set up a tax to support the poor (*zakat*), and to maintain religious trusts (*waqf*) and mosques. The

Enforcement of Sharia Act 1991 provides that the state must establish an Islamic economy and calls for the establishment of a supervisory commission to oversee the 'total elimination of *riba*'. Islamic taxation or *zakat* is enforced through the Zakat and Ushr Ordinance 1980.

Despite these attempts, the present legal situation is not very different from the situation at the beginning of the Islamisation process under Zia in 1977. During the 1980s, a number of judges declared the charging or payment of interest to be 'un-Islamic', and hence unlawful. In 2000, however, the Shariat Appellate Bench of the Supreme Court found that the previous decisions had been procedurally flawed and sent the matter back to the Federal Shariat Court for a complete retrial. To this day, the matter remains unresolved, with the case pending before the FSC and no indication as to when it is going to be heard. In the meantime, there have been several commissions which have investigated the viability of a financial and economic system based on Islam.

The principle of *zakat* forms an Islamic contribution to the concept of social justice and redistribution. The Zakat and Ushr Ordinance has introduced to Pakistan some features of an Islamic welfare state, in that the rich are asked to pay a tax on their wealth, which in turn is distributed to the poor.[77] Under the Zakat and Ushr Ordinance, a 2.5 per cent tax is imposed on the estate of every Muslim, which is then used to provide maintenance for the poor and needy. Local *zakat* commissions decide who is entitled to receive such public support. These commissions are also responsible for collecting the money, under the supervision of the Bureau of Zakat and Ushr of the Ministry of Religious Affairs (Shamim 2004). Following protests, Zia exempted Shias from the payment of *zakat*. *Ushr*, the religious tax on agricultural proceeds, is also covered by the 1980 Ordinance.

9.9 International treaty obligations and human rights

Compared with other Muslim countries, Pakistan has been slow in acceding to international human rights treaties. In the 1990s, under the two governments of Benazir Bhutto, Pakistan acceded to the Convention on the Rights of the Child CRC) in 1990, and to the Convention on the Elimination of All Forms of Discrimination against Women (CEDAW) in 1996. In respect of the latter, Pakistan stated that its ratification '[...] is subject to the provisions of the Constitution of the Islamic Republic of Pakistan'. However, in recent years Pakistan has shown more commitment to international human rights treaties. In April 2008 Pakistan signed the International Covenant on Civil and Political Rights and the U.N. Convention against Torture and Other Cruel, Inhuman or Degrading Treatment or Punishment and ratified the International Covenant on Economic, Social and Cultural Rights.

The elements of legally-implemented sharia in Pakistan conflict on a number of points with the corpus of internationally accepted human rights. Execution by stoning, amputation, the potential application of the rules of retribution, and flogging, for instance, all conflict with the international prohibition on torture or cruel, inhuman, or degrading treatment or punishment. In addition, a number of conflicts exist with the principle of equality, namely the unequal treatment of men and women and of Muslims and non-Muslims. This is the case with personal status, family and inheritance laws, and criminal law, both from a theoretical and a practical perspective. The sharia codes also tread a fine line with regards to the principle of freedom of religion. Although apostasy is not formally made punishable through the *Hudood* Ordinances, it does constitute an integral part of the classical doctrine and, as such, has an impact upon the legal status of people. Muslims who change their religion risk losing their civil rights; an apostate, for example, may not marry or acquire real estate. Blasphemy laws contravene the right to freedom of expression. And finally, the *Hudood* Ordinances appear in some cases to contravene the 1989 CRC agreement. According to classical sharia, adulthood begins with puberty. This means that young teens can, in principle, be tried as adults and may face *hadd* punishments.

In many areas of Pakistan, an atmosphere of religious intolerance prevails. Communities of religious minorities, such as Ahmadis, Hindus, and Christians, are sometimes the victims of physical violence and intimidation. Formal constitutional recognition of rights such as freedom of religion and the principle of equality have done little to abate this.

Amnesty International and other human rights groups and institutions such as the Human Rights Commission of Pakistan, regularly report on a wide range of human rights violations. It should be noted, however, that the vast majority of these rights violations are not directly, or even tangentially, related to sharia or sharia-based legislation. Rather, these violations have more to do with a culture of governmental lawlessness and impunity. Torture is a widespread phenomenon at police stations and in prisons. It is also of great concern that hundreds of people have been arrested in connection with the global war on terror and summarily handed over to the United States without even the pretence of first having received a trial in Pakistan. Every year, hundreds of women become the victim of tribal honour killings. There is frequent sectarian violence between Sunnis and Shias. The most oppressive aspect of Islamic criminal law is seen in the application of the blasphemy laws. Sometimes people are imprisoned on the basis of false accusations of blasphemy.

9.10 Conclusion

Pakistan, created as a result of the partition of British India into two independent states had a difficult start as a modern state. While the country consists mostly of Sunni Muslims, it is strongly divided along ethnic, socio-economic, and political lines. Issues of security, the army, and the police occupy a central place in Pakistani state policy due to decades of ongoing conflict, in Kashmir, in Afghanistan and its Pakistani borderlands, as well as the permanent state of tension with India. Poverty is large-scale and widespread. Women often face particularly difficult circumstances in this patriarchal and traditional society, as do religious minorities.

Pakistan has inherited a colonial legal system marked by the legal values, procedures, and laws of Great Britain. This means that private property law, civil and administrative law, criminal law, criminal and civil procedure, as well as most other areas of law continue to have a distinctly British character. Family and inheritance law are no exception: although many sharia rules apply to these legal areas, many aspects of these particular regulations have been codified using British legal terminology.

Following Pakistan's independence, the question whether or not sharia should play a larger role quickly gained prominence. The Pakistani national identity as 'the state for Muslims' has been an enduringly central issue for politicians and jurists. The tension between modernists and conservatives in how this identity should be formally and practically implemented has had a significant impact on political and legal developments. In the constitutions of 1956, 1962, and 1973, enacted under Prime Minister Zulfikar Ali Bhutto, Islam was allotted a central, but largely symbolic, role.

This changed in 1977, however, when Zia ul-Haq embarked on a policy of Islamisation, which included not just the promulgation of Islamic criminal laws, but also profound changes to the Constitution 1973, including the creation of the Federal Shariat Court in 1980. In order to Islamise the economy, in 1983 the collection and payment of interest was prohibited. And in 1985, a constitutional amendment was introduced granting Islam an even more central and pivotal role in the constitution. Islamisation could gain steam, in part due to the rise of political Islam in other countries.

Zia ul-Haq eagerly presented himself as the saviour of Islam, opted for a strict, conservative interpretation of Islam, and indeed made this interpretation the backbone of his political leadership. Many historians retrospectively see Zia's policy as an ill-disguised attempt at legitimising his *coup d'état* and subverting the democratic forces. It must be noted that the fundamentalist parties, on whose ideologies Zia based his political thinking, have consistently received few votes in successive elections.

Between 1985 and 1992, the judiciary played an increasingly activist role pertaining to the Islamisation of the legal system. Initially, judges contradicted one another freely, and legal insecurity increased. It was only in 1992 the highest judicial authorities proved themselves unwilling to allow the rule of law to be subjugated to exceedingly conservative interpretations of the sharia (Lau 2003, 2006).

Even in the 1990s, however, some Islamisation legislation was introduced, such as the Enforcement of Shari'ah Act in 1991, and the 1997 criminal legislation on retribution and blood money, whereas in North-Western Province in 2003 a provincial by-law was enacted on the enforcement of the sharia.[78]

Nonetheless, the tentative outcome of the Islamisation project has not at all yielded a favourable balance to the fundamentalists' advantage. The relatively liberal family legislation of 1961 has remained untouched, and the opportunities for women to independently obtain a divorce have been significantly expanded. The heaviest corporal punishments such as stoning and amputation have never been applied in Pakistan because the highest judicial authorities have consistently been opposed to their execution. The prohibition on interest is also not upheld by these same judges, and on this point, 'progress' for the conservatives has been limited to the establishment of a commission in 2002 to study the Islamisation of the economy in other Muslim countries. The 2003 NWFP Hisba Bill remained still-borne and, thus, without actual legal consequence. All in all, the Islamisation project has lost much of its former momentum.

The fate of the Zina Ordinance 1979 underscores this point. In the years following its promulgation, resistance to the Ordinance did not lessen. This was all the more so because of the tendency of ill-disposed men, sometimes with the help of the authorities, to use the law as a tool to harass wives they had abandoned or women who had been raped. In the majority of these cases the accused women were acquitted on appeal to the Federal Shariat Court because there was insufficient evidence for a conviction. However, until then many of the women charged under the Zina Ordinance had spent many years in jail, awaiting the outcome of their appeals. In November 2006, the Protection of Women Act was passed. This law improved the legal position of women in rape and adultery cases.

Islamisation of laws has also had unexpectedly positive effects with respect to the rule of law. After all, while the judicial authorities were grappling with the issue of Islamisation, another conflict continuously simmered in the background, one of no less importance to the judges: the battle against authoritarian government leaders and for the judiciary's own independence, for the rule of law, and for democracy. In this struggle existing legislation did not offer the judges much help because laws were under the control of the government and the government-dominated parliament. So, judges often called upon fundamental legal principles and began using Islamic concepts such as 'Islamic justice' and 'public interest' (Lau 2003). As is the case in India, a series of 'public interest' cases has also arisen in Pakistan. Unlike the secular system of India, however, this progressive development in Pakistan owes much to liberal interpretations of the sharia.

The process of establishing a truly democratic constitutional state and true enforcement of human rights still has a long way to go in Pakistan. From the *coup d'état* in 1999 until August 2008, Pakistan was ruled by Pervez Musharraf, an authoritarian military leader following a pro-American course, who had a moderate image as far as the sharia is concerned. He saw himself confronted with large socio-economic and political problems, as well as strong opposition from both democratic parties and fundamentalist groups. His aid in the American 'war on terror' was rewarded with much economic and military help for Pakistan. Nonetheless, this led – in addition to his persistent authoritarian leadership – to much criticism and discontent among the Pakistani population. This was reflected in the 2002 elections by the growth of protest votes cast for the conservative religious MMA alliance, although this coalition's share of the vote fell again in the 2005 local elections. Musharraf's reign came to an end in August 2008, when he was forced to resign or face impeachment proceedings to be brought by the government of the PPP, which ultimately emerged victorious in the 2008 national elections.

How the position and role of classical sharia will be further developed in Pakistan's national legal system will depend largely on the political choices to be made by the PPP, choices pertaining to socio-economic development, electoral results, political stability, relations with the West, Iran and China, and last but not least, to the Pakistani judicial authorities. At present, faced with the violent attacks carried out by Islamic extremists not just in the tribal areas but in the very hearts of Pakistan's cities, politicians seem to have lost any interest in pursuing a policy of Islamisation.

Notes

1 This chapter is a thorough rewrite, at the request of the editor of this book, of a chapter by M.G. Barends and J.M. Otto in a Dutch research publication prepared for the Scientific Council for Government Policy (WRR) in the Netherlands, published in Otto, Dekker & van Soest-Zuurdeeg (red.) 2006: 235-267.

2 Martin Lau is a Reader in Law at the School of Oriental and African Studies, University of London.

3 The East India Company had been granted the exclusive right to conduct business with and in India by the British Crown in successive Charters, the first dating back to 1600. This system came to an end in 1958 when the areas controlled by East India Company became the crown colony of British India.

4 Sati is the Sanskrit term to describe the practice of a Hindu widow to burn herself on the funeral pyre of her dead husband. The practice was outlawed in 1929, see the Sati Abolition Act, 1929.

5 'Proclamation by the Queen in Council to the Princes, Chiefs, and People of India' of 1 November 1858, British Library, BL/MSS Eur D620. A copy of the original text of the Proclamation of 1858 can be accessed on the website of the British Library at http://www.movinghere.org.uk/deliveryfiles/BL/Mss_Eur_D620/0/1.pdf (accessed February 2010).

6 The Code of Criminal Procedure 1898 and the Code of Civil Procedure 1908.

7 Khan (2001: 20) has the following to say about this: 'This Act provided for speedy trial of offences by a special court consisting of three High Court Judges. This Court could meet in camera to take into consideration evidence not otherwise admissible under the Evidence Act. No appeal was provided against the decision of the court. Provincial governments were also given wide powers in matters of arrest, searches and seizures, confinement of suspects, censorship, and so on.'

8 In Pakistan, the exclusion of agricultural land from the 1937 Act was only removed in 1962, see the West Pakistan Muslim Personal Law (Shariat) Application Act 1962. In India, the exclusion of agricultural land continues to apply in most states, thereby excluding preventing women from inheriting agricultural land (Agarwal 2005).

9 Hindu politicians only agreed to support the passage of the 1939 Act on the condition that it did not apply to Muslim wives who had converted to Islam prior to their marriage. In the 1930s there were concerns that Muslim mobs forced Hindu women to convert to Islam and to marry Muslim men against their will. As a result the 1939 Act contains a provision that section 4 of the Act does not 'apply to a woman converted to Islam from some other faith who re-embraces her former faith.' Hence, a Hindu woman who had converted to Islam continues to be able to dissolve her Muslim marriage simply by re-embracing Hinduism without any recourse to a court of law being required.

10 Section 7 of the Indian Independence Act of 1947 provided that 'As from the appointed day [August 15], His Majesty's Government in the United Kingdom have no responsibility as respects the government of any of the territories which, immediately before that day, were included in British India;...'

11 The Government of India Act, 1935, as adopted by the Pakistan (Provisional Constitution) Order, 1947.

12 The first Constituent Assembly to be convened was supposed to frame a constitution for the whole of British India. However, the Muslim League boycotted it on the ground that there should be two assemblies, drafting the constitutions of Pakistan and India. India's Constituent Assembly had adopted an Objectives Resolution on 22 January 1947 and its Constitution on 26 November 1949. By comparison, Pakistan's Constituent Assembly was created on the basis of a Notification of the Government of India on 26 July 1947, less than three weeks before independence, and convened for the first time on 10 August 1947. The Constituent Assembly adopted the Objectives Resolution on 12 March 1949 and its first Constitution on 2 March 1956.

13 The members of Pakistan's first Constituent Assembly had been determined through provincial elections in 1946-47. All Muslim seats except one were held by members of the Muslim League. The Muslim League was only open to Muslims. The twelve

million Hindus who remained in Pakistan after partition were represented by twelve members of the Congress Party, while the Schedules Castes (low-caste Hindus) were represented by three members of the Congress Party and one representative of the Schedules Castes Federation. Christians and Parsees did not have any representation in the Constituent Assembly. The number of non-Muslim citizens of Pakistan was much larger in 1947 than it is now: in East Pakistan at least one quarter of the population belonged to the Hindu religion. See Symonds 1950: 97-99.

14 Speech by S. C. Chattopadhaya, the leader of the Congress Party, see Choudhury 1967: 970.

15 The Government of India Act, 1935 as amended by the India Independence Act, 1947 and subsequent Pakistani amendments.

16 The Constituent Assembly had formed a Basic Principles Committee on 12 March 1949. The latter included a Board of Islamic Teachings (*Talimat-i-Islamiyah*) charged with giving advice on Islamic matters. Its recommendations were largely ignored by the Basic Principles Committee leading to the formation of a coalition of Islamic parties which agreed 22 fundamental principles of an Islamic state (Pirzada 2000: 18-19). The text of the principles is contained as Appendix B in Hassan 1985: 263-284.

17 *Riba* denotes the charging of interest in a financial transaction, such as a loan. The precise translation and indeed meaning of the term *riba* is, however, considered controversial. In Pakistan, the campaign to ban *riba* has been highly visible but largely unsuccessful. See Hassan, P. and Azfar, A. 2001.

18 Following independence, the Muslim League's hold over East Pakistan's politics became increasingly tenuous. In April 1954, provincial elections in East Bengal removed the Muslim League almost completely from the provincial legislative assembly, which was now dominated by a coalition of Bengali parties united under the slogan 'Bengal for the Bengalis'. After a spate of violence around Dacca, the provincial government was dismissed and East Bengal was ruled directly from Karachi. See Burks 1954: 544.

19 Report of the Court of Inquiry Constituted under Punjab Act II of 1954 to Enquire into the Punjab Disturbances of 1953.

20 In fact, the name had already been changed by presidential order to a simple 'Pakistan' shortly after the *coup d'état*, on October 11, 1958. Ibid: 195.

21 Apart from appeasing the Islamists, the first amendment to the 1962 Constitution also aimed to silence the legal community which had demanded that the fundamental rights were made justiciable, see Articles 30 and 98(2) of the 1962 Constitution. See Braibanti 1965: 81. However, the Islamic parties failed in their demand for a repeal of the MFLO 1961, see Pirzada 2000: 26.

22 See part 10, chap. 1, 1962 Constitution.

23 Since 1980, the Islamic Research Institute has been part of the International Islamic University, Islamabad.

24 Article 207, 1962 Constitution.

25 The most significant legal intervention came in the form of the Muslim Family Laws Ordinance of 1961, which reformed some aspects of Islamic family law, principally to improve the legal position of women. See Jahangir 1998.

26 See for instance *Mr Fazlul Quader Chowdhury v. Mr. Mohammed Abdul Haque* PLD 1963 SC 486.

27 See articles 227 to 231, Constitution 1973.

28 3rd Schedule, Constitution 1973.

29 Article 2, Constitution 1973.

30 See Article 106 (3) of the Constitution 1973. Article 106 (3) was amended in 2002 under the provisions of the Legal Framework Order 2002 and the Constitution (Seventeenth) Amendment Act 2003, removing any direct reference to who is

regarded as a non-Muslim for the purpose of seats reserved for non-Muslim minorities.

31 The definition of who is and who is not a Muslim was further refined in 1985 when the following text was added to Article 260(3) (b): '(b) "non-Muslim" means a person who is not a Muslim and includes a person belonging to the Christian, Hindu, Sikh, Budhhist or Parsi community, a person of the Quadiani Group or the Lahori Group (who call themselves "Ahmadis" or by any other name), or a Bahai, and a person belonging to any of the scheduled castes'. See section 6 of the Constitution (Third) Amendment Order 1985 as incorporated by section 19 of the Constitution (Eighth) Amendment Act 1985.

32 Article 58(2) b, Constitution 1973.

33 Ordinance XX of 1985, inserting new sections 298A and 298B to the Pakistan Penal Code 1860.

34 *Khurshid Bibi v. Muhammad Amin* PLD 1967 SC 97.

35 See for instance *Asma Jilani v. The Government of Punjab* 1972 SC 139 where the Supreme Court relied on Islamic principles of democracy to declare the *coup d'état* of Yahya Khan in 1969 unconstitutional.

36 See for instance *Nizam Khan v. Additional District Judge, Lyallpur* PLD 1976 Lahore 930.

37 The Constitution (Amendment) Order 1980.

38 See article 203B(c), Constitution 1973. For the first ten years, fiscal and banking laws were excluded from the jurisdiction of the Federal Shariat Court. This temporary bar came to an end in 1990.

39 See the Criminal Law (Amendment) Act 1997. Under this law the heirs of a murder victim determine the fate of the murderer and have the right to decide whether he should be punished, pardoned or be ordered to pay monetary compensation.

40 *Mahmood-ur-Rahman Faisal v. Secretary, Ministry of Law* PLD 1992 FSC 1.

41 *Mirza Qamar Raza v. Tahira Begum* PLD 1988 Kar 169.

42 *Irashad H. Khan v. Parveen Ajaz* PLD 1987 Kar 466.

43 *Bank of Oman Ltd v. East Trading Co. Ltd.* PLD 1987 Kar 404, p. 445.

44 *Hakim Khan v. Government of Pakistan* PLD 1992 SC 595, at p. 617.

45 *Hakim Khan v. Government of Pakistan* PLD 1992 SC 595 and *Mst Kaneez Fatima v. Wali Muhammad* PLD 1993 SC 909.

46 Reproduced in PLD 1991 J 1, at p. 142.

47 *Zaheeruddin v. The State* 1993 SCMR 1718.

48 The Oath of Judges Order 2000 was promulgated just one week before the Supreme Court was due to hear a case challenging the legitimacy of the military takeover.

49 See *Zafar Ali Shah v. General Pervez Musharraf*, PLD 2000 SC 869.

50 New Article 152A, Constitution 1973.

51 New Article 270 AAA, Constitution 1973.

52 Article 63, Constitution 1973.

53 *Watan Party vs. Federation of Pakistan*, PLD 2006 SC 697.

54 *Mr Justice Iftikhar Muhammad Chaudhry vs. President of Pakistan*, PLD 2007 SC 578.

55 *Pakistan Muslim League (N) v. Federation of Pakistan*, PLD 2007 SC 642.

56 *Pakistan Muslim League (N) v. Federation of Pakistan*, PLD 2007 SC 642, p. 673.

57 For a detailed analysis of these developments see Lau 2009.

58 The significance of the 3 November 2007 Order only became apparent two years later, when the Supreme Court ruled that the actions of Musharraf had been unconstitutional. See *Sindh High Court Bar Association vs. Federation of Pakistan*, 31 July 2009, judgment available on the website of the Supreme Court of Pakistan: http://www.supremecourt.gov.pk/web/user_files/File/const.p.9&8of2009.pdf, last accessed on 25 February 2010.

59 See the Revocation of Proclamation of Emergency Order 2007, Repeal of Provisional Constitution Order, Revival of Constitutional Order, Establishment of Islamabad High Court Order and grant of pension benefits to judges who had either refused or had not been invited by the government to take the oath under the PCO.
60 On the conflict about introduction of sharia law in the Swat valley see 9.5, subsection on the politics of Islamisation.
61 See BBC News, '"Taliban law" blocked in Pakistan': http://news.bbc.co.uk/2/hi/south_asia/6182395.stm, dated 25 September 2006.
62 See 'Bangladesh to return to its secular roots', Reuters News: http://in.reuters.com/article/southAsiaNews/idINIndia-46335820100221, dated 21 February 2010.
63 At the time of writing this chapter, Pakistan's parliament is debating the 18th amendment to the Constitution, which is supposed the Constitution 1973 to its original form, at least as far as the powers of the president are concerned. Changes to the Islamic additions effected under Zia's rule are not on the agenda.
64 Speaking about this period, the Pakistan Supreme Court commented in one of its judgments in 1991 that the 1990s had been 'a time of controversy and debate without precedence' (Lau 2003: 175).
65 See BBC, 'Taliban Law Blocked in Pakistan', 15 December 2006, at: http://news.bbc.co.uk/1/hi/world/south_asia/6182395.stm, accessed 25 March 2010.
66 The text of the SNA is available on a number of websites, see for instance Associated Press of Pakistan at: http://www.app.com.pk/en_/index.php?option=com_content&task=view&id=73492&Itemid=2, accessed April 2009.
67 According to Menski (1997), a number of noteworthy jurisprudential developments have occurred during the last decades. The most important of these developments is perhaps that the possibilities for women to have their marriage annulled under Article 8 have been significantly expanded upon. This has been the case since the landmark judgment in the *Khurshid Bibi* trial of 1967.
68 See Section 4 of the Muslim Family Laws Ordinance 1961.
69 See Pakistan Observer (2004), 'Majida urges provinces to name members for NCSW', http://pakobserver.net/200411/01/news/lahore03.asp, dated 1 November.
70 Dawn (2003), 'Law Commission seeks proposals: Effective inheritance law enforcement', *Dawn: The Internet Edition*, see http://www.dawn.com/2003/01/02/top11.htm, dated 2 January 2003.
71 *Daily Times*, dated 16 November 2006.
72 Inserted by Pakistan Penal Code (Second Amendment) Ordinance, XLIV of 1980.
73 See Section 295C of the Pakistan Penal Code (1860), inserted by the Criminal Law (Amendment) Act, III of 1986.
74 Muhammad Ismail Qureshi v. Pakistan PLD 1991 FSC 10.
75 The decision has not been reported as yet but see 'Pak SC rejects petition challenging death as the only punishment for blasphemy', Pakistan News Net, 22 April 2009, at http://www.pakistannews.net/story/492878.
76 'Pakistan reviews blasphemy law', The National, 5 September 2009, http://www.thenational.ae/apps/pbcs.dll/article?AID=/20090906/FOREIGN/709059901/1002.
77 Zingel (1998) argues that the central collection of *zakat* was used by the military regime in order to take over control from the religious establishment.
78 In 2003, the NWFP border province made headlines when the MMA-coalition that won the provincial elections decided to implement its own version of the law on the enforcement of the sharia. However, this attempt was blocked by the Supreme Court, which declared the bill to be unconstitutional, see In Re: Reference No. 1 of 2006 2007 SCMR 817.

Bibliography

Agarwal, B. (2005), 'Women's Inheritance: Next Steps', in *The Indian Express*, 17 October 2005, see http://www.binaagarwal.com/popular%20writings/Women's%20Inheritance_%20Next%20Steps%20IndianExpress_17Oct05.pdf (accessed February 2010).

Alavi, H. (1988), 'Pakistan and Islam: Ethnicity and ideology', in F. Halliday & H. Alavi (eds.), *State and ideology in the Middle East and Pakistan*, London: MacMillan: 21-47.

Ali, C.M. (1988), *The emergence of Pakistan*, Lahore: Services Book Club.

Ali, S.S. (2000), *Gender and human rights in Islam and international law*. The Hague: Kluwer Law International.

Amnesty International (2001), 'Pakistan: Insufficient protection of religious minorities', dated 15 May. See www.amnesty.org for annual reports on human rights in Pakistan.

Anderson, M.R. (ed.) (1989), 'Islamic law and the colonial encounter in British India', in C. Mallat & J. Connors (eds.), *Islamic family law*, London: Graham & Trotman: 205-223.

Barends, M. G. and J.M.Otto (2006), 'Sharia en nationaal recht in Pakistan', in J.M. Otto, A. J. Dekker & L.J. van Soest-Zuurdeeg (eds.), *Sharia en nationaal recht in twaalf moslimlanden*, Amsterdam: Amsterdam University Press: 235-267.

Bartleby (2010), 'Pakistan', in World Factbook, see http://www.bartleby.com/151/country/pk.html (2008 statistics) and https://www.cia.gov/library/publications/the-world-factbook/geos/pk.html (online edition). Washington, D.C.: Central Intelligence Agency.

Binder, L. (1961), *Religion and Politics in Pakistan*, Berkeley: University of California Press.

Braibanti, R. (1965), 'Pakistan: Constitutional Issues in 1964', *Asian Survey*, 5(2): 79-87.

Burks, A. (1954), 'Constitution-Making in Pakistan', *Political Science Quarterly*, 69(4): 544.

Chadbourne, J.D. (1999), 'Never wear your shoes after midnight: Legal trends under the Pakistan Zina Ordinance', *Wisconsin Law Journal* 17: 179.

Chadda, M. (1999), 'Talibinization of Pakistan's transitional democracy', *World Affairs* 3: 3.

Choudhury, G.W. (1955), 'Constitution-Making Dilemmas in Pakistan', *Western Political Quarterly* 8(4): 591.

Choudhury, G.W. (1967), Documents *and Speeches on the Constitution of Pakistan*, Dacca: Green Book House.

Derrett, J.D.M. (1963), 'Justice, equity and good conscience', in J.N.D. Anderson, *Changing Law in Developing Countries*, London: George Allen and Unwin Ltd: 114-154.

Dhavan, R., 'The Road to Xanadu. India's Quest for Secularism', in: G. J. Larson (ed.) (2001), *Religion and Personal Law in Secular India: A Call to Judgement*, Bloomington: Indiana University Press: 301-329.

Engineer, A.A. (1980), *The Islamic state*, New Delhi: Vikas Publishing House.

Engineer, A.A. (2006), *Muslims in India*, New Delhi: Gayan.

Esposito, J.L. (1998), *Islam and politics*, Syracuse: Syracuse University Press.

Esposito (ed.) (1987), *Islam in Asia: Religion, politics & society*, Oxford: Oxford University Press.

Ferguson, N. (2003), *Empire. How Britain Made the Modern World*, London: Penguin Books.

Fisch, J. (1983), *Cheap Lives and Dear Limbs: The British Transformation of the Bengal Criminal Law*, Wiesbaden: F. Steiner: 1769-1817.

Hassan, P. and Azfar, A. (2001), *Moving Toward an Islamic Financial Regime in Pakistan*, Cambridge, MA: Islamic Legal Studies Program.

Hassan, R. (1985), 'Islamization: An Analysis of Religious, Political and Social Change in Pakistan', *Middle Eastern Studies* 21(3): 263-284.

Hilton, I. (2002), 'Pakistan is being slowly Talibanised', *The Guardian*, dated December 11.

Husain, I. (2004), 'Evolution of Islamic banking in Pakistan', see http://www.meezanbank.com/articledetails.asp?aid=160.

Iqbal, A. (1986), *Islamization of Pakistan*. Lahore: Vanguard.

Imran, M. (2006), 'Clerics say no to changes in Hudood law, demand new CII', *Daily Times*, dated 7 July 2006, see http://www.dailytimes.com.pk/default.asp?page=2006\07\07\story_7-7-2006_pg7_11 (accessed February 2010).

Jahangir, A. (1998), 'The Origins of the MFLO: Reflections on Activism', in Shaeed, F., *Shaping Women's Lives: Laws, Practices and Strategies in Pakistan*. Lahore: Shirkat Gah: 93-106.

Jilani, H., E. Chodosh & T. Hussain (2002), 'Pakistan', in H.M. Kritzer (ed.), *Legal systems of the world*, vol. 3, Santa Barbara: ABC-CLIO: 1247-1251.

Kaushik, S. N. (1996), *Ahmadiya Community in Pakistan*, New Delhi: South Asian Publishers.

Khan, H. (2009), *Constitutional and political history of Pakistan*, Karachi, Lahore: Oxford University Press.

Kolff, D.H.A. (1992), 'The Indian and British law machines: Some remarks on law and society in British India', in W. Mommsen & J. de Moor (eds.), *European expansion and law*, Oxford: Berg: 201-235.

Lau, M. (1996), 'Indian tort law: A historical enquiry', *Delhi Law Review* 17: 24-40.

Lau, M. (2003), 'Article 2A: The objectives resolution and the Islamisation of Pakistani laws', in H.-G. Ebers & T. Hanstein (eds.), *Beiträge zum islamischen Recht* vol. 3, Frankfurt am Main: Peter Lang: 173-204.

Lau, M. (2006), *The role of Islam in the legal system of Pakistan*. Leiden: Brill.

Lau, M. (2007), 'Twenty-Five Years of Hudood Ordinances – A review', *Washington and Lee Law Review* 64(4): 1291-1314.

Lau, M. (2009), 'Pakistan', *Yearbook of Islamic and Middle Eastern Law (2007-2008)* 13: 275-292.

Malik, J. (1990), 'Waqf in Pakistan: Change in Traditional Institutions', *Die Welt des Islams*, 30: 63-97.

Mayer, A.E. (1995), *Islam and human rights: Tradition and politics*, Boulder: Westrick Press.

Mehdi, R. (1994), *The Islamization of the law in Pakistan*, Richmond: Curzon.

Mehdi, R. (2001), *Gender and property law in Pakistan*, Copenhagen: djof Publishing.

Mehmood, A. (2002), 'Islamisation of economy in Pakistan: Past, present and future', *Islamic Studies* 41(4): 688-689.

Menski, W.F. (1997), 'South Asian Muslim law today: An overview', *Sharqiyyat* 9(1): 16-36.

Metcalf, B. (2004), *Islamic Contestations: Essays on Muslims in India and Pakistan*, New Delhi: Oxford University Press.

Moten, A.R. (2003), 'Mawdudi and the transformation of Jamaat-E-Islami in Pakistan', *The Muslim World* 93: 391-414.

Naipaul, V.S. (1999), *Beyond belief: Islamic excursions among the converted peoples*, London: Abacus.

Nasr, S.V.R. (1994), *The Vanguard of the Islamic Revolution. The Jama'at-i Islami of Pakistan*, London: I. B Tauris.

Pearl, D. & W. Menski (1998), *Muslim family law*, London: Sweet & Maxwell.

Peters, R. (2005), *Crime and punishment in Islamic law*, Cambridge: Cambridge University Press.

Pirzada, S. (2000), *The Politics of the Jamiat Ulema-i-Islam Pakistan: 1971-1977*, Oxford: Oxford University Press.

Rahman, F. (1970), 'Islam and the Constitutional Problem of Pakistan', *Studia Islamica*, 32: 280.

Rehman, J. (2001), 'Minority rights and the constitutional dilemmas of Pakistan', *Netherlands Quarterly of Human Rights* 19(4): 417-443.

Rehman, I.A. (2003), 'Another fling at Shariat', *DAWN, The Internet Edition* (http://DAWN.com), dated 8 June.

Rudolph, S.H. and Rudolph, L., 'Living with Difference in India: Legal Pluralism and Legal Universalism in Historical Context', in: G. J. Larson (ed.) (2001) *Religion and Personal Law in Secular India: A Call to Judgement*, Bloomington: Indiana University Press: 36-68.

Singh, S. (2009), *Jinnah. India-Partition-Independence*, New Delhi: Rupa & Co.

Shamim, M. (2004), 'The Goal of Workers' Welfare and Policy Challenges', see http://www.paktiger.com/phpSpo/Admin/pdf/04-GoalOfWorkers.doc.

Symonds, R. (1950), *The Making of Pakistan*, London: Faber and Faber.

Talbot, I. (1998), *Pakistan: A Modern History*, New York: St. Martin's Press.

Wasti, T. (2009), *The application of Islamic criminal law in Pakistan*, Leiden: Brill.

Williams, R. V. (2006), *Postcolonial Politics and Personal Laws. Colonial Legal Legacies and the Indian State*, New Delhi: Oxford University Press.

Wolpert, S. (2000), *A New History of India*, Oxford: Oxford University Press.

Zingel, W.-P. (1998), 'Alleviating urban poverty – the Pakistan way', working paper, Department of International and Development Economics, South Asia Institute of Heidelberg.

10 Sharia and national law in Indonesia

Jan Michiel Otto[1]

Abstract

This chapter adresses the relationship between sharia and national law in Indonesia. The historical sections 10.1-10.4 examine the (pre)colonial pluralities of law, and subsequently relate how Indonesia has accommodated sharia in its laws, administration, and court system, from independence in 1945 until today. The sections 10.5-10.8 pay attention to the law presently in force. While the constitution does not mention Islam explicitly, the government is keen to coordinate religious affairs and prevent excesses. The Ministry of Religion plays an important role in this respect. Religious Courts, as branches of the national judiciary, mainly hear marital disputes, but have recently been given jurisdiction in economic matters as well. The Marriage Act of 1974 is the main sharia-based law; in its provisions Indonesia has kept a significant distance from the patriarchal norms of classical sharia. In 1991, an official Compilation of Islamic Law, drafted by scholars and judges, was promulgated. It contains three chapters – on marriage, inheritance, and religious endowments – which, beside the law, should serve as main reference for the Religious Courts. In the province of Aceh, with its special autonomy, sharia-based law also extends to certain criminal offences.

Table of contents

The Republic of Indonesia (1945) has a population of approximately 235 million people. It is the world's most populous Muslim country. The Indonesian archipelago is inhabited by many ethnic groups, the largest being the Javanese, who occupy the densely populated island of Java along with other ethnic groups, such as the Sundanese (West Java) and the Madurese (East Java). Muslims – primarily Sunnis – make up 86 per cent of the population. Other recognised religions are Protestantism (6%), Roman Catholicism (3%), Hinduism (2%), and Buddhism (1%). Virtually everyone in Indonesia speaks the official language, Bahasa Indonesia, although the many ethnic groups in the archipelago also have their own languages.

(Source: Bartleby 2010)

10.1 The period until 1920

Sharia and scholars between three fires[2]

Islam reached Indonesia around the thirteenth century through the influence of traders coming from India (Ricklefs 1981: 3-13). At that time, the archipelago was made up of various kingdoms, which at times cooperated with one another, but at other times went through periods of great conflict and warfare. Many centuries earlier, Indian traders had brought Hinduism to Java, which was to affect religion, culture, and the form of government for a long time (De Graaf 1949: 21). Hinduism influenced primarily the large states that emerged from central Java, namely Majapahit in the fourteenth century and Mataram in the fifteenth and sixteenth centuries.

These princely states were relatively well-developed with distinct social, political, and legal institutions (Ball 1981: 1-2). But Islam increased in its importance, spreading slowly but surely from settlements in the northern coastal regions of Java to the hinterland. Consequently, the Islamic religion, including the Islamic jurisprudence of the Shafi'ite school, blended with the religion, politics, and legal practices in the princely courts. A certain degree of fusion also took place between Islamic norms and the local customs and law-ways (*adat* law)[3] in rural areas (Lev 1972: 5). During the sixteenth century, the sultans of Yogyakarta and Solo converted to Islam. In their islamised principalities, they began to appoint, alongside a prime minister and a military commander, a religious scholar (*panghulu*), who was to be responsible for religious affairs, including the administration of Islamic justice (Cammack 2003: 114-115; Hisyam 2001).

The Dutch East India Company

In 1596, Dutch merchant ships arrived in search of spices. Initially, the Dutch East India Company (VOC), a powerful mercantile corporation, operated from small trading stations along the coast. For the Europeans living there, it established a comprehensive legal system based on Dutch models. With regard to the indigenous population, initially no colonial legal policy was deliberately pursued. In fact, only in 1747 – some one hundred and fifty years later – did the Company's Governor-General establish by decree the first court for the indigenous population of Java. The court, based in Semarang, was called the '*Landraad*'. It was chaired by a colonial administrator, and a few religious scholars (*panghulus*) were attached to it as advisers (Burns 1999: 61; Hisyam 2001). The management of the VOC itself was rather uninterested and ignorant about indigenous legal systems (Ball 1981: 17-25). This became clear when the VOC ordered various *compendia* of indigenous law to be drafted. Instead of accurate representations of the complex blending of *adat* law, Islamic law, and Javanese royal decrees that applied in practice, the colonial authorities clung to fallacious, one-sided assumptions; for example, it was wrongly assumed that the Islamic population was fully subject to religious, Islamic law only.[4]

The colonial state and sharia

When the VOC went bankrupt in 1800 and the Netherlands East-Indies were transferred to the Dutch state, the era of full colonial administration began. From the outset, colonial policy had consistently placed a central emphasis on maintaining a budget surplus (*batig slot*), but after 1800 the Dutch became increasingly concerned with the political and socio-economic situation in the colony. Influenced by events in Europe at the beginning of the nineteenth century, the colonial government also took its legislative duties more seriously.[5] A 'proto-constitution' was drafted and brought into force as early as 1803, calling for respect of indigenous laws, customs, and institutions (Burns 1999: 62; Ball 1982: 80). Under the leadership of General Daendels (1808-1811) and during the short interim period of British rule under Raffles (1811-1816), more territories on Java were brought under colonial rule. A dualist, yet coherent, administrative hierarchy was established, made up of Dutch civil servants on the one hand, and indigenous officials on the other hand. More courts were established for the indigenous population – still called *Landraad* – and presided over by high colonial officials called '*resident*', who were regional administrators. When a dispute between Muslims was brought before the *Landraad*, the *panghulu* served as an adviser regarding Islamic laws. However, his opinion was often disregarded because *panghulus* tended to cite primarily religious laws, regardless of whether or not these were applied in practice (Ball 1981: 69).

From around 1812, resistance against foreign domination started growing on Java. This resulted in the Java War (1825-1830), which in the end was won by the Dutch. Now colonial exploitation began in earnest (Ricklefs 1981: 111). The government implemented a repressive colonial agricultural policy that obliged Javanese farmers to use a set portion of their lands for the cultivation of crops for the colonial government, the so-called Cultivation System (*Cultuurstelsel*). Through this system the Dutch generated enormous wealth. Despite specific regulations calling for recognition of indigenous legal systems and the protection of local communities against abuses, colonial law served generally as an instrument for the government's extractive policy.

During this period, no satisfactory overall policy was made for the colonial administration of justice. As a consequence, also the position of the sharia remained unclear and ambiguous. The general ignorance of the Dutch East-Indies government with regard to *adat* and Islamic laws continued (Ball 1981: 35). Furthermore, according to a royal decree from 1830, the codified legislation of the Netherlands had to be applied in the Netherlands Indies to the extent possible (De Smidt 1990: 17-18). Thus, on 1 May 1848, ten major laws were brought into force in the colony, modelled after the innovative codifications of 1838 in the Netherlands. An 'Act on General Provisions of Legislation' divided the population into two groups: first, the Europeans and those with equal legal status; and, secondly, the natives and those with equal legal status (Art. 6). At first, all Christians were considered equal to the Europeans. The second category of natives and those with equal status included 'the Arabs, the Moors, the Chinese' as well as all others who were 'Mohammedans or Heathens'. While the codified civil and commercial legislation applied in principle to the Europeans, the native population was subject to 'the religious laws, social institutions and customs, insofar as these do not conflict with the generally recognised principles of fairness and justice' (Dekker & Van Katwijk 1993: 11-13). In 1854, the Netherlands Indies 'constitution' (*Regeringsreglement*) was promulgated; it further substantiated these provisions in Article 75(3).

The principle of legal dualism was by no means absolute. Indeed in public law there was a strong tendency towards unification. In 1867 a criminal code for Europeans was enacted, followed in 1873 by one for non-Europeans. Yet, the substance of both codes was identical, and as of 1918 all population groups would become subject to one unified criminal code. In 1879 labour law was also unified. But, in most matters of private law, legal dualism continued to prevail. When putting this system into practice, the colonial rulers were faced with the question of what these religious laws, social institutions, and customs actually came down to, and which agencies should be tasked with applying them. In the Dutch institutes where indigenous law was studied and taught to future colonial officials, the focus lay in discovering and finding 'Muhammadan law' (Otto et al. 1994: 732). Salomon Keijzer, a scholar of Islamic studies who lectured at the Royal Academy for colonial civil servants in Delft, argued that pure Islamic law should serve as the main reference in any attempt to understand the laws of the indigenous population. A colleague of his, the jurist L.W.C. van den Berg, described the indigenous laws on Java and Madura as 'deviations' from Islamic law.[6]

In 1882, the colonial government decided to formalise and regulate the existing administration of Islamic justice, and, as such, enacted an ordinance on the procedural law of Religious Councils, popularly known as the 'Council Agama'.[7] Thus, the colonial government put together non-salaried religious officials, led by a *panghulu*, in these councils and granted them jurisdiction over marriage, divorce, and inheritance, as well as over religious endowments (*wakaf*) (Noer 1978: 43). The council applied Islamic law. The religious scholars and other members of the council were now no longer appointed by the native ruler in their districts, but by the Dutch *resident*. The decisions of the Religious Council could only be executed following approval by the *Landraad*, which continued to be the main state court for the native population. Such ratification was in many, if not most, cases withheld, effectively relegating the status of the Religious Council to little more than an advisory body (Hooker 2003: 13). Despite the council's formal jurisdiction to decide on marital issues according to Islamic law, colonial legislators enacted the Mixed Marriages Ordinance of 1898, which decreed that Muslim women were allowed to marry non-Muslims. This measure, which conflicted directly with the prevailing interpretations of the sharia, was to remain in force until 1974.

The *panghulus* saw themselves placed 'between three fires': God, the colonial government, and local communities (Hisyam 2001). In practice, they cast themselves as mediators between the latter two groups, the government being keen to use their services. Some new Muslim movements, however, depicted the Religious Councils as corrupt and 'lackeys of the non-believers'. In addition, doubts were increasingly placed on their alleged expertise, by both the nascent Muslim movements and the colonial government itself, which had imposed certain standards precisely for this purpose. At the same time, other informal religious scholars began to gain prominence. Under the auspices of the Sultan of Yogyakarta, from 1905 some *panghulus* established their own Islamic schools (*madrasahs*) employing modern methods to educate staff for the Religious Councils. Eventually, *madrasahs* supported by new Muslim associations (see below) would spread across the island of Java.

Legislative policies, adat law and sharia in the late colonial state

Around 1900, various colonial administrators and scholars proposed the replacement of the existing legal dualism with a system of uniform private law codes based on the Dutch model for all inhabitants. They were of the opinion that the religious and customary laws were a source of legal uncertainty and that the corpus of different laws for different population groups created confusion (Ball 1981: 43). Others, however, believed that it would be wrong to apply the laws of the Dutch minority to the native majority, as it had its own laws. After a long political and academic struggle, the latter succeeded in convincing the Dutch parliament and government to stick to the pluralistic system and retain the indigenous law of the natives, rejecting proposals for the full unification of private laws. Around the turn of the century, *adat* law – Indonesia's version of customary law – became the key concept in the colonial analysis of indigenous laws. The first person to use the concept of 'adat-law' – in 1893 – was Snouck Hurgronje, an expert of Islam, Arabic and Indonesian languages and cultures.[8] Jurists, and one legal scholar in particular, the young law professor Cornelis van Vollenhoven who taught in Leiden (1901-1933), further developed this concept. To him and his many students and supporters, the recognition of *adat* law was the main objective of the so-called Ethical Policy initiative (1901). He argued in favour of extended indigenous land rights of native communities and protection from land grabbing by European and Chinese entrepreneurs. Much of the political and legal debates and literature on *adat* law deals with these issues of land tenure security.

However, in the context of Islamic legal development, the promotion of *adat* law could also be regarded as a deliberate effort to undermine Islamic law. Indeed, when Snouck Hurgronje coined the term, he happened to be involved in preparing a government strategy to address the rebellious, fervently Islamic, province of Aceh. In his opinion, the transformation of Islam and Islamic law into political factors had to be stymied, not only in Aceh, but throughout the colony. However, while it is true that in his view political Islam had to be resisted, he also argued that Islamic law should *not* be prevented from playing a role in regulating the private relations of Muslims. After 1900, Snouck Hurgronje worked in close collaboration with Van Vollenhoven who, assisted by dozens of field researchers and PhD students, scientifically developed, elaborated, recorded, and promoted the colony's customary law. As said, *adat* law was most important in the 'ethical' struggle for land tenure security, fitting in a new policy emphasis on the welfare and well-being of the indigenous population. Its key characteristic was that its norms were *actually* applied by local communities; thus, *adat* law was *living* law. As a consequence, it was reasoned that *adat* law would include only those norms of 'customary law', of 'princely decrees', and of 'religious law' that were actively practiced by the community.

The principle that sharia norms were considered the law in force only in as far they applied in practice – thus belonging to the living *adat* law – became known among legal scholars in Indonesia as the 'reception theory'.[9] This theory, however, was considered by orthodox and nationalist Muslims as a symbol of the subjugation of Islamic law to *adat* law. They accused the Dutch of engaging in divide-and-rule politics and of misusing the fact that *adat* laws differed from one place to another. Moreover, the repressive 'pacification' of Aceh reinforced both nationalist and Muslim resistance. As a consequence of these sentiments, various large Islamic popular movements were founded. In 1911, the '*Muhammadiyah*' was established. In 1912, the Islam Association (*Sarekat Islam*) followed, which would later be surpassed in importance by the NU established in 1926 (*Nahdatul Ulama*, lit. 'the awakening of the scholars'). The NU had its roots in the Islamic schools that taught sharia (Van Dijk 1988: 37-38). In 1923, an organisation of 'orthodox' Islamic intellectuals called '*Persis*' (*Persatuan Islam*, lit. Islamic Unification) was created (Hooker 2003: 28-32).[10] All sorts of differences of opinion existed between these new movements and the *panghulus*, but there was also a common goal: furthering the cause of Islam *vis-à-vis* the colonial government (Hisyam 2001).

10.2 The period from 1920 until 1965

The rise of nationalism, independence, and Sukarno's rule

In 1922, the colonial government established a commission for the reorganisation of the Religious Council. In addition to Muslim leaders and Javanese local rulers (*bupati* or *regent*), this commission included Hussein Djajadiningrat, the government's Deputy-Advisor for Native Affairs, and the professor of *adat* law Ter Haar (Lev 1972: 18). The work of this commission eventually contributed to the drafting and enactment of a regulation that came into force in 1937. This regulation changed the status, name, and composition of the councils on Java and Madura. It established '*Panghulu* courts', to be comprised of a religious scholar (*panghulu*) serving in the capacity of judge, who could be assisted by two assessors and a clerk. These would all be salaried positions in an effort to professionalise the courts. In addition, an Islamic Court of Appeals (*Mahkamah Islam Tinggi*) was established for the whole of Java and Madura. Under the same regulation, South

Kalimantan was provided with an equivalent court structure.[11] The new Religious Courts retained their authority to settle marital disputes. However, adjudication of religious endowments (*wakaf*)[12] and of inheritance law was removed from their jurisdiction. The regulation granted the secular General Courts (*Landraden*) full authority in matters relating to property. Understandably, the 1937 reform was seen as being anti-Islamic and sparked much resistance from Muslim movements, but to no avail (Cammack 2007: 148; Lev 1972: 19-24).

The end of colonialism and the birth pangs of independence

In 1942, Japan invaded the Netherlands Indies and took over the administration of the archipelago. All existing laws remained in force; therefore, the position of Islamic law remained largely unchanged. The Japanese did, however, concentrate the supervision of religious affairs into a single department of Religious Affairs instead of spread across various ministries as it had been previously (Lev 1972: 44).

From the end of 1944, when independence was in sight, a secret council of prominent Indonesians began meeting in order to advise the Japanese on administrative affairs. The agenda of these discussions included the position of Islam (ibid: 34-36). The visions of 'nationalists' and 'Muslim leaders' soon diverged on this issue, resulting in the council becoming deeply divided regarding the question of whether a future independent state of Indonesia should still have Religious Courts. A number of Muslim leaders hoped for an 'Islamic state' that would enforce the sharia for all Muslims. During negotiations in June 1945, their wishes were initially honoured in the so-called Jakarta Charter, which was intended as the preamble to the new constitution. This document stipulated that the new state would be based on the belief in God 'with the obligation to implement sharia for the adherents of Islam' (Cribb & Brown 1997: 15).

But in the following weeks, nationalist leaders Sukarno and Hatta changed their minds. When they pronounced Indonesia's independence on 17 August 1945 and read out and disseminated the first constitution, the cited words ('with the obligation to...') appeared to have been deleted. Sukarno and Hatta preferred a national state under a strong, unified leadership and with a secular, modernising orientation.

The ideological foundations of the Indonesian Constitution of 1945 lay in the five principles of the Pancasila. The Pancasila, which literally means 'five pillars', became part of the constitutional preamble. As such, it formed part of the highest source of law in the Indonesian state. The five principles were:

- belief in the One and Almighty God;
- just and civilised humanity;

- national unity;
- popular sovereignty governed by wise policies arrived at through deliberation and representation; and
- social justice.

This political formula incorporated the main ideological currents in Indonesia's political arena: Islam, internationally recognised principles of humanity, nationalism, traditional governance, democracy, and socialism. The general formulation of the first principle was meant to assuage the fears of the followers of other religions. Formally, no space was left for atheism or polytheism, but, culturally, religion in Indonesia was syncretic and tolerant.

Islamist rebellions, Islamic politics, administration, and law in the young republic

After independence, the Religious Courts remained in place, in accordance with the constitution's transitional provision that all laws and state institutions would remain unchanged as long as they did not conflict with the new constitution. The first twenty years of the young Indonesian republic, led by Sukarno from 1945 until the beginning of the New Order in 1965/1966, constituted a period of much military, political, and ideological tension and conflict. The struggle for independence undertaken against the Dutch lasted until December 1949. During this chaotic period, a number of insurrections against the republic occurred in various regions. In 1948, a mystic leader in West Java proclaimed himself to be the leader of an Islamic state based on the sharia and ruled by clergymen (Ricklefs 1981: 215-216). This *Darul Islam* insurgence sparked years of conflict with the government in the rural areas of West Java.

Starting in 1950, a rebellion against Jakarta also broke out in South Sulawesi, which aligned itself politically with *Darul Islam*. In 1953, Aceh joined in the insurgency (ibid: 232, 235). In 1956, army officers also rebelled in Sumatra and in 1957 in Kalimantan, the Moluccas, and North and South Sulawesi (ibid: 242). After a failed assassination attempt on Sukarno by Muslim extremists later that year, he began opting for a more dictatorial form of rule. The army supported him in this, as did his own nationalist party, 'Partai Nasional Indonesia' (PNI), and the communist party, 'Partai Komunis Indonesia' (PKI). Starting in 1957, he referred to his reign as 'Guided Democracy'. Relations with Aceh were restored in 1959 by giving the province a special legal status that granted it autonomy in matters of education, culture, and religion.[13] In West Java, the *Darul Islam* rebels were pushed back, but were not to fully give up their fight until 1965 (Van Dijk 1988: 40).

After independence, the Islamic mass organisation *Masyumi*, which had been founded during the Japanese occupation, had become the biggest political party. Initially, the NU, the *Muhammadiyah*, and other Muslim organisations worked together under the banner of *Masyumi*. Several prime ministers belonged to this coalition (Ricklefs 1981: 230). Following an internal conflict, however, between the 'pliable' conservatives and the 'strict' modernists, the conservative NU left the Masyumi during the 1950s and started working together with the nationalists and communists.

In 1955, general elections were held for parliament and for the *Konstituante*, the Constitutional Assembly of Indonesia. Masyumi, PNI, NU, and PKI became the biggest parties. In the *Konstituante*, which was inaugurated in 1956, Muslim politicians argued that the Jakarta Charter should be incorporated into the constitution, but this proposal was rejected by a small majority (ibid: 253). Sukarno, who adamantly continued his push for national unity, now tried to sway popular opinion in favour of the 'Nasakom' ideology, trying to unify three competing ideologies (*Nasionalisme*, *Agama* (religion), and *Komunisme* (ibid: 256). At this juncture, the communists were becoming more and more powerful, as the Muslim parties steadily lost ground.

On the administrative front, successive cabinets attempted to organise and regulate government and society following independence in 1945. A year later, in 1946, the Ministry of Religion was established (Lev 1972: 43). This new ministry opened local bureaus for religious affairs throughout the country, the so-called KUA (*Kantor Urusan Agama*). Oversight of the Religious Courts was also transferred in 1946 from the Ministry of Justice to the Ministry of Religion (ibid: 64). The ministry offered ample employment opportunities for supporters of the NU, and of the Masyumi, who, unlike other civil servants, mostly had their origins from pious, non-aristocratic circles (ibid: 53). Enactment of Law 22/1946 brought the contracting and registration of Muslim marriages and divorces within the administrative jurisdiction of the ministry (ibid: 54-57). The office of the salaried Civil Registrar, whose functioning followed national, uniform procedures overseen by the local bureaus for religious affairs, was also created. While the Ministry of Religion was viewed with hope by Muslim activists, it was seen with fear by others. Would it propagate Islam and undermine the state or would it control Islam on behalf of the state?

After the declaration of independence, nationalists made several attempts at abolishing the Religious Courts. The first was Act 19/1948, stipulating that the courts must be integrated into secular state courts. However, due to the ongoing struggle for independence against the Dutch, this law was not implemented and the Religious Courts simply continued to function as they always had, just now formally supported by the Ministry of Religion. Finally, in 1957, the cabinet enacted Government Regulation 45, authorising the formation of Islamic courts in every district in the outer islands where they did not already exist (Cammack 2007: 149). While the jurisdiction of these Religious Courts outside of Java appeared to be broader, as it included inheritance matters (ibid), in fact, it was more limited because its scope was decreed to be for 'the application of the laws living in society'. In essence, Regulation 45/1957 was a continuation of *adat* law policies, but now for the purpose of formation of a 'national *adat*' (Bowen 2003: 53).

The Supreme Court in Jakarta, led by the progressive Wirjono, was of the opinion that the position of widows under traditional *adat* law and Islamic law was too weak. Lev notes the court's argumentation, including reference to 'the equal participation of women in the national struggles' and 'the strong relationship between husband and wife' (1962: 213-222). In 1960, the Supreme Court ruled that 'adat inheritance law throughout Indonesia concerning the widow can be so formulated that a widow is always an heir to the separately owned property [...] of her husband.' Lev further notes, '[t]he essential point of this decision [...] is that the Supreme Court's view of justice has prevailed over the several adat views of justice [...]' (ibid: 222). This new nationalist legal discourse with regard to the position of sharia *vis-à-vis adat* law in Indonesia's national legal system came to expression in the plea of the eminent Muslim jurist Hazairin for the creation of a fifth Sunni school of Islamic jurisprudence, the *Madhhab Indonesia*. This would be based on an eclectic amalgamation of elements taken from the teachings of the four existing schools of jurisprudence complemented with Indonesian local *adat* practices, e.g. joint marital property (*harta bersama*).

10.3 The period from 1965 until 1985

The heyday of Suharto's New Order

On 30 September 1965 the army allegedly foiled an attempted leftist coup. This sparked off an immense power struggle, which eventually devolved into a huge massacre in which the army – backed by Muslim groups – imprisoned and murdered hundreds of thousands of communists and communist sympathisers. Sukarno lost his authority and on 11 March 1966 he signed a document in which he transferred executive powers to Suharto, who, in turn, ordered the Communist Party to be abolished. The following year, Sukarno was officially deposed and Suharto proclaimed himself president of the republic (Cribb & Brown 1997: 110-111). His rule, generally referred to as the 'New Order' (*Orde Baru*), was to last for 32 years.

Political control, bureaucratisation and two major laws

Under Suharto's rule only three political parties were allowed, all of which were controlled by the government. Golkar, a secular mass organisation initiated by the army in 1964 to unite all forces against the communist party, became the dominant ruling party. All civil servants were pressured to become members of Golkar. Existing Islamic parties were ordered to merge, thus becoming the United Development Party, or PPP (Partai Persatuan Pembangunan). The PPP together with the nationalist Democratic Party of Indonesia, or PDI (Partai Demokrasi Indonesia – the third and final political party permitted to operate under Suharto's regime – engaged in a very restrained form of opposition politics. With the help of his generals, Suharto created a stable, but repressive police state that aimed for quick economic growth. Indonesia's natural resources – oil, gas, and wood – were exploited at rapid rates. Suharto also set about to improve relations with the West and the international community.[14]

Suharto's politics of stability, control, bureaucratisation, and forced 'Pancasila-harmony' also affected Islam in Indonesia, which was initially allocated a secure, but limited role. The Ministry of Religion exercised political and administrative oversight of Islamic organisations, Islamic education, and the administration of Islamic justice. In the 1970s, the government made two major new laws to further define the position of the sharia, namely the Basic Act 14/1970 on the Judiciary and the Marriage Act 1/1974.

The Judiciary Act of 1970 specified that the national judiciary would be comprised of four sectors: general, administrative, military, and religious. In this context the word 'religious' (*agama*) in effect only referred to Islam.[15] Courts in all four sectors would be state courts, with both courts of first instance and appellate courts. The new law signalled the unification, strengthening and expansion of the state-led Islamic judicial sector (previously regulated in 1882, 1937, and 1957). The Religious Courts still required, however, approval from the General Courts for execution of their judicial decisions. Moreover, the new law of 1970 set forth that judgments of the Religious Courts were subject to review by the Supreme Court. Thus, the expansion notwithstanding, the subjugation of Islamic law was once again formally established. Initially, the Ministry of Religion resisted the Supreme Court's newfound authority over the Islamic courts and tried to keep the courts 'insulated from the pressures to conform to the imperatives of a national legal system' (Cammack 2007: 156). But, in 1979 when the Supreme Court actually exercised its jurisdiction over two cases originating in the Religious Courts, this was by and large accepted by the Ministry.

Before the 1974 Marriage Act was promulgated, various drafts had been discussed, none of which were ever approved. In particular, Islamic modernists and orthodox groups disagreed about draft provisions on polygamy and divorce. The orthodox preferred to leave everything to the uncodified sharia, but in 1973 modernists succeeded in pressuring the government to propose a bill that would strengthen the position of women in many respects and expand state supervision. Orthodox groups rose up in sharp opposition to these proposals, and massive, heated demonstrations were held around the parliamentary premises. After physical and political intervention of the army, the parliament reached a compromise, replacing a number of the proposals by less far-reaching reforms (Butt 1999: 122-123). Some of the new provisions about divorce were, however, so ambiguously worded that after an initial reading, one was still left unsure as to whether they entailed a modernist or a conservative solution. In any case, the government was now able to proudly declare that a unified marriage law covered all of Indonesia, and that the colonial Mixed Marriage Ordinance of 1898 had been abolished.

Generally speaking, the Religious Courts put themselves to their tasks of reviewing applications for divorce and polygamy. While cases of polygamy were rather exceptional, unilateral repudiation was common, although the statistics fluctuated significantly per region (Otto & Pompe 1988). However, because the new act was still weak in defining norms in several areas (e.g. the validity of unregistered marriages, grounds for polygamy and divorce, and guidelines on interreligious marriages) it did not end legal uncertainty.[16]

In the meantime, the government actively prosecuted groups of Muslim radicals that remained active after the disbandment of the *Darul Islam*. Ba'asyir, who would later gain notoriety as the alleged mentor of the perpetrators of the Bali bombings in 2002, was arrested in 1970 for his activities in the underground *Komando Jihad*. The prime objective of this organisation was the creation of an Islamic state. It was notorious for its bombing attacks on cinemas, nightclubs, and churches, in resistance to the regime of Suharto.

The Council of Indonesian Religious Scholars (MUI)

During the 1970s there was little trust between the government and the conservative religious leaders. In reaction to this, in 1975, Suharto, in his usual, crafty manner, attended to the creation of a national Council of Indonesian Religious Scholars, the *Majelis Ulama Indonesia* (MUI). First, twenty-six provincial councils were formed, which, in turn, instituted a national council. The status of the MUI was unclear: was it a private or a semi-state institution? One of the responsibilities of the

MUI was to assess the religious quality of laws (Bowen 2003: 229-231). The council also proclaimed unsolicited legal opinions (*fatwas*) that could be very controversial at times. In 1980, for example, the MUI declared itself against all marriages between Muslims and Christians, and, in 1981, it declared the attendance of Muslims at Christian celebrations to be sinful (ibid: 235). In the 1980s, the MUI was involved in the establishment of an Islamic banking sector. Some of its members also participated in drafting the 'Compilation of Islamic Law', an attempt to have religious scholars and jurists decide on a restatement of the sharia in force in Indonesia (see section below).

Through these measures Suharto provided a place for Islam during the New Order. The focus lay on control; what could be seen as islamisation of national law often came down to nationalisation of Islamic law. Because of the infamous *Ormas* legislation (1985), Islamic organisations, like others, were legally obliged to recognise the Pancasila state ideology as their highest norm and sole foundation. Any source of serious opposition against Suharto's rule, Islamic or otherwise, was harshly suppressed.

10.4 The period from 1985 until the present

The late New Order, the *Reformasi*, and recent developments

Suharto's pro-Islam policies and mounting criticism

Once major Muslim leaders had openly accepted the supremacy of the Pancasila, the proverbial hatchet between state and Islam could officially be buried. Rather than promoting political Islam, these leaders now turned their attention to 'cultural Islam' (Salim & Azra 2003b: 10). This, in turn, stimulated Suharto to embrace a pro-Islam policy. Incidentally, this came at a politically opportune moment, as Suharto had faced mounting criticism since the 1980s, and was, therefore, in crucial need of support from Muslim movements, notably in the elections of 1992 and 1993 (Hefner 2003: 155).

Criticism of Suharto's regime came from various corners. For years, the continuing violation of human rights by his regime had been openly condemned from abroad. In Indonesia, most people and organisations were more hesitant at voicing such criticism, partially out of fear, and partially because the achievements of Suharto for the country's stability and economy were still appreciated. When, however, the corruption of Suharto's family and inner circle rose to unprecedented heights, the support his regime enjoyed on the street level started to evaporate.

In the 1990s the regime's pro-Islam politics led Suharto's protégé Habibie, the Minister of Technology and Research, to form ICMI, a national association of Muslim intellectuals (*Ikatan Cendekiawan Muslim Indonesia*). The ICMI brought together pious Muslim intellectuals, giving them a useful political instrument (Schwarz 1999: 179). The association had its own think tank and a newspaper to better disseminate its ideas. The goals of ICMI were the improvement of the economic position of Muslims and the incorporation of Islamic values into official government policy (ibid: 175-176).

During the 1990s Islam also manifested itself increasingly in other areas. Islamic schools educated a new generation of students, trying to instil in them devotion, discipline, diligence, and moral ideals, all in the name of Islam. Within the bureaucracy Muslim civil servants were now permitted to openly present themselves as devout Muslims. Meetings were opened with an Islamic prayer, and speeches were preceded by Arabic prayer blessings. Suharto also became aware of this change of winds and he himself made the pilgrimage to Mecca in 1991. Both he and Habibie, who became vice president, increasingly emphasised the Islamic character of the New Order. Nonetheless, the Pancasila state ideology remained the fundamental guideline for Indonesia's governance, including in matters pertaining to religion. National religious harmony continued to be imposed and enforced from above, a kind of 'totalitarian tolerance' so to speak.

Meanwhile, in 1989 a new legislative centrepiece, Act 7/1989 on Religious Courts had been enacted. This law further regulated the position and functioning of the Religious Courts. Earlier drafts had sparked heated debates (Bowen 2003: 185-189). Many nationalists, members of the Christian minority, and professional jurists were strongly opposed to the law because they viewed it as an implicit acknowledgment and acceptance of an autonomous sharia sector within the national legal system. In contrast, the government and the army rather saw the law as a means through which to increase the state's influence over Islam.

For the content of the applicable law, the Religious Courts had to rely on the aforementioned Compilation of Islamic Law, which had already been completed in 1988, at a time when the debates about the Religious Courts' bill were still raging. The Compilation was drafted by many commissions made up of religious scholars, jurists, and other experts. In this way, the Indonesian government had ensured national unification and codification of major parts of the Islamic jurisprudence (*fiqh*), with the endorsement of both leading religious scholars and prominent judges. In 1991, Suharto issued a presidential instruction ordering his Minister of Religion to disseminate the Compilation to be used by state institutions '[...] as a reference to the greatest possible extent in resolving the issues it covers [...]' (Nurlaelawati 2010: 89). The minister then instructed all relevant state agencies to 'apply as much as possible the mentioned Compilation to complement the other legal regulations'. Nowadays the Compilation's rules are taught in schools and applied in Religious Courts. However, from studies of court decisions and interviews with judges, it appears that some judges still use *fiqh*-sources beyond the Compilation, as they want to be able to choose from a broad range of sources in order to arrive at just decisions that are also considered socially and religiously acceptable (ibid).

The Islamic revival taking hold in society in the late 1980s and 1990s also increased the demand for Islamic banking. Thus, in 1991, Suharto, who had hitherto been fearful of Muslim groups attaining financial power, agreed to the establishment of an Islamic bank. The founding of Bank Muamalat Indonesia (BMI) was intended both to strengthen the economic position of non-Chinese Indonesians as well as to serve as an example of corporate governance and honest banking.[17]

The fall of Suharto, winds of constitutional change, and the Islamic axis

When in 1997 the Asian Financial Crisis struck Indonesia, resistance against Suharto became massive and unstoppable. Students played a key role in these protests, demanding large-scale political reforms under the banner of *Reformasi*. Leading the resistance against Suharto were, among others, the NU leader and religious scholar Abdurrahman Wahid, a democratic-minded nationalist, and the more radical academic Amien Rais, leader of the *Muhammadiyah* movement. They dared to voice harsh criticism of the old president.[18] After large and protracted demonstrations, Suharto resigned in 1998. The *Reformasi* could then begin: democratisation, social justice, liberalisation, decentralisation, and possibly a chance for Islamic activists to wrest themselves free from the legacy of colonial and postcolonial state control.

Suharto was succeeded by Habibie, who swiftly pronounced a number of laws that regulated the upcoming processes of democratisation and islamisation. Law 22/1999 on regional autonomy, for instance, brought about a major political transformation of central-local relations. In addition, Habibie promulgated legislation concerning organisation of the pilgrimage (*hajj*), management of required almsgiving (*zakat*), and Islamic banking (Salim 2003: 228). It must be noted that these laws did not oblige Indonesians to undertake the *hajj*, pay *zakat* taxes, or open an Islamic bank account. They were procedural laws establishing an official legal framework for those Muslims who wanted to adhere to their religious duties in these fields (ibid: 229).

Habibie called parliamentary elections in the summer of 1999. Abdurrahman Wahid's PKB and Rais's PAN emerged as new Islamic parties. Together with the traditionally law-abiding PPP and a number of smaller Islamic parties, they formed the so-called 'Islamic axis' in Indonesia's newly elected parliament. Of the axis parties only the PPP and one of the smaller parties strove for the revival of the Jakarta Charter and the islamisation of the constitution. The big winner of the 1999 elections was, however, a secular party: the Partai Demokrasi Indonesia (PDI-P) led by Sukarno's daughter Megawati. Nonetheless, not she, but PKB leader Wahid became president as a result of the political manoeuvring of the Islamic axis led by Amien Rais. Megawati was chosen as vice president; Rais became speaker of the parliament.

President Wahid further restricted the role of the army in politics and initiated several major constitutional changes, strengthening human rights and the free press, empowering elected representative bodies, and safeguarding the independence of the judiciary. He also strongly opposed an Islamic state and the introduction of sharia, as he was of the opinion that religion and politics must remain separated (Bowen 2003: 240). Attempts to further islamise politics and laws did not, therefore, stand much of a chance under Wahid, despite his Islamic background and support base as the NU leader. A majority in parliament shared his viewpoints on these issues.[19] In 2000, several Islamic parties supported a bill on interreligious harmony. This draft proposed to outlaw mixed marriages and to set stricter conditions on the building of new churches in terms of a minimum number of adherents and the permission of inhabitants in the neighbourhood. In response to such developments, and especially when their churches were occasionally set on fire, Christians rose in protest (ibid: 239, 247). In the end, the bill was rejected.

Wahid felt so confident that he occasionally took stands diametrically opposed to those held by prominent *ulama* and the MUI. In the high-profile *Ajinomoto* case in 2002 the MUI had ordered tests of flavouring agents produced by the Ajinomoto company, and it was concluded that one product contained substances from the pancreas gland of pigs and was therefore considered forbidden (*haram*). President Wahid, drawing on other lab test results, decided that the substance was permissible (*halal*), and went on to declare that both the MUI and he were correct, and that the matter was a case of free interpretation (*ijtihad*). To the public it was no longer clear who held ultimate authority on religious matters in the country and who could make binding decisions in cases such as these (ibid: 233-234).

Decentralisation and local sharia-based regulations

Wahid had carried through with the decentralisation process started by Habibie in 1999, which strongly expanded the autonomy of the districts. For two provinces, Papua and Aceh, special autonomy laws were enacted that granted the provinces more authority in making their own provincial regulations. In Papua, these regulations referred to *adat* laws, while in Aceh, according to Act 18/2001 on Aceh, priority was paid to the sharia.

Act 18/2001 would form the legal basis for the provincial government of Aceh to issue a number of regional regulations called '*qanun*' (Arabic for law) on several contested issues. The central motive of the national government concerning Aceh is revealed by Ichwan (2007: 194-196) who demonstrates that both Abdurrahman Wahid and Megawati as presidents had instructed their minister of Religion 'to promote the initiative for creating security through a religious approach'. This played into the hands of the provincial branch of the MUI in Aceh, re-established in 2001 as MPU (ibid: 204), which had already played an active islamising role by issuing several *fatwas*. In particular, its *fatwa* ordering women to wear veils resulted in much uneasiness. But the government did not immediately take a stand on this thorny issue. As Bowen (2003: 231-233) noted, however, it became difficult to ignore the *fatwa*, particularly since in 2002 and 2003 the province's Sharia Office and the provincial parliament laid down Aceh's new sharia policy in a number of *qanuns* (Ichwan 2007: 205) (see 10.5).

Elsewhere in Indonesia, several districts enacted sharia-based regulations (*Perda Syariah*). Yet, in most areas, as a result of the 1999 decentralisation, it was not so much Islam that was undergoing a revival, but rather *adat*. Locally, rules of *adat* law dealt with issues of political authority and of land and natural resources. In the strongly Islamic province of Minangkabau, for example, the return of the *adat* was of a stronger political consequence than the return to Islamic beliefs. In other areas of the archipelago, the resurgence of traditional loyalties led to conflict. Consequently, ethnic and sectarian violence broke out in places such as Central Sulawesi and the Moluccas, where bloody fights between Muslims and Christians ensued.

Dynamics of Islam and politics from Abdurrahman Wahid to Megawati

Meanwhile, Wahid had come into conflict with parliament because of his increasing capriciousness and his rude and disdainful behaviour towards political opponents. Following accusations of mismanagement and involvement in corruption scandals, parliament pressured him into resignation for his 'grave' failure to abide to the 'main guidelines of state policy'. Megawati succeeded him as president in July 2001, with the leader of the Islamic PPP, Hamzah Haz, becoming her vice president.

Following the attacks of 11 September 2001 and the ensuing American attack on Afghanistan, the Indonesian government strongly endeavoured to prevent these foreign geopolitical developments from having negative repercussions on interreligious harmony at home. In October 2002, Indonesia itself was hit by a major terrorist attack targeting a nightclub on Bali, as a result of which many Australians and Indonesians died. In 2003, an attack on the Marriott Hotel in Jakarta followed, and the year after the Australian Embassy became the target of Islamic terrorism. Subsequent investigations focussed on local groups, national organisations, and branches of international Muslim terrorist networks.[20] A number of individuals were condemned to death, but the involvement of Ba'asyir, the alleged leader of the *Jamaah Islamiyah*, could not be irrefutably established.

During Megawati's presidency, which strongly relied upon a number of 'superministers', able technocrats, and military figures, including president-to-be Susilo Bambang Yudhoyono, various developments surfaced signalling the continuing islamisation of society. With the appointment of a vice president like Hamzah Haz, for example, who himself had three wives, the official state policy of rejecting polygamy, which had been adhered to for years, became a dead letter. Polygamy now occurred openly and trouble-free. In order to circumvent the restrictive provisions of the Marriage Act of 1974, men chose to have their polygamous marriages contracted solely by an imam. Earlier studies revealed that of all divorces about half took place without the involvement of the Religious Courts or prescribed law (Cammack et al. 2007: 120; Debating 2003; see also 10.6).[21] Thus, under Megawati, the government's control and supervision of religion seemed to lose some of its strength.

In addition, a fierce argument arose on the new draft criminal code when word spread that a new definition of adultery (i.e. all extramarital sexual relations) was adopted directly from *fiqh* sources. Minister of Justice, Yusril Mahendra of the small Islamist party PBB, was supposedly employing this tactic in order to win the support of the Muslim voters. However, it was the new fundamentalist Muslim party PKS, which was established in 1998, that grew very swiftly thanks to a young, well-educated and highly disciplined cadre of volunteers, engaging in social work in villages and urban kampongs. The party, based on the ideology of Hassan al-Banna (founder of the Egyptian Muslim Brotherhood), tried to come to power by using democratic ways, and would do quite well in several elections. Meanwhile, the practice of Islamic banking also expanded. The MUI successfully campaigned for further formalisation and regulation of interest-free banking (Bank Indonesia 2002).

Despite these developments, no clear-cut, massive process of political and legal islamisation took place. So far, islamisation appeared indeed to be more cultural than politico-legal in nature. In fact, from 2001 to

2004, a working group under the authority of the Minister of Religion drafted a new marriage act trying to improve the status of women. This so-called Counter Legal Draft aroused so much protest from orthodox Muslim organisations upon its publication, that it had to be withdrawn by the end of 2004 (Mulia 2007: 128-145). However, Islamist sentiments did not altogether get the upper hand among the population as a whole. Since the fall of Suharto in 1998, an overwhelming majority of Indonesian Muslims has come out in favour of secular and nationalist parties; this was confirmed in the 2004 parliamentary and presidential elections. The two parties that won the parliamentary election in April 2004 – Golkar (21%) and PDI-P (19%) – were both secular in orientation, as was the third party, Wahid's PKB (12%), which is allied to the traditionalist NU. In October, Susilo Bambang Yudhoyono (SBY) became Indonesia's first directly elected president. SBY is a nationalist with a military background and an experienced cabinet minister. He leads a small secular party, the Partai Demokrat. Yusuf Kalla, a Golkar politician and entrepreneur from NU circles, became his vice president.

The presidency of SBY (Susilo Bambang Yudhoyono)

Since the 2004 elections several legal changes have affected the existing, balanced relationship between sharia and national law. These reforms went in different directions. In 2004 the 1970 Act on the Judiciary was replaced by Act 4/2004, which transferred supervision of Religious Courts fully to the Supreme Court, thereby reducing the supervisory role of the Ministry of Religion to an advisory one. In 2006, Act 3/2006 on Religious Courts, amending the 1989 Act, strengthened the court's jurisdiction in inheritance cases between Muslims, and expanded jurisdiction over cases in sharia economy (*Ekonomi Syaria*).

In order to establish guidelines for the resolution of economic disputes in the Religious Courts, the Supreme Court issued in 2008 the Compilation of Economic Sharia Law (*Kompilasi Hukum Ekonomi Syari'ah*, usually abbreviated as KHES). In the same year, the Indonesian parliament promulgated Law 21/2008 on Islamic Banking. Together with Law 41/2004 on Religious Foundations (*wakaf*) and Law 38/1999 on Almsgiving (*zakat*) the KHES and the banking law have now met the demand for an economic system based on principles of Islamic justice (see 10.8). The *Ekonomi Syaria* regulations, however, are all of a voluntary, optional nature.

In this process of islamisation, state institutions with a predominantly nationalist and secular outlook, such as the Bank Indonesia and the Supreme Court, kept the say over legal developments. In the same vein, in the area of marriage law, the secular General Courts were given a role in registering interreligious marriages by Act 23/2006 on Civil Registration.

Act 11/2006 on special autonomy of Aceh replaced the 2001 Act on the subject. It further regulated the competence of Aceh's provincial government to issue *qanuns* as well as the jurisdiction of the special Islamic courts in the region (the Mahkamah Syari'ah). These powers went clearly beyond the 2001 Act. [22] The 2006 law confirmed and formalised regulatory practices that had emerged since 2002 in Aceh, notably the *qanuns* criminalising gambling and drinking and prescribing the corporal punishment of caning. It has broadened the jurisdiction of the Mahkamah Syari'ah by adding elements of criminal law (*jinayah*) and commercial law (*muamalat*) to it, as already was indicated in Qanun 10/2002. A legal debate has arisen about whether the *qanun* provisions on criminal matters now overrule the applicability of national criminal law, as laid down in the criminal code. The government and the Supreme Court have the power to annul Aceh's individual *qanuns* for 'going against the public interest or violating higher legislation, *unless the law regulates otherwise* [italics added]'. This may have occurred as the expansion of jurisdiction has been approved in a general way by national law. So far the *qanuns* have been limited to minor crimes. Human rights defenders have put forward that Aceh's *qanuns* and other sharia-based district regulations have encroached on human rights standards. This could subject such sharia-based regional regulations to review by the Constitutional Court.

What do these developments in Aceh mean for the existing relationship between sharia and national law? Lindsey & Hooker (2007: 252) consider Aceh's *qanuns* as potentially radical, but state that their implementation is considered by most Acehnese as symbolic rather than hard-line Islamist. They do note, however, that since the tsunami of December 2004, the *qanuns* have become more than just aspirational and that the new courts are more willing to exercise their expanded jurisdiction. Indeed, the first and widely publicised caning of gamblers in Bireuen in June 2005 has been repeated several times in other district towns.

In 2008, freedom of religion came under attack from Islamist organisations who were putting pressure on the government to pronounce a legal ban on the *Ahmadiyya*. The issue has been politicised since a 2005 MUI *fatwa* asking for a ban of this religious group, which considers itself Islamic, but which is not recognised by Sunni orthodoxy. Mosques and members of the group have been attacked by mobs on Lombok and elsewhere. While one government body advocated a legal ban, the president's legal advisors cautioned against it. In June 2008, a joint decree was issued by the ministers of justice and religion warning, on the one hand, Ahmadiyya adherents to return to true Islam or leave it, while warning radicals, on the other hand, not to attack the Ahmadiyya, or they would be sanctioned. Legally speaking, though, this decree did not have the effect of a ban.

This illustrates the way issues of sharia and law are played out in present-day Indonesia. Time and again they are politicised by Islamist groups. Actually, since 1998 the MUI has shifted from a pro-government role to a rather oppositional, Islamist stance. Meanwhile, the state, while deliberately giving in to some demands, has consistently tried to maintain a balance as well as overall control.

A notable instrument of this balancing effort are the Religious Courts that have become a recognised and established part of the national judiciary under supervision of the Supreme Court. Cammack (2007: 169) has compared the role of Religious Courts in the 1970s, when they were 'essentially informal and non-professional' to their present role. He writes:

> Despite their shortcomings [...] the unrestructured Islamic courts were generally successful in addressing the needs of those who used them. [...] It is my sense that the professionalization and bureaucratization of the Islamic judiciary has not fundamentally altered the essential institutional culture of the courts.

Cammack calls the Religious Courts 'a relative success story in Indonesia's otherwise dysfunctional legal system' (ibid). A 2008 study carried out by the Supreme Court and AUSAID revealed a high satisfaction rate among the courts' users – over 70 per cent of all clients and 80 per cent of the total applicants. It appears, however, that the poor still face serious barriers in accessing the Religious Courts (Sumner 2008: 4). Indeed, it is a sobering thought that whatever law-makers or judges may decide on the position of sharia in the national legal system, it does not affect a considerable part of the population since they are simply unable to afford a life within the limits of the law.

10.5 Constitutional law[23]

The words 'Islam', 'Islamic law', and 'sharia' do not feature in the constitution. Thus, Indonesia is not an 'Islamic state', and Islam is not the official state religion. Therefore, unlike in other Muslim countries, the supremacy of the national constitution over competing normative systems should be beyond any legal doubt. Yet, despite this presumptive clarity, one cannot consider Indonesia a fully secular state. The preamble of the constitution refers to the Pancasila state ideology as the highest source of law, within which the first 'pillar' or principle is identified as 'the belief in the One and Almighty God'. Further to this, atheism is not recognised, and in order to marry, one must declare his or her religion. The Ministry of Religion has also been specifically tasked with translation of the first pillar into state policy and practice.

The Indonesian legislator has largely defined the relationship between national law and sharia in the 1989 Act on Religious Courts[24] in procedural terms, and in substantive terms in the Marriage Act 1/1974 and in the 1991 'Compilation of Islamic Law'. The legislator has further created space for districts and provinces to experiment with sharia-related regional regulations through use of the Act on Regional Autonomy (Act 22/1999, amended and replaced by Act 32/2004). Exceptionally, in Act 11/2006 on Special Autonomy for Aceh, Jakarta has empowered this autonomous region to enact regulations (*qanuns*) that go so far as to include certain sharia-based criminal regulations and punishments such as caning. In 2009 the outgoing provincial parliament of Aceh even approved a new *qanun* prescribing stoning as a punishment for adultery; the legal status of this regulation, however, remains highly contested. Beside these elements of potential 'sharia-isation' of the law, it should also be noted here that during the post-1998 constitutional reform process human rights were given a prominent position in Indonesia's constitutional law.

This section will address in particular five key aspects of how sharia-based law has been given legal and institutional spaces in Indonesia's constitutional system, namely the Religious Courts, the Ministry of Religion, the Compilation of Islamic Law, human rights, and decentralisation.

Religious Courts

The Act on Religious Courts (1989) provides a uniform regulation of the position, support for, and competence of the Religious Courts (Cammack 2003: 96). There are three distinct levels of adjudication. In the first instance, each district has its own Religious Court, whose jurisdiction covers marital relations and inheritance issues of Muslims as well as the affairs of religious endowments (*wakaf*). On the provincial level, there are Religious Appellate Courts; at the apex is the Supreme Court in Jakarta. The 1989 law not only provides the Religious Courts with jurisdiction in matters of inheritance law, but also grants them the authority to execute their own rulings.

A gradual transfer of administrative supervision over the Religious Courts from the ministry to the 'one roof' jurisdiction of the Supreme Court has been initiated by Act 35/1999, and was finally effectuated in

2004.[25] Based on Law 4/2004 on the Judiciary, the Supreme Court now oversees the sector of religious jurisdiction as it has done for decades with its other, secular sectors of general (civil and criminal), administrative, and military jurisdiction. Presidential Instruction 21/2004 provides for the effectuation of this new policy for the Religious Courts.

While a Religious Court is essentially a state court, traditionally its judges have been trained as religious scholars (*ulama*). Most judges who presently work at these courts have a degree in sharia studies from the IAIN.[26] The law states that the judges of these courts must have earned a degree in law or in Islamic law from an institution of higher education. While most law degrees are obtained from secular faculties of law, a degree in Islamic law is provided by the sharia faculties of Islamic universities. Azra notes that the 2003 Advocates Act has also opened up the lawyer's profession to graduates of Islamic studies. Interestingly, the Faculty of Syariah at Jakarta's National Islamic University (UIN) has been renamed 'Faculty of Syariah and National Law'. Its former rector writes: 'Within this framework, Islamic law can be studied simultaneously with national law in ways that can serve to facilitate further development toward the development of a distinctly "Indonesian school of Islamic law"'(Azra 2007: 270).

In 2006, the 1989 Act on Religious Courts was amended to expand the courts' jurisdiction. Act 3/2006 provides that Religious Courts are currently the only competent court in inheritance cases between Muslims. The Act further grants the courts jurisdiction in matters of Islamic finance in the framework of 'Ekonomi syariah'. The Act also acknowledges the special jurisdiction of Religious Courts in autonomous regions, notably the Mahkamah Syariyah in Aceh, inaugurated in 2003 (Ichwan 2007: 193).

The Ministry of Religion

The Ministry of Religion provides supervision over Indonesia's varying religions, namely Islam, Catholicism, Protestantism, Hinduism, Buddhism, and, since 2006, Confucianism. As such, the ministry regulates Islamic education and the mosques, as well as the holy pilgrimage (*hajj*). The Ministry has offices in all provinces, districts, and towns, known as the Bureau of Religious Affairs (KUA, *Kantor Urusan Agama*). The Ministry has a Directorate for Islamic Affairs and the Development of Sharia. However, its previous tasks in developing the Religious Courts (Art.s 202-115 of the old Decree 1/2001) were removed since the abovementioned incorporation of these courts in the national judicial system in 2004.[27]

Together with the Ministry of Justice and the Supreme Court, the Ministry of Religion also exercises supervision over marriage registration. It prints marriage certificates, with a standard *taklik talak* clause, which provides women with the option of a divorce by 'automatic repudiation (*talak*)' in the event that they are deserted, neglected, abused, or not provided with financial support by their husband for a specified number of months (Cammack et al. 2007: 112). Together with the Supreme Court, the Ministry has directed the courts to interpret the marriage act in ways favourable to women (Mulia 2007: 130).

The Compilation of Islamic Law and its legal status

The 'Compilation of Islamic Law in Indonesia' (*Kompilasi Hukum Islam di Indonesia*) is a legal text intended to bring more legal certainty to the application of sharia-based law by the Religious Courts. Law 1/1974 on Marriage already stated in Article 2 that the requirements for marriage are based on religion (i.e. for Muslims on Islamic marriage law). Since the content of Islamic law is determined by the consensus of religious scholars, courts have had to rely on a wide range of *fiqh* texts.[28] This situation led to legal uncertainty, hence the government's desire for an authoritative restatement.

To obtain as much legitimacy as possible, the Compilation was drafted and discussed both by jurists representing state institutions, and by religious scholars well-versed in Islamic jurisprudence. The Compilation is constructed as a legal code with three sections: marriage law, inheritance law, and religious endowments (*wakaf*). It is comprised of 229 articles and an explanatory memorandum. Although it was officially launched in 1991, first by Presidential Instruction 1/1991 and subsequently through a ministerial decree, the Compilation is not a national law as such. Rather, it is presented by the government as a 'guideline' that the Religious Courts should 'take into account as much as possible'. The Compilation is formally presented as the Islamic law of Indonesia, which has been in effect in the Religious Courts (Ka'bah 2007: 87, 282). Through this construction, the government has been able to fend off accusations that it decides, by way of national law, about the interpretation of the sharia.

The Compilation stipulates that the eliciting of religious rules from the sharia is based on five sources: (a) standard texts from the Shafi'ite school of jurisprudence; (b) additional texts from other legal schools; (c) existing case law; (d) scholarly legal opinions (*fatwas*); and (e) the situation in other countries (cf. Hooker 2003: 23). While much of the contents reflect the mainstream Islamic thought of Indonesia's religious scholars, on a number of points, the Compilation has adopted a remarkably progressive stance.[29]

Since 1991, the verdicts of Religious Courts have increasingly referred to this Compilation. According to Justice Busthanul Arifin of the

Supreme Court, chairman of the drafting commission, the Compilation is an example of 'positive law'. Others insist that it is an authoritative restatement of existing legal practices, or of *living adat law* (Bowen 2003: 189-199). The renowned jurist Attamimi, on the other hand, argues that the legal design of the Compilation has limited its legal force (Mawardi 2003: 43-44). And, in fact, although the Compilation is now widely applied by the Religious Courts, it remains contested. Among its controversial features is a total prohibition of interreligious marriages. The Counter Legal Draft (see 10.4) testifies to a broadly perceived need for change to bring it in accordance with national and international human rights legislation (Mulia 2007: 133).

Human rights

Soon after the *Reformasi* of 1998, Act 39/1999 on Human Rights was enacted in order to clearly incorporate human rights standards and principles into Indonesia's domestic law. Subsequently, this was laid down in the Indonesian constitution. A new chapter now includes principles such as equality before the law (Art. 28(D)(1)) and non-discrimination (Art. 28(I)(2)). However, women's legal status under the sharia-based family and inheritance law violates these principles on several points. In addition, the constitution provides for the freedom of all citizens to have a religion (*agama*) and to practice it, as well as for the freedom of conviction (*kepercayaan*) (Art. 28(E)(2)). These freedoms are guaranteed by the state (Art. 29(2)).

The key question as to how the rights of equality and religious freedom can be reconciled has been dealt with in a typically Indonesian style, which, depending on one's point of view, can be described as balanced, or ambiguous. In 2007, the Constitutional Court in a ruling[30] on the Marriage Law of 1974 (see 10.6) concluded that on the one hand the law's articles on polygamy are justified by the freedom of religion as a fundamental right accorded to every Indonesian citizen, while on the other hand the law's limitations to polygamy were not deemed contrary to the freedom of religion.

The degree to which freedom of religion applies in Indonesia appears limited in more than one sense. First, the official state ideology of Pancasila, which speaks of 'the belief in the One and Almighty God', is fundamentally centred on the notion of theism, leaving no formal acknowledgment of or room for atheism or polytheism. Secondly, there are certain problems inherent to the state's official recognition of six religions: Islam, Protestantism, Catholicism, Hinduism, Buddhism, and Confucianism. Minority groups within Islam, such as the Ahmadiyya, suffer from legal problems. As mentioned in the discussion above, in June 2008, a Joint-Decree of the ministers of justice and religion called on the Ahmadiyya to stop practicing Islam in ways deviating from authoritative Sunni beliefs. Furthermore, in a formal legal sense, the six religions are all equal to one another, but in practice Islam occupies a much stronger and more prominent position. The corpus of national law includes several elements in the areas of marriage and criminal law that conflict with the principle of equality of Muslims and non-Muslims. Other difficulties are encountered in the area of administrative law. The 2006 Revised Joint Ministerial Decree on the Construction of Houses of Worship demands that religious groups wanting to build a house of worship first obtain the signatures of at least 90 members and 60 persons of other religious groups in the community stating that they support the establishment, as well as approval from the local KUA office.

Decentralisation

Beside the incorporation of human rights, yet another post-1998 constitutional reform was to fundamentally change the nature of the Indonesian state. The far-reaching Act on Regional Autonomy – the 1999 Act amended as Act 32/2004 – has not only granted expanded responsibilities and powers to districts and provinces, but also democratised their composition and decision-making. Many districts and provinces have used these new powers to locally introduce sharia-based regulations (*PerDa Syariah*). According to Lindsey, around 160 such *PerDa Syariah* were enacted in at least 24 of Indonesia's 33 provinces (2008: 107-108). Most of them target perceived religious, social, and moral wrongs, such as prostitution, alcohol and drugs, gambling, and pornography. Others promote and prescribe Islamic practices, such as religious rituals, Quranic education, and dress codes. Salim cites the example of Martapura on Kalimantan, where a district regulation prohibited publicly eating or drinking during the month of Ramadan (2003: 229). Although legally speaking, legislative power concerning 'religion' belongs to the central government and not to the regional government, these *PerDa Syariah* have not been formally contested by central authorities.

Corresponding to the nation-wide democratic decentralisation, Aceh and Papua have been granted even more autonomy resulting in a special legal status (see 10.4). Since 1999, the Indonesian government has resumed granting Aceh special autonomy in the religious, cultural, and educational sectors. The successive governments, from Habibie (1999) to Yudhoyono, have taken legal measures permitting Aceh the authority to 'enforce the sharia'.[31] While Act 44/1999 on the Special Status of Aceh had still been vague on this point, Act 18/2001 was already more specific, both in creating space for Aceh's own regulations (or *qanun*) and in setting the limits. The Act stated that: a) the province may not enforce sharia regulations conflicting with national laws (Art. 25); b) the sharia only applies to Muslims (Art. 25 § 3); and c) rulings from the sharia courts can be appealed before the Supreme Court in Jakarta, where they can be reviewed and, if necessary, annulled (Art. 26). On the basis of the 2001 Act, in 2002 and 2003 Aceh enacted several *qanuns* (hereinafter 'Q.'), such as Q. 10/2002 on Sharia courts, Q. 11/2002 on the Implementation of the Islamic creed, worship and symbolism, Q. 12/2003 on Intoxicants, Q. 13/2003 on Gambling, and Q. 14/2003 on Improper Relations between the Sexes (Ichwan 2007: 205).[32]

Act 11/2006 has replaced the Acts of 1999 and 2001 and significantly broadened the scope of sharia-based law in Aceh. Article 125 of this Act stipulates that implementation of sharia in Aceh covers the following areas: religion (*ibadah*); family law (*ahwal alsyakhshiyah*); private law (*muamalah*); criminal law (*jinayah*); the judiciary (*qadha'*); education (*tarbiyah*); and the mission, promotion, and safeguarding of Islam (*dakwah, syiar, dan pembelaan Islam*). Article 126 provides that every adherent of Islam is obliged to obey and carry out Islamic sharia. Everybody who lives or is present in Aceh is obliged to respect the implementation of sharia. According to Article 127, the provincial and local governments are responsible for the implementation of sharia. Article 128 provides that the Sharia Courts (*Mahkama Shar'iyah*) in Aceh form part of the national system of religious jurisdiction and are 'free from any external influence'. The jurisdiction, supervision, organisation, and procedures of these courts are further regulated in Articles 128-137 of the 2006 Act. In 2009, Aceh's legislature promulgated a regulation on Islamic criminal law, the validity of which is highly contested (see 10.7).

Indonesia's post-1998 constitutional law discontinued the authoritarian centralist system of Suharto's New Order, which strictly imposed on society an official, harmonious view of state-religion relations and stifled public debate in sensitive areas such as the relation between sharia and national law. The new, democratised constitutional law allows for debate and decision-making in multiple spaces about a broad range of subjects. Today these spaces range from national parliament to provincial and district legislatures, including the special case of Aceh; from the Supreme Court as the apex of the national court system to Religious Courts and General Courts throughout the country, including the special courts of Aceh; and the Constitutional Court acts as guardian of a constitution rejuvenated by references to all fundamental human rights. While the jurisdiction of Religious Courts has broadened, so has the supervisory role of the Supreme Court. In practice, in Indonesia, as in most other Muslim countries, the most pervasive influence of sharia remains in the area of family law.

10.6 Family and inheritance law

Marriage, divorce, and matrimonial property are regulated by Marriage Act 1/1974. Its provisions are elaborated upon by two Government Regulations (GR), namely GR 9/1975, which elaborates the substantive norms and procedures of the Act, and GR 10/1983 (amended by GR 45/1990), which contains special rules for civil servants. Both marriage law and inheritance law are addressed by the 1991 Compilation of Islamic Law (see 10.5). The text of the Compilation's chapter on marriage law matches the text of the 1974 Marriage Act in all respects, the only difference being that some Indonesian terms are replaced with equivalent Arabic words. There is no national legislation on inheritance law for Muslims. The competent court for disputes between Muslims concerning both marital and inheritance matters is the Religious Court. The Act on Religious Courts of 1989, as amended by Act 3/2006, contains procedural rules for marriage and inheritance law. More than 90 per cent of the caseload of the Religious Courts consists of divorce cases (Cammack et al. 2007: 164).

This section will first address four subjects of the marriage law, namely religion and validity, interreligious marriage, divorce and repudiation, and polygamy. This is followed by a short discussion about inheritance law. Finally this section will look into the role of Religious Courts and trends in case law deriving from these courts.

The 1974 Marriage Act represents a relatively liberal interpretation of sharia norms. It constrains the right of Muslim husbands to divorce their wives unilaterally by repudiation (*talak*). It also grants wives a variety of instruments through which to obtain divorce and sets clear limits on polygamy. The Act formulates substantive and procedural conditions that must be met for both divorce and polygamy. While decisions on these cases are entrusted to the Religious Courts, the review of their decisions is left to the national Supreme Court. Gradually, the Supreme Court has addressed many of the questions that Act 1/1974 and its government regulations had actually left unanswered. In doing so, the Supreme Court has established 'a regulatory regime which would certainly have met strong opposition if introduced transparently and directly in 1974' (Cammack et al. 2007: 111).

Article 2 and the validity of marriages

The Marriage Act declares in Article 2(1) that a marriage is valid when the two parties have concluded the marriage in accordance with their religion and conviction. In this way, national marriage law for Muslims is linked to sharia, and not to *adat*, which has, thus, been given a second-rate position. The Act further stipulates in Article 2(2) that all marriages must be registered according to the existing law.

Legal uncertainty has surrounded cases when a marriage was contracted in accordance with the religious rules, but was not officially registered as legally required. Was it still valid?[33] Yes, said the Islamists, the orthodox scholars, and their organisations. No, said the nationalists, the modernists, most jurists, and *their* organisations. The question is whether paragraph 1 of Article 2 supersedes paragraph 2 of the same article. Bowen maintains, to the contrary, that the Supreme Court has not developed a stable corpus of case law on the issue (2003: 182-185). Indecisively, the Supreme Court in 1991 sided with the no-camp, in 1993 with the yes-camp, only to switch sides again in 1995. According to Bowen, the debate continues (2003: 182-185). In any case, it is possible for unrecorded marriages to be registered retroactively.

The legal ambiguity pervasive in this area may also have negative repercussions on related subjects, such as polygamy, divorce and mixed marriages.

Interreligious marriages

Religiously mixed marriages remain one of the most problematic areas of the marriage law. The legality or validity of marriages between a Muslim man and a Christian woman or between a Christian man and a Muslim woman in accordance with Article 2 of the Marriage Law is sharply contested.

In the dominant interpretations of the sharia, the first case is permissible (Muslim man marrying a non-Muslim woman), but the second is not. Nonetheless, judicial decisions tend to show otherwise. In 1974, the Supreme Court held that a marriage between a Muslim man and a Christian woman is valid.[34] In 1986, the Supreme Court reviewed a case in which a Muslim woman had married a Christian man, holding that such marriage was also valid.[35] Oddly, though, in the latter case the Court reasoned that the woman was supposed to give up her religion by marrying a Christian.

A *fatwa* by the MUI (the Council of Indonesian Religious Scholars) in 1980 declared both cases of interreligious marriage to be forbidden. The Compilation also forbids any interreligious marriage. Consequently, during the course of the 1990s, mixed marriages have become increasingly difficult to legitimise. Yet, Justice Bismar Siregar of the Supreme Court stated in 1994 that he was opposed to mixed marriages as a Muslim, but that he did consider them legal as a judge (Bowen 2003: 242-248). The rejected Counter Legal Draft also states that the marriage between Muslims and Non-Muslims is permitted. The matter has taken a new turn with Act 23/2006 on Civil

Registration, which grants general courts the authority to legalise interreligious marriages.

In practice, the most common solution for Muslim-Christian couples wishing to get married is for the Christian spouse to convert to Islam. For a number of years, the organisation Paramadina, under the leadership of the late liberal religious scholar Nurcholis Madjid, made it possible for interreligious marriages to be contracted. The method used by this organisation was to first contract the marriage in accordance with Islamic precepts, and afterwards to marry the couple according to the other religion's norms. Subsequently, the couple could register the marriage at the civil registrar's office in the local government. Neither the husband nor the wife needed to convert in order to get married, and this option was, therefore, frequently used.[36] Civil registries are known, however, to have refused registration of interreligious marriages.

Divorce and repudiation

This subsection will explain that Act 1/1974 has established two different procedures for divorce. The first procedure assigns a central role to the husband and comes close to a formal repudiation of the wife before the court. The second procedure prescribes how the wife can obtain a divorce from the court. The provisions for both procedures reflect efforts to make a compromised text acceptable to both islamists and liberal reformers.

Two procedures

The drafters of the 1974 Marriage Act were forced to take a stance about the unrestricted unilateral repudiation (*talak*) of the classical sharia and options for women wishing to obtain a divorce on their own initiative. Remarkably, the word *talak* is neither mentioned in the Act, nor in its explanatory memorandum. Instead the Act regulates court procedures for 'divorce' (*perceraian*). It is only in the explanatory memorandum to GR 5/1975 regarding Article 14 that the legislator actually discloses that one of the legal procedures for a Muslim man to obtain a divorce is through repudiation (*cerai talak*). According to Article 38 of the 1974 Act on 'dissolution of the marriage' (*putusnya perkawinan*), a marriage can be dissolved only in three ways, namely by death, by divorce, or by a judicial decision. A Muslim man who goes through the divorce procedure by unilateral repudiation, even though he always has to address a judge, comes under the category of 'divorce by repudiation' (*talak*). In contrast, Muslim women, who according to sharia must also address a judge to obtain a divorce, come under the category of 'suing for divorce' (*gugat cerai*).

Divorce by repudiation (talak)

With regard to the first procedure, the Act states: 'Divorce can only be *effectuated in a court session* after the court has tried to reconcile the parties' (italics added). The procedure for divorce through repudiation or *talak* starts with a written application from the husband to the Religious Court, explaining the reasons for his request. The court reviews whether the conditions are met, and, if so, summons the petitioner and his wife for reconciliation. If the court fails to reconcile the couple, repudiation is pronounced by the husband or a representative before the court. After the session, the presiding judge draws up a declaration that records the divorce, which he then sends on to the Marriage Registrar. The wife retains the right to appeal the *talak*.

Article 39(2) stipulates that such divorce 'can only take place, if there are sufficient grounds which make impossible the consensus which ought to exist between husband and wife.' The explanatory memorandum to this article as well as Articles 19 and 14 of GR 9/1975 further define the reasons for divorce. They include adultery; addiction, including addiction to alcohol, opium use, or gambling; desertion; imprisonment; cruelty which inflicts damage; physical disability; and, finally, continuous conflict and disruption of the marriage.

Suing for divorce (gugat cerai)

The 1974 Marriage Act provides for dissolution through 'suing for divorce', as opposed to 'divorce by repudiation'. It contains several procedures for a judicial divorce to be obtained by the wife. The basic procedure is provided for in Article 20 of GR 9/1975. Largely the same procedures, requirements, and grounds apply as those in cases initiated by men (Art. 19). Many Religious Courts construe these procedures in such a way as to also comply with sharia rules about divorce options for women.

One option which is mentioned not in the law but in the Compilation (Art. 45) and which conforms to sharia rules and is often used in practice, is conditional repudiation (*taklik talak*). Prior to entering into a marriage, the groom assents to a number of conditions under which he would automatically repudiate his wife. These conditions would have to be proven in court. The practice of *taklik talak* is traditionally widespread in Indonesia – to the extent that the Ministry of Religion has incorporated them since 1955 into the standard pre-printed marriage certificate. The reasons for the use of *taklik talak* nowadays conform to the abovementioned legislative grounds for divorce.

A second possibility for divorce is the *syiqaq*, a mediation procedure that can be found in the classical sharia. A woman may use this procedure when requesting a divorce because of irreconcilable differences. A mediator representing the husband can pronounce a *talak* for him (Cammack et al. 2007: 114). A third form of divorce is the *fasakh*, which is more of a legal annulment than a divorce procedure. In the classical sharia, this procedure tends to be used in cases of physical or mental incapacity of the husband, a condition that is also listed in Article 19(e) of GR 9/1975. A fourth possibility involves payment of a financial compensation (*khuluk*) by the wife; Bowen calls this 'divorce by ransom' (2003: 208).

Because these types of divorce exist in both religious and legal sources, Religious Courts, when styling a dissolution *taklik talak, syiqaq, fasakh, or khuluk*, are able to adhere to both normative systems at the same time. In the eyes of conservative judges, the marriage legislation has created new procedures, but the substance is still deeply inspired by the sharia, which fundamentally grants the man stronger rights than the woman. Nationalists and liberal reformers naturally disagree, and they usually find the legislative texts as well as the Supreme Court rulings on their side (Cammack 2003: 106-107).

Polygamy

The 1974 Marriage Act states in Article 3(1) that in principle a man can be married to only one woman at the same time, and a woman to one man only. The explanatory memorandum to the Act confirms that 'the act starts from the principle of monogamy.' However, Article 3(1) also establishes that 'the [religious] court can give permission to a married man to marry more than one wife, if this is the wish of the parties concerned.'

The procedure for obtaining permission for a polygamous marriage is laid down in Articles 4 and 5 of the Act, and Articles 40-44 of GR 9/1975. In short, the man must submit a written application. The Religious Court will only give permission if it finds that one out of three substantive conditions is met:

- the wife cannot fulfil her duties as a wife;
- the wife is physically disabled or incurably ill; and/or
- the wife cannot give birth.

In addition, the law mentions in Article 5(1) three other requirements of a more procedural nature:

- the wife must give her consent, unless this is not possible, or the court does not deem it necessary;
- the man must prove that he is able to financially maintain his wives and children, with a declaration from his employer, the tax agency, or otherwise; and

– the man must declare that he will give his wives and children a fair and equal treatment.

Once the paperwork is filed, the court summons the petitioning husband and wives. If it finds that the law's conditions for polygamy are fulfilled, it issues a decision permitting the polygamous marriage. Without such decision, the Marriage Registrar at the KUA is forbidden to register the marriage. If a man marries a second wife without a judicial decision, he faces a fine. Likewise, the registrar who registers a polygamous marriage without prior court permission faces sanction, even imprisonment.

For civil servants, the law is more limited. Government Regulation 10/1983 (amended as GR 45/1990) forbids polygamous unions between two civil servants altogether. Civil servants who want to enter into a polygamous marriage with someone who is not state-employed must obtain written permission from his or her superior. For these types of marriages, another specified procedure is prescribed.

In practice, polygamy is fairly exceptional in Indonesia[37], and it accounts only for a very small part of the workload of the Religious Courts. However, its symbolic and political importance is considerable, deriving from the fact that it is considered as one of the milestones along the way to 'introducing the sharia' into national law.

Research of judicial decision-making in polygamy cases in the 1980s and 1990s suggests a difference in the holdings of lower Religious Courts and the higher courts who are asked to review cases on appeal. In a number of cases, courts wrongly granted permission for a polygamous marriage, but these were subsequently reversed by the Supreme Court (Otto & Pompe 1988: 14-15; Butt 1999: 128). This shows that the law on polygamy remains contested. During the post-1998 years of liberalisation new pro-polygamy voices came to the fore (Bowen 2003: 224-227). By contrast, in 2004, proponents of the Counter Legal Draft strived for a complete removal of polygamy (Mulia 2007) and President Yudhoyono declared that the abovementioned regulation, which bans polygamy by civil servants, is to be 'reactivated' (see 10.4). The Constitutional Court in its 2007 decision on polygamy mentioned above in the subsection on human rights (see 10.5) basically confirmed the balanced position of the 1974 legislation.

Inheritance law

There is no national legislation concerning inheritance law. The Islamic inheritance law in force for Muslims in Indonesia is laid down in the 1991 Compilation of Islamic Law. This is an almost identical copy of the dominant interpretations of sharia. The Religious Court has jurisdiction in inheritance affairs. Yet, several studies have revealed that it is rare for inheritance cases to be brought before the Religious Courts. Indeed, they form less than 1 per cent of the courts' workload (Cammack 2007: 164).

The Compilation includes the stipulation that when a person has sons and daughters, the sons will in most cases each inherit twice the share awarded each daughter. This contravenes a Supreme Court decision on *adat* inheritance law from 1961, which ruled that sons and daughters in modern Indonesia should inherit equal amounts. The abovementioned stipulation did not enter into the Compilation without controversy, and remains contested.

Yahya Harahap, a judge on the Supreme Court, argued for instance during the drafting process of the Compilation that an equal division of inheritance between men and women would not conflict with the Quran. The socio-economic position and role of women had changed, after all, therefore making the traditional allotment old-fashioned and outdated. The proposal offered by Harahap was, however, rejected by most religious scholars, who did not wish to diverge from the dominant interpretation (Cammack 1999: 30). Similarly, ex-Minister of Religious Affairs Munawir (1983-1993) frequently pleaded for an equal division.[38] He sometimes accused the *ulama* of hypocrisy in this matter (Bowen 2003: 161-165), maintaining that many religious scholars had told him in private that they would equally divide between their children. And, in fact, in practice, it appears that many Indonesians take measures to ensure that their property will be divided equally between sons and daughters because they consider this to be fairer than the prescriptions of Islamic inheritance law.

However, the way in which the Compilation dealt with inheritance issues, has left most classical rules unchanged. The few innovative parts deal with joint marital property (*harta bersama*) – a concept unknown in classical sharia – and inheritance by adopted children – who are typically not entitled to anything under Islamic inheritance rules. According to the Compilation, adopted children, even if they have not been named in the will of the deceased, are still entitled to up to one third of the total inheritance. Here Indonesia follows the model of the Egyptian inheritance law of 1946.

The 1989 Law on Religious Courts confirmed the longstanding freedom of choice of Indonesian Muslims to bring their inheritance disputes before either the secular General Courts (*pengadilan umum*) or the Religious Courts and to have them decided on the basis of national law, *adat* law, or Islamic law. Article 49 of this law attributed jurisdiction to the Religious Courts 'in cases relating to wills, inheritance [...] that are carried out according to Islamic law'. During parliamentary deliberations about the bill, this was interpreted as an implicit basis for freedom of choice. It was then decided to lay this down in the General Elucidation, thus stating that '[...] prior to the [initiation of the] case the parties can choose which body of law shall be used in the division of the estate' (Cammack 2007: 159).

In an amendment of the 1989 law, by Act 3/2006, this freedom of choice may have been reduced. At least, the general part of the elucidation of the new Act suggests so in its citation of a phrase from the elucidation of the old law that explicitly allows the parties' freedom to choose the applicable law and states that that phrase is abolished. On the other hand, the new Article 49 does not clearly confirm any such change. It does entrust the Religious Courts with the task and legal powers to settle inheritance disputes between people 'who adhere to the Islamic religion'. But, the elucidation of the new Article 49 states that the phrase 'people (or entities) adhering the Islamic religion' include those 'who have *subjected themselves voluntarily to Islamic law* concerning those matters which belong to the jurisdiction of Islamic courts [...]'. The latter clause suggests a continuation of the legal tradition of free choice of law in inheritance matters. But the old provisions that deprived the Religious Court of the power to decisively settle any dispute concerning property, have now been removed.

Practices and trends in the Religious Courts

As a Religious Court has jurisdiction over marriage and divorce as well as over inheritance matters and its legal position has changed with the politico-religious tide, this section concludes with some observations about three aspects of the changing role of Religious Courts. First, how strictly do the courts follow the Marriage Act and the Compilation? Secondly, to what extent are their decisions informed either by classical, undulated sharia or by modern concepts of justice and equality between men and women? And third, to what extent does the general public make use of the Religious Courts, and why?

According to Butt (1999: 128), in most cases, the Religious Courts appear to comply with the marriage legislation. Where they have deviated, for example in some polygamy cases (see above), the Supreme Court is there to correct them. In-depth knowledge about the jurisprudence of Religious Courts in Aceh is provided in *Islam, law and equality in Indonesia* by Bowen (2003). The author undertook an anthropological study spanning many years of practices and rulings of Religious and General Courts in rural Aceh. From the research, it appears that in family matters, the courts are primarily approached by women, and in most of these cases they rule in their favour. Bowen explains that both national legislation and Islamic law are more accommodating to the rights of women than the rural *adat* prevalent in Aceh (Bowen 2003:

84-88). While during the 1960s these courts had shown themselves to be very sensitive to the consensus of rural communities,

> [b]y the early 1990s, judges were emphasising the legal rights of the individual Muslim, usually the Muslim wife or daughter [...] Some judges, jurists and many others have attempted to construct an inclusive Islamic discourse that could take into account norms of gender equality, the traditions of *fiqh* and, selectively, adapt social norms (ibid 2003: 255-256).

The circulars and judgments of the Supreme Court in sharia-related cases also indicate incremental attempts at liberalisation. Cammack (2003: 109-110) cites Circular 2 of 1990, which emphasises that the role of the religious judge in repudiation cases is not that of a witness, whose task is merely to assess whether all conditions of the marriage law have been abided by, but rather that of a judge who must adjudicate in a matter involving two conflicting parties and who must resolve the issue with a judicial decision.

In the Nur Said case originating in Aceh, in which the brother of a deceased man demanded the entire inheritance, the Religious Court decided that not only the brother, but also the only daughter of the deceased would receive part of the inheritance. The Supreme Court, however, reversed this decision and argued that the child of the deceased must inherit everything, regardless of whether the child was a son or a daughter. Another inheritance case, *Warsih vs. Iim*, also demonstrates that decision-making by a Religious Court is certainly not a matter of a mechanical enforcement of sharia rules from the Compilation (Bowen 2003: 135-146). The judgment in this case does refer to the relevant article of the Compilation, but instead of directly implementing it, the argumentation is centred on a number of social norms. In the ruling, these norms are backed up by reference to 'the current Islamic law that is in force in Indonesia', which is taken from four legal sources: the Compilation, the traditions, the publications of a liberal Pakistani legal scholar, and finally a Shafi'ite *fiqh* book. The Compilation is, thus, complemented and legitimised by using other norms, carefully selected from among many possible sources in order to achieve a socially acceptable decision.

According to Nurlaelawati (2010: 143-144), judges in the Islamic courts have generally followed the provisions of the Compilation of Islamic Law in adjudicating cases before them. However, in some cases, judges have 'deviated' from the Compilation and referred to *fiqh* instead. Among the reasons is their intention to create public good (*maslahat*) or to guarantee satisfaction of the parties through their judgments. For reasons of legal justification, their decisions are then presented in such a way as to demonstrate conformity with the sources of Islamic law. Another reason, according to Nurlaelawati's evaluation, is that a number of judges simply have not accepted all the reforms of the Compilation. Thus, judges continue to produce legal uncertainty and anomalous decisions. In contrast, both Bowen (2003, 2007) and Cammack (2007) make a more positive assessment of the 'deviations', arguing that they are mostly made on the grounds of fairness, justice, public interest, or common good (see 10.4).

Cammack et al. (2007) estimate that at least in the 1970s and 1980s 'no more than about half of all Muslim divorces [were actually] processed through Islamic courts.' These findings are confirmed by a 2008 study of the Supreme Court and AusAID (Sumner 2008). Cammack et al. conclude that 'practical considerations of costs, convenience, and knowledge of the law's requirements are the principal reasons for non-compliance with statutory divorce procedures' as 'costs of adherence in terms of expense and inconvenience outweigh the perceived benefits' (ibid: 121). They found that ignorance of the law is a factor in the non-compliance of divorce procedures, though the Indonesian government and a number of NGOs have disseminated much information about it. Another factor is the unavailability of documentary proof of a marriage, as '[t]hose who enter into unapproved marriages will invariably secure an unapproved divorce should the marriage fail' (ibid: 123).

Cammack et al. also explain why Indonesian Muslims find compliance burdensome, writing:

> The simplest divorce requires at least three court hearings [... and moreover] entail[s] a certain amount of paperwork and bureaucratic annoyance. The parties must obtain a letter of residence from the local village head, and must present an original state-issued marriage certificate. For most litigants, the court staff translates the couple's wishes into a cognizable legal claim or claims, and complete forms that constitute the complaint or petition. Additional procedures are sometimes required to give notice to an absent spouse; the parties must secure the attendance of witnesses; and the court may require documentary evidence of the couple's property (ibid 122-123).

In addition, litigants must pay fees for obtaining documents and additional informal payments. It would appear, therefore, that non-compliance with the divorce rules contained in the Marriage Act of 1974 is primarily the consequence of neglect and avoidance, rather than principled rejection and refusal of the law itself (ibid: 125). Thus, the widespread evasion of statutory divorce requirements should not be interpreted as a dramatic failure of the marriage act. In the words of Cammack et al., the '[c]hanges to the law that require reasons for divorce and grant increased rights to wives are undoubtedly changing popular attitudes' (ibid: 127).

10.7 Criminal law

The current criminal code of Indonesia is not Islamic in nature and design, and based on the French-Dutch legal tradition. It does not incorporate *hadd* crimes, Islamic corporal punishments, or retribution-based sentencing. Apostasy is not a criminal offence under national law. This being said, Indonesian law does include a few crimes that relate directly or indirectly to Islam and sharia. Article 156 of the criminal code makes the spreading of hatred, heresy, and blasphemy punishable by up to five years in prison. Although the law applies to all officially recognised religions, it is usually invoked in cases involving blasphemy and heresy against Islam.

Today's criminal code is to be replaced by a new code. This draft bill, which has been worked on for decades, was presented to the president in January 2005, but has since been postponed and shelved several times. Its presentation to parliament scheduled for 2008 was once again postponed. The latest versions of the draft bill reflect the French-Dutch legal tradition, with little reference to sharia except for a few provisions pertaining to sexual morality and virtuous behaviour. These articles have been the subject of intense discussion for a number of years, in part due to connotations with the sharia concept of *zina*. For example, draft Article 484 makes extramarital sexual intercourse (*zina*) punishable with a prison sentence of up to five years or a substantial fine. This offence could also be interpreted as covering homosexuality and the living together of unmarried couples, while Article 486 of the draft bill makes unmarried cohabitation punishable with a sentence of up to two years or a proportionate fine. Incidentally, the penalisation of unmarried cohabitation is not a new development in Indonesia.[39] Many questions have been raised on the mutual relations between the two provisions and on the imminent problems that will undoubtedly arise concerning evidence in such cases.

The latest draft bill also prohibits kissing in public, a provision that has been included in the chapter regarding virtuous behaviour. In addition to many moral objections, doubts have been raised with respect to the viability of enforcement as well as the economic consequences in areas that largely survive on the tourist industry like Bali. The Islamic mass organisation NU has spoken out against these proposals, arguing that the inclusion of elements of sharia into Indonesian criminal law would undermine social cohesion and tolerance. Several orthodox Islamic parties and groups, on the other hand, have been eagerly propagating stricter legislation in these areas for years.[40]

Beside the contested drafts of a new criminal code, three subjects demand our attention here. First, the autonomous *qanuns* of Aceh; secondly, the criminalisation of behaviour that may disrupt interreligious peace; and thirdly, the Anti-Pornography Act.

The special status of Aceh province, regulated by a 2006 national law (see 10.4), has enabled the provincial government to make several crimes punishable under Islamic law. The criminal provisions of those provincial regulations or *qanuns*, take precedence over the criminal code, and thus form an important exception (Lindsey & Hooker 2007: 245-249). Since 2005, sharia-based sanctions such as public flogging have been applied occasionally in some of Aceh's district towns. Remarkably, since early 2007 no judicial order for such execution was issued in the area of the provincial capital Banda Aceh.[41]

On 14 September 2009 Aceh's legislative body, on the eve of its replacement by a newly elected council, passed a *qanun* on Islamic criminal law (*jinayat*) and criminal procedure law. Article 24, section 1 of this *qanun* regulates sanctions for adultery (*zina*). If it is proven that adultery has been committed by two married persons, they are to be stoned to death in a public place. In the case of unmarried persons, they will each receive 100 lashes. However, it is unlikely that this *qanun* is legally valid and can be implemented. The governor of Aceh, Irwandi Yusef, has declared his strong and continuous objection to the regulation. He stated that the regulation will never be implemented, that the newly elected council will revise it, and that he will not approve it.[42] According to Indonesian law, for the *qanun* to be valid the governor's consent during the making of a provincial regulation is required, as well as his approval of the council's decision to pass it. However, proponents of the new regulation have contested this and maintain that the *qanun* is already valid. Yet, the president of the Constitutional Court has stated that the validity of the new *qanun* is still problematic from a legal technical sense.[43]

Concerning the possible disturbance of interreligious harmony, a Joint Decree of the ministers of Justice and Religious Affairs, dating back to 1970, states that it is prohibited to convert people to a particular religion in a region where another religion is prevalent (Bowen 2003: 236). Bearing in mind that Islam is the most common religion by far, this decision can be seen as a form of official protection of Islam. A joint decree from 2008 by the same ministers, warns and directs adherents and leaders of the Ahmadiyya to refrain from religious practices that deviate from mainstream Islam. Referring to Act 1 (PNPS) of 1965 on the Prevention of Abuse and/or the Defiling of Religions, the decree further states that non-compliance may lead to legal sanctions. The same decree also warns opponents of Ahmadiyya to respect religious communities and to refrain from illegal actions against this group, under penalty of sanctions.

The 2008 Anti-Pornography Act, which was strongly promoted by Islamist circles, bans images, gestures, or talk deemed to be pornographic. The law has defined pornography very broadly as anything 'which may incite obscenity, sexual exploitation and/or violate the moral ethics of the community'. A section of the law allows members of the public to 'participate in preventing the spread of obscenity.' In the beginning of 2010, the Bandung police arrested four female dancers, who were showing their underwear during a 'sexy' New Year's dance performance, and two men involved in the management of the alleged performance. A senior Bandung policeman said the six could be charged under the criminal code or the anti-pornography law, depending on the prosecutors. Those convicted under the anti-pornography act can face a maximum jail term of fifteen years. Rights groups have already lodged a judicial review at the Constitutional Court demanding that the law be dropped.[44]

10.8 Economic law and religious foundations

Following Law 3/2006, which extended the jurisdiction of Religious Courts to economic sharia law, the Supreme Court issued a Compilation of Economic Sharia Law (KHES) as an attachment to Supreme Court Circular Letter 2/2008[45]. Just like the Compilation of Islamic Law (see 10.5), the KHES is not a law and does not impose rules on citizens. Its four chapters address the following topics:

1. Legal Subjects and Property (*subyek hukum dan harta*);
2. Contract (*akad*);
3 Almsgiving (*zakat*) and Gifts (*hibah*); and
4. Sharia-based accountancy (*Akuntansi Syari'ah*).

The 796 articles of the KHES are formally based on legal sources and principles of sharia, notably the Quran, the Sunna, custom (*'urf*), and consideration for the public interest (*maslahat*). In substance, this Indonesian version of economic sharia has been adjusted to the policies and rules of Indonesia's national banking system and to practices on the ground. Influence of sharia on Indonesia's economic law can also be found in laws regulating Islamic banking, Islamic taxation (*zakat*), and religious charitable foundations (*wakaf*).

Islamic banking law

In 2008, a new Sharia Banking Act was passed by parliament. Like its predecessor (Act 10/1998), Law 21/2008 acknowledges the principles of Islamic banking as constituting part of the national banking system[46] and establishes the supervisory authority of the central bank to ensure a healthy and proper regulatory environment surrounding the Islamic banking sector. In addition to the country's central bank (Bank Indonesia), the MUI (see 10.3) has certain powers concerning sharia banking.[47] The law provides for the MUI to lay down the relevant principles of sharia in *fatwas*. A committee composed of officials from Bank Indonesia, the Ministry of Religion, and 'sharia experts' is to incorporate these *fatwas* into the Bank's regulations. Observers have pointed out the danger of conflicting opinions between the two agencies. Nevertheless, there can be no doubt that the national policy and supervision of Islamic banking will primarily fall under the jurisdiction of Bank Indonesia. For example, a regulation issued in the summer of 2005 required that all rurally-based sharia banks draw up monthly reports in accordance with strict guidelines; these reports are to be submitted for approval by Bank Indonesia. Forms of Islamic insurance, stockbrokers, mortgage providers, and micro credit institutions have also quickly begun to expand and now also fall under the financial supervision of Bank Indonesia.

Almsgiving law or Islamic taxation

The Zakat Administration Law 38/1999 regulates the management of alms paid for the poor (*zakat*). This law does not establish an enforceable obligation for Muslims to pay *zakat*. Rather, it is targeted toward the unification, centralisation, and coordination of the numerous existing public and private *zakat* institutions. It is hoped that the act will increase the amount of *zakat* payments, direct *zakat* funds to social welfare for the poor, strengthen the legal basis of *zakat* collection, and boost participation levels and the religiosity of Indonesians in general (Salim 2008: 128). The law primarily deals with the tasks and powers of the National Zakat Agency (BAZNAS) for the management of *zakat*, but it also covers private *zakat*-related institutions. Furthermore, the law makes *zakat* a tax-deductible expense for both private individuals and firms. This has raised criticism that the law discriminates against followers of other religions for whom no similar tax-deductible regulations exist. Minister of Religion Munawir stated in 2001 that similar concepts existing in other religions shall be taken into consideration in the future; for the moment, however, priority lies with properly managing the *zakat* (ibid: 138).

Law on religious foundations (wakaf)

A *wakaf* is a religious foundation endowed by the founders with real estate and/or tangible goods to be used in the interest of the community. Act 41/2004 concerning *wakaf* established the independent Indonesian Wakaf Agency ('Badan Wakaf Indonesia', abbreviated as BWI) and charged it with the supervision of those who manage *wakafs*. Government Regulation 42/2006 provides the substantive and procedural rules for *wakaf* administration and corresponds with Part III of the Compilation of Islamic Law, also dealing with *wakaf*. Local offices of the Ministry of Religion, the so-called KUAs (see 10.2, 10.5), are responsible for the registration of *wakaf* and report to both the Ministry of Religion and the BWI. The BWI has the power to discharge or replace the *wakaf* management and to decide in matters concerning the status of a *wakaf*. The Minister of Religion and the MUI exercise advisory powers only. Jurisdiction in matters pertaining to *wakaf* rests with the Religious Courts.

10.9 International treaty obligations concerning human rights

We have pointed out above that some provisions in Indonesia's sharia-based national law are in conflict with its human rights law (see 10.5). In this section we examine whether Indonesia has ratified the main human rights treaties and whether, in doing so, it has entered into international legal obligations affecting its sharia-related domestic laws. In particular, we will note how the monitoring bodies of those treaties have assessed Indonesia's fulfilment of its duties under international law.

Indonesia ratified CEDAW in 1984, including its optional protocol. In doing so, the country made no reservations, and, therefore, agreed to the treaty principles affirming equality between men and women. Indonesia ratified the Convention Against Torture (CAT) in 1998 and, finally, in September 2005 the International Covenant on Civil and Political Rights (ICCPR). The National Commission for Human Rights (*Komnasham*) has played a major role in promoting such ratifications, and drawing attention to their legal consequences, such as Indonesia's obligation to report periodically to the monitoring bodies of those treaties. While the post-1998 democratic reforms have been hailed as remarkable improvements in human rights, concerns have been raised about stagnation in the law reform process regarding the status of women and about the introduction of sharia-based criminal law in Aceh.

In 2007, in response to Indonesia's periodic progress report, the international CEDAW Committee expressed its concern that

> the discriminatory provisions in the Marriage Act of 1974 [...] perpetuate stereotypes by providing that men are the heads of households and women are relegated to domestic roles.[48]

The Committee further noted that the law allows for polygamy and sets a legal minimum age of marriage at 16 for girls and that in general there is a 'lack of progress in the law reform process with respect to marriage and family law, which allows the persistence of discriminatory provisions that deny women equal rights with men' (CEDAW 2007). Since the time of the Committee's previous report on Indonesia, where similar concluding comments were made, amendments to the discriminatory provisions of the Marriage Act (1974) have not been undertaken. This prompted the Committee to request that the Indonesian government 'take immediate steps to revise the Marriage Act of 1974 in accordance with its obligations under the Convention', to which Indonesian representatives expressed their intention to amend the law without further delay (ibid).

Members of the Committee further urged Indonesia to address women and their role in marriage and family relations in a comprehensive strategy for the elimination of discrimination. It noted with particular concern that the government's decentralisation policy had 'resulted in the uneven recognition and enforcement of women's human rights and discrimination against women in some regions, including Aceh' (ibid). It also took note of 'the rise of religious fundamentalist groups advocating restrictive interpretations of sharia law, which discriminate against women, in several regions of the country' and concluded that:

> [The Indonesian government] has rescinded a number of local laws and regulations pertaining to economic matters such as taxes, but has failed to rescind local laws that discriminate against women on the basis of religion, including laws regulating dress codes, which are disproportionately enforced against women (ibid).

In 2008, the international Committee against Torture convened to monitor the implementation of the CAT in Indonesia.[49] They expressed deep concern that local regulations, such as the Aceh Criminal Code, adopted in 2005, introduced corporal punishment for certain new offences and furthermore that 'the enforcement of such provisions is under the authority of a "morality police", the Wilayatul Hisbah, which exercises an undefined jurisdiction and whose supervision by public State institutions is unclear' (ibid). The Committee also concluded that:

> the necessary legal fundamental safeguards do not exist for persons detained by such officials [and] the execution of punishment

> in public and the use of physically abusive methods (such as flogging or caning) [...] contravene the Convention and national law. In addition, it is reported that the punishments meted out by this policing body have a disproportionate impact on women (arts. 2 and 16). The State party should review all its national and local criminal legislations, especially the 2005 Aceh Criminal Code[50], that authorize the use of corporal punishment as criminal sanctions, with a view to abolishing them immediately, as such punishments constitute a breach of the obligations imposed by the Convention [...].

It is hard to assess the impact of such conclusions of international committees on domestic decision-making in Indonesia. While certain groups and institutions, including the departing provincial council of Aceh in September 2009, choose to ignore, if not defy, the calls from these international human rights committees, the latter's conclusions have certainly added weight to the claims of moderate politicians and human rights defenders and are reflected in the policies of Aceh's present governor who belongs to the local Partai Aceh, which presently has the majority, as well as in the post-2007 judicial policy in Banda Aceh.

10.10 Conclusion

Has Indonesia's moderate Islam, for which the country has been known since long ago, changed to the extent that puritan forces and interpretations of sharia have pervaded national law? Several developments point in that direction. The jurisdiction of Religious Courts has increased; new national laws on Islamic economic law – banking, taxation, almsgiving – have been promulgated; two major Compilations of Islamic law have been issued by the government; inter-religious marriages have become difficult to pursue and legally dubious at best; religious freedom for Ahmadiyya has been curbed due to pressure from puritan groups; and Aceh introduced sharia-based law even in criminal matters. It is also notable that through a variety of regional regulations (the so-called *PerDa Syariah*), individual freedoms enjoyed by citizens – to dress as they want, to move when they want, to eat and drink as they like, to pursue religious studies as they like – have been curtailed in quite a number of districts, towns and provinces.

Yet, in a recent book on islamisation of Indonesia's law, Salim has raised an important question about the essence of these legal changes, namely whether they can be qualified as islamisation or Indonesianisation? He argues that:

> The Islamization of laws in Indonesia [...] is not a real or complete introduction of shari'a. What on the surface appears to be the Islamization of laws in Indonesia is in reality a symbolic token for the most part. [...] [I]t is also an Indonesianization of sharia law that is currently taking place. This means that the Islamization of laws in Indonesia entails in part practical secularization of shari'a, namely human interference through parliamentary enactment in creating religious obligations that have non-divine character (Salim 2008: 177).

Salim is certainly right in stating that the introduction of sharia in Indonesia is not 'complete'. It should be realised that in Indonesia the bigger part of law has undergone little or no visible influence from Islam. Indonesia's constitution has remained secular, as have most of its codifications, whether in administrative law, criminal law, civil law, or laws of procedure. 'Islam' and 'sharia' lack a constitutional status as such.

Salim also states that the islamisation of laws in Indonesia is not a 'real' introduction of sharia. In his view, most of the abovementioned legal changes can also be interpreted as successful efforts by the state to incorporate, subjugate, and control Islamic law as a subsidiary part of national law and governance. Actually, I subscribe to this view, which, ironically, is probably shared by many discontented puritans as well. The powers of Religious Courts have indeed expanded. Yet, whereas these courts used to be supervised by the Ministry of Religion, a traditional bulwark of religious scholars, they have now come under the control of the Supreme Court, which of old has been a stronghold of professional jurists. Previously, Islamic banking, almsgiving, and the management of religious foundations were private matters, but they too are now regulated and supervised by national agencies.

From the above paragraph it may seem that islamisation of law should be understood simply as the outcome of a struggle between state institutions and religious scholars. Here, one should distinguish between two main politico-religious forces, namely moderates and puritans. Since Independence, the Indonesian government itself has been dominated by moderate nationalists. Both Soekarno and Suharto were essentially moderate Javanese Muslims, as were their successors. An important legislative achievement of Suharto's New Order regime was the 1974 Marriage Act. It was, and still is, the mainstay of sharia-based law. The 1974 law is a compromise between the government's previous drafts – which were decidedly more liberal – and the demands of a fierce puritan opposition. Despite ambivalent legislation and ongoing problems of implementation, the law brought an end to the unlimited freedom of Muslim men to divorce their wives at will and to take a second, third, or fourth wife as they liked. It assigned the Religious Courts the power to decide whether a man had good reasons for a divorce or a next marriage. The law also almost equalised divorce procedures for men and women. Thus, in spite of puritan resistance over the past quarter of a century, the law of divorce by the Indonesian courts has been gradually and quietly transformed (Cammack et al. 2007: 126-127).

The processes of legal change, to which Salim refers in the above citation as 'Indonesianization' of shari'a law and elsewhere 'nationalization of shari'a' (Salim 2008: 2), go a long way back indeed. In pre-colonial Java, the sultans of Yogyakarta and Solo converted to Islam and supervised the administration of justice by their religious officials (*panghulus*). The Dutch already began in 1882 to formalise Islamic councils, thus charging state-controlled bodies with the application of Islamic law, in subservience to the secular, general state courts. After Independence, Sukarno's new government first transformed the Dutch colonial office for religious affairs into a Ministry of Religious Affairs to supervise Islamic affairs. Since Islamist forces such as *Darul Islam* posed serious threats to the young republic, the government tended to fear puritans, and to fight the militants among them. Hazairin's scheme to establish as a fifth Sunni school of Islamic law, the so-called *Madhab Indonesia*, expressed the ambitions and hopes of moderate Muslim legal scholars that Islam, local *adat* and a national legal tradition could go hand in hand. Such ideas were not welcomed, though, by puritan scholars, who since the 1970s came under the increasing influence of transnational Salafist propaganda from the Middle East, especially from Saudi Arabia.

Under Suharto's New Order, the government first did its utmost best to control and oppress religious opposition. To this end, it set up the MUI as a national *ulama* organisation and the PPP as an Islamic political party, and it expanded and further formalised the Religious Courts as part of the national judicial system. In the 1990s, when opposition against his increasingly oppressive and corrupt regime mounted, Suharto started to provide support to Islamist movements and organisations such as ICMI. Several Islamic scholars including NU-chairman Abdurrahman Wahid played a leading role in the pro-democracy and pro-rule-of-law forces that led to Suharto's fall. Suharto's vice president and successor Habibie enacted several laws to regulate Islamic affairs (see 10.4).

The next presidents, Wahid himself, then Megawati, and presently Susilo Bambang Yudhoyono (SBY), arranged for a formidable increase in democracy and human rights. Indonesia ratified major human rights conventions without reservations, the army returned to the barracks, and the civil war between the army and the Free Aceh Movement was successfully ended with a peace agreement. Free elections on national and local levels now saw secular as well as Islamic parties bid for the public's favour.

Generally speaking, secular parties such as PDI, Golkar, and PD have been far more successful than Islamic parties such as PPP, PKB, PAN, and PBB. In elections neither of them has made sharia a big issue. In 1999 and 2004, nationalist parties like Golkar and PDI and the secular-oriented Islamic party PKB were the winners. In 2009, president Yudhoyono's Partai Demokrat won many votes. The Islamist PKS, which has become increasingly popular for its sense of decency and discipline, had success in 2004, but in 2009 it did not make the major breakthrough some had expected. It now seems to prefer the model of the Turkish AK party, which promotes democracy and economic growth, over the model of the more puritan Egyptian Muslim Brotherhood. As Azra noted, in the elections PKS leaders concentrated their political discourse on socio-economic subjects (2004: 12-14).

Remarkably, the promotion of sharia-based legislation, both in Aceh as well as in other provinces and districts, has largely been driven by non-Islamist parties such as Golkar and PDI (Bush 2008). Similarly, Aceh's turn to the sharia, based on 2001 and 2006 laws enacted in Jakarta, did not unequivocally express the strong demand of all Acehnese. On the contrary, when after the Peace Agreement the Free Aceh Movement had turned into a regular political party, and this newly formed Partai Aceh won the 2009 elections, they opposed the radical turn to sharia-based law. Governor Yusef Wanandi personally opposed the 2009 stoning regulation, which remains contested.

The election results confirm what had already been observed by socio-legal scholars. In spite of all attention drawn by puritan movements, and notwithstanding opinion polls reporting that a majority of Indonesians want to 'introduce the sharia',[51] legal development at the grassroots level is often marked by pragmatism. Backstage, throughout the country, numerous administrators, officials, judges, lawyers, and above all the common people are attempting in most cases to pragmatically utilise and blend the different normative systems in such a manner that they are able to achieve desirable solutions.

As Bowen (2003: 255-257) has observed in rural Aceh and elsewhere, Religious Courts in particular successfully attempt to construct an inclusive Islamic discourse that can take into account norms of gender equality (human rights) and the traditions of *fiqh*, as well as social norms prevailing in society. An obvious reason for common people to turn to the Religious Courts is their good reputation in terms of accessibility, integrity, and delivery of justice. For the time being, Religious Courts are preferred over General Courts, which are known for their corruption.

Indonesia is presently conducting a unique experiment with democratic law-making in the context of cultural islamisation. In this process, it has been responding both to Islamist pressure and the call to respect human rights.

On the one hand, puritan groups have become more vocal, more 'mainstream', and more influential than in the past. Some groups like FPI still use intimidation and violence to achieve their goals, unfortunately with incidental successes. Education programmes in the Middle-East and other exchanges with the Muslim world have created transnational networks and, as such, channels for dissemination of Saudi funds and puritan ideas. It also cannot be ignored that in the wake of Suharto's fall, Islam became for many Indonesians a symbol for the modern, self-conscious citizen and a political statement against New Order practices – against oppression and corruption, and for justice and human rights. While wearing the veil could indeed reflect oppression of women in some cases, for other women the veil became a symbol of seriousness, maturity, and social ambition (Brenner 1996).

On the other hand, the long tradition of most Indonesian Muslims being moderate traditionalists has not disappeared altogether. Many have associated themselves with their local *adat*, with local Sufi movements, with traditionalist and social service organisations such as the NU, and with the belief in the spirits of their ancestors and other spiritual forces. Among bureaucrats, politicians, military, police, judges, business, NGOs, academics, artists, intellectuals, journalists, and students, many favour national unity, economic growth, democracy, and human rights as the best path to socio-economic development. This large group has always been opposed to the strict implementation and enforcement of laws based on classical sharia.

In 2009, a team of Islamic scholars, representing two powerful mass movements, namely the NU and the Muhammadiyyah, and led by the late Abdurrahman Wahid, published a book entitled *Ilusi Negara Islam* (The Illusion of an Islamic State). This book carefully documents the ways in which Saudi-funded Salafi puritans have tried to infiltrate Indonesia's public and private institutions. It contains strong condemnations of such infiltration from both Islamic organisations, calling it an attack on Indonesia's society and culture. Judging from the above-mentioned election results, these views are actually backed by a pragmatic, silent majority that has consistently supported moderate parties and politicians.

As Azra (2004: 12-14) has argued, terrorist bomb attacks have led most Indonesians to strongly condemn radicalism and have instilled in them a resolute will to tackle this problem. At the same time, most Indonesians are not willing to sever the connections with their Islamic traditions. Against this background, the position and role of sharia-based law are bound to remain ambiguous and contested, moving back and forth in the decades to come as they have done in the recent past.

Notes

1 The author is professor of law and governance in developing countries at Leiden University, the Netherlands. He wishes to thank Adriaan Bedner, John Bowen, Mark Cammack, and Andrew Harding for their valuable comments on previous versions of this chapter. He also thanks Stijn van Huis for his extensive research assistance and his meticulous documentation of post-2007 legal developments, notably in the area of economic law.

2 An earlier version of the historical part of this chapter was published in Otto 2009b.

3 The term *adat* law (in Dutch *adatrecht*) was first used by Snouck Hurgronje in order to describe local customs (*adat*) that fulfilled a legal function; he referred to 'adats, which have legal effect' (Snouck Hurgronje 1893: 357). The argumentation for using *adat* law as a standard legal concept was developed by Van Vollenhoven, for example in *Het adatrecht van Nederlandsch-Indië* (1918: 8).

4 Javanese informants may possibly not have been very clear either, used as they were to present themselves to the outside world as adherents of a specific religion, while in private embracing a body of syncretic, pluralistic convictions (Ball 1981: 24). Today, this tendency has not altogether disappeared.

5 In the Netherlands, the Batavian Republic was proclaimed in 1795 in the wake of the 1789 French Revolution. In France, during the first years of the nineteenth century, Napoleon directed the unification and codification of customs and regulations and modernised the government, the economy, and the military. As France's political and cultural influence increased also in the Netherlands, the drive for codification also took hold there.

6 Both scholars were proponents of the legal theory of *receptio in complexu*, the total embracement of the complete corpus of religious Islamic law. Later on, this theory became subject to devastating attacks by Snouck Hurgronje.

7 Royal Decree of 19 January 1882, regarding the Religious Councils on Java and Madura, published in the official gazette (*Staatsblad*) 82-152 jo. 153. The official name of the councils was 'Priests Councils' (in Dutch *Priesterraden*).

8 From 1891 until 1898, he served as advisor to the Governor-General on 'Oriental languages and Muhammadan law' and from 1898 until 1906 he was the Adviser for 'Native and Arab affairs'. Subsequently, he was appointed as professor of Arabic in Leiden.

9 This reception theory formed a reaction to the older theory of *receptio in complexu*, as defended by nineteenth century authors (see *supra* n. 6).

10 In *Indonesian Islam*, Hooker (2003) compares *fatwas* by the Muhammadiyah, NU, and Persis with those of the national council of religious scholars (the MUI), which was established later (see 10.3).

11 Here the courts in first instance were called 'Kadi's Council' (*Kerapatan Qadi*) while the court of appeals was called 'High Kadi's Council' (*Kerapatan Qadi Besar), see* Cammack 2007: 147.

12 *Wakap or wakaf*: the Indonesian term for *waqf* (Arabic) or religious endowment. It refers to property that, in accordance with the rules of the sharia, is set aside for religious or social purposes and is administered by a kind of foundation.

13 This did not go as far as the recent autonomy laws on Aceh of 2001 and 2006.

14 Under Sukarno's rule, Indonesia left the United Nations in January 1965 in protest of Malaysia's becoming a temporary member of the Security Council. In September 1966, under Suharto, Indonesia reassumed membership (Cribb & Brown 1997: 86, 116).

15 See Article 10 of Act 14/1970; In Indonesia, since colonial times, the term 'religious jurisdiction' has referred to jurisdiction for Muslims.

16 The enactment of the implementing Government Regulation 9/1975 only partially resolved this uncertainty (see 10.6).

17 Progressive Indonesian jurists were involved in the drafting of regulations on Islamic banking, sponsored in part by USAID, the official American aid agency.

18 Both Wahid and Rais were to form political parties: Wahid the PKB, based on the older NU; and Rais, the PAN, which had more in common with the old Masyumi party.

19 In 2002 the PPP and other small Islamic parties proposed to revise the constitution in order to make Indonesia an Islamic state. In August of the same year, the MPR (People's Consultative Assembly) rejected this proposal, with the support of the NU and the *Muhammadiyah*.

20 The *Laskar Jihad* was the biggest and probably best organised movement among the Islamic militias. Another organisation, the Islamic Defenders Front (*Front Pembela Islam*, or FPI) executed countless attacks on bars, brothels, and nightclubs in Jakarta and its environs. The *Jema'ah Islamiyah* (JI) is mentioned in relation to the attacks on Bali, and the Southeast Asian cell of Al-Qaeda. For an overview of these three organisations see Van Bruinessen 2002. In 2003, the perpetrators of the Bali attack, all of them members of the JI, were convicted and sentenced to death. In 2005 Abu Bakar Ba'asyir, suspected to be the spiritual leader of the JI and of the attacks on Bali was convicted to thirty months imprisonment. Besides these three organisations, a number of networks, often operating underground, have taken up the fight for an Islamic state. They have once again united under the name *Darul Islam* or NII/TII (abbreviations for Islamic State of Indonesia/Islamic Army of Indonesia). In addition, local radical organisations have often been active, such as the *Laskar Jundullah* in southern Sulawesi (ibid). On 10 November 2008, the men who had carried out the Bali bomb attack, Amrozi, Imam Samudera, and Ali Gufron were executed. New suicide bombings took place on 17 July 2009 in two Jakarta hotels killing nine people. In September 2009, Indonesia's most wanted Islamist militant Noordin Top, the suspected mastermind of violent bomb attacks, was finally traced and killed during a police raid in Solo. The Economist concluded in late 2008 that 'Indonesia is, overall, edging away from radical Islamism. But the trend is not irreversible, and the authorities must avoid fostering fundamentalists by pandering to them' (Economist 2008).

21 To explain this, it is sometimes argued that court procedures are time-consuming, complicated, and expensive (Cammack 2007). Furthermore, a lack of knowledge of rights and duties is cited, despite the fact that the Ministry of Religion has local advisory offices that offer every prospective couple information about their rights and duties.

22 In the concluding section of this chapter, I will point out that throughout Indonesia politicians of secular nationalist parties have been involved in the introduction of sharia-related regulations. In the case of Aceh the party which represents most voters, the Partai Aceh, has spoken out against this islamisation of law.

23 An earlier version of sections 10.5 and 10.6 was published in Otto 2009a.

24 Amended first in 2006, and for the second time by Law 50/2009.

25 Act 35/1999 was aimed at making the judiciary more independent from the executive by removing some of the influence held by ministries with supervisory powers. While the other special courts were granted five years in order to prepare administratively for the changes, an exception was made for the Religious Courts following

protests by the Ministry of Religion and the MUI. According to appended Article 11 (A), section 2, no time limit was imposed on the Religious Courts (Salim 2003: 215-216).

26 IAINs (State Academies of Islamic Sciences) have for many years been the main institutes of higher education in Islamic studies. In 2002, a number of them were elevated so that they are now 'National Islamic Universities' (UIN).

27 For a more detailed description and analysis of the historical development of this ministry, see Boland 1982. For many years, the Directorate for the Development of Religious Courts did essentially fulfill the function of a court of appeals in religious affairs. Since 1965, the Supreme Court has formally become the national court of appeals in religious matters; nonetheless, the supervisory role of the directorate continued for many years (Hooker 2003: 37-38) until it was abolished with the complete transfer of the sector of Religious Courts to the Supreme Court in 2004.

28 In 1958, the Ministry of Religion issued a Circular Letter indicating thirteen *fiqh*-texts of the Shafi'ite school to be used by the Religious Courts. This canon has effectively been in use until present times.

29 This is, for instance, the case in the stipulation that in cases where the only child of deceased parents is female, she inherits the entire estate when both of her parents die. This progressive interpretation was also followed by the Supreme Court in judgments made in 1995, 1996, and 1998. In contrast, the widely held traditional interpretation of sharia was that in such cases, the brothers and sisters of the deceased would also inherit a portion of the estate. This has now been pushed aside (Bowen 2003: 195-199).

30 Decision 12/PUU-V/2007.

31 It remained unclear what the scope and meaning of this provision would be. Prosecutor General Marzuki made it known that it could only pertain to private law and not to criminal law. PKB leader Wahid was of the opinion that it was about the underlying principles of the sharia, and not about the actual content. What was clear was that various parties used this question to score political points, especially the PKB towards the PDI, and not so much to resolve the real problems afflicting Aceh (Salim 2003: 227).

32 For the content of these *qanuns* see Ichwan 2007: 205-214.

33 The legal requirement of registration, complete with a criminal penalisation, is not contested. However, negligence and liability to punishment do not immediately and in all cases imply that the marriage would be invalid.

34 Supreme Court decision 1650/K/Sip/1974, dated 13 November 1979, cited in Pompe 1991.

35 Supreme Court decision 1400K/Pdt/1986, dated 1989, cited in ibid.

36 Personal communication from a lawyer in Bandung, March 2005.

37 Practices of men secretly marrying their mistresses are not uncommon, though. In this way sharia is used by men to legitimise their unfaithful behaviour. This, in turn, often becomes a reason for the first wife to seek divorce.

38 Former Minister of Religious Affairs Munawir, for example, made no secret of the fact that in his testament, he had made sure that all heirs, whether male or female, would inherit the same amount, adding that many Islamic leaders had made the same arrangements (Bowen 2003: 159-165; Cammack 1999).

39 In the 1990s, several cases led to convictions. On the one hand the prosecutors called on an interpretation of Article 378 of the colonial criminal code, in which 'stealing' the honour of a woman was made punishable, and on the other hand they called on *adat* law (Pompe 1994). Unmarried cohabitation is socially unacceptable in many areas of Indonesia. In traditional areas, couples living together are sometimes attacked and beaten by furious crowds. It is plausible that the government, by

criminalising unmarried cohabitation, is trying to retain the initiative and to thereby prevent such incidents from recurring.

40 On this, see articles in *Tempo*, February 2005; *The Jakarta Post*, 11 October 2003; *Republika*, 30 March 2005.

41 Personal communication by Benjamin Otto, December 2009. A master student at Free University, Amsterdam, he carried out research about the implementation of Aceh's sharia criminal law in the capital Banda Aceh, during Spring and Summer of 2009.

42 'Standoff over Aceh Stoning Legislation', Jakarta Globe, 25 October 2009.

43 'Qanun Jinayat Perlu Diatur Teknis Hukumnya', Serambi, 15 September 2009.

44 '"Sexy Dancer" arrests condemned by Indonesian feminists', *Jakarta Globe*, dated 8 January 2010.

45 The Supreme Court had formed a committee to draft the Compilation of Economic Sharia Law. Experts of the central bank (Bank Indonesia), the MUI's national sharia board, experts in Islamic economic law, and judges of both Religious and General Courts shared their views during the drafting process.

46 Prior to 1992, it was not legally permissible to manage bank deposits without paying out interest (Hefner 2003: 153). Banking Law 7/1992 implicitly allowed Islamic banking, especially through implementing Government Regulation 72/1992, which paved the way for a dual banking system. At the initiative of the national council of religious scholars (MUI), 'the Bank Muamalat Indonesia' (BMI) was established. In the years until 1988, dozens of rural banks attained the status of 'rural sharia bank'. After 1998, the number of Islamic financial institutions rose sharply (Bank Indonesia 2002).

47 See Republika OnLine: http://www.republika.co.id/, dated 4 May 2005.

48 See CEDAW (2007), 'Concluding comments of the Committee on the Elimination of Discrimination against Women: Indonesia', para.s 18, 19. CEDAW/C/IDN/CO/5, dated 10 August.

49 See CAT (2008), Concluding observations of the Committee against Torture, Indonesia', para. 15. CAT/2/IDN/CO/2, dated 2 July.

50 Here the committee probably meant to refer to Act 11/2006 on the special autonomy of Aceh (see 10.4).

51 In June 2008 such polls were published by Australia's Roy Morgan Research. Esposito and Mogahed (2007) discuss similar Gallup polls, and explain why the press reports on such outcomes are usually misleading.

Bibliography

Azra, A. (2004), 'Indonesian Islam, election politics and beyond', *Niasnytt* 4: 12-14.

Azra, A. (2007), 'Islamic legal education in modern Indonesia', in R.M. Feener & M.E. Cammack (eds.), *Islamic Law in contemporary Indonesia: Ideas and Institutions*, 257-270. Cambridge (Mass): Harvard University Press.

Ball, J. (1981), *Indonesian law: Commentary and teaching materials*. Sydney: University of Sydney.

Ball, J. (1982), *Indonesian legal history, 1602-1848*. Sydney: Oughtershaw Press.

Bank Indonesia (2002), *The blueprint of Islamic banking development in Indonesia*. Jakarta: Bank Indonesia.

Bartleby (2010), 'Indonesia', in *World Factbook*, see http://www.bartleby.com/151/country/id.html (2008 statistics) and https://www.cia.gov/library/publications/the-world-factbook/geos/id.html (online edition, last accessed February 2010). Washington, D.C.: Central Intelligence Agency.

Boland, B.J. (1982), *The struggle of Islam in modern Indonesia*. Den Haag: Martinus Nijhoff.

Bowen, J. (2003), *Islam, law and equality in Indonesia: An anthropology of public reasoning*. Cambridge: Cambridge University Press.

Bowen, J. (2007), 'Fairness and law in an Indonesian court', in R.M. Feener and M.E. Cammack (eds.), *Islamic law in contemporary Indonesia. Ideas and Institutions*, 170-192. Cambridge (Mass): Harvard University Press.

Brenner, S. (1996), 'Reconstructing self and society: Javanese Muslim women and "the veil"', *American Ethnologist* 23(4): 673-697.

Bruinessen, M. van (2002), 'The violent fringes of Indonesia's Islam', ISIM *Newsletter* 11: 7.

Burns, P. (1999), *The Leiden legacy: Concepts of law in Indonesia*. Jakarta: Pradnya Paramita.

Bush, R. (2008), *Local Sharia regulations in Indonesian Districts – trending and implications*, paper presented at the workshop 'Studying Islam in Southeast Asia: State of the art and new approaches', organised under the auspices of the Australia-Netherlands Research Collaboration (ANRC), in co-operation with the International Institute for the Study of Islam in the Modern World (ISIM), Leiden, 7-8 July 2008.

Butt, S. (1999), 'Polygamy and mixed marriage in Indonesia: The application of the marriage law in the Courts', in T. Lindsey (ed.), *Indonesia: Law and society*, 122-144. Leichhart, New South Wales: The Federation Press.

Cammack, M. (1999), 'Inching toward equality: Recent developments in Indonesian inheritance law', *Indonesian Law and Administration Review* 5(1): 19-50.

Cammack, M. (2003), 'Indonesia's 1989 Religious Judicature Act', in A. Salim & A. Azra (eds.), *Shari'a and politics in modern Indonesia*, 96-124. Singapore: Institute of Southeast Asian Studies.

Cammack, M. (2007), 'The Indonesian Islamic judiciary', in R.M. Feener & M.E. Cammack (eds.), *Islamic Law in contemporary Indonesia: Ideas and institutions*, 146- 169. Cambridge (Mass): Harvard University Press.

Cammack, M.E., Donovan, H. & T. Heaton (2007), 'Islamic divorce law and practice in Indonesia', in R.M. Feener & M.E. Cammack (eds.), *Islamic Law in Contemporary Indonesia: Ideas and institutions*, 99-127. Cambridge (Mass): Harvard University Press.

Cribb, R. & C. Brown (1997), *Modern Indonesia: A history since 1945*. London: Longman.

Debating (2003), 'Debating polygamy's resurgence: Indonesians divided over meaning of Koran', *The Washington Post*, dated 28 November.

Dekker, A. & H. van Katwijk (1993), *Recht en rechtspraak in Nederlands-Indië*. Leiden: KITLV Uitgeverij.

Dijk, C. van (ed.) (1988), *Islam en politiek in Indonesië*. Muiderberg: Coutinho.

Economist (2008), 'Where "soft Islam" is on the march', *Economist* 386 (Issue 8562): 35-36.

Esposito, J.L & D. Mogahed (2007) *Who speaks for Islam? What a billion Muslims really think*. Based on Gallup's World Poll the largest study of its kind. New York: Gallup Press.

Graaf, H.J. de (1949), *Geschiedenis van Indonesië*. 's-Gravenhage/Bandoeng: Uitgeverij W. van Hoeve.

Hefner, R. (2003), 'Islamizing capitalism: On the founding of Indonesia's first Islamic bank', in A. Salim & A. Azra (eds.), *Shari'a and politics in modern Indonesia*, 148-167. Singapore: Institute of Southeast Asian Studies.

Hisyam, M. (2001), *Caught between three fires: The Javanese Pangulu under the Dutch colonial administration, 1882-1942*. Leiden: PhD thesis, Leiden University.

Hooker, M.B. (2003), *Indonesian Islam: social change through contemporary fatawa*. Crows Nest: Allen & Unwin.

Huntington, S. (1998), *The Clash of Civilization and the Remaking of World Order*. New York: Touchstone.

Ichwan, M. (2007), 'The Politics of Shari'atization: Central governmental and regional discourses of Shari'a implementation in Aceh', in R.M. Feener & M.E. Cammack (eds.),

Islamic law in contemporary Indonesia: Ideas and institutions, 193-215. Cambridge (Mass): Harvard University Press.

Ka'bah, R. (2007), 'Islamic law in court decisions and fatwa institutions in Indonesia', in R. M. Feener & M.E. Cammack (eds.), *Islamic law in contemporary Indonesia. Ideas and Institutions*, 83-98. Cambridge (Mass): Harvard University Press.

Lev, D. (1962), The Supreme Court and adat inheritance law in Indonesia, *American Journal of Comparative Law* 11:205-224.

Lev, D. (1972), *Islamic Courts in Indonesia: A study in the political bases of legal institutions*. Berkeley: University of California Press.

Lindsey, T. & M.B. Hooker (2007), 'Sharia Revival in Aceh', in R.M. Feener & M.E. Cammack (eds.), *Islamic law in contemporary Indonesia: Ideas and institutions*, 216-256. Cambridge (Mass): Harvard University Press.

Lindsey, T. (2008), 'When words fail. Syariah law in Indonesia: Revival, reform or transplantation?', in P.Nicholson & S. Bidolph (eds.), *Examining practices, interrogating theory: Asian comparative legal studies*, 196-220. Leiden: Brill.

Mawardi, A.I. (2003), 'The political backdrop of the enactment of the compilation of Islamic laws in Indonesia', in A. Salim & A. Azra (eds.), *Shari'a and Politics in Modern Indonesia*, 125-147. Singapore: Institute of Southeast Asian Studies.

Mulia, S.M. (2007), 'Towards a just marriage law: Empowering Indonesian women through a counter legal draft to the Indonesian compilation of Islamic law' in R. M. Feener & M. E. Cammack (eds.), *Islamic law in contemporary Indonesia. Ideas and Institutions*, 128-145. Cambridge (Mass): Harvard University Press.

NU (2003), 'NU rejects Sharia for criminal code', *The Jakarta Post*, dated 11 October.

Otto, J.M., A. Dekker & C. de Waaij (1994), 'Indonesian law and administration as reflected in 150 years of Bijdragen', *Bijdragen tot de taal-, land- en volkenkunde* 150(4): 728-754.

Otto, J.M. & S. Pompe (1988), 'Islamitisch recht in Indonesië. Inlijsting van de shari'a in het huidige nationale huwelijksrecht', *Recht van de Islam* 6, 9-23, Maastricht: RIMO.

Otto, J.M. (2009a), 'Islam, family law and constitutional context in Indonesia', in E. Cotran & M. Lau (eds.) (2009), *Yearbook of Islamic and Middle Eastern Law* (2006-2007) 13: 73-86. Leiden/Boston: Brill.

Otto, J.M. (2009b), 'The gradual incorporation of Islamic law in Indonesia's national legal system', in H. Purgstall (ed.), *Family, law and religion. Debates in the Muslim World and Europe and their implications for co-operation and dialogue*, 131-156, Austrian Association for the Middle East, Oberwart: Gröbner Druck.

Noer, D. (1978), *Administration of Islam in Indonesia*, Cornell Modern Indonesia Project. Ithaca (N.Y.): Cornell University.

Nurlaelawati, E. (2010), *Modernization, Tradition and Identity: The Kompilasi Hukum Islam and Legal Practice in the Indonesian Religious Courts*. Amsterdam: Amsterdam University Press.

Pompe, S. (1994), 'Between crime and custom: Extra-marital sex in modern Indonesian law', *Bijdragen tot de taal-, land- en volkenkunde* 150(1): 110-122.

Pompe, S. (1991), 'A short note on some recent developments with regard to mixed marriages in Indonesia', *Bijdragen tot de taal-, land- en volkenkunde*, 147(2/3): 261-272.

Ricklefs, M. (1981), *A history of modern Indonesia*. London: The Macmillan Press Ltd.

Salim, A. (2003), 'Epilogue. Shari'a in Indonesia's current transition: An update', in A. Salim & A. Azra (eds.), *Shari'a and politics in modern Indonesia*, 213-232. Singapore: Institute of Southeast Asian Studies.

Salim, A. (2008), *Challenging the secular state: The Islamization of law in modern Indonesia*. Honolulu: University of Hawaii Press.

Salim, A. & A. Azra (eds.) (2003a), *Shari'a and politics in modern Indonesia*. Singapore: Institute of Southeast Asian Studies.

Salim, A. & A. Azra (2003b) 'Introduction: The state and shari'a in the perspective of Indonesian legal politics', in A. Salim & A. Azra, *Shari'a and politics in modern Indonesia*, 1-16. Singapore: Institute of Southeast Asian Studies.

Schwarz, A. (1999), *A nation in waiting: Indonesia's search for stability*. New South Wales: Allen & Unwin.

Smidt, J.Th. de (1990), *Recht overzee: Een uitdaging*. Zwolle: W.E.J. Tjeenk Willink.

Snouck Hurgronje, C. (1893), *De Atjèhers: 1893-1894*. Leiden: E.J. Brill.

Sumner, C. (2008), *Providing justice to the justice seeker: A report on the Indonesian Religious Courts, acccess and equity study*. Jakarta: Mahkamah Agung and AusAID.

Vollenhoven, C. van (1918), Het adatrecht van Nederlandsch-Indië. Eerste deel. Leiden: E.J. Brill.

Wahid, A.(2009), *Ilusi negara Islam: Ekspansi gerakan Islam transnasional di Indonesia*. Jakarta: The Wahid Foundation a.o.

11 Sharia and national law in Malaysia

Andrew Harding[1]

Abstract

Malaysia is a multi-cultural Commonwealth country with a Muslim majority and a constitution based on the Westminster model, embodying federalism, multi-party democracy, constitutional monarchy, common law institutions and freedom of religion. Its legal infrastructure involves an increasingly contested bifurcation of jurisdiction between common law institutions – signally the civil courts and the legal profession – and the Islamic (Syariah) Courts, in which Islamic law is confined to personal law for Muslims. This divide is the legacy of the colonial legal system and the pre-independence accommodation between the different communities, which are increasingly defined by religion rather than race. This chapter traces the development of the complex relationship between the two systems in the context of Malaysia's evolving but strained constitutional structure and studies the terrain of the conflict between them in the context of a variety of deeply contested legal and political issues.

Table of contents

Malaysia is a multi-ethnic federal state with a population of approximately 25 million people, of whom about 60 per cent are Muslim and 40 per cent are non-Muslim. The group of non-Muslims consists of Buddhists (19%), Christians (9%), Hindus (6.3%), and Sikhs (0.4%). The members of the native tribes of East Malaysia (Sabah and Sarawak) and of the orang asli (original inhabitants) of West Malaysia (the Malaysian peninsula) profess animistic religions, although large numbers of Dayaks, Ibans, and Kadazans in East Malaysia have converted to Catholicism. The largest ethnic group in Malaysia are the Malays (50%), followed by the Chinese (24%), the indigenous people (11%), and the Indians (i.e. those of South Asian heritage, 8%). Bahasa Malaysia is the official language, but English, Chinese (Cantonese, etc.), Tamil, Telugu, Malayalam, Panjabi, Thai and several indigenous languages in Eastern Malaysia are also widely spoken.

(Source: Bartleby 2010)

11.1 The period until 1920

Colonial legal dualism and first codifications of Islamic law

Islam came to Malaysia[2] in the fourteenth century by means of Arab merchants and Sufi missionaries. When the Malacca sultanate was created in the early fifteenth century, its Hindu founder Parameswara converted to Islam. The royal houses of the Malay states, which culturally and politically derived from the Malacca sultanate, linked themselves symbolically with the Arab mainstream Islamic tradition, generally attempting to base their laws and governments on Islamic principles and Malay custom (*adat*). Hence, the Ruler of a state was head of both *adat* and Islam.

Nonetheless, for the purpose of this study it is important to realise that at the time there did not exist a sharp distinction between *adat* and Islam. It was simply not conceived that *adat* and Islam could be in conflict with each other. As Joseph Minnatur (1968) says,

> [i]n pursuit of justice and fair play, the adat considers itself to be in harmony with religious law. It declares:
>
> Customary law hinges on religious law,
> Religious law on the word of God.
> If custom is strong, religion is not upset,
> If religion is strong, custom is not upset.[3]

In reality, however, some of the *adat* principles actually contradicted Islamic law, especially with regard to the position of women[4], and in general one could claim that the restraining influence of *adat* prevented the full adoption of Islamic law.[5]

The pre-colonial legal system was, thus, influenced by Islamic law as well as *adat* law. The administration of justice varied from state to state and from time to time. Islamic law played an important role as the personal and religious law of Muslims (family law, succession, religious law relating to mosques, trusts (*waqf*), taxes (*zakat*), and so on), while *adat* played an important role in criminal law and in cases of property and inheritance, but only a marginal role in family law. The influence of *adat* was the strongest in the state of Negri Sembilan. Interestingly, there were no customary courts and conflicts were usually judged by the *khadi* (Muslim judge), demonstrating once again that *adat* and Islam were not viewed as being in conflict with each other. Parties were given the opportunity to appeal to the Sultan-in-Council. Although academic scholars describe the nineteenth century legal systems of Malaya as Islamic, in practice they were often very far from the Islamic ideal, though to a large degree this depended on the power and the inclination of the Ruler of a particular state (styled 'Raja' or 'Sultan'), as well as on the extent of adherence to *adat* in that state.

The legal system as a dualistic whole of Islamic law and *adat* continued to exist until the coming of the British administration at the end of the nineteenth century. The degree of pluralism further increased with the migration of people from South China and from the Indian subcontinent throughout the second half of the nineteenth and first half of the twentieth century. The pre-colonial nineteenth century legal system in the Malay states is exemplified by Terengganu, a state that has been – at least up to the state elections of 21 March 2004 – at the forefront of Islamisation. That legal system was summarised by British colonial official Hugh Clifford in his report to the Colonial Secretary entitled *An Expedition to Terengganu and Kelantan, 1895*. Clifford claimed that before his arrival, the powerful usurper Sultan Baginda Umar (1837-1876) had applied the sharia corporal punishments with harshness but impartiality. But by the time Clifford visited the state, the legal system, both civil and criminal, was being used by powerful aristocrats to exploit and terrorise the lower orders for their own benefit; there was no semblance of justice, Islamic or otherwise. The mere fact that Clifford commented on this, seems to suggest that it was quite unusual for Islamic law to be applied in an undiluted fashion.

The British established 'indirect rule' throughout the Malay states, which were technically protected states during the colonial period, and now form nine of Malaysia's thirteen states. The other four states – Penang, Malacca, Sabah and Sarawak – were already British colonies from around the late eighteenth or early nineteenth centuries.[6] Under the treaties concluded between the British Crown and the Rulers of the Malay states, the Ruler was obliged to receive and act on the advice of the Resident (the British advisor under Treaty provisions), except in relation to matters pertaining to 'Islam and Malay custom' (Maxwell & Gibson 1924; Kamali 2000). With their field of influence having become limited to 'Islam and Malay custom', the Malay ruling class started to embark upon regulating Islamic matters. To this purpose they used two British-introduced instruments: the State Councils and the positive law (Orders in Council) (Roff 1998: 212). According to Roff, much of the institutionalisation of Islam in Malaysia took place in this context and under the auspices of the British (ibid).

The eventual outcome (by about 1920) was a system that could be called 'colonial legal dualism', in the sense that judicature was divided between English 'common law' and Islam/*adat*. Common law became the general law, with Islamic law and Malay *adat* existing under its aegis together with Chinese customary law and other forms of customary and religious law. This description began to apply to the various Malay states at different dates between 1874 and 1920. It was only after 1920 that English law penetrated to such an extent that the description became wholly accurate. English-style legal institutions and legal principles were gradually introduced either through legislation (for example, the Anglo-Indian codes) or through judicial interpretation. Islamic law remained the personal and religious law of Muslims. In general, *adat* no longer played a role in criminal law after its replacement by the Federated Malay States Penal Code of 1915 (now Law No. 574, Malaysia). Of course this code only applied to the Federated Malay States (FMS), not the Unfederated Malay States (UMS), as discussed below.

The Malay Rulers of the different states did not in general resist the introduction of English legal institutions in the form of common law principles, courts, and English-style legislation and governance. Indeed several of them owed their thrones to British intervention in internal conflicts. In the colonies formed by the Straits Settlements English law was also introduced as the general law, but modified in its application to the different communities (Harding 2001, 2002). An important exception was that Islamic law was, by statute, applied as the personal law for Muslims.

However, the Malay Rulers did to some extent attempt to resist British efforts to integrate the nine Malay states. Only four states joined the Federation of Malay States (FMS) in 1895, namely Selangor, Negri Sembilan, Perak, and Pahang. The other five were known under the name 'Unfederated Malay States', consisting of Johor, Kelantan, Terengganu, Kedah, and Perlis. The process of progressive federalisation caused internal resistance because it was considered to be a disguised attack on the sovereignty of the Rulers (rather than on Islam as such, which was in fact unaffected by the 1895 federalisation and subsequent forms of centralised control).

In the period between the 1870s and 1920, the main effect of British intervention on Islam was that it tended to concentrate religious power in the hands of religious scholars (*ulama*), who depended directly on the Ruler for their positions. This group of conservative religious scholars was referred to as 'the Old Group' (*Kaum Tua*). As an indirect consequence of British colonial intervention, a recognisable split between these conservative legal scholars (*Kaum Tua*) and Muslim activists (*Kaum Muda*) began to appear (Tregonning 1962: 162). The *Kaum Muda*, also referred to by some as 'the Young Group', threatened the position of the *Kaum Tua* from about 1900 onwards (Peletz 2002: 53). They had strong links with the Middle East, Cairo in particular, and in opposition to the *Kaum Tua*, which was often associated with the ruling class, sought to achieve independence. They wanted to bring down the established authority and introduce Islamic modernism in its stead (Roff 1998: 214-215). In the judgement of a British District Officer who studied *adat* extensively in the early twentieth century, it is likely that in this context Islamic law would have replaced *adat* as the general law if British intervention had not checked it (Wilkinson 1908: 48-49). As we have seen, in the end the British successfully introduced British common law, leaving sharia to apply as personal law for Muslims only. This did not serve a *divide et impera* strategy, as was the case in other colonised countries. In fact, the British attempted to integrate as much as possible.

Another result of British intervention was a tendency to formalise the Islamic system of justice as a reaction to the injection of common law institutions. Indeed in the late nineteenth and early twentieth centuries the ruling Malay class and the *Kaum Tua*, under the 'guidance' of the British, began the process of formally codifying the Islamic system. This process included some codification of substantive law and 'reorganization and rationalization' of the Syariah (Sharia) Courts, of which the latter process had started to unfold around the 1890s (Peletz 2002: 47-63).[7] Codification of the Islamic system occurred both in the Malay States (federated and unfederated) and in the Straits Settlements, and covered criminal law as well as personal and family law. For example, the 1917 Code of Criminal Procedure of the state Kedah stipulated, on the basis of sharia, that a person who caused severe physical suffering could be punished with *diyya* (blood money). In 1916 the ruling Malay class and the *Kaum Tua* set up a Religious Council (*Majlis Agama Islam*) in Kelantan to ensure proper administration of justice in the field of Islam (see 11.2 below). This would also happen in Kedah in 1948 and in the other Malay states in 1949. The Religious Councils followed the Shafi'ite school in its legal interpretations, but in case the results of the interpretations were in conflict with the general interest, they could also make use of the Hanafi, Maliki, or Hanbali schools. The British, of course, made sure that these initiatives were within the boundaries of what they saw as acceptable judicial practice.

11.2 The period from 1920 until 1965

Consolidation and constitutional change

During the interbellum there were few changes in the relations between colonial common law, Islam, and *adat*, except for the above-mentioned reorganisation of the Syariah Courts, a process which continued during the 1920-1965 period. A policy of legal harmonisation was in general pursued, in which legal pluralism was accommodated within a common-law framework. The position of the common law also remained virtually unchanged between 1920 and 1965, although the legal institutions based on British law continued to spread in this period from the Straits Settlements to all the Malay States.

The Japanese occupation of 1941-1945 left no legal changes of lasting interest. It contributed, however, to a heightened sense of ethnic polarisation between Malays and Chinese in particular (Peletz 2002: 59). Hence, when the British attempted to establish a Malayan Union in 1946, which would have established a unitary state and accord more or less equal treatment to Malays, Chinese, and Indians under the constitution of this Union (Peletz 2002: 59), a Malay political opposition movement came into existence in which Islam played but a subordinate role to Malay nationalist sentiment. As a consequence of this resistance, in 1948, the Union was replaced by a federation of eleven states that formed the Federation of Malaya and consisted of a combination of the former Straits Settlements of Penang and Malacca and the nine other states located on the Malay peninsula, of which only four had joined the Federation of Malay States (FMS) in 1895 (see 11.1). Under the new federation, the Malays were given back some of their pre-war privileges (Peletz 2002: 60) and, crucially, traditional governance was reinstated in the Malay states.

In 1957 the Federation became formally independent with the proclamation of the Merdeka (Independence) Constitution. The former British colonies Sarawak and Sabah, both located on the island of Borneo, joined the Federation in 1963. This move was initially opposed by the Indonesian government and led to the so-called Indonesia-Malaysia Confrontation (*Konfrontasi*) of 1962-1966. Nevertheless, the Federation of Malaysia, comprised of fourteen states, came into being with the joining of the Federation of Malaya with Singapore, Sabah and Sarawak. Singapore separated from the Federation in 1965.

The Merdeka Constitution was drafted and adopted in 1957, when Islam was a much more peripheral issue than it is now, being much less important in the minds of the constitution-makers than emergency powers or the monarchy, for example. Essentially, the Report of the Constitutional Commission of 1957, a drafting body consisting of five Commonwealth jurists under the chairmanship of Lord Reid, a Scottish judge, formed the basis of the Constitution of the Federation of Malaya (1957) (the Merdeka Constitution), and later of the Federal Constitution of Malaysia (1963), which entered into force with the formation of Malaysia.

Concerning the role of Islam, the constitution entrenched the situation which had applied under British rule in the Malay States: in the Federation's political system this role was confined to the States and dealt with by the Ruler of a state in consultation with the Religious Council, of which the first had been installed in Kelantan in 1916 (see 11.1), and which were established in all states by 1949. Islamic law was, thus, outside the purview of the common law courts, but its sphere of operation was nonetheless ultimately constrained by the British legal structure. In terms of jurisdiction, Islamic law was confined to personal status law for Muslims, notably family law. In brief, it had no role, or only a ceremonial role, to play in the constitution. It was clear that an Islamic state as such was not contemplated and that the issue of making Islam the official religion of the Federation was merely a symbolic recognition of Malay Muslim identity.

Ironically, none of the Commissioners, who were appointed by their respective governments, was Malayan and only one of them, the Pakistani Judge Abdul Hamid, was Muslim. It seems likely, however, that the latter was included for his experience of constitution-making in Pakistan. His stance as a dissenter on several issues such as citizenship and fundamental rights was in fact generally based on constitutionalist, rather than Islamic, principles. In his note of dissent, he did express support, however, for making Islam the official religion of the Federation, which is now the position under Article 3.[8]

Abdul Hamid's view was in fact in accordance with the position of the multi-party Alliance, the predecessor coalition to the current Barisan Nasional (BN), then led by Tunku Abdul Rahman. The Tunku was in favour of Article 3 on the grounds that the provision was innocuous; would not prevent the state from being secular in nature; was similar to provisions in constitutions of other Muslim countries (Afghanistan, Iran, Iraq, Jordan, Saudi Arabia and Syria were cited); was found in the constitutions of some of the Malay States; and was agreed to unanimously by the Alliance, which also included non-

Muslim parties (Federation of Malaya Constitutional Commission 1956: 96).[9] The latter's acceptance of Islam as the official religion of the Federation was part of a political settlement in return of which they would obtain citizenship and the right to education in their mother tongue. In the constitution, Islam was thus proclaimed to be the religion of the Federation when it came into effect on 31 August 1957 (Harding & Lee 2007).

Islam *per se* was little discussed in the drafting process and there was no proposal that an Islamic state along the lines of Pakistan, for example, should be adopted. Despite the apparent failure to fully address in the constitution the religious predisposition of the majority of the population, the 1957 Constitution was approved by the federal and state legislatures and all key stakeholders. Islamic jurists, of whom there appear to have been rather few at that time, also appear to have supported (secular) constitutionalism. For example, the late professor Ahmad Ibrahim (1917-1999), the doyen of Islamic jurisprudence in Malaysia for many years and the founding Dean of the Khulliyyah (College) of Laws at the International Islamic University Malaysia (now named after him), wrote several pieces from a constitutionalist perspective, even though he was also a fervent advocate of Islamisation (Ibrahim 1977, 1989a, 2000).

The Constitutional Commission did not, however, have *carte blanche* in settling the constitution; it was tied by its terms of reference, which were agreed upon in London in negotiations between the Malay leadership and the British Government in 1956. Essentially, their brief was to give constitutional effect to: (1) the survival of the existing monarchies (the sultanates of the nine Malay States) and the federal system to which it was linked; (2) political agreements concerning special privileges for the economically disadvantaged Malays; and (3) citizenship and related rights of the non-Malays.

Thus, the constitution that emerged was an entrenchment of a social contract reached between the main communities. Otherwise, everything was left more or less as it had been under British rule, albeit with some advances in terms of democracy and constitutionalism more generally, for example in the enumeration of fundamental rights.

Resistance to British rule focussed on issues relating to ethnicity and unification rather than religion. Just as they resisted the federalisation attempts of the British in 1895, the Malays had again objected to the British attempt in 1946 to do away with the Rulers and the State governments, which were seen to be quintessential elements of Malay culture. They also objected to the granting of equal citizenship to the non-Malays. Thus, in spite of the constitutional enumeration of fundamental rights the process of federalism, independence and constitution-making also resulted in the special position of the Malays being recognised in terms of special privileges (e.g. quotas for university places, scholarships, places in the public service, and trade licences), and even as an exception to the general principle of equality before the law.[10] Hence, it was Malay nationalism, defined in relation to the Chinese and Indian communities, rather than Islam, defined in relation to Buddhism and Hinduism, that characterised the politics of this period. The historical facts about religion and law were entrenched in the 1957 Constitution, but not essentially changed by it.

Since the beginning of the Malayan Union of 1946 there have been two political currents among the Malays in Malaysia. The United Malays National Organisation (UMNO) of the Malay nationalists formed the largest political force in Malaya and was also the leading member of the Alliance (later Barisan Nasional – BN), which included non-Malay coalition partners.[11] UMNO was formed out of an independence movement that opposed the British Malayan Union proposal of 1946. Since independence, UMNO has ruled without interruption. The other primary political current, the Islamic party, Partai Islam Semalaysia (PAS), was founded in 1948, but its existence for the time being had little effect. This would change from the 1970s onwards (see 11.3 below). Suffice it here to mention that according to Roff (1998: 218) the PAS policy covered elements of thinking of both the old *Kaum Tua* and the younger, activist *Kaum Muda*, safeguarding Malay interests and promoting the establishment of an explicitly Islamic polity.

The previous section explains why in Malaysia Islam is within state, as opposed to federal, jurisdiction and within personal rather than public law. Islamic law operates as an exception to the common law, the latter being the general law as received (now) under the provisions of the Civil Law Act of 1956, which codified what was already the case and that which had previously been consolidated in similar provisions of different dates for the varying States (see 11.1 above). 'Law' according to the 1957 Constitution is the written law, common law, custom, and habits; Islamic law is explicitly excluded in this article, suggesting, oddly, that the constitution-makers did not consider it worth mentioning in this context.

One of the great tasks of Islamic law in Malaysia has been, and continues to be, the achievement of uniformity among the state jurisdictions. Since 1952 attempts have continued to be made to provide uniformity between the various State Enactments on Islamic law. The states were competent to make material and procedural legislation to support administration of justice according to Islamic law, but their competence was limited to personal and family law and to limited jurisdiction in related religious matters falling under the purview of criminal law. As explained elsewhere, this criminal jurisdiction is not general, but confined to personal law-related issues, such as in the case of *khalwat* (close proximity between unmarried persons of the opposite sex). The result is that while Islam is generally regarded as 'official' only in the ceremonial sense (although even this position is contested), there are actually fourteen different systems of Islamic religious administration and Islamic law, and each state (plus the Federal Territories) has its own Administration of Islamic Law Enactment and its own Islamic Family Law Enactment.[12]

In each state the Ruler retained a dual function as Head of Islam and primary authority responsible for the enforcement of *adat*. He was advised by the Religious Council (*Majlis Agama Islam*) (see 11.1), which was led by a jurist (*mufti*), who was also competent to promulgate formal religious legal opinions (*fatwas*) (Ishak 1989: 415). Since these *fatwas* were issued by the Religious Council they had official status. Moreover, a few years after independence, a State Department for Religious Affairs was established in each state that became responsible for the Syariah Courts and other syariah matters as well as for the appointment of judges and for the enforcement of Islamic law in general. According to Peletz, *adat* was not accorded a place within the jurisdiction of this Department and it '[...] received no institutional supports in any way comparable to those underwriting Islam' (2002: 60). State legislation concerned, for example, the registration of Muslim marriages and divorces. In these laws Islamic law was not in general codified; they merely provided the basis for enforcing Islamic law. Appeal could be made to the Ruler-in-Council, who had the authority to appoint a commission to handle the appeal. The state laws determined that the legal principles of the Shafi'ite school were applicable.[13]

With regard to the position of women, this varied according to whether Islamic law was or was not modified by *adat*. Under the matrilineal and democratic *adat perpatih* of Negeri Sembilan, women enjoyed extensive property rights and a married man joined his wife's family (see also note 4). *Adat temenggong*, prevailing in other states of Malaysia (see also note 4), was patrilineal and authoritarian in most of its forms. As such, the position of women was the same as their common position within Islam, except that under the rule of *harta sepencarian* ((division of) matrimonial property), divorcing spouses divided (and still divide) equally property brought into the marriage. While something resembling a women's movement can be discerned in the Straits Settlements in the early twentieth century, it was not until after World War II that women's rights became a major issue in the Malay States. An incident in 1951, in which functionaries of the ruling party UMNO spread a pamphlet stating that *adat* law with regard to property was not in accordance with Islam and was not justified towards men, stirred feelings of resentment in Negeri Sembilan, where *adat perpatih* was applicable (Ali 1963: 33; Hooker 1972, 1973: 509).

In summary, the position of sharia in relation to common law, as personal law for Muslims, in fact remained unchanged, notwithstanding the national struggle against the British attempts to form the Malayan Union (1946), the subsequent creation of the Federation of Malaya (1948), and the independence of the Federation with its new constitution (1957 and 1963).

11.3 The period from 1965 until 1985

The politics of ethnicity, nationalism, and religion

Although Malaysia had emerged by 1965 as a Muslim-majority state, the maldistribution of the benefits of economic development had not been solved by the special privileges of the Malays as authorised by the 1957 Constitution. Rural Malay disaffection surfaced in serious riots following favourable results for non-Malay parties in the 1969 elections. The riots, collectively known as the 'May 13 riots' resulted in the imposition of martial law under emergency powers for almost two years. Religion played no role in the May 13 riots.

The resumption of democratic normality in 1971 was conditional on renegotiation of the 'social contract' concluded in 1957. The special privileges of the Malays were extended and entrenched – so much so that they were placed beyond public debate and formed the basis of a New Economic Policy designed to give *bumiputera* (now defined as Malays and natives of Sabah and Sarawak) a 30 per cent share in the economy within twenty years (i.e. by 1990). In terms of religion and the legal system, these measures had the effect of increasing authoritarianism but did not affect the constitutional position of Islam.

During the late 1970s and 1980s Malaysian society experienced a resurgence of Islam in the wake of the Iranian revolution of 1979. This is referred to as the '*dakwah* (lit. call; missionary) movement' (Nagata 1984; Muzaffar 1987; Anwar 1987). During this period, the Islamic Party PAS, whose influence had previously been minimal, was able to press legal claims at the boundaries where Islam and the common law met. As a self-proclaimed 'true follower of both Malayan and Islamic principles', PAS worked for the establishment of a true Islamic state, in which only Muslims were to hold political power (Kamali 2000: 8). At the end of the 1970s PAS took over the state government of Kelantan, a State that was traditionally Islamic, for a short period of time. For hundreds of years Kelantan has been the Malaysian state with the closest relations with the Islamic world in general and the Middle East in particular (cf. Roff 1996). During PAS' tenure of its state government at that time, and again from 1990, PAS promoted Islamisation to the full extent possible given the limited powers of a state government in this regard.

The Islamic revival in Malaysia signified a challenge for the policy of harmonisation with which the government had until then been able to keep Islamic aspirations in check, or to a certain degree marginal. Events in the Middle East and the development of increasingly powerful Islamic movements in Iran and Pakistan, though, resulted in a stronger call for Islamisation in the political domain.

The ruling Barisan Nasional (BN), a coalition of parties representing different ethnic communities, led by Dr Mahathir Mohamed from 1981 to 2003, took its stand on the basis of Malay political dominance and economic development. With the aim of undercutting PAS' appeal, it mounted a modest programme of Islamisation of state and law: in the legal system, where the process of harmonisation of Islamic law and institutional reform was commenced; in education with the creation of an International Islamic University and assistance for Muslim students; and in banking with the creation of an Islamic banking system (Islamic Banking Act of 1983; Hidayat Buang 1998: 44).

Government policy under Mahathir, emphasising economic development, leaned towards 'Islamic values' such as discipline, reliability, integrity, cooperation, and hard work (Kamali 2000: 160), but this policy did not lead to radical changes in the position of sharia. The Islamic Family Law (Federal Territory) Act 1984, for instance, was aimed at unifying and modernising the personal and family law for Muslims. For example, it provided certain conditions to be complied with before a court could sanction polygamy. The attempt to create a uniform family law to be applied in each of the states was found by conservative elements to be too radical in its modernising measures and not in accordance with traditional sharia, as a result of which three states (Kelantan, Terengganu, and Perak) either rescinded their provision similar to the the Islamic Family Law (Federal Territory) Act 1984 or retained their own un-reformed law, so that merely the court's consent was required.[14] In the result, although the 1984 reformed law was speedily copied by various states, nothing was done to increase the actual scope of the sharia *per se*, which remained limited to personal status law for Muslims.

11.4 The period from 1985 until the present

Islamic revival and inter-religious conflict

During the late 1980s and early 1990s there was some discussion promoted by the then Lord President (chief justice) of the development of a 'Malaysian common law' that would incorporate Islamic values and other elements. Ultimately this discussion came to nothing; it was pointed out by the legal profession that the common law in Malaysia was already a 'Malaysian common law', as the law had developed from the original English model in line with the legal culture and social facts of Malaysian society. But it could hardly be said that Malaysian law had become in any real sense more Islamic as the imprint of British common law remained strong. Indeed, it was only in 1985 that appeals to the Judicial Committee of the Privy Council in London were finally abolished.

Under Mahathir, the Westminster system of government based on the 1957 Constitution had, however, become more authoritarian, with successive constitutional and legislative amendments giving more power to the government.[15] In 1988 the matter of jurisdiction over Islamic law cases came to a head, when the government decided to restrict the jurisdiction of the civil courts. An amendment to Article 121 of the constitution limited the jurisdiction of the civil courts regarding decisions of the Syariah Courts (see 11.5). As a result, Syariah Courts were granted much more independence in the field of personal law. This was done in the context of a constitutional crisis over government interference with the judiciary, which had become more activist in the brief period following the abolition of the appeal to the Privy Council in London.

Developments in three states

The period in question also marks the rise, and perhaps also the fall, of PAS. Having briefly taken over the government of the state of Kelantan in the late 1970s, PAS was able to capture the state again in 1990. After the election victory a coalition of PAS and an anti-Mahathir splinter party of the UMNO took over the administration of Kelantan. They possessed an overwhelming majority in the State Legislative Assembly and PAS' popular leader, Nik Abdul Aziz Nik Mat, became the Chief Minister. Kelantan subsequently commenced a program to incorporate Islamic principles into the law and government policy. These attempts at Islamisation first involved some small changes in the rules for the government apparatus, such as dress codes and stipulations concerning public entertainment and the sale of alcohol. The second initiative for new legislation, namely a *hudud* code of criminal law that introduced Islamic criminal offences and punishments, such as cutting off the right hand for theft, was extremely controversial. However, on November 25, 1993, the State Legislative Assembly unanimously approved the *hudud* law.[16] A chorus of dismay met the passing of the *hudud* law in Kelantan, not just from lawyers, non-Muslim groups and political parties, but also Muslim groups such as the Sisters in Islam, who vigorously objected to the discriminatory effect of several provisions against women and its inconsistency with the concept of fundamental rights in the constitution (Ismail 1995). The *hudud* law of Kelantan was even accused by some (who perhaps had their tongues firmly in cheek and were attempting, as they saw it, to call PAS' bluff) of being *insufficiently* Islamic in that it did not apply automatically to non-Muslims (who were allowed, however, to opt into the *hudud* law).

In Terengganu, where PAS took over the State government between 1999 and 2004, a *hudud* law was also passed. It should be mentioned that Terengganu PAS Chief Minister, Hadi Awang, was instrumental in the *hudud* episode. He also twice proposed in Parliament a bill providing for the death penalty for Muslims who apostatise. The *hudud* affairs in these two states developed into a new conflict between the PAS and the BN.

In the small northern state of Perlis, dominated by the BN, steps were made to solve the 'problem of apostasy' by the passing of the *Islamiah Aqidah* (Islamic religious belief) Protection Enactment in 2000. This law, *inter alia*, empowers the Judge in the Syariah Court to make an order detaining for up to one year in an *Aqidah* Rehabilitation Centre a person who attempts to change his or her religion if the person refuses to recant. Until now, this is the most extreme position taken with regard to the issue of apostasy. In none of the states is apostasy punishable by death, although Malaysia adheres to the Shafi'i school of law and according to prevailing Shafi'i interpretations apostasy should so be punished. There is presently a range of opinions both within the Muslim and non-Muslim communities as to the proper limits of Islamisation. Judging by the election results of 2004, and especially those of 2008, the majority view apparently supported by non-Muslims and many moderate Muslims is that Islamisation has proceeded far enough. While PAS gained votes from the BN, other secularist opposition parties made even greater gains, and even took over control of the state governments in Selangor, Penang, Perak and Kedah.

Dilemmas for the federal government

These developments placed the Federal Government in a politically difficult position: it was concerned about isolating PAS, which by then (although no longer) had become its main political rival and appeared to be fully Islamic. Thus, it maintained a policy of Islamisation that, as has been indicated above, was visible in the fields of education and in commerce and banking, policies which had begun in the early 1980s. At the same time, it did not wish to compromise economic growth, especially in circumstances in which its moral legitimacy from an Islamic standpoint might well be questioned.[17] In any case, it could not support *hudud* law without placing great pressure on the inter-racial, inter-religious nature of the ruling BN coalition itself and alarming the non-Muslim minorities, on whose support it increasingly depended. However, it could also not oppose *hudud* law without appearing to Muslims to be un-Islamic as alleged by PAS.

The electoral successes of PAS created a new environment for the discussion of the role of Islamic law. Beginning around 1999, for example, there was public debate about the concept of an Islamic state, which intensified and broadened following an announcement by the Prime Minister Dr Mahathir Mohamad in Parliament that Malaysia was an 'Islamic state'. Dr Mahathir even went so far as to say that Malaysia was a 'fundamentalist, not a moderate Islamic state', and that it was also a 'model Islamic state'.[18] These statements sparked great controversy. Catholic bishops and non-Muslim parties, for example, denounced them as creating a climate of fear and discrimination in a society that has always embraced religious and ethnic pluralism, and as being factually incorrect as an analysis of the Federal Constitution. On the other side, PAS criticised Dr Mahathir's statements as being false and not in accordance with Islam. An Islamic state, they said, is precisely what they wish to create if they get into power, and what they have been attempting to implement in Kelantan and Terengganu, albeit within the severe constraints of a federal constitution. For half a century PAS had based its politics on the idea that Malaysia should become an Islamic state. PAS sees the order established by the Federal Constitution of 1957 as secular, un-Islamic, corrupt, and, together with the common law, as an obstacle to the establishment of an Islamic state. PAS, however, covers many different opinions, and is as such forced to reach political accommodation with other opposition parties (which proved successful in the 2008 elections); for that reason it has refrained from explicitly making clear what an Islamic state would look like.

The constitution in fact has made precious little concession to the notion that the Federation has a Muslim majority. There is, for instance, no requirement that the Prime Minister must be a Muslim (otherwise for state Chief Ministers). Although Article 3 names Islam as the religion of the Federation, it has until recently always been agreed that this provision does not in any sense establish an Islamic state, but merely provides for the religious nature of state ceremony. Article 3 goes on to say 'but other religions may be practised in peace and harmony in any part of the Federation' (Kamali 2000: chapter 3). While Article 3 has historically been viewed as a provision with mere ceremonial significance, there is now a debate in which certain scholars argue that the article gives a mandate for the application of Islamic law as fundamental law, and in any case that Islam has more than mere ceremonial significance.

The 1999, 2004, and 2008 electoral events and jurisdictional struggles

The constitutional debate intensified into profound political struggle during a passage of events between 1997 and 2004. Despite the apparently calm rejection of the majority of the population in the 1999 elections of calls by PAS for reform, that election indicated some surprising developments. Large numbers of Malay/Muslim voters (traditional Government supporters) were angry with the treatment of former Deputy Prime Minister, Finance Minister and anointed successor to Mahathir, Anwar Ibrahim, who was dismissed, arrested, and charged with corruption and sodomy in 1988. They were also dismayed by the fallout from the economic crisis of 1997-1998 and defected to PAS, which based its campaign on a platform of furthering attempts to create an Islamic state. As a result, PAS not only substantially increased its representation in the federal *Dewan Rakyat* (lower house) from seven to 27 seats, enabling them to lead the parliamentary opposition for the first time in Malaysian history, but also retained control over Kelantan and additionally won control of Terengganu, another traditionally Muslim state.[19] The post-election period saw the Government attempting to control the spread of support for PAS by for example: restricting the publication of its newspaper *Harakah* to twice-monthly and only for party members; interfering with the political content of Friday sermons in the mosques; and presenting UMNO as the party of true, moderate Islam, and PAS as the agent of international terrorism (by claiming that PAS is supportive of international terrorist groups). In the meantime, PAS itself appeared to be undergoing a predictable internal power struggle in which the 'traditionalists' (principally the *ulama*) have been attempting to reassert themselves against the 'young professionals'.[20]

Attempts to Islamise the states under PAS control brought constitutionalism and the common law directly into question. Islam is a state as opposed to a federal subject, and the powers of the different States are severely circumscribed to the extent that implementation of such a programme requires the cooperation of the federal legislature in effecting constitutional amendments which, as matters stand, cannot obtain the support of the crucial two-thirds majority in lower and upper houses. In fact, the federal opposition itself, the Barisan Alternatif (Alternative Front), inaugurated in 1999 and now replaced in 2008 by the Pakatan Rakyat (People's Alliance), is made up of parties that hold directly contradictory views on the relationship between Islam, the common law, and the constitution. PAS, on the other hand, is restricted by the need to cooperate with the other opposition parties. And the post 9/11 environment has generally reduced their appeal in the eyes of the electorate. This was particularly evident in the federal and state elections of March 2004, when PAS' position was shown to have seriously eroded. It won only six seats in Parliament, losing its position as main opposition party to the mainly Chinese Democratic Action Party (DAP), and also lost Terengganu and only won its heartland state of Kelantan by the narrowest of margins following a recount. In contrast, the BN under the new Prime Minister Abdullah Ahmad Badawi increased its proportion of the vote from 54 per cent to 64 per cent. This reversal could be ascribed to a number of factors, including: PAS' failure to convince voters of its moderate intentions; the lack of any consensus between the opposition parties concerning the Islamic state issue; the subsidence of disquiet over the economy and the Anwar Ibrahim issue; and the 'honeymoon' popularity of the new Prime Minister, who was only the fifth in 47 years since independence.

The *hudud* matter has in effect been resolved by the *de facto* position that the state *hudud* laws of Terengganu and Kelantan cannot be enforced due to doubts as to their constitutionality. A case in which the Federal court was petitioned directly on the basis that the *hudud* law of Kelantan was beyond the power of a state to enact was taken to the Federal Court by a back-bench UMNO Member of Parliament and Kelantanese lawyer, Zaid Ibrahim; it was dropped in 2006 following the Prime Minister's intervention. Still, some experiments were performed in the field of Islamic governance within the existing constitutional limitations at the state level, particularly in Kelantan and Terengganu. These initiatives related for example to restrictions on the retail sale of food, public performances, and the implementation of a dress code. In the end, these experiments proved either illusory as with the *hudud* law, relatively trivial in their implications, or of short duration.[21]

Since the 2004 election there has been an intensified struggle around the issue of civil and sharia jurisdiction, based on the 1988 amendment to Article 121 of the constitution. While space precludes detailed discussion of the many important and problematical cases dealing with this crucial jurisdictional issue, suffice it to say that case law culminated in the long-awaited decision of the Federal Court in the *Lina Joy* case, which will be discussed in 11.5.

The 2008 elections have, however, turned upside down the political configuration of Malaysia. The BN lost its two-thirds parliamentary majority for the first time ever, lost control over five state governments (Kelantan, Kedah, Penang, Perak, and Selangor), and obtained only 49 per cent of the vote in Peninsular Malaysia. As an indication of opposition gains, the BN won only one parliamentary seat in the Federal Territory, whereas the opposition won ten. The opposition parties now have 82 out of 222 parliamentary seats, of which PAS has 23. Anwar Ibrahim's Parti Keadilan is now the largest opposition party. The BN's hold on government is water-thin, with many understanding these results as a rebuff for the BN amongst non-Malay voters in particular, partly due to its failure to resist over-ambitious Islamisation of the legal system, but also because of its failure to address other reform issues and to take charge of the economic situation. The overall result, despite PAS' increased representation, is to reinforce the multi-cultural imperative that lies at the roots of Malaysian society and to de-emphasise the Islamic state issue.

In the political and legal situation in Malaysia at this moment one can recognise the government's efforts towards inter-ethnic reconciliation and economic development. However, the historical basis and practical consequences of this reconciliation do not seem to be accepted by newer generations of Malaysian voters. For centuries Malaysian society has embraced a culture of mutual tolerance, and the principle of non-interference in religious affairs is deeply rooted. Pluralism has been a characteristic of many Islamic societies, but Malaysia is in this respect an outstanding present-day example because the country lies in a part of the world, Southeast Asia, where pluralism is a penetrating fact that deeply influences Islam along with other social phenomena.[22]

Yet, the position and role of sharia in national law has now become a matter of political conflict, as government and society are dealing with self-proclaimed followers of 'true Islam', such as PAS. The political situation is therefore now different from the country's longstanding experience, the very characterisation of this experience itself becoming contested. The 2008 elections have created new politics on both sides of the political equation, in which Islam is just one of several issues that appear to be profoundly intertwined. One small pointer might be that in the aftermath of the 2008 elections a problem arose under the State Constitution of Perak, where a DAP/PKR/PAS coalition has taken power. The problem centred around the fact that the constitution says that the Menteri Besar (Chief Minister) must be a Malay Muslim, but DAP is a mainly Chinese party and as such has no credible Malay/Muslim Members of the Legislative Assembly that might be appointed. Several possible solutions were canvassed, but in the end, the three opposition parties agreed that a leading PAS member, a Malay/Muslim, would be appointed even though PAS actually had fewer seats than either of its coalition partners. In the event this solution proved short-lived, and a controversial change in the state government occurred due to defections of assembly members and the head of state's dismissal of the Chief Minister in early 2009.

The abiding impression of the politics of this period is that much turbulence has occurred but very little actual movement on the underlying issues of religion and the identity of the Malaysian polity. As this chapter is finalised in January 2010 it is reported that arsonists set fire to eight churches over one weekend in different parts of Malaysia in incidents which are attributed to yet another legal/religious conflict, over a High Court decision allowing the use of the word 'Allah' in a Catholic magazine published in Malay to describe the Christian God.[23]

11.5 Constitutional law

As in India, Pakistan, and Bangladesh, Malaysia is one of those countries in which constitutionalism along Westminster lines is also a legacy of the British colonial past. The basic structure of the 1957 Constitution is still unimpaired, although there have been many, and frequently drastic, amendments. The result of this is a state termed semi-authoritarian or quasi-democratic, but nevertheless based on the principles of the rule of law. Interestingly, those who resist Islamisation trust the constitution, and even though they often also criticise it, they are reluctant to initiate any changes, as change itself is seen as a threat to their constitutional rights and status.

Malaysia has had to engage with Islam both legally, as an important topic to be dealt with as an aspect of the constitutional order, and philosophically, as an alternative conception of what the constitutional order might be. Four constitutional topics will be discussed below that have influenced that role and position of Islam in Malaysia.

Islam as the religion of the Federation

Article 3 of the Federal Constitution names Islam as the religion of the Federation. It has generally been agreed until recently (see 11.4 and below) that this provision does not in any sense establish an Islamic state, but merely provides for state ceremony. Article 3 goes on to say 'but other religions may be practised in peace and harmony in any part of the Federation'.[24] There is also no provision for the sharia to be a source, much less the primary source, of legislation. Yet, according to former Prime Minister Dr Mahathir, Article 3 is conclusive evidence of the existence of an Islamic state.

This matter was tested in the 1988 case of *Che Omar vs. Public Prosecutor*,[25] in which it was argued that the enactment of a mandatory death penalty was contrary to Islam and therefore unconstitutional. The Supreme Court (now the Federal Court) rejected this argument, holding that Article 3 was not a clog or fetter on legislative power. In doing so, the court drew a sharp distinction between private law, where Islamic law applies, and public law, where it does not, and referred to the basic facts of Malaysian history to explain this position. This position, however, has been expressly or implicitly rejected in a number of recent cases (e.g. *Kaliammal a/p Sinnasamy vs. Pengarah Jabatan Agama Islam Wilayah Persekutuan* [2006] 1 MLJ 685; *Subashini a/p Rajasingam vs. Saravanan a/l Thangathoray* [2007] 2 MLJ 798; also *Lina Joy* below).

Freedom of religion

Religious rights are constitutionally guaranteed in terms of the right to practise and profess any religion in peace and harmony; in the prohibition of discrimination on religious grounds; in the right of every religious group to establish and maintain institutions for the education of children in its own religion; and in the prohibition on requiring a person to receive instruction in or to take part in any ceremony or act of worship of a religion other than his own.

Article 11(1) provides that '[e]very person has the right to profess and practise his religion and, subject to Clause (4), to propagate it.' Article 11(4) allows the states to legislate for the control or restriction of the propagation of any religious doctrine among persons professing Islam. Thus Article 11, while safeguarding freedom of religion, draws a distinction between the *practice* and the *propagation* of religion. The states have in fact exercised their right to enact restrictive laws as envisaged by Article 11(4); and since the states include Penang and Melaka, former British colonies where Islam is not even the state religion, it seems that the restriction of proselytism has more to do with the preservation of public order than with religious priority as such. The restriction of propagation of non-Islamic religions among Muslims and state control over the propagation of Islamic doctrine may also serve the purpose of maintaining social stability.

Article 11 has very much been restricted in its scope by the decision in the abovementioned *Lina Joy* case, discussed in more depth below. In this case a Muslim woman attempted to convert from Islam to Christianity, but it was ruled she could only do so by an order of the Syariah Court. In its decision of 30 May 2007, the Federal Court elevated Article 3 to a higher status than Article 11, which provides for religious freedom.

Article 11(5) creates a further restriction on freedom of religion by providing that Article 11 does not authorise any act contrary to any general law relating to public order, public health or morality.[26] Freedom of religion is, however, bolstered by other provisions. Article 11(2), for example, states: 'No person shall be compelled to pay any tax the proceeds of which are specially allocated in whole or in part for the purposes of a religion other than his own.' Article 11(3) further provides that: 'Every religious group has the right (a) to manage its own religious affairs; (b) to establish and maintain institutions for religious or charitable purposes; and (c) to acquire and own property and hold and administer it in accordance with law.'

Similarly, Article 12(1) prevents discrimination on religious grounds in the administration of public education and scholarships. Article 12(2) gives every religious group the right to establish and maintain institutions for the education of children in its own religion, as stated above; the same clause adds that the States or the Federation may establish or maintain institutions providing instruction in Islam.

Legislation during an emergency, sanctioned by Article 150, and legislation against subversion under Article 149, may not interfere with freedom of religion, and may not interfere with the legislative powers of the states with regard to Islamic law. Thus, primacy is given by the constitution to religious rights even where the security of the state itself is at risk. This primacy has in effect been endorsed by the Supreme Court in *Jamaluddin Othman*, a *habeas corpus* case in which freedom of religion under Article 11 was held to override even the power of preventive detention under the Internal Security Act. The detainee, a Malay/Muslim who had converted to Christianity, was granted *habeas corpus* to secure his release from detention, which had been effected on the grounds that his alleged attempts to convert Muslims was a threat to national security.[27]

Islam as a state subject

Islam is recognised as a state subject under Schedule 9 of the constitution, in which the following competences of states are summarised:

> [...] Islamic law and personal and family law of persons professing the religion of Islam, including the Islamic law relating to succession, testate and intestate, betrothal, marriage, divorce, dower, maintenance, adoption, legitimacy, guardianship gifts, partitions and non-charitable trusts; Wakafs and the definition and regulation of charitable and religious trusts, the appointment of trustees and the incorporation of persons in respect of Islamic religious and charitable endowments, institutions, trusts, charities and charitable institutions operating wholly within the state; Malay customs, Zakat, Fitrah and Baitumal or similar Islamic religious revenue; mosques or any Islamic public places of worship, creation and punishment of offences by persons professing the religion of Islam against precepts of that religion, except in regard to matters included in the Federal List; the constitution, organisation and procedure of Syariah Courts which shall have jurisdiction only over persons professing the religion of Islam and in respect only of any matters included in

> this paragraph, but shall not have jurisdiction in respect of offences except in so far as conferred by federal law, the control of propagating doctrines and beliefs among persons professing the religion of Islam; the determination of matters of Islamic law and doctrine and Malay custom.

The courts have attempted[28] to clarify the way in which state and federal powers are divided with regard to religion in the 1988 case of *Mamat bin Daud and Others vs. Government of Malaysia*. The plaintiffs were charged under an amendment to the Penal Code, section 298A, which created a new offence of commission of an act on religious grounds whose effect was likely to cause disunity or disrupt harmony between people professing the same or different religions. They were charged with committing an act likely to prejudice unity amongst Muslims in that they acted as unauthorised *bilal* (one who gives the call to prayer), *khatib* (one who gives the sermon), and *imam* (one who leads the prayer) at Friday prayers. In response, the plaintiffs sought declarations that section 298A was *ultra vires* Article 74 of the Federal Constitution because in pith and substance it dealt with Islam, a state matter, and was therefore beyond the power of Parliament to enact. On a careful analysis of section 298A, a lengthy, complex and sweeping provision, the Supreme Court decided, by a majority of three to two, that the acts prohibited by the section had nothing to do with public order, a federal matter, but were directly concerned with religion, a state matter, and that therefore the plaintiffs were correct.

The dualistic administration of justice

The Syariah Courts administer personal status laws with respect to Muslims, but the ordinary criminal courts have jurisdiction over Islamic criminal matters provided for under the various Administration of Islamic Law Enactments. Following an amendment to the constitution in 1988 and subsequent amendments, notably that of 1994,[29] Article 121 provides for the jurisdiction of the High Courts, the Court of Appeal, and the Federal Court, but adds: '(1A) The courts referred to in clause (1) [i.e. the High Courts and inferior courts] shall have no jurisdiction in respect of any matter within the jurisdiction of the Syariah Courts.' Thus, Article 121 separates the jurisdiction of these courts (commonly known as the 'civil courts') and that of the Syariah Courts.

As indicated above, since the 2004 election there has been an intensified struggle around the issue of civil and sharia jurisdiction, based on the 1988 amendment to Article 121 of the constitution. Case law[30] culminated in the long-awaited decision of the Federal Court in the already mentioned case of *Lina Joy vs. Federal Territory Islamic Council* in a 2-1 decision on 30 May 2007. Professor Thio Li-ann summarises the position following this crucial decision as follows:

> The majority found that the [National Registration Department] had acted lawfully in requesting further documentary evidence such as a statement of apostasy from the Syariah Court and in rejecting a personal statutory declaration provided by Lina that she was a Christian. Following *Soon Singh,* the majority judgement delivered by Chief Justice Ahmad Fairuz opined that if a Muslim wanted to leave the religion of Islam, this entailed the exercise of a "right" under the context of Syariah law which had its own jurisprudence on apostasy. He reasoned in interpreting Article 11(1) that for a Muslim who practised and professed Islamic Law this was to be done in compliance with Islamic law which prescribed the method of converting into and out of Islam. Chief Justice Ahmad Fairuz reportedly observed: "You can't at whim and fancy convert from one religion to another."[31] One might observe that Lina Joy's battle to exercise free conscience for more than a decade is hardly whimsical. Thus, Islamic tenets were referenced in public law construction. By reason of Article 121(1A) apostasy as a matter relating to Islamic law lay within the exclusive jurisdiction of Syariah Courts.[32]

In an intellectually rigorous dissent demonstrating fidelity to constitutional supremacy, dissenting judge Richard Malanjum found that the NRD had acted without power in requiring such a certificate from a religious authority as this was an extraneous factor in the context of the existing Regulations. It was not the NRD's function to ascertain whether the appellant had properly apostasised. He found that the NRD policy failed the test of objective reasonableness and noted that even a reasonable policy 'could well infringe a constitutional right', as in the present case, where there was unequal treatment under the law. He argued that as apostasy involved 'complex questions of constitutional importance', including the federal-state division of legislative powers and fundamental rights, and noted that it was of 'critical importance' that civil superior courts 'not decline jurisdiction by merely citing Article 121(1A)'. He clarified that Article 121(1A) only protected Syariah Court jurisdiction in a matter 'which does not include the interpretation of the provisions of the Constitution'.[33] In displaying a rights protective consciousness, Malanjum HMP noted that where the prospect of curtailing fundamental rights was implicated, 'there must as far as possible be express authorisation for curtailment or violation of fundamental freedoms, which power should not be easily assumed by implication'.[34]

It is not surprising that this latest decision, which turns on a particular way of interpreting Article 121(1A) as well as definition of the substantive content of religious freedom, has provoked disquiet to the point of eliciting a statement from Prime Minister Abdullah Badawi that the Federal Court majority decision was not politically motivated and in reaffirming that Malaysia 'upholds the Constitution and supremacy of the law, otherwise, we would have become a "failed state"'.[35] Nevertheless, there is a sense that this regressive interpretation goes beyond a question of religious choice and forbodes a 'potential dismantling of Malaysia's [...] multi-ethnic, multi-religious character'.[36] Consequently, certain concerned citizens consider that political recourse is now the only option.

While the divided Federal Court decision goes some way in clarifying the ambiguities and gaps in protection surrounding interpretations of Article 121(1A) in relation to defining the jurisdictional ambits of civil courts and Syariah Courts, this is unsatisfactory in terms of principle, constitutional history and interpretive method. Further rationalisation of the dual court system is needed.

The preceding discussion should sufficiently indicate the bifurcated nature of Malaysian law under prevailing constitutional arrangements. In many ways the underlying issues that divide these two legal worlds have not until recently been explored and the engagement is slow and very controversial, the terms of reference being themselves a matter of disagreement.

11.6 Family law and inheritance law

While matters of civil law, including family law in general, fall under the jurisdiction of the federal government, Islamic personal and family law and *adat* law fall under the jurisdiction of the states (Harding 1996: 61-72). Muslim marriages are regulated by the Departments of Religious Affairs of the states. Besides satisfying the marriage requirements of the sharia, those Muslims who wish to enter into marriage must also complete administrative procedures and take a marriage course approved by the State's Department of Religious Affairs.

Even though Islamic family law matters are the most important affairs in which Syariah Courts are competent to judge, there is no uniform Islamic family law for all Malaysian states.[37] The most authoritative or exemplary statement of sharia-based family law is provided by the Islamic Family Law (Federal Territory) Enactments 1984-1994.[38] This law has been called an extremely important and guiding 'landmark legislation', based on the *siyasah shariyyah* (policy based on sharia) (Kamali 1997: 153-154). Its provisions, although resisted from some quarters, now form the basis of the law in most parts of Malaysia, with the exception of Kelantan, Terengganu, and Perak (Kamali 1997: 160; Ibrahim 1993). The law attempts to provide a better and uniform protection of property rights of married Muslim women. The law also aims to act as a model to be followed by the various state laws in ensuring that a Muslim woman's right to divorce and her subsequent rights relating thereto are regulated more fairly and consistently.[39]

Polygamy and registration of marriages

The Islamic Family Law Enactments 1984-94 determine in section 23(4) that polygamy is permissible according to Islamic tradition, albeit dependent on judicial approval. A Muslim man who desires a polygamous marriage must satisfy at least five conditions: the intended marriage must be 'reasonable and necessary'; the man must possess enough financial resources to support his family; his current wife must give her permission; the man must be capable of treating his wives equally; and the intended marriage may not harm the current wife or wives.

Despite these limitations, it must be noted that the regulations in various states have largely hollowed out the intent and purpose of the original 1984 law. The decision to approve of a polygamous marriage is made by the Muslim judge, the *khadi*. The Islamic Family Law Enactment is not very detailed in Kelantan and no mention is made of punishing polygamy lacking approval from the judge. In Terengganu, a similar regulation applies (Ahmad Ibrahim 1993: 299). The regulation in Perak provides that no person may enter into another marriage as long as the current marriage endures, unless a prior written approval from the judge is given (Kamali 2000: 65). In practice, judges presumably focus mostly on the question about whether the man can support his new wife (Kamali 2000: 162).

A 1994 law that amends the 1984 law allows for polygamous marriages without the approval of the judge, provided the marriage is in accordance with sharia; it leaves it up to the judge to decide whether or not to register the marriage. The disappearance of the prohibition of registering polygamous marriages lacking the judge's approval has turned back the clock, in that the inequality between sexes has increased.[40] This trend appears to be confirmed in 2002 in the northern state of Perlis. There, the authorities loosened the procedural and administrative requirements for polygamous marriages and permitted men to enter into a polygamous marriage without requiring permission from the first wife (Kent 2003).

In Malaysia under the Law Reform (Marriage and Divorce) Act 1976 every non-Muslim marriage requires registration; non-registration is a criminal offence, but does not render the marriage void or voidable. For

Muslims the registration of marriages is mandatory based on the 1984 law, in which neglecting to register a marriage is also a criminal office, punishable with a fine and/or detention.[41] A non-Muslim man who wishes to marry a Muslim woman must first convert to Islam.[42]

Divorce – unilateral and by mutual approval

The *talaq* or unilateral divorce by the husband is implicitly recognised by law, under the condition that he fills out a set form in which he mentions his reasons and that an attempt at reconciliation has been made. Section 124 of the 1984 law provides that pronouncing the *talaq* without the judge's approval is punishable, but it does not mention whether the marriage is subsequently dissolved or not (Kamali 2000: 86-87). Section 55(a) of the 1984 law as modified in 1994 holds that the judge must give approval after the *talaq* that has been enunciated without the judge's prior approval. If the judge then gives his approval, the *talaq* is considered to be in accordance with sharia. The judge must, however, make attempts at reconciliation for a maximum period of six months. If the judge then decides that there is an irreconcilable dispute in the marriage, the husband will be asked to pronounce the *talaq*, after which the divorce is registered.

In 2003 a remarkable case caused some fierce discussion. The occasion was a judgement by a Syariah Court that found a *talaq* in the form of an SMS message to be an adequate form of announcing a divorce. The religious advisor Abdul Hamin Othman agreed with the judgement, arguing that an SMS message is clear and unambiguous and therefore valid according to sharia law. The political elite and Islamic fundamentalists, on the other hand, fiercely opposed the judgement. According to Prime Minister Mahathir, it was in contradiction with Malaysian culture and the spirit of sharia law.[43]

Divorce based on mutual approval, or *khul'*, takes place when the woman starts the procedure by returning the dowry. In addition, section 52 of the 1984 law permits divorce by the woman on the following grounds: the husband is missing for more than one year; she has been living for three months without financial support; the husband is sentenced to prison for three years or longer; he does not fulfil his marital duties for one year; chronic impotence, but only in case the woman was not aware of this fact at the time of the marriage; a mental disease lasting longer than two years, leprosy or a transmissible sexual disease; when the woman opposes the marriage because it was effected by her father or grandfather before she had reached the age of sixteen, as long as the woman is under the age of eighteen and the marriage is not consummated; cruel treatment; the husband refuses sexual intercourse for four months; illegality of the consent to marry one of the women (for example because the consent was obtained by force or based on fallacy); or any other recognised ground for dissolution or nullification, such as *talak takliq* (breach of marriage contract) (Kamali 2000: 95-96). For non-Muslims a divorce is only possible when proclaimed by a competent court.[44]

Despite their acknowledgment that the Islamic Family Law (Federal Territory) Enactments 1984-94 comprise enlightened legislation, the Sisters in Islam handed in a list of complaints and reform proposals to the government in 1997.[45] The complaints concerned matters such as unnecessary delay when a woman asks for divorce (whereas the man can obtain a divorce immediately when he pronounces the *talaq*); unnecessary delay in mediation procedures when the husband does not appear; the lack of uniformity in the laws of different states, allowing husbands to choose the state that best suits their case;[46] attempting to evade the obligations of spousal support by moving to another state; and a lack of well-educated judicial and legal personnel, which presents an obstacle in the administration of justice and disproportionately affects women as they are most often the victims.

A Muslim woman whose husband unjustly divorced her can ask for a payment during the three menstrual cycle waiting period following divorce (*idda*) and gift on divorce payment (*muta*) periods. The judge determines the sum of the payment according to the 1984 act. Income or property obtained during the marriage through joint efforts is divided by the judge according to division of joint property (*harta sepencarian*, under *adat*). The judge can also divide income obtained through individual effort, by taking into consideration the extent to which the other party, for example through household work and care for the family, has contributed to the building of that income.

Inheritance

With regard to inheritance issues, Muslims follow uncodified Islamic law, based on the general rule that women receive half the share of what men in the same position would. In order to create a fair distribution of inheritance among all family members, it is usual in a will to follow the general rule of Islamic law that the testator does not have free possession of one third of his inheritance. Meanwhile adat, including matrilinear adat, is also still followed in inheritance matters.

11.7 Criminal law

The regular courts for criminal cases have jurisdiction over all acts punishable under the Penal Code, including acts which would be punishable if Islamic criminal law were applied. The Syariah Courts have some limited criminal jurisdiction, the precise scope of which is unclear given that the *hudud* laws have not been pronounced upon constitutionally. In general one could say that their criminal jurisdiction probably extends only to offences which are incidental to the Syariah Court's jurisdiction, e.g. failure to comply with a court order. However, some offences, such as *khalwat* (close proximity between unmarried persons of the opposite sex), are purely Islamic and are punishable only in the Syariah Court, as indicated below. As stated above, state laws make the spreading among Muslims of religious doctrines other than Islamic doctrines a punishable offence. And in the state of Perak, it is forbidden for non-Muslims to use a word from a list of 25 important Islamic words. The state has also forbidden the teaching of Islamic doctrine without written approval or in a manner that is not deemed to be in accordance with Islamic law. In some states it is forbidden to publish an Islamic book without permission. Additionally, state law prohibits *khalwat*. The Syariah Criminal Offences (Federal Territory) Act 1997 contains radical, but not atypical, criminal offences that are far-reaching in terms of restricting constitutional rights on freedom of religion and freedom of expression.[47] There is a religious police force which concerns itself specifically with the enforcement of rules such as these. As is explained above, *hudud* law is on the statute book in two states, but is not in practice enforced, is opposed by the Federal Government, and is probably unconstitutional. In one episode in 2005, which led to great public concern, the religious police raided a discotheque in Kuala Lumpur, isolated all the Muslim young men and women dancing there, including a well-known pop singer, and arrested them for being indecently dressed. They were later released and Prime Minister Badawi publicly stated that this incident should not have occurred.

11.8 Other areas of law, in particular economic law

The Islamic Banking Act of 1983, which emerged from the *dakwah* ('prayer') movement of the 1970s and gained influence especially since the creation of the Islamic Development Bank, forms the core of Islamic banking in Malaysia. The Malaysian Central Bank derived from this law its competence to supervise the Islamic banks. The Government Investments Law of 1983 granted the government competence to hand out state debentures on the basis of sharia principles. The subsequent creation of Bank Islam Malaysia Berhad (BIMB) was described by the Minister of Finance at that time as the first step in the government's endeavour to give Islamic values a place in the economic and financial system of the country (Razaleigh 1982). In 1991 the

Islamic Religious Council for the Federal Territories founded the 'Centre for Levying *Zakat*', with the task of informing the Muslim public of the obligation to pay Islamic taxes (*zakat*) and regulating the collection thereof. The two above-mentioned laws exist alongside legislation for the conventional banking system. Since 1993, when the 'programme for interest-free banking' was introduced, the existing banks have been encouraged to offer Islamic banking services in accordance with sharia. In 1997 the central bank also created the National Shariah Advisory Council (for the Islamic Banking System and Insurances), the highest sharia authority in this field in Malaysia.

11.9 Obligations with respect to human rights

The constitution contains a bill of rights which follows the standard pattern of 1950s de-colonising constitution-drafting and bears a strong similarity to its Indian equivalent. However, both religious rights and civil liberties, such a freedom of speech, are hedged around with loosely prescribed exceptions and provisos. For example Article 11, while allowing freedom of religion, restricts the propagation of non-Islamic religions among Muslims. The state also assumes control over the propagation of Islamic doctrine, and restrictions on apostasy for Muslims are regarded as constitutionally valid and indeed serving the purpose of maintaining social stability. The problem with these laws is that they are contrary to the spirit of freedom of religion and equality before the law, and place the adherents of other religions (or Muslims who hold to unorthodox religious tenets) at a disadvantage as compared with Muslims (or orthodox Muslims). Thus, in the long term, the maintenance of these restrictions may well have the effect of undermining the overarching principle of religious freedom, which, as may be seen, is a fundamental right that has historically existed at a higher level, in practice, than other fundamental rights. While Malaysia has not signed any of the international human rights covenants except the CRC and CEDAW, the latter of which has resulted in the inclusion of gender discrimination as an impermissible form of discrimination under Article 8 of the constitution, which deals with equal protection, it has clearly developed its own distinctive approach to human rights.[48] The language of cultural relativism 'Asian values' is never far from the lips of those in power when human rights issues are being addressed (Thio 1999; Langlois 2001).

Having said this, there have been some positive developments in recent years. In 1999 the National Human Rights Commission Act was passed, setting up the NHRC as a monitoring body without powers to deal finally or definitively with human rights concerns. This at least ensures a forum in which concerns can be raised and matters investigated

(Whiting 2003). Moreover, the Malaysian Bar has been unflinching over several decades in its determination to point out human rights failings and breaches of the rule of law and judicial independence, usually in effect leading the civil society charge against authoritarian government. While one can observe something of a split along religious lines between Muslim and non-Muslim lawyers, the more remarkable fact is the maintenance of long-term solidarity in spite of such internal cleavages.[49]

11.10 Conclusion

The constitutional balance can be said to have reverted in some ways to where it was before the tumultuous events following the economic crisis of 1997. The 1999 election result, an apparently conservative electoral reaction to those events, appeared to change the nature of the constitutional debate in Malaysia. The 2004 and 2008 election results appear to indicate that an Islamic state of the kind that PAS seeks to create is unacceptable to the generality of Muslim as well as non-Muslim voters. However, the issue of the Islamic state has re-emerged in the form of a struggle waged in the courts to define the respective jurisdictions of the civil courts and Syariah Courts.

With this caveat, after the dust of the intense political struggle of 1997-2004 had settled, there seemed, at least until the 2008 elections, to be little disturbance of the inter-ethnic, inter-religious, and political alignments and understandings that have obtained since 1957. To put the position simply, the liberal-democratic order implied in the 1957 Constitution has been partially maintained, but with two concessions: exceptional powers to the executive, which embodies Malay nationalism, inter-ethnic accommodation, and economic development, at the expense of democratic freedoms; and the privileging of Islam as a religion, and Malay/Muslims as a race (*bumiputera*) over other races (non-*bumiputera*) and other religions, at the expense of the democratic principle of equality before the law. Both of these concessions are, however, both problematical and increasingly contested.

If Malaysia manages to reach a new constitutional settlement acceptable both to Islamists and *reformasi* supporters (these are not of course mutually exclusive categories) it will have set a precedent of great interest and importance in the Islamic world and beyond. The success of the legal cultures of Southeast Asia over hundreds of years in absorbing and melding various legal worlds and concepts indicates that a syncretic, creative, and peaceful solution to the problem of Islam and constitutionalism is by no means impossible.[50] At present it seems as though such an ideal solution is fraught with both political controversy and intellectual confusion. Nonetheless, to describe the situation set out in this report as a 'clash of civilizations', while not without resonance in the Malaysian situation, would ignore the fact of peaceful cohabitation of Islam and other conceptions of state and law for more than one hundred years.

The apparent contemporary polarisation along religious lines, rendered complex by the new politics of 2008 and beyond, should not obscure this history. There have been and continue to be significant skirmishes at the borders, which are expressed principally in terms of legal struggles over territory or 'jurisdiction'. These skirmishes seem likely to veer towards an even more intense conflict. There are also, however, far-reaching compromises on both sides: Islam largely concedes, in practice and for the time being, that Islamic law is not fundamental in the constitutional order, while the constitutional order concedes that strict equality for Muslims and non-Muslims will not apply. But which society does not have such skirmishes and compromises, and are they not evidence of an underlying but significant degree of tolerance and acceptance of difference?

The Malaysian example is certainly one of conflict, but conflict has existed (apart from the May 13 riots of 1969) as purely political and litigious, not violent. Significantly, whereas the 1969 election resulted in ethnic rioting, in 2008, electoral results even more adverse to the government were accepted on all sides without any such incidents. Malaysia is also an example that shows the possibility of a tolerant, progressive, pragmatic, moderate, and consensus-based, if not always strictly democratic or egalitarian, Muslim-led government; and the sustained viability, over a century, of a dualistic legal system. The constitution and the institutions of the common law have indeed provided the means whereby accommodation between two fundamentally contradictory conceptions of legality has been achieved.

Notes

1 Professor of Asia-Pacific Law, University of Victoria, B.C., Canada. The author wishes to thank Ng Wei, David Chen, and Nadia Sonneveld for their support in research and their suggestions, as well as Jan Michiel Otto for his extensive and helpful comments and assistance.

2 This chapter uses the word 'Malaysia' to refer to the present-day Federation of Malaysia. The term 'Malaya' is used to refer to the Malay States and the Federation of Malaya in the period before Malaysia was created in 1963. The term 'Malay' is used for the language and ethnic group of Malay/Muslims living in Malaya/Malaysia.

3 See also Wilkinson 1970: 6 et seq.

4 *Adat perpatih* was the democratic *adat* law that was brought to the Malay state of Negeri Sembilan by immigrants from Minangkabau, West Sumatra. The more common form of *adat* was known as *adat temenggong*. According to *adat perpatih*, ancestral land passes via the female line (i.e. from mother to daughter). According to

tradition, the *adat temenggong*, which prevailed in other parts of Malaya, stems from the same matrilineal community of Minangkabau, but Hindu influences in this case changed *adat* to the extent that it now refers mostly to customs based on a patrilineal system. See also 11.2.

5 I say in general since the relation between *adat* and Islamic law varied (and still varies) a lot, depending on the state in question. In the state Negeri Sembilan, for example, *adat* played (and still plays) an important role, while Islamic law is more important in the state of Kelantan.

6 Singapore, Penang, and Malacca formed the so-called Straits Settlements between 1842 and 1941.

7 It is not easy to precisely establish the origins of Malaysia's Syariah Courts. Peletz argues that 'their precedents and genealogies qua religious symbols and judicial institutions can be traced back to the early modern period (which extends from the fifteenth to the eighteenth centuries)' (2002: 26).

8 This stipulation, the current Article 3 of the constitution, was originally not part of the design made by the Reid Commission but was later inserted during the review process in 1957.

9 Mohammad Hashim Kamali comments that 'the prevailing climate of opinion in the judiciary and elsewhere in the higher echelons of Government has not shown any decisive shift of policy to alter the original perception of the secular state as was expressed in the constitutional debate fifty years ago' (Kamali 2000: 35).

10 While the Chinese, and to a certain extent the Indians, controlled business life and the free professions, quotas were introduced to allow for positive discrimination favouring Malays. In the 1957 Constitution explicit mention was made of this exception to the principle of equality before the law (Art. 8(5), and more generally in Chapter X: Government Services).

11 Notably, the Malaysian Chinese Association and the Malaysian Indian Congress.

12 Hereafter there will be some generalisation because it would be too much to distinguish and cite all the different stipulations of fourteen jurisdictions for the purpose of this country study.

13 The reference to this school nowadays has consequences especially for *fatwa* jurisdiction, although the Syariah Courts in practice also follow the doctrines of the Shafi'ite school. Even with *fatwas* it is possible to consider principles of other schools, namely when this is done for the general interest. A *fatwa* can also involve *adat* and in some states the Council by law has to take *adat* into consideration when fulfilling its function. *Fatwas* are particularly important when it comes to determining the duties of Muslims. Compare Ahmad Ibrahim (2000).

14 Kamali (2000: 12-13, 64-65) suggests that a possible reason for the 'disobedience' of these states in adopting modernised family law legislation conforming to the original federal law of 1984 can be found in the fact that this law was primarily modelled after the Hanafi Madzhab of Pakistan and India, while most Malaysian states profess the Shafi'ite tradition. Ibrahim and Joned (1995) suggest that the fact that making Islamic laws is the prerogative of individual states has resulted in a lack of uniformity, despite attempts made by the federal government to unify the interpretation and the application of Islamic family law.

15 Compare Harding (1996). During this period the government coalition also retained the required two-thirds of the majority to amend the constitution.

16 Two members of the opposition also voted for the bill. For further analysis and comments on the *hudud* issue, see Kamali (1995). This book is summarised in a more accessible manner in Kamali 1998: 203. Compare Imam 1994: xxix; Ibrahim 1993: 14.

17 An interesting question arises here: what is the basis of political legitimacy in Malaysia? Is it traditional/Islamic, charismatic, legal-rational, or economic/

pragmatic? One could say that all these aspects are important for legitimacy or perhaps also that, cynically, those who are in power will use whichever aspect is most suitable in their situation. But it is undoubtedly true that the traditional/Islamic basis of legitimacy has long since been detached from the traditional monarchy.

18 CNN, 18 July 2002, see http://asia.cnn/2002/World/asiapcf/southeast/06/18/malaysia.mahathir/, consulted September 2, 2002. His successor as Prime-Minister, Abdullah Ahmad Badawi, made similar comments during the election campaign of March 2004.

19 Ironically enough, commentators attribute the political survival of Mahathir, who took over power in 1981 as an advocate of Malay rights, and the BN in the elections of 1999 to the votes of non-Muslims, which had the effect of compensating for the loss of Muslim votes to the PAS and other opposition parties. Non-Muslims voters must have realised that a vote against the BN could have led to the imposition of an Islamic state by a PAS-led government, although the cooperation of non-Muslims and non-Malay parties of the 'Barisan Alternatif' opposition coalition would have been necessary to actually gain power.

20 *The Sunday Times*, Singapore, 4 June 2000. The statutes of the party in the meantime have been amended in order to give the traditionalists more power at the state level. The PAS has also started a debate about the role of women in politics.

21 Although it appears to be an anomaly that Islam is an issue of the states within the federal structure of a country with a Muslim majority and where Islam is also the religion of the Federation, representatives of the PAS have admitted in a conversation with the author that the possibility to experiment and also eventually make mistakes at state level was actually an important acquisition.

22 Hefner & Horvatich (1997). It is entirely correct to refer to the 'Islam of Java', 'Aceh' or 'Malaysia'. Compare Kamali 2000: 3.

23 See http://english.aljazeera.net/news/asia-pacific/2010/01/201011022583880534l.html, dated 11 January 2010.

24 A prominent Muslim jurist told the author that the word 'but' in Article 3 is considered to be insulting towards Islam and that it must actually be read as 'and therefore'. Compare also Kamali 2000: chap. 3.

25 [1988] 2 MLJ 55. See, however, the contrary more recent case of *Meor Atiqulrahman bin Ishak & ors vs. Fatimah & ors* [2000] 5 MLJ 375 and the discussion and citations in Bari & Shuaib 2006: 5-10.

26 This clause came up in the case *Halimatussaadiah vs. Public Service Commission* MLJ [1992] 1: 513, in which it was declared that a disciplinary rule of the government that prohibited female employees from wearing the (*purdah*) (clothing covering the entire body), because it made personal identification impossible, was constitutional. For more comments and analysis, see also Zakaria 1993: xxv.

27 *Minister for Home Affairs vs. Jamaluddin bin Othman*, Supreme Court Review (SCR) [1989] 1: 311; [1989] 1 MLJ 369, 418.

28 See *Mamat bin Daud and Others vs. Government of Malaysia* [1988] 1 MLJ 119; 1988 LRC (Const) 46.

29 Constitution (Amendment) Act, A885 of 1994, creating the Court of Appeal. See, also on this article, Jusoh 1991; Ibrahim 1989a: 1; Ibrahim 1989b: xvii.

30 Space precludes the coverage in detail of several important and highly controversial cases, especially Shamala's and Subashini's cases: *Shamala a/p Sathiyaseelan vs. Dr Jeyaganesh a/l C Mogarajah* [2003] 6 MLJ 515; *Shamala a/p Sathiyaseelan vs. Dr Jeyaganesh a/l C Mogarajah* [2004] 2 MLJ 241; *Shamala a/p Sathiyaseelan vs. Dr Jeyaganesh a/l C Mogarajah* [2004] 2 MLJ 648; *Shamala a/p Sathiyaseelan vs. Dr Jeyaganesh a/l C Mogarajah* [2004] 3 CLJ 516; *Subashini a/p Rajasingam vs. Saravanan a/l Thangathoray* [2007] 2 MLJ 798; *Subashini a/p Rajasingam vs. Saravanan a/l*

Thangathoray [2007] 2 MLJ 705; *Subashini a/p Rajasingam vs. Saravanan a/l Thangathoray* [2007] 4 MLJ 97; *Subashini a/p Rajasingam vs. Saravanan a/l Thangathoray* [2008] 2 CLJ 1. See, however, also the case of Indira Gandhi, reported at http://www.malaysianbar.org.my/legal/general_news/conversion_case_indira_gandhi_gets_custody_of_her_3_children.html. For further discussion, see Whiting (2008) and Harding & Whiting (2010).

31 Hamid & Azman 2007.

32 Thio 2007; *Lina Joy* 2007, text in Bahasa Melayu, see http://www.malaysianbar.org.my/index.php.

33 Malanjum 2007, para.s 64, 65, 68.

34 Id., para. 84.

35 The Sun 2007.

36 Beech 2007, quoting Malik Imtiaz Sarwar.

37 In a letter from the *Sisters in Islam* to Prime-Minister Mahathir of August 1997 it was noted that 'Malaysia is the only country in the Muslim world in which every state has independent jurisdiction with regard to religious affairs, which leads to inconsistency and contradiction in the law, interpretation, and implementation', cited in Kamali 1997: 155-156.

38 The Federal Territories comprise Kuala Lumpur, the administrative centre Putrajaya, and the island of Labuan.

39 For non-Muslims, the Law Reform (Marriage and Divorce) Act 1976 unifies the law with respect to marriage and divorce issues with effect from 1 March 1983. The 1976 act moreover introduces reconciliation organs; these must attempt to solve within six months marriage problems brought before them by people who wish to divorce. Section 3(3) explicitly states that the law is not applicable to 'a Muslim or any other who is married according to Islamic law nor to a marriage in which one of the parties professes Islam'. Exemptions exist for natives of the states of East Malaysia, namely Sabah and Sarawak, or for aborigines of West Malaysia whose marriages and divorces are regulated by native customary law or aborigine customary law. Compare section 3(4); para. 384 of the 2004 CEDAW report concerning Malaysia; also 1976 Act, sections 55, 106.

40 In their joint letter to Prime-Minister Dr Mahatir, the *Sisters in Islam* and the Association for female jurists declared that 'the amendments made by several states to the original law have resulted in the man having the exclusive right to decide whether or not a polygamous marriage will take place.'

41 See part III on the registration of marriages of Muslims.

42 See *myGovernment: The Government of Malaysia Official Portal*, the part about marriage: accessible via http://www.gov.my/MyGov/Home/.

43 See http://timesofindia.com/articleshow/104860.cms.

44 A ground for divorce for a marriage between two non-Muslims would be conversion to Islam of one of the spouses during the marriage (1976 Act section 51). Conversion of a husband would have far-reaching legal implications for the woman who does not convert herself, particularly in the context of polygamy, for the right to maintenance and inheritance, and – in the worst case – divorce. The woman does have the right to request a divorce, on the condition that the petition must be started within three months after the conversion. In April 2004, in the case of *Shamala a/p Sathiyaseelan vs. Dr. Jeyaganish a/1 C. Mogarajah (Muhammad Ridzwan bin Mogarajah)*, of 13 April 2004, the court declared itself incompetent to adjudicate custody over the children of a woman whose husband converted himself and the children to Islam.

45 See Reform of the Islamic Family Laws and the Administration of Justice in the Syariah System in Malaysia. The memorandum was presented to the Malaysian government in March 1997. The proposal for the memorandum was formulated and

approved during the national workshop under the same name on 4 January 1997; the information is accessible via: http://www.muslimtents.com/sistersinislam/memorandums/04011997/htm.

46 See *Aishah Abdul Rauf vs. Wan Mohd Yusof Wan Othman* [1990] 3 MLJ ix. In this case the Syariah Court of Appeal of Selangor rejected a husband's request to marry a second woman because he could not sufficiently prove that his decision was 'reasonable and necessary'. Not long after, the man simply went to the state of Terengganu to marry his second wife there.

47 This law contains, among others, the following punishable offences: mistakes in worship (s.3), propagation of false doctrines (s.4), propagation of non-Islamic doctrines among Muslims (s.5), contempt or public disdain of religious authority (s.9), unauthorised giving of religious education (s.11), propagation of opinions that contradict *fatwas* (s.12), publications of religious writings that are in conflict with Islamic law (s.13), and even faults in fulfilling the obligation of Friday prayer (s.14) and encouraging others to fail to fulfil religious duties (s.17).

48 It must be noted here that although the constitution assumes equality of sexes in Article 8 and CEDAW is one of the few international human rights conventions ratified by Malaysia, the country has deviated from these stipulations with regard to testamentary ownership and the appointment of sharia judges, *muftis*, and *imams*. See Thio 1999.

49 Harding & Whiting 2010. This was written as a contribution to the American Bar Foundation's project on political liberalism, for which further information can be found at http://www.americanbarfoundation.org/research/project/32.

50 Compare An-Na'im 1999; Kamali 2000: chap. 15. This approach is reflected in the published work and the speeches of Anwar Ibrahim. In *The Asian Renaissance* (Singapore, Times Publishing, 1996), Anwar frequently refers to the necessity to promote democracy, civil society, and righteousness, whereby he uses an impressively extensive series of authors, Muslim as well as non-Muslim, Eastern as well as Western. Although Anwar does not answer specific constitutional questions, there can be no doubt that that he is an outspoken supporter of independence of the judiciary, democracy, and human rights; and there can also be no doubt about his ideas that these concepts are a significant part of the Asian traditions, including Islamic traditions. Furthermore, he fiercely rejects Eastern despotism. Recently it had become clear that the Parti Keadilan Malaysia (the Justice Party), led by Anwar's wife, Wan Azizah Ismail, has a principally constitutionalist agenda. Anwar's opinions probably differ from Western constitutionalism only in so far as he believes (and perhaps even wrongly) that constitutionalism is hostile with respect to religion. It could well be possible, and several commentators have already pointed this out, that the person who would be best capable of finding a solution to the contradiction between Islam and constitutionalism, is Anwar. Farish Noor (*South*, October 2000) even refers to 'the phenomenon of the *reformasi-Islamisasi*' and emphasises the possible explosive connection between these two concepts.

Bibliography

Ali, M.D. (1963), 'Islam and adat: Two forces in Malay society', *Intisari* 1: 33.

An-Na'im, A. (1990), *Toward an Islamic reformation: Civil liberties, human rights and international law.* New York: Syracuse University Press.

Anwar, Z. (1987), *Islamic revivalism in Malaysia: Dakwah among the students.* Petaling Jaya: Pelanduk.

Bari, A.A. (1999), 'Legal education and Islamisation', *IIUM Law Journal* 7: 83.

Bari, A.A. & F.S. Shuaib (2006), *Constitution of Malaysia: Text and commentary*, (2nd ed.). Petaling Jaya: Prentice Hall.

Bartleby (2010), 'Malaysia', in *World Factbook*, see http://www.bartleby.com/151/country/my.html (2008 statistics) and https://www.cia.gov/library/publications/the-world-factbook/geos/my.html (online edition, last accessed February 2010). Washington, D.C.: Central Intelligence Agency.

Beech, H. (2007), 'Malaysia's Crisis of Faith', *Time Magazine*, 30 May, see http://www.time.com/time/world/article/0,8599,1626300,00.html.

Buang, A.H. (1998), 'Islamic transactions in Malaysian courts', in A.H. Buang (ed.), *Islamic law in Malaysian Syariah courts: Practice and problems*, 44. Petaling Jaya: University of Malaya.

Clifford, H. (1992), *An expedition to Trengganu and Kelantan*. Kuala Lumpur: MBRAS.

Faruqi, S.S. (1999), 'Democratic constitutionalism in Islam and in the modern state of Malaysia', *Jurnal Fikrah* 2: 1.

Federation of Malaya Constitutional Commission (1956), *Report*. Kuala Lumpur: Government Printer.

Hamid, J. & S. Azman (2007), 'Malaysia's Lina Joy loses Islam conversion case', ABC News, 30 May, see http://www.abcnews.go.com/International/wireStory?id=3224695&ROS=true.

Harding, A.J. (1996), 'Islamic law in Malaysia', in *Yearbook of Islamic and Middle Eastern Law*, vol. 2, 61. Den Haag: Kluwer Law International.

Harding, A.J. (1996), *Law, government and the constitution in Malaysia*. Den Haag: Kluwer Law International.

Harding, A.J. (2001), 'Comparative law and legal transplantation in South East Asia: Making sense of the Nomic Din', in D. Nelken & J. Feest (eds.), *Adapting legal cultures*, 199-222. Oxford: Hart Publishing.

Harding, A.J. (2002), 'Global doctrine and local knowledge: Law in South East Asia', *International and Comparative Law Quarterly* 51: 25-53.

Harding, A.J. & H.P. Lee (ed.) (2007), *Constitutional Landmarks in Malaysia: The first 50 years, 1957-2007*. Kuala Lumpur: Malayan Law Journal/ LexisNexis.

Harding, A.J. & A. Whiting (2010), '"Custodian of Civil Liberties and Justice in Malaysia": The Malaysian Bar and the Moderate State', a forthcoming book chapter on file with the author.

Hefner, R.W. & P. Horvatich (eds.) (1997), *Islam in an era of nation states: Politics and religious renewal in Muslim South East Asia*. Honolulu: University of Hawaii Press.

Hooker, M.B. (1972), *Adat laws in modern Malaysia: Land tenure, traditional government and religion*. Kuala Lumpur: Oxford University Press.

Hooker, M.B. (1973), 'The challenge of Malay adat law in the realm of comparative law', *International and Comparative Law Quarterly* 22: 509.

Horowitz, D. (1994), 'The Qur'an and the common law: Islamic law reform and the theory of legal change', *American Journal of Comparative Law* 42: 233-543.

Ibrahim, A. (1977), 'Power to dismiss the Prime Minister or a Chief Minister in Malaysia', *Parliamentarian* 58: 34.

Ibrahim, A. (1989a), 'The Syariah Court and its place in the judicial system', *Syariah Law Journal* 5: 1.

Ibrahim, H. (1989b), 'The amendment to art. 121 of the federal constitution: Its effect on the administration of Islamic law', *Malaysian Law Journal* 2: xvii.

Ibrahim, A. (1993), 'Suitability of Islamic punishments in Malaysia', *IIUM Law Journal* 3(2): 14.

Ibrahim, A. (1999), 'Islamic law in Malaysia since 1972', in S.S. Ahmad (ed.), *Developments in Malaysian law*, 295-317. Petaling Jaya: Pelanduk Publications.

Ibrahim, A. (2000), *The administration of Islamic law in Malaysia*. Kuala Lumpur: IKIM.

Ibrahim, A. & A. Joned (1995), *The Malaysian legal system*. Kuala Lumpur: Dewan Bahasa dan Pustaka.

Imam, M. (1994), 'Islamic criminal law in Malaysia: Federal-state jurisdictional conflict', *Malaysian Current Law Journal* 1: xxiii.

Ishak, O. (1989), 'The making of fatwa in Malaysia', *Islamic Studies* 28: 415.

Ismail, R. (ed.) (1995), *Hudud in Malaysia: The issues at stake*. Kuala Lumpur: SIS Forum.

Jusoh, H. (1991), *The position of Islamic law in the Malaysian constitution with special reference to the conversion case in family law*. Kuala Lumpur: Dewan Bahasa.

Kamali, M.H. (1995), *Punishment in Islamic Law: An Enquiry into the Hudud Bill of Kelantan*. Kuala Lumpur: Institut Kajian Dasar.

Kamali, M.H. (1997), 'Islamic law in Malaysia: Issues and developments', in *Yearbook of Islamic and Middle Eastern Law* 4: 153-179.

Kamali, M.H. (1998), 'Punishment in Islamic law: A critique of the hudud bill of Kelantan, Malaysia', *Arab Law Quarterly* 13: 203.

Kamali, M.H. (2000), *Islamic law in Malaysia: Issues and developments*. Kuala Lumpur: Ilmiah Publishers.

Kent, J. (2003), 'Malaysian polygamy law under review', BBC News Online, 14 January, see http://news.bbc.co.uk/1/hi/world/asia-pacific/2659233.stm.

Langlois, A.J. (2001), *The politics of justice and human rights: Southeast Asia and universalist theory*. Cambridge: Cambridge University Press.

Lina Joy vs. Federal Territory Islamic Council et. al., decision of 30 May 2007, text in bahasa available on website of the Malaysian Bar, see http://www.malaysianbar.org.my/index.php.

Malanjum, R. (2007), dissenting judgment (in English), *Lina Joy v. Federal Territory Islamic Council et. al.*, decision of 30 May, http://www.malaysianbar.org.my/content/view/9223/27/.

Maxwell, W.G. & W.S. Gibson (eds.) (1924), *Treaties and engagements affecting the Malay states and Borneo*. London: Truscott.

Muzaffar, C. (1987), *Islamic resurgence in Malaysia*. Petaling Jaya: Fajar Bakti.

Nagata, J. (1984), *The reflowering of Malaysian Islam: Modern religious radicals and their roots*. Vancouver: University of British Columbia Press.

Roff, W. (1996), 'An argument about how to argue', in M.K. Masud, B. Messick & D.S. Powers (eds.), *Islamic legal interpretation: Muftis and their fatwas*, chapter 19. Cambridge: Harvard University Press.

The Sun (2007), 'Islam not above constitution says PM', 31 May, see http://www.malaysianbar.org.my/content/view/9186/2/.

Thio, L. (1999), 'Implementing human rights in ASEAN countries: Promises to keep and miles to go before I sleep', *Yale Human Rights & Development Law Review* 2: 1-86.

Thio, L. (2007), 'Jurisdictional embroglio: Civil and Religious Courts, turf wars and article 121(1A) of the federal constitution', in A.J. Harding & H.P. Lee (ed.) (2007), *Constitutional Landmarks in Malaysia: The first 50 years, 1957-2007*, chap. 14. Kuala Lumpur: Malayan Law Journal/ LexisNexis.

Tregonning, K.G. (1962), *Papers on Malay history*. Singapore: JSEAH.

US State Department (2004), Country Reports on Human Rights Practices 2003, 25 February, see http://www.state.gov/g/drl/rls/hrrpt/2003/27778.htm.

Whiting, A. (2003), 'Situating Suhakam: Human rights debates and Malaysia's National Human Rights Commission', *Stanford Journal of International Law* 39: 59-98.

Wilkinson, R.J. (1908), 'Law. Part 1: Introductory sketch', in R.J. Wilkinson, *Papers on Malay Subjects*. Kuala Lumpur: FMS Government Printer.

Wilkinson, R.J. (1970), 'Malay Law' (reprint), in M.B. Hooker (ed.), *Readings in Malay adat laws*, 6. Singapore: Singapore University Press.

Zakaria, Z. (1993), 'Religious freedom – Right to wear the purdah', *Malaysian Law Journal* 3: xxv.

12 Sharia and national law in Mali

Dorothea Schulz[1]

Abstract

The Republic of Mali is a multi-ethnic nation with an overwhelming Muslim majority and a constitution embodying a parliamentary system, multi-party democracy, and freedom of religion. Its legal infrastructure is strongly shaped by the legacy of the French Civil Code and the French principle of secularism (*laïcité*) and does not make room for any incorporation of Islamic law into the constitutional order.

Islamic law has never been strongly represented or institutionalised in any colonial or postcolonial state law. Its traces have become weaker, even if Islam, as an idiom of community building, has gained a new momentum since the late 1970s and a greater public prominence after the political liberalisation of the early 1990s. Mali's current positive legal system reflects several dilemmas and legacies deriving from a longer-standing legacy of colonial dual administration, from the particular power constellation between Muslim forces and the state, and finally, from the autocratic political heritage of its recent postcolonial history.

Mali's present-day legal system does not comprise a separate Islamic judicial sector, and sharia does not figure in any area of codified law. Nor did sharia play a role in the development or modification of Malian law. At the same time, democratisation and the empowerment of secularist forces within the government since the early 1990s has not put an end to Islam's imminent political force. At the level of positive law, however, the secular character of the constitution and of political parties is expressly maintained.

Table of contents

The Republic of Mali gained independence from France in 1960 and presently counts around 12.6 million inhabitants. Various ethnic groups live in Mali, including the Mande (Bamana, Maninka, Soninke) (50%), Peul (17%), Voltaic (12%), Songhai (6%), and the Tuareg and Moor populations (10%). Ninety per cent of Malians are Muslim, and nine per cent of the population professes an indigenous religion. Only one per cent of the population is Christian. French is the official language, but 80 per cent of the Malian population speaks Bamanakan and/or one of several other African languages.

(Source: Bartleby 2010)

12.1 The period until 1920

The coexistence of diverse politico-legal orders – a situation disrupted by French colonial administration

Precolonial centralised polities and diverse forms of local legal practice

Throughout the nineteenth century, the area of today's Mali was structured by various forms of politico-legal organisation. Some regions were under the tutelage of centralised polities. Although these polities are often referred to as 'kingdoms' (in scholarly publications as well as in local parlance), they differed from medieval European kingdoms with respect to their administrative and political organisation. They were based primarily on warfare, trade, and on the redistribution of booty and tended to be characterised by a high degree of instability. Royal and noble lineages and the principle of inherited leadership existed, but were often challenged by contending warrior entrepreneurs. Some of the ruling lineages were closely affiliated with lineages of Muslim scholars and traders, and had themselves adopted a Muslim identity. The majority of the population, in contrast, continued to subscribe to non-Islamic religious practices and belief systems.

Areas outside these centralised polities were by and large constituted by conglomerations of relatively autonomous village communities, which formed temporary and strategic military alliances against foreign aggressors. Here again, only few families considered themselves Muslim.

Starting in the late eighteenth century, populations in the southern triangle of contemporary Mali witnessed the emergence of a number of Islamic theocratic states. Among them were the empire of Macina (founded in 1810 and ruled by Sekou Amadou from 1755-1849) and the Tukulor empire of El Hadj Umar Tall (1794-1864), who, after his return from Mecca to his home base in the Futa Tooro (eastern Senegal), sought to create a warrior empire, which, however, due to the growing presence of the French colonial powers, never achieved a high degree of institutionalisation and stability. From 1852 onwards, El Hadj Umar gradually occupied south eastern Mali, which until then had been under the control of the empires of Kaarta, Macina, and Segu. The expansion of these theocracies did not bring with it a mass conversion to Islam. Widespread islamisation occurred only in zones under the immediate influence of these empires.

As a consequence of the varying degrees in islamisation, locally diverse legal orders and practices co-existed in many areas. In the northern regions, Islamic law (Maliki school of jurisprudence) was predominant in and near the urban centres such as Gao and Timbuktu where Muslims made up the majority of the population. In most regions of the French Sudan (Soudan Français), in contrast, customary practices of establishing 'law and order' were based exclusively on oral tradition, relatively fluid, and situationally contingent. Because Muslim communities existed as islands within non-Islamised populations, legal practice was characterised by a selective combination of Islamic and non-Islamic normative orders. This selective combination of normative orders was facilitated by the fact that only few people were literate and most normative principles were passed down orally. It is likely that many interpretations of Islamic law were inflected by customary legal principles. Only in towns where families of Muslim religious scholars had a political weight was this intermingling of different normative orders mitigated by the interventions of religious experts who watched over the correct application of Islamic legal conceptions.

The early days of French colonial administration

Earliest contact by the French colonial powers with the area of today's Mali dates back to the fifteenth century. But, actual colonisation of the region started only in the nineteenth century, in the context of a growing struggle among European powers over overseas colonial territories. Moving from the Senegalese coast to inner zones of Sahelian West Africa, French colonial troops gradually occupied a region that later was to constitute a major part of the Afrique Occidentale Française (AOF). French colonial occupation of the area started in the late 1850s and ended in 1892, with the subjection of El Hadj Umar's son Ahmadou Tall. In 1892, the 'French Sudan' (*Soudan Français*), the area comprising present-day Mali, was declared part of the French colonial empire; in 1902, it was incorporated into the administrative unit of 'Sénégambie et Niger' and, later, in the period between 1904 and 1920, into the 'Haut-Sénégal et Niger'.

12.2 The period from 1920 until 1960

The spread of Islam in the face of colonialism

The consolidation of colonial rule

The name 'French Sudan' (*Soudan Français*) was reintroduced for the area of today's Mali in 1920 and became a separate administrative unit in 1937. Colonial administration never affected local politico-legal and social structures to the same extent as in the case of the coastal French colonial territories. This is due to the fact that, apart from the commercial rice cultivation programme in southern Mali (region of Segu), colonial exploitation of natural resources was almost non-existent.

The majority of the Malian rural population, in particular in the South, converted to Islam only after the 1920s, that is, during the colonial period. The gradual conversion to Islam was facilitated by several factors. For a long time, Muslim faith had been associated with an erudite, cosmopolitan, and economically successful identity. Individuals and families critical of colonial occupation came to equate Islam with a modern, progressive orientation that constituted an alternative to the colonial normative and cultural order. The modernising, cosmopolitan outlook of Islam was reinforced under the influence of religious and economic entrepreneurs with intellectual and commercial ties to the Arab-speaking world. It allowed younger people to distance themselves from traditional political authorities as well as from an older generation of Muslim religious experts, many of whom had established a friendly relationship with the colonial authorities.

The role of Muslim authorities as brokers between local producers and the colonial state was significantly less important than in other West African countries, such as Senegal and Nigeria. Lineages associated with the Sufi orders, a prominent social form of Islam in West Africa, were influential in pre-colonial polities mostly in and around some urban areas (such as Timbuktu, Gao, Mopti, Djenne, Segu, Nioro), an influence that sometimes expanded in the colonial era. The three important Sufi brotherhoods – the Qadiriyya-Mukhtariyya, the Tijaniyya, and the Hamawiyya – emerged in doctrinal distinction from, and in political competition with, each other from around the late eighteenth century. Yet, today, their leading lineages and followers jointly constitute the basis of established or 'traditional' Islam. A crucial step in this fusion of representatives of the diverse doctrinal orientations into a group with a common structural position in contemporary Malian society was the active support of French colonial administrators for some of the Sufi lineages. French administrators considered them to be representatives of an established 'African' Islam capable of limiting the growing influence of a new group of Muslim entrepreneurs with strong intellectual and business ties to the Arab-speaking world.[2] The latter, labelled 'Wahhabi' by colonial administrators (and by many people today), consider themselves 'Sunnis'. Since their emergence in the 1940s, they have denounced some practices and beliefs associated with the Sufi brotherhoods as unlawful innovations, that is, as distortions of the original teachings of the Qur'an and Hadith. Although the Sunnis jointly opposed the representatives of the Muslim establishment, they never constituted a homogenous group.[3]

The French system of colonial administration invested the French Parliament with full legislative powers and with functions allowing for a direct administration of colonies, thus covering the domains of criminal law, of public matters, and of political and administrative regulation. In addition, the Governor General of 'French West Africa' (Afrique Occidentale Française or AOF), seated in Saint-Louis (Senegal), had the authority to promulgate legislation in the form of ordinances and of administrative orders.

A decree of 1903 by the Governor General of the AOF that stipulated that the French Civil Code should be applicable in French West Africa marked the formative period of colonial administration and the attempt of the French colonial powers to establish a legal system of general validity throughout this colonial territory. It established a dual colonial legal system with two distinct bodies of law and spheres of their application. French positive law (*Code Napoléon*) regulated the affairs of French citizens and 'assimilés', that is, French expatriates, non-African foreigners and those Africans who had acquired French citizenship (*citoyens*). The rest of the colonised population, the so-called 'French subjects' (*Sujets Français*), were adjudicated under the *Justice Indigène*, that is, according to various 'indigenous' or 'customary' laws among which Islamic law held a privileged position. The treatment of Islamic law as part of customary law served a *divide et impera* strategy that effectively contributed to the mutual neutralisation of competing local political factions and of the normative orders these different groups sought to establish as the dominant order. Colonial politico-legal practice thereby perpetuated the highly dynamic and conflict-ridden relations among different segments of the population.

Colonial attempts to control the normative regulation of social and political life were played out in, among other things, the absence of a separate Islamic or customary judicial sector. There was no direct and explicit incorporation of Islamic law into the constitutional order. The application of customary and Islamic law was limited to certain social domains, such as the customary regulation of marriage and inheritance matters. Yet, even if the regulation of these intra- and inter-familial matters remained by and large in the hands of male family members who exerted their authority in this domain, these matters did not remain fully outside colonial legislation. French politico-legal control interfered, for example, in the form of decrees such as the *Décret Mendel* (1939) and the *Décret Jacquinot* (1951), which set the minimum age for marriage and limited the amount of the bride-price, respectively.

Formal adjudication of disputes took place at the level of the district (*cercle*) and of the province. The third level of jurisdiction was the Court of Appeal in St. Louis (Senegal). The French administrator-judges working in the indigenous courts (*Tribunaux Indigènes*) relied on both customary law (including Islamic law) and modern law; they were supported in their work by advice from experts (*assesseurs*) in local legal norms and practices (Sall 1986; Hazard 1972). Some administrators invested great efforts in compiling and systematising 'local custom' as it appeared before their courts.

In regions with a Muslim majority, one of the two assessors or advisors to the judge was either an expert in Islamic jurisprudence or some other Muslim notable. As these Islamic experts turned into assessors, they lost crucial competences and decision-making powers with respect to the settlement of disputes over inheritance, land use, and slaves.[4] Because French magistrates had the authority for decision making in disputes centring around divorce, land use rights, succession, and so forth, their role had the effect of severely reducing the political power of village elders and Islamic notables. That being said, it is likely that a number of experts in Islamic law and in non-Islamic legal conventions, by contributing to the standardisation of different customary laws, were able to enhance their personal powers and to buttress the structural position of the group they represented. Furthermore, in spite of the seemingly overarching powers of colonial administrators, their possibilities to enforce their rulings were actually quite weak and, by and large, limited to the administrative centres and the immediate surrounding areas. Also, one has to keep in mind that, except for the areas where Islam had been established for centuries, Islamic legal norms and regulations were often strongly inflected by non-Islamic normative principles, such as in the domain of inheritance, marriage, and divorce matters. Accordingly, the endorsement of Islamic norms remained limited to areas under the influence of powerful lineages of Muslim religious specialists.

The times of the independence struggle

Islam never became a central rallying idiom for anti-colonial resistance in the Soudan Français. In the times of the independence movement (since the late 1930s), many representatives of traditional Islam joined the Parti Socialiste de Progrès (PSP), the basis of which was constituted primarily by the former political and religious establishment. The PSP was originally the more successful political party, but it lost political terrain to its competitor, the Union Soudanaise-Rassemblement Démocratique Africain (US-RDA), in the legislative elections of 1957. The latter adopted a more explicit socialist orientation and had its stronghold among segments of the population that were considered socially inferior (e.g. descendants of former serfs). Initially, the US-RDA also counted among its ranks a number of 'Wahhabi' activists and merchants.

After the official establishment of the internal autonomy of the French West African Colonial Territories in 1958, full legislative powers were transferred to the territorial legislative assemblies, created in the same year. Mali achieved independence as a member of the Malian Federation (which then comprised the French Sudan and Senegal); its first constitution was ratified in January 1959. After the failure and subsequent dissolution of the Malian Federation on 20 August 1960, Mali was declared an independent nation; its new constitution, adopted in September 1960, was a slightly revised version of the initial constitutional text.

Islam was not explicitly mentioned in either constitution. Article One simply states the indivisible, democratic, secular, and social character of the Malian Republic (Konaré 1982: 160). The legal system also did not comprise a separate Islamic judicial sector, and sharia did not figure in any area of codified law. Almost immediately after its independence, Mali became a member of the United Nations (September 1960).

12.3 The period from 1960 until 1985

From Keita's socialist single-party rule to Traoré's military regime

1960-1968: Keita's socialist single-party rule

The postcolonial evolution of the state legal system testifies to the persistent colonial legacy of a dual legal order, which established two distinct types of subjecthood (*citoyen* versus *sujet*). In the postcolonial context, the *Justice Indigène* was discontinued. But the duality of the colonial system was perpetuated in another form, that is, in the substantial gap between legal regulations on the one hand, and social practice and local law in a broader sense, on the other hand. The legacy of the dual colonial legal system is further reflected in the on-going, *de facto* exclusion of the majority of the population from basic citizenship rights. Most Malians – in particular those who live in remote, rural areas – have very limited, if any, access to courts and legal support. The reverse side of this situation is the judiciary's lack of legitimacy and means with which to enforce judgements.

The first President of Mali, Modibo Keita, pursued a socialistic policy. Although some 'Sunni' reformists had initially supported the cause of the US-RDA party that led Mali into independence, the reformists soon lost political terrain, as did their political opponents, the representatives of traditional Islam. The opposition of conservative Muslim forces to Keita's rule was certainly one reason why his party promoted a decidedly secular interpretation of the constitution. President Modibo Keita never went so far as to denounce the influence of Islamic clerics on local politics, but his secularist policy sought to neutralise them. However, his marginalisation of Muslim forces, especially of Muslim merchants, was only temporarily successful; it provided a seed of growing popular disaffection and passive resistance that would ultimately lead to the overthrow of his regime.

The first constitution of the Republic of Mali, adopted by the National Assembly in September 1960 by unanimous vote, was revised three times during the *de facto* single-party rule of the US-RDA.[5] The political system laid down in the constitution was a parliamentary democracy with a strongly centralised and personalised executive power. The division of legislative and executive powers was analogous to that of the French Constitution of 1958. Apart from the Supreme Court, a State Court (*Cour d'État*) combined constitutional, jurisdictional, and administrative functions with those of the Auditing Office (Lavroff & Peiser 1961: 172; Konaré 1982: 12). In the later years of Modibo Keita's rule (post 1965), amendments to the constitution reflected an ever increasing tendency towards monopolisation of political power and the downplaying of judicial independence and authority.[6]

The new constitution provided for the codification and legislative reform of several domains. The reorganisation of the judiciary in May 1961 put an end to the dualist colonial judicial system. However, adjudication on the basis of legal advice from assessors was still permitted, however, in yet unlegislated domains, such as in the area of inheritance. Revised versions of the colonial Criminal Code (*Code Pénal*) and the Code of Civil, Commercial, and Social Procedure (CPCCS) were enacted in August 1961, and the colonial Code of Criminal Procedure was reformed in August 1962. The penal code was subsequently modified again in 1967 and in 1972 in an effort to ensure the equal treatment (punishment) of men and woman under Malian law. Reforms established, for instance, that men too should be punished in the case of adultery, abandonment of spouses and children, and for refusal to provide financial support (Sall 1986: 387). The Code of Civil, Commercial, and Social Procedure was modified in 1972, under the military regime of Moussa Traoré (see below). New legislation also emerged in other areas, including, for example, laws on nationality and labour relations.[7] Sharia did not play a role in the formation or adaptation of Malian law.

The legislation of previously untouched domains occasionally put the new political power in a paradoxical situation. The US-RDA's version of an 'African path to socialism' was distinct from the atheist agenda of Marxism-Leninism. Islam was seen as an important source of both cultural values and socialistic values derived from traditional Malian culture. Subsuming Islam under the umbrella of an authentic, pre-colonial African heritage was part and parcel of the US-RDA's strategy of encompassing cultural and political difference, rather than excluding or marginalising certain cultural conventions at the expense of others. Yet, by appealing to a common nationalist agenda, Keita's regime reproduced the tensions inherent in the conception of a shared public interest as formulated by liberal Western political theory. Muslim identity and national identity were occasionally equated in official representations, but religion *per se* was treated as a matter of individual conviction and relegated to the realm of the private.[8] No legal or educational institutions or organisational structures were created that were directly inspired by, or served to promote, Islamic normative principles.[9]

The combination of a socialist programme with a legitimising rhetoric based on references to an authentic African cultural heritage confronted the state with contrasting, even mutually exclusive, objectives. This, and the particular role that Muslim authorities played in a struggle over legitimacy and control, is illustrated by the codification of family law. In 1962, the Law on Marriage and Guardianship (*Code de Mariage et de Tutelle*) was enacted. This codification was intended to support the programme of economic restructuration and development that Modibo Keita's socialist regime had designed. This programme of economic development revolved around the aim of transforming the notion of extended family as the basic unit of the traditional social order and of pre-capitalist relations of production. This required interference in social institutions that had remained outside the control of colonial administration. Moreover, it implied a substantive limitation of the prerogatives of gerontocratic authority. Given that the new nation was claimed to be based upon and to represent the perpetuation of 'primordial' African forms of social solidarity, this hardly authorised the new leadership to affect precisely these kinds of changes. From this dilemma, there resulted administrative reforms, which sometimes neutralised each other, and a potpourri of, sometimes incongruent, legal provisions (or the lack thereof).[10]

For instance, the Constitution of 1960 made women full citizens with equal civil and political rights. The *Code de Mariage et de Tutelle* of 1962 was based on a new, nuclear family model based on horizontal bonds between spouses. As such, the code laid down the full civil capacities of married women (Art. 36). Clauses such as the determination of the minimum marriage age and of the necessity of the wife's consent to the marriage crystallised the attempt to weaken the gerontocratic family complex based on the authority of male elders over the pro-creational capacities of women and daughters and over the productive capacities of sons.

The interference of the state with processes of decision-making within the family privileged the bond between the spouses and thus supported the emergence of new possible alliances within the family. However, the fact that the area of inheritance was never legislated reflected the continuing reluctance of the state to intrude into sensitive domains of everyday life. Consequently, fifty years post independence, there is an incongruence between the constitution, which guarantees women equal rights and full civil capacities, and Article 231 of the above-mentioned CPCCS which leaves the regulation of inheritance matters to locally diverse customary conventions – even where they are adverse to the principles of gender equality.

In rural areas, the substantial privileges of male elders (in some areas bolstered by references to Islamic principles and norms) were maintained principally because the relations of production remained largely unaffected by the changes imposed from above, in spite of the efforts of party representatives at the local level. For example, the limitation of the amount of the bride-price stipulated in the *Décret Jacquinot* of 1951 was generally disregarded, and no punitive measures were taken against it, partly because officials themselves continued with this practice. Arranged marriages, often of legal minors, also continued to be the rule. Likewise, although official registration of marriage was made a requirement, its application was nowhere enforced, allowing patriarchal prerogatives to be maintained.[11] Remaining traces of customary influence in the domain of marriage and divorce legislation reflect a reticence on the part of the US-RDA to police sensitive areas of patriarchal family control and to engage in conflict with religious authorities.

1968-1985: Traoré's military single-party rule

An alliance between representatives of the Muslim establishment and a new generation of Muslim businessmen was instrumental in the forming of a resistance to Modibo Keita's socialist policies, which ended with his overthrow by a group of officers of the Malian army in 1968.

Immediately after the putsch, an Ordinance (No. 1/1968, dated 19 November) suspended the Constitution of 1960 and established new, provisional structures of public powers that were to combine executive and legislative functions (effective until 1979). The result was the creation of the Military Committee of National Liberation whose president was to assume the function of the head of state.[12] A new constitution, approved by popular referendum (a novelty) on 2 June 1974, became effective only in 1979, with the creation of a new assembly, a government and the election of the leader of the military committee, Moussa Traoré, as the new president of the country, now under the single-party rule of the Democratic People's Union of Mali (*Union Démocratique du Peuple du Mali*, UDPM).

The new Constitution of 1974 emphasised its continuity with the secular nature of its predecessor and reconfirmed its adherence to the Universal Declaration of Human Rights (and civil liberties) of 1948. But in practice, Traoré granted Muslim groups special privileges, in spite of Mali's secular constitution. One motivation for Traoré's pragmatic revision of the former regime's decidedly secular orientation was the political weight of influential Muslim families, many of which had business connections to the Middle East. Granting this group special privileges allowed Traoré to extend his control over powerful segments of the religious establishment and their new opponents, the *arabisants*, that is, graduates from institutions of higher learning in the Arab-speaking world. Because of their higher religious education, the *arabisants* soon occupied leading posts in the state bureaucracy, especially in the Ministry of Interior (which comprises a Department of Religious Affairs) and the Ministry of Education. For this reason, they had strategic advantages over both the representatives of the Sufi orders and the older generation of 'Wahhabi' merchants. The foundation of the national 'Association Malienne pour l'Unité et le Progrès de l'Islam' (AMUPI), in the early 1980s consolidated state control over the activities of the various groups of Muslims. The organisation's official *raison d'être* was to reconcile 'traditionalist' forces of the Muslim camp with their principal contenders. The organisation allowed the government to monitor the funds that, starting in the late 1970s, flooded the country, under the orchestrated efforts of the Saudi government to extend their *da'wa* movement of proselytising to fellow Muslims in sub-Saharan Africa.

Over the years of Moussa Traoré's rule, Islam, sponsored by international public and private money, acquired a very visible presence in the form of infrastructure (such as mosques and *medersas*, that is, schools with a reformist pedagogy) and of a stronger discursive representation in the national political arena. Since then, influential Muslim merchants and religious experts have exerted a persistent and important informal influence on national politics. Legislation in the proper sense was not affected by these developments. Still, from about the second half of the 1980s, leading Muslim figures have been able to influence political decisions, such as the closing down of bars and sites of popular entertainment during the month of Ramadan.[13]

The 1974 Constitution also created a constitutional basis for military rule and extended the presidential powers to the president of the military committee. Changes in the new constitution involved a further weakening of the judiciary *vis-à-vis* executive power, and the reinforcement of executive powers *vis-à-vis* the legislature. For instance, the constitution undermined the independent status of members of the Supreme Court, by making their selection entirely dependent on the decision by the president (of the military committee and later that of the ruling party). Additionally, members of the Supreme Court were no longer elected for life (as stipulated in the Constitution of 1960), but for a limited period of time (Hazard 1972: 21). The establishment of a Court of State Security (on 15 September 1969, see Hazard 1972: 21f), in which members of the ruling military committee participated, can be seen in the same light. The above-mentioned strengthening of the executive power *vis-à-vis* legislative power manifested itself in amended legislative procedures; law proposals could previously be submitted by the president as well as by the parliament, but from now on the principal procedural power resided with the president (Sall 1986: 384ff). The president was also granted the power to appoint special delegates who should replace municipal councils.

The 1968 putsch had also marked a departure from the socialist economic policy of the previous regime.[14] Therefore, most of the legislative changes enacted in this period, by way of ordinances, addressed administrative, fiscal and economic matters. Almost no legislative changes were made with respect to penal and civil law.[15] This continuity is remarkable because it implies that the greater public prominence and political weight of Muslim authorities did not affect positive law, at least not in these legal domains.

A similar trend became evident in the proposed reform of family and personal status law, such as the 1962 Law on Marriage and Guardianship. A bill, submitted for discussion in 1973, did not reflect a greater influence of Muslim forces on this process. Instead, it illustrated a greater effort toward bringing Malian family and civil law into conformity with the international aspirations of the Malian state (for example the support of the U.N. Conventions of the rights of women and of children, Hazard 1973: 20, 22f). The proposed changes included the equal treatment of women and men with respect to inheritance matters, an attempt that implied a reassessment of both Islamic regulation and of non-Islamic customary conventions that prohibit women to inherit any share of family property (and occasionally even treat women as part of the inheritance). Another proposal was to change the legal status of illegitimate children, who were not recognised as such either by non-Islamic, customary law or by Islamic regulations. The draft law also laid down the legal status of adopted children, giving them the same rights as blood children to inheritance and the same obligation to support their aging adoptive parents. To date, this draft law has not been approved.[16]

12.4 The period from 1985 until the present

The new appeal of an Islamic idiom of political and social critique

Liberalisation and multi-party democracy under Konaré and Touré

The relative absence of substantial developments in the set-up of legal institutions and legal change throughout the late 1970s and 1980s reflects the general political stagnation that characterised the military regime and single-party rule under Moussa Traoré. One reason why the growing political weight of influential Muslims did not translate into an islamisation of the legal institutional framework is certainly the coterminous, growing influence of Western donor organisations to which Moussa Traoré turned increasingly throughout the 1980s in search for financial support.

Social protest movements directed against his regime surfaced intermittently after the early 1980s, yet were always bloodily repressed. Another reason why these protest movements did not lead to any substantive political institutional change under Moussa Traoré's government is that they originated almost exclusively in the urban youth. Only in 1989 did Moussa Traoré give way to the pressure of the democratisation movement. This movement, run by urban professionals, academics, and students was inspired by developments throughout Africa and in Eastern Europe and called for the introduction of a multi-party democracy.

In March 1991, a military coup under the leadership of Colonel Toumani Touré put an end to Moussa Traoré's single-party rule and to several weeks of bloody confrontations between the security forces and students and other supporters of the democracy movement. President Traoré's fall from power also marked the demise of the privileged political position that Muslim interest groups had occupied under his government. A *communiqué* of the national reconciliation council (*Conseil de Reconciliation Nationale*), led by Colonel Toumani Touré, suspended the Constitution of 1974 and dissolved the government. A transitional government under the leadership of Colonel Touré and his fellow militaries (*Comité de Transition pour le Salut du Peuple*) assumed provisional administration of public orders on the basis of an ordinance dated 31 March 1991. From the latter emerged a new constitution, which was adopted by popular referendum on 12 January 1992 (Pimont 1993: 462). Islam was again not mentioned in the constitution.

In 1992 the country's first democratic elections were held; only 21 per cent of the population participated. The newly-elected president Alpha Konaré and his party ADEMA (Alliance pour la Démocratie au

Mali) favoured a more stringent interpretation of Mali's secular constitution. They also ostracised the *intégristes*, who, as a recently constituted group of Muslims, capitalised on the liberalised public sphere and called for an introduction of 'the sharia', most often without specifying the exact contents of the reform to which they aspired.[17] Yet, President Konaré (as well as Toumani Touré who followed him in office in 2002) could not afford to antagonise prominent representatives of the Muslim establishment whose informal political influence is based on kin-related and clientelistic modes of followership.

In other words, the recent process of democratisation and of the empowerment of secularist forces within the government has not put an end to Islam's imminent political force. The latter never stopped to run like a red thread through Mali's political history as an independent nation-state. The ambivalent attitude towards Islam of current state and party officials is evident in their regular rituals of allegiance to Islamic values performed in the presence of influential figures of the Muslim establishment. At the level of positive law, however, the secular character of the constitution and of political parties[18] is expressly maintained.

The supremacy of the constitution was further established by the creation of a separate constitutional court charged with the assessment of the constitutionality of legislative change.[19] A major novelty in the 1992 Constitution is that it stipulates the replacement of the former presidential system with a parliamentary system, establishes a clearer separation of the legislative and executive powers, and substantially enhances the powers of the former *vis-à-vis* the latter.[20]

General tendencies of the past ten years

Since the political liberalisation of the early 1990s, Mali has witnessed an invigoration of Muslim actors who articulate a wide array of positions with regard to the extent to which Islam should provide the basis of the legal foundations of the political community. A numerically relatively minor group of actors, the *intégristes* mentioned above, denounced the prohibition of religious parties in 1991. At present, they seek to exert influence on public policy making and particular political processes, such as the reform of the judiciary and the draft family law. The debate over the reform of family law and of the judiciary is representative of several, sometimes paradoxical, trends. Contrary to their own claims that Islam should provide the normative basis of legal reform, their actual interventions are often guided by pragmatic concerns. Accordingly, these Muslim spokespersons often form strategic and shifting alliances with secularist representatives of the current government.

Women's rights activists constitute another group of actors that plays a prominent role in current controversies over the extent to which

Islamic regulations and values should be included in personal status law. While these women claim to defend the rights of women, their actual interventions reveal their preoccupation with interests and dilemmas of urban intellectual middle-class women; their public interventions, the ways in which they frame the issue of women's rights, and the kind of issues they address (e.g. female circumcision) also demonstrate that their activities and aims are importantly shaped by the current agendas of international governmental and non-governmental organisations.

Thus, current controversies over legislation and over the Islamic nature of national culture reveal how a local landscape of Muslim and secularist activism is fuelled and partly restructured by Western funding agencies (from e.g. the United States, France, Germany, and through European development funds) and by donors from Arab-speaking countries and other areas of the Muslim world (e.g. Libya, Saudi Arabia, Iran, Pakistan).[21] An expansive law reform project initiated in 1999 with the financial support of a number of international donor organisations (mainly U.S. and European funds) is indicative of this malleable climate. In aid negotiations with the government, these organisations were able to place this law reform at the top of the list of priorities.

The project's primary aim is to eliminate inconsistencies between the 1962 Family Law (*Code de Mariage et de Tutelle*), the 1972 CPCCS, labour legislation, and the 1992 Constitution, that have taken root as a result of the sometimes conflicting customary, Islamic, and state legal orders. Without explicitly specifying its agenda with respect to sharia-based law, the reform project is clearly intended to minimise the influence of puritan interpretations of Islamic norms. Furthermore, the reform project aims at creating institutional support for an extra-judicial arbitration system, the major function of which would be to deal with issues of property and land use.[22] It also includes measures to restrict practices of judicial corruption that are a principal reason for many people's tendency to evade the courts. Finally, it aims at improving people's opportunities for accessing courts and legal aid institutions.

Throughout the precolonial, colonial, and postcolonial history of contemporary Mali, sharia or sharia-based law never constituted a distinct, and even less so, overruling domain of relevant legal practice. To date, tendencies towards a dual legal order exist only at the level of norms, not in the form of separate court systems.

12.5 Constitutional law

Sharia-based law is not explicitly referred to in any part of the constitutional law in force. The pervasive and persistent secular character of the constitution was once again illustrated and bolstered by the provisions of 1991, which laid down the secular character of all political parties. The 1992 Constitution establishes the citizens' right to freedom of religion, as well as the equal status of adherents of different religious orientations before the law. Yet in reality, proponents of the two book religions, Christianity and Islam, have a greater political weight than those representing traditional African religions.

The Constitution of 1992 expands the list of 'fundamental rights and duties of humans and citizens' (*Droits et Devoirs Fondamentaux de l'Homme et du Citoyen*) elaborated upon in the Constitution of 1974. The preamble declares the determination to defend 'Rights of the Woman and Child' and subscribes to the Declaration of Universal Human Rights (1948) and to the African Charter of Human and People's Rights (1981).

At the same time, the constitution establishes a difference between the rights and liberties that are simply recognised as opposed to those that are guaranteed by law. Certain rights (e.g. to work, housing, vacation, and health and a healthy environment) are by their very nature difficult to assure, especially in the context of a country where these rights have been established only in recent times; as such, their non-application is not tied to any possibilities for legal recourse.

In the wake of the growing political salience of Islam, a major bone of contention between Muslim forces and state representatives is the degree of autonomy that practitioners of the different religions should have in regulating internal affairs of their religious community beyond state control. So far, state representatives have successfully fought off attempts by Muslim forces to gain greater control over community and intra-family affairs.

12.6 Personal status and family law

It must be noted that at the grassrooots level polygamy and other conventions in the sphere of marriage and family relations were never regarded as specifically Islamic practices. In most rural and urban zones of contemporary Mali, physical punishment, repudiation, and other practices reaffirming women's inferior status position and rights *vis-à-vis* elders and men are commonly accepted. These actions are occasionally attenuated by the intervention of mediators and kin. But the actions are nevertheless acknowledged as accepted custom. Whether this custom is defined as Islamic or non-Islamic is of little relevance, except in the case of urbanites who, influenced by a Saudi Arabia-sponsored missionary (*da'wa*) movement, recently adopted an explicit Muslim identity and distance themselves from others whose 'un-Islamic' practices they denounce. In other words, over the past twenty years, with the financial support of donors from the Arab-speaking world and, more recently, with political liberalisation, Islam has acquired a new political force and a salience as a symbolic language of legitimacy and normative distinction. In the course of this process, personal status law has become a bone of contention.

So far, family law is the only domain of legislation in which Islamic legal norms constitute an issue for debate. A new bill prepared in 2000 aims at the reform of the 1962 Marriage and Family Law (*Code du Mariage et de la Tutelle*). It forms part of the above-mentioned project on the promotion of democracy and justice in Mali funded by Western donor organisations and intended to enhance the effectiveness and credibility of the judiciary (see 12.6). The draft law aims to eliminate internal inconsistencies in the legal code arising from the sometimes conflicting principles of Islamic law and of conceptions derived from the *Code Napoléon*. The principal issues at stake are the fixing of a maximum amount of the bride-price, marriage registration, choice of the form of matrimony (i.e., monogamous versus polygamous), obligation of obedience to the husband, and choice of the site of residence.

Another goal of the project is to codify as yet unlegislated domains, such as that of inheritance. Muslim representatives who intervened during the publicly staged debates of the draft law in 2000 were guided not simply by a concern with the incorporation of Islamic legal norms in the positive law, but by an interest in gaining greater autonomy *vis-à-vis* the state in regulating affairs within the Muslim community. However, the government's effective neutralisation of Muslim interest groups in the drafting of a new family law is a clear indication of the current leadership's refusal to comply with these aspirations. In spite of the invigoration of Muslim political forces, their initiatives have not led to a greater presence or institutionalisation of Islamic legal norms, practice, institutions or practitioners within the family legislation.

This persistent exclusion is facilitated by the fact that Islamic legal adjudication was incorporated into the legal system of the colonial and later postcolonial state only as one form of customary law, which could be overruled by the legal principles laid down in the constitution.

12.7 Criminal law

The *Code Pénal*, revised several times since its initial legislation in the first constitution of independent Mali (September 1960), has not incorporated Islamic penal law. The latter also does not feature in the top priorities of the agendas of Muslim actors who call for the introduction of the sharia. Over the past eight years, only a handful of Muslim spokespersons have explicitly referred to elements of Islamic penal law in their public interventions, calling for example for public corporal punishment for the offense of adultery.

12.8 Other areas of law

Neither commercial and banking law nor civil procedural law have been influenced by Islamic legal conceptions.

12.9 International conventions and human rights

Mali ratified the Covenant on Civil and Political Rights (ICCPR, 1966) on 16 July 1974 (entry into force on 23 March 1976). It signed the Convention of Elimination of All Forms of Discrimination against Women (CEDAW, 1979) on 5 February 1985 (ratified on 10 September 1985; entry into force 18 October 1985). And, on 26 February 1999, it signed and ratified the Convention against Torture (CAT, 1984), which went into force on 28 March 1999.[23] Assessments of the second periodic report regarding CAT[24] and of the first periodic report regarding CEDAW[25] expressed concern about the invocability of the covenants (Art. 2), the persistence of slavery-like practices and hereditary servitude in the North, and the continued practice of female genital mutilation as well as the existence of laws discriminating against women with regard to marriage, divorce, inheritance, and succession.

The 1992 Constitution, together with other legislation, establishes a number of institutions and structures for the protection and promotion of human rights in such areas as equality of citizens before the law, equality of access to the courts, impartiality in decision making. The organisation of the judiciary should guarantee the independence of judges, the provision of remedies, and measures for the protection of citizens' rights against arbitrary action. However, the basic conditions that would ensure these rights are far from being realised. The limitations to this realisation do not reside in the legal texts *per se*, but in the political and social conditions that pose clear limitations to the application of legal provisions.

Mali's signing of the Platform of Beijing (1994) has led to a politicisation of certain governmental measures, such as the campaign to eradicate practices of female circumcision. While women's rights activists present this practice as a challenge to women's right to bodily integrity, its defendants present it variously as an Islamic or customary and authentic practice. Here again, references to the Islamic origins of this practice should be interpreted as a political gesture and as an attempt to bolster one's authoritative position by referring to the foundational texts of Islam. As with other domains where clear human rights abuses continue to take place, their commission and perpetuation generally have little to do with sharia or Islamic law.

12.10 Conclusion

In Mali, Islamic law has never been strongly represented or institutionalised in any colonial or postcolonial state law. Its traces have become weaker, even if Islam, as an idiom of community building, has gained a new force since the late 1970s and a greater public prominence after the political liberalisation of the early 1990s. Mali's current legal system reflects several dilemmas and legacies deriving from a longer-standing legacy of colonial dual administration, from the particular power constellation between Muslim forces and the political power, and finally, from the autocratic political heritage of its recent postcolonial history. Throughout the pre-colonial, colonial and postcolonial history of the Malian legal system, Islamic normative conceptions were acknowledged and incorporated as instances of traditional or customary regulations. Sharia or sharia-based law never constituted a distinct and separate domain of Mali's state legal system.

Mali's governments, past and present, have tended to exert great caution in intervening via legislation into sensitive domains of Muslim authority and of patriarchal family control. This cautious dealing with Islamic matters was realised to a limited extent by the first government of President Keita, but acquired a new salience under President Traoré. It was motivated by a pragmatic acknowledgement on President Traoré's part of the considerable political power and informal influence of Muslim authorities and interest groups. Discrepancies between the Constitution of 1974 (established by Traoré's government) and actual political practice exemplify his *realpolitik* in relation to Muslim political forces. The new constitution continued to establish the secular character of the constitution. Over the years, President Traoré granted Muslim interest groups special privileges. Still, the absence of legislative changes with respect to penal and civil law throughout the 1980s implies that the greater political weight and public prominence of Muslim authorities and interest groups had little real effect on positive law. This illustrates how Traoré's government carefully juggled competing interests and aspirations. He sought to appease Muslim authorities and thus to bolster the regime's shaky basis of political legitimacy.

President Traoré's *realpolitik* also needs to be related to dynamics emerging at the interface between national political processes and an international field of political interests. On the one hand, by granting special privileges to Muslim political actors, President Traoré gained greater control over local recipients of financial donations from the Arab-speaking world – donations that had begun flooding the country since the late 1970s under the orchestrated efforts of the Saudi government. On the other hand, Traoré's tendency to comply with the aspirations of Muslim political actors only to a limited extent, formed part of a gradual *rapprochement* to Western countries and donor organisations over the 1970s and 1980s. It illustrates the pragmatic orientation of Moussa Traoré's regime, which motivated it to depart from the anti-Western, socialist orientation of the previous regime of Modibo Keita.

The, as yet unaccomplished, project of legislating intra-family relations is another striking evidence of the pervasive effort of the different regimes to steer national policy-making in the triangle constituted by Muslim political influence at the national level, Saudi-orchestrated efforts to gain an influence on national politics, and finally the interests (and growing financial support) of Western donor organisations. Legislating this sensitive area of patriarchal control has historically been likely to destabilise the regimes' shaky foundations of political legitimacy by bringing state institutions and actors into conflict with Muslim and traditional political authorities. The fact that the respective draft law of 1973 has not been approved until today – forty years later – illustrates the persistent reticence by government and state officials to break with this pact.

The precarious power balance between party politicians, government officials and Muslim authorities who exert a considerable informal influence continues to shape administrative and legislative policy. The current relationship between Muslim actors and representatives of the secularist government could be appropriately described not as one of open conflict and confrontation, but as a struggle over representation in the national arena and over popular support and informal power. In some localities, Muslim authorities exert an important influence and, due to the lack of articulation between local, traditional forms of arbitration and the state legal system, may importantly shape the decisions of traditional authorities and, occasionally, of state employees.

Notes

1 Dorothea Schulz is currently a professor of anthropology at the University of Cologne. The author wishes to thank Amandou Keita for his comments.

2 French administrators, who feared a pan-Islamic resistance to European colonialism, sought to contain the influence of Arab Islamic reformist movements on what they labelled 'African Islam'. Therefore, the group of actors to whom I refer to as the current 'Muslim establishment' (and what, in popular parlance, is often called 'traditional' Islam) is a conglomerate of diverse Muslim actors who reacted to, and often

benefited from, the policy and discourse of French colonial administration; also subsumed under the rubric of 'established' Islam is a wide array of local ritual conventions, as well as beliefs and practices associated with Islamic esoteric knowledge (Brenner 1993, 2001).

3 Fissions within this group have been reinforced since the 1980s, when young Sunni intellectuals, who graduated from institutions of higher learning in the Arab-speaking world (the *arabisants*, cf. Otayek 1993), returned to Mali and entered into competition with the older generation of Sunni businessmen.

4 One important effect of the imposition of a colonial judicial system was that the former elite of Islamic scribes, that is, legal experts, were replaced by Sufi sheikhs who constituted a new, spiritual type of leadership. See Roberts 1991; Sarr & Roberts 1991.

5 The revisions entailed the suppression of the vice-president of government, a modification of the national flag, and the replacement of the State Court (*Cour d'État*) with a Supreme Court.

6 See e.g. the decree issued on 24 February 1968 to reduce the role of the judiciary (in this case, the *Cour d'Appel*) to that of an advisory body (ASAL 1968: 237; Prouzel 1979).

7 Such as the *Code de Nationalité* (February 1962), the *Code du Travail* (August 1962), the *Code de Prévoyance Sociale* (August 1962), the *Code Foréstier* (February 1968), the *Code sur l'État Civil* (February 1968), the *Code Électoral* (December 1968), and the *Code de Parenté* (July 1973) (Sall 1986: 382f). Sharia-based law did not play a role in the formulation of these codes.

8 This representation did not acknowledge the existence of non-Muslim minorities (Christians and those who engage in 'traditional' cults); nor did it account for the fact that Islam was more firmly entrenched in the northern societies of Mali.

9 The containment of Islamic influence was manifest in the field of education. Traditional and reformist institutions of Islamic learning were not granted the same status as French-language schools, and some of the reformist schools were integrated into the national educational system schools (Brenner 2001: 169-173).

10 The restructuring of the administrative organisation aimed at limiting the influence of traditional political authority by creating party structures at the village level. But for various reasons (e.g. generational conflicts and the lack of formation, training and legitimacy of these party structures), the impact of these party structures in transforming conventional administrative organisation and power structures remained very limited; rather, they contained the seed for the contestation that led up to the military putsch in 1968 (Prats & Le Roy 1979: 171-173).

11 The fact that women had relatively few possibilities to oppose an arranged marriage or to leave a husband against the will of their own families was, however, counterbalanced by the fact that kin-controlled marriage enhanced the stability of marriages because it rendered repudiation (whether justified by reference to Islamic or non-Islamic norms) more difficult. In contrast, today, in particular in urban areas where elderly control is weakening, the stability of the marriage union and a woman's possibility to forego repudiation depends to a larger extent on extra-familial resources she might mobilise in order to enhance her negotiating position *vis-à-vis* her husband.

12 Similar to the first constitution of independent Mali, the Ordinance allowed for the existence of multiple political parties. Only the Constitution of 1974 expressly laid down a single-party system.

13 Many Muslims strongly resented this decision by Moussa Traoré. This illustrates that although popular support for an Islamic basis of state legislation has increased in urban areas since the 1980s, the majority of Malian Muslims remained convinced that Islam should be treated as a personal faith and be relegated to the private realm.

Proponents of a strictly secularist constitutional order and politics were (and still are) Western-oriented intellectuals and individuals working on behalf of Western donor organisations (Brenner 1993).

14 Such as changes in taxation; the modification of commercial law to facilitate the development of a private commercial sector (ASAL 1969: 270); and the modification of legal texts that define the status of public enterprises and minimise the central controlling functions of the state (i.e. a planned economy according to a socialist agenda) and thus facilitate private investment (ASAL 1969: 268f).

15 Exceptions were: (a) the amendment of the criminal code, which provided a penitentiary regime for persons convicted of crimes against public property (1969); and (b) amendments to the criminal procedure code, which gave the army an investigatory role comparable to that of judicial police and also invested the criminal chamber of the Supreme Court with jurisdictional powers over crimes committed by high-ranking party officials (Hazard 1973: 20).

16 The current family bill, placed under considerable public scrutiny in 1999-2001, constitutes a modified version of this draft law. The fact that the draft law has been up for discussion for thirty years shows that the proposed changes concern highly sensitive issues.

17 Because they addressed the issue of legalising religious parties in most of their interventions, it seems that their frequently voiced intention to fight for 'the establishment of Islamic law as the basis of our constitution' was shorthand for their attempt to gather a following in a pluralised political field and to gain standing in a landscape of competing parties.

18 Also, the new constitution stipulates that multipartism cannot be subject to constitutional revision (Diarra 1995).

19 A constitutional court already existed in the form of the constitutional section of the Supreme Court (Constitution of 1974) or of the State Court (Constitution of 1960). The novelty in the 1992 Constitution concerns the strengthening of an independent judiciary. The new constitution provided for a reduction of the powers of both the executive (head of government) and the legislature (president of the assembly) over the selection of members of the Supreme Court and over the approval/ support of its decisions (Pimont 1993: 468).

20 The constitution establishes a 'bicephalous' executive power consisting of the head of state (*Président*) and the chief of government (*Premier Ministre*). It also introduces two new institutions: the Supreme Council of Regional Entities (*Haut Conseil des Collectivités Territoriales*, which bears resemblance to the French parliamentary system and its *Conseil de la République de la Constitution française*, and whose members are elected by direct popular vote to ensure the representation of the regional entities) and the *Conseil économique, social et culturel* (with purely consultative functions in the domain of economic and 'development' policy).

21 While many funds from the latter countries are channelled through projects of *da'wa* (Arabic, mission, call) and humanitarian aid, Western donor organisations (except for funds provided by Christian missionary services) generally present their loans as being directed towards the development of technical infrastructure and, more recently, of civil society and capacity-building.

22 Because these issues are not considered by Muslim authorities to fall into their area of expertise, it is likely that the establishment of these mediation institutions will not constitute a bone of contention between protagonists of legal reform based on sharia-law and their secularist opponents.

23 Other international treaties to which Mali has acceded are the CESCR, CERD, CRC, and the *Rome Statute of the ICC*.

24 The first report to CAT was submitted on 14 August 1979; the second on 3 January 2003.

25 Submitted on 13 November 1986. For the full evaluation of subsequent reports, submitted on 10 March 2004, see http://daccess-dds-ny.un.org/doc/UNDOC/GEN/N04/287/17/IMG/N0428717.pdf?OpenElement, on the second, third, fourth, and fifth reports.

Bibliography

Bartleby (2010), 'Mali', in *World Factbook*, see http://www.bartleby.com/151/country/ml.html (2008 statistics) and https://www.cia.gov/library/publications/the-world-factbook/geos/ml.html (online edition, last accessed February 2010). Washington D.C.: Central Intelligence Agency.

Brenner, L. (1993), 'Constructing Muslim identities in Mali', in L. Brenner (ed.), *Muslim identity and social change in Subsaharan Africa*, 59-78. Bloomington: Indiana University Press.

Diarra, E. (1995), 'Constitution et état de droit au Mali', *Revue Juridique et Politique. Indépendance et Coopération* 3: 252-284.

Hazard, J. (1972), 'Implementing law in post-Keita Mali's retreat from "Scientific Socialism"', *African Law Studies* 7: 1-26.

Konaré, A. (1982), *Les constitutions du Mali*. Bamako: Ministère des Relations Extérieures.

Lavroff, D.G. & G. Peiser (1961), 'La république du Mali', in D.-G. Lavroff & G. Peiser (eds.), *Les Constitutions Africaines*, 163-174. Paris: Éditions Pedone.

Megahed, H. (1970), *Socialism and Nation-Building in Africa: The Case of Mali (1960-1968)*. Budapest: Center for Afro-Asian Research of the Hungarian Academy of Sciences.

Pimont, Y. (1993), 'La constitution de la république du Mali', *Revue Juridique et Politique. Indépendance et Coopération* 3: 462-474.

Prats, Y. & E. Le Roy (1979), 'Les législations contemporaines: Mali', in G. Conac (ed.), *Les institutions administratives des états Francophones d'Afrique Noire*, 170-173. Paris: Economica.

Prouzet, M. (1979), 'Les procédures de révision constitutionnelle', in G. Conac (ed.), *Les institutions constitutionnelles des Etats d'Afrique Francophone et de la République Malgache*, 281-320. Paris: Economica.

Roberts, R. (1991), 'The case of Faama Mademba Sy and the ambiguities of legal jurisdiction in early colonial French Sudan', in K.R. Mann & R. Roberts (ed.), *Law in Colonial Africa*, 185-204. Portsmouth: Heinemann and James Currey.

Sall, Y. (1986), 'La codification et l'évolution de droit au Mali', *Revue Juridique et Politique. Indépendance et Coopération* 3-4: 376-390.

Sarr, D. & R. Roberts (1991), 'The jurisdiction of Muslim tribunals in colonial Senegal, 1857-1932', in K.R. Mann & R. Roberts (ed.), *Law in Colonial Africa*, 131-145. Portsmouth: Heinemann and James Currey.

13 Sharia and national law in Nigeria

Philip Ostien and Albert Dekker[1]

Abstract

The relations between sharia and national law in Nigeria have varied widely from time to time and from place to place within the country – which after all was first brought under a single administration only in 1914. In sections 1-4 of this paper the complex history of our subject is sketched, culminating in the programmes of 'sharia implementation' that began in 1999 in twelve of Nigeria's northern states. Sections 5-9 concentrate thematically upon the present day. Many details of the incorporation of sharia in the laws of Nigeria are discussed, including the Sharia Courts and the Sharia Penal and Criminal Procedure Codes now in place in the sharia states, the continuing application of uncodified Islamic personal law and other Islamic civil law throughout the north, the effects of sharia implementation on women and non-Muslims, and the constitutional questions the sharia implementation programmes raise. The conclusion, section 10, discusses the likely fate of Islamic criminal law in the sharia states, and gives some reason to think that sharia implementation has on the whole been a positive development for Nigeria.

Table of contents

The borders of present-day Nigeria were defined during the late nineteenth and early twentieth centuries, in the course of imperialist competition among Britain, France, and Germany for colonies in West Africa. Nigeria, a British colony, emerged as such in 1900, except that its eastern territories were augmented after World War I by accessions from the ex-German Cameroons. Nigeria was governed by the British until 1960, when it became an independent nation. It was then organised as a federation of its Northern, Eastern and Western Regions. It has since been divided into 36 states plus the Federal Capital Territory of Abuja. Its population in 2006, according to the census then taken, was about 140 million, the largest in Africa by far. Its ethnic diversity is extreme: the World Factbook conservatively says there are 'more than 250 ethnic groups'; the linguists list over five hundred living languages.[2] There are however three regional linguae franca, corresponding to the three largest ethnic groups: Hausa in the North, Igbo in the East, and Yoruba in the West. Moreover there has been a substantial dispersion of people of all ethnic and linguistic backgrounds throughout the country, and English, Nigeria's official language, is also widely spoken. According to the World Factbook, about 50 per cent of Nigeria's population is Muslim, 40 per cent Christian, and 10 per cent followers of African traditional religions. But these numbers are estimates only, as no accepted census since 1958 has gathered data on religious affiliation. Muslims predominate in the North, Christians in the East and West, although again there has been a substantial dispersion of people of all religious persuasions throughout the country.

(Source: Bartleby 2010, Lewis 2009)

13.1 The period until 1920

Partial Islamisation, partial Christianisation, and colonisation by the British

In the early years of the nineteenth century, the territory which became Nigeria was occupied by a heterogeneous assortment of peoples at many different stages of cultural and political development. Some – for instance the Yoruba and Benin kingdoms in the southwest and the Muslim emirates in the north – had strong central authorities whose writs ran far; most others were much more loosely and locally organised. Trade flourished along camel, donkey and headload routes criss-crossing West Africa and extending northwards across the Sahara and eastwards across the Sahel to the Nile. Trade along these routes involved some peoples but passed many others by. Warfare and slave-raiding were common. Slaves were traded within the country, and also exported, from the north to other parts of West Africa and across the desert to North Africa, and from the south to European slave traders at the Atlantic coast. From the end of the fifteenth century, Portuguese and later Dutch, French, and British merchants had established trading posts on the coast, where for three centuries the Atlantic slave trade thrived. But until the mid-nineteenth century European penetration northward into or beyond the mangrove swamps and rain forests of the coastal region was virtually nil, inhibited by disease. As the saying went: 'The Bight of Benin, oh the Bight of Benin, where few come out though many go in!'

Islam had reached the Borno region, in what is now north-eastern Nigeria, beginning as early as the eleventh century, from north and east across Sahara and Sahel. It came to Hausaland somewhat later, not only from north and east but from the west, from the empires of Mali and Songhay, where for several centuries Timbuktu was West Africa's most famous centre of Islamic learning. By the fifteenth century, Islam was established in the Hausa city-states – Kano and Katsina perhaps most famous among them. By 1750 it was the nominal, if only loosely observed, religion of the ruling and merchant classes in all those parts of the country (Hiskett 1984).

Islam received a new impulse in the north in the last quarter of the eighteenth century, through the activities of the Fulani revivalist and reformer Shehu Uthman dan Fodio. In twenty-five years of preaching and teaching the Shehu gained a large following, his 'Community', to the increasing alarm of the Hausa rulers whose corrupt and oppressive practices he condemned. Measures of repression only exacerbated the situation, finally triggering off the Fulani-led wars of *jihad*[3] (1804 to c. 1810 in Hausaland, and continuing elsewhere for many years thereafter) which established the 'Sokoto Caliphate' (Johnston 1967; Last 1967). Covering much of what subsequently became Nigeria's Northern Region, the Sokoto Caliphate was a loose confederation of emirates, all owing suzerainty to the Sultan of Sokoto. At least under its first leaders the Caliphate was inspired by religious zeal: by the desire to purify society of un-Islamic practices and to live solely according to the sharia. In particular, the Fulani 'made it their aim, in the states which they set up, to enforce Islamic law exclusively [...] and to outlaw customary and administrative law' (Schacht 1964: 86). There were some thirty emirates in all. The people under their rule were most of the many tribes of Northern Nigeria, some more or less Muslim and some not. The ruling houses were all Muslim and mostly Fulani. The Fulani failed in their war against Borno in the northeast, itself a Muslim empire of ancient vintage. When the British arrived, the only parts of the Northern Region not under the sway of one or the other of these two Muslim empires of Sokoto and Borno were the Igala, Idoma, Tiv, and Jukun areas in the south, the high plateau in the centre which now has Jos as its capital, and scattered pockets of peoples elsewhere. With these exceptions, throughout the North

> Islamic law [...] was still near its highest degree of practical application. Custom, if not entirely eradicated, had been pushed into the background, and the only existing tribunals were those of the *qadis* [Hausa: *alkalis*[4]] who were competent in all matters, including penal law. Only the customary land law remained valid and was enforced by the councils of the sultan and of the emirs (ibid).

British penetration of the Nigerian interior began with the second journey of Mungo Park across West Africa from Senegambia (1805-1806). Park passed through a slice of Nigeria on his way down the Niger River in 1806, but he died at Bussa before reaching the sea. It was only with the visits of Hugh Clapperton and his colleagues, first southward across the desert from Tripoli to Borno, Kano, Sokoto and back (1822-1825), and then from Badagry on the coast northward to Kano and Sokoto again (1825-1827), that real knowledge of the country began to be gained. British explorers then quickly confirmed the course of the Niger from Bussa to the sea, and its relation to the lower parts of the River Benue (1830-1831). But repeated attempts to sail or steam up the Niger/Benue system were frustrated by extremely high death rates from malaria. Finally, in 1854, William Baikie led an expedition up the Niger with no loss of life, protecting his men by administering quinine; this pioneering prophylactic use of quinine against malaria was a turning point in the European penetration of Nigeria and indeed of Africa. At the time of Baikie's expedition, another of the great European explorers of Africa – Heinrich Barth, in the service of the British Foreign Office – was nearing the end of his extended visit to the northern parts of the country. Like Clapperton on his first visit, Barth came south across the desert from Tripoli, spending five years (1850-1855) travelling in the region from Borno and Adamawa in the east to Kano, Katsina, Sokoto, Gwandu and all the way to Timbuktu in the west. Barth's *Travels and Discoveries in North and Central Africa* (1857-1859, five volumes) is one of the great works of scientific observation and analysis of the nineteenth century.

From the mid-nineteenth century, the British gradually extended their influence into Nigeria. In 1849 and 1852 they declared protectorates over the Bights of Benin and Biafra, at the southern coast. In 1861 they annexed Lagos. Trade with the interior (notably for palm oil, used among other things to lubricate the industrial revolution in Britain), Christian missionary activity, and political control, all gradually increased. At the Berlin Conference (1885), the British were granted a protectorate over the southern parts of Nigeria (comprising the later Eastern and Western Regions). In 1886, seeking to extend their dominions northward at the least possible expense, the British granted the National African Company, now renamed the Royal Niger Company, a charter empowering it to govern as well as to trade throughout the still vaguely-defined territories of the later Northern Region, all expenses of government to be paid out of revenues from trade. Treaties were signed between the Company and a number of northern rulers, including the Sultan of Sokoto, purportedly ceding extensive rights to the Company (Flint 1960: 89, 129-155). The Company, however, never managed to achieve 'effective occupation' of the North – the new criterion for international recognition of territorial claims laid down at the Berlin Conference – even along the banks of the Niger and Benue rivers where its trading posts were sited. In 1900 the British revoked the Company's charter and declared the Protectorate of Northern Nigeria, making Frederick Lugard High Commissioner. Units of Britain's West African Frontier Force then quickly defeated the forces of various lesser emirates where resistance to British rule was offered (1901-1902); Borno capitulated without a fight; and in 1903 Kano and Sokoto were taken, the latter only after a bloody battle (Muffett 1964). The North was administered separately until, in 1914, the Protectorates of Northern and Southern Nigeria were amalgamated with the Colony of Lagos under the name of the Colony and Protectorate of Nigeria. Lugard was the first Governor-General of the amalgamated Nigeria (1914-1919) as he had been the first High Commissioner of its Northern Region (1900-1906).[5]

Lugard is famous for his articulation of the sometime British policy of 'indirect rule', according to which colonial powers should not attempt to step directly into the shoes of indigenous rulers, but should govern through them. The British would rule, but local administration would be by native rulers, institutions, and laws found already in place, which would only gradually be modified or developed under British guidance. The testing-ground for Lugard's policies was initially Northern Nigeria under Lugard himself. When, in 1914, he became the first Governor-General of the whole country, Lugard extended his system of indirect rule to the Southern provinces as well (Perham 1937).

For Northern Nigeria, a major effect of indirect rule was to perpetuate and strengthen the rule of the Muslim emirates of Sokoto and Borno. In their search for indigenous authorities through whom to rule, the British did not go behind the ruling houses of the emirates to the peoples they ruled. On the contrary, the emirs and those already holding office under them were confirmed in power, under the name of 'Native Authorities', and emirate administration was sometimes even extended by the British to previously independent Northern peoples. 'A policy of preserving the very special identity of the Northern Provinces was consciously followed' (Perham 1937: 326). Under this regime 'the north entrenched itself in a policy of self-protective withdrawal from Western culture, whereas people in the south were deeply influenced by it' (Rasmussen 1993: 43). When, with the approach of independence, the principle of federalism was introduced into the government of Nigeria, and the Northern Region gained its own legislative and executive bodies, these in turn were initially dominated by the emirate ruling classes. The giant Northern Region, comprising about two-thirds of the land-mass of Nigeria and about one-half its population, dominated as it was by Muslims, and the much smaller but more modernised and Christianised Eastern and Western Regions, eyed each other with mutual distaste and suspicion as independence approached. The North, much slower to embrace Western education, feared that if self-government came too soon, Southerners would get all the best jobs in the North, if they did not actually dominate it. For their part the East and West feared domination at the centre by the more populous North, and a possible programme of Islamisation of the whole country by Northern rulers. But we have gone ahead of our story.

As to the law and its administration, indirect rule implied two systems (broadly speaking) of law, administered by two systems of courts. On the one hand there was 'native law and custom' – defined to include Islamic law – applied in most cases involving natives, in Native Courts staffed by native judges, according to native rules of procedure and evidence. In the North, consistently with emirate rule, most Native Courts were emir's or *alkali's* courts, and native law and custom was largely equated with Islamic law of the Maliki school. But even in the North, in the non-Muslim areas, and of course throughout the rest of the country, all of the more or less vague bodies of native law and custom of the many local ethnic groups were also applied in the Native Courts serving their territories. On the other hand there was 'English' law. Public law, including Orders in Council of the Government of Britain (in the case of Nigeria's colonial constitutions) and some of the enactments of the Governors-General, was of course 'English'. The British also enacted various other laws specific to Nigeria, including penal laws, and imported their statutes of general application, their doctrines of equity, and their common law. English law was applied in English courts staffed by British judges, according to British rules of procedure and evidence. On its private side, English law was originally intended for application primarily to non-natives, and most by far of all cases coming before Nigerian courts – upwards of 90 per cent, including, for a long time, criminal cases – were handled in the Native Courts according to native law and custom. The proviso was that no native law or custom should be enforced which was 'repugnant to natural justice, equity and good conscience [as determined by the British] or incompatible either directly or by necessary implication with any [English] law for the time being in force' (Keay & Richardson 1966: 233-238). Under this rule the penalties imposed in the Native Courts, in particular, were quickly brought under control. Mutilation – in the North whether as *hudud*[6] or as *qisas*[7] – was abolished; death sentences had to be carried out in a humane manner (Milner 1969: 263-264). Various means were used to enforce the repugnancy rule, including supervision of the Native Courts by British administrative authorities and finally, in 1933, rights of appeal from the Native to the English courts.

Islamic law never made the same impact in the southern parts of Nigeria as it had in the North. Islam did enter the South, notably what became the Western Region, where there is some record of Muslim communities already in the seventeenth century; Islam was well established in the Yoruba towns along the route to Lagos when the British began to extend their control there in the second half of the nineteenth century. But the character of the Islam practiced by the people of this part of the country was different from that of the North: faithful to that part of the sharia known as *ibadat*, which regulates matters of religious belief and worship, but much less concerned than in the North about *mu'amalat*, which regulates the conduct of Muslims in social life and is enforced in the *qadi*'s courts.

> The majority [of Southern Muslims] appear content to follow the religion of Islam more or less closely in matters of doctrine and ritual but to adhere to their tribal customs in such matters as marriage, divorce, adultery, guardianship and succession (Anderson 1954: 222).

The British found no Islamic courts in this region when they took over, nor were any established by them: 'no specifically Muslim court nor any formal application of Islamic law is known throughout the South, even in those areas where the proportion of Muslims is high' (ibid). This has remained true until quite recently. The establishment, beginning in 2002, of 'Independent Sharia Panels' in some Western cities, is a subject to which we shall return below.

13.2 The period from 1920 until 1965

The making of a nation; the settlement at independence of the place of Islamic law

Much of the story of this period has to do with the constitutional change that occurred with increasing rapidity after World War II, culminating in Nigerian independence in 1960. This subsumed a major change in the administration of Islamic law in the Northern Region that also took effect in 1960. We deal with these matters in turn.

Constitutional change 1920 to 1960

Indirect rule gave Nigerian officials considerable authority at local levels, subject to British supervision; but Lugard's constitution of 1914 gave them practically no say in the regional or national councils of government. Lawmaking was for the Governor-General alone. There was a Legislative Council, whose assent was required to some laws – but for Lagos only. The 'Nigerian Council', a national body which included a few Nigerian chiefs, was advisory and deliberative only, and all its 'unofficial' members were appointed by the Governor-General in any case. Executive power was concentrated in the Governor-General, his all-British Executive Council, his British Lieutenant-Governors for North and South, and all the officials of the British Colonial Service under them.

This arrangement was objected to by some Nigerians already in 1920. Not by Northern Muslims, but by Southerners – Christianised and Western-educated – who throughout the colonial period led the campaign for more say by Nigerians in government at the highest levels, more democracy in the selection of those Nigerians who would speak and act, more independence from British control, and the sooner the better. In 1920 such demands – in this case for fully competent Legislative Councils half composed of elected Africans, among others – were made by the West African National Congress on behalf of all Britain's colonies in West Africa. Later, in Nigeria, Nnamdi Azikiwe (from the East) and Obafemi Awolowo (from the West) came to the fore as leaders of what became the independence struggle. Northern leaders, with some exceptions, were never so anxious to see the British go.

The 1920 demands of the West African National Congress bore some fruit in Nigeria, resulting in new constitutional arrangements which took effect in 1922 and lasted until 1947 – longer than any other Nigerian constitution to date. After 1947 constitutional change became much more rapid. We can do no more here than summarise what in lived history was a complex and fraught process of political modernisation and nation-building. For details the reader is referred to the various works on Nigerian constitutional history, among the best of which are Elias 1967 and Nwabueze 1982.

a. The Clifford Constitution, 1922. This established a new 'Legislative Council of Nigeria', whose assent was required to certain laws. But a majority of its members were colonial officials, and of the unofficial members only four were elected (three from Lagos, one from Calabar), the rest being appointed by the Governor (as the Governor-General was renamed in 1919). Furthermore its jurisdiction extended only to the Southern Provinces and Lagos, the Governor alone retaining the power to legislate for the North. The all-British Executive Council and the rest of the apparatus of the colonial government remained in place.

b. The Richards Constitution, 1947. Pent-up demand for change, Azikiwe and Awolowo to the fore, was released after the war; the then-Governor, Sir Arthur Richards, had little choice but to make concessions. Under the new constitution he put in place:

- New 'Provincial Councils' were established, one each for what were now the Northern, Eastern and Western Provinces; these were the first regional bodies on which Nigerians were represented, each with majorities of 'unofficial' members largely selected by the Native Authority Councils from among themselves. The Provincial Councils were advisory and deliberative only, with an important exception: they each sent some of their unofficial members, selected by themselves, onward to the central Legislative Council. In the North a House of Chiefs was also established, which also sent some of its members to the Legislative Council.
- The central Legislative Council for the first time was given nationwide jurisdiction and a majority of unofficial members. But still only four of these were directly elected; the rest were nominated by the Provincial Councils (16), the Northern House of Chiefs (4), or the Governor (4). Meantime the old all-British central Executive Council survived as before.

Several points are worth noting. (1) While Southern politicians were far from satisfied with progress under the Richards Constitution, the Northerners struggled to master the new ways and to think how they would find enough qualified Northerners to fill all the posts that looming self-government would soon open up. (2) The tendency towards regionalisation is clear; this became full-blown federalism in 1954. (3) Of the twenty unofficial members of the new central Legislative Council that were nominated by regional bodies, nine – almost half – came from the North. This incipient predominance of the North in the national councils was in recognition of its predominance in size and more especially in population, but it was a matter of grave concern in the East and West.

c. The Macpherson Constitution, 1951. This was the first Nigerian constitution drafted in a process which included Nigerians themselves, starting with village, district and regional meetings, continuing with a General Conference in Ibadan in January 1950, and culminating in debates in the Provincial Councils, the Northern House of Chiefs, and the central Legislative Council. The result was the new constitution promulgated in July 1951.

- The three provinces were renamed regions. The Provincial Councils became much-enlarged and mostly-elected regional Houses of Assembly with real legislative authority. The Northern House of Chiefs was also enlarged and given legislative powers, and the Western Region got a House of Chiefs of its own. Regional Executive Councils were formed, with majorities of 'unofficial' members, now called Ministers, drawn from the Houses of Assembly and of Chiefs.
- At the centre, the Legislative Council became a much-enlarged and mostly-elected House of Representatives, with wide authority to legislate for the peace, order and good government of the whole country. Members of this House were still not elected directly, but by the Regional Houses of Assembly and of Chiefs from among themselves. The North was given as many elected members in the House of Representatives as the East and West put together. The old central Executive Council now became a Council of Ministers, with a majority of Nigerian Ministers drawn from the House of Representatives.

d. The Lyttleton Constitution, 1954. The 1951 constitution was widely understood to be a stepping-stone towards fuller democracy and self-government. Several crises hastened both its demise and the tendency towards a more robust federalism. One of these was precipitated in Lagos in early 1953, at a sitting of the House of Representatives, when a discussion of the timing of Independence threw the House into an uproar. The Northern standpoint – no definite date to be set yet – prevailed. The Northern members were then roughly treated by mobs in Lagos and all along their train-ride home, and a few weeks later serious fighting, rooted in the trouble in Lagos, broke out between Hausas and Igbos in Kano. This was the first major crisis of interethnic violence since the British occupation; unfortunately it presaged much more of the same to come. Northern leaders, much disturbed, seriously contemplated secession from Nigeria, but were deterred, it is said, by their lack of access to the sea. The Northern House of Assembly instead demanded a new constitution giving the regions much more authority and the central government practically none. Conferences in London (1953) and Lagos (1954) resulted in a new constitution popularly named after the then Colonial Secretary, Oliver Lyttleton:

- Nigeria officially became a federation of its three regions. Wide legislative, executive, and judicial powers were transferred to the regions; exclusive competence over a restricted list of subjects was reserved for the federal government.
- 'Official' members almost completely disappeared from the regional Houses of Assembly and the federal House of Representatives, which, except in the North, were now elected directly; in the North

'electoral colleges' based in the Native Authorities were still used except in some urban areas. In all regions the members of the federal House of Representatives were elected independently of the regional Houses of Assembly.

- Premiers were appointed in each region, from the party commanding a majority in the House of Assembly. The first Premiers were Nnamdi Azikiwe in the East, Obafemi Awolowo in the West, and Ahmadu Bello, Sardauna of Sokoto, in the North. The Premiers, responsible to the Houses of Assembly, took over the presidencies of the regional Executive Councils from the British Governors when regional self-government was achieved in 1957 (in the East and West) and 1959 (in the North).
- New High Courts were established for each region, with judges appointed by the regional governments. The regional Houses of Assembly were empowered to establish by law such other courts as they deemed expedient.
- At the centre, most British officials were withdrawn from the Council of Ministers in 1954; full Ministerial control, with a new federal Prime Minister at the head of the government, was achieved in 1957. The first Prime Minister was Abubakar Tafawa Balewa, the leader in the House of Representatives of the predominant Northern political party, the Northern Peoples Congress. Tafawa Balewa subsequently achieved international fame as the first leader of independent Nigeria.

e. Constitutional Conferences in 1957 and 1958. The Lyttleton Constitution of 1954 set the basic pattern of government which Nigeria was to take into Independence. Important steps forward, some already noted, were then taken at further constitutional conferences held in 1957 and 1958. A new upper legislative chamber, the Senate, was added at the centre. It was agreed that a Bill of Fundamental Human Rights, modelled on the European Convention on Human Rights of 1950, would be included in the Independence Constitution; the same basic provisions, from time to time expanded, have appeared in every Nigerian constitution since. Independence Day was set for the 1st of October, 1960, and other decisions were taken, on revenue allocation, the procedure for creation of new regions ('states') out of old should this be desired in the future, and other matters. Independence was well on its way.

Change in the administration of Islamic law in the Northern Region

Few changes were made in the system of Native Courts between 1920 and 1954. The various grades of courts, each with its own jurisdiction and powers, had already been established by statutes of 1906 and 1914.

From 1906 appeals were allowed from courts of lower grades to the Grade A courts of the emirs and chiefs. Until 1933 there were no appeals outside the Native Court system: British control was through the supervisory and quasi-appellate jurisdiction of the British administrative officers. The only other form of control exercised by the British was over the power of emir's courts to pass death sentences, which were made subject to review by the Governor. This was indirect rule, as applied to the Native Courts, at its height, involving, in the North, only the most minimal interference by the British in the administration of Islamic law.

This changed in 1933, when for the first time appeals were allowed from the Native Courts to the British Magistrate's and High Courts, a move designed to integrate the native and British courts. But there was an important exception:

> No appellate authority other than a native court of appeal could hear an appeal from a native court order relating to marriage, family status, guardianship of children, inheritance, testamentary disposition or administration of an estate (Keay & Richardson 1966: 39).

As the Native Courts also had exclusive original jurisdiction of such cases, exclusive control of these 'personal law' matters was kept in the hands of the Native Courts, a matter of particular concern to Northern Muslims. All other matters, including criminal cases decided under Islamic law, could and often did go on appeal to the British courts, which thus now began to interfere in the administration of Islamic law by the Muslim jurists best qualified to know it.

The unhappiness of the Northern *ulama*[8] with this situation is indicated by the fact that very soon after the regions were empowered (in 1954) to control their own court systems, the Northern House of Assembly set up a new 'Moslem Court of Appeal', whose appellate jurisdiction extended to *all* cases, civil and criminal, decided under Islamic law in the Native Courts. Appeals from the Native Courts in other cases went to the regional High Court. The introduction of the Moslem Court of Appeal 'was welcomed by Chiefs and Moslem jurists as a means of protecting Moslem law from encroachment as a result of appeal to "English" courts' (Keay & Richardson 1966: 56). But there were problems. The court had no permanent judges, but was merely constituted as needed from panels of *alkalis* and assessors learned in Islamic law. Moreover, Muslim suspicions of the High Court continued, because a right of further appeal from the Moslem Court of Appeal to the High Court was 'rendered inevitable since jurisdiction [of the Moslem Court of Appeal] extended to criminal matters' (ibid).

But with Independence fast approaching, pressures now came from other directions which overtook these problems. Chief among them were the fears of the non-Muslim minorities in the North – both indigenous peoples and Southern immigrants – about how they would be dealt with when the British were gone and they were left at the mercy of a powerful regional government and its Native Courts, dominated by Muslims. This was one of many issues looked into by the so-called Minorities Commission that was appointed after the 1957 constitutional conference and which held extensive hearings throughout Nigeria in the first half of 1958. In its lengthy report, submitted to the resumed constitutional conference in 1958 (Report 1958), the Commission rejected the demands of minorities in all the regions for subdivision of the country into more 'states' where some regional minorities could become self-governing majorities; the process of state-creation only began ten years later, on the eve of the Nigerian civil war. But the Minorities Commission did recommend, as one form of protection for minorities in all regions, the inclusion of a Bill of Fundamental Human Rights in the Independence Constitution. As we have seen, this was done.

Many felt that more radical reform was needed in the North, particularly in the matter of the continuing application there of Islamic criminal law. In this respect Northern Nigeria was out of step even with the rest of the Muslim world at the time:

> [T]he case of Northern Nigeria was, indeed, almost unique, for up till [1960] this was the only place outside the Arabian peninsula in which the Islamic law, both substantive and procedural, was applied in criminal litigation – sometimes even in regard to capital offences (Anderson 1976: 27).

The pressure to change this was intense.

> If the fears of the considerable Christian and animist minorities in the North were to be allayed, they needed to be assured that *Sharia* law would not be imposed upon them in the native and customary courts. [...] The Eastern and Western Regions were insistent that the [...] law which was administered in any part of the Federation [...] should respect the Fundamental Human Rights of Nigerians as set out in the constitutional instruments. [...] The U.N. Trusteeship Council had expressed reservations about the capacity of an independent Federal Government in Nigeria to uphold Fundamental Human Rights for the minorities without a radical reform of the law in the Northern Region. The British Government had made its position clear: reform of the legal and judicial systems in the North was a necessary

> preliminary to the granting of self-government to the Region (Richardson 2001: 209[9]).

The result of all this pressure was 'The Settlement of 1960' (Ostien 2006: 224-231), worked out and agreed to in general terms during 1958 and implemented in a spate of legislation all coming into operation on 30 September 1960, literally on the eve of Independence. Concluding that the North should keep up with the pace set by the Eastern and Western Regions in the race for independence, although it was less 'ready' than they, and that Northern independence, when it came, should after all be in federation with the East and West, the North's Muslim ruling class agreed to reform the legal and judicial systems of the Region, most notably by abrogating all the then-prevailing systems of criminal law, including Islamic criminal law, in favour of new Penal and Criminal Procedure Codes applicable in all courts of the Region to all persons without regard to religious or ethnic affiliation. Islamic personal law, and other Islamic civil law, continued in force for application in the Native Courts as appropriate, but parted company at the appellate level. Cases involving Islamic personal law went to the new Sharia Court of Appeal, whose jurisdiction was limited essentially to such questions. Cases involving other Islamic civil law went to the new Native Courts Appellate Division of the High Court. The Moslem Court of Appeal was abolished. The judicial powers of the emirs were curtailed; in subsequent years these powers were abolished completely. These concessions were balanced, to some degree, by the new prestige and privileges accorded to the Sharia Court of Appeal. It was made a permanent court with a standing membership and given a status equivalent to the Regional High Court. Its judgments, on matters within its jurisdiction, were made final and unappealable to any other court. Its jurisdiction was subject to extension beyond personal law matters, to questions of other Islamic civil law, at the instance of the parties to particular cases. Perhaps most importantly, its judges were given a seat on the Native Courts Appellate Division of the High Court, so that the North's Muslim jurists had a formal role in the application and development of all the law applied in the Native Courts, not limited to Islamic law. Beginning in 1959 and in the years following independence a huge effort went into making these new arrangements work properly (Ostien 2007: I, 57-133); and until the Settlement of 1960 fell apart in 1979, it seems that they actually did.

The First Republic

Under its Independence Constitution Nigeria became completely self-governing, but it nevertheless remained a 'part of Her Majesty's dominions'. In practice this meant, for instance, that Nigeria's Governor-General and the Governors of the Regions 'shall be appointed by Her Majesty and shall hold office during Her Majesty's pleasure and [...] shall be Her Majesty's representatives' in their respective jurisdictions; but the appointments were made, of course, on the advice of the federal Prime Minister and the regional Premiers. Appeals still lay from the Federal Supreme Court to the Privy Council. There were other badges and incidents of the continuing monarchy. In 1963 it was decided to do away with these vestiges and to convert Nigeria into a republic. Under the new constitution, which took effect on 1 October 1963, instead of 'The Federation of Nigeria' it became 'The Federal Republic of Nigeria'. The basic plan and most details of the constitution remained unchanged. The first Governor-General of independent Nigeria, Nnamdi Azikiwe, became the first President of the Republic. Other high officials also remained in place.

Unfortunately things did not go smoothly for the new country. The following brief summary may serve to give the uninitiated reader some idea of the range of problems that arose.

> The North-South and ethnic tensions, the politics of vindictiveness, oppression and thuggery, the Action Group crisis of 1962 [the party, rooted in the Western Region, split; after protracted violence and rioting and the apparent collapse of government in the Region the Federal Government declared a state of emergency and the Region was ruled by a federal administrator for about a year], revenue allocation disputes, the treason trials of Chief Obafemi Awolowo and twenty other members of the Action Group [accused of plotting to overthrow the Federal Government by force], the census controversy of 1962-1964 [the census, necessary to the allocation of seats in the House of Representatives, attempted twice, figures never accepted], the realignment of political parties before the 1964 federal elections [leaving the main party of the Eastern Region, led by President Azikiwe, in a weakened position], the 1964-1965 federal elections [boycotts in the East, violence, supplementary elections required], the dispute between the President and the Prime Minister over the 1964 elections, the Western Nigeria elections of 1965 and the civil violence that followed in the Region, contributed in varying degrees to hasten the fall of the First Republic and to the military takeover of January 1966 (Joye & Igweike 1982: 38-39).

13.3 The period from 1965 until 1985

Military coups, civil war, and the sharia debate of 1976-1978

Rule by the military, civil war, and the return to civilian rule

The military takeover proceeded in stages. On the night of 14-15 January 1966, a group of army majors, mostly Igbo by tribe, carried out coordinated assassinations of the Premiers of the Northern and Western Regions (Ahmadu Bello and Samuel Akintola), several other politicians, and a number of fellow-officers from the North and West. They also kidnapped and later killed the federal Prime Minister, Abubakar Tafawa Balewa. The next day the majors declared their allegiance to the General Officer Commanding, Major-General Aguiyi-Ironsi, also an Igbo but apparently not involved in the initial plot. President Azikiwe was out of the country at the time. On 16 January the Acting President, with the backing of the Council of Ministers, handed over administration of the country to the Armed Forces with Aguiyi-Ironsi at the head. The parts of the constitution relating to the legislative and executive branches of the federal and regional governments were suspended, the politicians were thrown out of office, and Military Governors were appointed for each region. Legislation thenceforward was by decree (federal) and edict (regional). The courts continued to function more or less as before.

Besides being an Igbo, Aguiyi-Ironsi pursued some unpopular policies, including dissolution of the regions and transformation of Nigeria into a unitary state. In July 1966, before this went very far in practice, there was a second coup within the military, this time led by Northern officers, in which Aguiyi-Ironsi and a number of other Igbo officers were killed. A young Northerner, Lieutenant-Colonel (later General) Yakubu Gowon, was installed as the new head of the Federal Military Government, and the federation was restored. Subsequently, in many parts of the North, there were pogroms against Igbos, precipitating a massive migration of Igbos back to the East.

The situation finally descended into civil war in mid-1967. On 30 May, Lieutenant Colonel Chukwuemeka Ojukwu, the Military Governor of the Eastern Region, declared the Region's secession from the Federation and its independence as a new nation under the name of 'The Republic of Biafra'. When discussions aimed at reversing this declaration went nowhere, the Federal Military Government commenced hostilities on 5 June. The war, which resulted in perhaps a million deaths, mostly in the East, ended in 1970 with the defeat of Biafra and its reincorporation into the country. Rule by the military continued.

One important by-product of the crises of 1966-1967 was the subdivision, so much talked of for such a long time, of Nigeria's regions into smaller states. In May 1967, in a futile attempt to stave off Eastern secession, General Gowon divided the country into twelve states, six of them in the North. This exercise was repeated in 1976, when seven additional states were created, four in the North. This process made the formerly monolithic North, in particular, much more palatable to the rest of the country. All the new states were legal clones of the regions from which they came, the laws and institutions of the old regions becoming the laws and institutions of the new states carved out of them, with much scrambling to staff all the new institutions thus created in the new states. State-creation had important effects on the administration of Islamic law in the states of the ex-Northern Region, to which we shall return shortly.

After the civil war General Gowon promised the early return of the country to civilian rule. Fulfilment of this promise always seemed to be put off, however, and, finally losing patience with the delays and with the mounting corruption throughout the government, in July 1975 another group from within the military deposed Gowon and replaced him as head of state with General Murtala Mohammed. In addition to taking drastic steps to combat corruption, Murtala quickly established a schedule for transition to civilian rule, and took the first step: appointment in late 1975 of a Constitution Drafting Committee (CDC) charged with preparing a new draft constitution for later consideration by a Constituent Assembly. Murtala was assassinated in February 1976, in yet another attempted coup from within the military, which this time failed. Murtala's successor was his second in command, General Olusegun Obasanjo (who subsequently served as Nigeria's elected president from 1999 to 2007). Obasanjo stuck to Murtala's transition schedule, handing the country back to an elected civilian government on 1 October 1979, under the new-modelled constitution of 1979.

The 1979 constitution preserved the federal structure of Nigeria – now with nineteen states plus the new Federal Capital Territory of Abuja (the capital was finally moved from Lagos to Abuja in 1991). But it made important changes in the system of government, the chief of which was to switch from the Westminster style inherited from Britain to a presidential system modelled on the United States. This change extended also to the state governments, so that in addition to an independently-elected president for the federation, with extensive executive powers laid down in the constitution, each state now also had an 'executive governor' elected independently of its House of Assembly. The new constitution also entrenched local government reforms decreed by the Military Government in 1976, guaranteeing a 'system of local government by democratically elected local government councils' (Art. 7); this was the final death-knell for emirate administration in the North. Many other adjustments were made. All of Nigeria's subsequent constitutions, including the 1999 constitution currently in effect, have been substantially identical to the 1979 constitution, with variations only at the margins.

The sharia debate of 1976-1978

The most contentious issue thrown up by the constitution-making process of 1976-1978 is directly related to our main subject here: it was the controversy over the proposal for a new Federal Sharia Court of Appeal. The call for such an institution was a by-product of the state creation exercises of 1967 and 1976. As we have seen, each new state inherited the laws and institutions of its parent region. In the North this meant (among other things) that in place of the one original Sharia Court of Appeal for the entire Region, there would now be, first six Sharia Courts of Appeal, and then ten, one for each of the states into which the Region was divided. All these new Sharia Courts of Appeal were legal clones of the original one for the Region; hence the judgments of each were final and unappealable to any other court. This raised the problem the proposed Federal Sharia Court of Appeal was intended to solve: the possibility of conflicts between the judgments of the Sharia Courts of Appeal of the states. They would all be adjudicating on the same class of cases – Islamic personal law. Inevitably cases involving the same legal issue would come before the Sharia Courts of Appeal of different states, and they would decide them differently, thus creating a conflict. But since the judgments of each of the courts were final, any conflict that might arise would be unresolveable. As early as 1972 it was proposed to create a new Federal Sharia Court of Appeal that would sit to hear appeals from the state Sharia Courts of Appeal and thus (among other things) to resolve any conflicts that might crop up between them. The CDC agreed with this proposal and included it in the draft constitution which it put before the country in 1976.

What happened is well known (Ostien 2006: 238-243 and authorities cited). The Report of the CDC, including the draft constitution, was published in September 1976 and became the subject of one year of public discussion and analysis. In October 1977 a mostly-elected Constituent Assembly convened to debate the CDC draft and to make such amendments as it saw fit. In one year of discussion Christian opinion on the Federal Sharia Court of Appeal had polarised and hardened, and in the Constituent Assembly the Christian delegates 'unleashed a storm of protest' against it (Hunwick 1992: 149). No compromise was found possible in protracted debate. In the end it was the Christians who had the votes, and in early April 1978, the Federal Sharia Court of Appeal was officially eliminated from the constitution. The Muslim members of the Constituent Assembly walked out the next day, maintaining their boycott for almost three weeks; only the intervention of the Head of State (Obasanjo) persuaded them to return. The Assembly then quickly wrapped up its work, adjourning finally on 5 June. After some further adjustments the constitution was officially enacted by a decree of 21 September 1978, to take effect on 1 October 1979.

State Sharia Courts of Appeal were indeed provided for, 'for any state that requires it' (Art. 240(1)); this was balanced by also allowing new Customary Courts of Appeal 'for any State that requires it', to which appeals in cases decided under customary law might be directed (Art. 245(1)). But the judgments of neither of these types of court were any more final, even in the fields of Islamic or customary personal law; all their judgments were made appealable to the federal Court of Appeal and thence to the Supreme Court. Thus the long-standing right of Muslim courts in the North to finally and autonomously decide all issues of Islamic personal law was lost. The possibility of extending Sharia Court of Appeal jurisdiction to questions of other Islamic civil law at the instance of the parties to particular cases was also lost. The right of judges of the Sharia Courts of Appeal to sit with judges of the High Courts to decide all other appeals from the Native Courts was also lost. In sum, the single high Muslim appellate court of days gone by, with wide territorial jurisdiction, finality in its judgments, and a voice in the decision of appeals by the High Court, was gone, replaced by many lesser offspring: no longer even clones of the former Regional Sharia Court of Appeal, they were lesser not only in their territorial reach and in their dignity, but also in their jurisdiction, powers, and autonomy. As the Muslims saw it, these new losses for Islamic law in Nigeria were the result, not of a negotiated settlement voluntarily entered into by the Muslim leadership, as in 1960, but of a humiliating defeat at the hands of Nigeria's Christians. As we shall see, various attempts were made in subsequent years, through the courts and the constitution, to repair the damage, until finally, in 1999, Zamfara State, seizing on a constitutional loophole, took the debate in a whole new direction.

Return to military rule

Nigeria was governed under the 1979 constitution for only a little over four years – 1979 to 1983. Shehu Shagari, elected president in 1979, was re-elected in 1983; but on 31 December 1983 the military stepped in once again, once again promising to clean up rampant corruption. General Muhammadu Buhari was installed as the new head of state, large parts of the constitution were suspended as before, and the country was ruled by decree and edict for the next sixteen years.

13.4 The period from 1985 until the present

Return to civilian rule at last; sharia implementation in twelve northern states

Constitutional developments

General Buhari is famous for his 'War Against Indiscipline', including the military tribunals he set up to pursue the recovery of public property looted during the Shagari era and to prosecute those who had stolen it. Many politicians were arrested and languished in prison awaiting trial; those tried and convicted were sentenced to serve long terms. But the tribunals became notorious for their arbitrary and highhanded behaviour, to the point that the Nigerian Bar Association instructed its members not to appear before them. Buhari's initial popularity faded as he resorted to ever more drastic methods to stifle criticism. It is said that the last straw was a threatened investigation into contracts awarded by the Ministry of Defence, which if pursued would have implicated senior military officers (Alli 2001). However that may be, in August 1985 Buhari was deposed by yet another coup from within the military, and replaced by General Ibrahim Babangida.

Babangida, like Murtala Mohammed a decade earlier, laid down a schedule for return of the country to civilian rule, complete with another Constituent Assembly convened (1988) to revise the 1979 constitution. But the last stage of Babangida's transition programme, the presidential election of 1993, was botched, and the country fell back into the hands of the military, this time under its worst tyrant to date, General Sani Abacha. Under the reign of Abacha (1993-1998), Nigeria drifted deeper into a morass of crime, corruption, and violence, resulting in its increasing international isolation. The 1995 hanging of human rights activist Ken Saro-Wiwa and eight of his companions, by orders of Abacha, led to widespread international condemnation. Nigeria was suspended as a member of the British Commonwealth and was targeted by economic sanctions imposed by the European Union among others. Abacha too announced a schedule for return of the country to civilian rule, convening yet another Constitutional Conference (1994-1995) for revision of the constitution, but he died in office before his sincerity on this point was tested.

Abacha died in June 1998. His successor was Major-General Abdulsalami Abubakar. Although Abubakar initially lacked even a modicum of support or legitimacy, and people feared for a continuation of the military dictatorship, he quickly took decisive steps towards the recovery of the Nigerian democracy (Nzeh 2002: 40-41). He released political prisoners, the international sanctions were lifted, and what many consider to be Nigeria's freest and fairest elections ever were held, to all local, state, and federal offices. On 29 May 1999, power was transferred to the new state governors and the new president, Olusegun Obasanjo. The 1999 constitution, which came into force the same day and under which the country is still governed, was essentially the 1979 constitution reinstated.

Nigeria is now continuing its longest period of uninterrupted civilian rule since Independence. Elections were held as scheduled in 2003; Obasanjo was returned to power for another four years. Elections were again held as scheduled in 2007. Although these elections were widely condemned as badly flawed, the presidency changed hands peacefully for the first time in Nigeria's history, and election tribunals, convened according to constitutional processes, have dealt with the irregularities apparently unswayed by political considerations. The new president, Umaru Yar'Adua of Katsina State, has pledged himself and his government to respect and enforce the rule of law.

Sharia and national law, 1985-present

The collapse of the Settlement of 1960 in the constitution-making process of 1976-1978 has been described. In the twenty years between 1979 and 1999 two types of attempts were made by Muslims to repair the damage. (1) A new field of constitutional litigation was opened up, focussed on the Sharia Courts of Appeal. New pressure had been put on Sharia Court of Appeal jurisdiction because judges of the Sharia Courts of Appeal no longer sat on the Appellate Division of the High Court. This meant that Muslims litigating, for instance, contract, tort, or land cases under Islamic law in the Area Courts (successors in the North to the Native Courts), who wanted specifically Muslim jurists to examine the matter on appeal, had no choice but to try for the Sharia Courts of Appeal. But the trouble now was that the possibility of extending Sharia Court of Appeal jurisdiction to such cases at the instance of the parties had been cut off; this was what a succession of cases held (Ostien 2006: 243-244). (2) The constitution being against them, the Muslims turned their attention to amending the constitution. The first attempt, decreed by General Babangida in 1986, deleted the word 'personal' wherever it occurred after the word 'Islamic' in the sections of the 1979 constitution touching on Sharia Court of Appeal jurisdiction. This theoretically should have done the trick, but the courts held otherwise, finding the amendment to be 'of no jurisdictional consequence and in practical terms [to have] achieved nothing' (ibid: 244-245). Under the Babangida and Abacha constitutions, the crucial section was therefore redrafted and simplified, unequivocally extending the jurisdiction of the Sharia Courts of Appeal to all 'civil proceedings involving questions of Islamic law where all the parties are Muslims'; but neither the Babangida nor the Abacha constitution ever came into force. When General Abubakar returned Nigeria to civilian rule in 1999, he disregarded the Babangida and Abacha constitutions almost entirely, simply reinstating the 1979 constitution (with some amendments not affecting our point here). The position looked hopeless.

It was at this point that Alhaji Ahmad Sani came into the picture. Sani was elected Governor of Zamfara State in the governorship elections held on 9 January 1999 – the first such elections after sixteen years of military rule. Zamfara State, in Nigeria's far north, has a predominantly rural population of about three million, of which 90 per cent or more are Muslim. Governor Sani was its first elected governor, the state only having been created (out of Sokoto State) in a new round of state-creation decreed by Sani Abacha in 1996. Governor Sani says that during his campaign,

> In any town I went to, I first started with *kafaral*, which is chanting *Allahu Akbar*[10] thrice. Then I always said, 'I am in the race not to make money, but to improve on our religious way of worship, and introduce religious reforms that will make us get Allah's favour. And then we will have abundant resources for development' (*Tell Magazine*, 15 November 1999: 19).

This promise was little noticed outside Zamfara during the campaign. But after his inauguration on 29 May 1999, Governor Sani proceeded to make it good – at least as to the religious reforms – and thus began a new chapter in the history of Nigeria's Muslims and of their relations with their non-Muslim neighbours and compatriots.

'Religious reforms that will make us get Allah's favour'. By this Governor Sani did not mean reforms of the religion, of Islam. He meant reforms of the laws and institutions of Zamfara State, to bring them more into conformity with Islam – in particular with Islamic law. 'Sharia implementation', as the reforms quickly came to be called, has been effected primarily by legislation at the state and local government levels, aimed at making the legislating jurisdictions, in various ways, more 'sharia compliant' than they had formerly been. After Zamfara showed the way, eleven other states – Bauchi, Borno, Gombe, Jigawa, Kaduna, Kano, Katsina, Kebbi, Niger, Sokoto and Yobe – followed with similar legislative programmes. Here is a summary of what has been done:

- The principal point conceded by the Muslims in the Settlement of 1960 – the abrogation of Islamic criminal law – has been reclaimed. Relying on their constitutional power to legislate on criminal matters, and their constitutional right to freely practice their

religion, all sharia states have reinstated Islamic criminal law, in the form of new Sharia Penal and Criminal Procedure Codes applicable to Muslims.
- Relying on their constitutional power to regulate their own court systems, all sharia states have established inferior Sharia Courts, with original jurisdiction to apply the full range of Islamic law, civil and criminal, to Muslims.
- Seizing on an anomalous clause in the constitutional language defining Sharia Court of Appeal jurisdiction – until 1999 little noticed – all sharia states have extended the jurisdiction of their Sharia Courts of Appeal to all matters, civil and criminal, decided in the inferior Sharia Courts. This move simply bypassed all the litigation relating to Sharia Court of Appeal jurisdiction, and all the attempted constitutional amendments, of the previous twenty years.
- A wide range of other legislation has been enacted aimed at particular 'social vices' and 'un-Islamic behaviour', like the consumption of alcohol, gambling, prostitution, unedifying media, and the excessive mixing together of unrelated males and females. Two states – Zamfara and Kano – uniquely among all Nigerian states – have even tackled the pan-Nigerian problem of corruption, setting up their own statutory Public Complaints and Anti-Corruption Commissions in accordance with Islamic principles.
- Other institutions have been established – Sharia Commissions and Councils of Ulama with important advisory and executive functions; boards for the collection and distribution *zakat*[11]; *hisbah*[12] organisations to monitor and try to enforce sharia compliance, but also to engage in mediation and conciliation within the society; and others; – all with the aim of deepening and enforcing the application of sharia law in the lives of the Muslims of the states that have established them.

Not all the sharia states have done all of these things, and what has been done has been done differently from state to state. Still, taken together, these interlocking measures – in theory at any rate – have restored the application of Islamic law to Muslims, in the states that have enacted them, to a state of completeness and a degree of autonomy from the 'English' legal system, that it has not had for over a century. In practice, of course, things have not always worked out as hoped. Extensive documentation of what has been done can be found in Ostien 2007.

Governor Sani's announcement of his sharia implementation programme exhilarated Nigeria's Muslims, and produced tremendous pressure on the governments of other northern states to follow suit. But it aroused fear and loathing among Christians, who expected the worst;

civil war was even predicted by some (Barends 2003: 19; Ostien 2002: 172-73). Everyone's worst fears seemed to be confirmed by the first amputation of a hand for theft already in March 2000, and then by the stoning cases of Safiyatu Hussaini (2001-2002) and Amina Lawal (2002-2003), which caused an uproar around the world.[13] In Nigeria serious fighting, killing and destruction of property, sparked off directly by agitation for and against sharia implementation, did break out, in Kaduna State, in February 2000, leaving hundreds, perhaps thousands, dead. Subsequent lesser outbreaks of violence elsewhere in the North, in the first year or two after sharia implementation started, perhaps resulted from it in part, and in part from all the other causes of inter-religious and inter-ethnic strife that have rankled for many years (see e.g. Boer 2003; Ostien 2009). Since those early days, however, the clamour has died down completely, to the point that sharia implementation was a non-issue, virtually never mentioned, in the state and federal election campaigns of 2007. Some of the reasons for this will be discussed below.

It remains to mention the 'Independent Sharia Panels' (ISPs) established in the South in the wake of sharia implementation in the North. As we have seen, there has never been any state-sanctioned application of Islamic law in the South. With no chance of changing this through legislation, Muslims in several southern cities (e.g. Lagos, Ibadan, and Ijebu-Ode) have set up what amount to private arbitration panels, to apply Islamic law in the settlement of disputes submitted to them by parties consenting to their jurisdiction and agreeing to abide by their judgments. These panels have gained recognition and status through the involvement of such national bodies as the Supreme Council for Islamic Affairs and the Supreme Council for Sharia in Nigeria. Intended primarily to resolve private disputes, especially in the field of personal and family law, the panels have sometimes also been drawn reluctantly into application of the penal law as well. In one famous case a self-confessed fornicator submitted himself to the ISP in his city, demanding the *hudud* punishment for his sin. Evidently never having been married, he was duly given his one hundred strokes of the cane. One wonders what would have happened had he been a married man.[14] Whether the courts would enforce the judgments of the ISPs, if asked to do so, is not known.

13.5 Constitutional law

In this section we deal with sharia-related matters arising under articles of Nigeria's constitution other than those on Fundamental Rights, which are dealt with in section 13.9. As much of the discussion, here and in section 13.9, pertains to various details of the new programmes of sharia implementation, it should be remarked at the outset that sharia implementation in northern Nigeria was not done in defiance of the constitution. In most sharia states, before they did anything, the governors appointed 'Sharia Implementation Committees' charged among other things to 'study what steps should be taken [and] to consider the constitutionality of the measures proposed' (Ostien 2007: II, 3). Then, in announcing their programmes, the governors explicitly acknowledged the supremacy of the federal constitution and laws. Governor Sani of Zamfara State said from the beginning that '[w]hatever I am doing must be [...] within the agreement signed by the people of Nigeria to live together which is referred to as the Constitution' (Nigerian *Guardian*, 6 December 1999: 69). Governor Kure of Niger State said that sharia law as implemented in his state would

> submit to the supremacy of the nation's constitution. [...] [H]e assured that where the system ran contrary to the provisions of the constitution, *shari'a* would bow to give the constitution the right of way. [...] He said that having vowed to preserve and protect the nation's constitution during his swearing in, his administration would do nothing to flout the provisions under any guise (Nigerian *Guardian*, 17 January 2000: 71).

Many other examples could be given. 'The Muslims of northern Nigeria are saying that they want to implement as much of their law as they possibly can within the constitution and laws of the federation. That attitude is entirely politically correct' (Ostien 2002: 167). The question remains, of course, whether the sharia implementation programmes, or any of them, do in any way go outside the bounds of the constitution and laws of the federation. Various aspects of this question are dealt with in the rest of this section and in section 13.9.

Sharia in Nigeria's constitution

Sharia finds its place in Nigeria's 1999 constitution only in a number of provisions relating to the Sharia Courts of Appeal of the Federal Capital Territory and of 'any State that requires it'; in fact, eighteen of the nineteen states of the ex-Northern Region have Sharia Courts of Appeal, the nineteenth, Benue State, sharing with Plateau. The constitution provides in detail for their establishment, the appointment and removal of their judges (since 1979 denominated 'kadis' in the constitution and laws), their jurisdiction, appeals from their judgments, and other matters relating to them (Chapter VII, on the judicature). For most purposes the Sharia Courts of Appeal are grouped with the

Supreme Court, the federal Court of Appeal, the state and federal High Courts, and the Customary Courts of Appeal. Thus, they are superior courts of record (Art. 6). The salaries of their kadis are set by the National Assembly and paid out of the Consolidated Revenue Fund of the federation (Art. 84). Their Grand Kadis (chief judges) may administer the oaths of office taken by state governors (Art. 185). Their Grand Kadis also serve on the National Judicial Council and the State Judicial Service Commissions, and all kadis may be (and many are) appointed to serve on Election Tribunals (III^{d} and VIth Scheds.). The Sharia Courts of Appeal and their kadis are familiar and accepted features of Nigeria's judicial landscape.

The existence of Sharia Courts of Appeal implies the existence of courts inferior to them in which Islamic law is applied and from which appeals to them may be taken. These were the North's Native Courts, which in 1967-1968 were reconstituted as 'Area Courts'. As we have seen, from 1960 the parts of Islamic law applied in these courts was limited to Islamic personal law and other Islamic civil law, Islamic criminal law having been abrogated. All appeals involving Islamic personal law went to the Sharia Courts of Appeal. Most appeals involving other Islamic civil law went to the High Courts until 1979, and all did thereafter. Since 1999-2000, in the twelve sharia states, the inferior courts in which Islamic law is applied have been reorganised once again: the Area Courts have been abolished and replaced by 'Sharia Courts', charged to apply the full range of Islamic law, civil and criminal, to Muslims. Appeals from the Sharia Courts in all types of cases have been directed to the Sharia Courts of Appeal.

Establishment of inferior Sharia Courts

The states may establish, below their superior courts, 'such other courts as may be authorised by law to exercise jurisdiction at first instance or on appeal on matters with respect to which a House of Assembly may make laws', and any court a House of Assembly can establish it can also abolish (Art. 6). Thus in the sharia states the Area Courts have come and gone and the Sharia Courts have replaced them. (This involved little change of personnel: most of the Area Court judges simply became Sharia Court *alkalis*.) Like the Area Courts before them, the Sharia Courts have criminal as well as civil jurisdiction, now to apply the new Sharia Penal Codes (see 13.7), as the Area Courts applied the Penal Code before. With all of this *per se* there appears to be no constitutional problem.

But there are problems with some provisions of the new Sharia Courts laws. Administrative responsibility for the Area Courts (and of the Native Courts before them) was in the hands of the Chief Judges of the High Courts. Now, in the sharia states, administrative responsibility for the Sharia Courts has been transferred to the Grand Kadis of the Sharia Courts of Appeal. Some of the Chief Judges have objected, resenting, perhaps, their loss of jurisdiction, and citing their *ex officio* chairmanship of the state Judicial Service Commissions, mandated by the constitution (III^{d} Sched. Pt. II C). This is perhaps not very convincing; nevertheless, as of October 2009, transfer of control from the Chief Judge to the Grand Kadi has yet to be accomplished in two sharia states (Borno and Katsina).

A more serious constitutional question is raised by the direction of all appeals from the Sharia Courts, in criminal as well as civil matters, to the Sharia Courts of Appeal, cutting out the High Courts completely. We consider this point next.

Expansion of Sharia Court of Appeal jurisdiction

Article 277 of Nigeria's constitution provides as follows (italics added):

> 277. (1) The Sharia Court of Appeal of a State shall, *in addition to such other jurisdiction as may be conferred upon it by the law of the State*, exercise such appellate and supervisory jurisdiction in civil proceedings involving questions of Islamic personal law which the court is competent to decide in accordance with the provisions of subsection (2) of this section.
> (2) For the purposes of subsection (1) of this section, the Sharia Court of Appeal shall be competent to decide

(a)
(b) } [specified questions of Islamic personal law, e.g. marriage,
(c) } divorce, guardianship, inheritance, etc.]
(d)
(e) – [any other question of Islamic personal law at the instance of Muslim parties to particular cases]

The question is whether subsection (2) lays down the *maximum* jurisdiction any Sharia Court of Appeal can have, or whether it lays down the *minimum* only, the states being free, under the italicised clause of subsection (1), to add any further jurisdiction they please. If the former, then the sharia states, by expanding the jurisdiction of their Sharia Courts of Appeal to matters well outside the bounds of Islamic personal law, have acted unconstitutionally. If the latter, then the sharia states have found a brilliant bypass to the constitutional roadblock, set up in 1979, which the North's Muslims then spent twenty years trying to remove.

If Article 277 is read by itself, the position of the sharia states looks strong. If it is read in the light of its history and of the rest of constitution, the position looks much weaker. Article 277 entered the constitution as Article 242 of the 1979 constitution, in identical terms except for a small difference in the wording of subsection (2)(e). There is no question but that the drafters of the 1979 constitution intended to limit Sharia Court of Appeal jurisdiction to questions of Islamic personal law only, and that the insertion of the italicised clause of subsection (1) was a draftsman's error that somehow escaped detection (Ostien 2006: 248-252). The other articles of the constitution dealing with the Sharia Courts of Appeal relentlessly use the phrase 'Islamic personal law'. To take just one example, the class of cases in which appeals lie from the Sharia Courts of Appeal to the federal Court of Appeal is defined as 'civil proceedings before the Sharia Court of Appeal with respect to any question of Islamic personal law which the Sharia Court of Appeal is competent to decide' (Art. 244(1)); but it cannot have been the intention to leave unappealable other types of questions that the state Houses of Assembly, if they were allowed, might empower their Sharia Courts of Appeal to decide. The High Courts of two states have already held that expansion of Sharia Court of Appeal jurisdiction beyond questions of Islamic personal law is unconstitutional.[15] In those states the old pattern has returned, appeals from the Sharia Courts in Islamic personal law cases going to the Sharia Courts of Appeal, appeals in all other cases going to the High Courts. More of the same is likely as time goes on.

Enactment of other elements of the sharia implementation programmes

Article 4(7) of the constitution provides that:

> The House of Assembly of a State shall have power to make laws for the peace, order and good government of the State or any part thereof with respect to the following matters, that is to say
> (*a*) any matter not included in the Exclusive Legislative List [...];
> (*b*) any matter included in the Concurrent Legislative List [...] to the extent prescribed [therein];
> (*c*) any other matter with respect to which it is empowered to make laws in accordance with the provisions of this Constitution.

We consider briefly the authority of the sharia states under this provision to enact four other elements of their sharia implementation programmes.

a. *Criminal law.* The power to create and punish criminal offences is vested in both the state and federal governments in Nigeria, within their respective spheres of authority (II^{d} Sched. Pt. III(2)). Thus the Penal Codes in force in all northern states are state enactments. There are of course limitations. No legislative body has power, 'in relation to any criminal offence whatsoever, [...] to make any law which shall have retrospective effect' (Art. 4(9)). Every criminal offence must be 'defined and the penalty therefore [...] prescribed in a written law', i.e. 'an Act of the National Assembly or a Law of a State [or] any subsidiary legislation or instrument under the provisions of a law' (Art. 36(12)). The new Sharia Penal Codes enacted by the sharia states comply with these broad requirements, except in one particular. Seven of the codes contain (with minor variations) the following provision, captioned 'General offences':

> Any act or omission which is not specifically mentioned in this Sharia Penal Code but is otherwise declared to be an offence under the Qur'an, Sunnah, and *ijtihad* of the Maliki school of Islamic thought, shall be an offence under this code and such act or omission shall be punishable: (a) with imprisonment for a term which may extend to five years, or (b) with caning which may extend to 50 lashes, or (c) with a fine which may extend to N5,000.00 [about € 22[16]], or with any two of the above punishments (Ostien 2007: IV, 60 n.e 118).

This incorporation by reference of otherwise undefined offences no doubt violates Art. 36(12), and would be struck down if challenged in a proper case. The other constitutional questions raised by the Sharia Penal Codes relate not to the power of the sharia states to enact them, but to issues of fundamental rights considered in section 13.9 below.

b. *Evidence.* Since 1979 the subject of evidence has been on the constitutional Exclusive Legislative List (II^{d} Sched. Pt. I §23), and therefore presumptively reserved for the National Assembly alone; and there is a federal Evidence Act, in force in Nigeria with few changes since 1945. At the same time, the North's Area Courts, and presumably the South's Customary Courts as well, have continued to apply, as the case may be, Islamic or 'native and customary' rules of procedure and evidence in civil matters coming before them, without regard to the Evidence Act; and now the new Sharia Courts are doing the same in criminal matters as well. Can this be correct?

As to civil matters there is clearly no problem. The Evidence Act by its own terms is inapplicable 'to judicial proceedings in any civil cause or matter in or before any Sharia Court of Appeal, Customary Court of Appeal, Area Court or Customary Court' (§1(2)(c)). It may be presumed that the term 'Area Court' will be read to include the new Sharia Courts as well. This exemption recognises the continuing duality of Nigeria's court systems and the continuing applicability, in the latter-day 'native' courts, of Islamic law and native law and custom, including the law and custom relating to procedure and evidence.

Criminal matters are a different question. The Evidence Act says that the North's Area Courts (we presume Sharia Courts are included), in criminal causes or matters, are to be *guided* by its provisions, except that they are *bound* by six specific sections all relating to burden of proof (§1 (3) and (4)). This distinction, between being guided and being bound, entered the law of the Northern Region in 1960, supposedly on an 'interim' basis, while the judges of the Native Courts became accustomed to the new Penal and Criminal Procedure Codes and the Evidence Act, all very different from the law they had been accustomed to applying up till then (Ostien 2007: I, 63-65 and IV, 181-182). But the distinction has persisted until the present, and has even been perpetuated in some of the new Sharia Criminal Procedure Codes enacted in the sharia states (Ostien 2007: IV, 195-197). Whether the principle of guidance, as used in §1(3) of the Evidence Act, leaves room for the application, in criminal cases in the Sharia Courts, of Islamic rules of evidence which are sometimes inconsistent with the Act, is a complex question on which we cannot enter further here.

c. *Zakat.* 'Taxation of incomes, profits and capital gains' is on the Exclusive Legislative List (II^{d} Sched. Pt. I §59). But eleven of the sharia states have set up official agencies for the collection and distribution of *zakat*, the Islamic 'alms' tax (see note 11). In most states payment remains voluntary, but in three defaulters can be prosecuted, and in one other *zakat* can be recovered as a civil debt. *Zakat* is a tax on wealth. The levy of *zakat* on their wealthy Muslims by the sharia states, if it is ever challenged, seems unlikely to be held inconsistent with the federal government's exclusive prerogative to tax incomes, profits and capital gains.

d. *The hisbah groups.* 'Police and other government security services established by law' are also on the Exclusive Legislative List (II^{d} Sched. Pt. I §45), and Art. 214(1) makes the point very clear:

> There shall be a Police Force for Nigeria, which shall be known as the Nigeria Police Force, and [...] no other police force shall be established for the Federation or any part thereof.

But seven of the sharia states have set up official *hisbah* organisations (see note 12) (in other states *hisbah* groups have organised themselves as NGOs), which, along with preaching, admonishing, and a good deal of mediation and conciliation, also do what looks like policing –

monitoring and trying to enforce sharia compliance. This has sometimes brought them into conflict with members of the public and with the police, particularly in Kano, where *hisbah* attempts to enforce bans on commercial motorcycles carrying female passengers resulted in late 2005 in serious clashes between *hisbah*, motorcycle drivers, and police (Nasir 2007: 110-111). Things came to a head in February 2006, when the federal government accused the Kano *hisbah* of being an illegal police force, purported to ban it, and arrested its Commander and his deputy, charging them with three counts of felonious membership and management of an unlawful society (Nigerian *Guardian*, 10 February 2006: 1). In response, two lawsuits against the federal government were promptly filed: Kano State sued in the Supreme Court, seeking a declaration that its *hisbah* organisation was legal, and the Commander and his deputy sued in the Federal High Court, seeking damages for unlawful arrest and illegal detention. The Supreme Court case was inconclusive: the court dismissed it as not within its original jurisdiction and said it should be refiled, if at all, in the Federal High Court (it never was). Kano was the clear winner in the other two cases: the *hisbah* Commander and his deputy were acquitted of the criminal charges, and in their own suit for illegal detention they won N500,000 (about € 2,222) each.[17] The Kano and other *hisbah* organisations are still very much in business.

The 'state religion' question

Article 10 of Nigeria's constitution provides that 'The Government of the Federation or of a State shall not adopt any religion as State Religion.' Have the sharia states, or any of them, violated this provision? This is a difficult question, because the measures taken differ significantly from state to state, most importantly in the scope of 'implementation of sharia' attempted, and also because no Nigerian court – certainly not the Supreme Court – has yet interpreted or applied Article 10 in any concrete case, so that one does not know what test the courts will use to determine whether a particular enactment or combination of enactments amounts to adoption of a state religion within the meaning of Article 10. Nevertheless, it is possible to say something on this point, at least in a negative sense: Article 10 does not imply a regime of strict separation between religion and state such as that obtaining in the United States and some other countries (Ostien & Gamaliel 2002). Its language is not so sweeping as the U.S. 'establishment clause', for instance;[18] and other parts of Nigeria's constitution, some mentioned already, imply a degree of accommodation, cooperation, and even of entanglement between religion and state that would be unimaginable in the U.S. For instance, Article 38(2), part of the fundamental rights provision on freedom of thought, conscience, and religion, clearly permits religious instruction to be given and religious ceremonies and observances to be conducted in the public schools, all of which is done everywhere in Nigeria but is strictly prohibited in the U.S. Articles 6, 247, 275-279, and 288, all touching on the Sharia Courts of Appeal, clearly permit the enforcement of at least large parts of the sharia in the public courts. The provisions on the Sharia Courts of Appeal bring out another point: Article 10 does not require even that all religious groups be treated identically by the state. The case of religion in the public schools obscures this, since Muslims and Christians both want it and both get it on equal terms. But they do not both want to live under their own religious law: only the Muslims want that, and under Nigeria's constitution they may to a large extent have it: Article 10, read in the light of Articles 6, 247, 275-279, and 288, permits the state and federal governments to accommodate *them in particular* in this way. But whether any or all of the sharia states have gone too far with their sharia implementation programmes, passing beyond the bounds permitted by Article 10, remains, until the Nigerian courts clarify what Article 10 means, a moot point (Peters 2003: 45).

13.6 Personal status, family, and inheritance law

This part of the law – 'personal law', to use the term often applied – is extremely complex, or should we say 'plural', in Nigeria.

Under the constitution, the federal government has the exclusive right to regulate 'the formation, annulment and dissolution of marriages *other than marriages under Islamic law and customary law* including matrimonial causes relating thereto' (II^{d} Sched. Pt. I §61, italics added). Accordingly there is a federal (originally English) Marriage Act dating from the colonial period, and a federal (also substantially English) Matrimonial Causes Act dating from 1970, the latter having replaced the prior rule that in matrimonial causes the courts should simply proceed 'in conformity with the law and practice for the time being in force in England'. Marriages under the Marriage Act must be officially registered. Matrimonial causes must be litigated in the High Courts.

But most marriages by far, and most dissolutions of marriage, and most issues closely related to marriage such as guardianships, child custody and, particularly for women, personal status and property rights, are governed not by the federal statutes at all, but by Islamic law or customary law. Islamic law is the classical Maliki *fiqh*,[19] with all its familiar features; customary law is as multifarious as are Nigeria's many ethnic groups. But in truth it is heterogeneous amalgams, of Islamic law with local custom, or of one set of customs with another, which are in practice applied; and none of it is codified. Administration is often informal, by family, clan, or community elders; few of the proceedings, including marriages and divorces, are officially recorded anywhere. If it comes to that, litigation is in the local Sharia, Area, or (in the southern states) the Customary Courts.

The constitution leaves regulation of inheritance entirely to the states. In all states there are statutes, again derived from English law, governing testate and intestate succession. These interact in various ways with the Marriage Act and with Islamic and customary law. Thus, for instance, the inheritance statutes usually apply only if one is married under the Marriage Act; but even if one is, one's power to dispose of property even by will may be limited by Islamic or customary law (Ezeilo undated: 3). But again, because most people are not married under the Marriage Act, most estates by far are disposed of, usually informally but sometimes through the local courts, under Islamic and/or customary law.

We have noted that in Nigeria's southern states Islamic personal law has never ousted customary personal law even among the Muslims (perhaps the new Independent Sharia Panels will begin to change that); so in practice it is only in the northern states that Islamic personal law is formally applied, in the Sharia Courts of the sharia states and in the Area Courts of other northern states in cases involving Muslims. The Area Courts also apply the appropriate customary personal law in cases involving non-Muslims, and there are statutory choice-of-law rules for 'mixed' cases.

As to non-Muslims in the sharia states, who might wish their own customary law to be applied in the adjudication of their disputes, the situation has become confused – the Area Courts, which used to apply customary law, having been abolished, the new Sharia Courts having jurisdiction to apply Islamic law only, and the Magistrate's and High Courts having historically been excluded from original jurisdiction of personal law matters arising under 'native law and custom'. In some places non-Muslims are nevertheless quietly being catered for in the Sharia Courts, the *alkalis* applying local customary law as if they were still the Area Court judges that most of them used to be. In other places the Magistrate's Courts come in, although their jurisdiction to do so too is questionable.

In the sharia states, appeals from the Sharia Courts should all go to the Sharia Courts of Appeal: it is anybody's guess what would happen to an appeal by a non-Muslim whose divorce or inheritance case had been decided by the *alkali* under customary law. In the non-sharia northern states, appeals from the Area Courts go to the Sharia Courts of Appeal in cases decided under Islamic personal law and to the High Courts or the Customary Courts of Appeal in cases decided under customary personal law. All appeals from the Magistrate's Courts go to the High Courts. High Court decisions have always been appealable further to the federal Court of Appeal and then to the Supreme Court, and similarly, since 1979, for decisions of the Sharia and Customary Courts of Appeal. The federal appellate courts both therefore do sometimes decide questions of Islamic and customary personal law.

The old patriarchies remain strong all over Nigeria, and accordingly much personal law and custom is skewed in favour of men. Many girls are married off at young ages to much older men, sometimes against their will (in Muslim cases, under the Maliki doctrine of *ijbar*, the overruling power of the father or guardian to act purely (theoretically) in the girl's best interest). Polygamy is lawful and remains common in all parts of the country under both Islamic and customary law. *Purdah*[20] is widely practiced among northern Muslims. Physical abuse of wives by their husbands is tolerated and even protected: §55(1)(d) of the Penal Codes of all northern states, now perpetuated in the new Sharia Penal Codes as well, provides that:

> Nothing is an offence which does not amount to the infliction of grievous hurt upon any person and which is done [...] by a husband for the purpose of correcting his wife.

Divorce is everywhere easier for men than for women (including the unfettered privilege of *talak*[21] for Muslim men), so they do it more often, and sometimes evade their putative obligations to wives and children in the process. But it is perhaps in the area of inheritance rights that women, especially in parts of the south, suffer the most – particularly widows, who under the customary practices of some ethnic groups are denied any right to inherit from their husbands, are sometimes themselves treated as heritable property, and are ritually humiliated and abused in the process (Sossou 2002 and authorities cited). Muslim women are generally not subjected to such extremes, but even they at best receive lesser shares than similarly situated males under the Islamic rules of inheritance. Much of this falls through the gaps of the fundamental rights provisions of the constitution. Finer-grained provisions, such as those embodied in the U.N. Convention on the Rights of the Child and the U.N. Convention on the Elimination of All Forms of Discrimination against Women, unfortunately do not apply: both conventions were ratified long ago by Nigeria, but neither has yet been domesticated, so neither yet has the force of law. We return to this subject in section 13.9 below.

Further details of any of Nigeria's bodies of personal law and custom are beyond the scope of this paper. Readers interested in Islamic personal law as applied in northern Nigeria in particular might well start with J.N.D. Anderson's long essay on Nigeria in his book on *Islamic Law in Africa* (Anderson 1954: 171-224). Anderson, himself deeply versed in the *fiqh* of all the major schools of Islamic law, made a tour of all parts of the then-Northern Region, conversing, often directly in Arabic, with the Sultan of Sokoto, many emirs, the chief *alkalis* and other court personnel, the Sudanese lecturers at the Kano School of Arabic Studies, and leading *ulama* (ibid: 183-184). The survey based on those discussions ranges over many aspects of Islamic law as applied in the various parts of the Region, including 'those modifications of the pure Shari'a in favour of local custom which are noticeable, in greater or lesser degree, in the day to day work of even the most staunchly Muslim courts' (ibid: 172). Let one example suffice:

> The maintenance due to a wife [...] is everywhere calculated by exclusive reference to the husband's means: and this, while reasonable enough, is directly contrary to the normal Maliki rule, as the better jurists in Nigeria fully realise. This provides a good example of a point on which customary law has everywhere triumphed (ibid: 208).[22]

No doubt the position has changed in some respects in the half-century since: probably not very much, but no one really knows because the sort of investigation made by Anderson, certainly on anything like the same scale, has never been repeated. That Islamic personal law as applied in northern Nigeria is still often contaminated by local custom antithetical to women is confirmed by the work of the Federation of Muslim Women Associations in Nigeria (FOMWAN), founded in 1985 (Yusuf 1993), and more recently by the attitude taken toward sharia implementation by Muslim women activists.

> Most Muslim women activists are working within the Sharia implementation paradigm: trying to use the [...] Islamic legal tradition to achieve more gender and social justice within Muslim families and communities. The enemy is "merely traditional practices" oppressive to women, which do not have – or should not have – the sanction of religion (Nasir 2007: 118, with details of the activist agenda at 100-105).

Sharia implementation

> has stimulated many women to a deeper study of Islamic law and its sources. [...] [This] has in turn fed back into the work of individual women lawyers and of NGOs like WRAPA and BAOBAB, of providing legal education and counsel and

representation to women in legal matters of all sorts – not only criminal cases, but especially family matters such as marriage contracts and divorce settlements, child custody, maintenance, and widow's inheritances (ibid: 99-100).

13.7 Criminal law

Nigeria's southern states apply criminal and criminal procedure statutes dating from colonial days, derived from English law. In all northern states, the Penal and Criminal Procedure Codes of 1960 are still in force, as variously amended by the states. And now, in the sharia states, running in parallel to the Penal and Criminal Procedure Codes of 1960, there are also *Sharia* Penal and Criminal Procedure Codes: the 1960 codes are applied in the Magistrate's and High Courts, the sharia codes in the Sharia Courts.[23] In this section we briefly discuss the new Sharia Penal and Criminal Procedure Codes. We can do no more than skim the surface of this interesting topic. For further details see Peters 2003 and Ostien 2007: IV.

The sharia codes are substantially based on the 1960 codes, with about 89 per cent of Sharia Penal Code sections coming from the Penal Code, and all of 99 per cent of Sharia Criminal Procedure Code sections coming from the Criminal Procedure Code (Ostien 2007: IV, 157-68 and 338-43). Particularly in the Sharia Penal Codes, however, there has been considerable alteration of Penal Code sections used, with the effect, together with new sections added, of infusing the Sharia Penal Codes with the letter and the spirit of Islamic criminal law of the Maliki school.

Thus, the substantive offences, covered in eighteen chapters of the Penal Code (312 sections), have been reorganised into just three chapters of the Sharia Penal Codes (290 sections on average). The three chapters are entitled 'Hudud and Hudud-Related Offences', 'Qisas and Qisas-Related Offences', and 'Ta'azir Offences'. The sections defining the classical *hudud* and *qisas* offences (see notes 6 and 7) have been redrafted in accordance with Maliki doctrine, and the classical punishments – amputation for certain thefts, stoning to death for certain acts of extra-marital sex, retaliation in kind for woundings and homicides unless waived by the victims or their heirs, and so on – have been imposed. Apostasy is not criminalised in any code,[24] but in some of them, in their sections on offences relating to religion, insulting the Prophet or defiling the Qur'an are made punishable by death. The defence of provocation to woundings and homicides, available under the Penal Code, has been eliminated from the Sharia Penal Codes, and other defences inserted, for instance, for acts 'done by a person compelled by necessity to protect his person, property or honour, or the person, property or honour of another from imminent grave danger'.

The '*ta'azir* offences'[25] have been copied wholesale from the Penal Code, but the punishments have been much adjusted, by tinkering with numbers of years of imprisonment or amounts of fines, and often by specifying a certain number of 'lashes' in addition or in the alternative to imprisonment or fine. The Penal Code already allowed judges considerable discretion in sentencing, including discretion to substitute caning or payment of compensation for any other punishment in most cases; the Sharia Penal Codes continue this broad discretion and expand it further, allowing also a sentence of reprimand, warning, exhortation, or boycott to be passed 'on any offender in lieu of, or in addition to any other punishment to which he might be sentenced for any offence not punishable with death, or offences falling under *hudud* and *qisas*'. This restores the almost unlimited discretion of the classical *qadi* in *ta'azir* cases, at least in the matter of sentencing.

There is considerable variation among the Sharia Penal Codes, some of it trivial, some of it less so. To give just one example: whereas most Sharia Penal Codes punish criminal breach of trust by a public servant with imprisonment, fine, and/or lashing, Kano punishes it with 'amputation of his right hand [...] and [...] imprisonment for not less than five years and stolen wealth shall be confiscated'. There has been a project on to 'harmonise' the Sharia Penal Codes (and also the Sharia Criminal Procedure Codes, among which there is less variation), so far without much success.

The Sharia Criminal Procedure Codes are almost completely copied from the Criminal Procedure Code of 1960, not, of course, without some changes. A number of CPC sections are left out, notably entire chapters on proceedings in Magistrate's and High Courts not necessary in codes to be used only in Sharia Courts. The Sharia Criminal Procedure Codes also all omit, unaccountably, a section of the Criminal Procedure Code prohibiting a court from taking cognisance of an adultery case except upon the complaint of the husband or guardian of the woman involved, or, if she is unmarried, of her father or guardian: this section, if present, would have stopped before they started most of the *zina* cases so far prosecuted, including the famous cases of Safiyatu Hussaini and Amina Lawal. The 'Harmonised Sharia Criminal Procedure Code' put forward by the Centre for Islamic Legal Studies of Ahmadu Bello University restores this section, and in Safiyatu's case the Sharia Court of Appeal of Sokoto State went even further, essentially restricting to the guilty person him- or herself the power to bring a *zina* case (Ostien 2007: IV, 189 and V, 15-16).

Only three sections are entirely new to the Sharia Criminal Procedure Codes. Two allow *alkalis* to order restitution or compensation in amounts beyond their powers to impose fines or civil damages (different grades of courts have different powers in these regards). The third relates to *qisas*:

> When a person is sentenced to suffer *qisas* for injuries the sentence shall direct that the *qisas* be carried out in the like manner the offender inflicted such injury on the victim.

This is closely related to the section on mode of execution of death sentences. The Criminal Procedure Code of 1960 had: 'When a person is sentenced to death, the sentence shall direct that he be hanged by the neck till he is dead'. The Sharia Criminal Procedure Codes have instead:

> [...] the sentence shall direct that: (a) he be beheaded; (b) in case of *qisas*, he be caused to die in the like manner he caused the death of his victim...; (c) in case of *zina*, he be stoned to death; and (d) in case of *hirabah* [see note 6], he be caused to die by crucifixion.

Before a sentence of *qisas* is passed, the court is to 'invite the blood relatives of the deceased person, or the complainant as the case may be, to express their wishes as to whether retaliation should be carried out, or *diyah* should be paid or the accused should be forgiven';[26] in some states the court is bound by the wishes expressed, in some it may apparently go against them if it 'sees reason' to do so.

Two other variations from the Criminal Procedure Code raise questions of conflict with other law. Under the CPC, 'an accused person shall be a competent witness in his own behalf in any inquiry or trial'. Most Sharia Criminal Procedure Codes, consistently with Maliki doctrine, have reversed this, saying 'shall not'. But the Evidence Act, by which the Sharia Courts are at a minimum to be 'guided', says 'shall'. The other conflict relates to numbers of witnesses required to prove particular facts. The Evidence Act says that 'no particular number of witnesses shall in any case be required for the proof of any fact'. But Kano's Sharia Criminal Procedure Code requires 'at least four unimpeached witnesses' in prosecutions for *zina* and 'at least two witnesses in other offences' (ibid: IV, 321). The Sharia Penal Codes of two other states go even further, extending the four-witness rule to other types of cases and distinguishing between witnesses depending on whether they are Muslim or non-Muslim, male or female – Niger doubles the number of witnesses required in many types of cases if they are females (ibid: 142). But this raises a final point. The laws establishing the Sharia Courts all lay down that '[t]he applicable laws and rules of procedure for the hearing and determination of all civil and criminal proceedings before the Sharia Courts shall be as prescribed under Islamic law.' Under this general directive the Sharia Courts in all states are applying a great many Islamic rules of procedure and evidence not contained in any enacted code but found only in the classical Islamic sources including the books of *fiqh*. The rules about numbers of witnesses are an example: they are expressed in only some of the codes, but are nevertheless presumably being applied in all the Sharia Courts. This opens up a wide potential for conflict of laws. How two of the conflicts that have arisen so far were resolved, is discussed in Ostien 2007: IV, 190-191.

The Sharia Penal and Criminal Procedure Codes have been in force for a number of years now. Many sentences shocking to modern sensibilities – of amputation of hands for theft, of other forms of mutilation as retaliation for injuries inflicted, of dire forms of execution, including stoning to death for *zina* and stabbing to death with the same knife the condemned man had used to kill his victims – have been imposed by the Sharia Courts (Weimann 2007 studies the cases from 2000 to 2004; more have accumulated since). What is notable, however, is how few of these sentences have actually been executed. Of the probably several hundred sentences of amputation of hands for theft, only three have been carried out, all very soon after sharia implementation started. None of the other sentences of mutilation appear to have been executed, no one has been stoned to death, and Sani Rodi, the double murderer sentenced to be stabbed to death, was hanged instead.

The reason for this is to be found in another provision of all Sharia Criminal Procedure Codes, which lays down that no sentence of the type under discussion can be executed unless and until the state governor expressly consents: and the governors are not consenting. The governors' immediate constituencies are the mostly-Muslim populations of their states, yes. But the governors, more than most other citizens, are brought face to face with the wider interests of their states within the Nigerian federation and internationally, where many pressures have been brought to bear against permitting the execution of types of sentences viewed in most of the rest of the federation and in much of the rest of the world as outmoded and inhumane. Moreover many of the sharia state governors – including Alhaji Ahmad Sani of Zamfara State, who started the sharia implementation ball rolling – have harboured ambitions for national office, including the presidency, and they must have recognised that to permit execution of the many sentences of amputation, stoning to death and severe forms of *qisas* that the Sharia Courts have imposed would ruin their hopes. The result has been that with the exception of the three amputations for theft carried out in the very early days of sharia implementation, the persons on whom such sentences have been imposed are being quietly dealt with in other ways.

Unfortunately, this often amounts simply to leaving them indefinitely in prison waiting (often for years, for small offences) for someone to do something about them. Nevertheless, the fact that the archaic punishments now reinstated in the laws of the sharia states, although they are being imposed as sentences by the Sharia Courts, are not actually being executed, is one important reason why the early Nigerian and world clamour over sharia implementation has so thoroughly subsided. We return to the problem of all those unexecuted sentences in section 10 below.

We have been discussing the Sharia Penal and Criminal Procedure Codes. But we must not leave the subject of criminal law without mentioning the assorted other statutes having penal implications enacted by various sharia states, or in some cases by local governments within the states. Aimed at 'sanitising society', these laws address subjects sometimes also touched on in the penal codes or other existing legislation: liquor, gambling, prostitution, the operation of cinema houses and video and film viewing centres, obscenity, certain sorts of extravagance, women's dressing, hawking by young girls, women riding on commercial motorcycles, unwholesome market practices, begging, and so on. For instance, four states, not content simply to revoke existing liquor licences and refuse to issue any more, have repealed their Liquor Laws entirely and enacted total bans on the manufacture and sale of liquor; Kano has also gone further to ban consumption – by anyone, not just Muslims – on pain of a fine of fifty thousand naira (about € 222) or up to one year's imprisonment or both; although this was enacted in 2004 it has yet to be enforced in the non-Muslim parts of Kano City and it is hard to see how it ever can be. In Gummi Local Government Area of Zamfara State, to try and cut down on frivolous expenditure and unseemly display, 'all forms of procession during wedding and naming festivities', including 'rallies with vehicles, motorcycles, bicycles, donkeys, horses, camels, etc.', and 'all types of musical concerts', including 'drumming, praise singing and dancing in whatever form and howsoever called', are prohibited on pain of a fine of three thousand naira or six months imprisonment or both. Zamfara State has added to existing national anti-corruption legislation by enacting its own Anti-Corruption Commission Law complete with a series of sections defining criminal offences and prescribing punishments. This miscellany of legislation is collected and analysed in Ostien 2007: III.

13.8 Other legal areas, especially economic law

Dividing the sharia up according to Western categories, we have discussed 'Islamic personal law' and 'Islamic criminal law'. On the private law side what is left over is what we have been calling 'other Islamic civil law', including all the rules that still govern the business relations and commercial transactions of millions of northern Muslims on a daily basis: 'sale, loan, bailment, security, hire, lost property, tort, agency, co-proprietorship to mention some of those that commonly come before the courts' (Report 1952: 121).

Like Islamic personal law, other Islamic civil law survived the Settlement of 1960, when Islamic criminal law was abrogated. Again like Islamic personal law, other Islamic civil law as applied in Nigeria has never been codified: it is still applied, primarily in the north's Sharia and Area Courts, on the basis of the Maliki *fiqh*, no doubt modified in favour of local custom in various ways in various places. The difference is that other Islamic civil law was not protected from exposure to the 'English' courts in the ways that Islamic personal law was. The High Courts have long had concurrent original jurisdiction, with the Native Courts and their descendants, of cases arising under all the 'other civil' part of 'native law and custom'; and as we have seen, appeals from the judgments of the Native and subsequently the Area Courts in all such cases, even when governed by Islamic law, were from 1960 directed to the High Courts, not to the Sharia Courts of Appeal.

The primary reason for this difference of treatment seems to have been a felt need in certain circles for uniformity in this 'other civil' area of law:

> Economic development may be retarded by a piecemeal system of law, and it may be fostered if there is one unified system of law which enables all persons in the territory to enter freely into commercial transactions. [...] Laws concerning trade and commerce should, in any event, be uniform throughout a territory. [...] The general law of torts or wrongs, and of restitution for money had and received, should be uniformly applicable to persons of all communities. [...] There should be a general law of contract [...] uniformly applicable to persons of all communities, races or creeds (Allott 1971: 6-8, quoting conclusions of the 1960 London Conference on the Future of Law in Africa).

Joined to the felt need for uniformity was the hope that the High Courts, and the federal appellate courts above them, could perhaps bring it about:

> It is vital that [this part of Islamic and customary law] should be moulded and developed by the superior courts so that it fits in, both with the social needs of the country, and with the rest of the law which is of statutory or exotic origin (Allott 1964: 192).

Whether the decisions of the superior courts have had the desired effect may be doubted. Whether any failure in this regard (as opposed to a thousand other factors) has retarded economic development may also be doubted. Perhaps Allott and his colleagues got the developmental cart before the horse. In Nigeria many subjects crucial to modern economic development – bankruptcy, banks, corporations, insurance, labour, patents, professional occupations, securities, trade and commerce with other countries and between the states, and more – are governed exclusively by federal legislation (1999 constitution, II^{d} Sched. Pt. I). As the economy develops, more and more of it will come under the sway of this legislation and of the lawyers and their common law which the legislation will inevitably carry along with it, and related litigation will go more and more to the High Courts only. In the meantime, most Nigerians, not having reached that stage, are still content to order their affairs in accordance with the law they know, which in the Muslim north is the 'other Islamic civil law' we have been discussing. The programmes of sharia implementation have brought little new in this regard: the venue of litigation changed from Area Courts to Sharia Courts, and, more problematically, the redirection of appeals to the Sharia Courts of Appeal instead of the High Courts. As we have seen (see 13.5), the expansion of Sharia Court of Appeal jurisdiction in the sharia states, beyond the subject of Islamic personal law, to other Islamic civil law and to Islamic criminal law as well, has already been declared unconstitutional by the High Courts of two states, and in the end will probably fail altogether unless the constitution is amended.

A great deal of business in the north is conducted in open-air markets in all the cities and towns. Among the hopes expressed for sharia implementation was that it would purify practices in these markets.

> [U]nscrupulous people have filled our markets and nobody can stop them from what they are doing. [...] The above [particularly the practices of self-imposed middlemen, discussed at length] are the main problems facing us and we hope that as the implementation of Sharia takes shape in this State, such practices will in time be wiped out [...] because they are harmful to both Islam and to Muslims. [...] Government should ensure standard measuring units in terms of weights and volume for goods to ensure fairness in business transactions. Price and quality control task forces should be established at various levels to supervise and enforce strict adherence to Islamic laws on business transactions (from memoranda to the Bauchi State Sharia Implementation Committee, in Ostien 2007: II, 52, 91, 96).

These goals of sharia implementation are being pursued by various organisations that have been charged with these tasks. In Kano State, for instance, the Sharia Commission is to 'initiate and implement policies that will sanitise business transactions in our markets and ensure orderly relationships among the general public in accordance with dictates of Islamic injunctions' (Kano State Sharia Commission Law 2003: §4(iv)). In Zamfara State the Markets Affairs Committee of the Joint Aid Monitoring Group on the Application of Sharia 'is responsible for enlightening the dwellers in our markets on the provisions of Sharia in their respective business transactions. It also mediates and resolves amicably any case between buyers and sellers, ensures the use of Government-approved measures/scales in our markets, monitors any transaction in the market and refers any breach of Sharia law in buying and selling to the appropriate authority' (Joint Aid Monitoring Group, undated). At least one local government, in Yobe State, has enacted a by-law 'to make provision for the prohibition of certain un-Islamic practices such as non-maintenance of standard grains measure, middlemanship and other matters related thereto'; other matters prohibited by this law include 'any act of slaughtering and selling of meats of donkeys, horses, pigs, dogs and other categories of prohibited animals' (Ostien 2007: III, 230-233). Obviously none of this involves new applications of sharia but attempted purging from old applications of corrupting local custom.

We have already mentioned (see 13.5) the attempts in most sharia states to revivify and institutionalise the collection and distribution of *zakat*, with four states going so far as to make payment mandatory and enforceable in the courts (it is not known that any such action has so far been taken). The institutions charged with administering *zakat* are variously the Ministries of Religious Affairs, the Sharia Commissions, or, in six states, new Zakat Boards set up especially for the purpose, but in all cases working with and through the emirate councils, the local governments, and local committees going all the way down to village level. Good is being done. For instance Zamfara State's Zakat Board reports that between 2000 and 2005 it collected N106,855,630.63 (about € 474,915) in *zakat* from which about 35,000 destitute persons benefited, plus 49,590 bags of grain from which almost 124,000 benefited. With the money the sick are being treated, low-cost housing is being built or refurbished, small capital and equipment are being provided to help people start businesses, marriages are being facilitated, debts are being paid off, wayfarers are being assisted, and so on (Zamfara State Zakat and Endowment Board 2006). Several of the new boards also have charge of pious endowments (*awqaf* or *wakfs*), which they are to encourage and to administer as trustees. This is a fairly recent departure: in the early 1950s Anderson found that in Northern Nigeria 'there are no endowments or trusts of the sort termed *ahbas* or *awqaf*, except in so far as mosques are concerned' (Anderson 1954: 217).

Land law is a subject apart. The basic document is the federal Land Use Act, dating from 1978, Chapter L5 of the Laws of the Federation of Nigeria 2004. According to the explanatory note, the Act

> vests all land comprising the territory of each State (except land vested in the Federal Government or its agencies) solely in the Governor of the State, who would hold such land in trust for the people and would henceforth be responsible for allocation of land in all urban areas to individuals resident in the State and to organisations for residential, agricultural, commercial and other purposes, while similar powers with respect to non-urban areas are conferred on Local Governments.

There are thus 'statutory rights of occupancy', granted by the governors, and 'customary rights of occupancy', granted by the local governments. One might have rights under Islamic law *to* either of these forms of R of O, e.g. by inheritance or by prescription. Or one might have rights under Islamic law *under* a customary R of O, such rights being included in the bundle the R of O itself comprises. But here an important historical fact comes in again: even under the Sokoto Caliphate, 'the customary land law remained valid and was enforced by the councils of the sultan and of the emirs' (Schacht 1964: 86, already quoted in section 13.1 above); in the early 1950s Anderson found that '[i]t is in the matter of land tenure that native law and custom has won its most decisive victory over the general ascendancy of the Shari'a in the Muslim Emirates of Northern Nigeria' (Anderson 1954: 184). In other words the strict Islamic sharia has never had much influence on land law as actually practiced even in the Muslim parts of the North. Whether that influence is waxing or waning at the present time we cannot say.

Finally, we come to Islamic banking and insurance, both subject to federal regulation. *Takaful* is a form of insurance that is 'sharia compliant'.

> [Nigeria's] main *takaful* provider, African Alliance Insurance (AAI) [...] began offering life and family *takaful* in 2003 and quickly attracted thousands of applications. This prompted a host of other Nigerian financial organisations to apply to the National Insurance Commission for licences to underwrite *takaful* products (Ford 2007).

Similarly, the Central Bank of Nigeria, responding to a growing demand, has granted permission to a number of banks to offer sharia compliant accounts and other products, and in doing so has showed itself responsive to a growing demand for this kind of banking. Nigeria's first 'fully-fledged Islamic bank', to be known as Jaiz Bank International, has been in the works for some time, but is still trying, it seems (October 2009), to raise the minimum capital reserve required under the banking regulations before it can start in business.

13.9 International treaty obligations and human rights

Since 1960 all of Nigeria's constitutions have included a chapter on Fundamental Rights; this is a standard bill of civil and political rights derived primarily from the European Convention on Human Rights of 1950, enforceable in the courts. Another chapter on 'Fundamental Objectives and Directive Principles of State Policy', articulating broad social, economic, environmental and other aspirations, is not justiciable. In 1981 Nigeria also ratified the African Charter on Human and Peoples' Rights; the Charter was then domesticated in Nigeria in 1983, and has now become Chapter A9 of the Laws of the Federation 2004. This raises a point to which we shall return, which is that in Nigeria, no treaty has the force of law domestically unless and until it is enacted by the National Assembly, then ratified by a majority of the state Houses of Assembly, and finally signed by the president (Art. 12 of the constitution). Nigeria has in fact ratified or adhered to most of the world's human rights instruments, but in some cases domestication has been difficult (Obiagwu & Odinkalu 2003: 229). There is a National Human Rights Commission, mandated to 'deal with all matters relating to the protection of human rights as guaranteed by [the constitution, the African Charter], the Universal Declaration on Human Rights and other international treaties on human rights to which Nigeria is a signatory' (§5 of the National Human Rights Commission Act 1995, now Chapter N46, Laws of the Federation 2004).

In any case the main problem in Nigeria, as in many other countries, is not with the rights but with their realisation. Violation of even the most basic civil and political rights by state organs and their agents, to say nothing of social and economic rights, is a commonplace of everyday life throughout Nigeria. We needn't rehearse these problems here. At least two organisations – the U.S. Department of State and Human Rights Watch – issue annual reports on human rights practices in most countries of the world, including Nigeria; the sad story can be read in those reports.[27] Here we have space only to mention some of the human rights issues raised by the sharia implementation programme in particular.

Criminal law

The reinstatement of Islamic criminal law is the obvious place to start. Three issues immediately suggest themselves. (1) In the sharia states, parallel penal codes are now being applied, under which, for the same crime, different punishments are prescribed for different people depending solely on their religion. This seems clearly to violate the constitutional ban (Art. 42) on discrimination based solely on religion. (2) Article 42 also bans discrimination based on sex, but as we have seen discrimination between male and female witnesses has been reinstated, implicitly under the Sharia Courts Laws and explicitly in some of the Sharia Penal and Criminal Procedure Codes. Notoriously, certain sorts of evidence apply against females only; hence several women, pregnant out of wedlock, have been convicted of *zina* and sentenced to death, while the equally guilty men, denying everything, got off scot-free. (3) The archaic punishments now reinstated seem to many to violate the constitutional ban (Art. 34) on cruel, inhuman or degrading punishment or treatment. This provision has hardly been applied by the Nigerian courts. But courts elsewhere have held that it means, among other things, that punishment must not be disproportionate to the offence; and death for adultery, or amputation of a hand for theft of a cow, today seem disproportionate. Lawful punishments may not be carried out in an unlawful manner; and although the death penalty is lawful in Nigeria, its infliction by stoning, stabbing, or crucifixion should be beyond the bounds. Some punishments have in some jurisdictions been declared unlawful *per se*: the death penalty in South Africa; flogging in the European Union. What of amputation of hands and other forms of mutilation? The Nigerian courts might outlaw these if given the chance in proper cases.

But the interesting point about all these issues is that the courts are not being given the chance to address them, because they are not being raised by parties with standing to do so – i.e. defendants in criminal cases in the Sharia Courts. Most such defendants are not represented by counsel and have no conception of their constitutional rights. Even where counsel – in most cases themselves Muslims – do come in to defend, they are not raising issues that might strike at the very heart of the sharia implementation programme. Why they are not has been discussed in a paper by one of the lawyers who represented Safiyatu Hussaini and Amina Lawal (Yawuri 2007: 133, 139). Meantime, as we have seen, actual execution of the punishments in question has been very rare, the executive and judicial officials of the sharia states, between them, finding ways to limit the many kinds of damage this would cause.

Women

The classical Islamic law of personal status, the family, and inheritance, still applied in Nigeria, discriminates in various ways against women. These issues, some touched on in section 13.6 above, are well known and need no further discussion here. A number of the new enactments of the sharia states also specifically affect women. Most of these have to do in one way or another with trying to keep unrelated males and females apart, or, where they do mix together, with trying to make the females less sexually attractive to the males. Thus, some jurisdictions have made the *hijab*[28] compulsory for all female Muslims ten or more years old appearing in public. Even where no law requires it, the *hijab* has become quasi-compulsory through regulations governing state institutions, including schools, and, outside such institutions, through pressure exerted by *hisbah* groups. Attempts have been made to keep males and females separated in taxis and buses, and to keep females off of commercial motorcycles (all operated by men); the result of the attempts of the Kano *hisbah* to enforce the ban there on commercial motorcycles carrying female passengers has already been described. The regulation of hawking by young girls, a matter of concern in the North for some time because it exposes the girls to unscrupulous men ready to pay for sex or have it by force, has in some states been tightened. Some jurisdictions have tried, without much success it seems, to stop social mixing of Muslim males and females at events like weddings and naming ceremonies (also targeted by sumptuary laws as we have seen). Whether any of this violates the human rights of the women is debatable. In any case women apparently do not feel particularly oppressed by most of it, except where it has impinged on their livelihoods or mobility or on their traditional modes of socialising and enjoyment; there the women have resisted or simply ignored it (Nasir 2007: 105-118). As we noted in section 13.6, Muslim women activists have not so much objected to sharia implementation, as they have tried to work within it, to effectuate rights of women under the sharia which 'merely traditional practices' have denied them (ibid: 100-103).

One such right is the right to education; and here we come to the case of a human rights instrument which Nigeria has ratified, but has not yet been able to domesticate. The U.N. Convention on the Rights of the Child (CRC) was ratified by Nigeria in 1991. The CRC's most controversial provision (in Nigeria) puts the minimum age for marriage at eighteen years. But in Nigeria's Muslim north particularly, girls are often married off much younger, even as early as nine or ten. This obviously keeps them out of school; it also contributes to a serious public health problem in the north, vesico-vaginal fistula, which results from early pregnancy and child-birth. In 2003 the National Assembly took the first step towards domestication of the CRC by enacting it, over considerable (male) Muslim opposition, as the Child Rights Act. Many prominent Muslim women and women's organisations, among others, have since campaigned for ratification of the Child Rights Act by the states. But, despite their efforts, the necessary nineteen states have still (October 2009) not ratified.[29] The fate of the U.N. Convention on the Elimination of All Forms of Discrimination against Women (CEDAW) has been even worse. Although Nigeria ratified CEDAW in 1985, to date no bill for domestication has even been enacted by the National Assembly for ratification by the states.

Non-Muslims

What of the effects of sharia implementation on non-Muslims? In treating of this topic one must be wary of reports in the popular press, allowing for the errors and exaggerations of reporters who are often ill-trained and undisciplined and writing for a credulous public ready to believe anything bad about Islam. Thus, for instance, early reports that all churches in Zamfara State would be demolished and everyone made to learn Arabic were sheer nonsense – which nevertheless did their work of inflaming Christian alarm. One must also try to distinguish between continuing manifestations of long-standing problems for non-Muslims, more specifically Christians, living in the northern states, and anything new resulting from sharia implementation in particular. The various forms of official discrimination against non-Muslims sanctioned by the classical sharia have since Independence been officially in abeyance.[30] Nevertheless, for many years there have been problems, ranging from difficulties with whether and where a church may be built, up to periodic outbreaks of communal violence sparked off by some incident usually involving not only religion but ethnicity and 'place of origin' as well. One variant of this, in Hausaland, is 'indigenous' Hausa Muslims vs. 'settler' Igbo or Yoruba (or other) Christians. In Plateau State, where there were serious outbreaks in 2001, 2004 and 2008, it is rather 'indigenous' Plateau Christians (from one tribe or another) vs. 'settler' Hausa or Fulani Muslims; and so on, there are many such problems all over the country. These problems can unfortunately be said to be 'normal' right now in Nigeria (see e.g. Human Rights Watch 2006; Ostien 2009).

Bad as all that is, the further question is, what new problems for Christians or other non-Muslims living in the sharia states have been added by the programmes of sharia implementation? This is less clear. Non-Muslims are for the most part expressly exempted from the new laws, which are frequently said by the authorities to be 'for Muslims only'. Most importantly, non-Muslims are not subject to the Sharia Penal Codes or to the jurisdiction of the Sharia Courts (unless they consent in writing), and it appears that these rules are being strictly observed. Non-Muslim women and girls are not subject to the rules aimed at separation of the sexes. Sharia-related laws that do affect non-Muslims, such as the new ways of regulating liquor and prostitution, are often approved of by Christian leaders, and in any case are well within the constitutional authority of the states to enact (Ostien & Umaru 2007).

This does not mean that there has not been some additional trouble for non-Muslims in the sharia states resulting from sharia implementation, especially in its early days when the zeal of irregular Muslim enforcers was at a high pitch. For instance, in some places lawless attempts by self-appointed *hisbah* groups to enforce new liquor laws resulted in wanton destruction of property. Christian women sometimes suffered from attempts of over-enthusiastic youths to enforce the *hijab* and separation of the sexes in public transportation. In one famous case, the director of a *federal* medical centre in Bauchi State imposed a new uniform of trousers and *hijab* on his nursing staff, and sacked eleven Christian nurses who refused to comply (they were subsequently reinstated). But most of this sort of thing died down fairly quickly, as the authorities got the social forces unleashed by sharia implementation under better control. Other problems are less acute. Many sharia states are spending considerable sums on new programmes and institutions specifically for Muslims, probably not balanced by proportionate spending on non-Muslims.[31] Non-Muslim access to justice may in some places have been impeded by conversion of the old Area Courts, open to everybody, into Sharia Courts primarily for Muslims. Nevertheless, for some time Christians living in the sharia states have been complaining, not so much about sharia, as about all the many other troubles with Nigeria. The fact that non-Muslims living in the sharia states have not had to face significant new or additional continuing burdens resulting from sharia implementation specifically, is a second important reason (along with non-execution of the archaic penalties being imposed on some Muslims) why the early Nigerian clamour over sharia implementation has so completely died down. Although it continues as an official programme of a number of northern state governments, and is still advancing on various fronts, sharia implementation has nevertheless become largely irrelevant to the national discourse.

13.10 Conclusion

How are the sharia implementation programmes in northern Nigeria likely to develop in the next five to ten years? Let us begin our answer by going back to the matter of the sentences of *hudud* and *qisas* being imposed by the Sharia Courts but never executed, the convicts instead languishing in prison, sometimes for many years, serving time to which they were not sentenced and never knowing their fate. How is this outcome – acceptable to no one – likely to be resolved?

We consider three possibilities.

(i) *The governors, under pressure from ardent and impatient sharia implementers, will at last give their consent to execution of these sentences. The large backlog of pending sentences will be carried out, as will new sentences as they are imposed.*

Probability: practically nil.

This would stir up the Nigerian and world-wide clamour all over again, and result in all sorts of sanctions against any state that tried it. More importantly, there is now little sentiment among Muslims even in the sharia states for such a course. After several years of experience with it, most see that sharia implementation, even in all the useful forms it is taking, will not quickly cure all social ills, as many at first believed. Real progress will require the deepening of religious knowledge and practice among the people; the state also has much work of its own to do; and it will take a long time. Meantime, of all the forms of sharia implementation that have been tried, bringing back Islamic criminal law has proved least useful of all as a means of social betterment, in practice falling in its harshest aspects only on the poor, who need help more than punishment, while the richer and more powerful, despite all their evident sinning, escape unscathed. Few in any social stratum want to see mutilations resume or anyone stoned to death; the governors will not consent.

(ii) *The sharia states will continue to muddle along under the penal legislation now in place, finding various ways to limit and mitigate the damage.*

Probability: high over the near to medium term.

Outright repeal of the Islamic penal legislation so recently enacted would be politically impossible. But three states (Borno, Gombe and Yobe), even eight or nine years after enactment, have not yet even begun to apply their Sharia Penal Codes. In other states the use of the Sharia Courts to try criminal matters is declining, the charging authorities – the police and the public prosecutors – preferring to charge even Muslim accused persons in the Magistrate's and High Courts especially in serious cases. Where they do try criminal matters, the Sharia Courts, recognising that they will not be carried out, are imposing *hudud* punishments less frequently than at first, finding reasons in the doctrine to dispose of such cases in other ways. In *qisas* cases complainants are encouraged to accept *diyah* in lieu of *qisas*; at least one state (Kano) has made this more attractive by enacting that the state must pay if the defendant and his family cannot.

But still: there remain those large backlogs of unexecuted sentences, the convicts still languishing in prison waiting for something to happen, and more will doubtless accumulate. What to do with these cases is very much under discussion in the sharia states. One idea is that the governors, in the exercise of their constitutional prerogative of mercy, should substitute less severe forms of punishment for the ones imposed, or remit the punishments after some suitable time served, or pardon the convicts completely; in fact in 2005 twenty-one persons sentenced to amputation of their hands for theft were set free by the governor of Sokoto State in this way, and the same may also be quietly happening elsewhere. Another idea is that where the governors refuse to act, the courts, or one of them, perhaps the High Court or the Sharia Court of Appeal, should bail the convicts after some time served – presumably subject to revocation in the unlikely event that the governor should at some point decide to execute the sentence after all. Something like this has happened in the case of the Niger State couple, Fatima Usman and Ahmadu Ibrahim, found guilty of *zina* in 2002 and sentenced to stoning to death. They appealed to the Sharia Court of Appeal, which admitted them to bail pending the outcome. While the appeal was pending the jurisdiction of the Sharia Court of Appeal to decide it was called into question by the High Court (see note 15 and accompanying text). The appeal therefore has never been decided by the Sharia Court of Appeal, but it has also never been transferred to the High Court. The couple are still out on bail, and they are unlikely ever to hear from the authorities about this matter again. None of this is very tidy, but for the time being it will probably continue.

(iii) *The federal courts will rule that the penal legislation now in place is unconstitutional. The penal law of all sharia states will revert to what it was before sharia implementation started. All persons still in prison under sentence of hudud or qisas will be released and no more such cases will arise.*

Probability: quite high in the not too distant future.

Consider only the problem of running parallel penal codes in the same jurisdiction, under which different punishments for the same crime are prescribed for different people depending on their religion. This clearly violates the anti-discrimination provisions of the constitution. The probability that it will be challenged in the courts is increased by the fact that the burden of the discrimination falls not only on Muslims, who might not be inclined to complain: sometimes it falls on non-Muslims, who for some crimes can be punished more harshly under the Penal Codes than Muslims can be under the Sharia Penal Codes (Ostien 2007: IV, 14). It is likely, therefore, that before too long somebody will raise this issue, that it will eventually reach the federal Court of Appeal and the Supreme Court, and that they will rule that different penal codes for people of different religions will not do: each state must have one and only one penal code applicable in all courts to all persons regardless of their religion. Which code will that be? We may be sure that non-Muslims will never tolerate application of the Sharia Penal Codes to them. Furthermore, it is the Sharia Penal Codes that expressly discriminate on the basis of religion: for that reason they will likely be struck down, and the Penal Code of 1960, always intended for universal application and still the law in all sharia states, will once again cover the whole field. When this happens, any persons still in prison awaiting execution of sentences of *hudud* or *qisas* under the then-outlawed Sharia Penal Codes will be released, and this problem will finally, and correctly, have been resolved.

It will have been resolved, moreover, in a way palatable to the vast majority of the north's Muslims. They will have done their utmost in the cause of sharia. The responsibility – or the guilt – for saying 'no' once again to the application of Islamic criminal law will fall on the federal constitution and the distant federal judges who administer it. The judges, Muslims and non-Muslims all concurring, will give clear and convincing reasons – reasons that in no way impugn Islamic criminal law *per se* – why under the constitution the Sharia Penal Codes may not be run in parallel with the Penal Codes and must be dropped. Muslims will resign themselves to this as a matter of necessity under present historical circumstances – there being no possibility, in the foreseeable future, of withdrawing from the federation or changing the constitution. Resignation will be easier because of the evident inutility, even unfairness, of trying to apply Islamic criminal law in its full rigor under present social conditions. This is moreover but a very small part of the whole fabric of the sharia, historically often in abeyance even in Muslim lands. Letting it go for the indefinite future once again, perhaps with some sense of relief, the north's Muslims will pray for better times ahead, when, God willing, it will come to pass that circumstances will not be so much against them.

So much for the likely fate of Islamic criminal law, which always tends to monopolise the discussion. Two important points stand out, which also apply to all the other, more useful, forms that sharia implementation is taking. One is the psychological and symbolic importance of having tried so comprehensively to bring Islamic law and Islamic institutions back into the governance of these large Muslim populations, after the depredations of the British and of the post-colonial era. The other is the practical education in modern principles of governance and politics which the continuing sharia implementation effort is bringing with it.

Sharia implementation had to be tried: to work through the obsession, to honour and reconnect with the north's Islamic past, and to restore the Islamic sharia to an honourable position in the Nigerian public space. Being tried, sharia implementation is doing all those things. At the same time, it is teaching many useful lessons all around – about how democracy and constitutionalism and federalism work and what it takes to make them work; about the real causes of social problems; about which programmes of amelioration and improvement will go how far and what more might be needed; and about who is serious and who is not, among others. On all of these subjects sharia implementation has revitalised and complicated the public discourse involving sharia, including bringing in new voices, notably those of women, whose assertions of their own Islamically correct positions against oppressive male practices are making themselves felt. The new Islamic institutions – sharia courts, councils of *ulama*, sharia commissions, *zakat* boards, *hisbah* organisations, and so on – which will still be there when the Sharia Penal Codes pass into history, are providing useful opportunities, for many people, for the responsible expression of Islamic learning and piety and the beneficial application of Islamic precepts in all aspects of life.

These are all good things about sharia implementation: ways in which it has been a positive development for Nigeria itself and for many of its people. These good things are going some distance in their various directions towards helping to resolve some of the 'troubles with Nigeria'. Unfortunately Nigeria's troubles are legion, and, along with the north's most sincere Muslims, it will also take the sustained and co-operative efforts of many other people of all religious and ethnic persuasions all over the country to even begin to address them. Perhaps, if it doesn't just 'fizzle out' as President Obasanjo predicted it would, sharia implementation may at least provide good examples, so sorely needed in Nigeria, of what can practically be done by committed public officials working with ordinary citizens to improve the unfortunate circumstances in which so many of the people are living.

Notes

1 Philip Ostien taught for many years in the Faculty of Law of the University of Jos, Nigeria; he is the author or editor of a number of works on the laws and legal institutions of northern Nigeria and the programmes of sharia implementation that began

there in 1999. Albert Dekker is a reference librarian with the Van Vollenhoven Institute for Law, Governance and Development of Leiden University.

2 World Factbook: see Bartleby 2010: Nigeria. Linguists: see Lewis 2009: Nigeria.

3 *Jihad*: 'struggle' or 'striving', in Islam usually meant in the sense of 'striving in the way of Allah', which may range from personal striving to correct one's own faults to armed warfare against those labeled as unbelievers.

4 *Qadi*: an Islamic judge charged to apply the sharia in cases brought before him. *Alkali*: Hausa form of *al-qadi*.

5 A note on terminology: the Northern Region was sometimes called the Northern Province or Provinces, and similarly for the South = the East + the West. The names the British gave to their high officials in Nigeria also changed from time to time. At the center, Governors-General of the whole country (1914-1919) became Governors (1919-1954) and then Governors-General again (1954-1963). In the regions High Commissioners (1900-1908) became Governors (1908-1913), then Lieutenant Governors (1914-1932), then Chief Commissioners (1932-1951), then Lieutenant Governors again (1951-1954), and finally Governors again (1954-1966).

6 *Hudud*: punishments prescribed by Allah for specific offences, namely, in Maliki law, *zina* (roughly, sex outside of marriage; punishment: either one hundred lashes if the offender has never been married or stoning to death if the offender is or has ever been married); *qadhf* (wrongful accusation of *zina*; punishment: eighty lashes); *sariqah* (theft meeting certain conditions; punishment: amputation of the right hand for the first offence and further amputations for subsequent offences); *shurb* (drinking wine, and by extension imbibing other intoxicants; punishment: eighty lashes); *hirabah* (roughly, armed robbery; punishment ranges from amputation of right hand and left foot up to death by crucifixion depending on circumstances); and *ridda* (apostasy from Islam; punishment: death).

7 *Qisas*: retaliation in kind for woundings or killings: an eye for an eye, etc.

8 *Ulama* (sing. *alim*, scholar): Islamic scholars; those learned in the theology and law of Islam and the literature, mostly in Arabic, proper to these disciplines.

9 In this quotation from Richardson, the order of the last two sentences has been reversed, in hopes of enhancing clarity.

10 *Allahu Akbar*: Allah, God, is great, or the greatest.

11 *Zakat*: the Islamic 'alms' or religious tax, payable annually, in cash or in kind, on most forms of wealth, and meant in various proportions for the support of specified classes of people including the destitute, the poor, those in debt, those in bondage, strangers stranded on the way, new converts to Islam, those 'striving in the way of Allah' including e.g. Qur'anic teachers, and those who administer the tax itself.

12 *Hisbah*: enjoining what is good and forbidding what is wrong according to the sharia; by extension, those who enjoin and forbid.

13 The first amputation was performed on 22 March 2000, when the right hand of Bello Buba Jangebe of Zamfara State was cut off for theft of a cow. Jangebe had declined to appeal the sentence, accepting it as his just desserts under divine law. See e.g. Nigerian *Guardian* of 24 March 2000. The complete records of proceedings and judgments of the courts in the Safiyatu Hussaini and Amina Lawal cases, in English, together with other information and analysis, are given in Ostien 2007, Vol. V.

14 This episode was reported in Abdulfattah Olajide, 'Shariah Gains More Ground in Yorubaland', *Weekly Trust*, 15 November 2002, see http://www.corpun.com/ngj00211.htm.

15 *Mai Tangaram vs. Mai Taxi*, High Court of Borno State, case no. BOM/5A/2002, ruling dated 28 June 2002 (unreported), notice of appeal filed but appeal abandoned; and *Ibrahim Haruna Kuta vs. Ahmadu Galadima*, High Court of Niger State, appeal no. NSHC/MN/6A/2003, ruling dated 12 September 2004, reported in *Law Report of*

Northern Nigeria 2004, 398, appealed on other grounds, CA/A/151/2004, appeal decided 15 March 2006, see http://courtofappeallibrary.gov.ng/index.php?option=com_sobi2&sobi2Task=sobi2Details&catid=3&sobi2Id=325&Itemid=.

16 This and subsequent conversions of naira to euros have been calculated at the rate of 225 to 1, around which the actual rate fluctuated in October 2009.

17 The Supreme Court case is reported, see *Attorney-General of Kano State vs. Attorney-General of the Federation* (2007) 3 NILR 23, see http://www.nigeria-law.org/Attorney-General%20of%20Kano%20State%20v%20Attorney-General%20of%20the%20Federation.htm. For the victory of the Commander and his deputy in their civil suit, see *Daily Triumph*, 29 March 2007, internet edition see http://www.triumph-newspapers.com/archive/DT29032007/right293207.html. The acquittal in the criminal case was reported to one of the authors in a visit to the Kano State Hisbah Board in March 2008.

18 The establishment clause is the first clause of the First Amendment to the U.S. constitution: 'Congress shall make no law respecting an establishment of religion....' The U.S. Supreme Court has read this very broadly: 'Not simply an established church, but any law respecting the establishment of religion is forbidden. [...] The Amendment's purpose was not to strike merely at the official establishment of a single sect, creed, or religion. [...] It was to create a complete and permanent separation of the spheres of religious activity and civil authority.' *Everson vs. Board of Education*, 330 U.S. 1, 31 (1947) (Rutledge, J., dissenting). Or, as Justice Black, writing for the majority, said in the same case: 'In the words of Jefferson, the clause was intended to erect a "wall of separation between Church and State."' Ibid: 16.

19 *Fiqh*: Islamic jurisprudence; the detailed working out of the sharia and its proper application in various circumstances.

20 *Purdah*: the seclusion of women, particularly married women.

21 *Talak*: pronouncement by the husband that he divorces his wife. No special form of words is necessary, nor are witnesses; the mere pronouncement effects the divorce.

22 Cf. Yusuf 1982: 46-47: 'local [customs] among the Hausa and other Moslem societies have become a major source of Islamic law in the Northern States' (giving many examples). Doi 1984 gives interesting details of the lives of Nigeria's Muslims in all parts of the country, including chapters on 'The Life-Cycle of Hausa-Fulani Muslims', 'The Life-Cycle of Yoruba Muslims', 'Sufism and Mystical Practices in Nigeria', and 'Syncretism in the Belief and Practices of Muslims in Nigeria'. The 'Izala' movement, very active in the 1970s and 1980s, was in many ways an effort to purge Nigerian Islam of its syncretism, see Umar 1993 and Loimeier 1997.

23 The situation is actually more complicated than this sentence suggests, in ways it is perhaps unnecessary to explain here: see Ostien 2007: IV, 6-7, 185-186. But the reader should be aware that the following discussion is subject to a variety of exceptions and qualifications.

24 Unless it has unconstitutionally been incorporated by reference under the section on 'General offences' included in some codes, see discussion in 13.5 above.

25 *Ta'azir* offences: in classical Islamic law, offences defined and punished at the virtually unfettered discretion of the *qadi* in particular cases coming before him. In modern penal law these are defined and the punishments are prescribed by statute. Outside northern Nigeria the word is more usually transliterated as *ta'zir*.

26 *Diyah*: compensation that may be paid to the victim of a wounding, or to certain of the victim's relatives in cases of homicide, if the victim or the relatives elect to forego *qisas* and accept the *diyah* instead. Elaborate rules specify the amounts to be paid for which types of injuries. Acceptance of *diyah* in lieu of *qisas* is encouraged; even more meritorious is the free pardon of the perpetrator by the victim or the relatives.

27 For the latest reports on Nigeria, both covering 2008, see U.S. Department of State (2009) and Human Rights Watch (2009).

28 *Hijab*: a covering worn over other clothing, drawn tightly around the face and draping loosely down to the knees.

29 There is even debate among the constitutional lawyers as to whether what has been done so far, by the National Assembly and by the states that have acted on the Child Rights Act, amounts to steps towards "domestication" of the CRC within the meaning of Art. 12 of the constitution at all. Our thanks to Dakas C.J. Dakas for drawing this controversy to our attention, on the complexities of which we cannot enter further here.

30 One example: in *Tela Rijiyan Dorowa vs. Hassan Daudu* 1975 NSNLR 87, the Muslim judge of an Area Court in Sokoto rejected the testimony of a non-Muslim against a Muslim on the ground that it was 'not acceptable in Islamic law'. On appeal the High Court, per another Muslim judge, reversed, holding that under Maliki law the evidence of a non-Muslim against a Muslim is acceptable in all cases of necessity, and in Nigeria 'the necessity [...] has always been with us. This is because this country [...] is not a Muslim country but a country where a large number of its inhabitants are Muslims. Business transactions are bound to occur and have always been occurring between Muslims and non-Muslims. Equally disputes leading to litigations of Muslims against non-Muslims, as in this case, and vice versa must happen and have always been happening. In a large cosmopolitan community as exists in Sokoto engaging in a multitude of commercial transactions it would be impossible to do justice in litigation if a distinction is drawn on the religion a witness adheres to before he could give evidence in a given case. It would [also] be unconstitutional for any law enforced in this country to provide for the rejection of any witness because of his religion' (quoting Art. 28(1) of the 1979 constitution prohibiting discrimination on the basis of religion).

31 To take the extreme case of Zamfara State: there is a Ministry of Religious Affairs dealing almost exclusively with Muslim matters, including the organisation of Islamic preaching and teaching across the state, a Council of Ulama, a Sharia Research and Development Board, a Qur'anic Recitation and Memorization Board, a Religious Preaching and Establishment of Jumu'at Mosque and Idi Praying Ground Commission, a Hisbah Commission, and a Zakat and Endowment Board (all to be documented in forthcoming volumes of Ostien 2007). All of these have their own offices, vehicles and other equipment, paid staffs, and operating budgets.

Bibliography

Alli, M.C. (2001), *The federal republic of Nigerian army: The siege of a nation*. Ikeja: Malthouse Press.

Allott, A.N. (1964), 'The place of African customary law in modern African legal systems', in L. Brown & M. Crowder (eds.), *The proceedings of the first international congress of Africanists* (held at Accra, 11-18 December 1962), 190-196. London: Longmans, Green and Co. Ltd.

Allott, A.N. (1971), 'A note on previous conferences on African law', in University of Ife Institute of African Studies, *Integration of customary and modern legal systems in Africa* (proceedings of a conference held at Ibadan on 24-29 August 1964), 4-16. New York: Africana Publishing Corporation.

Anderson, J.N.D. (1954), *Islamic law in Africa*. London: HMSO.

Anderson, N. (1976), *Law reform in the Muslim world*. London: Athlone Press.

Barends, M.G. (2003), 'Fears of a civil war in Nigeria may not be unfounded', *DevISSues* 5 (1): 18-19.

Barth, H. (1857-1859), *Travels and discoveries in North and Central Africa: being a journal of an expedition undertaken under the auspices of H.B.M.'s government in the years 1849-1855*, 2nd ed. London: Longman, 5 volumes, extracted in A.H.M. Kirk-Greene (ed.), *Barth's travels in Nigeria: Extracts from the journal of Heinrich Barth's travels in Nigeria, 1850-1855*. London: Oxford University Press, 1962.

Bartleby (2010), 'Nigeria', in *World Factbook*, see http://www.bartleby.com/151/country/ni.html (2008 statistics) and https://www.cia.gov/library/publications/the-world-factbook/geos/ni.html (online edition, last accessed February 2010). Washington, D.C.: Central Intelligence Agency.

Boer, J.H. (2003), *Nigeria's decades of blood 1980-2002*. Belleville, Ontario: Essence Publishing.

Doi, A.R.I. (1984), *Islam in Nigeria*. Zaria: Gaskiya Corporation Limited.

Elias, T.O. (1967), *Nigeria: The development of its laws and constitution*. London: Stevens & Sons.

Ezeilo, J. (undated), *Laws and practices relating to womens' inheritance rights in Nigeria: an overview*. See http://www.wacolnigeria.org/lawandpractices.doc.

Flint, J.E. (1960), *Sir George Goldie and the making of Nigeria*. London: Oxford University Press.

Ford, N. (2007), 'Islamic banking strides across Africa', *African Business*, June 2007, see http://findarticles.com/p/articles/mi_qa5327/is_200706/ai_n21290326.

Hiskett, M. (1984), *The development of Islam in West Africa*. London: Longman.

Human Rights Watch (2006), *"They do not own this place": Government discrimination against "non-indigenes" in Nigeria*. See http://hrw.org/reports/2006/nigeria0406/.

Human Rights Watch (2009), *World report 2009: Country summary: Nigeria*. See http://www.hrw.org/sites/default/files/related_material/nigeria.pdf.

Hunwick, J.O. (1992), 'An African case study of political Islam: Nigeria', *The Annals of the American Academy of Political and Social Science* 524(1): 143-155.

Joint Aid Monitoring Group (undated), 'Joint aid monitoring group on the application of sharia in Zamfara state at a glance'. Unpublished document in the possession of P. Ostien, to be published in a forthcoming chapter of Ostien 2007.

Johnston, H.A.S. (1967), *The Fulani empire of Sokoto*. London: Oxford University Press.

Joye, E.M. & K. Igweike (1982), *Introduction to the 1979 Nigerian constitution*. London: Macmillan.

Kano State Sharia Commission Law (2003), *Kano State of Nigeria Gazette* No. 5, Vol. 35, 13 November 2003, pp. A7-A12. The complete law will be published in a forthcoming chapter of Ostien 2007.

Keay, E.R. & S.S. Richardson (1966), *The native and customary courts of Nigeria*. London: Sweet & Maxwell and Lagos: African Universities Press.

Last, M. (1967), *The Sokoto Caliphate*. London: Longman.

Lewis, M.P. (ed.) (2009), *Ethnologue: languages of the world*, Sixteenth edition. Dallas: SIL International. Online version: http://www.ethnologue.com/, with Nigerian languages given at http://www.ethnologue.com/show_country.asp?name=ng.

Loimeier, R. (1997), *Islamic reform and political change in northern Nigeria*. Evanston: Northwestern University Press.

Milner, A. (1969), 'Sentencing patterns in Nigeria', in A. Milner (ed.), *African penal systems*. London: Routledge and Kegan Paul.

Muffett, D.J.M. (1964), *Concerning brave captains; being a history of the British occupation of Kano and Sokoto and of the last stand of the Fulani forces*. London: Andre Deutsch.

Nasir, J.M. (2007), 'Sharia implementation and female Muslims in Nigeria's sharia states', in P. Ostien (ed.), *Sharia Implementation in Northern Nigeria 1999-2006: A Sourcebook*, vol. III, 76-118. Ibadan: Spectrum Books Limited. See also http://papers.ssrn.com/sol3/papers.cfm?abstract_id=1470239.

Nwabueze, B.O. (1982), *A constitutional history of Nigeria.* London: Longman.

Nzeh, C.C.O. (2002), *From clash to dialogue of religions: A socio-ethical analysis of the Christian-Islamic tension in a pluralistic Nigeria.* Frankfurt am Main: European University Studies.

Obiagwu, C. & C.A. Odinkalu (2003), 'Nigeria: Combating legacies of colonialism and militarism', in A.A. An-Na'im (ed.), Human rights under African constitutions: Realizing the promise for ourselves, 211-250. Philadelphia: University of Pennsylvania Press.

Ostien, P. (2002), 'Ten good things about the implementation of sharia in some states of northern Nigeria', *Swedish Missiological Themes* 90 (2): 163-171. See also http://papers.ssrn.com/sol3/papers.cfm?abstract_id=1458996.

Ostien, P. (2006), 'An opportunity missed by Nigeria's Christians: The 1976-78 shari'a debate revisited', in B. Soares (ed.), *Muslim-Christian encounters in Africa,* 221-255. Leiden and Boston: Brill. See also http://papers.ssrn.com/sol3/papers.cfm?abstract_id=1464339.

Ostien, P. (ed.) (2007), *Sharia implementation in northern Nigeria 1999-2006: A sourcebook.* Vol. I: *Historical background;* vol. II: *Sharia implementation committee reports and related white papers;* vol. III: *Sanitizing society;* vol. IV: *The sharia penal and criminal procedure codes;* vol. V: *Two famous cases.* Ibadan: Spectrum Books Limited. See also http://www.sharia-in-africa.net/pages/publications/sharia-implementation-in-northern-nigeria.php.

Ostien, P. (2009), 'Jonah Jang and the Jasawa: Ethno-religious conflict in Jos, Nigeria', *Muslim-Christian Relations in Africa,* August 2009, online publication hosted at http://www.sharia-in-africa.net. See also http://ssrn.com/abstract=1456372.

Ostien, P. & J.D. Gamaliel (2002), 'The law of separation of religion and state in the United States: a model for Nigeria?', in S.O.O. Amali et al. (eds.), *Religion in the United States of America,* 14-32. Ibadan: published for the American Studies Association of Nigeria by Hope Publications Ltd. See also http://papers.ssrn.com/sol3/papers.cfm?abstract_id=1458421.

Ostien, P. & M.J. Umaru (2007), 'Changes in the law in the sharia states aimed at suppressing social vices', in P. Ostien (ed.), *Sharia implementation in Northern Nigeria 1999-2006: A sourcebook,* vol. III, 9-75. Ibadan: Spectrum Books Limited: See also http://papers.ssrn.com/sol3/papers.cfm?abstract_id=1460769.

Perham, M. (1937), *Native administration in Nigeria.* London: Oxford University Press.

Peters, R. (2003), *Islamic criminal law in Nigeria.* Ibadan: Spectrum Books Limited.

Rasmussen, L. (1993), *Christian-Muslim relations in Africa: The cases of northern Nigeria and Tanzania compared.* London: British Academic Press.

Report (1952), *Report of the native courts (northern provinces) commission of inquiry.* Lagos: Government Printer.

Report (1958), *Report of the commission appointed to enquire into the fears of minorities and the means of allaying them.* London: Her Majesty's Stationary Office.

Richardson, S.S. (2001), *No weariness: The memoir of a generalist in public service in four continents, 1919-2000.* Wylye, Wiltshire: Malt House Publishing.

Schacht, J. (1957), 'Islam in Northern Nigeria', *Studia Islamica* VIII: 123-146.

Schacht, J. (1964), *An introduction to Islamic law.* Oxford: Clarendon Press.

Sossou, M. (2002), 'Widowhood practices in West Africa: The silent victims'. *International Journal of Social Welfare* 11 (3): 201-209.

Umar, M.S. (1993), 'From sufism to anti-sufism in Nigeria', in L. Brenner (ed.), *Muslim identity and social change in sub-Saharan Africa.* Bloomington and Indianapolis: Indiana University Press.

U.S. Department of State (2009). *2008 human rights report: Nigeria.* See http://www.state.gov/g/drl/rls/hrrpt/2008/af/119018.htm.

Weimann, G.J. (2007), 'Judicial practice in Islamic criminal law in Nigeria 2000 to 2004 – A tentative overview', *Islamic Law & Society* 14 (2): 240-286.

Yawuri, A.M. (2007), 'On defending Safiyatu Hussaini and Amina Lawal', in P. Ostien (ed.), *Sharia Implementation in Northern Nigeria 1999-2006: A Sourcebook*, vol. V, 129-139. Ibadan: Spectrum Books Limited. See also http://papers.ssrn.com/sol3/papers.cfm?abstract_id=1470205.

Yusuf, A.B. (1982), *Nigerian legal system: Pluralism and conflict of laws in the northern states.* New Delhi: National Publishing House.

Yusuf, B. (1993), 'Da'wa and contemporary challenges facing Muslim women in secular states – A Nigerian case study', in N. Alkali et al. (eds.), *Islam in Africa: proceedings of the Islam in Africa conference*, 276-295. Ibadan: Spectrum Books Limited.

Zamfara State Zakat and Endowment Board (2006), 'Achievements so far recorded 2000-2005'. Unpublished document in the possession of P. Ostien, to be published in a forthcoming chapter of Ostien 2007.

14 Towards comparative conclusions on the role of sharia in national law

Table of contents

14.1 Introduction

Preliminary analysis

This chapter draws some preliminary conclusions from the country studies. It does not yet attempt to present a comprehensive analysis of all issues addressed in the country studies. More extensive work is needed to expose and analyse the rich harvest of these studies. A publication including full comparative analysis is planned for the near future.

Different uses of the term sharia

Many people assume and propagate that sharia is a uniform thing, a fixed, unchangeable set of norms that is binding upon all Muslims. On the other hand, we can all see a diversity of schools and interpretations of Islam. In section 1.2 it was suggested that this contradiction stems from conflating the different ways in which the term 'sharia' is used. The twelve country studies have illustrated the co-existence of these different uses of the term sharia beyond any reasonable doubt. Whereas sharia in Saudi Arabia equals a set of puritan interpretations, which have kept the legal status of women quite similar to the times when its rules were developed by the classical scholar al-Hanbali, in Egypt, Morocco or Indonesia sharia manifests itself quite differently, for example in moderate, contemporary interpretations which provide for a better legal position of women in marriage law.

The chapters provide abundant historical evidence of shifts in the interpretation of sharia as well as of a great variety in orientations both among and within national legal systems. To pick just one example, we trace Iran one century back, when it witnessed a movement that culminated in the Constitutional Revolution of 1905-1911.

> Mirza Mohammad Hossein Na'ini (1860-1936), the most high-ranking cleric to support the movement, provided for instance religious arguments for the rejection of absolutism and a defence of constitutionalism. In contrast, the main clerical opponent of the constitution, Sheikh Fazlollah Nuri, argued that ideas of democracy and freedom, the reforms advocated by the constitutionalists, and the establishment of a parliament to enact legislation, were in contradiction with Islam. (Mir-Hosseini *intra*, see 8.1)

The common assumption that sharia is *binding*, i.e. that Muslims are exclusively subject to classical sharia, is also based on misconceptions. This book illustrates that since the early Islamic states of the eighth and ninth centuries sharia always existed alongside of other normative systems which could be as binding as or even more binding than particular versions of sharia. Whilst religious scholars have always argued that God's divine law is binding upon believers, in practice the application of the doctrine has often been made subordinate to other norms, for example to the state's definition of the public interest, or to local custom. This is also the case in states that are supposed to have 'completely' islamised their laws, like the Sudan.

> At present, the Sudan possesses a legal system that is characterised by a high degree of legal pluralism. The heritage of the common law is, despite the ups and downs of twenty years of Islamisation efforts, still clearly visible in two important aspects: first of all, certain laws of the time of the condominium are still valid, and, secondly, more recent legislation can be traced back to the condominium in terms of organisation and wording. Most significantly, despite efforts of the Bashir government to marginalise it, customary law is still of major importance in the rural areas of the Sudan. It is estimated that as much as 80 per cent of all cases in the Sudan are judged in accordance with customary law. (Köndgen *intra*, see 5.10)

The essentialist trap

Misconceptions about the 'unchangeable' and 'binding' nature of sharia are not just isolated opinions. They are indispensable building bricks of an essentialist perspective, which conceptualises 'the sharia', 'the Islamic law', 'the Islam', the Muslim people', 'the Muslims' as fixed and delineated entities. In this perspective, particular provisions in authoritative texts are held to represent the essence of a whole Islamic civilisation, an Islamic culture, and a living Islamic legal system. Such essentialism is, in the first place, the trademark of puritans in the Muslim world. In addition, it provides the main rationale for Islamophobia in the West. The simple reduction of the values and norms of millions of people to a few daunting notions, is a familiar tool in the discourse of ethnic politics. Clearly, essentialists are not impressed by the fact that such reduction often leads to generalised assumptions – for example, 'women do not work under Islam' as Ibn Warraq put it in *Why I am not a Muslim* – which are in stark contrast with transparent social realities.

The puritan discourse of how sharia has been incorporated in national law, is equally essentialist: the incorporation has been all wrong, corrupt and Western, and only complete replacement with 'true sharia' can bring salvation. As explained in section 1.5, this is only one of several ways to look at the incorporation of sharia.

'Structural death' or 'incorporation' of sharia?

A different view of incorporation holds that the sharia's actual structures of authority – including the jurisconsult (*mufti*), the judge (*qadi*), and the law professor (*sheykh*) – and the discursive and cultural practices that had always existed within the sharia, met their 'structural death in the nineteenth and early twentieth centuries' (Hallaq 2009: 15-16). For those who have been worried about the recent expansion of sharia, it is perhaps surprising to learn from a leading academic scholar in this field that sharia, as an organic system, is no more; in his previous work Hallaq (2003) found this an understandable reason for 'Muslim rage'. His analysis is shared by Feldman who writes about the sharia: 'Most devastating, the one institution that historically played a central role in establishing and maintaining the rule of law in Islamic states has been destroyed' (Feldman 2008: 126). He deplores this big role reversal, which transferred final authority in legal matters to the state, calling it plainly a 'disaster' (ibid: 7).

The country studies in this book confirm that most Muslim states – with the exception perhaps of Saudi Arabia – have indeed replaced those age-old structures and practices with new legal institutions which are shaping and reshaping the legal rules of the present. Indeed we could conclude with Cammack that '[T]he acquisition by the modern state of a virtual monopoly over law-making presents the Islamic legal tradition with one of its most basic challenges' (Cammack 2005: 190).

At the same time, the vast majority of contemporary Muslim-majority states, confronted with the imposing heritage of sharia, decided to preserve important elements. They probably realised that this also is what most of their citizens prefer and expect. In *Who speaks for Islam,* Esposito and Mogahed (2007) confirm on the basis of large-scale opinion polls, that there is widespread support 'for sharia in the Muslim world' (Esposito & Mogahed 2007: 35). However, the desired sharia seems not to be of the classical and static type, and does not fully depend on the old structures of authority. For according to Esposito and Mogahed, the Gallup data demonstrate that clear majorities of respondents throughout the Muslim world find that women should have the same legal rights as men (ibid: 51). Generally, the support for democracy and human rights is also significant (ibid: 47). Muslims seem to entrust key decisions in law and governance to the 'new' legal institutions of the state, rather than to the old structures of sharia authority.

> Significant majorities in many countries say religious leaders should play no direct role in drafting a country's constitution, writing national legislation, drafting new laws, determining foreign policy and international relations, or deciding how women dress in public or what is televised or published in newspapers. Others who opt for a direct role tend to stipulate that religious leaders should only serve in advisory capacity to government officials. (Esposito and Mogahed 2007: 50)

In section 14.5 we will further explore how governments, in matters of incorporation of sharia, are often forced to steer a middle course between the main opposing forces and their discourses, namely puritans, religious scholars, tribal and community leaders, and human rights critics at home and abroad. Struggles and negotiations are conducted in several governance arenas, of which the 'new' legal institutions, government, parliament, judiciary, and, last but not least, the bureaucracy, play crucially important roles. It remains here to say that the preservation of important elements of sharia, whether in the puritan or moderate form, continues to be a factor which cannot be ignored in any discussion of legal systems in most Muslim countries.

Not an overview of human rights violations

The country studies in this book sadly confirm the well-known fact that in most developing countries violations of human rights occur frequently and systematically. Up-to-date information on such violations is available from websites and reports of monitoring committees of international human rights treaties, of governments and non-governmental organisations like Amnesty International, Human Rights Watch, or Freedom House. However, unlike many assume, violations in Muslim countries often have little to do with sharia. Abiad (2008: 173-175) even concludes on the basis of another comparative research of Muslim countries, that 'it is not Sharia which is preventing the implementation of human rights', but a 'lack of political will' of the governments (ibid: 173). In contrast, Abiad argues, 'the very nature of Sharia demonstrates the potential of reform in the interest of human rights' (ibid: 173).

Our study finds that a number of violations is directly related to norms and practices based in Islamic legal traditions. The fact that similar violations elsewhere may be based on Christian, Hindu, Buddhist or other convictions and ideologies, does not diminish that relation. In many cases, such human rights violations are condoned by the state, and in certain cases they are even officially justified by sharia-based state law.

Although this book does not systematically list human rights violations, as there is no need to reiterate the existing reports, the authors' chapters are thoroughly informed, if not motivated by the said concerns. In our probing of national law, we have, often implicitly, explored and assessed the human rights protection systems available in the respective countries. It is in view of the sharia-related violations of human rights that this study has defined four areas of main concern (see 1.3). Discrimination of women, freedom of religion (apostasy), and cruel corporal punishments are among the concerns investigated. Other important concerns, for example the legal position of non-Muslims and non-orthodox Muslims, of atheists, and of homosexuals, could not be included in this study.

Structure of the chapter

Following these words of introduction, the second section (see 14.2) will summarise historical changes in the relationship between sharia and national law. The section will start with developments in most recent decades, and then unfold the trends and changes which took place in relevant historical periods, going back in time. In section 14.3 we will consider the law presently in force in the twelve countries under review and draw preliminary comparative conclusions about the four concerns identified in the introduction, i.e. the supremacy of sharia; the legal status of women; degrading corporal punishments; and the compatibility of sharia with human rights. The next section (see 14.4) will compare the twelve countries under review in respect of the degree to which sharia-based rules, especially those of a puritan orientation, have actually been incorporated in their respective legal systems. The final section 14.5 will look at the incorporation of sharia as a problem of governance. It will consider several aspects of governance: how has the state been incorporating sharia amidst many other concerns with development and governance; the pressure of puritan politics and the religious establishment of scholars; customary law and its complex relationship with sharia; attitudes of the West; and, in conclusion, it will look at the conditions under which the relation between sharia and national law may further develop on the long and winding road to justice.

14.2 Understanding the present by the past

The twelve country chapters in this book examine historical changes and trends in the relationship between sharia and national law. For the purpose of comparison they use a common periodisation. Section 1.6 explains why the years 1800, 1920, 1965 and 1985 were selected as turning points.

1985 up to the present: taking stock of recent developments

One of the most striking findings of this study is that the first wave of stringent islamisation of law, which took place between 1972 and 1985 in no less than four countries, was not followed by a similar second wave. As the country studies demonstrate, since the mid 1980s core countries of the Islamic revolution such as Iran, Pakistan, the Sudan – as well as Libya – have shown second thoughts about some of their early legal reforms. Actually, most of the countries under review have shown a sense of moderation, by either rolling back on some of the earlier reforms (Iran), or moving – slowly or rapidly – towards constitutionalism (Saudi Arabia, the Sudan, Afghanistan, Turkey), continuing liberalisation of marriage laws (Egypt, Morocco, Pakistan), restraint in the execution of cruel corporal punishments (Pakistan, Malaysia, Nigeria), significant progress in democracy and human rights (Indonesia), or just maintaining the *status quo* (Mali). Their record in ratification of human right treaties confirms this trend (see 14.3).

In Afghanistan, the puritan Taliban regime was replaced with a constitutional regime, though by military force. In Indonesia, after Suharto's fall in 1998 a regime emerged, which was much more devoted to the rule of law, democracy and human rights. Liberal reforms of marriage law were notably carried through by innovative legislation in Egypt (2000) and Morocco (2004), by amendments of the civil code of Iran (see 8.6), and by case law in Pakistan (see 9.6). The expansion of sharia criminal law in particular, which had caught worldwide attention in 1979 (Pakistan) and in 1983-1984 (the Sudan), lost much of its practical application. This became clear also in North Nigeria, where sharia criminal law had been introduced only in 2000/2001. In Iran the orthodox fervor of the revolution and its massive support base have declined over the last decade; even the conservative Council of Guardians had to tolerate a more pragmatic body above it. Saudi-Arabia announced a major judicial reform in 2008 and appointed its first female cabinet minister in 2009.

Despite this evidence of moderation, there were also some signs of reverse trends. The most evident examples include: the introduction of retribution punishments in Pakistan (1997); the rolling back of marriage law reform in Malaysia (1994); the abovementioned introduction of sharia criminal law in Northern Nigeria (2000) and in other sub-national entities, including Indonesia's remote province of Aceh. In Iran, as Mir Hosseini describes (see 8.6), at the time of writing parliament is revising a conservative draft Family Protection Law, which women's rights defenders have chosen to call an 'Anti-Family Bill', and a bill making apostasy a criminal offence.

On balance, however, trends of moderation and gradual liberalisation seem to outweigh the trends in opposite direction. This conclusion goes against the publications of influential academics such as Huntington and Lewis, and strongly suggests that the alarmist report published by Freedom House in 2005 stating that the world in the last 25 years has witnessed the rapid replacement of liberal Western law by extreme sharia, is at best incorrect (Marshall 2005).

1965 to 1985: the rise, flowering and effect of the Islamic revival in law

The remarkable Islamic 'Revolutions' of Iran and Pakistan (1979), and the Sudan (1983) were the result of both domestic as well as international processes. Development policies had been rather unsuccessful in those countries. The centralised, authoritarian, mostly socialist, ideology of the 1960s was showing cracks, and so were the reputations of ruling political elites. Governments and politicians felt a strong pressure from traditional elites, such as religious scholars and tribal chiefs, and had to respond, even if only for tactical reasons. During this period religious scholars and puritans made their voices better heard throughout the Muslim world, and in Iran under Khomeini the clergy even seized power.

The international impact was tremendous, especially in the Muslim world. Islamists everywhere were encouraged to gear up their opposition against governments. Their puritan ideology featured three elements: a broad and bitter critique of the government in power; an outspoken dislike of the West because of its political, military, and economic dominance and of what is seen as its moral decadence; and a competing governance model, i.e. the 'Islamic state', which should 'introduce the sharia' and replace 'Western law'. General Zia-ul-Haq, who seized power in Pakistan in 1979 and General Numeiri, who had long been in power in the Sudan, both sensed the legitimising effects of this ideology, and decreed islamisation of law.

Because Islam in most Muslim countries is Sunni, whereas Islam in Iran is Shii, most puritan movements were more open to Sunni missionary movements. These were often sponsored by Saudi Arabia, while the Egyptian Muslim Brotherhood served as a model for political programmes and organisational methods. The aversion of the Brotherhood and similar movements to the West dated back to the times of its founding in 1928 by Hassan al-Banna; only a while ago most Muslim countries had been under European colonial rule. After struggling for independence they were liberated from foreign rule, and yet many felt that Western domination had still not disappeared.

1920 to 1965: decolonisation, developmental ambitions of new states, and their limits

In this period colonial rule came to an end, with a first wave of independence of Muslim countries in the 1920s, and a second after 1945. Modernisation, or 'development' as it came to be called after 1950, became a declared goal for almost all new governments. Reforms in the Muslim world were sometimes quite radical.

> [I]n 1920 [...] the Ottoman Empire collapsed and the Turkish Republic rose from its ashes. The founder of the Republic, Kemal Atatürk, tolerated the continued existence of Islamic law in the Republic for only a very short period of time. Especially during the period 1924-1929, a number of voluntary receptions of codes of law from Western countries gave Turkey its civilian, secular character. The Constitution of 1924 confirmed the principle of laicism as a key foundational principle of the Republic. After the 1930s, the influence of the sharī'a on national law evaporated. (Koçak *intra,* see 6.10)

Inspired by the Turkish example, strong modernist rulers, such as Reza Shah in Iran and King Amanullah in Afghanistan, also distanced themselves from the religious establishment and classical sharia in order to create strong nation-states with modern legal systems. In Egypt, the first post-independence cabinets opted for more gradual modernisation. The same goes for Morocco, which had become a French Protectorate in 1912. In the Arab paeninsula King Abd al-Aziz was building the nation-state of Saudi Arabia, having just united, as Van Eijk puts it 'the cosmopolitan Hijaz' in the West 'with his own conservative Wahhabist followers in the Najd' (see 4.2).

From the 1950s onwards, almost all newly independent states embraced the ideology of development, cherishing the twin goals of nation-building and socio-economic progress. Consequently, countries such as Egypt, Indonesia, Pakistan, the Sudan, Malaysia, Mali, Morocco, and Nigeria, also set out to build for themselves a modern national legal system, as an instrument for social transformation. Especially after World War II, socialism, with its atheistic standpoint, exerted much influence in developing countries. 'Arab Socialism', emphasising equality – also between men and women – became a dominant ideology in the Middle East under the leadership of Egypt's President Nasser. Under the new nationalist but authoritarian regimes, the displacement, nationalisation and reform of sharia, which had started in the nineteenth century (see below), were accelerated. Nasser, for example, closed the religious family courts in 1955, placing jurisdiction for marital and inheritance cases under the umbrella of a unified, national judiciary.

> [...] the Nasser government saw the existence of the separate family courts as a legacy of Ottoman colonisation [...]. (Berger and Sonneveld *intra*, see 2.2)

The religious scholars who had once been the leading authorities of sharia, found themselves in a third-rank position; tribal and community leaders, who had been in charge of customary law for so long, were also marginalised.

However, by the mid-1960s it appeared that many states had achieved less security and socio-economic development than they had hoped for and promised. The fact that leading politicians, civil servants and army officers used their public positions for private gain, began to create widespread resentment. Also, government's attempts to unify and modernise sensitive areas of law, such as family law and property law, bringing them in accordance with rule-of-law standards, caused considerable resistance (Allott 1980). Ethnic conflicts, separatist movements, military coups and other conflicts threatened the stability of many young states.

Although modern legislation existed on paper, its implementation and enforcement proved disappointing. As the people expressed dissatisfaction with their governments, traditional leaders saw opportunities to regain lost powers. Many people loosing faith in the state resorted to the mosque and the imam, even if only for Friday prayers, for marriages, burials, and rituals. Prominent religious scholars, like the Iranian Ayatollah Khomeini, bided their time in seminaries. Perhaps the time was ripe for a successful counter-movement against the changes that had begun to overtake the Muslim world more than 150 years earlier.

1800 to 1920: European expansion, modernisation, colonial pluralism, and the rise of nationalism

When Napoleon and his famous mission arrived in Egypt in 1798, sharia had been the prevailing legal system for more than thousand years (see 1.6). The Ottoman Empire had carried on this tradition throughout the Middle East for centuries. But around 1800 processes of rapid modernisation were set in motion under the influence of European expansion, and '[T]he whole complex edifice that supplied religious authority in Islam started to crumble' (Abou el-Fadl 2007: 35).

The introduction of European legal concepts took place in two ways. In the Ottoman Empire, Egypt and Persia it was a matter of deliberate efforts by local elites and voluntary reception, whereas in Asia and Africa the process occurred rather through colonial legislation and adjudication. Colonial expansion of European law occurred in the countries under review which are today known as Indonesia, Malaysia, Pakistan as well as Mali, Morocco, Nigeria, and the Sudan. Indigenous rulers, chiefs, and religious office-bearers were incorporated in colonial structures led by European non-Muslims, and thus moved to a secondary position.

The advance of modern law also sealed the fate of classical sharia. The Tanzimat reforms in the Ottoman empire introduced large scale codification in all important areas of law. Secular courts were introduced to adjudicate cases on the basis of national law codes. Meanwhile modernist religious scholars like the polyglot al-Afghani and Muhammad Abduh in Egypt – which was still under formal Ottoman authority – proclaimed the reopening of the gate of free interpretation of sharia (*ijtihad*), and prepared for cautious codification and modernisation of sharia-based marriage law.

Meanwhile, in the British, French and Dutch overseas territories, colonial governments enacted a massive amount of new legislation, which had nothing to do with sharia. New secular courts were established, whilst sharia courts and other indigenous courts were regulated and restricted. In areas, where European law overlapped with sharia or customary law, new forms of mixing took place. In Britain's colonies an enlightened 'Anglo-Muhammedan' law emerged through legislation and case law. In Indonesia and other colonies, the government elevated 'customary law' to serve as the law of the indigenous population, whereas sharia was recognised only in so far as it was part of living customary law. So, in different ways sharia law and institutions were restricted or even pushed aside. A citation from the chapter on Nigeria gives a good example of the advance of European law.

> Public law, including Orders in Council of the Government of Britain (in the case of Nigeria's colonial constitutions) and some of the enactments of the Governors-General, was of course 'English'. The British also enacted various other laws specific to Nigeria, including penal laws, and imported their statutes of general application, their doctrines of equity, and their common law. English law was applied in English courts staffed by British judges, according to British rules of procedure and evidence. On its private side, English law was originally intended for application primarily to non-natives, and most by far of all cases coming before Nigerian courts – upwards of 90 per cent, including, for a long time, criminal cases – were handled in the Native Courts according to native law and custom. The proviso was that

> no native law or custom should be enforced which was 'repugnant to natural justice, equity and good conscience [as determined by the British] or incompatible either directly or by necessary implication with any [English] law for the time being in force' (Keay & Richardson 1966: 233-238). Under this rule the penalties imposed in the Native Courts, in particular, were quickly brought under control. Mutilation – in the North whether as *hudud* or as *qisas* – was abolished; death sentences had to be carried out in a humane manner (Milner 1969: 263-264). Various means were used to enforce the repugnancy rule, including supervision of the Native Courts by British administrative authorities and finally, in 1933, rights of appeal from the Native to the English courts. (Ostien *intra*, see 13.1)

A remarkable exception to these patterns of European legal expansion was Saudi Arabia. No Western power had the ambition to conquer this vast desert land, so that the power of the ruling Saudi tribes could remain connected with radical-puritanical Wahhabi doctrine, as it had been since the eighteenth century. Under Wahhabi influence classical sharia prevailed unimpaired as law.

Back to the present

It is safe to say that the main historical turning point in the relation between sharia and national law occurred as the state in the nineteenth and twentieth century appropriated the leading part in legal development, a role hitherto played by the religious scholars (*ulama*). As explained in the introduction, before 1800, in the Muslim world, a ruler's power to make laws was derived from the sharia-principle of *siyasa*, which required that the laws remained within the limits of sharia (see 1.6). The authority to decide whether this was the case, rested, according to sharia, with the scholars – a system which is often regarded as the classical Islamic version of constitutional checks and balances (Feldman 2008). This led to a situation in which legal systems in the Muslim world consisted of two branches – scholars' law and state law – which could come together at the top in the Sultan-Caliph, and below him in state-appointed *qadis* and *muftis*.

After the Ottoman reforms and the European colonial administration of justice had prepared the ground for the take-over by the nation-state, from 1920 onwards a growing number of independent Muslim states began to introduce their own policies regarding incorporation. It was not their main concern, though. The governance challenges for the newly independent, developing, Muslim countries were daunting. From the 1950s until the 1970s separatism, civil wars, and military coups were frequent. Despite the fact that many states succeeded in stabilising society, and making progress in many areas (agriculture, industry, education, public health), partly with the help of oil revenues, much went wrong too.

There seems to be consensus on the idea that in that period most developing states suffered from major governance failures. Political elites made policies for the common people without giving them a political voice. Bureaucracies blocked and frustrated private entrepreneurship. Individual rights were systematically subordinated to the public goods of 'stability' and 'development'. Politicians who now had the power to manage vast public funds became self-serving, and corruption increased. Most countries were unable to maintain effective courts, which were to control illegal practices and provide remedies. And, finally, there was a serious underestimation of people's attachment to tradition in the form of symbols, structures and authorities of religion and custom.

In response to the above-mentioned governance failures a range of domestic and transnational actors, began to promote democratisation, privatisation, human rights, anti-corruption measures, and rule-of-law policies, all with different motives. Also part of this counter-movement were the *ulama* and their supporters, who called for religious and cultural authenticity. The latter translated into the broad transnational trend often indicated as the Islamic resurgence or awakening, or the advent of political Islam. While the diversity among islamist movements was enormous, most of them shared the twin goals of introducing an 'Islamic state' as well as 'the sharia', instead of the pre-existing constitutions and laws which were considered 'bad' and 'Western'. The next section discusses the effects of the efforts to islamise national law, since Iran's 'Islamic revolution' of 1979. How did the Muslim countries under review deal with the various demands to radically change their constitutional, family and criminal laws? And are the alarmist assumptions about the islamisation of law, so common in the West, actually justified?

14.3 Concerns and issues, preliminary findings

In the introduction I identified four widely shared concerns about islamisation of law, and divided them in concrete issues. This section will consider what preliminary conclusions can be drawn about these concerns and issues on the basis of our country studies.

Supremacy of sharia

Scope

To which extent has sharia influenced the national legal systems as a whole? Most country studies demonstrate clearly that most areas of law have not been pervaded by sharia-based law. Saudi Arabia is the main exception, followed at a distance by Iran, and then perhaps by the Sudan. The majority of moderate governments strives to ensure that national law meets modern socio-economic needs. This has meant that in many areas governments did not replicate classical sharia. Perhaps surprisingly, Ayatollah Khomeini himself shared this view.

> In order to facilitate legislation considered to be socially necessary, even if it was in conflict with sharia, Khomeini gave a fatwa in 1981 granting parliament the authority to proclaim such legislation with absolute majority votes. Subsequently, the Guardian Council ignored this fatwa and refused to approve much legislation promulgated on the basis of it. Khomeini responded in 1984 with another fatwa authorising parliament to create legislation based on the Islamic principles of social necessity (*zarurat*) and expediency (*maslahat*) with a two-thirds majority.
> (Mir-Hosseini *intra*, see 8.3)

> Khomeini had written that the Leader's mandate is absolute, that he can even order the suspension of the primary rules of Islam (for example regarding prayer or pilgrimage) if the interests of the Islamic state (*maslahat-e nezam*) demand it. Clearly, when Khomeini had to choose between the sharia and the survival of the state, he chose the latter (Arjomand 1992: 156-158).
> (ibid, see 8.4)

In addition, it becomes clear that in eleven of the twelve countries the impact of the colonial legal heritage of civil law and common law has remained substantial (see Table 2 in 1.4). This does not apply only to 'sharia-neutral' areas of law – such as environmental law, labour law or telecommunications law, where no influences of *fiqh*-texts are found – but also to the politically 'delicate' areas where *fiqh* has traditionally played an important role, such as family and inheritance law. Harding's observation about Malaysia that

> The constitution and the institutions of the common law have indeed provided the means whereby accommodation between two fundamentally contradictory conceptions of legality has been achieved. (Harding *intra*, see 11.10)

could also apply to legislation and the rulings of supreme courts in other common-law countries as well as in civil-law countries. In Egypt, a civil law country, the scope of sharia, potentially widened by the 1980 amendment of Article 2 of the constitution, is in fact delineated by the Supreme Constitutional Court, which

> has laid down a few important ground rules: first, it is the only court allowed to rule on (in)compatibility of Egyptian legislation with the sharia; and, second, only legislation implemented after 1980 must conform to the principles of the sharia. Furthermore, the Constitutional Court holds a restrictive view of what is encompassed by obligatory rules of sharia and, consequently, accords the legislature a wide margin of legislative freedom. (Berger and Sonneveld *intra,* see 2.4)

Territory

To which extent has sharia-based law been enacted at sub-national levels, notably in specific states, provinces or districts? In the 1990s waves of democratic decentralisation led to the empowerment of sub-national entities – states of a federation, provinces, districts, towns. Some of them decided to enact sharia-related regulations, usually to promote Islamic 'virtue' in religious and social behaviour. Certain states in federations such as Malaysia, Pakistan, and Nigeria, as well as provinces and districts in Indonesia issued regulations with criminal provisions, prescribing dress codes for women and men, or compulsory lessons in religion. Some prohibited the consumption of food and drinks during Ramadan, the consumption of alcohol, or 'indecent behaviour', notably extramarital sex. On the latter, a much disputed regulation in Aceh, Indonesia, even put a death penalty by stoning, in September 2009. In reality such regulations are not systematically enforced, in the first place because it would be practically impossible to do so, and secondly because the legal basis of such regulations is often contested. As national legal institutions are usually slow and reluctant to interfere in such cases, issues are mollified, and legal uncertainty prevails.

Basic norm

To which extent have constitutions introduced sharia as the highest or basic norm of legal systems? In five of the twelve countries, the constitution holds provisions which establish an 'Islamic state' (see Table A.2 in Annexe). In seven of the twelve countries, constitutional articles declare Islam to be the state religion (ibid). Six countries proclaim sharia as 'a source' or even 'the source' of the national legal system or declare that all legislation must be tested for its accordance with sharia (see Table A.3 in Annexe).

However, the suggestion of sharia supremacy created by such provisions must be questioned, since at the same time, many provisions in the same constitutions testify to supremacy of the constitution itself and of the rule-of-law standards laid down therein. As a result, constitutional laws in Muslim countries often seem to have a 'dual basic norm'. This gives the national legal systems of these countries an inherently ambiguous character.

Legal decision makers

This issue is about who ultimately decides the rules in a legal system: religious scholars or the office holders of the state? Iran provides us with the only example of a national legal system where ultimate decisions are the prerogative of a religious scholar, the Leader; other important state offices in Iran must also be fulfilled by religious scholars, such as six of the twelve seats of the Guardian Council which can veto laws which parliament has approved, as well as the chief of the Supreme Court. In Saudi Arabia religious scholars often enjoy a veto in the legislative drafting process; especially the *fatwas* of the Council of Senior Ulama and of influential government-employed *ulama* have 'a near legislative effect' (see 4.5). Judicial office is accessible only to graduates from the sharia colleges. Sharia legal opinions (*fatwa*) by jurisconsults (*mufti*) are important constitutive elements in the interpretation of the law.

As to the other ten countries, most important decisions in the respective legal systems are made by office holders of the state instead of religious scholars.

Islamic codification

The issue here is twofold, the first whether the area, in which sharia is most influential, i.e. family law, is regulated by uncodified sharia law or by codified national law, and the second whether due to recent islamisation policies pre-existing law codes, based on Western models, were thrown overboard and replaced by fully islamised codes.

According to Table 3 (see below) Islamic family law is codified into national legislation in eight of the twelve countries; secular marriage law is codified in three others namely Turkey, Mali and the Nigerian federation. Uncodified sharia is applied in marital affairs only in Saudi Arabia, and North Nigeria.

A full scale islamisation of existing law codes seems to have taken place in two countries mainly, the Sudan and Iran, not in the others.

It must be noted that Saudi Arabia has made some important steps to codify hitherto uncodified areas of law into national legislation, namely its constitutional law in the Basic Ordinance of 1992, and its criminal procedure law in the code of 2001.

Table 3 *Codification of Islamic family law in twelve countries*

Country	*Codification: Yes/No*	*Year*
Egypt	Yes	1985,2000
Morocco	Yes	1958, 2004
Saudi Arabia	No	-
Sudan	Yes	1991
Turkey	-[1]	-
Afghanistan	Yes	1977
Iran	Yes	1931, 1935, 1992, etc.[2]
Pakistan	Yes	1961
Indonesia	Yes	1974, 1975
Malaysia	Yes	1984, 1994
Mali[3]	No	-
Nigeria[4]	No	-

1 In 1917 a Family Code was enacted, based on sharia. In 1926 it was replaced by a secular Civil Code including family law, based on the Swiss Civil Code.
2 A procedural Marriage Law of 1931 is still valid. Substantive family law is codified in the Civil Code of 1935, which was changed several times since the Islamic revolution, namely in 1982, 1991, and in the early 2000s. The Family Protection Law of 1967 was changed in 1975, suspended in 1979. In 1992 an Amendments to Divorce regulation was enacted. In 1996 a Family Courts Law was enacted. In the early 2000s 21 bills became law. In 2010 a new controversial Family Protection bill is debated.
3 In 1962 Mali enacted a secular code of family law, which was elaborated in 1975.
4 A federal Marriage Act of colonial origin is still in force, as well as a 1970 federal Matrimonial Causes Act.

Islamic courts

Have states established separate Islamic judiciaries[1] that have taken on the functions of secular state courts? We noted that in four countries, namely in Malaysia, Indonesia, the Sudan and North Nigeria, there are broadening mandates and powers of separate 'religious' or 'Islamic' courts.[2]

Islamic ruler

Is the 'Islamic ruler' with his apparatus essentially authoritarian and without a check on his power, i.e. does 'oriental despotism', to use Wittfogel's famous term, still prevail? Among the Muslim countries under review, monarchs and dynasties are not common anymore. Of the twelve countries, ten are republics, and two are monarchies, namely Saudi Arabia and Morocco; in both countries the king is powerful and authoritarian.

In all countries, with the exception of Saudi Arabia, national parliamentary elections are held. In several countries the office of president is also elected. For example, in Iran people elect the president, who can be impeached by Iran's parliament. Iran's Leader is elected by the Assembly of Experts, who can also depose him. In the Sudan, the ruling military dictatorship called elections in Spring 2010, ensuring democratic legitimacy of his regime. As in most developing countries, political culture in the Muslim world is still marked by authoritarianism, albeit in varying degrees.

Legal status of women

Of all areas of law, family and inheritance law are most influenced by classical sharia. Turkey which has adopted a civil code based on a Swiss model, is the exception to this rule. Sharia-based family law discriminates against women on a number of issues. However, family laws in many Muslim countries have gradually taken distance from classical sharia to the benefit of women; repudiation and polygamy are restricted by procedural and substantive requirements which are laid down in legislation, case law, and in (standard) marriage contracts. Such provisions vary in their severity and effectiveness.

Repudiation (unilateral divorce by the man)

Is a man's right, bestowed upon him by classical sharia, to repudiate his wife at will, unilaterally, and without having to give a reason, still valid? Unilateral repudiation is restricted in six of the countries, and prohibited in one, Turkey. In five of the twelve countries under review the man can still on his own authority cast off his wife, with no or hardly any restriction (see Table 4).

Polygamy

Has the man maintained his right, as provided for by classical sharia, to conclude multiple marriages with up to four wives, without the need for permission of the first wife or of state authorities? In only three of the twelve countries under review a man may freely marry a second,

Table 4 *Family law: unilateral repudiation of wife by husband, in twelve countries*

	Not or hardly limited	*Several procedural and/or substantive limits*	*Prohibited*
Egypt		x	
Morocco		x	
Saudi Arabia	x		
Sudan	x		
Turkey			x
Afghanistan	x		
Iran		x	
Pakistan		x	
Indonesia		x	
Malaysia		x	
Mali	x		
Nigeria	x		

third, or fourth wife on his own authority and without any restrictions or formalities. In other countries polygamy is legally controlled and restricted by the state, usually by family courts or councils.

Divorce, initiated by women

Does a woman have the possibility to obtain a divorce from a court? In ten of the twelve countries women can apply to the court for divorce – whether or not the divorce is based on grounds established in her marriage contract; frequently the law gives women considerable space.

Inheritance

Do female heirs inherit half of what male heirs in a similar position would inherit? Inheritance law has distanced itself much less than marriage law from classical sharia. Formally, women in most of the countries under review have indeed the right to one half of the heritage of a man in an equal position. Some country studies, however, like Morocco and Indonesia, refer to research suggesting widespread discontent with such discriminatory law, and presenting evidence that in practice people manage to find ways to leave equal shares to their daughters as to their sons.

Cruel corporal punishments

Enactment of hadd-offences

Have national criminal laws enacted the classical sharia-based provisions that prescribe heavy corporal punishments for five specific *hadd*-crimes, namely extramarital sex, accusation of extramarital sex, robbery, theft, and consumption of alcohol; and have they added, as some schools prescribe, apostasy as a sixth *hadd*-offence? Of the twelve countries, there are five where these *hadd*-offences are partially or fully enacted in national law, i.e. Pakistan, Iran, the Sudan, Saudi Arabia, Afghanistan (see Table 5 below). Four countries have not done so, namely Egypt, Morocco, Turkey, Mali, and the Nigerian federation. While Indonesia, Malaysia as well as Nigeria have a long tradition of national criminal law without such provisions, they were introduced in the 1990s by several Malaysian states, and in the 2000s by eleven Northern Nigerian states, as well as by the remote Indonesian province of Aceh. Concerning apostasy, see below and Table A.6 (in Annexe).

Executions of heavy corporal punishments

To which extent is it common practice to actually administer cruel corporal punishments, such as stoning and amputation. According to the country studies, at the time of writing, only Saudi Arabia is still

Table 5 *Twelve times hadd-punishments in law and actual executions, in twelve countries*

	Hadd-punishments in the law[1]	*Stoning and/or Amputations carried out*[2]
Egypt	No	-
Morocco	No	-
Saudi Arabia	Yes	No recent stonings, amputations continue
Sudan	Yes	Declined strongly
Turkey	No	-
Afghanistan	Yes, but legality disputed	No
Iran	Yes	Irregularly[3]
Pakistan	Yes	No
Indonesia	No	-
Malaysia	No, except in certain states	No
Mali	No	No
Nigeria	Yes, in Northern states	No stoning, amputation strongly declined

1 The penal code of Saudi Arabia is completely based on sharia, including *hadd*--punishments. In the other "yes" nations the punishments can be found in the following legislation: the Sudan, penal code of 1991, articles, 78, 26, 146, 157, 168, 171; Afghanistan, penal code of 1976; Iran, penal code of 1996, articles 63-203; Pakistan, *hudud* ordinances of 1979; Malaysia, *hudud* laws in two member states, Kelantan and Terengganu; Nigeria, penal codes of eleven Northern states.

2 In some nations, whipping has taken place regularly, e.g. in Pakistan, particularly in the early 1980s.

3 In July 2005, two boys were hanged after being convicted for homosexuality. This execution shocked many, the more so since Iran had suspended applying corporal punishment, such as stoning and amputations, since 2002. It should be noted that hangings are anyway not in line with the traditional *hadd*-punishments, as mentioned in classical sharia. Since 2005, when the new conservative government under Ahmadinejad came in, amputations and to a lesser extent stoning were carried out again.

executing the *hadd*-punishment of amputation. As Table 5 shows, in the other countries where such punishments are legally in force, such executions are reportedly very rare to non-existent.

Retribution and blood money

Have national criminal laws enacted classical sharia-based provisions that entail the retribution (*qisas*) of violent offences, such as murder and assault, according to the principle of an 'eye for an eye', or its being bought off with 'blood money' (*diyya*). Such provisions are not found in seven of the twelve legal systems. In five countries, Saudi Arabia, the Sudan, Iran, Pakistan, and North Nigeria, such provisions are in force; the legal situation in Afghanistan is uncertain.

Violations of human rights

This fourth area of concern is different from those mentioned above in that here we are concerned with the extent to which international human rights standards are accepted, affect national laws, and are adhered to in practice.

Joining international human rights treaties

Have Muslim countries actually accessed, ratified, and implemented the major human rights treaties, and are they subjected to regular evaluation and benchmarking? The country studies confirm that since the 1990s governments of Muslim countries have abandoned their previously dismissive attitude towards human rights. Becoming signatories to international treaties and adopting human rights in national constitutional law, Muslim countries have made important steps in a process of convergence between their national laws – whether formally referring to sharia or not – and human rights standards. Table 6 below details the year of signature, accession, and ratification for three key human rights treaties by each country reviewed.

Table 6 *Signing, years of accession and ratification of human rights treaties in twelve countries*

	ICCPR[1]		*CEDAW*[2]		*CAT*[3]	
	Signed	Ratification, Accession, Signing year	Signed	Ratification, Accession, Signing year	Signed	Ratification, Accession, Signing year
Egypt	Yes	1982 R	Yes*	1981 R	Yes	1986 *A*
Morocco	Yes	1979 R	Yes*	1993 R	Yes	1993 R
SaudiArabia	No	-	Yes*	2000 R	Yes	1997 *A*
Sudan	Yes	1986 *A*	No	-	Yes	1986 s
Turkey	Yes	2003 R	Yes	1986 R	Yes	1988 R
Afghanistan	Yes	1983 *A*	Yes	2003 R	Yes	1987 R
Iran	Yes	1975 R	No	-	No	-
Pakistan	Yes	2008 s	Yes	1996 R	Yes	2008 *A*
Indonesia	Yes	2006 *A*	Yes	1984 R	Yes	1998 R
Malaysia	No	-	Yes*	1995 *A*	No	-
Mali	Yes	1974 *A*	Yes	1985 R	Yes	1999 *A*
Nigeria	Yes	1993 *A*	Yes	1985 R	Yes	2001 R

* *Reservation(s) related to sharia*

(Source: http://treaties.un.org/Pages/ViewDetails.aspx?src=TREATY&mtdsg_no=IV, last accessed on March12, 2010)

1 International Covenant on Civil and Political Rights (1966)

2 Convention on the Elimination of All Forms of Discrimination against Women (1979)

3 Convention against Torture and Other Cruel, Inhuman or Degrading Treatment or Punishment (1984)

Freedom from discrimination
To which extent do laws and practices discriminate against women in family and inheritance law, as well as against other groups? Table A.4 (see Annexe) shows that the constitutions of eleven of the twelve countries under review embrace the principle of equality – the exception being Saudi Arabia. Two countries, Iran and Egypt, make express reservations for conformity with Islamic rules.

However, as the country studies demonstrate, a host of particular rules in national laws and case law conflict with the constitutional guarantee of equality, not to speak of social practices on the ground. Of the frequent practices of discrimination – a hard fact of life in most countries – a number is sanctioned by national and local sharia-based laws and regulations. In most countries efforts to completely remove such discriminatory provisions run up against fierce puritan and conservative resistance (see 14.5).

Freedom of religion and apostasy
Is leaving one's faith criminalised as apostasy and punishable with heavy penalties? As shown in Table A.5 (see Annexe) eleven of the twelve constitutions guarantee freedom of religion, the exception being Saudi Arabia. Seven out of twelve countries have not criminalised apostasy (see Table A.6). In two countries, Saudi Arabia and the Sudan, apostasy is a crime, and in Iran, at the time of writing, a bill of similar import is pending (see 8.7). In Afghanistan it is unclear and disputed, while in at least one state in Malaysia, it is punishable, though the subject is heavily contested.

14.4 Comparing and ordering national legal systems

This section will attempt to classify the twelve countries' legal systems according to the degrees in which they have been impacted by sharia-based law, notably of puritan orientation, by introducing a rough, threefold division. The first category consists of systems where sharia-based law of a puritan orientation pervades most areas of law. Saudi Arabia and Iran fit into this category. A second category consists of secular legal systems, in which sharia has no role whatsoever. Turkey is a prominent example. This leaves us with the majority of legal systems, a middle group of 'mixed systems' as our third category. In these legal systems sharia-based law has no overall dominance but plays a significant role in one or more areas of the law. We will begin with Saudi Arabia and Iran, followed by the large middle group in order of decreasing level of puritan islamisation. We will conclude with Turkey.

Puritan orientation towards classical sharia

Saudi Arabia and Iran have, each in their own way, a strong orientation towards classical sharia. For Saudi Arabia sharia is the basic norm, while Iran wants to combine the two competing norms of what is called Islamism *(eslamiya)* and the republicanist state *(jomhuriyat)* (see 8.4). In these two countries conflicts between sharia-based law and human rights are most prevalent and acute.

In the traditional, closed, autocratic kingdom of Saudi Arabia, under supervision of the royal house and the powerful *ulama*, uncodified sharia of a puritan orientation has remained the backbone of the country's legal system until the present day.

> Saudi Arabia not only has a unique legal system, compared to Western systems, but also compared to other Muslim countries. The Saudi model is perhaps closest to the classical form of shari'a adherence and application which developed after the establishment of Islam on the Arabian peninsula in the early seventh century. [...] While the revealed law has always been – and remains – the general law of the land, the government also issues important 'regulations'. However, Islamic jurisprudence remains the first point of reference in cases concerning personal status, crime, civil contracts, property, etc. Judges have resorted primarily to the Qur'an, the Sunna, and *fiqh*-books in their quest for justice. A judge [...] enjoys great discretionary power and is not bound by doctrine of precedent. Religious scholars are also permitted to give their opinions on the application of shari'a by giving legal advice (*fatwa*). *Fatwa*s are of legal importance in Saudi Arabia and judges take them into consideration. (Van Eijk *intra*, see 6.10)

The Islamic Republic of Iran (1979) is led by a supreme Leader, who, with support from other high clerics, maintains sharia in the Shiite tradition. Contrary to Saudi Arabia, Iran established a tradition of parliamentary elections and law-making, codification, and a centralised judiciary (1906-1907). Today's Iran is shaped by a revolutionary response to the last Shah's repressive regime.

> Ruled by clerics, it combined not just religion and the state, but also theocracy and democracy. The founders made two broad assumptions: first, that what makes a state 'Islamic' is adherence to and implementation of the sharia; secondly that, given free choice, people will choose 'Islam' and will, thus, vote for clerics as the interpreters and custodians of the sharia. When they

> framed the constitution, the founders included both theocratic and democratic principles and institutions. The Constitution clearly recognises the people's right to choose who will govern them. But some institutions, including Parliament and the presidency, though elected by direct popular vote, are nevertheless subordinated to clerical oversight and veto. This contradiction remained unresolved but unproblematic while Ayatollah Khomeini was alive and able to mediate it [...]. (Mir-Hosseini *intra*, see 8.10)

However, 'after over a decade of the experience of Islam in power, Islamic dissent began to be voiced among "insiders" and became a magnet for intellectuals whose ideas and writings now formed the backbone of the New Religious Thinking.' In the 1990s they sought new directions, and. [...] 'armed with Soroush's theory of the relativity of religious knowledge, they wanted to create a worldview reconciling Islam and modernity, and argued for a demarcation between state and religion.' (ibid, see 8.4). Such debates among Iran's religious scholars display a dynamism which differs considerably from the static conservatism prevailing in Saudi Arabia. In recent years,

> [...] the notion of sharia as an ideal enabled the reformists in Iran to argue for democracy and the rule of law and to challenge patriarchal and despotic laws enacted in the name of Islam. They did so by appealing to Islam's higher values and principles, and by invoking concepts from within Islamic legal theory, notably the distinction between sharia as 'divine law' and jurisprudence (*feqh*) as the human understanding of the requirements of the divine law. (Mir-Hosseini, *intra*, see 8.10)

Large middle group

Of the nine countries of the large middle group, the Sudan, Pakistan, and Afghanistan are more oriented toward classical sharia and puritan orientations. Yet, they belong to a category different from the first two countries in that their basic norm combines the 'introduction of sharia' with more explicit and broader adherence to rule-of-law standards. In these countries, the basic norm seems more dualist and ambiguous.

In the Sudan, many of the legal codes were replaced by Islamic codes in 1983-1984. Because the non-Islamic South would not accept this, war under a military dictatorship prevailed for many years. However, the 1998 Constitution established a remarkably pluralistic basis for the law, which was reconfirmed in the 2005 interim national constitution (INC) following the Comprehensive Peace Agreement. At present 'a non-Muslim could, theoretically, become president of the whole of the Sudan (Art. 53)' and the Sudan has a constitutional court to uphold its moderate constitution (Köndgen *intra*, see 5.5).

> Only a few of the INC's articles make direct reference to Islam. Article 1 (INC) states that the Sudan is a multi-racial, multi-ethnic, multi-religious, and multi-lingual state. Thus, *de jure* Islam is not the state religion. (Köndgen *intra*, see 5.5)

Accordingly,

> The INC also guarantees men and women equal rights in the areas of civil, political, social, cultural, and economic rights (Art. 32). These guarantees, however, contradict to some degree other Sudanese legislation. Equal rights for men and women are especially relevant with regard to shari´a-based parts of the Criminal Act (1991) and in consideration of family and inheritance laws, which are known to be disfavourable to women in a variety of ways. (ibid)

Pakistan was founded in 1947 as a republic for Muslims, but islamisation of the constitution and other laws had to wait until the 1970s (see 9.3-9.5). Islamic criminal law, including the law of retribution, applies today, but family law, codified in the Muslim Family Laws Ordinance of 1961 was not further islamised. In both areas of law, judges in the higher courts have carried out an intense battle of ideas – often by use of impressively reasoned common law arguments – to maintain a moderate position. Among other things, they were able to strengthen the legal status of women in divorce matters and to prevent severe *hadd*-punishments; also they called the legislative ban on interest into question.

> How the position and role of classical sharia will be further developed in Pakistan's national legal system will depend largely on the political choices to be made by the PPP, choices pertaining to socio-economic development, electoral results, political stability, relations with the West, Iran and China, and last but not least, to the Pakistani judicial authorities. At present, faced with the violent attacks carried out by Islamic extremists not just in the tribal areas but in the very hearts of Pakistan's cities, politicians seem to have lost any interest in pursuing a policy of Islamisation. (Lau *intra*, see 9.10)

Afghanistan's constitution has a dual basic norm and progressive human rights provisions. It bears the marks of years of intense international and national negotiations in the wake of the 2001 Bonn Accords. Yet, the liberalisation of marriage laws has been very limited. In criminal matters it is unclear to what degree sharia or any codified criminal law is now in force. Customary law plays a major role in property dealings and a considerable role in family law and criminal matters as well. For the time being, the political and security situation hinders the effectiveness of any legal system, whether based on sharia or another source.

> The result is disjointed legislation, with many gaps and unregulated areas of law. Röder calls the legal landscape 'a patchwork' of various norms (Röder 2009: 257). [...] a fragmented *mélange* of secular, customary, and religious law variously applied according to local acceptance of central legislation and modified by shifting conditions of governmental authority. [...]. The limited practical value of Afghanistan's statutory laws has to be attributed to the decline and demise of central political authority in Afghanistan as a result of the civil war, but also to the lack of training of legal professionals and the inability to adapt statutory law to Afghanistan's particular circumstances. This means for instance that judges either do not know the law well, or know it, but are reluctant to apply it. (Yassari and Saboory *intra*, 7.10)

> Any reform of the legal system to bring it in line with international human rights standards or with the provisions of the new constitution will require as an essential prerequisite the existence of a stable, functioning, and capable state, both able and willing to enforce laws (Lau 2003: 4). At present, this is sadly not the situation in Afghanistan. (Yassari and Saboory *intra*, see 7.9)

As compared to the three abovementioned countries, the constitutions and laws of both Egypt and Morocco seem relatively stable. Their criminal laws have stuck to their European models without sharia-based provisions. Similarly, their civil laws, in French fashion, have remained unchanged, while the marriage laws in both countries have been strikingly modernised.

Morocco's 2004 reform of the family law codification, almost fifty years after its first enactment, marked the end of a long and intense domestic debate.

> The debate on family law was waged almost entirely in Islamic terms. Progressive groups frequently referenced the applicability of universal human, women's, and children's rights and the

> importance of international women's conferences and conventions, but they never dared to voice the possibility of viewing Moroccan family law from a secular perspective. By constantly referring to *ijtihad*, the modernists placed themselves within the Islamic tradition. [...] While Islamic family law has gained renewed meaning as a political symbol, 'human rights' (*huquq al-insan*) as a concept has become the most important political discourse in present-day Moroccan society, as a means of both legitimising and criticising government policy. (Buskens *intra*, see 3.4)

In Egypt, the relation between sharia and national law is marked by strong opposing forces. On the one hand, puritan political pressure is exerted to stretch the meaning of Article 2 of the constitution which states that the principles of sharia are the source of legislation. On the other hand, we see a Supreme Constitutional Court acting as guardian of the rule of law, and a new marriage law, which is

> one of the most radical reforms also being Egypt's first law of the twenty-first century. Article 20 of Law 1/2000 effectively provides for the right of women to unilaterally divorce their husbands through a court procedure called *khul'* (Sonneveld 2009; see also 2.6). This is exceptional for two reasons. Firstly, while the law was presented as a law of procedure, it, in actual fact, contains rules of substantive law. Secondly, although the article on *khul'* was presented as being in accordance with the sharia, it is not part of the corpus of any of the four Sunni schools of jurisprudence. [...] This law therefore brought about an expansion of the authority of the legislature with regard to interpretation of the sharia. (Berger and Sonneveld *intra*, see 2.4)

Two other countries of the 'large middle group', namely Nigeria and Malaysia, are federations with large non-Muslim population segments, which enacted rather progressive constitutions that ascribe only a limited place to Islamic law. Both countries have a strong common law tradition. Sharia plays an important role in matters of family law. In both countries leading politicians at sub-national state level promised to introduce sharia-based criminal legislation at the time of elections, won, and kept their promise. In Nigeria, this process happened on a much larger scale and more systematically than in Malaysia. In both countries the jurisdiction of sharia courts was extended at the cost of general courts.

In Malaysia, according to Harding, between the sharia courts and the civil courts there 'have been and continue to be significant skirmishes at the borders, which are expressed principally in terms of legal struggles over territory or 'jurisdiction' (see 14.10). There is, for example, a difference of opinion in the federal courts over the question as to whether the states have the power to introduce sharia criminal law, and execute punishments. In Harding's view:

> The success of the legal cultures of Southeast Asia over hundreds of years in absorbing and melding various legal worlds and concepts indicates that a syncretic, creative, and peaceful solution to the problem of Islam and constitutionalism is by no means impossible. At present it seems as though such an ideal solution is fraught with both political controversy and intellectual confusion. (Harding *intra*, see 14.10)

However, the very fact that these conflicts are debated, and often eventually decided, in the courtroom makes the author conclude that the mechanisms of the common law are capable of structuring and moderating the fundamental conflicts between sharia and the rule of law (ibid.).

In 2000 and 2001 eleven states in Northern Nigeria went so far as to implement Islamic criminal law and entrust its application to Islamic law courts. While this is a major legal shift, it should be noted that the judiciary still has allowed no stonings, and since 2002 no more amputations. The federal government has decided to allow islamisation for as long as, in its judgment, the constitution is not actually violated.

> Governor Sani [of the northern state of Zamfara, JMO] 's announcement of his sharia implementation programme exhilarated Nigeria's Muslims, and produced tremendous pressure on the governments of other northern states to follow suit. But it aroused fear and loathing among Christians, who expected the worst; civil war was even predicted by some [...] Everyone's worst fears seemed to be confirmed by the first amputation of a hand for theft already in March 2000, and then by the stoning cases of Safiyatu Hussaini (2001-2002) and Amina Lawal (2002-2003), which caused an uproar around the world. Since those early days, however, the clamour has died down completely, to the point that sharia implementation was a non-issue, virtually never mentioned, in the state and federal election campaigns of 2007. (Ostien *intra*, see 13.4)

The legal systems of the two remaining countries of the large middle group, Indonesia and Mali, are more secularly oriented. The word Islam does not appear in Indonesia's constitution, while Mali's constitution states that it is a secular republic. Both systems, founded on a colonial heritage of continental law, Dutch and French respectively, allow only limited space to sharia, mainly in family and inheritance law.

Indonesia has a codified Marriage Law (1/1974), which assigns considerable powers to the state Religious Courts to decide about cases of divorce and polygamy. The 1991 Compilation of Islamic Law is to back up the work of the Religious Courts with an Indonesian restatement of *fiqh*-rules. In 2006 a similar compilation was issued for the area of economic law. While until 1998 Indonesia's ruling elites, whether colonial or postcolonial, tried to control, bureaucratise and direct people's religious orientations,

> Indonesia is presently conducting a unique experiment with democratic law-making in the context of cultural islamisation. In this process, it has been responding both to Islamist pressure and the call to respect human rights. (Otto *intra*, see 10.10)

This experiment has led to many local and provincial regulations aiming at the promotion of Islamic virtue and the prevention of vice.

> Remarkably, the promotion of sharia-based legislation, both in Aceh as well as in other provinces and districts, has largely been driven by non-Islamist parties such as Golkar and PDI (Bush 2008). Similarly, Aceh's turn to the sharia [...] did not unequivocally express the strong demand of all Acehnese. On the contrary, when after the Peace Agreement the Free Aceh Movement had turned into a regular political party, and this newly formed Partai Aceh won the 2009 elections, they opposed the radical turn to sharia-based law. (ibid.)

In Mali, 'Sharia did not play a role in the formation or adaptation of Malian law' as '[I]slamic law has never been strongly represented or institutionalised in any colonial or postcolonial state law.' (see 12.3, 12.10).

> One reason why the growing political weight of influential Muslims did not translate into an islamisation of the legal institutional framework is certainly the coterminous, growing influence of Western donor organisations to which Moussa Traoré turned increasingly throughout the 1980s in search for financial support. (Schultz *intra*, see 12.4)

The way in which people equate their local customs with sharia also needs to be taken into consideration.

> It must be noted that at the grassroots level polygamy and other conventions in the sphere of marriage and family relations were never regarded as specifically Islamic practices. In most rural and urban zones of contemporary Mali, physical punishment, repudiation, and other practices reaffirming women's inferior status position and rights *vis-à-vis* elders and men are commonly accepted. These actions are occasionally attenuated by the intervention of mediators and kin. But the actions are nevertheless acknowledged as accepted custom. (Schultz *intra*, see 12.6)

Efforts to pass a new bill on family law have been frustrated for many years, due to the conflicting views of puritans and moderates, and of Western and Islamic donors.

Secular system

In Turkey sharia is completely removed from the national legal system. Secularism or kemalism is constitutionally anchored, and a constitutional court watches out for any violations. An Office for Religious Affairs supervises religion and education. The first three articles of the constitution (1982) formulate 'fundamental principles described as 'immutable provisions' in Article 4'. They stipulate that

> Turkey is a constitutional parliamentary democracy with a wide range of human rights [...] Articles 1, 2, and 3 [...] outline the constituent characteristics of the system which include it being a democratic, laic, constitutional state that respects human rights.[...] The republic remains loyal to Atatürk's nationalism and the fundamental tenets set forth in the preamble, which states that 'as required by the principle of laicism, there shall be no interference whatsoever by sacred religious feelings in state affairs and politics [...]. (Koçak *intra*, see 6.5)

The secular legal system, however, is often tested by individuals, groups and political parties demanding more space to profess their Islamic religion, for example by wearing a headscarf. The judiciary and the army's general staff remain on guard to protect the state against what they see as a direct threat.

As this section has shown, the differences between countries in how they have incorporated sharia in their national legal systems – or not – are considerable. In view of such overwhelming diversity an essentialist approach seems beside the point. The future modalities of incorporation of sharia do not primarily depend on puritan rage, or on transnational human rights activism. The leading part is played by national office-bearers – politicians, law-makers, judges and bureaucrats – who, interacting with civil society amidst opposing and complex ideological forces, will continue to struggle, negotiate, and decide about the guiding principles and rules of incorporation.

14.5 Governance

Policy re sharia and contemporary challenges of governance

It may be the case that this book has created the impression that problems of sharia-based law appear as priority issues on cabinets' agendas throughout the Muslim world all the time. In reality, far more frequently discussed are issues of security and stability, economic growth, public finance, poverty reduction, education, public health, housing, decentralisation, elections, and foreign relations. No different than anywhere else, Muslim governments aim for the three goals of stability, prosperity, and social justice. Governance efforts to reach these goals require a degree of democracy, sound administration, and an effective legal system, whether derived from *fiqh*-sources or not.

Perhaps in Saudi Arabia and Iran sharia is so central to all policy concerns that political decision-making immediately touches upon issues of sharia-based law. In most Muslim countries, however, political debate about sharia and national law is often just simmering in the background, only to flare up when attention is called to specific events and issues. High profile cases of 'Islamic crimes', a new marriage bill, puritan violence, skirmishes about judicial competences, inter-religious conflict, are all of great political sensitivity.

Governance in such areas comes down exactly to how Hyden et al. define it, namely as "the formation and stewardship of the formal and informal rules that regulate the public realm, the arena in which state as well as economic and societal actors interact to make decisions" (Hyden et al. 2004: 16). Governance decisions, as Hyden et al. elaborate, are made in six different arenas of governance, i.e. government, civil society, political society, bureaucracy, economic society, and the judiciary (ibid: 18-22). The country studies in this book have explored many of these arenas, and show that the Muslim state has taken many different shapes: just caliphate, despotic sultanate, colonial empire state, independent state, authoritarian state, socialist state, developmental state, sharia state, democratic state, aid state, corrupt state, failing state, rule-of-law state.

In section 14.2 we concluded that during the first decades after World War II most developing countries suffered from several serious governance failures. In response, a 'new governance' emerged in the developing world during the last few decades. Therefore, contemporary policy discussions on incorporation of sharia take place in a governance context which has changed. First, market forces have been released and created in many countries an entrepreneurial middle class with a vested interest in the rule of law. Furthermore, democratisation and elections have changed political landscapes significantly. Demands for respect of individual human rights cannot be neglected by governments without strong criticism. Corrupt behavior is openly discussed, yet still omnipresent. Domestic and international programmes to strengthen judiciaries in order to promote the rule of law are in full swing (Carothers 2006). And, finally, religion, notably Islam, has returned to the center stage. No doubt, this new governance cannot be a cure for all policy problems, but it certainly shows a learning curve.

As for the relationship between sharia and national law, the experiments with puritan governance in Iran, the Sudan, Pakistan, Afghanistan, and North Nigeria have provided an opportunity to experience the 'introduction of the sharia' in contemporary states. The chapters by Mir-Hosseini, Lau, and Köndgen, describing Iran, Pakistan, and Sudan – the forerunners in this process – strongly suggest that the era of revolutionary Islamic law reform is past its peak. Ostien's chapter emphasises that for Nigeria the learning experience of islamisation is essentially a good thing, and that within a decade since its inception, the introduction of sharia has already become a non-issue. Yet, there is no reason to expect that political pressure to incorporate sharia in national law will altogether wither away.

Governments, puritans and scholars: clashes and compromises[3]

In every country study in this book, sooner or later the puritans pop up; for example, the Mahdi in nineteenth century Sudan, the Muslim Brotherhood in Egypt, the *mullahs* who deposed king Amanullah of Afghanistan, Khomeini and his Ayatollahs, the Saudi rebels occupying the Grand Mosque in Mecca, the MMA-coalition in Pakistan, and the PAS party in Malaysia. No region, no era in Islamic history escapes completely the presence of the puritans.

Time and again they display the same features, these men – and women – of ideals, imagining a better society and government. Quite a few are individual models of selflessness, devoted to 'the cause' and to providing social services. Both characteristics are rare in developing societies, where most people struggle to make ends meet. In doing so they act as catalysts of popular discontent. A minor segment is militant, and ready to die as martyrs. All of this is part of their appearance as true and pious Muslims.

Most governments fear puritans. Puritan groups are often well-organised, have large numbers of active followers and transnational networks, their own media, and (inter)national financiers. They also are among the few organised movements who speak about the real and serious problems that disrupt society in most of these countries: poverty, lack of security, education, and health; invasion of the government into everyday life; and corruption, urbanisation problems, social and cultural changes, partly under foreign influences (Halliday 2003: 118). Although many of them are young students, one can find senior members in religious institutions, the bureaucracy, the judiciary, the army, and the business sector. While puritans are often capable of infiltrating those institutions, state intelligence units are often able to detect and arrest them.

In the struggle to change the existing relationship between sharia and national law, puritan movements deploy their activists along a number frontlines, which largely coincide with the main concerns and issues discussed in previous sections (see 14.3).

Another important party in this struggle is the religious establishment of scholars. Many scholars have an ambivalent relationship with the puritan movements: they feel criticised by them, and they see them as unskilled in *fiqh* and overzealous. But, at the same time, they see them as the front soldiers, who could pave the way to an Islamic state in which they, the scholars, will finally play a leading role again. In spite of their marginalisation from the national legal system, scholars retain important functions. They are senior staff at the ministries of religion. They sit on local, regional and national bodies as the official representatives of religion, and issue *fatwas* about many different subjects, from Islamic banking to euthanasia. As judges in family courts, many of them have earned a reputation of fairness and ability to find reasonable solutions for problematic cases. As preachers, they lead the Friday prayer and are called to attend to the important 'rites de passage' – birth, marriage, divorce, death – and to act as people's moral compass in the problems of daily life. Some of them do this also on radio, TV, or the Internet. In addition, they oversee educational institutions, the management of *waqf*-land, the annual pilgrimage, and the collection of Islamic alms (*zakat*). On all issues discussed in section 14.3, scholars take positions based on their interpretation of the *fiqh*. Most governments hope that such positions will support state policies and laws, as the scholars' religious blessing is most welcome to enhance the state's legitimacy.

Besides puritans and religious scholars, the ideological spectrum of Muslim countries is beset with feminist movements, human rights groups, and explicitly liberal Muslim groups. While deciding upon sharia-related issues, governments have to consider the – often conflicting – demands of the conservative *ulama*, the puritans, the modernists, the religious minorities, the feminists, and so on. Inevitably, they will invoke disappointment and anger from one party or the other. In order to take the wind out of the puritans' sails, to appease the clergy, and to reconcile the various goals of development and good governance, clever compromises are needed. The country studies in this book testify to the impressive balancing capacities of law-makers, administrators and judges, using the dual basic norm and legal ambiguity to the best of their knowledge.

The complex relationship between sharia and custom

Meanwhile, governments in developing Muslim countries also have to deal with communities, clans, and tribes which make up much of the social structure of their countries. Alongside the rise of Islam, sharia brought a series of religious, social and legal reforms to a patriarchal and often brutal society, where Arab tribal customs constituted the prevailing law. In spreading their religion, Muslims set out to replace local traditions with sharia as the prime normative system. However, customary norms were not simply washed away, being deeply rooted and closely connected with kinship, power, and economy. In certain areas consensus emerged by mutual acceptation and adaptation. As the scholars developed sharia, they took local norms into account. Islamic jurisprudence recognises custom (*orf*). Leaders of clans, tribes and local communities converted to Islam and added sharia to the repertoire of norms they applied. In other areas, tensions grew between such leaders, their customs and old-established authority structures on the one hand, and the Islamic authorities with their firm beliefs, their message of reform, and their more uniform and elaborated justice system on the other hand. Both harmony and conflict between sharia and custom are played out throughout this book.

Puritans especially tend to hold local custom and local culture in low esteem. They disapprove of pre-Islamic norms, they denounce casual dress, close companionship between unmarried women and men, they dislike the widespread respect for Sufism, for saintly figures, for music and dancing, branding it all as un-Islamic. Their zealous promotion of puritan ideas, however, has yielded not only political successes, but also a variety of counter-movements. In a book entitled 'The Illusion of the Islamic State' (*Ilusi Negara Islam*) the late former president of Indonesia, Abdurrahman Wahid, strongly condemns the infiltration of Saudi-funded transnational puritan movements in Indonesia, accusing them of 'cultural genocide' (Wahid 2009: backcover).

In contrast, there is also evidence from countries in both Africa and Asia that there is a strong demand for sharia as a substitute for arbitrary and repressive tribal justice. In fact this is a historical role of sharia. As Yassari explains 'the status of Afghan women under customary law is worse than the status afforded to them under the most conservative interpretation of Islamic law' (see 7.10). Ostien suggests that activists who seek to improve the legal status of women in Nigeria take recourse to sharia for the same reasons:

> That Islamic personal law as applied in northern Nigeria is still often contaminated by local custom antithetical to women is confirmed by the work of the Federation of Muslim Women Associations in Nigeria (FOMWAN), founded in 1985 (Yusuf 1993), and more recently by the attitude taken toward sharia implementation by Muslim women activists (see 13.6).

Ostien's findings confirm the recent findings of Stiles (2009) about Tanzanian Muslim women who discovered that Islamic justice provides them with individual rights (*hakki*), opening the desired road to freedom from a tribal life without rights. Today, amidst much understandable criticism of sharia, it is often forgotten that the only alternative which is available in many places, is unfortunately not an effective and fair state justice system, but rather a semi-functional customary system.

Often it is difficult to entangle the religious from the customary. Does sharia justify customs such as female circumcision, or honour killings, or are these local traditions, which the sharia disapproves of? In spite of authoritative *fatwas* denying the Islamic nature of such customs, for example the one on circumcision issued by Egypt's supreme religious authority, the Sheykh al-Azhar (see 2.9), such practices continue. At grassroots level, people often do not know nor mind the precise normative foundation of their behaviour, as long as it is part of 'our tradition'.

Similarly, it is sometimes difficult for outsiders, including Western journalists, to distinguish Islamic court rulings from primitive mob-justice or repulsive misuse of authority by local policemen or other officials. If primitive clan members kill a woman accused of extramarital sex by stoning her, as has happened repeatedly in Pakistan – in flagrant violation of sharia's basic procedural and evidence rules – Western media are often quick to link it to what they call 'Islamic law'.

Since tribal and community leaders are real power holders in many areas of the Muslim world, they often are instrumental for national political stability. In their communities they are 'big men', who solve problems and settle conflicts by applying traditional or indigenous law. They manage the relations between the local and the national, acting as intermediaries between the police, the army, business, and as vote-brokers in elections. In times of trouble they can become small or big warlords, turning their clan members into fighters. Governments, for the sake of stability, must therefore also keep the tribal leaders satisfied, and be careful not to disregard their wishes and 'their traditions'.

Attitudes of the West

Our country studies confirm that the relationship between sharia and national law is highly dependent on domestic politics. Transnational relations within the Muslim world is another important factor. In addition, the West remains involved in this matter, as certain sharia policies are in part motivated by a rejection of the West and others by appeasement. At the time of writing, two decades of extreme Western *hubris* that started with the fall of the Berlin wall, seem to be coming to an end. The Western banking system has undergone an unprecedented financial crisis. China, India and other economies have emerged successfully; Muslim countries such as Indonesia, Turkey and Saudi Arabia have joined the G-20. Regime change in Iraq and Afghanistan, as conceived by the West, has been far more difficult than expected. Western foreign policy regarding the Muslim world also seems unable to solve the democratisation dilemma: on the one hand, the West pushes for free elections; on the other hand, it is not always ready to accept the outcome.

A more productive attitude regarding problems in the Muslim world will require refreshing the knowledge base, and adapting positions. An important lesson from the country studies is that, as Buskens puts it, the far-reaching debates on family law are waged almost entirely in Islamic terms. Even progressive groups do not dare to present their views from a secular perspective. By constantly referring to *ijtihad* they place themselves within the Islamic tradition. Meanwhile 'human rights' (*huquq al-insan*) as a concept has become a very important political discourse, as a means of both legitimising and criticising government policy (cf. 3.4).

Some authors, such as Lau on Pakistan, state that politicians in the Muslim world have lost interest in pursuing a policy of islamisation, due to the violent attacks, for which Islamists claimed responsibility. Perhaps the effect of those attacks on domestic policy is greater than most human rights interventions by the West; this would count in favour of Western foreign policies of restraint. Reading through the country studies in this book, one cannot but agree with Zakaria (2003: 155), who comes down on the side of caution in the democratisation dilemma, and turns against rapid and large-scale democratisation as was advocated by the Bush administration. In this connection he warns against 'ugly ethnic forces' and argues for 'a longer period of state-building.' He feels that in certain situations elections can be held only after 'civic institutions, courts, political parties, and the economy have all begun to function. As with everything in life: timing matters.' He advocates 'a certain sophistication' in this regard, warning that '[t]he haste to pressure countries into elections [...] has been, in many cases, counterproductive.'

In any case, the international quest for justice in the Muslim world deserves to be pursued with political sophistication, and a solid knowledge base (Carothers 2006). If human rights are to be 'everyone's right', they should not be in conflict with the beliefs of 1.5 billion people (Brems 2001). In the international monitoring procedures to oversee the implementation of human right treaties there should be some recognition for the difficult dilemmas faced by governments of Muslim countries who often cannot but respond to the fact that the majority of their citizens do hold sharia in a positive light.

Perhaps the West could provide useful technical and financial assistance for the strengthening of human rights protection systems. For, the 'supply side' of justice systems, i.e. the quality of legal process, requires much investment and leadership. Whereas legal institution-building is in the first place a domestic affair, international legal cooperation, with professional assistance from other Muslim countries as well as from Western countries, can probably be of help, if carried out well.

The long and winding road to justice

While 'good' governance can mean different things to different people, there is consensus that rules and governance are good when they contribute to stability, prosperity and justice. 'Justice' is the keyword in Western treatises about the rule of law and human rights. Justice (*'adl*) is also the core concept in Islamic jurisprudence (*fiqh*). This book demonstrates that under certain conditions both concepts of justice do actually coincide in the established practice of moderate interpretation of sharia, which is manifest in laws, rulings and legal practices in Muslim countries, as well as in religious discourse (see 1.5).

Moderate practice has a long tradition in Islam. Akbar, a Mughal emperor in India (1591) who was leading a vast Muslim empire in an age when in Europe the 'Inquisitions were in full swing', promoted freedom of religion and 'insisted that we should be free to examine whether reason does or does not support any existing custom, or provides justification for ongoing policy'. This Muslim emperor figures in Amartya Sen's *The Idea of Justice* also as a fierce proponent of the freedom of religion (Sen 2009: 36-39). Recent studies of sharia by Abou el-Fadl (2005), Ardjomand (2008), Feldman (2008), and Hallaq (2009) all highlight the old 'Islamic constitutional state' and the 'Circle of Justice', providing many historical examples of what contemporary Western lawyers would call 'legality', 'due process', and, indeed, 'justice'. Islamic legal history is more than what puritans often suggest it is. As Hallaq demonstrates in his 2009 work, the historical archives of sharia and ruler's law contain many treasures to be discovered and valued as the building bricks of a strong moderate tradition.

In the long term the processes of state formation and socio-economic change will probably contribute to the convergence of sharia and the rule of law. Essentially, for legal development there is no main route other than through the state, its laws, its legal processes and institutions. Meanwhile, the emancipation of women, the democratisation of politics, and the increase in respect for human rights are developments that cannot be denied or halted. After nationalisation and adaptation of sharia, we are now witnessing its democratisation and constitutionalisation. Sharia-based laws, therefore, are increasingly adapted – by legislatures and courts – and applied in accordance with the prevailing sense of justice, as our country studies demonstrate.

This puts huge responsibilities on the legal institutions that have been established for these purposes. The country studies in this book suggest that most legislatures, bureaucracies and courts in the Muslim world have made considerable progress in a few decades time. Harding, referring to Malaysia, argues that modern legal institutions are, in principle, able to bring 'the problem of Islam and constitutionalism' to a peaceful solution, even though their work is complicated by political controversies and intellectual confusion. In countries such as Turkey, Pakistan, and Egypt, fairly independent courts play key roles in accommodating or even solving fundamental conflict. The very fact that these conflicts are dealt with in a legal procedural manner, is a clear sign of hope that, as Harding puts it, the mechanisms of modern law are capable of structuring and moderating many of the fundamental conflicts between sharia and the rule of law (see 14.10). Generally speaking, though, the state of legal institutions in the developing world is far from ideal, and much remains to be done, but at least they are there, and channel conflicts.

While professional jurists operate from the end of national law, much work lays also ahead at the other end, i.e. for religious scholars to make constructive use of the intellectual heritage of the *fiqh*. Mir-Hosseini shows how in Iran *ulama* have taken the lead in intense discussions about ways to make interpretations compatible with contemporary aspirations, notably with human rights. Scholars therefore are increasingly trained in the new methodologies, as Hallaq discusses in the last chapter of his latest book. Egypt's Ashmawi, Syria's Shahrur, Kuwait's Abou el-Fadl, Pakistan's Fazlur Rahman, Iran's Soroush, Indonesia's Hazairin, were raised and studied in different Muslim countries, but they all share a strong desire to reconcile sharia with modernity (Hallaq 2009: 500-542).

Puritans will remain a social and political force to reckon with. In recent decades they have been associated with radicalism and violence, without any credible and feasible perspective on justice for all (Fuller 2003). Perhaps their recent recourse to human rights and democracy will open up more constructive and successful routes. In any case, they will keep reminding the world that sharia remains a cornerstone of Islam. And as long as the state's legal systems keep suffering from serious shortcomings, many people will feel a strong desire for better governance, for a better system of law. In such circumstances, God's law, the sharia, will remain an obvious reference for legal development, or at least, a source of moral and political inspiration, as has been proposed by An-Na'im in his visionary *Islam and the Secular State* (2009).

Vikør, in conclusion of his historical analysis of sharia, sees in most Muslim countries

> 'both a dichotomy between 'state law' and an independent 'Sharī'a' and – as under the medieval siyāsa – a merger of them through the incorporation of Sharī'a-based rules into the codified laws of the state.' (Vikør 2005: 346-347).

It is this incorporation, this merger, which has been the main theme of this book. If the collaborative efforts of all contributors have provided the reader with a realistic and balanced overview and a deeper insight into the relationship between sharia and national law, our main objective has been achieved. Hopefully, this book will also serve as a useful foundation for further comparative research, moving into three directions, as to include analyses of landmark decisions by the courts, of field studies on local sharia-related practices, and, finally, initiate additional socio-legal studies of the sharia-based laws of other Muslim countries.

Notes

1 As we learned from the country studies, the terms 'Islamic court', 'sharia-court' or 'religious court' are labels which in themselves contain little relevant information, not any more than 'national court' or 'general court' for that matter. Some 'Islamic' or 'religious courts', like in Indonesia, are actually state courts, subordinate to a supreme court of a basically secular set-up. Elsewhere, for example in Saudi Arabia or Iran, courts are not given such label, but the law they apply and their legal interpretations are clearly based on *fiqh*.

2 The next phase of this research project will address developments in the case law of religious courts. Based on the country studies so far, our overall hypothesis is that

higher courts tend towards more moderate interpretations as compared to the sometimes strict interpretations in the rulings of lower courts.

3 See for an analysis of 'the clash within the Islamic civilisation', Trautner (1999).

Bibliography

Abiad, N. (2008), *Sharia, Muslim States and International Human Rights Treaty Obligations: A Comparative Study*. London: British Institute of International and Comparative Law.

Abou El-Fadl, K. (2007), *Islam and the challenge of democracy*. Princeton (NJ): Princeton University Press.

Allott, A. (1980), *The limits of law*. London: Butterworth.

An-Na'im, A.A. (2008), *Islam and the secular state: Negotiating the future of Sharia*. Cambridge (MA): Harvard University Press.

Ardjomand, S.(ed.) (2008), *Constitutional Politics in the Middle East. With special reference to Turkey, Iraq, Iran and Afghanistan*, Oxford: Hart Publishing.

Von Benda-Beckmann, F. (1983), *Op zoek naar het kleinere euvel in de jungle van het Rechtspluralisme*. Inaugural lecture, Agricultural University, Wageningen.

Brems, E. (2001), *Human rights: Universality and diversity*. Den Haag: Martinus Nijhoff.

Cammack, M. (2005) in Bearman, P., R. Peters, and B. Weiss (eds.) (2006), *The Islamic School of Law : Evolution, Devolution, and Progress*. Cambridge: Harvard University Press: 175-190.

Carothers, T. (2006), *Promoting the rule of law abroad: in search of knowledge*. Washington (DC): Carnegie Endowment for International Peace.

Esposito, J.L. and D. Mogahed (2007), *Who speaks for Islam? What a billion Muslims really think. Based on Gallup's World Poll – the largest study of its kind*. New York: Gallup Press.

Feldman, N. (2008), *The Fall and Rise of the Islamic State*. Princeton: Princeton University Press.

Fuller, G. (2003), *The future of political Islam*. New York: Palgrave Macmillan.

Hallaq, W. (2003), 'Muslim rage and Islamic law', *Hastings Law Journal* 54 (6): 1705-1719.

Hallaq, W. (2009), *Sharia: Theory, Practice, Transformations*. Cambridge: Cambridge University Press.

Halliday, F. (2003), *Islam and the myth of confrontation: Religion and politics in the Middle East*. London: Tauris.

Huntington, S.P. (1998), *The clash of civilizations and the remaking of world order*. New York: Touchstone.

Hyden, G., J. Court and K. Mease (2004), *Making sense of governance: empirical evidence from sixteen developing countries*. Boulder (CO): Lynne Rienner Publishers.

Lewis, B. (2002), *What went wrong: western impact and Middle Eastern response*. Oxford: Oxford University Press.

Lewis, B. (2003), *The crisis of Islam: Holy war and unholy terror*. London: Weidenfeld & Nicholson.

Marshall, P. (ed.) (2005), *Radical Islam's rules: The worldwide spread of extreme Shari'a law*. Lanham, MD: Rowman & Littlefield.

Sen, A. (2009), *The Idea of Justice*. Cambridge: The Belknap Press of Harvard University Press.

Stiles, E. (2009), *An Islamic Court in Context. An Ethnographic Study of Judicial Reasoning*. New York: Palgrave Macmillan.

Trautner, B.J. (1999), *The clash within civilisations: Islam and the accommodation of plurality. Empirical evidence and contemporary reformist approach*. Bremen: Institute for International and Intercultural Studies.

Vikør, K.S. (2005), *Between God and the Sultan: a history of Islamic law*. London: Hurst.

Wahid, A. (ed.) (2009), *Ilusi Negara Islam. Ekspansi Gerakan Islam Transnasional di Indonesia.* Jakarta: The Wahid Institute.

Warraq, I. (1995), *Why I am not a Muslim.* Amherst, NY: Prometheus Books.

Zakaria, F. (2003), *The future of freedom: Illiberal democracy at home and abroad.* New York: Norton.

Annexe: Tables

Table A.1 *Twelve countries by socio-economic indicators*

Country	*GDP/PPP Capita (US $ 2008)*	*Life expectancy (M/F 2007)*	*Literacy rate, adult total (% of people aged 15 and above)*	*Official development aid (US $ Mln. 2007)*
Egypt	5460	68-72	66 (2007)	1,083
Morocco	4330	69-73	56 (2007)	1,090
Saudi Arabia	22950	71-75	85 (2007)	-131
Sudan	1930	56-60	-	2,104
Turkey	13770	69-74	89 (2007)	797
Afghanistan	..	..-..	-	3,951
Iran	10840	69-73	82 (2006)	102
Pakistan	2700	65-66	54 (2006)	2,212
Indonesia	3830	69-73	92 (2006)	796
Malaysia	13740	72-77	92 (2007)	200
Mali	1090	52-57	26 (2007)	1,017
Nigeria	1940	46-47	72 (2007)	2,042

Source: The World Bank.
Data reports available:
http://web.worldbank.org/WBSITE/EXTERNAL/DATASTATISTICS/0,,contentMDK:20535285~menuPK:1192694~pagePK:64133150~piPK:64133175~theSitePK:239419,00.html (accessed March 2010)

Table A.2 *Islamic state and state religion, in twelve countries*

	Islamic state[1]	*Islam as state religion*[2]
Egypt	No	Yes
Morocco	Yes	Yes
Saudi Arabia	Yes	Yes
Sudan	No	No
Turkey	No	No
Afghanistan	Yes	Yes
Iran	Yes	Yes
Pakistan	Yes	Yes
Indonesia	No	No
Malaysia	No	Yes
Mali	No	No
Nigeria	No	No

[1] As a basis we took the standard text "nation A is an Islamic state." This clause can be found in the constitution of Morocco in the preamble; in Saudi Arabia article 1. Variants of this provision include: Afghanistan, article 1, "Afghanistan is an independent, unitary, and indivisible Islamic republican state"; Iran, article 1, "The form of government of Iran is that of an Islamic Republic"; Pakistan, article 1, "Pakistan shall be a Federal Republic to be known as the Islamic Republic of Pakistan." Concerning those nations that are not Islamic states, the formulations of interest are: Egypt, article 1, "The Arab Republic of Egypt is a democratic state based on citizenship. The Egyptian people are part of the Arab nation and work for the realization of its comprehensive unity.". Sudan, article 1, defines its own nation as "(...) a country of racial and cultural harmony and religious tolerance." Turkey "is a democratic, secular and social state governed by the rule of law" (article 2). Indonesia is founded on "the belief in One and Only God" (preamble and article 29, sub 1). (Source: http://www.law.cornell.edu/world, accessed on 10 March 2010)

[2] As a basis we took the standard text "Islam is the state religion of state A." These statements are to be found in the constitutions of: Egypt article 2; Morocco article 6; Saudi Arabia article 1; Pakistan article 2. Variants of the standard text are: Afghanistan (article 2): "Islam is the sacred religion of Afghanistan"; Iran (article 12): "The official religion of Iran is Islam and the Twelver Ja'fari school"; and Malaysia (article 3, sub 1) "Islam is the religion of the Federation". Of the nations that do not mention Islam as the state religion, Sudan is of particular interest: in article 1 it is stated: "Islam is the religion of the majority of the population and Christianity and traditional religions have a large following". (Source: http://www.law.cornell.edu/world, accessed on 10 March 2010)

Table A.3 *Sharia as main source of law, in twelve constitutions*

	Sharia as 'a' or 'the' main source[1]
Egypt	Yes
Morocco	No
Saudi Arabia	Yes
Sudan	Yes
Turkey	No
Afghanistan	Yes
Iran	Yes
Pakistan	Yes
Indonesia	No
Malaysia	No
Mali	No
Nigeria	No

[1] *The constitutional articles referred to are: Egypt, article 2; Saudi Arabia, article 1; Sudan, article 65; Afghanistan, article 3; Iran, article 4; Pakistan, article 2A in relation to article 227.1*

Table A.4 *Principle of equality in twelve constitutions*

	Principle of equality	*Direct limitations based on sharia*[1]
Egypt	Yes	Yes
Morocco	Yes	No
Saudi Arabia	No	-
Sudan	Yes	No
Turkey	Yes	No
Afghanistan	Yes	No
Iran	Yes	Yes
Pakistan	Yes	No
Indonesia	Yes	No
Malaysia	Yes	No
Mali	Yes	No
Nigeria	Yes	No

[1] *Egypt (article 11): "The State shall guarantee harmonization between the duties of woman towards the family and her work in the society, ensuring her equality status with man in fields of political, social, cultural and economic life without violation of the rules of Islamic jurisprudence." Iran (article 20): "All citizens of the country, both men and women, equally enjoy the protection of the law and enjoy all human, political, economic, social, and cultural rights, in conformity with Islamic criteria." Malaysia (article 8, sub 1) "All persons are equal before the law and are entitled to the equal protection of the law." Article 8, sub 5 states: "This Article does not invalidate or prohibit: a) any provision regarding personal law; b) any provision or practice restricting office or employment connected with the affairs of any religion, or of an institution managed by a group professing any religion, to persons professing that religion." The Pakistan constitution (article 25, sub 1-3) is very specific on the principle of equality for women: "All citizens are equal before the law and are entitled to equal protection of law. There shall be no discrimination on the basis of sex alone. Nothing in this Article shall prevent the State from making any special provision for the protection of women and children." (Source: http://www.law.cornell.edu/world, accessed on 10 March 2010)*

Table A.5 *Freedom of religion in twelve constitutions*

	Constitutional freedom of religion	*Formal limitations based on Sharia*[1]
Egypt	Yes	No
Morocco	Yes	No
Saudi Arabia	No	Yes
Sudan	Yes	No
Turkey	Yes	No
Afghanistan	Yes	No
Iran	Yes	No
Pakistan	Yes	No
Indonesia	Yes	No
Malaysia	Yes	No
Mali	Yes	No
Nigeria	Yes	No

[1] Even though none of the nations researched, except for Saudi Arabia, directly and explicitly limits freedom of religion on the basis of sharia, most of the Muslim nation are not neutral on religion. Many nations have Islam as a state religion. Examples are Morocco (article 6): "Islam shall be the state religion. The state shall guarantee freedom of worship for all." Afghanistan (article 2): "The religion of Afghanistan is the sacred religion of Islam. Followers of other religions are free to perform their religious rites within the limits of the provisions of the law." Many Muslim nations have a dual norm on this point. Pakistan (article 20) has constitutional freedom of religion: "Subject to law, public order and morality: a) every citizen shall have the right to profess, practice and propagate his religion; and b) every religious denomination and every sect thereof shall have the right to establish, maintain and manage its religious institutions." At the same time, Pakistan has in its constitution taken this right from the Ahmadiyya movement). The constitution of Indonesia includes freedom of religion (article 29, sub 1 and 2): "The State shall be based upon the belief in the One and Only God" and "The State guarantees all persons the freedom of worship, each according to his/her own religion or belief." Its post-1998 amendments confirm this in Article 28E, stating "(1) Each person is free to worship and to practice the religion of his choice,[...] (2) Each person has the right to be free in his convictions, to assert his thoughts and tenets, in accordance with his conscience. (3) Each person has the right to freely associate, assemble, and express his opinions. Yet the Indonesian state recognizes only a few religions. The implication is that freedom of religion is limited to these religions.
(Source: http://www.law.cornell.edu/world, accessed on 10 March 2010)

Table A.6 *Twelve criminal laws on illegality and punishment of apostasy*

	Illegality of apostasy	*Actual convictions and executed punishments*
Egypt	No	No
Morocco	No	No
Saudi Arabia	Yes[1]	Not recently[2]
Sudan	Yes	Not since 1985
Turkey	No	No
Afghanistan	Disputed	No
Iran	Yes, disputed	Very rarely[3]
Pakistan	No	No
Indonesia	No	No
Malaysia	Yes, some states, disputed	Very rarely[4]
Mali	No	No
Nigeria	No	No

[1] *The penal law of Saudi Arabia is completely based on sharia. The death penalty applies in cases of conviction of apostasy. If apostasy is proved, the execution will take place. In Sudan (article 126, penal code) apostasy is also punishable by death.*
[2] *The U.S. International Religious Freedom Report (2009) said the following: "Conversion by Muslims to another religion (apostasy) and proselytizing by non-Muslims are punishable by death under the Islamic laws adopted by the country, but there have been no confirmed reports of executions for either crime in recent years." US International Freedom Report at http://www.state.gov/g/drl/rls/irf/2009/127357.htm accessed on 25 February 2010.*
[3] *In recent years there have been few confirmed reports on persecution of those who have converted to Christianity. Concerning executions because of apostasy, in November 2009 a Kurdish freedomfighter named Fattahian was hanged supposedly for enmity against God and apostasy.*
[4] *In some states, such as Terengganu, Kelantan and Perlis, regulations were enacted to make apostasy punishable. In Perlis the Islamiah Aqidah (Islamic religious belief) Protection Enactment was passed in 2000. 'This law empowers the Judge in a Syariah Court to make an order detaining for up to one year in an Aqidah Rehabilitation Centre a person who attempts to change his or her religion if the person refuses to recant. Until now, this is the most extreme position taken with regard to the issue of apostasy.' Moreover, the constitutionality of such regulation is contested (Harding intra, see 11.4).*

Glossary

Adat – Custom (Malaysia, Indonesia).

Adat law – Customary law (Indonesia).

Alim (pl. *Ulama*) – Those who have been trained in religious sciences; religious scholar. Also *'Alim.*

Amir – Traditionally, a military commander, leader, governor. In modern times it denotes membership in the ruling families of the monarchs and means 'prince'.

Amir al-mu'minin – Literally 'commander of the faithful'; title first attributed to the second caliph, Umar ibn Al Khattab (634-644) and adopted by numerous Muslim leaders throughout history, including the king of Morocco. In Sudan called *Qa'id al-mu'minin.*

Awqaf (pl.) – See *waqf* (sing.).

Bad – Dari word for the practice of the exchange of women between families when a crime is committed as compensation for the crime (Afghanistan).

Baraka – Blessing conferred by God upon humankind. In popular Islam manifest in the ability to perform miracles.

Bilad al-siba – Literally 'the area of rebellion (dissidence)'; areas in Morocco that were beyond the scope of control by the central authority.

Caliph – Term adopted by dynastic rulers of the Muslim world; transliteration of *khalifah,* meaning 'successor' referring to the successor of prophet Muhammad as political-military ruler of the Muslim community.

Da'wa – Missionary work; God's way of bringing believers to faith and the means by which prophets call individuals and communities back to God.

Da'wa movement – Missionary movement. Seeks greater application of Islamic laws and values in national life and articulates a holistic Islamic perspective of social, economical and spiritual development. Also *Dakwah* movement (Malaysia; Indonesia).

Dahir – Royal decree (Morocco); legal rule proclaimed as a decree by a sultan.

Darar – Legal term meaning harm, damage, physical or psychological injury. Generally used in the context of divorce; constituting a valid ground for judicial divorce initiated by women. In Iran: *'Osr va haraj*: 'hardship and harm'.

Diyah – See *Diyya.*

Diyanet – Office of Religious Affairs, within the administrative structure of the state as per 1982 (Turkey).

Diyya – Financial compensation payable to the victim or the victim's next of kin in case of a crime against a person, such as homicide, infliction of wounds or battery in place of retribution (*qisas*) Commonly referred to as 'blood money'. Also, *Diya* (Sudan), *Diyah* (Dari, Afghanistan), *Diyat* (Nigeria) *Diyet* (Turkey).

Ejtehād: – See *Ijtihad.*

Faqih (pl. *fuqaha, foqaha*) – Expert in Islamic jurisprudence (*fiqh*).

Faskh or *fasakh* – Annulment of marriage based on legally valid grounds.

Fatwa – Legal opinion issued by Islamic religious scholars.

Fiqh – Islamic jurisprudence; the total product of human efforts to understand the divine will. Also *feqh.*

Fuqaha' (pl.) – See *faqih* (sing.).

Gharar – Uncertainty in contracts, prohibited in Islamic law.

Hadana – Care of child by the mother, as distinct from legal guardianship (*wilaya*), which in general belongs to the father. After divorce, in general custody belongs to the mother, at least until the child is considered no longer in need of a woman's care.

Hadd – See *Hudud*.

Hajj – Yearly pilgrimage to Mecca in Saudi Arabia. The *hajj* is one of the five pillars of Islam. All adults, if able, are required to perform it at least once in a lifetime.

Halal – Permissible according to sharia.

Hanafi – Sunni school of jurisprudence.

Hanbali – Sunni school of jurisprudence.

Haram – Forbidden according to sharia.

Hijab – A covering worn by women over other clothing, drawn tightly around the face and draping loosely down to the knees.

Hijra – Emigration of Prophet Mohammed from Mecca to Yathrib (later Medina) in 622 AD. This event marks the beginning of the Islamic calendar.

Hirabah – Violence not sanctioned by Islamic law of war, including *hadd* crimes such as armed robbery, or banditry, as defined under Islamic law. Also, *Hiraba* (the Sudan).

Hisbah – Community morals; by extension the maintenance of public law and order and supervising market transactions.

Hodūd – See *Hudud*.

Hudud (sing. *Hadd*) – Punishments fixed in the Qur'an for crimes considered as violations of God's limits, namely theft, extramarital sex, unproven/wrongful accusation of extramarital sex, armed robbery, consumption of alcohol – and, according to some schools of thought, apostasy; one of four categories of crimes/punishment in Islamic penal law. Also, *Hodud* (Iran); *Hodūd* (Dari); *Hudood* (Pakistan).

'Iddah – Three-month period during which a divorced woman cannot marry another man in order to make sure that she is not pregnant by

her ex-husband. Men are required to continue maintaining their ex-wives when the divorce is revocable (*talaq al-raji*).

Ijbar – Doctrine under Maliki law providing for the overruling power of the father or guardian to act purely (theoretically) in the girl's best interest. In Nigerian context, *ijbar* manifests itself for example in the marrying off of young girls to much older men.

Ijtihad – Independent interpretation of the Quran and Sunna. Traditionally, only allowed when Quran and Sunna are silent on a particular issue. Also *Ejtehād* (Iran, Afghanistan).

Ijma' – Consensus or agreement among religious scholars. One of the four legal sources of Islamic law.

Jezye or *jizyah* – A special poll tax levied from non-Muslims in Islamic societies. Traditionally, meant as a compensation for not entering the military service.

Jihad – 'Struggle' or 'striving', in Islam usually meant in the sense of 'striving in the way of Allah', which may range from personal striving to correct one's own faults to armed warfare against those labeled as unbelievers.

Jinayah – Islamic penal law.

Jirga – local or regional assembly. Took, still take, primary role in dispute settlement for tribal groups (Pakistan, Afghanistan).

Jomhuriyat – Republic, 'republicanism' (Iran).

Kafala – Agreement with third party to financially support a family, in practice a form of adoption, where children retain membership to their original family.

Khalwat – Close proximity between unmarried persons of the opposite sex. Criminal offence under Islamic law in Malaysia, and Aceh, Indonesia.

Kholᶜ – See *Khul'*.

Khul'– A form of divorce by mutual consent in which the wife asks her husband to repudiate her in exchange for waiver of her financial rights (e.g. waiver of alimony payments or return/forfeit of dower). Also, *Ibra'* (Egypt); *Khol*[c] (Afghanistan); *Khuluk* (Indonesia).

Khuluk: See *Khul'*.

Liwat – Hetero- or homosexual anal intercourse. Also *Lawat* (Iran).

Madhhabs – Muslim schools of jurisprudence.

Madrasa or Madāres (Dari), *Madrasah* (Indonesia); *Medersas* (Mali), *Medrese* (Turkey) – Religious schools; religious colleges for higher studies.

Maharim – See *mehrem.*

Mahr – Islamic dowry, part of the 'wife's dues', may be paid at once or split into two payments, one upon marriage and one part later. One of the requirements for a valid marriage.

Majlis – Council. Also *majelis.*

Majlis al-shura – Consultative council, legislative council. See *shura.*

Malik – King.

Maliki – Sunni school of jurisprudence.

Marja' (pl. *maraje'*) – Spiritual guide, recognised after a long process of acquiring respect for his teaching and scholarship; especially after qualifying as an *ayatollah* by writing a legal treatise or manual (*resaleh*) – a model for those who have chosen to follow him in religious matters (Iran).

Marja'iyat – Ultimate authority of the *Marja* (Iran).

Marsum – Royal decree.

Maslaha – Public interest; a basis for law. Also *maslahat.*

Medersas – See *madrasa.*

Mehrem – A male relative of a woman who is religiously banned from marrying that woman under any circumstances.

Mecelle or *Mejelle or Majalla* – The Ottoman civil code (late 1800s). Although the *Mecelle* only remained in force in Turkey until 1926, in other parts of the former Ottoman Empire it remained in use for much longer. The *Mecelle* codified civil law, excluding family law. The substance of the code was based on the Hanafi legal school (*madhhab*) that enjoyed official status in the Empire. However, using the method of preference (*takhayyur*), it also incorporated legal opinions that were considered more appropriate to the time, including some derived from non-Hanafi *madhhab*.

Misyar marriage – Ambulant marriages, or marriages in which spouses agree that the wife will continue to live with her parents, thus freeing the husband of his obligation to provide marital domicile for her.

Mojāhedīn (or *Mujahidin*) movements – Literally, movements who engage in *jihad*. Refer to Islamic resistant groups. See also *jihad*.

Mojtahed or *mujtahid* – scholar qualified to perform *ijtihad* or independent interpretation of the sources of Islamic law.

Muamalah – Commercial law. Also *muamalat*.

Mufti – 'Official interpreter of Islamic law' or a member of the community of religious scholars (the *'ulama*), who is competent to give his authoritative legal opinion (*fatwa*) on a particular issue. The term *mufti* can have multiple meanings. In the Egyptian context a state *mufti* refers to the position held by the highest (supreme) advisor on Islamic matters to the state, also known as the 'grand mufti'. Also *Müftü* (Turkey).

Muhtasib – Holder of the office of *al-hisbah*; market inspector (Morocco). Also see *hisbah*.

Mullah – Islamic cleric. The principle interpreters of Islamic law for Shiis (Afghanistan, Iran).

Musharaka – Generic term in Islamic commercial law for business partnership.

Murabaha – Islamic banking principle in which a bank purchases a good on behalf of the client and later resells it to the client at a marked-up price.

Mudaraba – Legal contractual arrangement under Islamic law between two partners for profit sharing.

Muta' – Obligatory financial compensation to be paid by the husband following the dissolution of marriage on the basis of his repudiation if the wife did not play a role in bringing about the repudiation and did not consent to it. Also *Mut'a* (Sudan, Iran); *Sigheh* (Iran).

Nafaqa – Husband's duty to provide maintenance to his wife and children, at least consisting of housing, food and clothes.

Nasab – Spiritual lineage or genealogy.

Neẓām-nāme – See *Nizam* (Saudi Arabia).

Nizam – Ordinance or regulation; order, system, organisation. Intended to infer 'man-made law', as opposed to that deriving from Allah. Compare *qanun*.

Nizamiyye – System of state courts.

Ojrat al-methl – 'Exemplary wages', or monetary compensation for the work a woman has done during marriage (i.e. raising children and housework, which she is not obliged to do by classical jurisprudence) to be paid by the husband, provided that the divorce is not initiated by her and is not caused by any fault of her own (Iran). Compare *muta'*.

Örf – See *'Urf*.

Orfi courts – State courts that had jurisdiction over matters involving the state (Iran).

Osr va haraj – See *darar*.

Pancasila – Translating as 'five pillars', Pancasila refers to the five principles of state ideology, mentioned in Indonesia's constitutional preamble.

Panghulu – Religious scholar (Indonesia).

Purdah – The seclusion of women, particularly married women.

Qadhf – Wrongful/slanderous accusation of illicit sex (Nigeria), *hadd* crime. Also, *Qazf* (Iran).

Qadi – An Islamic (Muslim) judge charged to apply the sharia in cases brought before him: Also *Khadi* (Malaysia), Kali, *Alkali* (Nigeria).

Qanun – Laws and regulations enacted by a government. Originally intended as supplement to Islamic law in matters it left insufficiently regulated. Also *Kanun* (Turkey).

Qes,ās, – 'Retaliation' in Dari. Also, *Qisas, Qeses.*

Qisas – Retaliation in kind for woundings or killings: an eye for an eye, etc. Also *Qesas* (Iran); *Qes,ās,* (Afghanistan), Qeses.

Qiyas – Analogical reasoning. A method to deduct legal prescriptions from the Qur'an and Sunna.

Rajm, Rajam or Rejm – *Hadd* punishment by stoning of an adulterous woman.

Riba – Arabic for 'interest' in fiscal setting. Prohibited in Islamic law.

Ridda – Apostasy from Islam. *Hadd* crime.

Salaf – Early pious Muslim from the first three generations following the time of the Prophet Mohammed, or Islamic forefathers.

Salafiyya movement – Name given to a reform movement led by Jamal al-Din al-Afghani and Muhammad Abduh at the turn of the twentieth century. Emphasised restoration of Islamic doctrines to pure form, adherence to Qur'an and Sunna, rejection of the authority of later interpretations, and maintenance of the unity of the *ummah*. Viewed political and social reforms as essential requirements of revitalisation of the Muslim community. In the late twentieth century, the term came to refer to puritan reformers.

Salafism – See *Salafiyya movement.*

Sariqah – Theft meeting certain conditions under Islamic law . *Hadd* crime. Also, *Sariqa* (the Sudan); *Serqat* (Iran). There are two types: *sariqah al sughra* crimes that are punishable with the amputation of the right hand and *sariqah al kubra* crimes punishable with cross-amputation of the right hand and the left foot.

Shafi'I Sharif (sing.) *ashraf, shurafa* (pl.) – Man claiming descent from prominent ancestors usually the Prophet Mohammed through his grandson Hassan; position of governor (Saudi Arabia).

Shiqaq – Reconciliation procedure after enduring marital discord, providing one of the bases for the dissolution of marriage initiated by women. Two arbiters (*hakam*), one of both families of the spouses, attempt to reconcile the couple. When reconciliation fails the marriage is dissolved.

Shubha – An illicit act that seems a licit one, or legal doubt. In Islamic law a ground to reduce severity of punishment in criminal cases. Under Moroccan law a valid ground for establishment of descent in cases where there is a formal lack of a valid marriage but the couple are maintaining conjugal relations.

Shura – Consultation as basis of governance, based on quranic injunction to Muhammad to consult with his followers. By some religious scholars seen as the Islamic basis for democracy.

Shurb – Drinking wine, and by extension imbibing other intoxicants. *Hadd* crime. Also *Mosker* (Iran).

Siyasa shar'iyya – Regulatory authority of the state as recognised by Islamic law. Also *siyasa, al-siyada.*

Sufism – Islamic mysticism. Sufis strive to constantly be aware of God's presence, stressing contemplation over action, spiritual development over legalism and cultivation of the soul over social interaction.

Sukuk – Islamic bonds. An Islamic product or service now being offered by conventional banks in Saudi Arabia, although traditionally such constructions would not have been permissible, as bonds typically involve interest-based constructions.

Sunna – Traditions and teachings of the Prophet Muhammad.

Ta'azir – See *ta'zir.*

Tafriq – See *tatliq.*

Takaful – Form of insurance that is considered 'sharia compliant'.

Takhayyur – Method of selection of legal sources of Islamic jurisprudence (*fiqh*) that enabled Muslims to follow legal interpretations of Islamic schools of jurisprudence (*madhhab*) other than their own.

T,alaq – Traditionally, unilateral divorce by the husband without having to produce legal reason, effective upon his pronouncement of the divorce. *Talaq* that are revocable in the waiting period of the wife (see *iddah*) are called *talaq al-raji*. The third time a *talaq* is uttered for the same marriage becomes irrevocable and is called *talaq al-bain*. Also *T,alāq* (Dari), *Talak* (Indonesia).

Tarbiyah – education.

Tariqat (pl. *tariqas*) – Religious Sufi association. Also *tarekat, tarikat*.

Taqlid – Imitation or tradition. Refers to the obligation to conform to a single school of Islamic jurisprudence (in Sunni Islam: the Hanafi, Hanbali, Maliki, and Shafi'i schools).

Tatliq – Judicial form of divorce based on valid grounds, including a breach of the marriage contract. In many countries valid divorce grounds are incorporated in standard marriage contracts. Also *Tafrīq, taklik, takliq*.

Ta'zir offences – Punishment for crime not measuring up to the strict requirements of the *hadd* punishments, although they are of the same nature or those for which specific punishments have not been fixed by the Qur'an. In classical Islamic law, offences defined and punished at the discretion of the *qadi* in particular cases coming before him ('right to censure'). In modern penal law these are defined and the punishmentsare prescribed by statute. Also *Ta'azir* (Nigeria); *Ta'zirat* (Iran); *Tazir* (Turkey).

'Udul (sing. *'adl*) – Professional Islamic witnesses who write down documents for all matters in which Islamic law applies.

Ulama (sing. *alim*, scholar) – Islamic scholars; those learned in the theology and law of Islam and the literature, mostly in Arabic, proper to these disciplines. Also, *'Ulama* (e.g. Saudi Arabia), *Ulama'* (the Sudan), *'Ulama'* (Morocco).

'Umma' – 'Community of all Muslims'.

'Urf – Custom. Also *Örf* (Turkey).

Urfi marriages – Unregistered marriages that while often considered valid are not legally recognised by the courts and are thus in legal limbo (Egypt); also 'unregistered, traditional marriages' (*'Urfi*, the Sudan).

Ushr – A religious tax on agricultural proceeds.

Velayat-e faqih (Iran) – Guardianship of the *faqih*, or expert in Islamic jurisprudence.

Wakf – See *waqf*.

Wali – Male guardian for the bride required to make a marriage valid in Islamic law.

Walwar – 'Bride price' (Dari), or transfer of money from the groom to the bride's family. Customary tribal tradition in Afghanistan whereby the groom or his family has to pay to the head of the bride's household a sum of money (or commodity) to reimburse the parents of the bride for the financial loss they suffered while raising their daughter.

Waqf – A domain constituted into a pious endowment; charitable trust.

Wilaya – Legal guardianship over children. In general hold by the father or his family.

Zakat – Required almsgiving that is one of the five pillars of Islam.

Zina – Unlawful sexual intercourse; fornication; adultery. *Hadd* crime, that must be established by testimony of four adult male witnesses. Also *Zena* (Iran).

About the contributors

Maurits Berger is a lawyer and Arabist. He holds the chair of Islam in the contemporary West at the Institute for Religious Studies at Leiden University, and is a senior research associate with the Clingendael Institute for International Relations in The Hague. He has written extensively on Sharia and Islamic law in the Arab as well as the Western world, and translated the Moroccan family law into Dutch.

Léon Buskens is Professor of Law and Culture in Islamic Societies, both at the Faculty of Humanities as well as at the Law Faculty of Leiden University, including the Van Vollenhoven Institute. He completed his degree in anthropology at the University of Nijmegen and in 1993 obtained his Ph.D. in Leiden with a thesis on Moroccan family law. His research focuses mainly on the relationship between Islamic norms and practises.

Albert Dekker is coordinator of the library of the Leiden University Law Faculty, with particular focus on the collection of the Van Vollenhoven Institute. The collection includes many works on modern and colonial Indonesia. He graduated in law and library sciences in Groningen. He has published law & development bibliographies in the Van Vollenhoven Publication Series and authored and co-authored two index volumes on the law and jurisprudence of the Netherlands Indies, published by the Royal Institute of Linguistics & Anthropology.

Esther van Eijk is a Ph.D. Candidate at Leiden University in the Netherlands, studying family law in Syria. She completed degrees in law and Arabic at Leiden University and specialises in Islamic law. She contributed to a variety of projects, including a publication on the UN Declaration on the Elimination of Violence Against Women, and the Sharia and National Law project, carried out by the Van Vollenhoven Institute.

Andrew Harding is Professor of Asia-Pacific Law at the University of Victoria, BC (Canada). He is a former Head of Department and Professor of Law in the Law School, School of Oriental and African

Studies (SOAS), University of London and formerly taught at the Faculty of Law, National University of Singapore, and as a Visiting Professor at Harvard Law School. He is the author of 'Law, Government and the Constitution in Malaysia' (1996). He is co-editor of 'Constitutional Courts: A Comparative Study' (2009), and 'New Courts in Asia' (2010). He is presently working on books on Thailand and Malaysia for the Hart Publishing series 'Constitutional Systems of the World', of which he is also co-general editor.

Mustafa Koçak is currently the Professor of Public Law and Founder Dean of the Okan University Faculty of Law in Istanbul, Turkey. He studied law at the University of Istanbul, held positions as lawyer and journalist and was a temporary researcher at the law faculty of the University of Glasgow. He did research into the history of Turkish (constitutional) law, sovereignty, political parties and human rights.

Olaf Köndgen is currently preparing a Ph.D. dissertation on Islamic criminal law in the Sudan (University of Amsterdam). He holds an M. A. in Islamic Studies from the Free University of Berlin and worked as Senior Acquisitions Editor on Islam and the Middle East for Brill Academic Publishers in Leiden. He published on political and economic issues related to the Sudan, Egypt, Jordan, Lebanon and Israel.

Martin Lau is a Reader in Law at the School of Oriental and African Studies, University of London, where he teaches courses on South Asian law. He is a regular visitor to Pakistan and has published widely on the country's legal system.

Ziba Mir-Hosseini is an independent consultant, researcher, and writer on Middle Eastern issues, based at the London Middle East Institute and the Centre for Middle Eastern and Islamic Law, both at SOAS, University of London; since 2002 she has been Hauser Global Law Visiting Professor at New York University. She specialises in gender, family relations, Islamic law and development, and is a founding member of Musawah Global Movement for Equality and Justice in the Muslim Family.

Philip Ostien is an independent scholar, working from Madison, Wisconsin, USA. He received his Ph.D. in philosophy from the University of Pennsylvania, and also holds J.D. and LL.M. degrees from the University of Iowa. Having taught at the University of Iowa and practiced law in Des Moines, Iowa, in 1991 he joined the Faculty of Law of the University of Jos, Nigeria, where he taught (with some interruptions) until his retirement in 2007. He is the author or editor of a number of works on the laws and legal institutions of northern Nigeria and the programmes of sharia implementation that began there in 1999.

Jan Michiel Otto is Professor of Law and Governance in developing countries and director of the Van Vollenhoven Institute for Law, Governance, and Development. He studied law at the University of Leiden and wrote his Ph.D. thesis on public administration in rural Egypt. Since 1983 he has conducted comparative studies of law, governance, and development in Asia, Africa and the Middle East.

Mohammad Hamid Saboory is an independent consultant, providing services to several NGOs in Europe and North America on legal reform and development issues related to Afghanistan. He holds an M.A. in International Relations from Syracuse University and an M.A. in Middle/Near Eastern Studies from New York University. He studied law in Kabul and as researcher contributed to projects run by the Max-Planck Institute for Comparative and International Private Law in Hamburg.

Dorothea E. Schulz is professor of anthropology at the University of Cologne. Her expertise is on Islam in Africa, the anthropology of religion, gender studies, media studies, public culture, and the anthropology of the state. She is currently a professor at the University of Cologne. She obtained her Ph.D. from Yale University, USA, and her habilitation (second docoral degree required for promotion in the German academic system) from the Free University, Berlin. She taught at Cornell University, New York, and Indiana University, Bloomington, USA. Her regional expertise is in West Africa (particularly Mali) and East Africa (Uganda).

Nadia Sonneveld is a senior researcher on the implementation of Islamic law in practice affiliated with the School of Oriental and African Studies (SOAS), University of London, and the Van Vollenhoven Institute, University of Leiden. While earlier research focused on Egypt and Indonesia, she now focuses on comparative research in a number of Muslim majority countries. She graduated in law in 2009, Arabic in 2002 and cultural anthropology in 2000.

Nadjma Yassari is a senior fellow at the Max-Planck-Institute for Comparative and International Private Law in Hamburg, where she heads the Department for the Laws of Islamic countries. She was born in Iran and studied law in Austria, France and the United Kingdom. Her main fields of research are private national and private international law of Islamic countries, in particular the Arab Middle East, Iran and Afghanistan with a special focus on family and inheritance law. Since April 2009 she is leading a Max-Planck Research Group investigating the scope and limits of contractual freedom in Islamic family law.

FSC
www.fsc.org
MIX
Papier | Fördert gute Waldnutzung
FSC® C083411

Kolibri 360 GmbH
Ferdinand-Jühlke-Straße 7
99095 Erfurt, Deutschland
produktsicherheit@kolibri360.de